WOMEN, GENDER, AND TRANSNATIONAL LIVES: ITALIAN WORKERS OF THE WORLD

Edited by Donna R. Gabaccia and Franca Iacovetta

Scholars in the United States have long defined the Italian immigrant woman as silent and submissive – a woman who stays 'in the shadows.' In this transnational analysis of women and gender in Italy's worldwide migration, the contributors challenge this stereotype, using international and internationalist perspectives, feminist labour history, women's history, and Italian migration history to provide a woman-centred, gendered analysis of Italian workers.

Analysing the lives of women in Italy, Belgium, France, the United States, Canada, Argentina, and Australia, the contributors offer realistic and engaging portraits of women as peasants and workers and uncover the voice of female militants. Most importantly, through a comparative approach to the study of women's migration over the nineteenth and twentieth centuries, this volume examines not only the work and activism of migrant women but also the experiences of those women who remained in Italy. The result is a rich volume that ranges from the white widows of Sicily to union organizers in the United States, from anarchists in Argentina to Fascist-era activists in Canada.

Groundbreaking and original, this erudite collection of thirteen essays brings a fascinating new perspective to women's studies and migration history.

(Studies in Gender and History)

DONNA R. GABACCIA is Charles H. Stone Professor of American History at the University of North Carolina at Charlotte.

FRANCA IACOVETTA is a professor in the Department of History at the University of Toronto.

STUDIES IN GENDER AND HISTORY

General Editors: Franca Iacovetta and Karen Dubinsky

Women, Gender, and Transnational Lives

Italian Workers of the World

Edited by

DONNA R. GABACCIA *and* FRANCA IACOVETTA

UNIVERSITY OF TORONTO PRESS
Toronto Buffalo London

Printed in Canada

ISBN 0-8020-3611-2 (cloth)
ISBN 0-8020-8462-1 (paper)

Printed on acid-free paper

National Library of Canada Cataloguing in Publication

Main entry under title:

Women, gender and transnational lives : Italian workers of the world /
edited by Donna R. Gabaccia and Franca Iacovetta.

(Studies in gender and history series)
Includes bibliographical references and index.
ISBN 0-8020-3611-2 (bound)   ISBN 0-8020-8462-1 (pbk.)

1. Women – Italy.   2. Women employees – Italy.   3. Women   immi-
grants – Italy.   4. Women alien labor.   5. Women immigrants –
Political activity – History.   6. Italy – Emigration and immigration –
History.   I. Gabaccia, Donna R., 1949–   II. Iacovetta, Franca, 1957–

DG453.W65 2002   305.4′0945   C2002-902129-4

University of Toronto Press acknowledges the financial assistance to
its publishing program of the Canada Council for the Arts and the
Ontario Arts Council.

University of Toronto Press acknowledges the financial support for
its publishing activities of the Government of Canada through the
Book Publishing Industry Development Program (BPIDP).

To our mothers,
Marjorie Anne Krauss Gabaccia
and
Dalinda Carmosino Lombardi Iacovetta

Contents

Illustrations follow page 216

Preface

Italian women as 'workers of the world' may not be a familiar image for our readers. Italy's women have often seemed foreign to Anglo-Americans, who imagine Latin and Catholic patriarchs controlling women's lives, leaving them – unlike their supposedly more emancipated English-speaking 'sisters' – silent, submissive, and at home 'in the shadows.'[1] To Italian readers, by contrast, focusing on women's history as workers threatens to separate women artificially from men, ignoring what they both shared historically, whether family loyalties or shared subordination in a world dominated economically by northern Europeans and North Americans.

When we decided to attempt a woman-centred but gendered analysis of the twenty-seven million migrants who left Italy in the nineteenth and twentieth centuries, we suspected we might challenge conventional portraits of Italian women. Building on the historiography on Italian women immigrants in the United States, we were most interested in the relationship between work and female agency, but we were determined to follow women's activities wherever they led us. Thus, we insisted on seeing both the majority of females who 'waited' (while men went abroad) and the minority of females among the emigrants as integral actors in what was arguably the single largest international migration system of the world's modern era. We wanted to view the global social networks created by massive male emigration from Italy through female eyes.[2] Our hope was not just to make women more visible in a migration literature focused on male migrants but to pinpoint also the origins of persistent stereotypes of Italy's women in a literature disproportionately focused on immigrants to the United States.

Still, we were surprised by what we found. In the same spirit in which Italian women on five continents confronted exploitation at home and at work, our book highlights the complex, transnational lives of feisty, and at times frustrated, but always formidable and fascinating women. If our contributors had to work hard and long to create this volume, they certainly drew inspiration from the hard-working women they studied.

This book is the result of international collaboration at its best. It originated in 1996 when U.S. historian Donna Gabaccia (who, together with Fraser Ottanelli, was editing a collection of essays on Italian workers around the world) approached Canadian historian Franca Iacovetta to discuss their project's difficulties in integrating research on women.[3] We then decided to plan a second project that – while focused on questions of gender in women's work, labour organizing, and radicalism – would also touch issues such as family and household, sexuality, community, politics, and identities. If we could not easily integrate women into a history of Italian radicalism, then we would write a gendered feminist history of their lives and labour both together and in struggle with men. As we turned our attention to this new project, we noticed immediate changes in our networks of collaboration: perhaps unsurprisingly, male participation dropped off somewhat. But the boundaries around our field of research also broadened to include unpaid as well as waged work, the lives of peasants in Italy as well as of emigrants around the world, and activism outside as well as within traditional labour, political, and radical movements.

It is scarcely original to observe that economic globalization has recently pushed feminist and labour historians like us to attempt to rewrite world history 'from the bottom up.' Although hardly a new historical development, globalization is again transforming the relationship between wealthier Northern and poorer Southern nation-states and – as in the past – is again pushing people from the South to earn wages in the North. But while today's international labour migrations are relatively gender-balanced, the ones we intended to study in the past were heavily male-dominated – an intriguing difference that has not yet found the analytical and theoretical attention it deserves from scholars of international migration.[4]

Fortunately, feminist scholars are no strangers to building intellectual networks across national boundaries. For almost ten years, our individual scholarly development had shared certain key features – not the least an on-going critique of the dominant stereotypes of Italian immigrant women in North America as docile, anti-union, housebound women controlled by men or victimized by a deeply patriarchal Latin culture.

We were also on a similar intellectual trajectory, first articulated in Gabaccia's second book, *Militants and Migrants*, from writing the social history of the immigrant experience (or, what Iacovetta has called the 'new' immigration history) to approaches that were broadly transnational.[5] A generation of scholarship spearheaded by historians Rudolph Vecoli, Herbert Gutman, John Bodnar, and Dirk Hoerder had already sought to understand the homeland experiences of immigrants and to be sensitive to the 'mental maps' of migrants within an 'Atlantic economy.'[6] As socialist feminists, we had also grappled – alone and together – with ways to integrate the insights of women's historians and historians of gender into immigration history and the social and labour history of working-class immigrants.[7] Finally, in choosing a transnational approach, we were guided by our subjects – migratory people who had sketched strategies for family survival and proletarian struggle on an international canvas.

Our approach had to be collaborative: no one scholar could tackle the full range of women's experiences worldwide. We aimed to present national case studies – of Italy, the United States, Argentina, France, Belgium, Canada, and Australia – in ways that would facilitate multinational comparison while also drawing explicit connections among national histories. We were challenged to satisfy historians' penchant for the specificity of time and place while still allowing for transatlantic (and cross-pacific) comparisons over relatively long periods of time. We requested essays that were case studies of specific regions of out-migration, particular occupational clusters in a given city or town, or particular workplaces, strikes and boycotts, or the individual and collective biographies of female activists. But we also asked collaborators to 'talk across national boundaries' and we thank them for their willingness to do so. They showed intellectual generosity and goodwill, sharing with each other their research findings, revising their own research priorities, reappraising their conclusions in light of other contributions, and generally engaging in genuine intellectual debate. Perhaps this is why all the essays we received revealed the enormous complexity of women's identities well before our own postmodern age. The women we studied were simultaneously wives and mothers, peasants, workers, Catholics, radicals, and internationalists who nevertheless intensely loved their particular homeplaces. National identities triumph mainly in national historiographies, we concluded; comparative and transnational approaches paint a more complex picture of lives lived beneath and beyond the power of nation-states to dictate human subjectivity.

Yet our collaboration also shed interesting light on how the writing of history – its methods, preferred theories, and genres – is still also, to a large degree, national. As we read and responded to early drafts of the essays collected here, we began to discuss how national cultures shaped our contributors' questions, interpretations, and ways of reporting on their research. We already knew that women's history was not firmly anchored in universities outside the English-speaking world. But since we, as English-speaking North Americans, lived and worked in a professional world where 'gender history' was increasingly associated with discourse theory and postmodernism, and increasingly and sharply differentiated from social-historical or materialist approaches, we were surprised when none of our contributors felt compelled to identify themselves or to situate their work in either camp. Not all our contributors may have entirely shared our material feminist perspective, but all acknowledged the critical role of material conditions – notably hard physical labour and material want – in shaping women's lives. Our many multilingual contributors paid exquisitely close attention to language and to discourse while interpreting them in historical context. As North American scholars continue to ponder the disagreements that flourish among them, and in particular to question whether gender analysis must be considered inherently either materialist or postmodern, we wish to recognize that our perspective has much in common with that of our North American colleagues in feminist and labour history, and that we are encouraged by recent efforts to transcend the division.[8]

Regrettably, our project did not benefit from a tightly focused conference or workshop; there were no special grants to ease us through the exciting but time-consuming and even expensive phases of organizing and editing the project. Fortunately, however, we were able to draw on existing national and international professional networks. Over the course of five years, ten contributors met in various combinations to deliver papers – at the 1996 Tampa conference of the 'Italians Everywhere' Project; at the Wayne State Labor History Conference in Detroit; the Canadian Historical Association in St Catharines, Ontario, and in Quebec City; the American Historical Association in Washington, DC; the Berkshire Conference on the History of Women in Chapel Hill, North Carolina; and the American Studies Association in Washington, DC. As editors we reported on the project in Paris, Cambridge (U.K.), Amsterdam, New York, Winnipeg, and Toronto. For conference commentaries and suggestions for contributors we thank Craig Heron, Andrée Lévesque, Bruno Ramirez, Carina Silberstein, Elisabetta Vezzosi, and Seth Wigderson, and for joining us mid-project, we are indebted to José Moya and Angelo Principe. For access to the world of international feminist scholarship, we also thank the newsletter of the International Federation for Research in Women's History.

Certainly there were times when we wondered if we could ever finish, given the difficulties of long-distance communication – email notwithstanding – among contributors who spoke and wrote in differing languages and scholarly styles. That we were able to transcend these difficulties reflects, we believe, shared feminist commitments and the looser 'hold' of national historiography on feminist history, especially when compared to labour history. None of our collaborators, we were pleased to note, expressed concern that comparative or transnational history carried professional risks or was the latest 'scholarly fad' of scholarship in the United States. We suspect many of our contributors had wearied of complaining about the marginality of gender analysis in migration studies: collaboration was a proactive response we shared with other feminist projects.[9]

Fortunately, too, our decision to publish in English also struck our contributors as a desirable strategy for reaching the widest possible audience in women's and gender history. To publish in Italy and in Italian would have meant severely limiting our audience; by far the largest group of historians of women and gender work in the English-speaking world, and English has become the most important language of international scholarly communication in migration studies too. In choosing to edit the one French and three Italian essays only after they were translated into English, we leaned heavily on the expert skills of our history colleague and friend Gabriele Scardellato, who combined precision in translation and editing with a sensitivity for history and historical argument. Without Gabe, this project would have taken much longer to complete. We are truly indebted to him for guiding us through various stages of the revision, editing, and production of a manuscript.

Finally, we hoped that by publishing in Canada instead of in the United States, we would further extend the professional 'reach' of transnational approaches to the study of Italian migration. Books linked to the 'Italians Everywhere' project have now been published in Europe (University of College of London), the United States (University of Illinois), and Canada. We hope to see a fourth collaboration find a French publisher in the years ahead. For their encouragement, enthusiasm, and support, we want to thank, at University of Toronto Press, retired editor Gerry Hallowell, former editor Jill McConkey, and our new colleague Len Husband; Frances Mundy and John St James for their editorial work and accommodation to our requests; as well as Karen Dubinsky, co-editor of the Studies in Gender and History series. In submitting this manuscript to this series, we hope to contribute to its mandate to be international in scope.

Our project benefited from a long feminist tradition of building and nurturing networks of international intellectual exchange. On a personal level, we take pride in having helped in modest ways to sustain the networks that made this project possible and in contributing to the impressive array of studies that have made feminist scholarship a less marginal endeavour than it was thirty years ago. Collaboration confirmed our feminist convictions that the personal and political are intertwined and that friendship and scholarly collaboration can overlap.

Not surprisingly, then, we wish to acknowledge the many colleagues who gave us advice, provided feedback on papers, and generally supported our efforts at global history and comparative feminist scholarship: Christiane Harzig, Nancy Green, Nancy Hewitt, Dirk Hoerder, Gregory Kealey, Fraser Ottanelli, Roberto Perin, Ian Radforth, Bruno Ramirez, Matteo Sanfilippo, Pam Sharpe, and Michael Miller Topp. For assistance with illustrations we thank Gabe Scardellato, Matteo Sanfilippo, Mario Carini, Joel Wurl (of the IHRC), Father Maffeo Litti (of the CSER in Rome), the National Archives of Argentina, the Fondazione Sella in Italy, and Famee Furlane of Toronto. For the good humour and patience they showed us during a particularly intense writing and editing stint at the Iacovetta-Radforth cottage, we owe special thanks to Christiane Harzig, Dirk Hoerder, and Ian Radforth. They had the good sense to leave us alone to work and the good grace to wine and dine us at the end of each long day and to force us – every once in a while – to enjoy a bit of afternoon sun on the dock. Franca adds special thanks to the Toronto Labour Studies Group, Mariana Valverde, and Cynthia Wright for their continuing support for this and other ongoing projects. Donna again thanks her faithful gang of five – Dorothy, Jeanne, Jeffrey, Tamino, and Thomas. And, as usual, too, they know the reasons why. Finally, at *Labour / Le Travail*, where we published an early research report on the project, we were very fortunate to benefit from the cogent advice and comradely support of Greg Kealey, the (founding) editor of the journal, shortly before he stepped down from that position. In his many years as the journal's editor, Greg amply demonstrated how a male editor can nurture collegial relations between men and women scholars and encourage productive dialogue between labour and feminist historians.

Donna Gabaccia, Charlotte, North Carolina
Franca Iacovetta, Toronto, Ontario

NOTES

1 The terms 'of the shadows,' 'in the shadows,' and 'out of the shadows' appear repeatedly in studies of Latin women. For Italy, see Anne Cornelisen, *The Women of the Shadows* and Donna Gabaccia, 'In the Shadows of the Periphery: Italian Women in the Nineteenth Century,' in Jean Quataert and Marilyn Boxer, eds., *Connecting Spheres: Women in the Western World, 1500 to the Present* (New York: Oxford University Press, 1987). For a Mexican example, see Vicki Ruiz, *Out of the Shadows* (New York: Oxford University Press, 2000). See also Angelo Principe's essay in this volume.

2 For a critique of the usefulness of the term see Donna Gabaccia, *Italy's Many Diasporas* (London: University College of London Press; Seattle: University of Washington Press, 2000) and Gabaccia and Fraser Ottanelli, 'Diaspora or International Proletariat?' *Diaspora* 6, 1 (Spring 1997).

3 The book became Gabaccia and Ottanelli, eds., *Italian Workers of the World: Labor, Migration and the Making of Multi-Ethnic States* (Urbana: University of Illinois Press, 2001).

4 For some preliminary thoughts on the topic, see Gabaccia, 'Women of the Mass Migrations: From Minority to Majority, 1820–1930,' in Dirk Hoerder and Leslie Moch, eds., *European Migrants: Global and Local Perspectives* (Boston: Northeastern University Press, 1996). For those seeking the foundational statements on women and international migration, see Caroline B. Brettell and Rita James Simon, eds., *International Migration: The Female Experience* (Totowa, NJ: Rowman & Allanheld, 1986) and Annie Phizacklea, ed., *One Way Ticket: Migration and Female Labour* (London: Routledge & Kegan Paul, 1983).

5 Gabaccia, *Militants and Migrants: Rural Sicilians Become American Workers* (New Brunswick, NJ: Rutgers University Press, 1988); Franca Iacovetta, 'Manly Militants, Cohesive Communities and Defiant Domestics: Writing about Immigrants in Canadian Historical Scholarship,' *Labour / Le Travail* 36 (Fall 1995).

6 See, e.g., Rudolph Vecoli, 'Contadini in Chicago: A Critique of the "Uprooted,"' *Journal of American History* 51 (1964): 404–16; Herbert G. Gutman, *Power and Culture: Essays on the American Working Class* (New York: Pantheon Books, 1987); John Bodnar, *The Transplanted* (Bloomington: Indiana University Press, 1985); and Dirk Hoerder, *Labor Migration in the Atlantic Economy: The European and North American Working Classes during the Period of Industrialization* (Westport, CT: Greenwood Press, 1985).

7 Gabaccia, *From the Other Side: Women, Gender, and Immigrant Life in the U.S., 1820–1990* (Bloomington: Indiana University Press, 1994); and Iacovetta, *Such Hardworking People: Italian Immigrants in Postwar Toronto* (Montreal: McGill-Queen's University Press, 1992).

8 For example, see Ava Baron, ed., *Work Engendered: Towards a New History of American Labor* (Ithaca: Cornell University Press, 1991), esp. Mary H. Blewett's 'Manhood and the Market: The Politics of Gender and Class among the Textile Workers of Fall River, Massachusetts, 1870–1880'; and Nancy A. Hewitt, 'In Pursuit of Power: The Political Economy of Women's Activism in Twentieth-Century Tampa,' in Nancy A. Hewitt and Suzanne Lebsock, eds., *Visible Women: New Essays on American Activism* (Urbana: University of Illinois Press, 1993). On the latter point, see, e.g., Mariana Valverde, 'Some Remarks on the Rise and Fall of Discourse Analysis,' *Histoire sociale / Social History* 33 (2000); Franca Iacovetta, 'Post-Modern Ethnography, Historical Materialism, and Decentring the (Male) Authorial Voice: A Feminist Conversation,' ibid. 32 (2000); Kathryn McPherson, Cecilia Morgan, and Nancy Forestell, eds., *Gendered Pasts: Historical Essays in Femininity and Masculinity in Canada* (Toronto: Oxford University Press, 1999); and Carole Turbin, 'What Social History Can Learn from Postmodernism and Vice Versa. Or, Social Science Historians and Postmodernists Can Be Friends,' *Social Science History* 22, 1 (Spring 1998): 1–6.
9 See Pam Sharpe's collection *Women and International Labour Migration: Historical and Global Perspectives* (London: Routledge, 2001).

WOMEN, GENDER, AND TRANSNATIONAL LIVES:
ITALIAN WORKERS OF THE WORLD

Introduction

Donna R. Gabaccia and *Franca Iacovetta*

In turn-of-the-century Buenos Aires, the Italian-born immigrant Ana María Mozzoni reminded female readers that 'the priest who damns you,' 'the legislator who oppresses you,' 'the husband who reduces you to an object,' and 'the capitalist who enriches himself with your ill-paid work,' were all men. At almost the same time, in far-off Illinois, immigrant women from Italy and Belgium formed the Luisa Michel women's circle. Arguing that motherhood could be revolutionary, the women began to translate a children's story that would help them to teach their children 'the love of their own freedom together with the respect for the freedom of others.'

Radical female voices like these were not limited to a fleeting early-twentieth-century moment. In the 1930s, Virgilia D'Andrea – morally branded by Italy's state authorities for her free-love union – exhorted her working-class audiences to 'exterminate all capitalists because they suck the blood of the working class.' Her contemporaries, the socialist seamstresses and sisters Angela and Maria Bambace drew inspiration from an immigrant mother in New York who joined them on union rounds with a rolling pin under her arm, while in Canada Maria Cazzola was dubbed 'the mother of Italian-Canadian anti-Fascism.' Across the ocean in Belgium, Italian workers in the 'Woman's Peace Group' protested Italy's invasion of Ethiopia with their own logo declaring, 'Mothers of Italy, mothers of Abyssinia, mothers of the entire world shout: we don't want war.' Among them were Italian women who would later die in the Nazi concentration camp at Malthausen.[1]

When we first embarked upon a collaborative project to integrate women and gender into a history of the 'Italian workers of the world,' we did not expect that female resisters, radical exiles, rank-and-file militants, and community-based activists would eventually become the focus of so many of the essays we solicited.[2] It is not that we did not wish it to be so. Still, at most, even we believed that collaborative research on Italian women living on four continents, and in seven countries, would mainly shed new light on the complex link between women's work and family identities while adding insight into how women developed national identities in the twentieth century. At project's end, we remain fully aware that women radicals constituted a small minority of Italian women around the world, but take delight nonetheless in highlighting the many defiant peasants, workers, and seasoned radicals our contributors discovered.

Recovering the lives of the militant minority among Italy's women forced us to view the majority with fresh eyes. What explained the radicalism of this female minority, and why had we and other scholars not noticed it? Acknowledging its existence required us to re-examine the historiography on Italian migration and especially writings on immigrant women in the United States. It required us to reassess the significance of peasant work, culture, and patriarchy and the lives of the women who 'waited' while men migrated abroad.[3] It forced us to think about how family loyalties encouraged activism rather than passivity. In this volume, parts I (on women in Italy) and II (on women's work abroad) provide readers with some context for interpreting the female militants described in part III. Part IV then encourages readers to think about the differing ways that outsiders have constructed Italian women's identities – sometimes as workers, sometimes as familists, but rarely as militants – in two receiving countries; in these essays, readers will glimpse migrated women's evolving and sometimes defensive understandings of themselves across the twentieth century.

Transnational Studies and North American Paradigms

The United States is known around the world as the paradigmatic 'nation of immigrants.' Its very large and comparatively well-funded university system has produced the largest cohorts of scholars developing the fields of immigration and women's history. The voices of these researchers – usually in English – dominate scholarly discourses on international migration and on immigrant women. As their footnotes reveal, our contributors learned much from the important work of specialists on

Italian immigrant women in the United States.[4] Much of that literature focuses on the relationship between women's waged work and their family loyalties; so do many of our contributors. The influence of research on immigrant women and gender in the United States has been particularly pronounced in Canada and Australia and among Italian colleagues who are also Americanists.[5] Nevertheless, as editors, we initially feared and wanted to avoid the undeniable power of the 'immigrant paradigm' of U.S. history to predetermine interpretations of Italian women's life, work, and identities in the many places they lived.

To some degree it is, of course, justifiable to treat the United States as paradigmatic. It is an undeniable demographic fact that two-thirds of the sixty million Europeans who emigrated between 1820 and 1920 chose the United States as their new home. In the twentieth century, however, many other countries around the world – including France, Switzerland, Australia, Canada, and Argentina – have all had proportions of resident foreigners that equaled or surpassed those of the United States. In part that was because the United States in 1924 chose to harshly restrict, rather than welcome, new immigrants. Its immigration policy remains heavily restrictive even today.

When we turn to the history of Italy's migrations, the risks of applying interpretations of immigrant women in the United States more broadly become particularly obvious. Only about a third of Italy's emigrants migrated to the United States and Canada between 1870 and 1970. And at least half of those returned again to Italy. Furthermore, those who went to the United States were somewhat different from the migrants heading for European or Latin American destinations. For one thing, more migrants to both North and South America were female (about a third), and more men and women travelled there in family groups. Proportionately many more in the transalpine migrations were men (70 to 90 per cent). More Italians migrating to the United States, Canada, and Australia originated in Italy's southern provinces – almost 90 per cent of the emigrants from Sicily, for example, went to the United States – while migrations to Latin America and transalpine Europe included more central and northern Italians (who were the majority of all emigrants before 1945).[6]

For all these reasons, we consciously limited the number of contributions on Italian immigrant women in the United States in our collection, and we chose to examine Italian migration, work, and even labour militancy as transnational phenomena that linked life in Italy simultaneously to several 'receiving countries' in Europe, Australia, and the

Americas.[7] In our collection, just three of twelve essays focus exclusively on the United States. In choosing a transnational approach, we built on a deeply rooted and now flourishing scholarly tradition of studying Italy's migrations from global perspectives. Earlier researchers have imagined Italy's migrants as 'gli italiani nel mondo' (Italians 'in' or 'of' the world) who created an 'Italia fuori d'Italia' ('Italy outside of Italy,' sometimes called in English 'Little Italies' or in Italian 'altre Italie' – other Italys), or they have described them as key elements in an international proletariat – the 'workers of the world' – or as part of a 'proletarian mass migration.'[8] More recently, scholars have investigated and also critiqued the possibility that Italy's migrants formed if not a single diaspora then at least an evolving collection of transnational, multi-sited social networks that resembled diasporas in important ways. Most of these networks emanated from particular village communities, but some were networks of exiles and their followers, linked by shared political ideologies such as anarchism, socialism, communism, Fascism, and anti-Fascism.[9] We were also convinced that a transnational approach could contribute, however modestly, to current efforts to rewrite world history 'from the bottom up,' from the vantage point of women, workers, consumers, and peasants rather than as a history of civilizations, world systems, or international relations.

Using a transnational method to analyse Italy's migrations, and women's lives within them, has many advantages. One is the opportunity it opens to consider the impact of emigration on Italy as a 'sending nation,' an issue rarely tackled in research focused exclusively on immigration. Several essays in this collection suggest that migration simultaneously transformed female lives in Italy and abroad, often in broadly similar ways. More important, our decision to include case studies from many sites of Italian life constituted a methodological challenge to immigration history as it is usually written in the United States and Canada. Ours was a comparative method that immigration historian Nancy Green has called 'diverging'; the historiography on immigrant women in the United States has instead been dominated by 'converging' comparisons of two or more immigrant groups in single American cities. Green argues that convergent comparisons highlight cultural differences, and that scholars who choose this method invariably explain variations in immigrant women's work, family, or educational patterns as evidence of the continuing power of cultures, rooted in immigrants' homelands, on women's lives abroad. Diverging comparisons such as ours, by contrast, show women of roughly similar cultural background responding to a wide variety of circumstances, thus highlighting cultural flexibility, change over time, and the influence of the specific characteristics of the receiving society in provoking social and cultural change.[10] Historians of immigrant women in the United States have most frequently compared Italian and Jewish immigrant women, with results we will discuss below. Our diverging comparisons should, instead, help North American (and other) scholars appreciate what is, and is not, distinctive about their own 'nation of immigrants' and about their own national interpretations of women, as Italians and as immigrants.

When Men Go Away: Women Who Wait and Work

Our collection opens with three essays – two by scholars in Italy, Maddalena Tirabassi and Andreina De Clementi, and one by North American Linda Reeder – that focus on the men and women of Italy as workers, family members, and potential migrants. In surveying the diversity of gendered divisions of labour in rural Italy, the essay of Paola Corti, in part II, can also usefully be consulted. While Tirabassi focuses on the development of a negative national and bourgeois discourse on peasant morality and women's work that extended throughout Italy in the late nineteenth century, the other three essays point to regional variations in family practices and gendered divisions of labour. De Clementi examines several agricultural districts in continental southern Italy (Calabria – an area that sent many migrants to the United States), while Reeder examines a region – the central and western parts of the island of Sicily – that occupies a special place in North American analyses of immigrant women's culture. Corti instead focuses on Piedmont in northwest Italy, a region that – along with the northeastern districts around Venice – had emigration rates equalling or surpassing those of the Italian south until the Second World War, but that sent many more emigrants to other European countries and to Latin America. Collectively, these four essays confirm the importance of regional differences in Italy; outside of the country's elite, there was no one national culture. At the same time, however, they warn scholars against simplistic contrasts between a premodern Italian south inhabited by competitive and conservative familists and cloistered women and a prosperous, industrializing Italian north of emancipated, wage-earning men and women with few economic incentives to emigrate.

Tirabassi's essay introduces English-speaking readers to a nineteenth-century national discourse in Italian that rendered peasant women in all rural districts – from north to south – as beasts of burden, lacking decent moral instincts and living in irregular households scarcely deserving the name 'family' precisely because they were *not* governed by a powerful, male patriarch and not ensconced in private, domestic, or female-dominated spaces. Tirabassi draws on Italian government surveys of rural life after 1870; their investigators were, with few exceptions, middle-class professional men and intellectuals from northern Italian cities, and they were shocked and puzzled by the lives, work habits, and families they observed among peasants even in their own countryside. Their gaze was shaped by class privilege, a disdainful view of rural life that had deep roots in Italy's urban culture and a pronounced moral disdain for the exhausting physical labour expected of rural women throughout the country. This female labour, observers claimed, left rural women with no time or energy to fulfil their 'natural' obligations as mothers, nurturers, or creators of homes. (Later female observers – of whom the best known to historians is probably Amy Bernardy, the daughter of a U.S. ambassador and an Italian mother – did not offer substantially different portraits.) In their eyes, rural women were as shameless as the more migratory rural men who 'abandoned' their agricultural work to women in order to migrate. The bourgeois investigators often seemed to believe that the only solution to Italy's agricultural crises was to immobilize men and force them to return to the fields, thus returning them to positions of patriarchal authority over rural women and children.

Surprisingly, bourgeois Italians saw patriarchy collapsing in the same Italian countryside where American scholars would later claim to find the roots of immigrant women's conservative gender ideals. The biases of the Italian observers described by Tirabassi were not entirely unlike the Social Darwinist prejudices of Anglo-American reformers, or early historians of immigration in the United States, who found disorganization, pathology, and alienation everywhere in immigrant communities. In the 1970s, to a very real degree, the social historians of immigrant Italians in North American mounted a defence against just such charges. Thus, when influential historians such as Robert Harney, in Canada, wrote of migrant men without women, they often stressed men's strongly felt family values and the role village gossip and kin relations played both in protecting women in a separate domestic sphere in Italy and in guaranteeing that men would provide for them with wages from abroad before returning to assume authority over them.[11] Studies of Italian immigrant women and working families, including those penned by feminist labour and migration historians, similarly highlighted the sexual

safety and conservative, 'old world,' or Catholic moral values that en-
cased Italian wives, mothers, and daughters – to their own considerable
satisfaction – within domestic worlds at home and abroad.[12] In defending Italian immigrants' moral reputations, these studies acknowledged
the centrality of a family-based work ethos in Italy but nevertheless
created caricatures of their own. Historians responded to moral critiques of family disorganization with portraits of women whose lives
seemed more like those of the housewives of urban and bourgeois
Anglo-America than of the peasants of Italy.

In exploring the lives of Italy's peasants and artisanal workers, the
essays by Reeder, De Clementi, and Corti allow readers to contemplate
the complexity of Italian regionalism in the nineteenth century. For at
least one hundred years scholars have differentiated the 'backward'
Italian south from the 'progressive' Italian north. The origins of this
divisive discourse are in Italy; they were by no means the product of
Anglo-Americans' flights of fantasy. In the years after Italian unification,
southern and northern intellectuals came to agree that the south ('the
mezzogiorno') was a backward, rebellious, ungovernable, impoverished,
and racially less evolved region and thus a threat to the civic well-being of
the new nation.[13] Yet, as Tirabassi reminds readers, Italy's north was also
heavily agricultural until well into the twentieth century.[14] In the face of
truly overwhelming evidence of emigration from northern and central
Italy, Italian officials and social scientists nevertheless began to describe
emigration as symbolic of the collapse of economy, morality, and order
in the south. Immigration officials in the United States carried this
understanding of an Italian regional divide to absurd extremes. Beginning in 1899 they expanded the boundaries of Italy's south to include all
national territory up to the Po River, thus making even Genoa a 'southern' city. Their decision raised the proportions of 'backward' southern
immigrants entering the United States substantially, to about 80 per
cent, fuelling their claims that Anglo-Saxon America was being 'overrun'
by racially inferior and backward southerners.

Studies of immigrant women in the United States have further simpli-
fied the influence of southern Italian culture by seizing on the domestic
ideology of a single and atypical, if also important, southern Italian
region – Sicily – as typical of the entire south.[15] Linda Reeder's essay
introduces readers to some of the peculiarities of this fascinating island
region when she describes the extreme difficulties women experienced
in trying to work productively for their families in Sicily, and the extreme
hostility faced by the poorest women constrained to leave their large

urban villages to work in the far-off wheat fields. By contrast, almost everywhere else in southern Italy women clearly worked with and without wages – in family groups of subsistence producers and as employees in both smaller and larger-scale commercial agriculture. This was certainly true of much of Calabria as described by De Clementi, and of the northwestern region of Piedmont described by Corti. Overall, as Tirabassi's essay demonstrates, women in Italy in 1880 and 1900 were actually more likely to work for wages than were women in the United States, and most earned wages in agriculture; unlike many northern European countries, furthermore, Italy's rates of female employment declined rather than increased with industrialization.

In Tirabassi's research, we see confirmed for most of Italy, outside central and western Sicily, the early observations of feminist historians Louise Tilly, Elizabeth Pleck, and Alice Kessler-Harris, who argued in the 1970s and 1980s that the worlds of work and family were not separate spheres – one public, one private – even in the industrialized world.[16] In making the same case for rural Italy, north and south, Tirabassi demonstrates that peasant women's lives did not neatly fall into private or public worlds and that the 'casalinga' (housewife) performed a wide-ranging array of work (including wage labour and fieldwork) that fell well outside middle-class understandings of female domesticity. Rural Italian women's domestic worlds were neither hermetically sealed prisons from which women escaped upon migration into wage earning and autonomy as individuals nor female-dominated havens of skilled household manager-housewives or 'mothers of civilization' – the Anglo-American bourgeois model for female power.

Peasant women were no rural 'angels of the house.' Their hard physical labour and their earthy and pragmatic notions of reciprocity between men and women shaped a female consciousness not yet excavated effectively by modern feminist analysis. Here, the research of Italian scholars – like that of Tirabassi, De Clementi, and Corti – deserves far more attention than it has received in English-speaking North America. Taken together, their essays show that in most of southern and northern Italy, peasants did not distinguish non-waged and wage-earning work or work 'in' or 'outside' the family: all work, whether performed by men or women, regardless of location, was 'for' the family and all – man, woman, or child – were expected to 'make sacrifices' for group well-being as needed. They also reveal how misleading it is to apply the term 'casalinga' (housewife) to a peasant woman working as a subsistence producer. A major finding of these essays is that wage-earning was not new for the women who left Italy. 'Home-based' peasant producers routinely joined seasonal harvest gangs or worked for periods on commercial estates, or as more skilled rural artisans (also 'home-based') such as tailoresses and embroidery sewers.

All the evidence included in this volume suggests that decisions about which family members would migrate and which remain at home reflected shrewd calculations about work opportunities – in both subsistence production and for wages – at home and abroad and for both men and women. At 60 to 80 per cent male, sex ratios in Italy's migrations between 1870 and 1914 fell between the heavily male-dominated migrations of indentured labourers from India and China (which were 90 per cent or more male) and the more gender-balanced migrations of refugees fleeing famines or pogroms in Ireland or Jewish Russia (which were roughly half female).[17] However justified by the raw numbers, studies that focus exclusively on Italy's male migrants have helped to generate wrong-headed generalizations, when not cruel caricatures, of the hardworking and shrewd women of Italy as passive dependants, or 'housewives,' waiting in idleness for remittances sent by emigrated men who 'provided' for women and children.

In fact, in many parts of Italy, men could migrate in large numbers only because women could feed their families themselves. Corti's description of northwestern Italy during the nineteenth century reveals a local alpine economy where peasant families had access to their own small pieces of land but had long been engaged in seasonal migration to provide much-needed cash. There, the field labours of older women freed both men and younger women to migrate. Men took seasonal jobs in construction or industry in neighbouring transalpine Europe (including Switzerland, France, and Germany). Younger women migrated either to textile mills in nearby cities such as Biella, Turin, and Milan, to the rice fields of the Po Valley, or to the urban kitchens, textile mills, or fields of nearby littoral France. In this setting, women were occasionally the pioneer migrants, outnumbering men, and they offered a wide range of occupational skills to neighbouring countries like France. Overall, however, women remained a relatively small proportion of emigrants from the northwest, and the majority of women in this region remained in Italy.

In Sicily, the focus of Reeder's work, fewer peasants controlled their own land, and men had effectively excluded women from wage-earning on the large landowners' commercial estates, but women also enjoyed more power over their own dowries and owned more property than in parts of Calabria. Because Sicilian women faced taboos against field-work, they could not easily feed their families when men departed. As a result, more residents of Sicily migrated as family groups and sex ratios among emigrants from Sicily were far more balanced than those from Piedmont or Calabria, the subject of De Clementi's essay.

In Calabria, emigration rates and emigrant sex ratios varied sharply with local customs of inheritance and land ownership, and with family cultures that encouraged particular forms of reciprocity linking men and women and parents and children in kin groups in several house-holds. De Clementi criticizes the ways in which earlier scholars, notably American political scientist Edward Banfield, treated Italy's south as 'the time that land forgot,' where pre-modern folk preferred superstition and family security to 'modernity' and the modern liberal state. Such studies, as De Clementi astutely observes, used the supposedly backward and primitive southern Italian women as a convenient 'foil' to northern European and American women allegedly released from the shackles of patriarchy by the dual progressive forces of capitalist economic develop-ment and liberal democracy. Rejecting this patronizing snapshot of rural society, and its overly positive view of proletarianized work in industrial settings, De Clementi stresses instead that both economic changes and state formation encouraged peasant families to renegotiate inheritance rules and their children's marriage contracts, encouraging temporary male emigration. As new inheritance rules and fiscal policies imposed by the Italian state pushed regions of customary subsistence-production (especially in arable southern scrub lands) further toward the market-place and especially toward the pursuit of cash income, migration pro-vided an infusion of money to revitalize traditional mechanisms of survival and reproduction. In turn, these new inheritance arrangements allowed daughters to get their economic share (in the form of a movable dowry) without making claims on the land or patrimony. For the majority, De Clementi concludes, peasant families saw America as a resource that could shore up their subsistence-oriented way of life. But migration also altered young men's attitudes toward parental authority and marriage, changing the very traditions – including gender roles and parent–child relations – it was intended to shore up. The returning migrants set off 'small earthquakes' of change in marriages and families, including, eventually, permanent migration of youthful nuclear family groups, mak-ing the lives of those who remained more like the lives of migrants who settled abroad as families.

De Clementi and Reeder provide little evidence that male emigration created opportunities for individualism among southern Italian women. While both note the stresses that prompted emigration and some of its more negative consequences for women – including significantly increased agricultural responsibilities – they also emphasize the importance of continued solidarity between husbands and wives, and what De Clementi calls the 'avalanche' of remittances sent home to wives for safekeeping or investment in land and housing. A dependent wife whose purchases of food or extravagances endangered investment in the family's future would have enjoyed little respect in such communities.

Reeder offers an even more positive assessment of male emigration for wives left behind in Sutera, Sicily. While emigration certainly produced casualties (such as women whose bigamist husbands never returned or called them over), the majority of Sutera's white widows did not sink into poverty, sexual depravity, or madness (as bourgeois moral critics feared). With no access to credit, women managed to finance a husband's migration by turning to kin and neighbours for loans or they sold their dowries. Some women also acted as informal moneylenders. While men from Sutera toiled in American coal mines and cities, argues Reeder, women tried to acquire the economic, social, and cultural accoutrements associated with the local elite – two-storey houses, land, small businesses, and literacy – by managing the family's savings and interests. The general direction of change in the lives of women who emigrated and those who remained in Italy thus seemed remarkably similar. Reeder argues that both acquired more education, higher material standards of living, and some of the pleasures of participating in a modern, consumer economy. Whether or not one agrees with Reeder's argument that female entrepreneurship was a path into the rural middle classes, rising rates of female literacy certainly had far-reaching consequences. So did Sicilian women's entry into the consumer market, as purchasers of iron beds and the latest gadgets bought through catalogues.

Women, then, did much more than wait when men emigrated. In many areas, they fed themselves and their children so that the cash earnings of emigrated men could be used to purchase the land or housing that promised to shore up a changing way of life. In Sicily, where work options were particularly limited, women pursued a strategy often chosen by immigrants facing racial prejudice in foreign job markets – they turned to entrepreneurship, if only on a petty level. Collectively, our contributors suggest that the mobile, male 'workers of the world' – who seemed the ultimate proletarians to observers such as Marx – were in fact still firmly moored in subsistence and artisanal modes of production. Migration encouraged the feminization but also the survival of subsistence production in Italy; it limited the impact of economic globalization and its social consequences, which have been summarized (for men) as 'proletarianization' and (for women) as 'emancipation.'

Culture and Economy: Women Were Labour Migrants Too

Just as the essays focused on Italy strongly suggest the need to move beyond conventional portraits of rural women's work and domesticity in Italy, the essays in part II help readers to sort out the influence of culture and economic opportunity on women's work as they began to leave Italy. Most research on the employment of Italian immigrant women in North America has rightly focused on industrial work. Part II of our collection instead recovers small and important, if hitherto unnoticed, streams of female labour migrants (as in Corti's study of late-nineteenth-century migrations from Piedmont to southern France) and the active lives of immigrant businesswomen and professional midwives (as Vecchio does for Wisconsin). We do not ignore women as industrial workers, of course. Readers interested in the topic will find that Anne Morelli's contribution to part III and Roslyn Pesman's contribution to part IV advance scholarship on women's industrial employment by analysing the years after the First World War, and by focusing on Italian immigrant women working in Belgium and Australia.

As Nancy Green would have predicted, comparing Italian women's work in many locations sheds new light on issues dominating the historiography on Italian immigrant women in the United States. That historiography describes Italian immigrant women's reluctance to work for wages outside their families (especially compared to Jewish women), notes in particular their almost total rejection of work as domestic servants in the kitchens and homes of middle-class, Anglo-American women, and attributes both patterns to the moral conservatism discussed above. In sharp contrast to those in the United States, however, Italian women in Italy, France, and Latin America worked in large numbers as domestic servants; there, domestic service typically followed agriculture or industry as the largest employer of Italian women. Corti's essay on the Italian-French border, with its mention of Piedmont's migrating servants and wet nurses, confirms the earlier arguments of Louise Tilly that single, rural Italian women frequently migrated relatively short distances from countryside to city in order to take jobs as domestics.[18] As Latin American specialists such as Carina Silberstein, an early project participant, have documented, Italian women in Argentina also generally accounted for a large group of urban laundresses in this period. Canada even recruited Italian women as domestic servants in the years following the Second World War; government schemes met with limited success, but some Italian immigrant women became lifetime (live-out) domestic workers.[19]

Analyses of the millions of Irish and Scandinavian domestic servants who migrated to the United States as young, single women have suggested that their preference for domestic service reflected a desire for female autonomy and a step toward emancipation that Latin patriarchy precluded for Italian women.[20] Rather than see Italian women's avoidance of domestic service in the United States as a 'missed opportunity,' our contributors suggest that women from Italy were more often motivated to migrate by the higher wages available in industry.[21] Only then could families transplanted to a high-cost consumer economy like that of the United States be sure of the multiple incomes required to replace the contributions of women's unpaid subsistence production in Italy. It continues to strike us as a peculiarity of Anglo-American thought to regard domestic service – rather than waged industrial work – as a foundation for immigrant women's autonomy or emancipation. Certainly in Italy's overwhelmingly urban culture – where even in Sicily peasants lived in 'villages' of thousands of residents – craft and industrial production were widely regarded as more appropriate work for women than agriculture. And in all of Italy the artisan – whether male or female – enjoyed a higher status than the peasant or domestic servant because they worked under 'civilized' and autonomous conditions – that is, in town, controlling their own labour rather than in the fields or kitchen, submitting to a 'boss.' Essays by Tirabassi, Corti, Vecchio, and (in part III) Jennifer Guglielmo show that Italians universally respected the lady tailor (sartina) and a few other skilled female trades, including midwifery.

Still, opportunities for women to work in industry varied considerably from place to place worldwide, as they did also in Italy. Demand for labour in world markets of the nineteenth century was as sex-specific as it had been centuries before, when European landowners' preferences had generated male majorities in the African slave trade even though the agricultural workers of western Africa had been largely female. Italian women found few work options at the construction sites that employed the largest groups of male 'birds of passage' from Italy to Europe and the Americas in the nineteenth century. Nor did mining towns in the Lorraine of France or the Ruhr of Germany or the steel-

and metal-working cities of the United States lure women with jobs. In Marseilles, Buenos Aires, New York, and Montreal, by contrast, textile mills, canneries, and garment shops provided female wages high enough to draw women out of transnational family economies initially based on the somewhat different, but solid, financial expectation of men earning where wages were high (abroad) in order to spend where prices were low (in Italy). Thus, during the mass emigrations of the late nineteenth and early twentieth centuries, Italy's women left home mainly when they could find work in the most modern, industrializing sector of the world economy. Work in the garment industry, in particular, gave even women with limited skills claims to the respected title of 'sarta.' Waged work in garment, textile, and cigar factories was the single most important occupational 'niche' for Italian immigrant women in North and South America and Europe.[22] Yet as part IV also shows, while some saw this waged work as increasing both the financial well-being of their families and their own autonomy (for example, to choose their own husbands), others viewed it instead as wage slavery, destroying the autonomy that peasant workers enjoyed and shackling them instead to 'bosses' and 'machines.'

Corti's essay reveals the wide range of employments – in French agriculture, domestic service, and industry – that transformed women from Piedmont from subsistence workers in family enterprises to individual labour migrants. Through painstaking data analysis and demographic reconstruction made possible by an international collaboration of French and Italian scholars working on borderland migrations, Corti maps an especially interesting – because unusual, if not unique – migration stream of skilled, labouring women from the northwestern Italian province of Cuneo in Piedmont to the French Department of the Maritime Alps in France. Never random movements, these female labour migrations – like men's – involved networks of personal and family relationship with mediators – 'bosses' acting as conduits of information and recruiters of labour. Corti's case study of Grasse, an industrializing city in the predominantly agricultural region of Nice, shows that female immigration (a good deal of it from Piedmont) was large enough already in 1861 to be recorded officially. Corti examines the large female presence, particularly of young single women (who often travelled with sisters or other female or male kin) among the streams of agricultural wage workers who took on seasonal jobs in the countryside near Grasse. She introduces also Grasse's immigrant urban working women, who toiled in a wide range of occupations, including as domestics and manual labourers, cooks, seamstresses, hotel workers, and gardeners. In addition, there was an important cluster of female silk spinners – sojourners – who travelled to Grasse and neighbouring villages and valleys to spin linen and hemp or to take jobs in textile workshops.

Over the course of the nineteenth century, a migration of female silk workers developed in response to the changing economic situation of the border region Corti studied. The emerging manufacturing regions on the French side of the border drew highly skilled female workers from Italian areas of declining proto-industrial production seeking more secure work and wages. Their migrations provoked predictable debates about the dangers of female emigration and the evils of French 'sweat-shops.' Corti describes a migration organized not only by the parents (who received the girls' wages) but also through a system of female 'labour bosses.' These contractors recruited women, acted as mediators between parents and employer and otherwise created female links in these all-female migration chains. The role and status of this female figure – called 'maestra' (the female equivalent of maestro, master, or teacher) – is indeed intriguing, and her presence invites comparisons with the double-edged function of the male 'padrone' (who was often despised but needed by male workers who paid him deference and cash). Corti's findings should also prompt further research on what she calls 'a strongly hierarchical female world stratified according to age and by domestic or family status and clearly bounded by education and skill.' In highlighting the beneficial consequence of skilled female migration for the women themselves, including higher rates of literacy and educa-tion, Corti's female silk spinners and Reeder's 'white widows' are more similar than their differing conditions of life would ordinarily suggest.

Vecchio turns her gendered lens to the better known and more intensely studied Italian immigrants in the United States, focusing in particular on Milwaukee, Wisconsin, a town that offered relatively limited opportunities for women to work in industry. Vecchio's study of immigrant businesswomen builds on Reeder's discovery of entrepre-neurship as a common response of Sicilian women to limited opportuni-ties for wage-earning. Her concern, however, is to explore how gender roles and domestic values shaped the work opportunities and lives of Milwaukee's many Italian female greengrocers, restaurateurs, and dry-goods store owners and to compare them to professionally trained mid-wives who serviced the women in the Italian immigrant communities of Milwaukee and surrounding areas. While acknowledging that both groups provided services necessary to first-generation Italians living within their ethnic enclave, Vecchio ultimately stresses differences between entrepreneurs and professional midwives in their educational backgrounds, routes of entry into work, and commitments to domesticity. According to Vecchio, the work histories of the Italian businesswomen she unearthed, particularly those who operated home-based enterprises, were very influenced by women's domestic responsibilities. By contrast, the small group of Italian midwives, most of whom had attained professional training in Italy and saw themselves as transplanted professionals, sometimes put work above family expectations. Businesswomen were shrewd, and often combined child-minding (in some cases with grandchildren) with store-keeping at home, and they found ways to pass on their entreprises to daughters and in some cases sons. But the professionally trained Italian midwives, suggests Vecchio, were pioneer 'career women' who brought to the United States a professional ethos that could on occasion override family needs. As individuals, the midwives Vecchio describes shared a willingness to challenge tradition along with the militant women and collective activism among industrial workers introduced in part IV.

In the twentieth century, as the global economy evolved, wage-earning options for women in industry expanded. This was especially true outside Italy (where, to repeat, women's representation in the waged workforce was declining with industrialization). Thus, after 1914, gender ratios among Italy's emigrants, even to Europe, became modestly more balanced (60 to 70 per cent male). According to Pesman, Australia actively recruited migrants from Italy as settlers in family groups, but nevertheless recognized and perhaps even expected that both women and men would work for wages. Fearing the sexual menace and potential disorderliness of unattached men, Australia's rulers apparently hoped that family migration could guarantee a permanent supply of European industrial workers as the immigrants had children in Australia. By contrast, Belgium after the Second World War, as described by Morelli, specifically negotiated for male 'guest workers,' expecting most men to return home again; because Belgian policy also allowed the guest workers to arrange for the migration of wives and children under specific circumstances, permanent settlement soon occurred. And as women migrated, they flocked into Belgium's labour-starved 'light' industries, extending the niche of Italian immigrant women as industrial workers into the postwar era. Unsurprisingly, then, Italian women's migration usually meant a relatively swift and almost universal move from subsistence production into industrial employment and petty enterprise – experiences that also shaped their distinctive histories as emerging labour militants at home and abroad.

Foreign and Dangerous Women

Part III introduces the many female militants that we discovered world-wide, with essays on Argentina, Belgium, and the United States. Here, our comparative method significantly revises a historiography on Italian immigrant women in the United States that compares their relative passivity to the feisty political and labour-movement activism of their Jewish immigrant counterparts and attributes Italian women's behaviour to their rural backgrounds, familism, and Latin or Catholic moral conservatism.[23] At the same time, the essays remind readers that for women from Italy, as for many others in the Latin world, women's struggles for power and influence were collective ones, and often – although not always – 'maternalist.' Such struggles linked improvements in women's well-being to improvements for their families and entire communities; theirs were not battles for autonomous individualism, as Anglo-American feminists were more likely to understand women's liberty.[24]

For almost half a century, scholarship on Italian immigrant workers in the United States, both male and female, has remained to a considerable degree under the lockhold of American political scientist Edward Banfield's analysis of southern Italian culture as familist and amoral. (The observation also applies to the Canadian literature, which reveals many U.S. influences in approach and method.) Banfield explicitly argued that southern Italians, as 'amoral familists,' were concerned only with the interests of their own nuclear families and thus hostile to collective action and ideology of all kinds. As a result, they were also incapable of shouldering the civic responsibilities of modern, liberal democracy. An American academic, Banfield spent a single year in southern Italy where – having never written previously about Italian culture – he developed his repeatedly dismissed but never completely demolished concept of the region's amoral familism. Revealing the worst excesses of Western imperialist ethnography, Banfield erroneously attributed both the region's economic stagnation and the material conditions of class exploitation and oppression to a devastating regional 'culture of poverty.'[25] Even in the 1990s, Banfield's work provided the foundation for analyses that attributed the peculiarities of Italian civil life and politics to the cultural distinctiveness – and incapacities – of its south.[26]

Feminist historians in the United States have given Banfield's concept of familism a more positive twist by insisting on its conservative morality. But ultimately their portraits of passive Italian immigrant workers reflect more their choices of research methods and topics than any obeisance to Banfield.[27] Most conclusions about Italian immigrant women's passivity as workers emerged from studies of early garment workers' strikes orchestrated by the Jewish women who dominated the rank and file in garment shops and unions, including the International Ladies Garment Workers' Union (ILGWU) in the first decade of the twentieth century.[28] Indeed, the history of New York City female garment workers in this period remains almost exclusively focused on the first major garment strike in the city, the famous 1909 'Uprising of 20,000.' During this strike Jewish women workers responded to the reluctance of the male leaders of the ILGWU to support them by aligning themselves with middle-class progressives and feminist activists in the Women's Trade Union League (WTUL).[29] Scholars were quick to assert that Italian women were unorganized and unsympathetic to the union movement because only 6 per cent (approximately 2000) of the strikers were Italian women at a time when they constituted almost 34 per cent of the shirtwaist-industry labour force.[30]

Given the limited chronological and geographic range of this historiography, it is perhaps not so surprising that our contributors discovered so many female immigrant Italian militants. For twenty years, historians of Italian men have substituted a more nuanced portrait of labour militancy among southern Italian peasants, revealing 'familists' who were perfectly capable of collective action and even class consciousness.[31] In the first years of the twentieth century, however, Italian immigrant men in the United States were active mainly outside the mainstream of the American labour movement and more often in the radical Industrial Workers of the World (IWW) than in the American Federation of Labor (AFL, of which the ILGWU was an affiliated union). Italian immigrant men at that time were still most often anarchists, syndicalists, and revolutionaries, not labour reformers or democratic socialists – strategies that held more appeal for Jewish immigrants. Even in the United States, we know the same was true of the few Italian women radicals to appear in the existing scholarship – such as the bohemian, photographer, and international communist activist Tina Modotti in the United States, Mexico, and Europe, and the anarchist Gabriella (Ella) Antolini in the United States.[32] The essays in part III easily demonstrate that Italy's female militants could be found everywhere Italians migrated, but that they – like Italian men – more easily found common ground with other workers in labour movements shaped by anarchist, syndicalist or, later, communist ideals, not those of central European and German social democracy or Anglo-American labour reform.

Although arranged chronologically, part III begins and ends with studies of Italian women outside the United States. Moya's pioneering work on Argentine cities and Morelli's sweeping survey of militants across twentieth-century Belgium offer excellent case studies against which to evaluate the North American paradigms of Italian women workers as docile, fearful, or submissive. Their work complements Samuel Baily's early comparative work on Italians in the labour movements of Argentina and Brazil and French research that traces the leadership roles of Italians in the emerging labour movements of turn-of-the-century France. In these countries – unlike the United States, Canada, and Australia – Italians played leading roles in creating national labour movements and encouraging internationalist models of proletarian mobilization. It would have been surprising had no women worked among them.[33]

As Moya notes, Italian women's radicalism in turn-of-the-century Argentina needs to be understood against the backdrop of distinctive migration patterns and of Italian leadership in workers' movements, in particular a thriving anarchist movement that – following Errico Malatesta – embraced rather than rejected labour organization. Moya documents women's impressive presence within this anarchist movement as rank-and-file community activists, as compelling orators before large crowds, as writers of political pamphlets, and as organizers of schools, libraries, theatre troupes, reading groups, labour unions, strikes, and boycotts. Moya offers a sensitive, multilayered, and nuanced analysis of the appeal of anarchists' messages of human liberation. These differed considerably from those of liberal, Anglo-American feminists in their critique of both marriage and wage slavery, in an equal-rights philosophy that stressed personal liberty and dignity and economic independence, in an emphasis on mutuality, solidarity, and 'sociability,' and in an 'insistence in linking the public and the personal, in identifying economic and cultural forms of oppression.' Italian anarchist understandings of liberation apparently allowed women to act 'politically' in the sites – the factory, street, storefront, and home – and in the relationships – to bakers, butchers, and landlords and to husbands and fathers – that mattered most to them.

Morelli shifts our attention to Belgium later in the century, and to the Italian migrations that bracketed the Second World War. Her focus is on communist immigrant women, their work, and their complex relations to their husbands and male comrades. Through a series of intriguing portraits of Italian women who juggled the myriad duties of wife, mother, worker, political ally, and activist, Morelli explores the overlapping but

sometimes also contradictory pressures for foreign females simultaneously fighting capitalist injustice and patriarchal oppression. Her portraits explore seemingly paradoxical links among work, family, and
community ties and the complicated gender politics that marked relations between men and women who were partners both politically and
personally. By exploring the lives both of women who were already
political activists before leaving Italy and of those who became radicalized
in Belgium, Morelli asks readers to rethink the traditionalism supposedly implicit in women's responsibility for leftist 'welfare work.' She also
reminds us that activism motivated by family solidarity did not inevitably
render women submissive to men, and that it transformed communist
organizing among workers in Catholic countries like Belgium and Italy.[34]
Her female subjects often ignored men's commands – whether to join
the party or to stay at home – in order to find their own path to power as
migrants, women, workers, and party activists.

In focusing on women's activism, Moya and Morelli develop new
themes for the national historiographies of Argentina and Belgium,
where labour activism among immigrant women has scarcely been explored. Three essays that focus mainly on the United States (by Caroline
Waldron Merithew, Jennifer Guglielmo, and Robert Ventresca and Franca
Iacovetta) instead tackle portraits of female passivity in an already
influential historiography. Merithew's study of anarchist women in
Illinois and Ventresca and Iacovetta's biography of the anarchist
D'Andrea also provide evidence of transnational linkages among anarchist women on several continents. Both essays underscore the appeal
to women of anarchists' collectivist theories of human liberation while
uncovering the diversity of women's opinions on free love, marriage,
and motherhood.

In her illuminating case study of Italian- and French-speaking immigrant women from Italy, Belgium, and France, Merithew broadens
our knowledge of a distinctive form of immigrant female anarchism
that until now has been defined largely through the biography of
Emma Goldman. While a small minority of Italian anarchist women
shared Goldman's brand of anarcho-feminism and the majority respected
Goldman and denounced as patriarchal and capitalist the legal and
religious rules of marriage, most nevertheless articulated a form of
maternalist radicalism that Merithew aptly calls 'anarchist motherhood.'
Immigrant anarchist mothers formed broad-based alliances within late-
nineteenth and early-twentieth-century Illinois's multi-ethnic coal communities and they sought to sustain the revolution through the next

generation by teaching their children a revolutionary ideology that reflected both their local circumstances and their internationalist commitments. Merithew's work helps us to see that women's activism in mining communities was not limited to supporting male strikers. She explores the feminist practice of housewives and daughters in mining and industrial communities who fought back on the streets, taunting police and strike-breakers, and becoming – what contemporaries called immigrant women radicals of the striking community of textile workers in Lawrence, Massachusetts – 'radicals of the worst sort.'[35]

Ventresca and Iacovetta's biography of Virgilia D'Andrea reminds us that women, too, could be political exiles, living and working in small but often influential and usually beleaguered communities of anarchists, socialists, communists, and anti-Fascists, often fleeing from country to country, especially in the interwar years when Mussolini's dictatorship drove his enemies abroad. Like the women in Moya's and Merithew's essays, D'Andrea was a committed anarchist, inspired in her youth by the ageing Malatesta. The transnational dimensions of D'Andrea's life as exile and intellectual are particularly obvious, as is her role in connecting the worlds of ideology and politics on two continents. Although clearly deeply sympathetic to the immigrant workers among whom she worked, D'Andrea's life seems less rooted than theirs in a geographically-based community. At the same time, D'Andrea's political profile, poetry, propaganda work, chronic ill health, and deep-seated homesickness raise important questions about the politics of free love and about how male allies viewed their female comrades. In a different way from Merithew's 'anarchist mothers,' D'Andrea's life makes a fascinating contrast to the iconic Emma Goldman. It should also encourage scholars to explore the still-neglected role of poetry, literary traditions, and cultural nationalism in the history of Italian radical politics around the globe. D'Andrea's short but complex life is best understood, the authors conclude, not as a series of contradictions but instead as a reflection of the transnational life of a radical exile rooted in attachments to Italian internationalist ideologies and to a beloved 'homeplace.'

Guglielmo's work on Italian female activists in New York City's garment industry from the 1890s to the 1940s is the most direct challenge in our collection to U.S. historiography. Although her research could scarcely have been undertaken without the ground-breaking and truly important work of earlier feminist labour historians, Guglielmo moves beyond static portraits of Italian immigrant women as reluctant activists that are based only on the 1909 New York shirtwaist-makers' strike. Guglielmo suggests it was the tension between the Industrial Workers of the World (IWW) – with its many Italian leaders – and the more conservative AFL and its socialist-dominated garment workers' unions that provides the best explanation for Italian women's behaviour in that strike. Moreover, her essay reminds us of other contemporaneous strikes in which Italian women were present, active, and even leaders. Her perceptive analysis of 'one of the most explosive labour uprisings of the era' – the 1913 garment strike in which striking workers abandoned the International Ladies Garment Workers' Union (ILGWU) for the more militant IWW and staged a women's 'riot' – is especially important. It suggests that Italian women's activism differed in form and locus, not intensity, from that of Russian and eastern European Jewish women.

Paying close attention to the evolution of female immigrant activism over time, Guglielmo's work shows that Italian-American female militancy changed over the course of the twentieth century, but remained nurtured by ethnic loyalties and networks of family and community. Like Moya, Merithew, Morelli, and Principe, Guglielmo profiles a multi-generational array of fascinating female militants living in the middle of a deeply felt ethnic, left-wing culture. In describing how immigrant mothers passed on a radical heritage and a repertoire of strategies to their daughters, Guglielmo shows us the radical implications of female bonds of solidarity and the importance of kitchens and neighbourhoods in reproducing a radical culture and its ideals. Like their Russian, Lithuanian, Polish, German, Greek, Irish, and Spanish counterparts, Italian women who became labour organizers endured ridicule, arrest, and even violence at the hands of police and employers. Guglielmo's research also hints at the ethnic and racial divisions that have marked the twentieth-century history of the garment workers' unions. Rooted in family and community ties, and in struggle with the Yiddish-speaking Jewish immigrants who initially dominated the ILGWU, Italian women's activism developed in part as a movement for Italian ethnic autonomy. The stance later made immigrant workers and their children complicit in the exclusion of the next generation of Puerto Rican and African-American garment workers. Guglielmo thus begins to tackle, and to make gender-specific, the challenge raised by recent race-studies theorists and by labour historians interested in whiteness as a socially constructed identity.[36]

Analyses of radical women's lives reveal the value of viewing female militants as gendered subjects and exploring gender politics and practice on the left. The papers by Moya, Morelli, and Ventresca and Iacovetta all illuminate an apparent paradox. Because women were considered less threatening, they could often carry out their subversive activities while men, who were usually accorded more notorious reputations and thus subjected to more serious surveillance, were for long periods imprisoned and/or under house arrest. (As with other recent scholarship, we also see in these essays the importance of records generated by police, surveillance, and intelligence workers for reconstructing radical history.)[37] All the essays of this section show that individual women might achieve notoriety in their own right but that they typically became radicals and practised their radicalism as members of families. Central to their identity as daughters, wives, and mothers was their location in and sense of belonging to a family and to communities of subversives. Rather than reject familism as an influence on the lives of Italian women, then, these essays change our understanding of what familism means and revise our understanding of its consequences for collective action.

As We See Ourselves, As Others See Us

However important and complex their linkages, family, work, and struggle were only three elements from which women crafted identities for themselves in Italy and with which they redefined those identities as they migrated to other countries around the world. As Tirabassi's essay in part I suggested, international migration seems to have opened opportunities for dramatic debates over women's sexuality on both sides of the Atlantic. As the story of Nestore's wife reminds readers too, women workers were often simultaneously communists and Catholics, activists and mothers, rebellious and accommodating family members. And, as Guglielmo's essay emphasizes, the development of class consciousness in the United States could not easily be separated from immigrant women's emerging ethnic identities – as hyphenated 'Italian-Americans' – and racial identities – as whites. Furthermore, regardless of where women lived in the twentieth century, nation-states in an era of recurring total warfare on a global scale demanded allegiance and loyalty to the nation from women, even when those women did not enjoy full rights of citizenship.

Given the complexity of women's lives, is there any way to understand how some elements of female experience became more central than others in the evolution of women's identities in one country or another? Why, for example, did familism, Catholicism, and the reproduction of the ethnic group come so largely to define the identities of immigrant women in North America, while class consciousness, political ideology, and a new national identity as Belgian seem more important to women like Nestore's wife? We end our collection with two essays that should help to focus readers' attention on issues related to identity formation – in Canada before the Second World War and in Australia after the war's end. Read in conjunction with earlier essays, they point to the considerable power of national states, national cultures, and national elites – sometimes including feminist scholars – in selecting the elements that become salient in outsiders' views of peasant, immigrant, and working-class women. In turn, and to a considerable extent, immigrant women have found themselves constrained to develop identities in struggle against national discourses that negate key elements of their day-to-day lives. Future research on immigrant women workers, these essays suggest, ignore the nation and national differences in the construction of women's identities only at great cost.

More than any other author in our collection, Angelo Principe attempts to convey the full complexity of immigrant women's lives in Canada in the first half of the century, placing in wider perspective the accounts of the small but important radical minority of women explored in part III. The women Principe describes were workers as well as members of families, communities, and churches; most were working-class, some were upwardly mobile, a few were quite prosperous. There were militants among Canada's immigrant women but, unsurprisingly, the militants were a small minority. In addition – and of critical importance for his analysis – the immigrant women of Canada sympathized with both Fascists and anti-Fascists.

The Fascist era appears to have been critically important in the formation of immigrant women's identities in Canada, as it was also in the lives of the minority of militant women described by Morelli for Belgium and by Ventresca and Iacovetta for the United States. Given the differing character of working-class movements of the Anglo-American and French worlds it is scarcely surprising that Fascists enjoyed more influence over identity-formation in Canada (and also in the United States) than they did in Belgium, where vigorous anti-Fascism characterized the multiethnic Belgian labour movement. The consequences for women immigrants of these struggles seem to have been very significant indeed. While both Fascists and anti-Fascists in Canada created new arenas of activism for women, Fascist notions of womanhood differed sharply from anti-Fascist ones. Fascists abandoned the earlier national discourse on the immorality of peasant women to instead praise the plebeian woman as mother and reproducer of the nation – contrasting her healthy, rural, and prolific motherhood to the celibacy and limited fertility of nervous, emancipated, urban, wage-earning women.

Principe's essay suggests that while models for female ethnic and national identity were sharply contested in Canada, those contests occurred largely within an Italian-speaking community. Women from Italy did not seem to draw too directly on models of womanhood from the larger Anglo-Celtic or French worlds of native-born Canadians. A woman like Grace Bagnato – who by the 1930s had given birth to more than a dozen children – best illustrated the procreative role of women encouraged by the pro-natalist Fascists, especially once they had again – for the first time since Italy's unification – made the Roman Catholic church the state religion of Italy. Anti-Fascist proletarian leftists like Cazzola, 'the mother of Italian-Canadian anti-Fascism,' offered an alternative, indeed defiant, model of motherhood that Virgilia D'Andrea or the anarchist maternalists of Illinois mining communities might have praised. Principe's discussion of women's political lives during the interwar decades reminds us that battles between radicals and Fascists were also battles over female national and – in the Canadian context – ethnic identity.

Along with Ventresca and Iacovetta's analysis of D'Andrea's cultural nationalism, Principe's work carries abroad to Canada into the interwar years Reeder's suggestive comments on the development of national identities among Sicily's white widows. In differing ways, both provide examples of what Victoria De Grazia has termed the 'nationalization' of Italian women – a transformation that Fascism hastened and intensified wherever Italians had settled around the world. But whereas in Italy it was the nation of Fascist Italians that claimed women's reproductive capacities as mothers of 'the Italian race,' in Canada it was the ethnic group – 'Italo-Canadians' – that women were to reproduce by devoting themselves to their families and homes.[38] Raising questions about reproduction, gender, and the politics of nation-making, Principe's work should encourage future researchers to take seriously the multidisciplinary, literature on nationalism, post-colonialism, and subaltern peoples originating in the work of Benedict Anderson, Edward Said, and Gayatri Spivak.[39]

Pesman's study of postwar Australia also focuses on the power of nations and national states in the formation of identities among migratory women. Far more than Principe, however, Pesman emphasizes instead the considerable power of the receiving country to define the identities of newcomer women. Pesman writes of the years after the

Second World War, as emigration from Italy again rose, and as Italians were forced to seek new destinations in a world of harsh immigration restrictions in countries such as the United States. (In fact more Italians went to Canada and Australia than to the United States after the war. And by far the largest number of Italy's emigrants in those years were men 'guest workers' in other European countries such as France, Germany, Switzerland, and Belgium.) By war's end the power of national states had arguably reached its twentieth-century peak. In the Western democracies, national campaigns against economic depression and military campaigns against Fascism had strengthened the bond between 'welfare' and 'warfare' governments and their citizens. In this context, the receiving nation was in a strong position to impose its own understandings on the identities of newcomers, women among them, from a nation so recently defeated in the worldwide wars against Fascism.

Pesman's study shows how the economic needs of their nation shaped Anglo-Celtic Australians' views of women from the Mediterranean. Encouraged by government-assisted passages and other incentives, family migration to Australia was significant, as it also was to Canada during these years. Like their Canadian counterparts, post-1945 Italian and other foreign-born immigrant women, including married women and mothers, joined the Australian paid labour force in large numbers.[40] Yet unlike the emerging ethnic discourse on womanhood in Canada (or the United States) in the interwar years – with its focus on women's devotion to family and home – Australians instead positioned women from Italy as industrial wage workers and as the largest single component in a collective group called the 'non-English-speakers.' Here, readers will also want to compare the very differing dynamic of identity-construction in Belgium, where immigrants from Italy were also regarded as essential contributors to the revival of the Belgian national economy. The difference lies in the fact that Belgians seemed little concerned about the language or politics of the new immigrants; having cooperated with Italian immigrants in a multi-ethnic movement against Fascism in the interwar years, they obviously expected not only wage-earning but labour activism from the new female arrivals.

Pesman is particularly adept at revealing the role of scholarship, and especially sociology, in constructing the identity of Italian women in Australia. She notes, for instance, the importance of contemporary Australian politics and the (not entirely unproblematic) shift, under the influence of second-wave feminism, to write women-centred histories of immigrants. Pesman explores the gap between representations (by feminists and others) of Italian immigrant workers and their social experiences, and she demonstrates the tensions emerging between the English-speaking second-generation daughters of Italians and the Anglo-Celtic scholars who still often serve as their historians. While Australian scholars continue to view 'non-English-speaking women' and their daughters as victims of patriarchy and capitalism, second-generation women continue to think of themselves as foreign but also as active – as females who fight (or at least talk back to) those who attempt to interpret them. Complex issues related to cultural preferences for individualism or group solidarity and to the impossibility of measuring patriarchy or female autonomy cross-culturally are obvious in these debates, as they are also in the sometimes-troubled dialogue of 'rich world' and 'third world' feminists.[41]

By introducing historical perspectives and methodologies to an Australian literature dominated by social scientists, Pesman – like many of our contributors – focuses on a critical distinction. On the one hand, she recognizes and understands the central role that family loyalties and finances played in Italian women's identities and work lives. On the other, she avoids falling into the trap of either writing a non-gendered family history that obscures women's roles and lives while celebrating them (as do some male migration historians) or of viewing women as oppressed by a false collective consciousness that negates individual identity for women. Women from Italy – indeed many women of peasant, working-class, and Latin background – define their individual identities, and the completeness of those identities, through the extent and intensity of their connections to others, not through independence from such connections.

Pesman's focus on the role of scholars and feminists in creating immigrant women's identities may very well have its counterpart in North America too. Our discussion of Tirabassi's essay in part I suggested that peasants, as immigrants to North America, initially responded to a national Italian discourse that stigmatized them as immoral. Their elaborate defences of their own moral propriety inevitably reproduced the terms of the critics they deplored, however, so that women sometimes insisted with considerable vehemence that they were indeed completely devoted to domestic work and children, under the surveillance of patriarchal fathers and husbands. In short, they represented themselves – to borrow Banfield's terms – as familists but not as amoral familists. In Canada, according to Angelo Principe, Fascists proved more effective than anti-Fascists in linking this defensive discourse to their own cause.

Four decades later, the new immigration history of the United States also understandably seized on these themes – readily found in immigrant oral histories and memoirs – without recognizing either their defensiveness or their transatlantic origins. In the new immigration history of the 1970s, Italian immigrants' cultural conservatism, familism, and respect for female domesticity imbued humble and impoverished, but defensive, migrants with modest resources, choices, and, not least of all, human dignity.[42] We believe the essays in this collection provide a firm foundation for historicizing these debates and contribute to the efforts of women of Italian descent to 'fight back' against discourses of womanhood that have obliterated many dimensions of their past and present lives.

Where Do We Go from Here?

Have we solved the complex riddle of identity formation among women from Italy as they migrated around the world? Of course not. Like any good collaborative project, this collection of essays answers many questions but raises even more. Thus, while we were pleasantly surprised by our collective discovery of so many activists, we cannot yet compare fully Italian women's activism across the globe. We need to know much more about individual biographies and the chronologies of strikes, organizing, and political action in Europe, Latin America, Canada, and Australia before the better-studied case of the United States can be interpreted from a truly global perspective. Only then can we conclude with any certainty how the foundations of and restraints on women's activism differed from Italian men's, or whether it was the national context, as much as gender or ties of family and community solidarity, that explains variations in women's militancy around the world. Only then can we begin to understand why the descendants of the women we study here have such noticeably different identities, in which work and militancy also occupy such different places, in Australia, France, Italy, or Canada.

We should also note that certain aspects of our original research agenda remained unfulfilled, in part because questions of labour activism became so central to the collective enterprise. We need to know more about how women from Italy became consumers and what that did to the 'power of the purse' enjoyed by many women in peasant subsistence production. Indeed, the evolution of subsistence production on women's changing identities – 'from peasant to housewife' – is worth far more attention than our contributors were able to give it.

We would also encourage readers to contemplate further how women developed national identities during migration and began to function as citizens in the many nations where they lived. Recent studies typically show that migrants 'became Italians' while abroad, and that some receiving nations (through guest-work programs, for example) explicitly encouraged them to maintain that identity rather than to become full citizens in their new homes. Other receiving countries instead imagined themselves as 'nations of immigrants' (or 'nations of immigration') and fully expected immigrants to become citizens. In these countries too, immigrants adopted national identities but in widely differing ways, ranging from the hyphenated identities of the English-speaking world to the blended national identities of Brazil and Argentina, to the unitary and culturally homogeneous expectations of republican France. It is also unlikely that migrant women and men developed national identities in exactly similar fashion in any of these countries. Women's claim to citizenship was more often based on motherhood and on physical labour; they have rarely been soldiers, and in many parts of the world where Italians lived and worked (including Italy), women were not voters until after the Second World War. The full implications of gender differences for the creation of multi-ethnic nations around the world, not just the United States, surely deserve the kind of international scrutiny we have given other topics here.

We hope too that this volume encourages readers to rethink sexuality and pan-Mediterranean codes of honour, shame, and sexuality that link Catholic, Orthodox, and Islamic cultures. In debunking conventional notions of a deeply patriarchal Latin culture, we have sought to move beyond caricatured portrayals of sexually controlled and submissive women. But our analysis also raises a suggestion worth further exploration: namely, that fear of female sexuality in the Mediterranean reflected the assumption that women had strong sexual appetites and that, if left unsupervised, women naturally followed their sexual urges. Such an understanding of female sexuality was fundamentally at odds with that of Anglo-American culture, with its view, throughout much of the nineteenth and twentieth centuries, of passionless females. Analysis of sexuality in the formation of identities among Italian women strikes us as a very valuable project that can problematize Anglo-American assumptions in cross-cultural perspective. Comparative analysis could also help us to see what, if anything, is peculiarly Anglo-American about 'queer theory,' the historiography on sexuality, and the meaning of gender itself.

Finally, we believe that scholars of migration need to think carefully about how women in countries as diverse as Italy, Brazil and Argentina, France, Germany, Australia, Algeria and Tunisia, and the United States and Canada acquired racial identities. All these countries received significant numbers of migrants from Italy; all linked nation-building differently to race and also defined race differently, emphasizing sometimes colour, sometimes culture, and sometimes descent and biological reproduction as its foundations.[43] At present we can only outline the relationship between gender and the formation of racial identities for the United States, where hyphenated identities among immigrants' descendants and irrational notions of 'one drop' of 'black blood' defined a woman as white or non-white.

As the North American literature on 'whiteness' proliferates, the questions about the racial identities of immigrant women also expand.[44] Were Italian immigrant women also 'in-between' people, and if so where did their in-between racial status matter?[45] On the job? In their unions? In their interactions with social settlement workers? At school? In their own communities? Italian men may have been firmly 'white on arrival,' as Thomas Guglielmo has recently argued, for as European immigrants they could acquire citizenship and have immediate access to the full rights of citizenship. But the full rights and full obligations of citizenship remained closed to women and to racial minorities through much of the twentieth century, and American law continues to classify women as a distinctive category of citizen down to the present.[46]

Jennifer Guglielmo's work suggests that struggles within multi-ethnic unions and community organizations in places such as New York's East Harlem may hold the keys to the emergence of immigrant women's sense of themselves as white Americans. Earlier work on immigrant women suggests, somewhat differently, that it was in struggles with native-born American women, many of them feminists, over reproduction, sexual morality, and family roles and relations, more than work and citizenship, that immigrant women came to understand themselves as different from racial minorities. By 1900, white American women had already developed sharply differentiated understandings of their relationship to African-American and to foreign-born women. American women tended to see foreign women as the victims of their own men and of forms of foreign patriarchy more primitive and violent than those of white, Protestant America. They saw immigrant women as exploited, overworked drudges for the men of their group. They saw them in need of help, protection, and uplift from their modern, white, better-educated American sisters, the female professionals then just emerging and – to a considerable extent – defining liberal American feminism.

Their goal for immigrant women was not emancipation but American domesticity. Nowhere in their panoply of racialized images of the foreign-born woman was the equivalent of the African-American Jezebel, the mouthy woman, the powerful African-American matriarch, who stood as partner, or worse, dominator of her man, her family, and her community, or the Black woman who enjoyed her own sexuality and pursued pleasure within the constraints of American racism.[47]

Yet readers who have fully digested the essays in this collection will have encountered many such feisty, powerful, openly sexual women in the transnational circuits created by Italy's millions of migrants. They will have seen such women living, talking, and fighting in Italian communities around the world. They will also have found some clues, at least, to how these dimensions of female experience were excised both from women's identities and from the historiography on Italian immigrant women in North America. In short, scholars and feminists have been active participants in constructing ethnic and racial identities for newcomers – something that we, as scholars, must continue to ponder in assessing our own work. We must also consider the importance of national forms of scholarship and politics, including feminist politics, in guaranteeing that the identities of Italian immigrant women in North America differ from those of their sisters, mothers, and nieces in Italy, Europe, and Argentina. In the same spirit in which our contributors entice readers to rethink and re-theorize the many connections and networks that shape Italian women workers' lives around the world, we invite interested readers, in closing, to join our collaborative initiative with their own new research.

NOTES

1 These women appear, in order, in essays in this volume by José Moya, Caroline Waldron Merithew, Robert Ventresca and Franca Iacovetta, Jennifer Guglielmo, Angelo Principe, and Anne Morelli.

2 For a preliminary statement on the collaborative project, see Donna Gabaccia and Franca Iacovetta, 'Women, Work, and Protest in the Italian Diaspora: An International Research Agenda,' *Labour / Le Travail* 42 (Fall 1998): 161–81.

3 The image of the 'women who wait' comes from Caroline Brettell, *Men Who Migrate, Women Who Wait: Population History in a Portuguese Parish* (Princeton: Princeton University Press, 1986).

4 Our discussions of the North American literature on Italian immigrant

women refer to one or more of the following works: Virginia Yans-
McLaughlin, *Family and Community: Italian Immigrants in Buffalo, 1880–1930*
(Ithaca: Cornell University Press, 1977); Betty Boyd Caroli et al., eds., *The
Italian Immigrant Woman in North America* (Toronto: Multicultural History
Society of Ontario, 1978); Judith Smith, *Family Connections: A History of
Italian and Jewish Immigrant Lives in Providence, Rhode Island, 1900–1940*
(Albany: State University of New York Press, 1985); Elizabeth Ewen,
*Immigrant Women in the Land of Dollars: Life and Culture on the Lower East
Side, 1890–1924* (New York: Monthly Review Press, 1985); Kathie Kasaba-
Friedman, *Memories of Migration: Gender, Ethnicity, and Work in the Lives of
Jewish and Italian Women in New York, 1870–1924* (Albany: State University of
New York Press, 1996); Miriam Cohen, *Workshop to Office: Two Generations of
Italian Women in New York City, 1900–1950* (Ithaca: Cornell University Press,
1993); Gabaccia, 'Italian American Women: A Review Essay,' *Italian Ameri-
cana* 12, 1 (Fall/Winter 1993); Rose Laub Coser, Laura S. Anker, and
Andrew J. Perrin, *Women of Courage: Jewish and Italian Immigrant Women in
New York* (Westport, CT: Greenwood Press, 1999).

5 On these influences in the literature on Italians arriving in Canada before
the Second World War, see, e.g., the various Canadian essays in Caroli et al.,
The Italian Immigrant Woman in North America; John Zucchi, *Italians in To-
ronto: Development of a National Identity, 1875–1935* (Montreal: McGill-Queen's
University Press, 1988); and Franc Sturino, *Forging the Chain* (Toronto:
Multicultural History Society of Ontario, 1991).

6 Our calculations are based on Italian emigration statistics in Gianfausto
Rosoli, ed., *Un secolo di emigrazione italiana, 1876–1976* (Rome: Centro Studi
Emigrazione, 1978).

7 Arguments for 'transnational' analysis first emerged in anthropology. See
Nina Glick Schiller, Linda Basch, and Cristina Blanc-Szanton eds., *Towards a
Transnational Perspective on Migration: Race, Class, Ethnicity, and Nationalism
Reconsidered* (New York: New York Academy of Science, 1992). As we argue
in notes 8 and 9 below, historians of international migration used transnational methodology throughout the 1980s, but instead called it 'international,' 'comparative,' or 'Atlantic.' Other attempts at gendered global
analyses also appeared in the 1980s. See Joan Smith et al., *Households and the
World Economy* (Beverly Hills, CA: Sage Publications, 1984) and Joan Smith
et al., *Creating and Transforming Households: The Constraints of the World
Economy* (New York: Cambridge University Press, 1992). Even more attentive
to women are Sharon Stichter and Jane L. Parpart, *Women, Employment and
the Family in the International Division of Labour* (Philadelphia: Temple University Press, 1990); Joan Nash and Patrícia Fernández-Kelly, *Women, Men and*

the International Division of Labor (Albany: State University of New York Press, 1983); and Lourdes Benería, ed., *Women and Development: The Sexual Division of Labor in Rural Societies* (New York: Praeger, 1982).

8 Robert Foerster, *The Italian Emigration of Our Times* (New York: Arno Press, 1968, orig. pub. 1919); Ernesto Ragionieri, 'Italiani all'estero ed emigrazione di lavoratori italiani: Una tema di storia movimento operaio,' *Belfagor, Rassegna di Varia Umanità* 17, 6 (1962): 640–69. Beginning in the 1980s, first Italian and then English-speaking scholars adopted the insights of these path-breaking earlier studies. See, e.g., Bruno Bezza, *Gli italiani fuori d'Italia, Gli emigrati italiani nei movimenti operai dei paesi d'adozione 1880– 1940* (Milan: Franco Angeli, 1983); Dirk Hoerder, *Labor Migration in the Atlantic Economy: The European and North American Working Classes during the Period of Industrialization* (Westport, CT: Greenwood Press, 1985); and Gabaccia and Ottanelli, *Italian Workers of the World: Labor, Migration and the Making of Multi-ethnic States* (Urbana: University of Illinois Press, 2001).

9 The term diaspora seems to have been first applied to Italian migrants by George Pozzetta and Bruno Ramirez, eds., *The Italian Diaspora* (Toronto: Multicultural History Society of Ontario, 1990). We have also sometimes worked critically with the concept of diaspora: see Gabaccia and Ottanelli, 'Diaspora or International Proletariat? Italian Labor Migration and the Making of Multi-ethnic States, 1815–1939,' *Diaspora* 6, 1 (Spring 1997): 61– 84; Gabaccia and Iacovetta, 'Women, Work, and Protest'; and Gabaccia, *Italy's Many Diasporas: Elites, Exiles, and Workers of the World* (London: University College of London Press, 2000).

10 Nancy L. Green, 'The Comparative Method and Poststructural Structuralism: New Perspective for Migration Studies,' *Journal of American Ethnic History* 13, 4 (Summer 1994): 3–32, esp. 14–16.

11 Robert Harney, 'Men without Women,' in Betty Boyd Caroli, Robert F. Harney, and Lydio F. Tomasi, *The Italian Immigrant Woman in North America* (Toronto: Multicultural History Society of Ontario, 1977), 79–102. In Canada this article, along with Harney's related essays on the padrone system and male sojourning, have been reprinted in several anthologies and are widely used in general survey histories of Canada as well as in (im)migration courses.

12 Historian Virginia Yans-McLaughlin offered a particularly vigorous defence of immigrant families against American critiques of them as disorganized and pathological; in doing so, she also criticized Oscar Handlin's seminal interpretation of the immigrants as alienated and 'uprooted' persons. See *Family and Community*, 18–20. See also her debate on Italian women's work and domesticity, 'A Flexible Tradition: South Italian Immigrants Confront a

New Work Experience,' *Journal of Social History* 7 (1974): 449–55; and Louise A. Tilly, 'Comment on Two Papers on British and American Working Class Families,' *Journal of Social History* 7 (1974): 452–9.

13 John Dickie, *Darkest Italy: The Nation and Stereotypes of the Mezzogiorno, 1860–1900* (New York: St Martin's Press, 1999).

14 On women's work in northern Italy, readers can also usefully consult Franco Ramella, *Terra e telai: Sistemi di parentela e manifattura nel Biellese dell'Ottocento* (Turin: G. Einaudi, 1983); Elda Gentili Zappi, *If Eight Hours Seem Too Few: Mobilization of Women Workers in the Italian Rice Fields* (Albany: State University of New York Press, 1991); and Patrizia Audenino, *Un mestiere per partire: Tradizione migratoria, lavoro e comunità in una vallata alpina* (Milan: Franco Angeli, 1990).

15 See, e.g., Ewen, *Immigrant Women in the Land of Dollars*, 30–7.

16 Elizabeth Pleck, 'Two Worlds in One: Work and Family,' *Journal of Social History* 10 (Winter 1976): 178–95; Louise A. Tilly and Joan W. Scott, *Women, Work and Family* (New York: Holt, Rinehart and Winston, 1978), esp. chaps. 2–3; Alice Kessler-Harris, *Out to Work: A History of Wage-earning Women in the United States* (New York: Oxford University Press, 1982).

17 The main source for data on Italian migration arranged by receiving country is Walter F. Willcox, *International Migrations* (New York: National Bureau of Economic Reserch, 1931).

18 Tilly, 'Comment on Two Papers.'

19 Judith L. Sweeney, 'Las lavanderas de la ciudad de Buenos Aires en la segunda mitad del siglo XIX,' *Jornadas de historia económica* 6 (Rosario, mimeo, 1985), cited in Alicia Bernasconi and Carina Frid de Silberstein, 'Le altre protagoniste: Italiane a Santa Fe,' *Altreitalie* 9 (January–June 1993): 116–38; Loraine Slomp Giron, 'L'immigrata in Brasile e il lavoro,' *Altreitalie* 9 (Jan.–June 1993): 108–9; Franca Iacovetta, 'Primitive Villagers and Un-educated Girls: Canada Recruits Domestics from Italy, 1951–52,' *Canadian Woman Studies* 7, 4 (Winter 1986); Stepanie Weisbart Bellini, 'The Kitchen Table Talks: Immigrant Italian Domestic Workers in Toronto's Post-War Years,' MA thesis, Memorial University of Newfoundland, St John's, July 2001.

20 Joy K. Lintelman, '"Our Serving Sisters": Swedish-American Domestic Servants and Their Ethnic Community,' *Social Science History* 15 (Fall 1991): 381–96; Hasia Diner, *Erin's Daughters in America: Irish Immigrant Women in the Nineteenth Century* (Baltimore: Johns Hopkins University Press, 1983).

21 An argument also made many years ago by Steven Steinberg in *The Ethnic Myth: Race, Ethnicity, and Class in America* (New York: Atheneum, 1981), esp. chap. 6, 'Why Irish Became Domestics and Italians and Jews Did Not.'

22 Gabaccia, *Italy's Many Diasporas*, 75–8.

23 Given the near invisibility of Italians, especially women, in studies of labour

and the left in Canada, we hope, too, that these essays, along with Principe's contribution, inspires research on the subject! This lack of attention to the Italian left stands in sharp contrast to a well-established literature on Finns, Ukrainians, Jews, and other ethnic groups on the Canadian left, including feminist scholarship, where important contributions include works by Varpu Lindstrom (Finns), Ruth Frager (Jews), Frances Swyripa (Ukrainians), and Linda Kealey's comparative study *Enlisting Women for the Cause: Women, Labour, and the Left in Canada, 1890–1920* (Toronto: University of Toronto Press, 1998). In addition to Principe's pioneering contributions, published and unpublished, most of the published research on Canada's militant Italians is found in studies on the Fascist era, including, most recently, essays in Franca Iacovetta, Roberto Perin, and Angelo Principe, eds., *Enemies Within: Italian and Other Internees in Canada and Beyond* (Toronto: University of Toronto Press, 2000), and in a small number of essays dealing with multi-ethnic strikes, including Carmela Patrias, 'Relief Strike: Immigrant Workers and the Great Depression in Crowland, Ontario, 1930–1935,' in Franca Iacovetta, ed., *A Nation of Immigrants: Women, Workers, and Communities in Canadian History* (Toronto: University of Toronto Press, 1997) and Robert Ventresca, 'Cowering Women, Combative Men? Femininity, Masculinity, and Ethnicity in Two Southern Ontario Towns, 1964–66,' *Labour / Le Travail* 39 (Spring 1990): 125–58. For a more detailed discussion and citation of studies of Canada's ethnic left, see Iacovetta, 'Manly Militants, Cohesive Communities, and Defiant Domestics'; F. Iacovetta, Ian Radforth, and Michael Quinlan, 'Immigration and Labour: Australia and Canada Compared,' in the special issue *Australia and Canada – Labour Compared*, co-published in *Labour / Le Travail* 38 (Fall 1996): 90–115, and *Labour History* 71 (Australia); and F. Iacovetta and R. Ventresca, 'Italian Radicals in Canada: A Note on Sources in Italy,' *Labour / Le Travail* 37 (Spring 1996): 205–20.

24 Ann Bravo, 'Solidarity and Loneliness: Piedmontese Peasant Women at the Turn of the Century,' *International Journal of Oral History* 3 (1982); Donna Gabaccia, 'Immigrant Women: Nowhere at Home?' *Journal of American Ethnic History* 10, 4 (1991): 72.

25 Critics of Edward Banfield, *The Moral Basis of a Backward Society* (Glencoe, IL: Free Press, 1958) are many and varied, but see as an example Sydel F. Silverman, 'Agricultural Organization, Social Structure and Values in Italy: Amoral Familism Reconsidered,' *American Anthropologist* 70 (1968): 1–20.

26 See, e.g., Robert D. Putnam, *Making Democracy Work: Civic Traditions in Modern Italy* (Princeton: Princeton University Press, 1993).

27 For comparisons of Jewish and Italian labour activism, see Ewen, *Immigrant Women in the Land of Dollars*, ch. 14.

28 See Susan Glenn's discussion of this historiography in *Daughters of the Shtetl: Life and Labor in the Immigrant Generation* (Ithaca: Cornell University Press, 1990), 191–4; and Maxine Seller, 'The Uprising of the Twenty Thousand: Sex, Class and Ethnicity in the Shirtwaist Makers' Strike of 1909,' in Dirk Hoerder, ed., *Struggle a Hard Battle: Working Class Immigrants* (DeKalb: Northern Illinois University Press, 1986).

29 Key interpretations include Nan Enstad, *Ladies of Labor, Girls of Adventure: Working Women, Popular Culture and Labor Politics at the Turn of the Twentieth Century* (New York: Columbia University Press, 1999); Annelise Orleck, *Common Sense and a Little Fire: Women and Working-class Politics in the United States, 1900–1965* (Chapel Hill: University of North Carolina Press, 1995), 41–50, 57–63; Glenn, *Daughters of the Shtetl*, 177, 213; and Ann Schofield, 'The Uprising of the 20,000: The Making of a Labor Legend,' in Joan Jensen and Sue Davidson, eds., *A Needle, a Bobbin, a Strike* (Philadelphia: Temple University Press, 1984).

30 Helen Marot, 'A Woman's Strike: An Appreciation,' *Proceedings of the Academy of Political Science* 1 (October 1910): 119–28; Glenn, *Daughters of the Shtetl*, 191.

31 Besides Gabaccia and Ottanelli, *Italian Workers of the World*, cited above, see Rudolph J. Vecoli, 'Italian Immigrants in the United States Labor Movement from 1880 to 1929,' in Bruno Bezza, ed., *Gli italiani fuori d'Italia*, 153–306; and Bruno Ramirez, 'Immigration, Ethnicity, and Political Militancy: Patterns of Radicalism in the Italian-American Left, 1880–1930,' in Valeria Gennaro Lerda, ed., *From 'Melting Pot' to Multiculturalism: The Evolution of Ethnic Relations in the United States and Canada* (Rome: Bulzoni Ed., 1990), 115–41. For Canada, see Ramirez, 'Ethnic Studies and Working-Class History,' *Labour / Le Travail* 19 (Spring 1987): 45–8 and Iacovetta, Radforth, and Quinlan, 'Immigration and Labour Compared.' See also Samuel Baily, 'The Italians and the Development of Organized Labor in Argentina, Brazil, and the United States, 1880–1914,' *Journal of Social History* 3 (Winter 1969–70): 123–34; and his *Immigrants in the Lands of Promise* (Ithaca: Cornell University Press, 1999).

32 On Modotti see, e.g., Patricia Albers, *Shadows, Fire, Snow: The Life of Tina Modotti* (New York: Clarkson Potter, 1999) and Elena Poniatawska, *Tinisima* (London: Faber, 1996). On Antolini see Paul Avrich, *Sacco and Vanzetti, The Anarchist Background* (Princeton: Princeton University Press, 1991), 107–21. See also Jean Scarpaci, 'Angela Bambace and the International Ladies Garment Workers Union: The Search for an Elusive Activist,' in George Pozzetta, ed., *Pane e Lavoro: The Italian American Working Class* (Toronto: Multicultural History Society of Ontario, 1980).

33 Baily, 'The Italians and the Development of Organized Labor.'

34 Her work parallels in intriguing ways the research of Carole Turbin on the militancy of Irish immigrant women in the United States: *Working Women of Collar City: Gender, Class, and Community in Troy, New York, 1864–86* (Urbana: University of Illinois Press, 1992).

35 See, for the United States, Ardis Cameron, *Radicals of the Worst Sort: Laboring Women in Lawrence, Massachusetts, 1860–1912* (Urbana: University of Illinois Press, 1993); and, for Canada, Ventresca, 'Cowering Women, Combative Men?'

36 David Roediger and James Barrett, 'In Between Peoples: Race, Nationality and the "New Immigrant" Working Class,' *Journal of American Ethnic History* 16 (1997): 3–44.

37 Scholars writing the social and gender history of Italian radicals and labour activists in France and in North America have found particularly useful (though also frustrating) the Casellario Politico Centrale (CPC) files. While the CPC files predate Fascism, the case files from the Fascist era are especially voluminous. Since the files track Italian 'subversives' in Italy and exiles abroad, the CPC collection facilitates a diasporic and transnational approach. With few significant exceptions – including D'Andrea – women ppear in these files as members of families. The richer files also capture the ways in which the state pathologized female 'subversives' as political and simultaneously sexual and moral transgressors. For further descriptions of the CPC files, and demonstration of their value for writing radical history, see, e.g., Iacovetta and Ventresca, 'Italian Radicals in Canada.'

38 Victoria DeGrazia, *How Fascism Ruled Women* (Berkeley: University of California Press, 1992).

39 Gayatri Chakravorty Spivak, 'Subaltern Studies: Deconstructing Historiography,' in Donna Landry and Gerald McLean, eds., *The Spivak Reader* (New York: Routledge, 1996). For recent efforts to apply (and in some cases modify) post-colonial, subaltern, and cultural-studies approaches to the role of immigration and refugee policies and of citizenship criteria and restrictions to nation-building in North America, see, e.g., Lisa Lowe, *Immigrant Acts: On Asian American Cultural Politics* (Durham, NC: Duke University Press, 1996) and essays by Nandita Rani Sarma, Sunera Thobani, Cynthia Wright, Shahrzad Mojab, et al. in Tani Das Gupta and Franca Iacovetta, eds., in the special issue 'Whose Canada Is It? Immigrant Women, Women of Colour and Feminist Critiques of Multiculturalism,' *Atlantis: A Women's Studies Journal* 24, 2 (Spring/Summer 2000).

40 Readers interested in these and other comparisons can consult the special issues 'Canada and Australia Compared' in *Labour / Le Travail* 38 (Fall 1996)

and *Labor History* 71 (November 1996), which includes Iacovetta, Quinlan, and Radforth, 'Immigration and Labour Compared.'

41 See, e.g., Chandra Talpade Mohanty, 'Under Western Eyes: Feminist Scholarship and Colonial Discourses,' in Mohanty et al., *Third World Women and the Politics of Feminism* (Bloomington: Indiana University Press, 1991) and Ruth Pierson and Npuri Chauderie, eds., *Colony, Nation, Empire* (Bloomington: Indiana University Press, 1999).

42 Most influential on this point was the award-winning work of Yans-McLaughlin, *Family and Community*. For an early critique of what she termed feminists' 'history as empathy,' see Jean V. Scarpaci, 'La Contadina: The Plaything of the Middle Class Woman Historian,' *Journal of Ethnic Studies* 9 (Summer 1981): 21–38.

43 Here we would like to call attention to a collection of essays, edited by contributor Jennifer Guglielmo together with Salvatore Salerno on Italians and racial politics in the United States, *Are Italians White? How Race Is Made in America* (forthcoming with Routledge.)

44 Besides Roediger and Barrett, 'In Between People,' see David Roediger, *Wages of Whiteness: Race and the Making of the American Working Class* (London: Verso, 1991); Roediger, *The Abolition of Whiteness: Race, Politics, and Working Class History* (New York: Verso, 1994); Noel Ignatiev, *How the Irish Became White* (London: Routledge, 1995); George Lipsitz, *The Possessive Investment in Whiteness: How White People Profit from Identity Politics* (Philadelphia: Temple University Press, 1998); and Matthew Frye Jacobson, *Whiteness of a Different Color: European Immigrants and the Alchemy of Race* (Cambridge: Harvard University Press, 1998).

45 Besides Barrett and Roediger, 'In Between People,' see Robert Orsi, 'The Religious Boundaries of an Inbetween People: Street Feste and the Problem of the Dark-Skinned "Other" in Italian Harlem, 1920–1990,' *American Quarterly* 44 (September 1992).

46 Thomas Guglielmo, 'White on Arrival: Italians, Race, Color, and Power in Chicago, 1890–1945' (Unpublished PhD dissertation, University of Michigan, 2000); 'White on Arrival,' paper presented at the 'Defining Whiteness? Race, Class and Gender Perspectives in North American History' conference, Toronto, October 2000. See also Rudolph J. Vecoli, 'Are Italians White?' *Italian Americana* 12 (Summer 1995): 149–61; Thomas Guglielmo, 'Toward Essentialism, Toward Difference: Gino Speranza and Conceptions of Race and Italian-American Racial Identity, 1900–1925,' *Mid-America* 81, 2 (Summer 1999): 169–213; and David Richards, *Italian American: The Racializing of an Ethnic Identity* (New York: New York University Press, 1999). The 'in-between' status of Italians was one of the themes that provoked

debate and discussion at the 'Defining Whiteness' conference held at the University of Toronto (with special guests David Roediger, James Barrett, Donna Gabaccia, and Elizabeth Grace Hale).

47 Gabaccia, *From the Other Side: Women, Gender, and Immigrant Life in the U.S., 1820–1990* (Bloomington: Indiana University Press, 1994), 115–23.

PART I

When Men Go Away: Women Who Wait and Work

1 When the Men Left Sutera: Sicilian Women and Mass Migration, 1880–1920

Linda Reeder

By 1910 hundreds of thousands of Sicilian men had left their homes for the Americas.[1] As politicians and critics watched the men flock to Italian ports, they expressed concern about the long-term effects of the exodus on the island and the nation. How could Italian industry grow if the industrious left? How could the military protect the nation if the bravest men were overseas? In these debates, the women who remained behind – Sicily's so-called white widows – became the symbols of the heavy price exacted by male migration. Social critics described how young men arranged marriages only to raise the money to buy a transatlantic steamship ticket, and then quickly abandoned their young wives for America, forcing these poor women to turn to relatives, fieldwork, or prostitution.[2] Not only infidelity but also insanity were the inevitable consequences of male emigration. Regional newspapers ran stories of emigrants who returned home to find their wife living with other men, pregnant with a lover's children, or worse. The *Giornale di Sicilia* reported that Carmelo S. came home to find his wife in jail, serving a sentence for infanticide; a few months later he was on trial for killing his wife's lover, the father of the dead child.[3] By the end of the First World War, popular novels commonly described how migrants' wives and mothers went mad when they realized their men were never coming home. In 'La Mèrica,' a heartbreaking story by Maria Messina, Catena forbids her husband, Mariano, to emigrate unless she and her son accompany him. They fight for weeks, until he books passage for the family, but as they pass through customs in Palermo, Catena is diagnosed with trachoma and forced to return home. The local pharmacist treats her eyes with caustic poultices and she goes blind. Mariano never writes or returns, and Catena goes insane.[4] While politicians, writers, and journalists may have disagreed over whether migration was ultimately beneficial or harmful to the island, they all agreed that when the men left, many of the women who remained behind sank into poverty, sexual depravity, or madness.

These pervasive and powerful images of emigrants' wives and mothers rarely reflected the reality of women's experiences. Here, I focus on a specific case study – Sutera, a small town located in western Sicily – to explore how women who remained behind experienced transnational migration. My research shows that far from being abandoned by husbands seeking to satisfy selfish dreams of adventure and wealth, these women, like their counterparts who journeyed to the new world, actively participated in the process of transatlantic migration. In Sicily, migration was a strategy to improve a family's material condition.[5] Despite the hardships that migration entailed, everyone agreed that American money offered the greatest possibility to better the family's social and economic position at home. Rural residents, I argue, hoped that higher wages earned in the Americas would enable them to purchase the trappings of wealth: two-storey houses, land, or small businesses were the minimum requirements needed to claim membership in the local elite. Although important, property ownership was but one of many qualities associated with wealth; honour, respect, large families, and literacy also differentiated local gentry from the rest of the townsfolk. In carrying out a family emigration strategy, men and women performed different roles; the men went overseas, while the women who remained behind helped to finance and organize the trip. While the men worked in the coal mines and cities of North America, Sutera's 'white widows' worked to acquire the economic, social, and cultural characteristics associated with the local elite.[6]

In some respects, male migration from Sicily appeared to reinforce traditional patterns of female behaviour, encouraging rural women to have many children and discouraging them from seeking agricultural wage work. In other instances, however, migration created new economic opportunities, as evidenced by Sutera, where the women married to migrants were more likely to participate in property markets, buying and selling land and houses, than women whose husbands stayed home. Migrant money also encouraged rural women to purchase mass-produced goods, enabling them to provide visual evidence of their upward social mobility and linking them to a growing national consumer economy. Furthermore, as the women of Sutera worked toward their goals, they redefined their relationship with the nation-state. A sense of national belonging emerged through greater contact with government agencies and the educational system. Transoceanic migration provided the means and incentive for rural Sicilian women to carve out new social, economic, and civic spaces in the community, the nation, and beyond. These women's stories also help us better understand the choices that immigrant Italian women made in the United States. Indeed, there were striking similarities between the women's experiences in families that settled in the Americas and those that welcomed their migrating men home. For migrant and non-migrant women alike, Sicilian social and cultural codes shaped decisions concerning family size and work, and the emerging relationship between rural women and the Italian state affected the impact of mass migration on attitudes toward the nation-state on both sides of the Atlantic. Whether women left their home-towns, or chose to stay behind, the experience of mass migration profoundly transformed their lives.

Sutera, Sicily

In the shadows of Mount San Paolino, Sutera overlooks the highway that runs from Palermo to Agrigento. In 1901, it boasted 5892 residents.[7] Like most Sicilian agro-towns, Sutera had the physical aspects of an urban community. The houses were built close together, one on top of another along narrow winding streets. There were four churches, three squares, dry-good stores, and workshops. Few trees or gardens grew near the houses; families planted fruit and vegetables on the outskirts of town. From the main square the town appeared encircled by a swath of green, separating the houses from the desolate, treeless countryside that stretched out toward the horizon.[8] Scholars have speculated that Sicilian settlement patterns came about, in part, as a consequence of the dangers endemic to the lowlands. Malaria, marauding armies, and bandits made living in the countryside a decidedly dangerous proposition. Along with the physical difficulties, the feudal system that accompanied Norman rule in the late eleventh century shaped the region's urban development. From the twelfth century onwards, local aristocracy seized the best lands for their own vast estates, and pushed residents out of the small villages established by the Arabs. Despite the abolition of feudalism in the beginning of the nineteenth century, and the numerous land reforms after Italian unification in 1860–1, agricultural land remained concentrated in the hands of absentee landlords.[9]

Class and gender shaped daily life in early-twentieth-century Sutera.[10] On any given weekday morning, it was easy to identify the gentry, professionals, and artisans; they were the only men in town, apart from the unemployed, elderly, and infirm. These men, who lived off their rents or skills, constituted the local elite, bourgeoisie, and craftsmen. Most men worked as day labourers or sharecroppers in the surrounding wheat fields, and were gone for days on end.[11] Rural workers left town before dawn each Monday morning and returned home late the following Saturday afternoon, then spent Sunday looking for work for the following week. Women's lives were not as visibly marked by class. Most women, regardless of social position, stayed home, their status reflected in their daily chores, making the family's clothes, hauling water, cooking, or cleaning. Wealthy women supervised the servants, looked after household affairs, and perhaps took time to read for pleasure or to visit with friends and family. The wives of agricultural workers spent their days spinning, weaving, and caring for their children and their houses while their husbands worked in the fields.

As other contributions to this volume document, throughout much of rural Italy, including the regions of the south, women performed agricultural work, whether as members of peasant families or as seasonal wage-earners on commercial estates, or both. An island with many distinctive features, Sicily differed markedly from Italy's other rural regions in this respect: its long-standing taboo against female agricultural work and male control over fieldwork meant that agricultural work, paid or unpaid, was not an option for most Sicilian women, including those in Sutera, rich or poor.[12] The distances that separated the fields from the towns and the dangers associated with the countryside discouraged all, except the most desperate, women from seeking work in the wheat fields.[13] In his 1907 report for a parliamentary inquiry (*inchiesta*) on Sicily, Senator Giovanni Lorenzoni noted that travellers often saw single women working in the citrus groves and commercial gardens along the coast, but inland such women seemed to disappear. In the regions dominated by large landed estates there was a strong cultural code stipulating that 'honest women should not work in the fields for wages.' That work was reserved for 'the most miserable women; those abandoned by their husbands, or widowed, or girls who suffered some disgrace.'[14] Respectable women worked alongside their men only during the harvest when all available labour was needed. But though the cultural taboos against women earning agricultural wages were stronger in central Sicily than anywhere else in Italy, there were always some women compelled by personal or familial circumstances to seek this work.

Men and women lived and worked in separate spaces, but their worlds were complementary, and both men and women worked together toward buying their own house and owning enough land to live comfortably from the rents.[15] Chronic underemployment, low wages, and the land-tenure system, however, meant few families could ever realize their dreams. In 1876, the politician and social critic Sidney Sonnino wrote that Sicilian peasants had two options to improve their lives: organize or emigrate.[16] Suteresi tried both. Before 1900, residents seemed uninterested in seeking their fortunes overseas. In 1893, for example, the townspeople joined agricultural cooperatives (*fasci*) and tried to break up the large estates by force.[17] But when the Italian army brutally suppressed the *fasci*, destroying what little hope there was to improve the economic conditions on the island, residents began to listen to the stories of plentiful jobs and high wages in North America. By 1899, emigration seemed to be the only way that a rural worker could hope to improve his family's economic and social position. Between 1899 and 1901 over two hundred people sought permission to emigrate.[18] Just as interest in emigration began to grow, sulphur was discovered in Mount San Paolino. Although few Suteresi sought work in the mines, the mining concessions brought in tax revenues that bolstered the local economy and slowed outward migration. When the mine collapsed in 1905, leaving hundreds homeless and one dead, residents began to leave once more. In 1906 more than two hundred people left, and nearly three hundred set sail the following year.[19]

The typical migrant from Sutera was a married man, between 23 and 45 years of age, who had spent his life working in the wheat fields and who now travelled with brothers, uncles, or cousins;[20] few migrant men left with wives and children, although most of the women who did emigrate were married. Very few single women chose to leave town.[21] Both the men who migrated and the women who remained home viewed emigration as a temporary condition. The stories they heard from neighbours, friends, and relatives told of a land where a hard-working, frugal man could save nearly four thousand lire (a little less than $1000) in five or six years. Southern Italians in the Birmingham area of Alabama, for example, earned an average of eight dollars a week, as compared to a weekly wage of about two dollars back home, assuming a day labourer could find steady work.[22] This meant that within a few years, a family earning American wages through a male migrant could save enough to buy a new house, invest in land, or open a business in Sutera – an accomplishment that eluded even the most industrious. Most men left with every intention to return, and nearly 70 per cent of them did so.[23]

In some respects the pattern of migration from Sutera, which witnessed high rates of male migration and repatriation, differed from that of surrounding agro-towns. In Sicily, where family migration, as defined by the presence of women and children among the migrants, was generally higher than in other Italian regions, women constituted 25 to 30 per cent of all migrants. In contrast, far fewer Suteran women migrated.[24] The number of returning migrants in Sutera was also significantly higher than regional or national rates, though historians have estimated that nearly half of all southern Italian emigrants returned.[25] While the timing and geography of emigration account for the distinctive sex ratios and return rates in Sutera, they do not make the town exceptional. In the surrounding hill towns, men began to leave around 1900 and their numbers grew each year. Over time, migrating men decided to settle overseas and called for their families to join them in the new world. In Sutera, early outward male migration slowed as the local economy improved with the discovery of sulphur. Although residents began emigrating overseas again after 1905, migration rates fell sharply less than a decade later in the wake of war and Fascist policies. The relatively short period of intense emigration from Sutera (1905–13) meant that significant numbers of Suteresi did not settle permanently in immigrant communities in the United States before the First World War, and so fewer migrants called for their wives and children. Another factor contributing to the unequal sex ratios among migrants was the destination of most Suteresi, who after 1905 headed for the mills and mining towns of Alabama, Pennsylvania, and New York rather than New York City, Chicago, or Boston. The absence of significant Italian-American communities meant there was little incentive to bring families over during the first few years, and the high proportion of male migrants and the prevalence of rural destinations probably contributed significantly to the high repatriation rates reported throughout Sicily and the South.

In March of 1910 Paolino C. left his wife, Giuseppa, and their two children to find work in the United States. A year later he returned home for a few months, and had already returned to Pennsylvania when his wife gave birth to their third child. Paolino and Giuseppa had most likely planned to use migration as a means to improve their lives shortly after their marriage in 1907. During the next two years they saved enough money to buy a steamship ticket.[26] Giuseppa's consent was officially visible on her husband's passport application. According to the 1901 emigration law, married men had to provide written proof that they were not abandoning any dependants. Local officials took this regulation to heart and commonly requested wives' written permission on passport applications.[27] In stilted, bureaucratic language, the mayor of Sutera commonly included written declarations from wives supporting their husbands' passport applications. When Giuseppe C. requested permission to emigrate the mayor wrote on the application, '[H]is wife, on her part, declares her consent ... in the hope that he will find work and can send his savings to his family for their sustenance.'[28] A wife's support, however, went beyond formal consent, as she probably helped finance and organize her husband's trip. As an agricultural worker, Paolino made only about 250 lire a year, so to make the migrant dream a reality he turned to Giuseppa for emotional and material support.

Female financial participation in the migration process arose from the customary economic and social roles women played within the family economy. Ethnographers had long noted that Sicilian women generally controlled the household budget; men turned their earnings over to their wife or mother at the end of the work week or, if they were sharecroppers, when they sold their harvest. Women oversaw the family's savings, and husbands and wives jointly decided on all major expenses, from buying land and mules to purchasing boat tickets to the Americas.[29] A family needed to raise nearly 200 lire to send one person to North America (not including living expenses overseas). A day labourer in Sutera made little more than 250 to 300 lire a year, and a sharecropper made even less.[30] Saving enough money for the voyage would have been difficult without a wife's cooperation. When a family's savings proved insufficient to cover the costs of the trip, women often turned to their relatives and neighbours for loans. In villages like Sutera it was not uncommon for women to act as informal moneylenders, even though official institutions excluded them from taking out loans.[31]

Giuseppa's influence on migration patterns was not limited to helping finance her husband's voyage; a few months after her husband left, she arranged for her brother to join him in Pennsylvania.[32] A close analysis of migration patterns suggests that women, whether they migrated themselves or stayed home, acted as links in the informational network and as agents in the formation of emigrant groups. The kin networks provided village women with information about the Americas that influenced a family's decision when and where to send someone overseas. When the men from Sutera began to migrate, women turned to the female relatives, friends, and neighbours they had long relied on to help with daily chores, childbirth, arranging marriages, and now with gathering information about conditions overseas. Women shared stories of their brothers' and husbands' experiences in the Americas.[33] The presence of women also can be seen in the familial relationships that linked male migrants; indeed female kin networks could link seemingly unrelated migrants. Through their financial position and their role as kin-keepers in the family and the village, rural women influenced who left, where they went, and with whom they travelled.[34] The women who remained in Sutera were not left behind, but rather chose to stay home and watch over the family's interests.

Whether a woman's cooperation was coerced or not is difficult to tell. Tales of women forced to sell their dowry to raise money for emigration, or even murdered by family members to whom they refused money were widespread, suggesting perhaps that not all women were willing participants. In 1905, Senator Lorenzoni reported on a resident of Solarino who killed his aunt and benefactress because she refused to give him the money he needed to emigrate.[35] In Milocca, a husband's flight to the United States drove his young wife to suicide. On 23 June 1913, Graziella Li Giovanni dressed for church and shot herself in her father's house in Racalmuto after her husband emigrated. According to the *Giornale di Sicilia*, 'a year earlier the young Graziella, more from a desire to please her family than any sense of affection, married a peasant from Milocca. The marriage was not a happy one. Very soon the couple fought and separated: ultimately the husband abandoned the conjugal roof and emigrated to America.' Left alone Graziella returned to her mother and father's house to recover. However, even in Racalmuto, 'it seems that malicious tongues attacked her honour' and drove her to suicide.[36] Graziella's story reminds us that some men used transoceanic migration to end an unhappy marriage, abandoning their wife to a tragic fate, but this was by no means a typical scenario. For Sutera, there is little evidence that women in general were forced to sell dowries or otherwise raise money for a boat ticket against their will. There is no evidence of women murdered or even left poverty stricken. And wives of migrants do not appear on village poor rolls.[37] At least one woman was not afraid of challenging her husband's decision to emigrate. In September 1920, Francesca G. appeared in the Palermo police department with a formal request to stop her husband, Ignazio N., from sailing to the United States. It is not clear whether she located her husband, but the incident suggests that she was not afraid to use any means necessary to stop him from leaving.[38]

Perhaps the most telling evidence of female participation in the decision-making process underlying male migration was a refusal to join a husband overseas. In letters dictated to city officials, women explained how they had willingly agreed to a temporary separation hoping to improve the material conditions of life at home, but they had not agreed to emigrate. When one man sent his wife a prepaid ticket for herself and their daughter, she purportedly told him that 'she would never cross the sea to join him, and that if he wanted to see his family he had to come to Sutera.'[39] For these women, migration remained a means to support, not uproot, their families. Other women did join their husbands overseas, either temporarily or permanently, but whether they sailed for America or refused to leave, Sicilian women influenced the process of mass migration.

Female participation in the migration process could also redefine customary ideas of family, work, and citizenship. Having invested in their own dreams of bettering their families' material conditions through transoceanic migration, the wives of migrants worked hard to make that dream come true. At the beginning of the twentieth century, Sicilians measured status by property and behaviour: land, housing, children, and honour all marked a family's position within the local community.[40] A two-storey house in the centre of town attested to hard work and good fortune, but if the family's behaviour did not correspond to accepted cultural codes, they had little chance of furthering their position through business or social networks. Even before couples had saved enough money to purchase the physical trappings of material success, the wives of emigrants worked to strengthen the family's reputation at home.

In Sicily, honour was more than a measure of personal morality, virtue, or integrity. Not only was individual honour enmeshed in the entire kin group, where one person's behaviour had the power to sully the reputations of the extended family, but honour and respect were needed to compete for scarce economic and social resources. An honourable man was a good husband and a good father, who made sure his daughters married well and his sons found gainful employment. A family's honour was measured largely by a man's ability to protect and supervise female sexuality. Women were the repositories of honour and the public measure of a family's reputation.[41] Transatlantic migration could strain a family's ability to conform to cultural ideals, as men found it difficult to fulfil their familial roles while so far away, thereby leaving the women to ensure that the family suffered no loss of respect in their husbands' absence. Any suggestion of betrayal, dishonesty, or adultery weakened a woman's social position. Since women faced harsher punishments than men for any perceived or actual transgression, most women, especially 'white widows,' scrupulously avoided any activity that could bring dishonour to their families. No amount of American money could redeem a woman's family's honour or reputation once the town labelled her a fallen woman and her husband a cuckold. It would be difficult to arrange prestigious marriages for her children or for her husband to succeed in business once he returned. These women had every reason to shield their families from malicious gossip while their husbands were gone, lest they compromise the success of the entire venture. As a result, migration did not lead to an explosion of illegitimate children or divorces as many feared. On the contrary, the number of illegitimate children born in Sutera fell during the peak years of migration (1900 to the First World War): from 3 per cent to 1.3 per cent of registered births.[42]

The same social and cultural ideals encouraged these women to have many children. In rural Sicily, large families had long been a mark of distinction. Elite families had an average of six children in the early 1880s, and lower rates of infant mortality among the wealthy ensured that most of their children would survive.[43] Agricultural workers had an average of five children per family in the late nineteenth century.[44] The numerous children of a rich man were proof of his personal power and vast wealth. Not so for the poor, as the following proverb suggests: 'Two or three children are a pleasure, seven or eight a torment.'[45] In response to changing social and economic conditions, marital fertility among the elite began to decline toward the end of the nineteenth century (falling, on average, from six to four children in Sutera), but the cultural association between wealth and children did not disappear. Large families remained a visible sign of prosperity until after the the First World War, one that migrating men and their wives eagerly embraced as they sought to claim a place alongside the gentry. Among couples married during the last decade of the nineteenth century, the women whose husbands emigrated had an average of one child more than those women whose husbands never left home.[46] Only after 1905, when cultural codes associating fecundity with respectability weakened, did the birth rates of migrant families fall sharply. Rather than depressing legitimate fertility rates, as so many Italian critics and politicians had predicted, emigration provided the means for couples to have larger families.

Evidence from Sutera confirms John Briggs's argument that accepted assumptions about Italian fertility have distorted our understanding of how transoceanic migration affected family size. U.S. scholars have assumed that Italian immigrant women who settled in the United States, having come from a culture that encouraged marriage at a very young age and large numbers of children, clung to these old world traditions, and thus continued in North America to have as many children as possible. It is true that fertility rates among southern Italian migrants in the United States were significantly higher than all other immigrant groups,[47] but this was not a consequence of early marriage or uncontrolled fertility; rather, it was a reflection of a family's attempt to realize the migrant dream of upward mobility shaped in the homeland. In Sutera, most women married in their early twenties; only the wealthy married at a very young age. In the United States, Briggs found that Italian immigrant women tended to marry a year or two earlier than non-immigrant women. This pattern also held true for female migrants from Sutera, as well as for wives of emigrants who chose to stay home. Women whose husbands emigrated were, on average, two years younger when they married than those whose husbands stayed in Sutera.[48] It was not the personal act of immigration that encouraged younger marriages and more children, but the process of migration that influenced marriage and fertility patterns. Motivated by familial dreams of social improvement, transnational migration affected family planning on both sides of the Atlantic. In new world immigrant communities and in old world agro-towns, fertility patterns changed only when the cultural link between wealth and family size broke.

In Sutera, the association of large families with social status gradually weakened as rural residents from all classes adopted the changing behaviour of the elites. A noticeable decline in fertility rates occurred in the 1920s among the island's labouring classes as they joined the gentry and artisans in limiting family size.[49] Significantly, the birth rates fell more sharply among women married to migrants. Birth and marriage records show that women who married after 1905, and whose husbands worked in America, had on average three children; in comparison, women with husbands overseas who had married earlier, between 1895 and 1904, had five children. Among women whose husbands stayed in Sutera the number of children fell from four to three in the same period. In Sutera, emigration reinforced changing cultural attitudes toward family size.

The reproductive choices of southern Italian female immigrants followed similar patterns, although the forces of change differed. In the United States, successful immigrants replaced the local gentry as the measure of status. Migrants who earned enough to buy their own house, or start their own businesses had realized the Italian-American dream. As Susan Watkins has argued, fertility decline among immigrant women at the turn of the century was linked to residence, occupation, length of time in the United States and their ability to speak English.[50] Those who stayed the longest, had acquired at least a limited ability to speak English, and had skilled jobs or owned their own businesses were more likely to limit family size. Moreover, the smaller family associated with this new Italian-American elite became the model for success, and influenced the decisions of the more recent immigrants. As in Sutera, changing definitions of success and wealth influenced marriage and fertility patterns. Large families were not a sign of rural folk clinging to old world traditions, but rather an indicator that traditions were changing on both sides of the Atlantic. Like their sisters back home, the women emigrants, having adopted the social and cultural codes that linked smaller families to wealth and status, had fewer children.

In Sicily, the traditional social and cultural codes that enjoyed much influence in the decades before mass migration also contributed to women's general reluctance to seek agricultural work, despite the limited opportunities available to women to earn cash and the rising wages for field labour that might have enticed them to take on wage-earning jobs as rural workers. Throughout most of the nineteenth century, Sicilian women had found employment in the textile industry, or sold their homespun cloth and their needlework on the market, but by the end of the century, opportunities for island women to earn cash diminished. By the 1880s, the Sicilian cloth industry had virtually disappeared, unable to compete with the cheaper mass-produced northern textiles flooding the markets, and industrial and household looms disappeared.[51] During the 1880s, a third of the married Sutera women described themselves as spinners or weavers, whereas in the 1890s only two women appear in the marriage records as *filande* (spinners).[52] Across the island rural women withdrew from wage work, yet, despite the loss of income, Sicilian women continued to avoid paid agricultural work, except during the harvest. The number of women employed in agriculture continued to fall, even as agricultural production rose after 1895 as a consequence of protectionist tariffs and increased domestic demand.[53]

The prevalent belief that only disreputable and abandoned women worked in the fields kept the wives of migrants out of agriculture. If a woman whose husband had gone overseas trudged to the fields, a hoe over her shoulder and a child in her arms, she publicly announced her husband's failure, damaging forever her own and her family's reputation. No matter how much money her husband sent home, a woman who sought work in the fields was counted as among the abandoned women, the 'poor, the widows and the beggars ... whose husbands had left for America.'[54] Emigration led to widespread labour shortages and higher wages for both men and women across Sicily – for example, between 1886 and 1906, wages for women and men had risen by nearly 50 per cent – but women married to migrants still did not enter the workforce. In Caltanissetta, the percentage of working women employed in agriculture instead declined, as did the percentage of women workers in the agricultural workforce during the peak years of emigration.[55]

Cash, Commerce, and Rising Expectations

Contrary to the expectations of many politicians and critics, then, mass male migration did not transform rural Sicilian women into wage workers, but it did provide the means and incentive for rural women to enter commercial activities.[56] Migration furnished the necessary investment capital and stimulated consumer demand. Most migrants from Sutera managed to earn within a few years enough money in the mines and plants of Alabama and Pennsylvania to improve significantly their family's economic condition. In Alabama a man could expect to earn between $300 (1500 lire) and $400 (2000 lire) a year and his income increased with the length of his stay. Lodging, food, and fuel cost a frugal man about $200 a year; the rest he could save or send home to his wife.[57] Between 1904 and 1907 emigrants sent back thousands of lire; for example, deposits in one rural cooperative bank in Sutera, the Cassa Rurale di San Paolino, rose by over 50,000 lire.[58] Throughout the province, millions of lire poured into postal savings accounts and rural banks each year.[59] If a woman received even 500 lire annually, she could probably save at least 200 lire for a house or land – far more than if her husband was working as a day labourer or sharecropper at home.[60] Before the First World War, a two-storey, four-room house in the centre of town cost between 600 and 1000 lire. Within three years a family could conceivably save enough money to purchase a new house, and in another two or three years they might have put enough away to open a store or invest in land.[61]

Access to cash and the growth of rural commerce created more economic opportunities for women. Not only did remittances improve the financial condition of migrants and their families, but the higher wages that accompanied the shrinking labour force at home improved the economic condition of all villagers. Rising wages and better agricultural contracts translated into greater disposable income throughout the region, and greater demand for consumer goods.[62] Since commerce was considered a perfectly respectable occupation for women, and the consumer market was expanding, the wives of migrants often chose to invest their savings in a small business, usually a dry-goods store. In the decade 1901 to 1911, the number of working women engaged in commercial activities in the district rose from 8 to 10 per cent; by 1920, the figure was 24 per cent.[63] Though a few women opened a small store while their husband was still overseas, most waited until after his return. When Calogero F. returned to Sutera, he and wife Maria M. invested the 6000 lire he had earned abroad in a small dry-goods store and a house in the centre of town. Maria ran the shop while her husband travelled to neighbouring towns to buy supplies. Years later her son fondly remembered his mother as an 'excellent businesswoman' who kept the shop profitable. Even those women whose husbands never returned from 'La Mèrica' could take advantage of the monies sent home, as did the woman who opened the first coffee bar in Sutera.[64] Not all businesses thrived, and the small-scale nature of the enterprises did not industrialize the local economy. Still, remittances from overseas enabled rural women to create a space for themselves as entrepreneurs in the growing cash economy, without directly challenging accepted ideas about female work.

Female migrants from Sutera adopted similar strategies in response to the needs and opportunities they found abroad. The women who settled with their husbands in Alabama and Pennsylvania did not enter the mines or mills, but chose to contribute to the family income in more traditional ways, or by exploiting new employment opportunities. A 1911 investigation of immigrant life in the U.S. South found that over 98 per cent of southern Italian women (over 16) living in the Birmingham area did not work for wages,[65] and only one out of nearly two hundred women surveyed worked as a domestic servant, a disreputable occupation in Sicily. If a husband's wages proved inadequate, the family sent the children out to work and took in lodgers, which placed the burden of an extra mouth to feed and clothes to wash on the wife. It was female labour that made the extra money, even if official statistics did not consider boarders' rents to be income earned by women.[66] The few entrepreneurial opportunities available to Italian-American women in the Birmingham area, combined with long-standing cultural codes, shaped patterns of female work. Like agricultural work, mining (even female-specific jobs such as sorting), was unacceptable to respectable women, and the wives of immigrants refused to work in those industries. By contrast, taking in boarders, like opening bars or theatres back home, meant carving out a new economic space that nevertheless did not conflict with existing attitudes toward women's work.

Transnational migration also enabled women in Sicily to enter the consumer economy through the real-estate market, since negotiating property transactions was not a new role for rural women. In contrast with other regions of Italy, Sicilian women traditionally had access to property.[67] In the 1870s, when the housing records in Sutera begin, village women were registered as sole or part owner of a third of the buildings and 13 per cent of the land.[68] Before 1900, most rural women commonly acquired property as part of their dowry, through inheritance, or as a family gift. The common division of the family patrimony reflected the prevailing belief that fieldwork was for men and housework for women. One result of the island's economic shift from exporting wheat to exporting labour was the devaluation of land as the sole measure of wealth. The growing importance of cash and liquid assets in the family economy in turn changed inheritance and dowry patterns. Between 1890 and the First World War, fewer women received land and houses from their family on the eve of their wedding; more often, they brought money, trousseaux, or gold to the marriage. The number of women who appear in the records registering property given to them as a marriage gift or inheritance fell from 37 per cent in the 1890s to 28 per cent by 1909. At the beginning of the twentieth century, only women who had the means to purchase property appear in the provincial registers, and emigration provided many of these women with the necessary cash.

The story of Rosario M. and Paolina B. illustrates the ways in which women married to migrants used family savings to realize familial dreams of social mobility. Rosario left Sutera in December 1908 to work in mines on the outskirts of Birmingham, Alabama, and within a year he had sent home enough money to pay off his debts and build a two-storey, two-room house in the centre of town. Paolina bought the land, contracted the labour, and oversaw construction. By November 1909 she had registered their new house.[69] But even though a house brought stability and security, land brought wealth. Thus, when Rosario returned a few years later, the couple began to search for a plot of land.

Finding land, however, proved more difficult. Most of the surrounding fields were still part of large estates, owned by one family who refused to sell any portion of their property, thereby seriously limiting what even townsfolk with money could buy. Most of the migrants who returned to Sutera intended to invest their hard-earned savings in land, yet few could find affordable fertile acreage, in part because the process of migration itself had wildly inflated land prices.[70] Despite growing cash reserves, few Suteresi, male or female, could buy extensive tracts of land, as was the case for Paolina and Rosario. Typically migrants first used their savings to build or buy a larger house, and then looked for land or business opportunities. Like large families, home ownership symbolized the success of migrant men and their wives – but it did not seriously challenge, let alone dismantle, the region's inequitable land-tenure system.

Family reconstructions and property records in Sutera suggest that women married to migrants were far more likely to be engaged in these commercial property transactions than women whose husbands stayed home. For the period 1900 to 1909, these records show that 80 per cent of women who were the wives of migrants purchased or built houses, while only about half of those active in the housing market were married to non-migrants.[71] In contrast to their mothers and grandmothers, wives of migrant men who earned wages in the United States could, in addition to housing and feeding their children, participate in the market as buyers and sellers. Nearly one quarter of women married to migrants who acquired property invested the family's savings while their husbands were still overseas.[72] In short, these women had some control over the money from abroad and on decisions about how and when to spend it. In Sicilian agro-towns, remittances constituted the largest source of capital for most residents. Historians are only starting to recognize the importance of this money in the economic development of the region.[73] Rural women were active players in the development of this new cash economy, even though cultural codes excluded them from waged work.

As they sought to purchase the physical accoutrements of the bourgeois world, most wives of emigrants did not settle for just any house, but searched for roomy, two-storey structures, preferably with a small separate kitchen, just like the houses owned by the elite. When these women could not find an acceptable house, they built their own, rather than purchase a smaller house. The average house registered by the wives of migrants was twice the size of the houses owned by women whose husbands did not migrate, and its net worth was substantially higher: between 1900 and 1909, such houses were worth on average twice the value of the houses owned by women whose husbands did not migrate.[74] Grander houses, in turn, encouraged women to purchase material goods;

government officials often noted that families who financed a new house with migrant money also bought new furniture and utensils. In this way, iron bedsteads, mirrors, ornate dressers, Singer sewing machines, and even carpets found their way into the most remote villages.[75] Money earned overseas by the men gave rural women in Sutera the opportunity to purchase goods for their homes and the space to display their new possessions, and thereby enjoy the benefits of an expanding consumer society, as their counterparts did overseas.[76] In Sutera, mass migration appears to have accelerated a process that began in the mid-nineteenth century – the transformation of the household from a centre of production to one of consumption.

Confronting the State

A family's struggle to improve its material conditions through migration, as we have seen, redefined meanings of motherhood and work for Sicilian women, though it did not directly challenge traditional gender roles. Yet, this struggle did serve to reposition rural women within both local communities and the nation-state. Nor did it affect only those women who migrated. Women who chose to remain home also established new ties to the state as a consequence of migration.[77] In Sutera, the acquisition of the cultural and material trappings of success made possible by transatlantic male migration fostered a new relationship between rural women and the nation-state. Indeed, male emigration, by encouraging women to negotiate with government agents, the schoolhouse, and the mass media, facilitated (often for the first time) the entry of rural women into the national community as citizens.

During the peak years of migration the women of Sutera increasingly turned to local and national agencies to negotiate family business. The exigencies of migration required women to assume new responsibilities and the expanding state bureaucracy became an important tool enabling women to fulfil their familial duties. Women used city hall and national ministries in their efforts to ensure that international migration improved their economic and social conditions. Although motivated by familial dreams, this new relationship generated a sense of national belonging among rural women. Beginning in 1860–1, the presence of the new Italian state in rural Sicily had been concerned chiefly with conscription, public security, and taxation; it had tried to mobilize Sicilian men into the nation as taxpaying citizens and soldiers. Rural women had little direct contact with government representatives, and their ties to local government rested on informal kin networks rather than a formal sense of civic inclusion. Apart from the event of marriage, women had had little reason to enter public spaces. During the last decade of the nineteenth century, however, the position of women in public life began to change. Sutera's women, for example, began to take over their husbands' legal obligation to register all newborn children at the registry office within three days of birth. As more men took on wage work abroad, they were often absent when their children were born and thus could not themselves register the births. In the 1880s, women accounted for only 5 per cent of the people who registered births, and not one woman appeared as an official witness. Between 1890 and 1900, women registered nearly a third of the births, and women witnessed nearly half of the recorded births. By 1910, women reported nearly 40 per cent of all births.[78] The appearance of women in city hall marks the creation of at least one place where women were officially recognized by the state as legitimate representatives of their families, even if it did not signal a shift in women's civic inclusion. As men left, women used their growing access to city hall to build different relationships with governmental officials; they increasingly saw agencies and institutions as effective tools for keeping the family together and improving its social and economic conditions.

Emigrants' wives turned to local officials for assistance with a variety of personal and financial needs. Overseas communications and transatlantic banking, for example, required institutional resources. If a woman's husband stopped sending her money, she went immediately to the mayor for information. When Giuseppa T. lost contact with her husband, Carmelo M., she stomped into city hall and asked the mayor to write to the consulate in Birmingham, Alabama. Without abandoning their kin and migrant networks, women now also saw the state as a legitimate means to force husbands to fulfil their duties.[79] Women like Onofria V. also saw the state as a means to redress economic difficulties; when the 1100 lire her husband sent her failed to arrive, she went directly to the mayor's office, and at city hall she dictated letters to the Ministry of Foreign Affairs and police headquarters in Naples. Noting that the money represented her husband's 'extraordinary privation and the work of three years far from his family in a strange land,' she demanded that they investigate the Credito Italiano, one of the largest banks in the country. She pressed her case until the matter was successfully resolved.[80] Transoceanic migration transformed local government into a conduit linking national agencies and migrant communities overseas. By encouraging these 'white widows' to use state resources for personal or familial gain, male migration helped to bring them into the nation as active participants. Nor was the Sutera situation unique. Across the island women turned to local and national government to protect familial interests. The archives of the Ministry of Foreign Affairs contain numerous complaints by Sicilian women against steamship companies. Many women appeared as plaintiffs in lawsuits brought against these companies, demanding reimbursement for the cost of the voyage, for instance, because they or their children had been denied entrance to the United States by customs officials.[81] By encouraging rural women to use governmental agencies to defend their family's interests, migration fostered an independent relationship between rural women and the state without violating the codes of behaviour that still seriously defined their daily lives. Eventually this relationship translated into a reluctant affinity with Rome and the Italian nation. Interestingly, it was a relationship based on their roles within the family as wives and mothers, rather than as active enfranchised citizens – a concept that would become fundamental to a Fascist definition of female citizenship.[82]

Women from Sutera brought their new relationship with government officials to the Americas. Upon hearing that her husband had been killed in a job-related accident in Boyles, Alabama, Onofria R. set out to collect her pension, eventually travelling to Alabama to file the claim. Although she could not speak English, she successfully fought for her widows' pension. Such examples help to explain the attitude of Italian emigrant women in the United States toward the state. As relevant studies show, Italian women in 'La Mèrica' turned to state agencies when they could no longer contend with abusive husbands, chronic unemployment, or sudden illness. Historian Miriam Cohen writes that Italian women turned to government officials 'in defiance of what all Italians had learned and believed about government.'[83] Yet, from the other side of the ocean, the attitudes of Italian immigrant women in Boston and New York appear as a continuation of a relationship that had emerged in Italy over previous generations. A transnational approach makes it clear that, on both sides of the Atlantic, women's utilization of government resources was a means to protect family interests and not a mark of faith or trust in the state.

Schooling and Literacy

Male emigration served to incorporate rural Sicilian women into the national body. The schoolhouse was another space where rural women encountered representatives of the Italian nation. Fifty years of government legislation and reform to improve public schooling had had little effect in Sicily by 1900, when nearly 70 per cent of the adult population was functionally illiterate.[84] Attendance in elementary and adult schools was sporadic, reflecting family economic needs and the agricultural calendar. Although rural residents recognized the importance of book learning, and considered education a sign of status, it was not essential to family survival. Before emigration began, the spoken word was the chief means of communication. Labour contracts generally took the form of verbal agreements, and most business transactions did not require written or spoken Italian.

The ability to read and write became more important when a family member was overseas and letters and telegrams became the major form of communication for families separated by the Atlantic. School records from Sutera show that enrolment of women in night courses rose significantly as men began to migrate. Between 1895 and 1905, female enrolment in adult education classes remained unchanged, and enrolment averaged around thirty students. Also, classes often closed at midyear due to lack of attendance. After 1905, attendance rose rapidly, and by 1907 the number of women enrolled in night courses had risen by 40 per cent.[85]

Migration encouraged women to enter the classroom for a variety of reasons. Economic necessity, concerns for privacy, and familial dreams of upward mobility combined to make learning to read and write an imperative. Translation services had to be paid for in cash or kind, and the intervention of a third party exposed a family's private affairs to outsiders. Most Suteresi wanted to keep their personal relations and financial situation within the immediate family, and only reluctantly went to the local priest or the mayor for help in reading a letter from overseas. According to Lorenzoni, in villages across Sicily and southern Italy migrants wrote to their wives urging them to learn to read and write and to 'keep their children in school at any cost.'[86] The women of Sutera and Milocca seem to have acted on their husbands' advice. Not only did enrolment in female adult classes grow, but so did attendance in elementary schools.

Literacy itself also became part of the realization of the migrant dream. In the nineteenth century, only the local gentry could read and write and afford to send their children to school beyond the third grade. School diplomas were visible signs of a family's successful transition from peasant to bourgeois status, and reading for pleasure was a privilege normally reserved for bourgeois women whose family status afforded them time for such leisurely pursuits. Anthropologist Charlotte Gower Chapman noted that in Milocca, Sicily, roughly 'a dozen people read for pleasure, mostly women, some of whom read religious pamphlets and others the few old novels which they might have or the serial story in the newspapers.'[87] Furthermore, literacy and a common language (Italian) opened new worlds for rural women as they began to read newspapers, novels, and religious tracts. For the first time ever, women of Sutera gained access to new ideas and information about Italy and faraway lands that was not filtered through fathers, husbands, or sons. In the daily newspapers women could read about life in Alabama, earthquakes in Calabria, African safaris, national political scandals, and international crises.[88] Serialized stories gained in popularity among a newspaper's female readership, and publishers chose stories that appealed specifically to women. In Sicily the historical romances of Luigi Natoli commonly appeared in *Giornale di Sicilia*. The written word integrated rural women into Benedict Anderson's 'imagined community' of newspaper readers.[89]

The magazines and newspapers that appeared in Sutera reinforced the new female consumer role in rural Sicily. Literacy gave women direct access to catalogues and a wealth of advertisements, while remittances enabled them to purchase mass-produced goods. By 1908 a woman in Sutera could order walnut armoires, dining room tables, iron bedsteads, carpets, mirrors, and even tile stoves. Although the lack of electricity kept gramophones and lights out of most rural homes, sewing machines, sofas, tables, and pianos appeared in the village and quickly became a family's prize possession.[90] Just as imported furnishings altered rural living spaces, ready-made clothing changed local dress. By 1906, rural women could order the latest Parisian fashions directly from stores in Palermo or Agrigento. If a particular style was not available, women could order a pattern from Butterick, and silk and satin cloth made in northern Italy or imported from Paris, to make their own. The appearance of mass-produced consumer goods in rural Sicilian towns eroded regional distinctions.[91] Newspaper articles, stories, furniture, and clothes began to erase the difference between the country bumpkin and city sophisticate.

The cultural, social, and economic impact of migration on the lives of rural women strongly influenced the transformation of rural women into consumers. Remittances enabled the women of Sutera to modernize their homes and to purchase new furnishings and fashionable clothes just like urban women. By the 1920s, Sicilian women were demanding access to the comforts of the modern urban world, better housing, running water, new clothes, and entertainment. Migration reinforced the emerging identification of rural women as housewives overseeing a consumer household, rather than as agricultural or industrial wage workers. Participation in consumer culture affected the position of women in civic life. As cultural critics and historians have recently suggested, the creation of public commercial spaces, based on mass communication and commodity exchange, serve as a means to include previously excluded peoples in national life.[92]

This case study of women in Sutera, Sicily, who remained home as their husbands searched for work in Alabama, Pennsylvania, and New York, confirms the wisdom of a transnational approach to migration by showing that transoceanic migration involved all family members and changed the lives both of those who migrated and of those who remained behind. The experiences of Sicily's so-called white widows also underscore the importance of a gendered perspective: we cannot fully understand the migration process, or patterns of repatriation, assimilation, settlement, or employment, without accounting for the influence that women in the homeland exerted on male migrants and on decisions made both overseas and at home. Transoceanic migration was deeply gendered. The influence of women who remained behind but actively sought to realize the migrant dream of a better life at home also helps to explain some of the seemingly conservative effects that migration had on rural communities. The Sutera case also suggests that migration may have served as an alternate route by which humble people from 'peripheral regions' could acquire capital. Although many island villages did not experience industrialization directly, peasants used the industrial economy to realize their own goals, many of which reflected pre-industrial definitions of wealth and success. The process of migration, like industrialization, redefined the economic position of both men and women, within both the family and community. Migration created a female consumer culture among rural women even though they had been pushed out of the wage labour force. The lives of Sicily's 'white widows' also raise questions regarding the political evolution of Italy and the role women played in efforts to create a unified state. Male migration also encouraged rural women to establish strong ties to the state long before they had the right to vote, and in this and other ways the Sutera, and Sicilian, example sheds light on gendered aspects of Italy's political evolution into a nation-state. Finally, the white widows of Sutera, though they lived their lives in small isolated villages, actively participated in the major economic, political, and cultural changes that occurred in Europe at the turn of the century.

NOTES

1 Ministero degli Affari Esteri (MAE), Commissariato Generale dell'Emigrazione (CGE) 'Sicilia: Emigrati italiani partiti negli anni 1876–1925, classificato per sesso e per età,' in *Annuario statistico della emigrazione italiana 1876–1925* (Rome: Commissariato Generale dell'Emigrazione, 1925), 183 (hereafter *Annuario statistico*).

2 Antonio Mangano, 'The Effect of Emigration upon Italy,' *Charities and Commons* 20, 5 (2 May 1908): 179; U.S. Congress, Senate, *Reports of the Immigration Commission*, vol. 12, *Emigrant Conditions in Europe: Italy*, S. Doc, 748, 61st Congress, 3rd session (Washington: Government Printing Office, 1911), 227; Giovanni Lorenzoni, *Inchiesta parlamentare sulle condizioni dei contadini nelle province meridionali e nella Sicilia*, vol. 6, *Sicilia*, 1, part 3, 509 (hereafter Lorenzoni, *Inchiesta*). For a discussion of the criticisms and concerns surrounding transoceanic migration see Giuseppe Bruccoleri, *L'emigrazione siciliana: Caratteri ed effetti secondo le più recenti inchieste* (Rome: Cooperativa Tip. Manuzio, 1911), 5–6; Pasquale Villari, 'L'emigrazione e le sue consequenze in Italia,' *Nuova Antologia* 127 (January 1907): 33–56; Biagio Puntero, *L'emigrazione: Conferenze tenute nella sala gialla del palazzo municipale in Caltanissetta. La sera 21 maggio 1910* (Caltanissetta: Tip. Ospizio Prof. di Beneficenze, 1911); Angelo Mosso, *Vita moderna degli italiani* (Milan: Fratelli Treves Editori, 1906); and Francesco Colletti, *Dell'emigrazione italiana* (Milan: Ulrico Hoepli, 1912). See also the article by Maddalena Tirabassi in the present volume.

3 'Cronaca Siciliana: I Drammi dell'adulterio,' *Giornale di Sicilia*, 4–5 February 1908, 5.

4 Maria Messina, 'La Mèrica,' in *Piccoli gorghi* (Palermo: Sellerio, 1988), 127–37.

5 Robert Foerster, *The Italian Emigration of Our Times* (1919, repr. New York: Arno Press, 1969), 22–43; Michael Piore, *Birds of Passage* (New York: Cambridge University Press, 1979), 56.

6 In making this point, I do not want to suggest that even the most successful migrant actually attained the same power and influence enjoyed by the landed elite and local bourgeoisie. However, the acquisition of the physical and cultural characteristics of the elite did mean that the children of these former sharecroppers and tenant farmers had the tools eventually to

reshape the social hierarchy of Sutera. Access to education, professions, and state resources would translate into influence and power in the postwar world.

7 Ministero di Agricoltura, Industria e Commercio (MAIC), Direzione Generale della Statistica (DGS), *Censimento della popolazione del regno al 10 febbraio 1901*, 1 (Rome: Tip. Naz. Bertero, 1902), 80. All population statistics include Milocca and Sutera. Although Sicilian towns were relatively large as compared to northern European villages, they generally resembled such villages; inhabitants were employed in agriculture and there was little industry. See Rudolph Bell, *Fate and Honor. Family and Village* (Chicago: University of Chicago Press, 1979), 9–10 for a discussion of definitions of village and town.

8 Stefano Sonnino, *Inchiesta in Sicilia* (1876, repr. Florence: Valecchi, 1974), 11; Lorenzoni, *Inchiesta*, part 2, 111.

9 Jane Schneider and Peter Schneider, *Culture and Political Economy in Western Sicily* (New York: Academic Press, 1976), 32–6; Francesco De Stefano and Francesco Luigi Oddo, *Storia della Sicilia* (Bari: Editori Laterza, 1963), 176–84; Lorenzoni, *Inchiesta*, part 2, 222–35.

10 Donna Gabaccia, *From Sicily to Elizabeth Street: Housing and Social Change among Italian Immigrants, 1880–1930* (Albany: State University of New York Press, 1984), 35–40.

11 Archivio Comunale di Sutera (ACS), 'Inchiesta sulle condizioni igeniche e sanitarie dei comuni del regno, 1885,' cat. IV, cl. 3. fasc. 1. According to this report, 88 per cent of the male population worked in agriculture, 4 per cent as artisans, and the remaining 8 per cent formed the local elite, civil servants, professionals, and clerics. For a description of fieldwork see Sonnino, *Inchiesta*, 12.

12 For more details, see the introduction, where Donna Gabaccia and Franca Iacovetta discuss Italian regionalism, rural women's waged and non-waged agricultural work throughout Italy's northern and southern regions, and the 'peculiarities' of Sicily, a major source of migrants for the United States. See also the detailed discussion of rural women's work in the essays by Andreina De Clementi (on the continental south, including Calabria), Maddalena Tirabassi (on rural districts across Italy), and Paola Corti (on Piedmont, in northwest Italy).

13 Sonnino, *Inchiesta*, 58–9. Most studies of Sicilian life note the difference between female agricultural wage work on the island and that on the mainland. In the northern regions of Piedmont and Lombardy women were expected to work as hard, if not harder than men, and women constituted half of the agricultural labour force in 1881. Similarly, in Calabria and

Campagna it was not unusual to see women working in the fields. For a
general overview see Donna Gabaccia, 'In the Shadows of the Periphery:
Italian Women in the Nineteenth Century,' in Marilyn Boxer and Jean
Quataert, eds., *Connecting Spheres: Women in the Western World, 1500 to the
Present* (New York: Oxford University Press, 1987), 173. For more informa-
tion on female labour patterns in the north see Patrizia Audenino, *Un
mestiere per partire: Tradizione migratoria, lavoro e comunità in una vallata alpina*
(Milan: Franco Angeli, 1990); see also Paola Corti, ed., *Istituto 'Alcide Cervi'
Annali 12/1990: Società rurale e ruoli femminili in Italia tra ottocento e novecento*
(Bologna: Il Mulino, 1992) and other essays in this volume dealing with
women's rural work in Italy.

14 Lorenzoni, *Inchiesta*, part 3, 16.
15 Ibid., part 4, 462–4; Gabaccia, *From Sicily*, 40–5.
16 Sonnino, *Inchiesta*, 242.
17 Francesco Renda, *I Fasci Siciliani* (Turin: Einaudi, 1977), 6–114, 342.
18 ACS, 'Registro delle domande di nulla osta 1890–1903,' cat. XIII, cl. 1–3,
    fasc. 2.
19 ACS, 'Prospetto dei movimenti avvenuti nella popolazione residente, 1901–
    1910,' cat. XII. Figures compiled by Dr Mario Tona; Lorenzoni, *Inchiesta*,
    part 5, 787.
20 In Sutera, women and children accounted for about 15 per cent of emi-
    grants from the village before 1930.
21 Migration statistics from Sutera are based on a database compiled from
    birth records, marriage records, passport registers, and draft records in the
    municipal archive of Sutera, along with passenger lists from ship records,
    1908–10, located at the New York Public Library. The file contains informa-
    tion on 714 migrants. There are ninety female migrants. One-third of the
    women are under fifteen years of age. Of the women over fifteen, thirty-six
    are married, eight are single. The civil status of sixteen of the adult women
    is unknown. The rest of the migrants are men.
22 U.S. Congress, Senate, *Reports of the Immigration Commission*, vol. 71, *Immi-
    grants in Industries, Part IV, Iron and Steel Manufacturing Industry in the South*,
    S. Doc, 633, 61st Congress, 2nd session (Washington: Government Printing
    Office, 1911), 173 (hereafter *Iron and Steel Manufacturing Industry in the
    South*).
23 Southern Italian emigrants in Alabama earned approximately $8.00 a week,
    nearly $400 a year. See *Iron and Steel Manufacturing Industry in the South*,
    173–4. In 1915 a two-room house in Sutera cost approximately 1000 to
    1500 lire. A one-room house sold for 600 lire. Housing prices are based
    on recorded sales in the Ufficio Conservatore dei Beni Immobiliare in

Caltanissetta. To read about migrants' intentions to return see Lorenzoni, *Inchiesta*, part 5, 812. Calculations of the rate of repatriation in Sutera are based on the migrant file.

24 *Annuario statistico*, 183, 193. While it is important to note that Sicily had the lowest percentage of individual migrants and much higher proportion of family groups among emigrants, the number of men migrating alone rose between 1901 and 1914.

25 Betty Boyd Caroli, *Italian Repatriation from the United States, 1900–1914* (New York: Center for Migration Studies, 1973), 49–50; priests in the surrounding parishes noted similar rates of return.

26 New York Public Library, 'S.S. San Giovanni Palermo–New York, 31-3-1910,' *Passenger Lists*. On his arrival in New York City, Paolino C. declared he had paid for his ticket by himself, and was in possession of $15.

27 MAE, *Norme legislative e regolamentari concernenti la concessione di passaporti per l'estero* (Rome: Tip. Naz. di G. Bertero, 1905), 6, 24–6. In 1905 the law was amended: a migrant no longer had to provide official proof of his wife's consent. However, women retained the right to invalidate their husbands' passport applications.

28 ACS, 'Domanda di nulla-osta, Giuseppe C., 1901,' cat. XIII, cl. 3.

29 Lorenzoni, *Inchiesta*, part 4, 463; Giuseppe Pitrè, *La famiglia, la casa, la vita del popolo siciliano* (Palermo: A. Reber, 1913), 33–4. Charlotte Gower Chapman, *Milocca: A Sicilian Village* (Cambridge: Schenkman, 1971), 38.

30 Lorenzoni, *Inchiesta*, part 3, 21, 34–5, 136. On average, day labourers worked between 150 and 200 days out of each year. The average daily wage for hoeing, sowing, and plowing was 1.9 lire. ACS, 'Risposte ai quesiti contenuti nella circolare prefettizia, 3 ottobre 1901, div. 3 # 11030-riguardanti l'inchiesta pel contratti di lavoro,' cat. XI, cl. 2, fasc. 2a; 'Patti agrari Sutera, 15 agosto 1911,' cat. XI, cl. 1a, fasc. 4a; 'Relazione periodica agraria aprile–luglio 1905,' cat. XI, cl. 1a, fasc. 4a.

31 Archivio Comunale di Ficarazzi, 'Memo: Al sindaco giugno 18, 1937,' cat. XIII, cl. 1; Audenino, *Un mestiere*, 152–3.

32 New York Public Library, 'SS. San Giorgio, September 16, 1910,' *Passenger Lists*; ACS, *Atti di nascita, 1882*, #89; *Atti di nascita, 1884*, #130.

33 Gower Chapman, *Milocca*, 109.

34 Analysis of female-related migrants is based on family reconstructions and passenger lists.

35 Lorenzoni, *Inchiesta*, part 4, 690.

36 'Stoico suicidio a Racalmuto: Abbandonata dal marito e colpita nell'onore,' *Giornale di Sicilia*, 22–3 July 1913, 2.

37 ACS, 'Elenco delle famiglie povere del comune /capoluogo/ chi hanno

diritto all'assistenza gratuita ed alla alimentazione per l'anno 1912,' cat. II,
cl. 4, fasc. 1.

38 ACS, 'Memo: Dalla questura di Palermo al sindaco di Sutera, settembre
1920,' cat. XIII, cl. 3, fasc. 1.
39 ACS, 'Memo dal R. agenzia consolare d'Italia, Birmingham, Alabama,
12 novembre, 1915,' cat. XIII, cl. 1, fasc. 1.
40 The lack of industrial development in the island, combined with the linger-
ing consequences of feudalism that shaped land-tenure patterns, ensured
that property ownership remained the most important measure of wealth.
See De Stefano and Oddo, *Storia della Sicilia*, for a description of Sicilian
society and economy. For discussions of honour and respect in Sicily see
Schneider and Schneider, *Culture and Society*, 86–102; Bell, *Fate and Honor*,
2–3; and Jane Schneider and Peter Schneider, 'Going Forward in Reverse
Gear: Culture, Economy and Political Economy in the Demographic Transitions of a Rural Sicilian Town,' in John R. Gillis, Louise A. Tilly, and David
Levine, eds., *The European Experience of Declining Fertility, 1850–1970* (Cambridge: Blackwell Publishers, 1992), 154.
41 Schneider and Schneider, *Culture and Political Economy*, 87–9.
42 ACS, *Atti di nascita 1890–1914*.
43 ACS, *Atti di nascita 1880–1885*, and *Atti di matrimonio, 1880–1885*. The
average birth-per-marriage ratio provides a rough estimate of marital
fertility. These calculations are based on 374 family reconstructions.
44 ACS, *Atti di nascita 1880–1920*; Schneider and Schneider, 'Going Forward,'
147. John Briggs found similar rates in the Abruzzi; see 'Fertility and Cultural Change among Families in Italy and America,' *American Historical
Review* 5 (December 1986): 1132–3.
45 Gower Chapman, *Milocca*, 80–1; Jane Schneider and Peter Schneider,
'Demographic Transitions in a Sicilian Rural Town,' *Journal of Family History*
9 (Fall 1984): 250.
46 The birth-per-marriage ratio, family size, and marriage ages are based on
the *Atti di nascita 1890–1914* in Sutera. The total number of births among
the migrant population was 699, and the total number of marriages was
183. Among those residents who did not emigrate there were 3003 births
and 629 marriages.
47 John W. Briggs, 'Fertility and Cultural Change,' 1134.
48 ACS, *Atti di matrimonio, 1890–1904*. The average age of brides at first marriage, where the groom has never been married before, is calculated from
603 marriages.
49 Schneider and Schneider, 'Going Forward,' 157–73.
50 Susan Cotts Watkins, *From Provinces into Nations: Demographic Integration in*

Western Europe, 1870–1960 (Princeton: Princeton University Press, 1991), 113–14.

51 Enrico La Loggia, *Storia della Sicilia post-unificazione* (Palermo: Industria Grafica Nazionale, 1958), 13–22; Donna Gabaccia, 'In the Shadows of the Periphery,' 166–76; Jole Calapso, 'La donna in Sicilia e in Italia: La realtà e la falsa coscienza nella statistica dal 1871 ad oggi,' *Quaderni Siciliani* 2 (March–April 1973): 13–20.

52 ACS, *Atti di Matrimonio 1880–1900*.

53 Gianni Toniolo, *An Economic History of Liberal Italy* (New York: Routledge, 1990), 103–4.

54 In 1910 Caterina Bennetti-Ventura described the few women she saw working in the fields as 'poor widows, or miserable beggars or women who had husbands in America.' Bennetti-Ventura, *Trine e Donne Siciliane* (Milan: Ulrico Hoepli, 1911), 179.

55 MAIC, DGS, *Censimento 1901*, vol. III, 272–320; MAIC, DGS, *Censimento della popolazione del regno d'Italia al giugno 1911*, vol. III (Rome: Tip. Naz. di G. Bertero, 1914), 331–2.

56 Giovanbattista Raja, *Il fenomeno emigratorio siciliano con speciale riguardo al quinquennio 1902–1906* (Palermo: Tip. Imp. Affari Pubblicità, 1908), 54–72; Giuseppe Bruccoleri, *La Sicilia di oggi: Appunti economici* (Rome: Athenaeum, 1913), 94–9.

57 *Iron and Steel Manufacturing Industry in the South*: for wages see 176–9; for information on the standard of living see 207–27.

58 ACS, 'Cassa rurale dei depositi e prestiti, AS. Paolino' di Sutera, 31 Aug. 1904, cat. II, cl. 4a, fasc. 1a; Lorenzoni, *Inchiesta*, part 2, 714. In 1907 the mayor of Sutera noted that the money migrants sent home had 'noticeably improved their economic position.' ACS, 'Notizie statistiche,' private library of Dr Mario Tona.

59 Lorenzoni, *Inchiesta*, part 5, 816. In 1906 1,201,591 lire were deposited by emigrants in the province of Caltanissetta. In 1907, the amount reached nearly 2 million lire.

60 The cost of living in Sutera was far lower than in the United States. Most families lived off pasta, bread, and vegetables made from crops they grew themselves or gathered in the fields and woods. Meat was only served at Christmas, Easter, or in case of illness. A family could feed itself for around fifty dollars (250 lire) a year and manage to save at least 250 lire each year.

61 Ufficio Conservatore dei Beni Immobiliare, *Registri dei Case-Sutera*, vol. 641, no. 527, 1915. Francesco F. bought a two-floor two-room house for 600 lire. Smaller houses sold for as little as 100 lire. After the First World War real

estate and land prices rose sharply. A modest two-floor house sold for about 2000 lire.

62 Luciano Cafagna, 'Italy 1830–1914,' in Carlo M. Cipolla, ed., *The Emergence of Industrial Societies* (New York: Fontana Books, 1976), 303; Toniolo, *An Economic History*, 100–4. Although remittances did not stimulate industrial economic growth in the region, they did contribute to the movement away from an agricultural economy.
63 MAIC, DGS, *Censimento 1901*, vol. 3, 272–320; *Censimento 1911*, vol. 3, pp. 331–2; *Censimento della popolazione del regno al 31 dicembre 1921*, vol. 13 (Rome: Stabilimento Poligrafica per L'amministrazione dello Stato, 1927), 508–25. In 1929, Charlotte Gower Chapman noted that female shopkeepers were well respected in the village of Milocca, a town that had been governed by Sutera until 1926, and were addressed as Donna, a title reserved for elite women. Gower Chapman, *Milocca*, 50–4.
64 Interview, Summer 1991.
65 *Iron and Steel Manufacturing Industry in the South*, 662.
66 Ibid., 180–2, 671. Note that boarders are persons who receive room and board; lodgers paid only for a room.
67 Ida Fazio, 'Transmissione della proprietà, sussistenza e *status* femminili in Sicilia (Capizzi, 1790–1900),' in Corti, *Istituto 'Alcide Cervi' Annali 12/1990: Società rurale*, 181–99.
68 Archivio dello Stato-Caltanissetta (ASC), *Catasti dei terreni-Sutera 1870–1879; Catasti dei fabbricati-Sutera 1870–1879.*
69 New York Public Library, 'S.S. San Giorgio: December 10, 1908,' *Passenger Lists*; ASC, *Catasto dei fabbricati-Sutera*, partita #2271.
70 Lorenzoni, *Inchiesta*, part 5, 839.
71 ASC, *Catasto dei fabbricati-Sutera 1900–1920.*
72 Ibid.
73 Bruno Ramirez, *On the Move: French-Canadian and Italian Migrants in the North Atlantic Economy, 1860–1914* (Toronto: McClelland and Stewart, 1991) has done some important preliminary work on this front.
74 ASC, *Catasto dei fabbricati-Sutera 1900–1914.*
75 Lorenzoni, *Inchiesta*, part 5, 832–3.
76 For a discussion of consumption and migration within the Jewish immigrant community see Anna R. Igra, 'Male Providerhood and the Public Purse: Anti-Desertion Reform in the Progressive Era,' in Victoria de Grazia, ed., *The Sex of Things: Gender and Consumption in Historical Perspective* (Berkeley: University of California Press, 1996), 188–211. For a general discussion of working-class women and consumption see Kathy Peiss, *Cheap Amusements:*

Working Women and Leisure in Turn-of-the-Century New York (Philadelphia: Temple University Press, 1986).

77 In the United States, Sicilian women's identities changed as they settled into their new communities – defined by non-Italians as Italian, within the community as southern Italian or Sicilian, and within the Sicilian community by their village. Transoceanic migration shifted the way these women saw themselves in relation to nation-states – a process that emerges in the biography of Rosa Cavatelli, Maria Hall Ets, *Rosa: The Life of an Italian Immigrant*, 2nd ed. (Madison: University of Wisconsin Press, 1999).

78 ACS, *Atti di nascita 1880–1910*.

79 ACS, 'Memo dal sindaco al consolato d'Italia, 12 ottobre, 1915,' cat. XIII, cl. 1, fasc. 1.

80 ACS, 'Dal sindaco al questura di Napoli, 1907,' cat. XV, cl. 8a.

81 MAE, CGE, 'Commissione Arbitrale d'Emigrazione della Provincia di Caltanissetta 1906–1913,' busta 10, fasc. 122; and 'Commissione Arbitrale di Palermo,' busta 29, fasc. 11.

82 Victoria de Grazia, *How Fascism Ruled Women* (Berkeley: University of California Press, 1992). As de Grazia notes, the position of women under Fascist rule was defined by maternity, their identification with tradition, and their willingness to subordinate their individual or even familial needs to the good of the state. Fascist definitions of citizenship swept aside ideas of equality or liberty central to socialist and feminist equal-rights movements, and replaced them with corporatist ideas of male and female citizenship. I do not want to suggest, however, that the emerging relationship between Sicilian rural women and the nation-state meant that they supported Fascism, only that their claims on the state were never based on individual rights as active citizens.

83 Miriam Cohen, *Workshop to Office: Two Generations of Italian Women in New York City, 1900–1950* (Ithaca: Cornell University Press, 1992), 110; see also Linda Gordon, *Heroes of Their Own Lives: The Politics and History of Family Violence in Boston, 1800–1960* (New York: Viking Press, 1988), chaps. 8–9. For a first-hand account see Maria Hall Ets, *Rosa*.

84 ACS, 'Scuole seriale e festive per adulti analfabeti 1905–1906,' cat. XII, cl. 2, fasc. 9. For a history of education in Sicily see Gaetano Bonnetta, *Istruzione e società nella Sicilia dell'ottocento* (Palermo: Sellerio, 1981).

85 ACS 'Scuola Seriale 1895,' cat. IX, cl. 2, fasc. 9; ACS, 'Istruzione di scuole rurale e festivi per adulti analfabeti, 16 luglio 1905,' cat. IX, cl. 2, fasc. 9; Stefano Jacini, *Atti della giunta per l'inchiesta agraria e sulle condizioni della classe agricola*, vol. 13, 1, fasc. 1, Relazione del Commissario Abele Damiani (Rome: Forzani Tip. del Senato, 1884), 121.

86 Lorenzoni, *Inchiesta*, part 3, 531–2; see also Foerster, *The Italian Emigration*, 460–1, and John Briggs, *An Italian Passage: Immigrants to Three American Cities* (New Haven: Yale University Press, 1978), 55–6.
87 Gower Chapman, *Milocca*, 20.
88 *Giornale di Sicilia*, 7–8 Sept. 1905, 2; 17–18 Sept. 1905, 3; 4–5 Jan. to 13–14 Mar. 1908, 4; 5–6 June 1912, 4.
89 Benedict Anderson, *Imagined Communities* (London: Verso Press, 1983); Cotts Watkins, *From Provinces*, chaps. 6 and 7.
90 Gower Chapman, *Milocca*, 19, 131.
91 Lorenzoni, *Inchiesta*, part 4, 470.
92 Victoria de Grazia, 'Empowering Women as Citizen-Consumers,' in *The Sex of Things*, 275; see also Judith G. Coffin, 'Consumption, Production, and Gender: The Sewing Machine in Nineteenth-Century France,' in Laura L. Frader and Sonya O. Rose, eds., *Gender and Class in Modern Europe* (Ithaca: Cornell University Press, 1996), 111–41.

2 Gender Relations and Migration Strategies in the Rural Italian South: Land, Inheritance, and the Marriage Market

Andreina De Clementi

TRANSLATED BY GABRIELE SCARDELLATO

In 1908, a young immigrant man named Saverio wrote to his wife in southern Italy from Westfield, Connecticut, U.S.A. His brief message home, though formulaic, suggests how gender expectations shaped the mass migrations from Italy while also challenging men and women to relate to each other in new ways. 'I ask your forgiveness for not having written,' Saverio wrote before explaining his silence: 'I have not worked for more than two months because of the presidential elections ... and many projects have been stopped.'[1] Saverio presented himself to his wife, after a long and apparently anxious silence, as the victim of politics and the economic instability that accompanied American democracy.

In fact, however, it was not the presidential election of 1908 that frustrated Saverio's efforts to fulfil his obligations to his family in Italy. Rather, the U.S. economy was recovering from the severe financial panic in 1907, when unemployment levels soared temporarily. The numbers of new immigrants arriving in the United States from Italy and other countries plummeted immediately in 1908, but for those like Saverio who found they had entered an economy in crisis, the search for work was far more difficult than the reports of earlier migrants, returned to their home villages and eager to demonstrate their successes, may have led them to expect.

Unfortunately for Saverio, his competence as a breadwinner remained in question well after the presidential elections had come and gone. Eight months later, in March 1909, Saverio again apologized to his wife for a long silence, although he no longer blamed his economic woes on an American political transition, which had in fact proved an easy one, from one Republican party president to another. 'Beloved wife, you must forgive me,' he wrote in words bordering on despair, 'I have put off writing because I have been without work for seven months.'[2] Significantly, Saverio apologized to his wife, in both cases, for his silence, not for his unemployment. Evidently, his wife was somehow able to feed and house herself without money from Saverio during these months, although we do not know how. We can assume also that Saverio felt sufficiently embarrassed about his unemployment that his sense of failure caused the silences for which he apologized.

Theorists tell us that gender shapes all human movements; migration is surely no exception, though it has perhaps received less attention from historians of gender than some other dimensions of human life. In this essay, I establish how notions of masculinity and femininity, and of men's and women's roles, helped produce the apparently marginal role of women in the mass migrations from the rural Italian south. It bears stressing that my focus, though comparative, concentrates on the regions of the continental south, and thus does not include the island of Sicily, where some different patterns emerge. (One contrast concerns women's differing access to agricultural work; while large numbers of women in parts across the continental south performed agricultural work – as did their counterparts in the rural north – far fewer women did so in Sicily – for reasons that Linda Reeder examines elsewhere in this volume.)[3] I also examine how migration, and the departure of large numbers of men, altered the roles of women in southern peasant society during the mass exodus. These linked themes require a fresh, and gendered, look at Italy's south, its structures of rural life, and its peasant families and economies.

Italians and Americans alike view the Italian south as the paradigmatic region of Italian emigration. Indeed, when Italians refer to the mass migrations of the years from 1870 to 1914, they are almost always referring to the great exodus from the south to the Americas that occurred during the first twenty years of the twentieth century. Quantitatively, these migrations were certainly impressive, even though (as other essays in this collection note) regions outside the south also contributed more than their share of Italy's emigrants. Between 1870 and 1914, the four leading emigration regions of the Italian south (including the Abruzzo, Campania, Calabria, and Basilicata, and excluding Puglia and the islands of Sicily and Sardinia) totalled some four million emigrants. More than three-quarters of those migrating to the United States were from south-

TABLE 2.1
Percentage of females among migrants from
Italian south by region, 1876–1925

Abruzzo/Molise	19
Campania	27
Puglia	21
Basilicata	30
Calabria	19
Sicily	29
Sardinia	15

Source: Annuario statistico dell'emigrazione
italiana dal 1876 al 1925 (Rome: Ed. del
Commissariato dell'emigrazione, 1926),
table V.

ern Italy and Sicily; around half of the migrants to Argentina and Brazil were from these regions. Argentina and Brazil also witnessed a consistent migration from the Veneto in the northeast.

Migrations from the Italian south were of two types – permanent and temporary (or 'sojourning'). In the latter pattern, migrants travelled to the Americas several times for brief work campaigns that lasted from four to eight years. Not surprisingly, both migration patterns reflected conventional expectations about gender and age. Most permanent migrants were young couples with or without children, while most temporary migrants were men. U.S. immigration officials noted that the largest group of south Italian male migrants were married men like Saverio, but that younger and unmarried men formed an important minority. Sojourning by male 'birds of passage' (or *golondrinas*, swallows) was so extensive that permanent demographic losses to southern Italy proved to be much lower – only two million – than total emigrations from the region had threatened.

The two types of migration were also linked through gender relations. Men like Saverio generally returned to Italy several times and many resettled there permanently after twenty or more years of sojourning. Men also became permanent migrants when whole families resettled abroad, often after interludes of male sojourning. South Italian women thus typically left their native villages in far smaller numbers than men (see table 2.1). When they did emigrate, women left as permanent migrants intending not to return, and they followed the paths of fathers and husbands who had sojourned abroad several times themselves. In some cases, the women's fathers or uncles had been sojourning for decades. Between 1909 and 1928, 115,451 women (or about 20 per cent of all women emigrants to the United States) returned to Italy. During the same period, the number of male returners (847,235) was much greater, as were male rates of return (60.33 per cent).[4]

Volumes have been written about the Italian south and its mass emigrations, but little of it from a feminist perspective.[5] At least until the 1960s, Anglo-American researchers tended to see the region as an enormous anthropological deposit of a European past that had everywhere else disappeared, leaving Italy's Mezzogiorno – 'the land that time forgot' – as much a part of the Third World as the Samoan Islands or Amazon forest.

The economic stagnation of this European periphery was attributed to a distinctive culture of poverty that discouraged economic initiative and political democracy. Edward Banfield's influential but wrong-headed book on one south Italian village in the 1950s particularly emphasized southern Italians' familist indifference to individual initiative and responsibility, and their distrust of the liberal state, modern education, voluntary association, and civic cooperation.[6] Whether intentionally or not, the backwardness of the region and its familism became associated with orientalist images of secluded, superstitious, and oppressed women. These provided a convenient counterpoint to the autonomy and competence of more fortunate northern European and American women supposedly released from patriarchy by economic development, wage-earning, and liberal democracy.[7]

More recently, historians in Italy and in the English-speaking world have become more interested in explaining how and why this notion of an exotic, different, and backward Italian south emerged during the political unification of Italy. While this new research has not completely dispelled older stereotypes, it has opened up avenues for new approaches to the study of women, gender, and the mass southern migrations. In particular, new interpretations of the Italian south encourage us to assume a critical stance toward any exoticized images of southern women that suggest women's limited mobility resulted directly or simply from their domestic segregation and/or from men's efforts to control their sexuality.

Rural Life and Change in the Italian South

By the end of the nineteenth century, the governing classes of Italy had begun to outline the characteristics that made the Mezzogiorno different from the rest of the country. They undoubtedly exaggerated these differences, as they did also the levels of economic and industrial development in Italy's north.[8] Still, it is useful to view Italy's Mezzogiorno as a particular kind of peasant society that is indeed different from industrial societies.

As theorists of peasant society A.V. Chayanov, Karl Polanyi, and Theodor Shanin have pointed out, peasant rural life is as much driven by reproductive as productive goals. Indeed, in societies where almost all production is subsistence (that is, intended for consumption by members of a family household), where the main work group is structured by kin relations, and where cash wages are the exception rather than the rule, the distinction between production and reproduction is not easy to draw. The main concern of families in peasant societies is to keep all members of the family fully employed, and to maintain a delicate balance between family resources (usually land), family labour, and family consumption. Making a profit is not the essential motor of a peasant economy; the survival and reproduction of a family group – often viewed in linear terms – is.[9]

Italy's Mezzogiorno was still a peasant society in 1900, but it also was buffeted considerably by change during the complex process of Italy's political and economic unification. In various ways most of these changes forced peasants into the marketplace for goods without substantially expanding their opportunities to earn the cash they needed there. The market increasingly rendered subsistence production an impossible basis for an alternative 'good life.' Peasants' efforts to preserve some elements of the self-sufficiency and autonomy they enjoyed as subsistence producers merely highlighted their increasing economic marginality and revealed how badly the market had broken the once sturdy bones of subsistence production.

A short catalogue of the main economic changes occurring in rural Italy in the nineteenth century provide the foundation for understanding how migration and gender eventually entwined in the rural Mezzogiorno. The impact of these changes varied considerably from region to region, and even from village to village. Thus, for example, the regions of the continental Italian south featured here (especially parts of Basilicata and Calabria) seem – and were – quite different, socially and economically, from the Sicilian region examined by Linda Reeder.[10] Many domestic and proto-industrial forms of production – including textiles, a traditionally female craft – collapsed in the south in the aftermath of unification, as Italy's liberal trade policies opened southern marketplaces to textiles produced elsewhere in Italy and in Europe. Dependence on agriculture thus actually increased. In some southern regions, especially along the coasts, production for the market (usually wheat, citrus, grapes, oil, or nuts) expanded. But in many other areas, the majority of peasant families continued to sell only surpluses not required for family food consumption rather than changing their cultivation habits so as to purchase food with cash generated by commercial agriculture.

Little cash circulated in areas of subsistence agriculture. Debts in this peasant society were incurred and discharged without recourse to cash – a discrete quantity of seed borrowed today against an abundant amount to be harvested later. Credit was otherwise virtually unavailable, and usury flourished. Many kinds of transactions were made in kind. Rent was rendered in wheat, making it necessary always to set aside a portion, if not all, of a family's land holdings for this purpose. Services – whether by doctor, wise-woman, or priest – were also paid in kind. Cash purchases had to be limited, even as peasants became aware of what cash could buy: some wanted a suit, a pair of shoes, new tools, salt, or a bit of olive oil. But consumption was also limited by taxes, the most important, and inescapable, drain on limited cash incomes in areas of subsistence production. After unification, the very light taxes of the old Bourbon monarchy gave way to the much more rigorous demands of the national administration, which simply imposed the tax traditions of Piedmont on the rural regions of the Italian south, exacerbating peasant complaints.

Although it is difficult to judge the amount of conscious planning involved, Italy's new national state clearly used fiscal policy to expand the place of the market in the Italian economy and to weaken, if not destroy, a peasant economy viewed as backward and illiberal.[11] Some improvements accompanying economic change and unification did occur, and were reflected in declining mortality rates that sent local populations soaring. Still, it seems an inescapable conclusion that this rural and now highly indebted majority, was destined for, but also deeply opposed to, proletarianization and to lives as full-time wage-earners.

For many centuries, peasant labour in the Italian south had been transformed into a commodity for sale only at particular times of the year, notably for the harvest. Even days of labour on a neighbour's lands, or help in slaughtering a pig, had no price, but were instead parts of labour exchanges within and between families. For those families with no agricultural surplus to sell, the only way to obtain cash was to join the gangs of migrant agricultural labourers. As increasing numbers did so, they set in motion the dynamic that would eventually send millions to the far-off Americas. Finally, and contrary to every appearance, not even the land was part of a self-regulating market.

Even by century's end, very little money circulated within the rural southern economy. To obtain cash, it was necessary either to shift family labour devoted to subsistence production toward production for the market or to join the migrant agricultural work gangs seeking wages elsewhere. Many peasant families initially viewed migration to the Americas as a way to earn cash and thereby shore up an older way of life. For others, however, migration rather quickly became a way to abandon a peasant society and a way of life that no longer seemed desirable or even viable.

Gender, Land, Inheritance, and Migration

A sense of permanent economic crisis rooted in political change was already widespread in southern Italy by the time that Saverio wrote his despairing notes home to his wife in 1908 and 1909. Although migration became a very popular response to the myriad threats the market posed for peasant families, by no means all or even the majority of southern Italians chose to migrate. Rates of emigration varied significantly with age and gender, with men outnumbering women and working-age persons outnumbering children and older persons. One village might have a high emigration rate while a village in the next valley over had a low one.

Economists and historians alike have noted how landowning patterns, which defined status and social mobility in peasant societies, influenced patterns of migrations.[12] Few, however, have examined how gender relations shaped landowning patterns, or studied the influence of distinctive inheritance systems on both. As a result, they may have missed significant factors in explaining the region's patterns of migration. A few very wealthy families owned large estates, while peasant households combined subsistence production on very small parcels of land they owned with wage-earning and sharecropping on large estates. Many such estates specialized in wheat or oil production, with the surplus intended for sale. Occasionally, as occurred on the plain of Eboli (Campania), 'natives' reared water buffalo or sheep, while migrant labourers from other districts worked on the large estates. In these areas, land was rarely for sale, and few peasants owned enough land to guarantee their own subsistence needs.

Studies of the mainland south argue that emigration rates were highest from regions with widespread landowning, and considerably lower in areas of concentrated landholding and large estates.[13] Differing rules of inheritance produced and perpetuated the differences between these two kinds of peasant societies as they faced the economic changes of the nineteenth century. Linked to differing gender ideologies, and to differing family structures, inheritance rules also helped to produce differential emigration rates for men and women, and to make male sojourning particularly characteristic of regions of subsistence production. According to available case studies, the traditional Italian south was characterized by two systems of inheritance. One can be considered a partible but patrilineal system, where the family patrimony passed to male heirs and every effort was made to avoid dividing plots of land into parcels that could not guarantee subsistence in the next generation. The second system divided family patrimonies, and expected daughters and sons to inherit equally.[14]

Patrilineal transmission of property to sons characterized the hilly and mountainous areas of the southern scrub lands, where land was widely distributed and subsistence production common, albeit under siege from the changes described above. Here the focus of peasant society was the continuity of a family lineage that often coupled land with the family name. Very strong attachments between the family line of fathers and sons and their houses and plots of land were common; the land was viewed as the 'seat' of family life and the ideal was for these attachments to persist over several generations.[15] In regions like these, daughters had a right to a dowry rather than to a share of the family patrimony of immovable properties. At marriage, daughters received a trousseau (usually of clothes and household linens) and a sum of money. Dowries were important symbols of family well-being, but not symbols of family identity comparable to land or houses.[16] According to a contemporary observer, 'The more well off is the family of the bride, the greater is the amount of money,' whereas in marriages among the poor, 'the trousseau often is or outweighs the dowry.'[17] In these areas, women simply did not inherit land. The payment of cash dowry money might be spread out over time. Given the high death rates of much of the *ancien régime*, women sometimes died without children; in these cases her dowry reverted to the family members (her parents or brothers) who had been responsible for paying it.[18]

Despite their frequency, however, such deaths were unpredictable, and could not be relied upon to relieve fathers or brothers of the financial burdens posed by women's dowries. Avoiding the cash costs of dowries thus remained a singular preoccupation, leading, for instance, to a limited but not uncommon matrimonial strategy of double marriages of brother and sister with sister and brother. Such marriages in effect cancelled accounts without requiring the transfer of any cash payments. The marriage of one woman and her dowry proceeded on the assumption that the marriage of the second woman and her dowry (of equal value) would occur at a later date. This arrangement gave a family breathing space in accumulating cash reserves.[19] Not surprisingly, then, the principle of endogamy reigned supreme in these regions, where families so feared dispersing the family patrimony that even couples without children favoured masculine inheritance. Women in these circumstances named their husbands as their immediate heirs, while men 'postponed' their wives' inheritance, and 'jumped over' their sisters so that property reverted to their brothers.[20]

By contrast, in south Italian wheat-growing districts and areas with large estates and concentrated patterns of landholding, men and women were on an equal footing for property inheritance, which more commonly consisted of houses rather than lands. Here, the demand for labour could be intensive – that is why the plain of Eboli attracted immigrants. The need for labour encouraged Ebolians to obtain it through definitive inducements to outsiders. And no argument could be more persuasive than an offer of a marriage that included a house and sometimes a bit of land as a dowry. Women in these regions could sometimes become the guarantors of a successful agricultural enterprise. Poorer families sought mainly that the property to be inherited by a bride complemented that of the groom: cash payments, lands, houses, trousseaux, and wage-earning potential all might be significant factors in arranging marriages. In any case, women frequently held lands, houses, livestock, and agricultural implements.[21] The remains of this inheritance system, for example, left visible traces in the household census for Pisticci in the latifondial district of Matera. There, in 1961, 53 per cent of the taxable population was made up of women, 60 to 75 per cent of whom were titular heads of households.[22]

As anthropologist Jack Goody observed, methods of dividing property are also methods for separating and valuing people. It seems quite possible that some regions of southern Italy assigned much higher social value to women than others. In the districts of the large estates, where access to immovable goods was awarded to both men and women, women could often have 'a say in the formulation of marriage contracts.'[23] Such female authority was virtually unimaginable in the districts of patrilineal inheritance in the hills and mountains. There, gender inequality was sanctioned in a thousand different ways, beginning even before birth. The hereditary arrangements of the village of Solofra (Campania), for example, dictated different treatment of sons and daughters born after their father's death: a dying father might quickly arrange special ceremonies in the event of the premature death of his as yet unborn male heir. Nothing of the sort was done for daughters.[24]

Despite occasional efforts to establish gender equality in inheritance rights reaching as far back as Frederick II of Swabia,[25] patrilineal inheritance continued to characterize south Italian areas of small landholdings until Italian unification. The system had its own internal problems, of course. Its purpose was to guarantee the integrity of plots of land and the patrilineages associated with them. After unification, the imposition of Piedmont's civil code – which required inheritance by all children – left fewer escape routes. The tenacity of resistance to these changes was marked. Understandably, with few local options for wage-earning in commercial agriculture or on large estates owned by others, inheritance by daughters again appeared as a threat to the unity of family name and plot of land. Only cash earnings, and the purchase of land, could solve this problem, and cash was scarce in these regions.

Piedmont's inheritance code allowed for two related options. One was a straightforward equality among all heirs; this was automatically enforced in the event of an intestate death.[26] The second allowed division of property into two equal parts, of which one portion would be distributed equally amongst all the children, and the remainder left to the discretion of the writer of the will. In the latter case, females divided with their brothers one-half of the patrimony, but they could be, and often were, excluded from the other half. Agricultural families in areas of the arable, southern scrub land, already struggling because of population growth starting at the end of the eighteenth century and the economic crises described above, sought to minimize the most pernicious effects of the new inheritance law. They used every means at their disposal to continue older practices under the new legal codes. One solution was to give half the father's property to one son (not always the oldest), thus preserving the unity of family name with the parental house or a significant plot of land.[27]

Still, when faced with a growing population of children who more often than in the past survived infancy, peasants' efforts to come to terms with the new inheritance laws were indeed difficult and constantly threatened the splitting up of landholdings into tiny 'handkerchiefs.' The proliferation of small landholdings insufficient for maintaining a family's subsistence needs has been widely remarked in studies of such regions. This trend in turn forced families to try to rent or lease additional lands or to pursue seasonal wage labour. Female dowries constituted an ongoing aggravation under these conditions, and proverbs regularly disparaged daughters, and their dowries, for bankrupting their fathers and brothers. With mortality rates declining, and the numbers of daughters to be dowered increasing, fathers were forced to multiply their efforts and to stain with their sweat the proverbial seven shirts in order to scrape together a dowry. The payment of dowries in cash seemed the only sensible way of avoiding an unsustainable fragmentation of patrimonies while leaving in place the traditional distinction between male and female goods: land for sons and trousseaus and money for daughters, a safe balance at the death of the parents. But the limited amount of cash circulating through areas of widespread landholding and small-scale subsistence production made this obvious solution virtually unobtainable.

Satisfactory solutions to such inheritance problems were hard to find and both real change and serious resistance marked areas of subsistence production and widespread landholding through the late-nineteenth-century Italian south. After the liberalization of the country's inheritance laws, the goal was no longer the recovery of the dowry but rather the task of preventing plots of land – no longer solely male possessions – from escaping the control of an identifiable patrilineage. This concern may also explain why so many marriages among cousins occurred in these regions in the nineteenth century.[28] Such 'cross-cousin' unions (to use the anthropologists' term) could also ensure that the land granted to daughters could remain in the kinship group. Demographic growth expanded what had previously been the nucleus for identification – the family plot – and placed kinfolk in newly supportive roles alongside members of the immediate lineage traced from father to son.[29] Thus, if inheritors (usually married siblings) got along and kin solidarity remained firm, a family holding could remain undivided in practice, at least initially.[30] There was, for example, no expectation that all the heirs would have their homes on the land they inherited; on the contrary, most southern Italian towns were a patchwork of scattered small holdings around a village. Completely unconnected to residence, undivided holdings required only that kin agree how to cultivate collectively or divide crops, with the result that five or more families might at times share the harvest of a single olive tree.

Yet, even these solutions simply delayed the inevitable, because the heirs sooner or later – even years after the death of the testator – partitioned the holding in some way in anticipation of the needs of the next generation. At this stage, most typically, women agreed to sell their rights to their brothers. Often, the sale was little more than symbolic given the tenuous condition and value of a land holding divided among so many heirs and, more importantly, the trivial benefit any family could expect a tiny parcel to contribute to family subsistence. Thus, new inheritance rules imposed by the Italian state, along with many of its other fiscal policies, pushed regions of traditional subsistence production further toward the marketplace, and especially toward the pursuit of a cash income through wage-earning.

Emigration became the trump card in this context, and high levels of emigration, unbalanced sex ratios, and male sojourning all characterized migration from areas of widespread landholding. A true ace up the sleeve, even given a rapidly growing population, emigration could provide an infusion of money, which would revitalize the traditional mechanisms of survival and reproduction under new rules of inheritance. Daughters could receive their due without making their claims on the patrimony and brothers could neutralize their sisters' claims to the land that ensured survival of men's family name through its attachment to immovable property. Male sojourning reminds us how closely bound many men felt to their plots of land. Maintaining the family lineage, and plot of land, could be accomplished in myriad ways. Parents might encourage unmarried sons to migrate in order to earn the cash needed for their sister's dowries, or to purchase additional lands so they could subsequently marry and continue the lineage on their own, new landholdings. Alternatively, the pursuit of a cash income could 'push' into permanent emigration those sons with few hopes of inheriting a plot of land capable of sustaining a family. Male sojourning was possible, furthermore, because particular forms of patriarchal family structures associated in the past with the traditional inheritance system allowed the fathers and brothers of migrants to maintain the appearance of propriety and supervision of women left behind like the wife of the unemployed Saverio.

Male Migration, Gender, and South Italian Families

The association of land and landholdings with men was powerful where landowning had been limited to men and a family plot descended through the male line. The foundations of the traditional inheritance system spoke clearly on that point. The imposition of Piedmont's code of inheritance could not alone make land into 'women's business.' It had long been men's concern to receive land, preserve it, and increase its size. Thus, when the unity of family lineage and landholding seemed threatened, it was also the responsibility of men to prevent the loss of the resources they needed for their families' subsistence in a village, a house, or a field that symbolized their presence in the local community.

A headlong tumble into the ranks of landless wage-earner was not perhaps so threatening to southern Italian men because of the diminished standard of living it implied. In fact, differences in the standards of living of wage-earners, renters, sharecroppers, and owners of tiny parcels of land could be very small. More profoundly frightening was the abandonment of a cluster of obligations and reciprocity among men and the family work groups they supervised. These exchanges were inseparable from subsistence production. They began with matrimonial exchanges, and continued through the reciprocal exchanges of labour and locally produced goods that consolidated social ties among kin and neighbouring families. Proper fulfilment of these exchanges was an integral part of higher social status for a landowning peasant, and an integral part of his social identity. Fulfilling these exchanges may have carried more weight than any of the new opportunities for consumption that cash earned through wage-earning could now purchase in local marketplaces. Temporary male emigration was therefore an undertaking of a given duration. It had to generate cash for dowries, debts, taxes, or land purchases, but it could not remove men too long from the performance of the social exchanges that maintained their status within local communities. The length of any sojourn and its geographical distance, moreover, did not differentiate it significantly from more customary seasonal dislocations long associated with local and regional labour migrations; being catapulted into the strange cultures of the Americas would have been traumatic only for the first men pioneers who ventured there: '[M]igration lost its semi-dramatic character: one went back and forth to America quite easily ... Leaving was no more scary ... Peasants did not go towards the unknown: many had already been in America three or four times. In Basilicata, where emigration was a long lasting phenomenon, traveling to America was soon considered less difficult than traveling to Florence.'[31]

The philosophy that underlay male sojourning was an attitude of 'bite and run.' It required men to suffer significant deprivations and make real sacrifices in order to accumulate a sum that was enough to re-establish the good fortune of the respected family name. Having earned a targeted sum, a man could end his 'campaign' and return as quickly as possible to the homeland. Few men, or their families, initially intended overseas male sojourning to result in their permanent migrations abroad.

Whether men's intention to return remained fixed, and whether they began to entertain thoughts of leaving southern Italy more permanently, depended largely on two variables: the point in the life cycle when men emigrated, and the family structure to which they belonged. As the example of Saverio reminds us, men's sojourns occurred at specific historical moments. They also occurred at particular moments in the histories of specific families, and of marital relations: before or just after marriage, in response to the birth of a child or the death of a father, the upcoming marriage of a sibling, and so on. Even though the possibility of emigration to and wage-earning in the Americas persisted over three generations, or a good century, the expectations, experiences, and philosophy of male sojourning changed surprisingly little over time. Evidently, both single and married men began their sojourns with the intention of shoring up family structures already severely weakened by rising family size, economic crisis, and state intervention in local traditions of inheritance. It also seems clear that migration fundamentally altered many of the familial traditions, including gender roles and parent–child relations, that it was intended to shore up.

Gerard Delille's research on southern Italian family structures allows us to see connections among landholding, inheritance patterns, family structures, and male patterns of migration. According to Delille, the Italian south divides into two general areas. One, characterized by multiple extended families encompasses Cilento and the Tyrrhenian strip of Calabria. The other, dominated by nuclear families, covers the zone from the Naples-Salerno boundary to the Calabrian slope and down to the Ionian Sea. Although Delille's meticulous reconstruction (drawn primarily from the *stati delle anime,* or parish censuses) ends on the eve of Unification, he has argued that the two family types persisted into the first half of the twentieth century.[32] By contrast, other sources, albeit much less comprehensive and more subjective than Delille's, date significant changes in family structures to the first decade of the twentieth century. Clearly, the tempo of change in south Italian peasant family structures deserves more scrutiny. Here I attempt mainly to demonstrate how family structure influenced the chronology and the migration strategies of married men.

Delille divided Calabria in two. The Cosenza-Tyrrhenian portion of the region, with its centre at Paola, was populated by extended families. In the Ionian portion of Calabria, nuclear households prevailed. This division was confirmed by the early investigation of rural life by the Italian national state. The middle-class, and often northern Italian, men who performed this survey were deeply concerned about possible breakdowns in family morality and a loss of patriarchal authority that they feared accompanied the rise of wage-earning and market relations among peasants. Their model peasant family was not that of the urban bourgeois family, but remained the multigeneration family supposedly characteristic of Tuscan sharecropping, where a single patriarch (father or eldest brother) firmly ruled all other members of a large household of cultivators.[33] In 1883 a government investigator reported on the persistence of extended families in Cosenza, where parents controlled their children's salaries and looked after 'the governance of the family.'[34] By contrast, the investigator in the Catanzaro area (on the opposite side of Calabria) noted with concern, 'Family ties are very casual,' by which he meant that children left the household when they married. Under such conditions, he insisted, 'elderly parents, too weak to work, remained abandoned in misery.'[35]

Although these descriptions may be exaggerated through moralizing eyes, they do represent two different structures and expectations of family life. One was more lineal and extended; the other more nuclear. The first was associated with subsistence production, male inheritance, and widespread landholding, and the other with wage-earning, commercial agriculture, partible inheritance by all children, and concentrated landholding. Each also was associated with distinctive patterns of emigration. We know, for example, that the district around Paola was one of the most ancient reservoirs for emigration from Calabria, while in the area around Catanzaro emigration developed only belatedly. The extended family and its needs no doubt generated high rates of male emigration and sojourning. Such was the case in post-unification Basilicata, whose similarly extended family structure invited the following comment: 'The family ... has traditions of tenacious unity; the father of the family receives the bulk of the inheritance as the sole head and the other brothers are constrained to remain helpful and subdued [to him].'[36] This situation even elicited sarcasm from local critic Enrico Pani Rossi, who did not deny the diffusion of the extended family in this region, but noted many solitary meals and ostentatious and self-punishing forms of religiosity. 'The family, according to a local bright light,' he noted, 'has no cohesiveness.'[37] Unlike those who glorified the traditional patriarchal peasant family, Rossi insisted on deviation from a new, middle-class, and nuclear model. He also warned his readers that 'husbands are much rarer than bachelors.'[38] A glance at the 1861 census for Basilicata – which recorded 266,557 bachelors, 188,214 husbands, and 38,188 widows and widowers – suggests that Rossi was correct in seeing a linkage between extended families and low rates of marriage for those who could not inherit land. That many of these 'bachelors' were young, dependent children, however, points to the polemical nature of Rossi's observations. Still, bachelorhood was a common fate for young men in areas of the Italian south where extended families and efforts to preserve a family patrimony despite state demands for partible inheritance coexisted. Indeed, the parliamentary inquiry directed by Stefano Jacini[39] reaffirmed this linkage, noting that, as head of the family, the father, and in his absence the first-born son, 'organizes the day's work, assigns various undertakings, pays necessary tributes, sees to the needs of the family and attends to all its business.'[40] Early emigration and a tendency toward permanent departure could easily be the fate for those men excluded from inheriting and thus from marrying; they were destined to seek better fortunes elsewhere.

Male emigration, however, did not always produce the expected goal of shoring up extended families under the dominance of fathers. In fact, it encouraged the autonomy of sons and the spread of nuclear families through regions where they had previously been little known, and even disparaged. Returning male migrants set off small earthquakes of change in their marriages and families. Having experienced autonomy as migrant workers, sons found it difficult to submit again to paternal authority. Also, the father's authority lost its lustre when he no longer controlled the wages a son could earn as an individual. The nuclear household waited at the door.

By 1910 emigration had been under way in most regions of widespread landowning for a more than a generation. Observers recorded the consequences. In Basilicata, where extended families had once been common, change was particularly obvious. 'In general,' wrote the engineer and government investigator Azimonti, 'newlyweds begin their own households. The exception is families with only one child in which case the only offspring remains at home.'[41] Francisco Saverio Nitti, a careful student of the 'southern problem,' echoed this observation.[42] Another contemporary study recorded a state of affairs that had been harshly

stigmatized only forty years earlier. The region of Potentino was exceptional because of its high marriage rates, which the author attributed to
'the wish of youth to be independent of the paternal family. By and
large,' he added, 'new couples formed their own households and, in the
case of smallholders, they prefer to separate their own minuscle holding
from that of their parents and their in-laws, rather than live and work
together, as is customary in many regions.'[43] Nuclear households also
seemed to have won out in Calabria,[44] and in Abruzzo, where 'emigration tends to replace the extended patriarchal family with the small,
bourgeois-type household. The separation of savings from the paternal
patrimony creates many small and distinct economic units, which substi-
tute themselves in the place of the ancient patriarchal economy.'[45]

Although new, these nuclear households of young marrieds remained
integrated into a network of kin and neighbours still governed by older
rules of solidarity and mutual assistance. It was expected that an emigrant husband like Saverio would remain responsible from afar for the
maintenance and financial security of his wife and children. Nevertheless, events did not always work out as they should. As in Saverio's case,
the interval between the farewell and the first remittances could be
longer than anticipated. Contemporaries also feared that, as Tirabassi
and Reeder document, young wives might be driven by financial need
into irregular sexual relations resembling prostitution or concubinage.[46]
Although rates of illegitimacy did not increase in Italy's south during the
era of the mass migrations, widespread anxiety about female sexuality
and wives' fidelity certainly made departing husbands suspicious and
desirous of a guarantee of marital fidelity. For all these reasons, men like
Saverio often entrusted their wives and children to the supervision and
care of their parents and brothers.

The nature of the relationship between the wife 'left behind' and her
husband's family drew on long traditions of extended family life. While
few wives any longer moved physically into the homes of their in-laws or
brother-in-laws, they did become part of the patrilineage that produced
food and ate it together, gathered around the same table – as an archaic
saying suggested 'to one loaf of bread and to one bottle of wine.' Emigrés
recognized that their newly-wed wives paid considerable psychological
debts in this situation. 'I can imagine,' the migrant Michele wrote to his
wife, 'the life that you are living, you and my beloved children, and your
mortification ... [Let me know] if my brother has ever denied you
anything that you needed ... I will tell my brother that I am very indebted
to him, because I have left my family on his shoulders.'[47] As this suggests,

the husband breadwinner was expected to repay his brother for any costs of feeding and maintaining the wife 'left behind.'

Many of the female-headed nuclear-family households that census takers claimed to find in the south[48] in reality were still parts of extended families that continued to engage collectively in subsistence agriculture for their own consumption. The difference was that they no longer cohabited as they might have in the past. The spread of nuclear households thus was limited in its significance; such households were residential groups, while work and consumption continued within extended family groups that remained organized as a patrilineal group of fathers, sons, and brothers. Furthermore, since this group administered the woman's dowry, it was to them that the wives could be entrusted. Dowry traditions had rendered wives almost extraneous to their family of origin, who had lost all say, and delegated them to the interests and identities of a new patrilineal group. Young men desired the autonomy and independence of nuclear-family households when they married, but fears about their wives' sexuality made temporary emigration particularly difficult for them. Immediately, they resolved their dilemma by subjecting their wives to the regime of patriarchal supervision that they themselves had tried to escape.

Yet, in other ways emigration favoured the position of brides left in Italy. Supervision by the husband's parents or brothers reinforced a married couple's solidarity. Wives usually emerged rather quickly as the most trustworthy and diligent custodians of the funds forwarded from America for investment on behalf of the nuclear family group. One economist reported that 'the majority of the savings are deposited in the Postal Savings Banks with deposit books in the name of the women.'[49] Absent husbands were as apt to distrust the loyalty of their fathers and brothers as the fidelity of their wives. Often they entrusted only to their wives such important tasks as the payment of debts, arrangement of contracts, divisions of inheritances, dowries of daughters, and purchases and sales: in short, all of those activities that required a clear understanding between the delegator and his delegate. Women became frequenters of the post office, the bank, and the notary office as they took on a wide range of extra-domestic responsibilities and social relations once jealously guarded by males. The women that Anne Cornelisen later called 'the women of the shadows' had become deputies of their husbands, but in that capacity they had freed themselves in significant ways from the direct surveillance and control of the patrilineal extended family.

Obviously, female solitude was not always dedicated to marital fidelity.

While male emigration reduced the number of homicides, the incidence of female crimes – adultery, infanticides, and petty thievery (including 'abusive' gleaning on property belonging to others) – all increased during the mass migrations. One student of Calabria's agriculture insisted, with an ambivalence about masculinity that associated bravery with violence, that '[t]he extraordinary exodus of these years [1899–1901] dragged to the other side of the ocean the youngest and bravest, those who are most liable to commit those violent acts for which Calabrian delinquency sadly is known.'[50] Even a knowledgeable observer like Francesco Coletti attributed women's abusive gleaning, in particular, to the gap between the departure of married men and the arrival of their first remittances.[51] Overall, however, the many new nuclear families of the south withstood this formidable period of financial 'crunch'; the avalanche of remittances provides the best proof of increased solidarity between husbands and wives during the mass migrations.

It would be a mistake to view these changes in gender and intergenerational relations as transitions to modern individualism, even on the part of the migratory men. Most men did not emigrate as individuals but with their peers, and the absence of women did not mean the absence of family ties among men. The 693 migrants who left one town in Campania between 1886 and 1901 included only two women, but included at least five groups of twenty adult male kinsmen.[52] As Paola Corti's contribution to this volume reminds us, 'women are labour migrants too'; we should not forget that men's migrations were shaped by family ties even when they departed without wives, daughters, or sisters. Married men took with them their own sons as well as adolescent nieces and nephews, while single men joined their brothers or cousins. Official statistics ignored the ties of fictive kinship (*comparatico*) important to southern Italians; these featured in the emigration of minors, as Corti shows for 'mistress spinners' and their 'girls' emigrating to France from Piedmont.[53] Throughout the Italian south, boys as young as five and six years old had long been employed as animal herders, thereby literally becoming adults while 'in pasturage.' In districts with histories of herding migrations (transhumance), boys became involved in all-male groups of herders that reproduced family relations, with the older men as 'fathers,' 'uncles,' and 'brothers' in a world almost completely apart from women.[54]

Far from indicating the beginnings of male individualism, emigration remained a collective experience – from the first pioneers to chain migration. Among the pioneers, many sons emigrated as an act of filial loyalty, and married men as a way of continuing their obligations to family solidarity and the plot of land that supported it. For most, so-journing was also a collective experience, though it took many forms, from the sometimes-fraudulent activities of labour recruiters to the carefully arranged plans worked out among relatives and fellow-townspeople ready to receive newcomers and provide them with work and housing. The reunification of the family that had remained behind was a final outcome of the many solidarities strengthened during migration.[55] Thus, one important outcome of chain migration was the homogeneous and cohesive neighbourhood of Italians in North and South America, unrivalled by other ethnic groups. In Cleveland, for example, migrants from the Sicilian municipalities of Patti and Palermo clustered together, as did those from Benevento and Campobasso. Seventy per cent of the Italians of Cleveland in 1900 originated in these areas; ten years later the figure had risen to 84 per cent. By contrast, only 60 per cent of the Romanians and Slovakians in the city originated from distinctive homeland clusters. Italians undertook their travels as parts of extended chains that numbered from thirty to one hundred people. Romanian villages, by comparison, rarely sent more than five persons to Cleveland, and Slovakian villages sent only four.[56]

The importance of family migration for Italy's male sojourners emerges clearly from Weinberg and Eberle's case study[57] of Giovanni, whose first sojourn from Roccaspinalveti to South America in 1912 began a chain that continued in successive waves until 1960. Two years after he had arrived in Bahia Blanca (Argentina), Giovanni was joined by his brother Leonardo and, after the interruption of the First World War, another brother Domenico and his wife Mariannina. After the Second World War, the chain was re-established when, in 1947, a third brother, Nicola, arrived. In 1952, Domenico sponsored a nephew, Guerrino, and one year later a brother-in-law, Giuseppe. Also in 1952, Nicola, who in the meantime had been joined by his wife and children, sponsored two brothers-in-law, Tito and Elverino, and his father-in-law Angelo and his entire family. In 1954, Tito arranged for the arrival of his wife, son, and nephew. Giuseppe, one of Angelo's sons, first 'brought over' his wife and five children, and then in 1960 arranged for the emigration of three paesani (fellow villagers). At the same time, the other Giuseppe had arranged for the emigration of a nephew (also called Giuseppe) with his wife and two children.

Over the course of fifty years, an isolated teenager became head of a genuine migration dynasty, an extended family of thirty-nine men and women distributed across three generations.[58] The chain was organized around three brothers and their own families – a possible echo of older patrilineal principles of kinship in south Italian inheritance systems. But the chain also included three fellow villagers and the in-laws (father and brothers-in-law) of the original group of brothers. Thus, the chain also incorporated the men's wives' relatives; kinship linked these migrants bilaterally while also relegating women to the role of passive subjects, subordinated to male mobility. In short, even migration chains resulting in permanent transplantation of whole family groups, including women, remained controlled by men.

The Consequences of Male Sojourning: Demography, Work, and Marriage in Southern Italy

Especially during the first fifteen years of the century, the peninsular Italian south experienced an unparalleled departure of adult males. So significant was this male exodus, especially among working-age persons between 15 and 40 years of age, that the southern Italian population became increasingly feminized (see table 2.2). The 1901 census calculated for Calabria 38,000 wives with departed husbands and for Basilicata 11,000. In 1905 the number of Calabrian women living as 'pseudo-widows' grew to 50,000.[59]

Not surprisingly, male migration left its long-term mark on the work patterns, demography, and marriage customs of the south. It bears stressing, however, that the women entrusted by their husbands to brothers and fathers scarcely lived in idleness or hunger as they awaited a husband's remittances. This conventional portrait of 'women who wait' must be challenged. Given that most women remained immersed in extended families that organized production and consumption even when they did not always share a residence, a woman like Saverio's wife very likely was not dependent on his remittances for her food. In Calabria alone, 29.1 of every 100 families lacked male heads of households. Male departures reduced the sizes of peasant families, and the numbers of workers in each. In Campania, for example, agricultural families averaged 4.3 members, but this figure fell in areas of intensive emigration: in Ariano di Puglia, the average was only 3.97, in San Angelo dei Lombardi, 4.08, in Piedimonte Matese 3.64, and in Sala Consilina 3.82.[60] Increasingly, the entire weight of agricultural work and subsistence production fell on those who remained behind in southern Italy, and this meant women, the elderly, and the very young – and not just the fathers or brothers of the sojourners.

TABLE 2.2
Males per 1000 females

	Abruzzo	Campania	Basilicata	Calabria
1861	957	966	951	965
1871	951	985	954	970
1881	936	978	922	958
1901	915	943	895	894
1911	863	931	901	869
1921	904	953	939	913

Source: *Statistiche sul Mezzogiorno d'Italia; 1861–1953* (Rome: SVIMEZ, 1954), 23.

Parliamentary enquiries from the 1900s amply document women's agricultural labour, and also link it to the departure of men. 'The most noteworthy fact brought about by emigration,' wrote Azimonti in his report on rural conditions in Basilicata, 'is the expansion, even in those municipalities where it was not customary, of the work of women and young children, in the cultivation of the soil.'[61] Francesco Nitti said the same for Calabria and warned about the dangers of hard physical labour for women who were pregnant or who had recently given birth.[62] Ernesto Marenghi similarly observed that women 'normally' worked until the 'last days' of their pregnancy, and returned to it 'almost immediately' after giving birth. 'There have even been cases of pregnancies,' he added, 'that have resulted in births in the field.'[63] Observers evidently worried mainly that women's hard labour in the field would result in infant mortality and abortion.

Marenghi also elaborated on the new chores Calabrian women now acquired. Where manual labour was scarce, they were forced to become responsible not only for harvesting (a traditional female activity) but also for hoeing, reaping, and mowing. In the woods of Serra San Bruno women carted away the coal before dawn, while in Bagnara 'they work without relief to transport barrel hoops, loading and unloading wagons and boats, carrying on their heads loads of from 50 to 80 and more kilograms.'[64] Writings from Abruzzo specified that women no longer restricted their attentions to their own landholdings, but now did not hesitate to work for daily wages on the holdings of others.[65]

That so many writers distinguished women's past and present work might suggest that emigration transformed dependent women into workers for the first time. But this was not the case. On the contrary, although domestic spinning and weaving had partially occupied women, they had nevertheless already been responsible for an onerous round of household labour that included washing laundry in the river, baking bread, and hauling water. The hilltop location of many villages required people to journey from their settlement to the valley below where a river allowed them to replenish their water supply. Significantly, the task of 'fetching water' was assigned to women, who loaded and carried heavy jugs and also used donkeys to transport barrels.[66] Often, women also devoted themselves to marketing any food surpluses; at Campodigiove, for example, an observer noted that 'in addition to domestic activities,' the women 'trade in nearby locales, carrying on their heads firewood to sell in Sulmona and other loads for other places, thus providing skimpy sustenance for their families.'[67]

Women's agricultural labours now became almost ceaseless. As one observer noted, the absence of men from Causano from October to July, meant that 'agriculture is completely entrusted to their women who plough, hoe, sow and lead animals to their grazing.' In wintertime, he added, they again resumed womanly tasks, 'tend[ing] to the spindle, the needle and to weaving wool and hemp cloth.'[68] Another agreed, noting that the women of the countryside (Sepino, Molise) were so industrious 'that they do not hesitate to wield the hoe and the spade with the men.'[69] Evaluations of women's labours were mixed. In Calabria, for example, one observer worried, 'When a woman worked with a hoe, she had reached the bottom rung on the social ladder – hoeing being a task that was quintessentially male.'[70] Gender-based divisions of labour thus revealed both a measure of flexibility and a persistence in ideas that certain jobs ought to belong to one sex or the other. Exact notions of who should perform which jobs, however, differed, and changed from one locale to another. And even with extraordinary female effort, many traditionally male tasks could only be covered in part because women's older tasks had still to be accomplished. One could decide to forgo gleaning or gathering olives, but not domestic duties or child-rearing. The result was that many women found themselves having to work for two. Some female tasks – notably domestic spinning and weaving – disappeared completely.

Almost everywhere women took the place of beasts of burden or performed tasks generally regarded as unpleasant, even if this required them to become sojourners themselves. Between autumn and spring, for example, 300 charcoal burners and woodcutters from the area of Avellino and Sora (Lazio) sojourned in Terra di Lavoro. Seventy of them were women. Among 315 charcoal burners gathering in Irpinia from the mountains of Isernia, Molise, and Basilicata, there were 140 women.[71]

Women travelled long distances from their homes to devote themselves to intensive cultivation (vines and olives in particular) and to hoeing and sowing wheat. In Puglia, tens of thousands of agricultural labourers descended on the large farms in the summer; in coastal Terra d'Otranto 4000 came to a September harvest. During the last months of the year 3700 women and 3000 men participated in the harvesting and grinding of olives and the first tasks of cereal cultivation. The olive harvest employed 1500 women (from a population of 5000) in the area around Rossano in Cosenza: 1000 of 2000 harvesters in the countryside of Reggino and 1600 of 4000 in the countryside of Catanzaro were women. Still, women remained marginal to the largest migration streams of the region, even after so many men had departed for the Americas. According to the calculations of the labour office, even in moments of great poverty, women made up less than 10 per cent of local migrants. If the shortfall of manual labour succeeded in toppling many other gender-based barriers, the same could not be said for the temporary harvest migrants: reaping remained a firm male prerogative, in part because (much as in Sicily) areas of large wheat estates often had extremely strict divisions of labour. Further, women struggling to complete their traditional tasks while taking on some of the work of the departed men in their families had few incentives to add seasonal harvest migration to their long list of responsibilities.

On the other hand, a few pockets of industrialization in the south privileged the recruitment of women workers, many of whom were drawn by domestic jobs in the military establishments of Gaeta. The new Neapolitan industries also had taken on female workers from nearby towns, and some forty women moved from Nola to work in the spinning mills of Sarno (Salerno).[72] In the region of Ariano (Avellino), the light industry of cloth making was also still in women's hands.[73]

Contemporaries tended to associate, in negative terms, a wide range of demographic changes with male emigration. Certainly male sojourning caused demographic disturbances, and often surprising ones. In much of southern Italy, the birth rate declined but marriage rates increased. While the first seems unsurprising, the other is harder to explain. Even the fact that the mortality of infant girls exceeded that for boys was attributed at the time to male emigration. The demographer Giorgio Mortara noted that maximum levels of infant mortality coincided with the boom of male departures during 1886–7, while its decline in 1890–5 corresponded to a lull in departures associated with the economic depression of the Americas during those years. 'Among the explanations that come to mind,' he wrote, the 'most plausible' one 'argues that males are the objects of the greatest amount of loving care from the parents and families who raise them.' Furthermore: 'With the growth of migration the economic worth of males has become ever more apparent, the parents of those born legitimately and the mothers of the illegitimate are forced to base greater hopes on them than on females. Moreover because of emigration, there is an overabundance of women, and a scarcity of men. No doubt it is for these reasons that everywhere it is male progeny who are thought to result in the prosperity of the family.'[74] In this case, the pattern of male sojourning seemed to reinforce, if not to exacerbate, traditions of viewing women as of little social value, as was true in the areas of patrilineal extended families and male inheritance described above. The reasons for the lower value assigned to women rather than to men may have changed, but the imbalance itself remained unchanged.

In contrast to regions of the centre and north of Italy, where the number of the unmarried surpassed married persons only around the year 1911, southern marriage rates seemed to vary positively with rates of male migration and return.[75] Table 2.3 provides some preliminary evidence. Contemporaries attributed increasing marriage rates in these regions to the spread of partible inheritance, which uncoupled marriage from a family patrimony and allowed little room in local communities for persons who were unwed. Second, they attributed increased marriage to the interactions between the male migration cycle and the marriage market. Many young men wanted to marry before they left the country. In his survey of rural Calabria, Giorgio Mortara noted, 'Those who are considering emigration often are forced to marry when very young, either to ensure themselves of the woman they have selected, or to entrust her with control of their interests at home; or simply in order to ensure her fidelity.'[76] With the consolidation of immigrant enclaves in America, however, young bachelors could also expect to find wives among the daughters of townsfolk from the preceding generation of migrants. Whether in New York, Cleveland, San Francisco, or Latin America, endogamy remained the ironclad rule, which distance did not diminish. One survey of New York's Italian parish of Our Lady of Pompei, formed in Greenwich Village in 1892, found that a very high percentage, more than 83 per cent, of the spouses came from the same town. The rate remained unchanged until the end of the century, then declined to 50 per cent in the 1920s and 1930s.[77] As more young men considered making a match in the Americas, parents in southern Italy responded in

TABLE 2.3
Number of marriages per 1000 inhabitants

	Abruzzo	Campania	Basilicata	Calabria
1903	7.2	7.3	8.2	7.4
1904	8.2	7.8	8.2	8.4
1905	9.1	8.1	9.0	8.1
1906	8.5	8.1	9.0	8.1
1907	8.3	7.9	8.4	8.0
1908	9.6	8.6	9.1	9.7
1909	8.7	7.9	7.8	8.5

Source: Statistiche sul Mezzogiorno, 77.

predictable ways, and women of marriageable age began crossing the ocean in increasing numbers. In her enquiry into the 'Terra di Lavoro,' Giuseppina Scanni had been astonished in San Benedetto (Abruzzo) by a witty tobacconist with a sharp tongue who told her that young women 'would wait for ages; if they would want to get married in San Benedetto, only one would get married every ten years; instead they go to America and there marriage is a snap: there even hunchbacks get married!' From the entire district of Caserta (not an unusual case) departing families took with them any female relatives or friends who wished to be married in America.[78] As the last wave of male sojourning ended during the crisis of the First World War, a new migratory current of women began to form, travelling via female networks to the other side of the ocean. This was not so much a family migration, like that of the women who had earlier followed their fathers or husbands, but was instead a migration of women expecting to establish new families without the direct intervention of their parents, and without dowries, with no expectation of return to southern Italy or to the plots of land, inheritance patterns, and family structures outlined here. We cannot detail the extent of this phenomenon, but it is certain that these new female arrivals contributed to the consolidation of Italian communities in the United States and to the reduction of male sojourning and return migration in the post–First World War period.

NOTES

1 Letter from Westfield, 23 July 1908. The letters quoted here are part of the author's private collection.

2 Letter from West Farmes, 28 March 1909.
3 In addition to Linda Reeder's essay (chapter 1), see also the relevant discussion in the introduction. Other essays dealing with rural women's paid and unpaid agricultural work include Maddalena Tirabassi and Paola Corti (chapters 3 and 4).
4 Massimo Livi Bacci, *L'immigrazione e l'assimilazione degli italiani negli Stati Uniti secondo le statistiche demografiche americane* (Milan: A. Giuffrè, 1961), 26.
5 See Francesco Barbagallo, *Lavoro e esodo nel Sud, 1861–1971* (Naples: Guida, 1973); Francesco P. Cerase, *Sotto il dominio dei borghesi: Sottosviluppo ed emigrazione nell'Italia meridionale, 1860–1910* (Rome: B. Carocci, 1975); Ercole Sori, *L'emigrazione italiana dall'Unità alla seconda guerra mondiale* (Bologna: Il Mulino, 1979); and Fortunata Piselli, *Parentela e emigrazione.* (Turin: G. Einaudi, 1981).
6 Edward C. Banfield, *The Moral Basis of a Backward Society* (Chicago: Free Press, 1958).
7 This sterotype is very old, and we can still find it in more recent times in the anthropological researches of Ernesto de Martino, *La terra del rimorso* (Milan: Il Sagiatorre, 1961) and in Carlo Levi, *Cristo si é fermato a Eboli* (Turin: Einaudi, 1945), about his confinement in a Basilicata village during the Fascist period.
8 See chapter 4, by Paola Corti.
9 Alexander V. Chayanov, *On the Theory of Peasant Economy* (Homewood, IL: R.D. Irwin, 1966); Karl Polanyi, *The Great Transformation* (New York: Farrar & Rinehart, 1944); Theodor Shanin, *Defining Peasants: Essays concerning Rural Societies, Expolary Economies, and Learning from Them in the Contemporary World* (Oxford: Basil Blackwell, 1990).
10 See chapter 1.
11 Maurice Aymard, 'Autoconsommation et marchés: Chayanov, Labrousse ou Leroy Ladurie?' *Annales: Economies, Sociétés, Civilisations* 38.
12 *Inchiesta parlamentare sulle condizioni dei contadini nelle province meridionali e nella Sicila* (Rome: Tip. Naz. di G. Bertero, 1909–10).
13 Pino Arlacchi, *Mafia, contadini e latifondo nella Calabria tradizionale: Le strutture elementari del sottosviluppo* (Bologna: Il Mulino, 1980); Josef J. Barton, *Peasants and Strangers: Italians, Rumanians and Slovaks in an American City* (Cambridge: Harvard University Press, 1975).
14 The wording is that proposed in W. Goldsmith and Evalyn Jacobson Kunkel, 'The Structure of Peasant Family,' *American Anthropologist* 73 (1971): 1058–76.
15 C. Belli, 'Famiglia, proprietà e classi sociali a Montefusco nella prima metà del XVII secolo,' in *Mélanges de l'École Française de Rome. Moyen Age–Temps*

Moderne 95 (1983); F. Luisa, 'Solofra fra il 1640 e il 1676 nei capitoli matrimoniale e nei testamenti,' in ibid. 299–338; Giuseppe Civile, *Il comune rustico* (Bologna: Il Mulino, 1990).

16 Georges Augustins, 'La position des femmes dans trois types d'organisation sociale: La lignée, la parentele et la maison,' in G. Ravis Giordani, ed., *Femmes et patrimoine dans les sociétés rurales de l'Europe Méditerranéenne* (Paris: CNRS, 1987), 30.

17 Civile, *Il comune rustico*, 34.

18 Belli, 'Famiglia, proprietà e classi sociali,' 370.

19 G. Delille, 'Classi sociali e scambi matrimoniali nel Salernitano: 1550–1650 ca.,' *Quaderni Storici* 33 (1977): 983–97.

20 Luisa, 'Solofra fra il 1640 e il 1676,' 333.

21 A. Villone, 'Contratti matrimoniali e testamenti in una zona di latifondo: Eboli a meta del "600,"' in *Mélanges*.

22 John Davis, 'An Account of Changes in the Rules for Transmission of Property in Pisticci, 1814–1961,' in J.G. Peristiany, *Mediterranean Family Structure* (Cambridge: Cambridge University Press, 1976), 291.

23 Villone, 'Contratti matrimoniali,' 247.

24 Luisa, 'Solo fra il 1640 e il 1676,' 238.

25 Davis, 'An Account of Changes.'

26 An 'intestate' death occurred without a legal will having first been composed.

27 Civile, *Il commune rustico*, 37.

28 G. Delille, *Famiglia e proprietà nel Regno di Napoli* (Turin: G. Einaudi, 1988), 333.

29 Georges Augustins, 'Division égalitaire des patrimoines et institution de l'héritier,' *Archives Européennes de Sociologie* 1 (1979): 127–41.

30 G. Augustins, *Comment se perpétuer: Devenir des lignées et destins des patrimoines dans les sociétés paysannes européennes* (Nanterre: Société d'ethnologie, 1989), 363.

31 Francesco S. Nitti, 'Inchiesta sulle condizioni dei contadini in Basilicata e in Calabria (1910),' in *Scritti sulla questione meridionale* (Bari: Editori Laterza, 1958), 154.

32 G. Delille, 'Famiglie contadine in Italia,' in *Storia universale della famiglia*, vol. 2, ed. It. (Milan, 1990), 535–70.

33 Donna R. Gabaccia, *Italy's Many Diasporas* (London: University College of London Press, 2000), 84.

34 *Atti della Giunta per l'inchiesta agraria sulle condizioni della classe agricola*, vol. 9, pt. 1 (Sala Bolognese: Arnoldo Forni, stampa 1986), 120.

35 Ibid., 214.

36 Giacomo Racioppi, *Storia dei moti di Basilicata e delle province contermini nel 1860* (Bari: Giuseppe Laterza, 1909), 4.
37 E.P. Rossi, *La Basilicata, Studi politici, amministrativi e di economia pubblica* (Verona: Coi Tipi di G. Civelli, 1868), 83.
38 Ibid.
39 *Atti della Giunta per l'inchiesta agraria.*
40 *Atti della giunta per l'inchiesta Agraria*, vol. 9, pt. 1, 63.
41 *Giunta parlamentare d'inchiesta sulle condizioni dei contadini nelle province meridionali e nella Sicilia*, vol. 5 (1910), 66.
42 'In the normal course of things, the newlyweds form their own families; firstborn children are accustomed to remain in the paternal home after they are married.' Nitti, 'Inchiesta,' 310.
43 Giorgio Mortara, *La popolazione di Basilicata e di Calabria all'inizio del secolo ventesimo* (Rome: Tip. Naz. Di G. Bertero, 1910), 113.
44 *Giunta parlamentare d'inchiesta sulle condizioni dei contadini*, vol. 5, 588–9
45 Ibid., vol. 2, pt. 1, 271.
46 Francesco Coletti, 'Classi, società e delinquenze in Italia nel periodo 1891–1900 con particolare considerazione per le classi rurali,' in Coletti, ed., *La popolazione rurale in Italia e i suoi caratteri demografici, psicologici e sociali* (Piacenza: Federazione italiana dei consorzi agrari, 1925), 101.
47 Letter from Houston, 22 August 1926.
48 Mortara, *La popolazione di Basilicata e di Calabria*, 101.
49 L.A. Caputo, 'Di alcune questioni economiche della Calabria,' *Giornale degli economisti* (December 1907).
50 Dino Taruffi et al., *La questione agraria e l'emigrazione in Calabria* (Florence: G. Barbèra, 1908), 863.
51 Coletti, 'Classi, società e delinquenze.'
52 Civile, *Il comune rustico*, 215.
53 See chapter 4.
54 Paul Scheuermeier, *Il lavoro dei contadini* (Milan: Longanesi, 1980; orig. pub. 1943), vol. 1, 2.
55 J.S. MacDonald and Leatrice D. Macdonald, 'Urbanization, Ethnic Groups and Social Segregation,' *Social Research* 4 (1962).
56 Barton, *Peasants and Strangers*, 53–4.
57 F. Weinburg and A.S. Eberle, 'Los Abruzeses en Bahia Blanca: Estudio de cadenzas migratorias,' *Estudios migratorios latinoamericanos* 8 (1988).
58 No information is provided about the original composition of Giovanni's family; we cannot know what family criteria or decision-making selected him as the initial migrant.
59 Mortara, *La popolazione di Basilicata e di Calabria*, 101, and Taruffi et al., *La questione agraria*, xxxvii.

60 Mortara, *La popolazione di Basilicata e di Calabria*, 90.

61 *Giunta parlamentare d'inchiesta sulle condizioni dei contadini*, vol. 5, 84.

62 Nitti, 'Inchiesta,' 281

63 *Giunta parlamentare d'inchiesta sulle condizioni dei contadini*, vol. 5, 268.

64 Ibid.

65 Ibid., vol. 2, pt. 1, 95.

66 M.P. Divino, 'La donna nell'onciario di Motta Placanica,' in Mirella Mafrici, ed., *Il Mezzogiorno settecentesco attraverso i catasti onciari*, vol. 2 (Naples: Edizioni scientifiche italiane, 1986), 227.

67 F. Cirelli, *Il Regno delle due Sicilie descritto e illustrato* (Naples, 1853), vol. 4, 94.

68 Ibid., 356–7.

69 Ibid., 102.

70 Ibid., 2, 10.

71 Divino, 'La donna nell'onciario di Motta Placanica.'

72 Taruffi et al., *La questione agraria*, 98; *Giunta parlamentare d'inchiesta sulle condizioni delle contadini*, vol. 4, 534.

73 Giuseppina Scanni, 'L'emigrazione delle donne e dei fanciulli dalla provincia di Caserta,' *Bollettino dell'emigrazione* 12 (1913): 11.

74 Mortara, *La popolazione di Basilicata e di Calabria*, 216.

75 *Statistiche sul Mezzogiorno d'Italia; 1861–1953* (Rome: SVIMEZ, 1954), 28.

76 Mortara, *La popolazione di Basilicata e di Calabria*, 113.

77 This percentage was remarkably high if we note that only those originating from the same village were counted, and not those coming from the region or province. Patrizia Salvetti, 'Una parrocchia italiana di New York e i suoi fedeli: Nostra Signora di Pompei (1892–1933),' *Studi emigrazione* 73 (1984). For Cleveland, see Barton, *Peasants and Strangers*, 58; for Brazil, Chiara Vangelista, 'Genere, etnia e lavoro: L'immigrazione italiana a Sao Paulo dal 1880 al 1930,' *Annali di Istituto A Cervi* 12 (1990): 361.

78 As one reported, 'In New York, or perhaps in Boston there is almost always an aunt, godmother, a woman friend, who runs a boarding house and who offers to find a good husband from amongst her boarders for her towns-woman who has remained behind in Italy.' The latter sent a photograph and in this way found a fiancé who would send her the price of her ticket. Scanni, 'L'emigrazione delle donne e dei fanciulli,' 13–16.

3 Bourgeois Men, Peasant Women: Rethinking Domestic Work and Morality in Italy

Maddalena Tirabassi

TRANSLATED BY GABRIELE SCARDELLATO

In 1908, the Italian government's General Commissariat for Emigration asked Amy Allemand Bernardy, the cosmopolitan daughter of the American consul in Florence and an Italian mother, to investigate the life of Italian women and children in the United States.[1] An astute observer despite the vast class chasm that separated her life from that of poorer migrants, Bernardy wrote two detailed reports for the Commissariat, focusing on the work choices and morality of Italian women in America.

Bernardy's inquiries raised two issues that would become central to scholarly study of Italian immigrant women in the United States (and to the smaller body of Canadian work dealing with the pre-1945 era).[2] She reported with fascination, but some disappointment, that Italian immigrant women rarely became domestic servants as Irish and Swedish immigrant women did.[3] Italian women's aversion to domestic service, she argued, reflected 'the principal characteristic of female migration from Italy ... women's dependence on relatives.'[4] Travelling in family groups and in no need of independent housing, most young southern Italian immigrant women preferred factory work.[5] They even worked over seventy poorly paid hours weekly in canneries with children as young as four helping them. Furthermore, '[t]here are women who return to these labors only three days after the birth of a baby.'[6] Like most bourgeois women, Bernardy wanted immigrant women, ill-equipped to run a 'mechanized' household with telephone and modern culinary standards, to develop American domestic skills, and thus favoured placements 'in service' to middle-class American women who could teach them.[7] Bernardy also linked women's work choices to moral concerns:

while critical of the southern Italian man as an 'intensely jealous' husband who 'does not allow [his wife] to go into others' houses,' she saw greater moral dangers in women's own homes and families, where, she wrote with horror, 'cases of incest are much more prevalent than one might have thought possible.' '*Syphilis insontium*,' she continued, 'is to be found among Italian families in New York with terrifying frequency.'[8] For Bernardy, male boarders endangered the morality of immigrant women and their daughters more than domestic work in American households.

The vigour with which Italian-American scholars for thirty years have repeatedly reasserted the moral conservatism and domestic orientation of Italian immigrant women workers must be considered in part an unconscious response to moral critiques penned by bourgeois observers like Bernardy.[9] Scholarship on Italian immigrant women in North America remains more or less ensnared within moral discourses on domesticity and sexuality peculiar in some ways to the bourgeois world of Anglo-Americans.[10]

This paradigm matters because the study of Italian immigrant women in the United States has disproportionately defined women's place throughout the Italian diaspora. U.S. scholars pioneered the study of both immigration and women's history – a praiseworthy initiative – but with some problematic consequences. Certainly, the United States attracted more Italian immigrants than any other single country in the years between 1870 and the First World War, but patterns of migration from Italy to the United States were quite distinctive. While the majority of Italy's emigrants were from the north and centre (many of whom went to Europe and Latin America to work), over three-quarters of Italians migrating to the United States were instead from the south and Sicily. Women were better represented in migrations to the United States than to Europe, and they also were more likely to travel there in family groups.

It is thus best not to generalize too quickly from research on Italian women in the United States to the majority of Italian women. At home in Italy, in Latin America, and in France, women encountered job opportunities, ideals of domesticity, and moral codes different from those of middle-class Americans. As students of immigrant women have demonstrated, the worlds of work and family did not always form separate 'private' or 'domestic' and 'public' spheres, even in industrial settings.[11] Child-rearing responsibilities were not everywhere the overwhelming focus of women's domestic duties. Nor was domesticity everywhere the linchpin of the sexual control of women. Women's domestic labour in Italy was disproportionately onerous, and domestic social relations were sometimes violent and oppressive, but nonetheless gender- and generation-crossing forms of domestic work underwrote the economic well-being of entire families. Rural Italian women's domestic worlds were not isolated prisons from which they escaped into independence via wage-earning. But neither were they female-dominated havens for highly skilled and chaste housewives as bourgeois Americans, much like Bernardy, more often believed. North American historians of late-nineteenth- and early-twentieth-century Italian migration have largely accepted, rather than critically scrutinized, the serious gender biases that lay at the heart of a negative national and bourgeois discourse on peasant morality and women's work during this era. In examining the pathological portraits that late-nineteenth-century Italian government surveyors drew of the ever-toiling rural women they observed, this essay also draws attention to two related aspects of peasant women's work lives throughout rural Italy (excluding Sicily)[12] that have failed to penetrate the immigration literature: their significant presence in a range of both non-waged and waged forms of agricultural work. Given that the influential U.S. historiography on Italian immigration has been shaped in part by scholars' uncritical use of these Italian sources as they pertain to women,[13] it seems clear that moving beyond the U.S. paradigms on Italian immigration requires us in part to rethink the faulty stereotypes of women perpetuated in that scholarship. Revealing the inaccuracies, class prejudices, and bourgeois moralizing that informed portraits of Italian rural women during the era of mass migrations to the United States offers a critical first step.

Visible Work: Female Wage-Earning

The largest group of women touched by migration actually remained behind in Italy while men ventured forth. Work experiences in Italy also provide the baseline against which emigrants' work choices elsewhere can be assessed. Reconstructing the history of women's lives in Italy is no simple task, but a growing literature produced by Italian scholars offers critical insights and thus deserves more attention than it has received in the U.S.-dominated literature on immigrant women.[14] Italy was a largely agricultural nation with few large employers and a relatively weak yet highly centralized record-keeping state. Furthermore, most women were illiterate and poor. Nevertheless, as recent scholarship on Italian peasant

TABLE 3.1
Composition of the Italian labour force by gender (in thousands), 1871–1931

	Women	Men	% Female
1871	5,005	9,258	35.1
1881	6,564	10,176	39.2
1891	n/a	n/a	n/a
1901	5,350	11,103	32.5
1911	5,127	11,275	31.3
1921	5,247	13,036	28.7
1931	3,903	13,359	22.6

* No census of the Italian population was taken in 1891.
Source: Istituto Centrale di Statistica, Sommario di statistiche storiche dell'Italia, 1861–1975 (Rome: ISTAT, 1976).

women, diet and consumption, and domestic work[15] suggests, female wage-earning was common.

Two problems seem particularly intractable in understanding women's work. The first is that regional variations were far more complex than the usual 'north/south' distinction invoked in studies of migration. Italy, before and after unification in 1861, was a country with almost no articulated or systematic trade, transport, or political connections among its many and strikingly diverse regions. Women's work, like that of men, differed with terrain, crops raised, altitude and location, and micro-history. The second problem is that Italy, like most modern nations, gradually came to see wage-earning and the exchange of cash for labour as the definers of work in its records, notably the decennial census. Before the Second World War, however, wages and other cash income provided only a part of rural Italians' basic needs for housing, clothing, food, and shelter. Subsistence production remained critical to individual and familial well-being, performed without wages by both men and women.

The Italian censuses of the nineteenth century likely under-reported subsistence activities, especially those done by women without wages.[16] The census takers were men who identified women mainly by their subordinate civil status. Worse, as Maria Casalini has noted, they considered 'women's work' as 'supplementary' to that of the male head of the family, and thus 'ignored it even for those women who worked in factories.'[17]

Nevertheless, the Italian census shows that more than 30 per cent of the Italian labour force from 1871 to 1911 was female – a surprisingly

TABLE 3.2
Composition of the female labour force by section, 1871–1931(per cent)

	Agriculture	Industry	Domestic service	Total
1871	60.7	27.1	12.2	100
1881	54.5	33.6	11.8	100
1891	n/a	n/a	n/a	n/a
1901	59.8	25.6	14.6	100
1911	58.0	26.9	15.1	100
1921	59.4	23.7	16.9	100
1931	39.4	32.1	28.5	100

* No census of the Italian population was taken in 1891.
Source: Istituto Centrale di Statistica, Sommario di statistiche storiche dell'Italia, 1861–1975 (Roma: ISTAT, 1976).

high proportion, little different from that in the more industrialized countries of northern Europe (see table 3.1). Rather than increasing with industrialization, however, women's representation in the Italian labour force began to decline significantly in the 1920s. Industrialization began in earnest in Italy only around 1900; by the 1920s, the negative impact of Fascist economic policies, the regime's intensified glorification of domesticity and maternity, changes in record-keeping, and sharp drops in male migration all influenced levels of female employment. Yet, even in the 1920s, the representation of women in the Italian labour force was not noticeably aberrant – it left Italy in fourth place among European nations.[18]

Italy's census figures, though flawed, challenge the assumption that female employment increases with industrialization. Italy was a predominantly agricultural country during the mass migrations, and women's wage-earning patterns reflected that reality. Before 1921 roughly 60 per cent of wage-earning women worked in the agricultural sector; only after 1931 did the number of women employed in the service and industrial sectors surpass those engaged in agriculture (see table 3.2).

The regions with high rates of female employment – most of them clustered in the north and centre – had high representation of women in agriculture. According to the 1891 and 1911 census, the representation was highest in Piedmont, with 83 women for every 100 men engaged in agriculture. In the northern and central regions of Liguria and the Marche the ratio of women to men was roughly 70, followed by Lazio (in the centre) with 49 and – in the south – Calabria with 45, Puglia with 36, and Sicily with 28.7.[19] These figures may reflect the more commercialized nature of agriculture in the north, and the more frequent use of paid labour in commercial agriculture. In the south, by contrast, cultural prohibitions against female work in Sicily emerged as commercial agriculture expanded, and men almost completely replaced women as harvest workers.[20]

The result, ironically, was that industry was the only important employer of women in much of the south – a pattern associated not with high rates of female employment, but rather with rates well below those of the north, and declining over time. In Sicily in 1881, for example, women employed in industry (mainly textiles and tobacco) far surpassed in number those employed in agriculture. According to Simona Laudani, women in Sicily played an important role in the production of goods in the pre-industrial era, often in cottage industry, but were then excluded during industrialization. From 1881 to 1901, some 190,000 women were dismissed from the textile and tobacco industry in Sicily. It is not clear whether the industries that employed women collapsed or whether men replaced women.[21] Throughout much of the south collapsing cottage industries left women spinners and weavers without employment after 1881, and the numbers of women workers declined accordingly.[22]

In the north, the growing textile industry of Piedmont and Lombardy improved job opportunities for women. The work of Franco Ramella has shown how migrations of varying distances and durations allowed many northern families to guarantee employment for all family members.[23] The oldest and youngest women worked close to home in agriculture or organized cottage production of silk worms for nearby silk spinning and weaving mills. Younger women took jobs in these mills while older and younger men sought seasonal work beyond the Alps, in Switzerland, France, Austria, and Germany.[24]

While agriculture and industry were the major employers of Italy's wage-earning women, the production of clothing, domestic service, and the professions also had some importance. Uneven but steady feminization of garment production occurred in Italy over the course of a century. Analysing the 1881 census, Maura Palazzi found 12.2 tailoresses and 3.5 tailors per 1000 in Piedmont, whereas in Calabria there were 8.1 tailors and only 1.4 tailoresses. The percentage of women rose everywhere thereafter. The number of garment businesses increased, and by 1911 had reached 17,526, of which 513 had more than ten employees. Lombardy and Piedmont were the main centres of industrial production of clothes. As the garment industry and female employment in this sector increased, Italian society became fascinated with the figure of the *sartina* (seamstress).[25]

A recent study of Turin – which, thanks to its proximity to France, was the capital of Italian fashion – reveals both the risks and opportunities opened by this new female occupation. The *sartina* worked twelve or more hours a day in difficult conditions, and occupational ills affecting the eyes, spinal column, and lungs were common. Public discussion sparked by the newly formed National Society for the Protection and Mutual Aid of Young Women Workers focused equally on the moral health of the girl workers. More emancipated than their peers, and often living away from their families in urban centers, the *sartine* were relatively well educated and described as insatiable readers of feuilletons (cheap romance novels). Such girls seemed to live between the worlds of their rural or petty bourgeois families and that of the better-off women whose dress they could emulate. Women active in charity did not hesitate to relate the moral dangers (abortions and illegitimate births) that followed from girls dressing 'up.' But in the narratives that anthropologist Vanessa Maher collected from workers in Turin's garment industry during the first half of the twentieth century, women remembered the liberty and happiness of their lives.[26]

Domestic service actually became more important as an employer of women during the mass migrations. In the seventeenth and eighteenth centuries, employers in Italy had normally employed men as domestic servants. Most female servants in Italy were all-purpose household workers, not wet nurses or child-minders. The employment of domestics for child-minding began to decline in noble and bourgeois households in the second half of the eighteenth century. Well into the late nineteenth century, bourgeois families most commonly sent their infants to rural wet nurses rather than hiring rural women in the city.[27]

Only in the nineteenth century did women begin to replace men as both live-in and part-time servants.[28] The numbers of female domestics in Italy increased during the era of mass migrations from 391,985 in 1881 to 400,948 in 1901.[29] In much of the centre and north, the search for work as domestics, along with seasonal employment in agriculture, was an important instigator of short-distance female migration. Most domestics were young, unmarried women who had emigrated from the countryside to live with their employers; like their northern European counterparts, they usually saw employment as a temporary phase before marriage.[30] In southern Italy, by contrast, very few households hired domestics. Concerns about sexual purity clearly influenced women's choices. According to Giovanna Da Molin, '[I]n Southern society, to go into service was considered humiliating and a disgrace; in some cases it was almost better to starve.'[31] Domestic service became a life-long occupation for men and women, not a specialty of young, unmarried women.

Among major professions, only teaching and midwifery were open to women in Italy during the period of mass emigration. In fact, the feminization of teaching proceeded more rapidly in Italy than it did in France. Already in 1871, there were 13,730 female teachers in Italy, representing 42 per cent of all teachers in the country. By 1901 the figure was 68 per cent, with 35,344 female teachers, and their representation would increase to 78 per cent in 1922. This phenomenon probably reflects the character of Italy's nascent system of public schools, which were largely limited to teaching young children for a few years. Higher education, where men were more likely to be employed, remained extremely limited.[32]

The medicalization of birth in these years also resulted in the professionalization of midwifery in Italy. Whereas most Italian midwives in the mid-nineteenth century had been untrained women of the lower classes, the number of midwifery schools increased with government support after unification, as did the numbers of midwives themselves, from 9432 in 1871 to 13,886 in 1901.[33] In many southern communities with few schools or students, the midwife was the only female professional.[34] And in Italy as a whole, the female professional was still an anomaly, not a model of female independence and achievement for ambitious girls. For most girls and women in Italy during the mass migrations, work meant subsistence production and, to a more limited extent, wage-earning in commercial agriculture. Much of subsistence production, furthermore, remained invisible, and closely tied to women's other domestic responsibilities.

Domestic Work, Invisible Work

While the Italian census made waged work 'visible,' most Italian women's work remained invisible, unpaid, and tied to a domestic world of family ties and subsistence production. The two extensive agrarian inquiries commissioned by the Italian parliament – the Inchiesta Jacini, which surveyed all of rural Italy, and the Inchiesta Faina, which considered only the southern regions in the years of mass exodus and return – shed light on this invisible female work. The two inquiries offer valuable

insights into material conditions of rural life, debunk common stereotypes of Italian family life, and help us to understand the everyday life
of the *donna contadina* (peasant woman).[35]

Whereas the Italian census established the centrality of agricultural
work for northern and central Italian women, these inquiries demonstrated its importance everywhere, even in the south, where women
rarely appeared as agricultural wage-earners in the census. While they
listed wages that women sometimes earned in agriculture (which equalled
about 50 per cent of men's wages), the investigators for the Jacini
inquiry describe most women working without pay to produce food
for their families. They estimated that women did roughly one-half to
two-thirds the amount of agricultural labour of men in most southern
regions. Local variations were sharp, however. In Campania, Fedele de
Siervo reported women weeding, sowing, and picking olives, and concluded that it equalled about a quarter of the work expected of men
during the year. In the district of Caserta, however, women's work was
reported to be equal to that of men. De Siervo also noted, with disap-
proval, that 'women who must work in the field go there every morning
carrying on their heads a cradle with their child in it.'[36] Describing
conditions in 1885 in Cittaducale, a small village in Abruzzo, Antonio
Piccinini found women performing tasks heavier than most tasks allot-
ted to men, including carrying large, heavy faggots of wood. He also
found women working in the fields with men in summertime and doing
up to half the work of the men during that season. [37] In Campania, de
Siervo observed in 1882, '[w]omen are more often beasts of burden
than workers,' but he also reported them weeding, sowing, and picking
olives: he estimated that they did about a quarter of the work of men.

The investigators were well aware that their observations contradicted
published reports that recorded very low numbers of women doing
fieldwork.[38] As bourgeois men, these government investigators believed
that such heavy workloads endangered women's health and reproductive capabilities. Later (in 1902 and 1907), Italian legislators would try to
protect the health of working mothers, but since so many of these
women were not wage-earners, but rather worked within family groups,
such efforts had limited effect.[39]

As part of subsistence production, agricultural chores were domestic
chores and thus not easily separated from women's other tasks. Even
where women worked in the fields like men, however, they faced domestic tasks no man undertook. Investigator Piccinini, for example, observed that while men were unemployed during many winter months

because of the weather, women turned to wintertime chores like spinning wool, making canvas, and weaving. Whether for family use or regional cottage industries census enumerators ignored such domestic chores. Women also worked year-long producing cloth and clothing and, together with younger children, caring for small animals and gardens. They also were exclusively responsible for laundry, mending, and food preparation.[40] Rural women, in other words, worked full time but housekeeping and child-minding were not their main occupation, or even their second priority.

Just as Italian record keepers hesitated to list women working without wages as employed, they seemed confused about applying the label *casalinga* or housewife to rural women.[41] A description of peasant dwellings demonstrates just how poorly a concept like housework, or housewife, fits the lives of Italy's rural women, whether in the north or south. In areas outside the northern city of Verona, one observer described rural homes that were little more than cane walls and covered with reeds and straw. Houses in the nearby mountains, he noted, were sturdier, but also dirtier.[42] Indeed, all the investigators for the Jacini inquiry emphasized how dirty rural homes were, and one explained that, in the Veneto, women's work in the fields left little time for housework.[43] Others noted that no one remained inside such houses, except to protect themselves from inclement weather and to obtain some privacy for sleeping. Farther south, in Abruzzo, an investigator found a stone house of only one room for an entire family and its pigs and chickens. A heap of straw served as a bed for many children. In Puglia an observer reported with concern that 'the pig was almost always in the same room' as family members who shared beds in their dirty houses.[44] The same situation obtained in Campania and in Salerno, where many farm families also lived in straw houses.[45]

Cooking was only a slightly more time-consuming chore. The foods prepared daily were simple and monotonous. Differences between north and south, and within regions, were significant. In the north, in the countryside around Turin, peasants ate large quantities of polenta (cornmeal mush) and some wheat bread, supplemented with a little cheese, salad, and vegetables for their noontime meal. In the evening they ate a thick soup of beans, grains, and sometimes a little pasta or rice. Sausage appeared on the table only on feast days.[46] In the south, day labourers ate three times a day, but took at least one meal, of bread and vegetables for lunch or vegetable soup in the evening, in the fields. The employer might provide a bit of wine during harvest season as part of a man's wages. In Calabria, peasants eating together at home enjoyed bread, olive oil, and vegetables at noon, and an evening meal of polenta or beans or potatoes. Meat was eaten only for major festivals in the south, whereas breads of legumes and wild greens often appeared on the table.[47]

The parliamentary investigators were more interested in the adequacy of peasants' diet than in women's work as food providers. Finding diets dominated by cereals and bread plus oil, salt, and vegetables, they concluded that peasant diets provided adequate calories but little pleasure or variety.[48] They further agreed that southern men's diets were better than those of women and children because they more often worked far from home and received meals with wine as part of their pay. Women and children, by contrast, supplemented their monotonous diet by stealing wild fruits and vegetables, an act that modern liberal Italy (unlike the aristocratic and semi-feudal states that preceded it) defined as petty theft even when plants grew, uncultivated, on private property.[49]

Unfortunately, the women's own impressions of their work as food providers are not contained in the government inquiries, although the cleaning, storage, and sometimes milling of grain (in hand mills) clearly consumed considerable time, as did baking in some areas. The most commonly eaten foods (mushes and thick soups) might require long cooking but little attention, and few rural women had the opportunity to develop a large repertory of specialized dishes. One can glean from the inquiries peasant women's focus on providing sufficient quantities of food, not elaborating their skills as cooks.

Government reports also say comparatively little about child-rearing; the investigators mainly comment about fertility, birthing, and the nursing of very young children.[50] This absence might well reflect the fact that peasant women did not devote the bulk of their attention to the care of children. In order to give birth, a peasant woman interrupted her work for at most one or two weeks. In Campania, a surveyor for the Faina inquiry in 1909 found women taking their children to the fields with them until they were 18 to 24 months in age. Earlier, breastfeeding generally had continued until the child was 12 or 18 months old, but at the end of the nineteenth century 11 per cent of rural women breastfed for as long as 31 months, perhaps to avoid pregnancy or to keep children with them while they worked.[51] Once children could walk, reported the same investigator, they were sometimes cared for by 'old women' who earned money by babysitting 'ten or twelve children in one room,' or, in many cases, simply left alone. Significantly, domestic accidents were one of the main causes of child mortality.[52] An observer reported 'accidental homicides caused by fire, hot water burnings, falls, pig bites and so on.' He added that once a child reached the age of five or six, and began to work as a helper for another member of the family, a mother's responsibility as child-minder was essentially over. She could again turn her undivided attentions to the endless list of domestic tasks that nevertheless seem oddly unsuited to the category of 'housework.' [53]

Male Emigration and Women's Work

Even as the Jacini investigators surveyed the Italian countryside in the 1870s and early 1880s, emigration was changing the lives of Italians in rural districts, especially in Genoa, a few scattered areas of the south, and more generally throughout the Italian north. By the first decade of the twentieth century, the reports of the Faina investigators allow us to trace the impact of emigration on women's lives in the rural south. Women's work changed significantly with male emigration.

It is quite likely, for example, that the high rates of female employment, and the heavily female agricultural work forces in northern districts – which appeared in both census listings and the Jacini reports – reflected the early beginnings of temporary male emigration across the Alps from these regions. Agricultural employment for women was often temporary, and was thus associated in the north with significant internal migrations of women, for example to the rice fields of the Po Valley.[54] In the north, women were mobile locally while men were mobile internationally. In quite sharp contrast, regions like Sicily – with their declining opportunities for women to work in agriculture and industry – sent proportionately more women abroad together with male migrants in family groups.

By the first decade of the twentieth century, observers in the south noted a similar impact of male emigration on female work. In all the regions affected by emigration, women's agricultural contributions increased. Emigration improved a family's cash income, but the cash sent by husbands was typically used to pay debts or to buy a small house or a piece of land, or was saved – not to support women and children in idleness. With men gone, women had to work even harder in order to guarantee the family's subsistence. In Campania, surveyor Oreste Bordiga observed, with moral concern, that where emigration had 'noticeably reduced the male population,' women, in replacing men even for the most arduous tasks, had become 'beasts of burden subjected to labor that is incompatible with their sex, with their physiognomy, and with the duties of maternity and of breastfeeding.'[55] In Abruzzo and Molise, landowners also substituted female for male workers; here the infant mortality rate went from 3.7 per 1000 in 1895 to 4.37 in 1904, mainly as a consequence of 'heavy work undertaken during the last phase of pregnancy.'[56]

Not surprisingly, the Faina investigators viewed male emigration as detrimental to women. They criticized men whom they claimed married a week before leaving, returned after two, three, five, or sometimes even ten years, and then left again after only one or two years. As one cynical observer claimed, a man intending to emigrate married so as to secure the ownership of a wife, and to have someone in the village to manage his savings to prevent them from being used by his father's family. Meanwhile, women supported themselves, and their families, at home.[57]

In other ways, however, emigration had a positive impact on women's work lives in rural Italy. As Reeder's contribution to this collection shows, emigration encouraged women to stay in school and it also improved housing. In Puglia, an observer found that 'peasant dwellings tend to improve in the villages with the strongest and oldest emigration.'[58] Investigators described the houses of *americani* (those returned from sojourns in the Americas) as white and clean, with a rigid separation between the living areas and the stables, tile floors, and real kitchens.[59] They boasted plastered walls, brick floors, proper windows, a separate kitchen, an internal staircase, and two upstairs rooms. Some had balconies and shutters, sturdy wooden doors, and a tiled roof.[60] In some villages, returnees introduced acetylene lighting or made inquiries about obtaining electrical service in towns that still lacked piped water or sewage. The contrast between these homes and the 'old black homes, piled on top of each other and separated only by torturous, dark little streets' impressed upper-class observers.[61]

The Faina inquiry investigators also attributed to heavy emigration significant improvements in the diet of peasants, who now ate meat sauce on macaroni weekly on Sundays; they more often kept and slaughtered pigs, increasing the amount of meat they consumed.[62] Local elites complained about these changes; from Molise, one wrote of inflation resulting when the wives of the emigrants 'arrive at the marketplace and buy up all the fresh fish newly arrived from Termoli, regardless of price.'[63] Migration may have allowed peasants in certain areas to create what we now recognize as the popular regional cuisines of Italy.[64] Peasants around Vasto developed a taste for hot peppers, while enthusiasm for macaroni spread throughout the south. In the north, peasants substituted more rice, and wheat bread, for the ubiquitous polenta, and they began eating more meat (pork, rabbit, chicken) and cheese.[65] In Campania, a surveyor recalled an incident at an open market, where a *contadina* (peasant) was selling eggs. On seeing this an acquaintance told her that 'an americano's wife must eat and not sell her eggs.'[66] Increasingly, then, Italian women of the popular classes were developing the domestic skills that made them *casalinghe* (housewives) rather than peasants.

Discourses of Domesticity

The domestic lives of Italy's rural women differed substantially from those of their middle-class counterparts, both in Italy's cities and in the United States. Tellingly, the investigators of the Jacini and Faina inquiries wrote about Italian peasant domestic life in moral terms quite unlike those used for the middle classes of either country. Their views of the domestic relationships of peasant men and women also differed particularly sharply from American observers of Italian immigrants. American observers saw Italian immigrant women as the victims of Italian male patriarchy; they attributed to men's rule over women the failure of Italian immigrant women to take 'appropriate' jobs as domestic servants. Meanwhile, in Italy, observers instead noted nervously that patriarchy had already collapsed in most villages. While Amy Bernardy in New York seemed concerned mainly to remove boarders from women's domestic world, and to guarantee women employment in all-female domestic settings, the Jacini and Faina investigators instead saw domestic order endangered by men's departure from the domestic world.

This is not to say there were no signs of female subservience or patriarchal authority in the rituals of everyday peasant family life in Italy. In a small village near Avola, an investigator noted that wives addressed their husbands with 'voi,' the formal form of address, and served men their meals before themselves sitting at the table. When a man left on Monday morning for his week's work in the distant fields, he put into sacks 'all the bread he finds, leaving the family to feed itself on fine bran.'[67] Men could and did beat their wives and children in rural Italy, as in most other rural parts of Europe and the Americas.

Such domestic rituals, however, did not convince government investigators that patriarchal authority reigned in peasant households. Bourgeois Italians idealized rural families that worked collectively under firm, patriarchal authority, as did the sharecroppers of central Italy, especially in Tuscany. There, at least in the past, the male head of the household, usually the father, organized and supervised all family labour, with the assistance of his wife (the *massaia*).[68] Sharecropping households might include twenty persons that formed stem families (parents plus one married son and his family). Other households were joint ones, where several married brothers cooperated under the leadership of their father or the eldest brother.[69] The government investigators found few families like this anywhere in rural Italy by the late nineteenth century. Most families were nuclear and relatively small. Worse, men were often absent, and women determined their own work routines, at times even working for wages under the supervision of other men. Work for wages in commercial agriculture and in local industries had, observers believed, begun to tear rural families apart, mainly by drawing men out of the domestic world. Married men left behind women and children overworked and without proper supervision. Unmarried men returned unwilling to submit to their father's authority, or to marry local women. In short, male migration was completing the destruction of patriarchal peasant families.

Bourgeois observers wrung their hands over the collapse of traditional patriarchy, and with it of the morality of the poorest Italians. Whether in Italy's northwest or south they reported incessantly that family ties were 'nonexistent,' 'loose,' or 'weak.'[70] They dismissed sentimental attachments among family members, claiming that men mourned a dead mule more than a dead wife. In Campania, wrote de Siervo, 'the family is not based on sentiments but on reciprocal economic interests.'[71] They worried as much, or more, about a father's declining control over his sons as over his wife or daughters. Observers noted that children sometimes denied their elderly parents food and they descried 'limits or nonexistence of children's respect for their parents or parents' concern for their children.'[72] A Jacini investigator proclaimed, with horror, that women in the Abruzzo were the real rulers of their families; men too often worked far away to seem firmly 'in control' of the domestic world, as bourgeois Italians wished them to be.[73] Even a sympathetic Sicilian folklorist agreed, seeing matriarchal elements in island families and in women's control of both their own dowries and of a family's savings.[74] Government investigators in the south did not find that mass emigration or return had substantially changed the tenor of family life, and continued to denounce it in harsh terms.[75]

Like Bernardy, the investigators for the Jacini and Faina inquiries reported widespread adultery, prostitution, illegitimate births, incest, and rape in many Italian provinces. Significantly, all the surveyors were men and their notes reveal a degree of misogyny. For instance, Abele Damiani, reporting from Sicily, insisted that rapes were rare in the region because women more often accepted than rejected men's advances.[76] Like Bernardy, these observers associated terrible housing conditions with incest and sexual promiscuity. They saw parents, children, and grown-ups sharing beds or sleeping together in the same room as evidence of sexual perversion.[77]

With regard to the alleged moral failings of women, investigators blamed male emigration for the collapse of patriarchy and the ensuing 'crimes against the good order of the family.' In Abruzzi, one observer noted with horror that adultery in particular had increased, and he attributed the problem to the weakening of marriage ties caused by 'the abandonment of wives by their emigrant husbands for long periods of time.'[78]

In Campania, another investigator stressed the impact of emigration on recent marriages, and expressed some sympathy for the young wives, about whom he wrote: 'Left alone shortly after their wedding, surrounded by a thousand temptations, often by that of need, on other occasions not distracted by work, because the faraway husband provides for them, they are in the least favourable conditions to remain chaste.[79] In many cases, he added, the wives no longer received news or financial support from the emigrant husband.[80] Another concurred, describing the wives of emigrants as 'still overflowing with youth but often impoverished or stunted in life, and exposed every day to a thousand temptations by those in search of amorous adventures.' The dramas of adultery, hidden pregnancies, abandoned children, abortions, and infanticides, he added, visibly multiply.[81]

Italy's statistics on illegitimacy, infanticide, and criminality did not, in fact, support the investigators' alarmist conclusions. Increases in all these measures of social stress were relatively small during the mass emigrations. Nevertheless, we should not dismiss these writings as mere products of the terrified imaginations of misogynous bourgeois observers. Violence, rape, and incest were real elements of rural Italian domestic life, and they would not disappear with emigration abroad.[82] They serve as a reminder that the lives of Italy's rural peasants were as difficult and constrained – and as troubling to bourgeois observers – as were the lives of the poor of other nations and of other times. Still, when subsequent American observers explained immigrant immorality as a consequence of urban life or as a reflection of a stern patriarchy rooted in conservative Italian peasant customs, their claims were less statements of fact than elements of distinctive American discourses on domesticity.

As they emigrated abroad, Italian men and women negotiated lives between two conflicting discourses of domesticity. Women's choices about work in the United States are probably best interpreted not as a continuation of old world habits but rather as complex responses to conflicting Italian and American expectations and judgments of domesticity and female morality. Women could not simultaneously fulfil American expectations that work as domestic servants was the most appropriate choice for them while also countering Italian concerns that collapsed patriarchal authority diminished their moral worth. Ultimately most chose to fulfil Italian ideals. Ironically, eschewing domestic work may have allowed Italian immigrant women to claim for the first time the moral mantle of a woman properly under the control of the patriarch of her family. But it also opened them to American charges of immorality, since their extended families – with boarders and male kin living under the same roof – violated American expectations of a morality maintained by women in a female-dominated and female-controlled domestic sphere.

Furthermore, the creation of the kind of domesticity idealized by Italians was accomplished only with resources available in America. A father's wages could provide for his subsistence but they could not support a family of idle wife and children. Pressures on women to produce without wages, and to bring cash into the family, continued. Women's wage-earning in household sweatshops and canneries also continued to reproduce in the modern United States the close linkage in rural Italy of subsistence production, family work groups, and wage-earning with domesticity. Women's insistence that work, and even wage-earning, belonged in the domestic arena, tied to family work groups, remained an important challenge to the U.S. discourse of domesticity that clearly demanded the separation of the two. Thus, domesticity for immigrant women was, from the first, strongly marked by 'ethnic' difference: as with housing and cuisine choices, it also represented the fulfilment of Italian, rather than American, domestic ideals.

Conclusions

It is only in recent years that scholarship on Italian immigrant women has deliberately challenged the hagiography of the Italian family in America as one supposedly dominated by a sense of honour and united like the five fingers of one hand in the face of life in a strange country. For first-generation Italian-American women, there was continuity (pre- and post-emigration) in at least one aspect of their lives – its harshness. Whether dealing with fieldwork or household management in Italy, or piecework at home in ethnic neighbourhoods in America, women's workdays continued to be too long, the work often rendered invisible, and always underpaid. Yet America did give peasant women from southern Italy access to a domesticity strongly marked by ethnic features. Not accidentally, the first sign of 'domestic' improvement was in household cuisine, with the introduction of foodstuffs into daily life that normally had been reserved for Italian feastdays. Later came the purchase of a home, another dream of Italian peasants. Female wage-earning was not necessarily new to Italian immigrant women in the United States, although, ironically, family solidarity in that country was perhaps not as seriously challenged as in Italy, where a husbands's work at a considerable distance from home meant constant separation. Eventually, intergenerational differences would emerge, including among second-generation daughters who would challenge, even reject, aspects of a familialist work ethos and older forms of perceived female subjugation. For these single young women the factory was attractive because it provided an opportunity for socialization against the sombre confines of the family and the ethnic group that also characterized young working women in the industrialized Italian north.[83]

NOTES

1 Amy Allemand Bernardy, 'Inchiesta sulle condizioni delle donne e dei fanciulli negli stati del Nordest della Confederazione Americana,' *Bollettino dell'emigrazione* 1 (1909); 'Inchiesta sulle condizioni delle donne e dei fanciulli negli stati del Centro e dell'Ovest della Confederazione Americana,' *Bollettino dell'emigrazione* 1 (1911). The emigration agency was housed in the Ministry of Foreign Affairs. On Bernardy's life and work, see Lina Del Romano, 'Amy Allemand Bernardy e l'emigrazione italiana nel Nord America' (University of Pescara thesis, 1993–4) and Anna Gasparini, 'Amy Allemand Bernardy, studiosa dell'emigrazione italiana in Nord America,' *Il Veltro* 34, 1–2 (1990): 169–79.
2 Most of the early work on Italian immigrant women in the U.S. focused on their wage-earning patterns: Louise Odencrantz, *Italian Women in Industry: A Study of Conditions in New York City* (New York: Russell Sage Foundation,

1919); Miriam Cohen, 'Italian American Women in New York City, 1900–1905: Work and School,' in Milton Cantor and Bruce Laurie, eds., *Class, Sex and the Woman Worker* (Westport, CT: Greenwood Press, 1977); Virginia Yans-McLaughlin, 'A Flexible Tradition: South Italian Immigrants Confront a New Work Experience,' *Journal of Social History* 7 (Summer 1974): 429–51; Luisa Cetti, 'Donne italiane a New York e lavoro a domicilio (1910–1925),' *Movimento Operaio e Socialista* 3, 7 (1984): 291–303; Luisa Cetti, 'Work Experience among Italian Women in New York, 1900–1930,' *Rivista di Studi Anglo-Americani* 4–5 (1984–5): 493–508. On Canada see Franca Iacovetta, 'Writing Women into Immigration History: The Italian-Canadian Case,' *Altreitalie* 9 (1993): 24–47.

3 Bernardy 1909, 13.

4 Ibid., 7–9.

5 Ibid., 131; Bernardy 1911, 39.

6 Bernardy 1909, 65, 67.

7 American social workers organized domestic economy courses to teach immigrant housewives to shop, to cook with a gas stove and to prepare proper meals for small children, with primary attention to hygiene; see Maddalena Tirabassi, 'Prima le donne e i bambini,' *Quaderni storici* 42 (December 1982): 464, and Tirabassi, 'Italiane ed emigrate,' *Altreitalie* 9 (1993): 139–51. On the domestication of women, see Donna Gabaccia, *From the Other Side: Women, Gender and Immigrant Life in the U.S., 1830–1990* (Bloomington: Indiana University Press, 1994), 115–23. See also Bernardy 1909, 13, 131; and 1911, 31, 35.

8 Bernardy 1909, 80–1.

9 Paul J. Campisi, 'Ethnic Family Patterns: The Italian Family in the United States,' *American Journal of Sociology* 53 (July 1948): 443–9; Lydio Tomasi, *Italian American Family Life* (Staten Island: Center for Migration Studies, 1972); Virginia Yans-McLaughlin, *Family and Community: Italian Immigrants in Buffalo, 1880–1930* (Ithaca: Cornell University Press, 1977), 18–19; see also Yans-McLaughlin, 'Patterns of Work and Family Organization: Buffalo's Italians,' *Journal of Interdisciplinary History* 2 (Fall 1971): 299–314.

10 Sophonisba Breckinridge, *New Homes for Old* (New York: Harper, 1921); Barbara Klaczynska, 'Why Women Work: A Comparison of Various Ethnic Groups, Philadelphia,' *Labor History* 17 (Winter 1976): 73–88; Florence Teicher Bloom, 'Struggling and Surviving: The Life Style of European Immigrant Breadwinning Mothers in American Industrial Cities,' *Women's History International Forum* 8, 6 (1985): 609–20. On Canada, see Iacovetta, 'Writing Italian Women into Migration History.'

11 Elizabeth H. Pleck, 'A Mother's Wages: Income Earning among Married

Rethinking Domestic Work and Morality in Italy 125

Italian and Black Women, 1896–1911,' in Michael Gordon, ed., *The American Family in Social Historical Perspective*, 2nd ed. (New York: St Martin's Press, 1978), 367–92; Alice Kessler Harris, 'Women's Wage Work as Myth and History,' *Labor History* 19, 2 (Spring 1988): 287–307.

12 On the differences between continental Italy and the island of Sicily, see the relevant discussion in the introduction and Linda Reeder's essay (chapter 1) on Sutera, Sicily, in this volume.

13 For a more detailed discussion on this theme see the editors' introduction and my discussion below.

14 Besides the works cited below, the reader can usefully consult Michela De Giorgio, *Le italiane dall'Unità ad oggi* (Bari: Laterza, 1992); Giovanna Fiume, *Madri: Storia di un ruolo sociale* (Venice: Marsilio, 1995); Ilaria Porciani, ed., *Le donne a scuola: L'educazione femminile nell'Italia dell'Ottocento* (Florence: Il sedicismo, 1987); Paola Nava, *Operaie, serve, maestre e impiegate* (Turin: Rosenberg, 1992); and Adele Maiello, Franco Ragazzi, and Paola Toni, *Dal filo al file: Un secolo di immagini del lavoro femminile in Liguria* (Tormena: Miscellanea, 1995). Studies of emigration that give good attention to women and gender include Fortunata Piselli, *Parentela e emigrazione: Mutamenti e continuità in una comunità calabrese* (Turin: G. Einaudi, 1981); Andreina De Clementi, 'I ruoli scambiati: Donne e uomini nell'emigrazione italiana,' in De Clementi and Maria Stella, eds., *Viaggi di donne* (Naples: Liguori, 1995), 171–95; A. De Clementi, 'Madri e figlie nelle emigrazione americana,' in Angela Groppi, ed., *Il lavoro delle donne* (Bari: Laterza, 1996), 421–44; Nicoletta Franchi, 'Donne emigranti: Il caso di Pontebuggianese,' *Farestoria* 28 (1996): 52–61; Nicoletta Serio, 'Italiane in rotta per l'America: Emigranti e studiose dell'emigrazione,' *Il Veltro* 34, 1–2 (1990): 181–201; Maddalena Tirabassi, 'Trends of Continuity and Signs of Change among Italian Migrant Women,' in Roberto Maccarini, ed., *Le stelle e le strisce: Studi americani e militari in onore di Raimondo Luraghi* (Milan: Bompiani, 1998), 283–98; Elisa-betta Vezzosi, 'L'immigrata italiana alla ricerca di un'identità femminile nell'America del primo Novecento,' *Movimento operaio e socialista* 7, 3 (1984): 305–19; and Patrizia Audenino, 'Le custodi della montagna: Donne e migrazioni stagionali in una comunità alpina,' in Paola Corti, ed., 'Società rurale e ruoli femminili in Italia tra Ottocento e Novecento,' special issue, *Annali dell'Istituto Alcide Cervi* 12 (1990): 265–88.

15 Corti, 'Società rurale e ruoli femminili'; P. Corti, 'L'emigrazione e consuetudini alimentari: L'esperienza di una catena miratoria,' in *Storia d'Italia: Annali*, vol. 13: L'alimentazione (Turin: Einaudi, 1998), 683–719; Giovanna Da Molin, *La famiglia nel passato: Strutture familiari nel regno di Napoli* (Bari: Cacucci, 1990), 504.

16 Groppi, *Il lavoro delle donne*, 8, 11; Ornello Vitali, *La popolazione attiva in*

126 Maddalena Tirabassi

agricoltura attraverso i censimenti italiani: 1881–1961 (Rome: Failli, 1968), 13; Maura Palazzi, *Donne sole* (Milan: Bruno Mondadori, 1997), 357; Alessandra Pescarolo, 'Il lavoro e le risorse delle donne in età contemporanea,' in Groppi, *Il lavoro delle donne.*

17 Maria Casalini, 'Il servizio domestico femminile nella Firenze dell'Otto-cento,' *Passato e presente* 23 (1990): 138.

18 Victoria De Grazia, *How Fascism Ruled Women: Italy, 1922–1945* (Berkeley: University of California Press, 1992), 168.

19 Palazzi, *Donne sole,* 357.

20 Simona Laudani, 'Trasformazioni agricole e condizione femminile in Sicilia,' in Corti, 'Società rurale,' 113–28.

21 Simona Laudani, 'Tra autoconsumo e mercato: Le attività tessili della donna siciliana nell'Ottocento,' *Memoria* 30 (1990): 34.

22 Donna R. Gabaccia, 'In the Shadows of the Periphery: Italian Women in the Nineteenth Century,' in Marilyn J. Boxer and Jean H. Quataert, eds., *Connecting Spheres: European Women in a Globalizing World, 1500 to the Present,* 2nd ed. (New York: Oxford University Press, 2000), 194–203.

23 Franco Ramella, *Terra e telai: Sistemi di parentela e manifattura nel biellese dell'Ottocento* (Turin: Einaudi, 1981).

24 As some women also did; see Paola Corti's essay in this collection (chapter 4).

25 Palazzi, *Donne sole,* 151–5.

26 Maria Bellocchio, *Aghi e cuori: Sartine e patronesse nella Torino d'inizio secolo* (Turin: Centro Studi Piemontesi, 2000).

27 Daniela Perco, *Balie da latte: Una forma peculiare di emigrazione temporanea* (Feltre: Comunità Montana feltrina, Centro per documentazione della cultura popolare, 1984).

28 Marzio Barbagli, *Sotto lo stesso tetto* (Bologna: Il Mulino, 1984, 392); Perco, *Balie da latte;* Daniela Todesco et al., *Ciòde e ciodéti: Un'emigrazione stagionale di donne e ragazzi dal bellunese al trentino* (Feltre: Comunità Montana feltrina, Centro per la documentazione della cultura popolare, 1995), 10; Adriana Dadà, 'La mostra collettiva sull'emigrazione femminile da ponte Buggiane-se: Itinerio didattico di ricerca storica sociale,' *Farestoria* 30 (1997): 77–80); Angiolina Arru, 'I servi e le serve: La particolarità del caso italiano,' *Journal of Family History* 15,4 (1990): 545; Arru, 'Il matrimonio tardivo dei servi e delle serve,' *Quaderni storici* 68 (1988): 469–96; Arru, 'Protezione e legitti-mazione: Come si usa il mestiere di serva nell'Ottocento,' in Lucia Ferrante, Maura Palazzi, and Gianna Pomata, eds., *Ragnatele di rapporti* (Turin: Rosen-berg and Sellier, 1988); Arru, 'Donne e uomini nel mercato del lavoro servile,' in Groppi, *Il lavoro delle donne,* 247–68; Giovanna Da Molin, 'Family Forms and Domestic Service in Southern Italy from the Seventeenth to the Nineteenth Centuries,' *Journal of Family History* 4 (1990): 503–27.

29 Pescarolo, 'Il lavoro e le risorse delle donne,' 223; Barbara Armani and Daniela Lazzari, 'Padroni e servitori a Lucca, 1871–1914,' *Quaderni Storici* 68 (1988): 519–40.

30 Margherita Pelaja, 'Mestieri femminili e luoghi comuni: Le domestiche a Roma a metà dell'Ottocento,' *Quaderni Storici* 68 (1988): 497–518.

31 Da Molin, *La famiglia nel passato*, 519, 521.

32 Simonetta Soldani, 'Lo stato e il lavoro delle donne nell'Italia liberale,' *Passato e presente* 24 (1990): 41; see also Soldani, 'Maestre d'Italia,' in Groppi, *Il lavoro delle donne*, 368–97.

33 Soldani, 'Lo stato e il lavoro delle donne,' 38; see also Luisa Accati, 'Introduzione,' in Luisa Accati, Vanessa Maher, and Gianna Pomata, eds., *Parto e modernità: Momenti dell'autobiografia femminile* (Bologna: Il Mulino, 1980), 333–45.

34 Barbagli, *Sotto lo stesso tetto*, 392; Todesco, *Ciòde e ciodéti*, 10; Adriana Dadà, 'La mostra collettiva.'

35 Stefano Jacini was the director of the inquest, published as *Atti della Giunta per l'inchiesta agraria e sulle condizioni della classe agraria* (Rome: Forzani, 1881–5). Eugenio Faina was the director of the inquest published as *Giunta parlamentare d'inchiesta sulle condizioni dei contadini nelle province meridionali e nella Sicilia* (Rome: Tip. Naz. di G. Bertero, 1909–10).

36 *Atti della Giunta per l'inchiesta agraria*, vol. 7, 197.

37 Ibid., vol. 12, 158–9.

38 Ibid, vol. 7, 262.

39 Pescarolo, 'Il lavoro e le risorse delle donne,' 386.

40 *Atti della Giunta per l'inchiesta agraria*, vol. 12, 158–9.

41 Gabaccia, 'In the Shadows of the Periphery.'

42 *Atti della Giunta per l'inchiesta agraria*, vol. 5, 278–9.

43 Ibid., vol. 4, 7.

44 Ibid., vol. 12, 469–71.

45 Ibid., vol. 7; Caterina Rapetti, *Archivi familiari: Storie, volti e documenti dell'emigrazione lunigianese* (Lunigiana: Rapetti; Florence, Nuova grafica fiorentina, 1986), 48–9; Donna Gabaccia, *From Sicily to Elizabeth Street: Housing and Social Change among Italian Immigrants, 1880–1930* (Albany: State University of New York Press, 1984), 18–21.

46 *Atti della Giunta per l'inchiesta agraria*, vol. 8, 644.

47 Ibid., vol. 9.

48 Ibid., vol. 12, 465.

49 Ibid., vol. 13, 27, 523.

50 Besides the work of Livi Bacci (see note 51), see Anna Maria Birindelli, 'Emigrazione e transizione demografica,' in Valerio Castronovo, ed., *Studi sull'emigrazione. Un'analisi comparata: Atti del Convegno storico internazionale*

sull'emigrazione, Biella 25–27 settembre 1989 (Milan: Electa, 1991), 353–65; J.L. Rallu, 'Permanences des disparités régionales de la fécondité en Italie?' *Population* 1 (1983): 29–59; Luigi Di Comite, 'Teoria e prassi della transizione demografica,' in *Studi in Onore di Paolo Fortunati* [Università di Bologna, Istituto di Statistica] (Bologna: CLUEB, 1974); Di Comite and Eros Moretti, *Divari demografici regionali e declino della fecondità* (Milan: Franco Angeli, 1990); John Briggs, 'Fertility and Cultural Change among Families in Italy and America,' *American Historical Review* 91, 5 (December 1986): 1129–45.

51 Massimo Livi Bacci, *Donna, fecondità e figli: Due secoli di storia demografica italiana* (Bologna: Il Mulino, 1980), 315; see also Bacci, *A History of Italian Fertility during the Last Two Centuries* (Princeton: Princeton University Press, 1977).

52 M. Livi Bacci, *L'immigrazione e l'assimilazione degli italiani negli Stati Uniti secondo le statistiche americane* (Milan: Giuffré, 1961), 86.

53 *Inchiesta Parlamentare sulle condizioni dei contadini*, vol. 4, 264.

54 Elda Zappi, *If Eight Hours Seem Too Few: Mobilization of Women Workers in the Italian Rice Fields* (Albany: State University of New York Press, 1991).

55 *Giunta parlamentare d'inchiesta sulle condizioni dei contadini*, vol. 4, 259.

56 Ibid., vol. 2, 192–3.

57 Ibid., vol. 2, 244; vol. 6, 360–70; Vito Teti, 'Note sui comportamenti delle donne sole degli "americani" durante la prima emigrazione in Calabria,' *Studi Emigrazione* 85, 24 (1987): 13–46. See also Andreina Di Clementi's essay in this volume (chapter 2).

58 *Giunta parlamentare d'inchiesta sulle condizioni dei contadini*, vol. 3, 498–500; vol. 5, 57.

59 Ibid., vol. 6, 832; see also Reeder's essay in this volume (chapter 1).

60 *Atti della Giunta per l'inchiesta agraria*, vol. 5, 504.

61 Ibid., vol. 2, 186–7.

62 *Giunta parlamentare d'inchiesta sulle condizioni dei contadini*, vol. 3, 438.

63 Ibid, vol. 2, 159.

64 Piero Bevilacqua, 'Emigrazione transoceanica e mutamenti dell'alimentazione contadina calabrese fra Otto e Novecento,' in *Quaderni storici* 47, 2 (1981): 520–55; Vito Teti, 'La cucina calabrese è un invenzione americana,' *I viaggi di Erodoto* 12 (1991): 58–73.

65 Paola Corti, 'Il cibo dell'emigrante,' *Il Risorgimento* 44, 2 (1992): 363–78.

66 *Giunta parlamentare d'inchiesta sulle condizioni dei contadini*, vol. 6, 363.

67 *Atti della Giunta per l'inchiesta agraria*, vol. 13, 672; Barbagli, *Sotto lo stesso tetto*, 498–501.

68 *Atti della Giunta parlamentare per l'inchiesta agraria*, vol. 3, 656. In other parts of central Italy they were called *reggitore* and *reggitrice*; ibid., vol. 1, 237–9.

69 The key theoretical reading on the peasant stem family is Lutz Berkner,

'The Stem-Family and the Developmental Cycle of the Peasant Household:
An Eighteenth Century Austrian Example,' *American Historical Review* 77
(1972): 398–418. See also David I. Kertzer, *Family Life in Central Italy, 1880–
1910: Sharecropping, Wage Labor, and Co-residence* (New Brunswick, NJ: Rutgers
University Press, 1984); Piero Melograni and Lucetta Scaraffia, *La famiglia
italiana dall'Ottocento ad oggi* (Bari: Laterza, 1988); and Chiara Saraceno,
Anatomia della famiglia: Strutture sociali e forme familiari (Bari: De Donato,
1976). On joint families, see William A. Douglass, 'A Joint-Family Household in Eighteenth Century Southern Italian Society,' in David L. Kertzer
and Richard P. Saller, eds., *The Family in Italy: From Antiquity to the Present*
(New Haven: Yale University Press, 1991), 286–303. In the 1870s and 1880s,
the joint household of brothers – which a Jacini commissioner termed 'a
very curious type of patriarchal republic' – existed mainly in Val d'Aosta and
other parts of Piedmont. See *Atti della Giunta per l'inchiesta agraria*, vol. 8,
641, 656.

70 *Atti della Giunta per l'inchiesta agraria*, vol. 11, 1132–3.
71 Ibid., vol. 7, 181, 332.
72 Ibid., vol. 13, 389; vol. 9, 214.
73 *Giunta parlamentare d'inchiesta sulle condizioni dei contadini.*
74 Giuseppe Pitrè, *La famiglia, la casa, la vita del popolo siciliano*, vol. 25 of
Biblioteca delle tradizioni popolari siciliane (Palermo: A. Reber, 1913), 36.
75 *Atti della Giunta per l'inchiesta agraria*, vol. 13, 35, 389; vol. 7, 214.
76 Ibid., vol. 13, 35.
77 For general studies of Italian sexuality in this period, see Maria Pia Di Bella,
'La sessualità femminile tra rappresentazioni e pratiche nelle storie di vita
delle contadine italiane,' in Corti, *Società rurale*, 361–71; and Bruno Wanroj,
Storia del pudore: La questione sessuale in Italia 1860–1940 (Venice: Marsilio,
1990).
78 *Giunta parlamentare d'inchiesta sulle condizioni dei contadini*, vol. 2, 271.
79 Ibid., vol. 4, 536.
80 Ibid., 612.
81 Ibid., 591.
82 Maddalena Tirabassi, *Il Faro di Beacon Street: Social workers e immigrate negli
Stati Uniti (1910–1933)* (Milan: Franco Angeli, 1990), 199–201; Linda
Gordon, *Heroes of Their Own Lives: The Politics and History of Family Violence,
Boston, 1889–1960* (New York: Viking, 1989).
83 Tirabassi, *Il Faro di Beacon Street*; Giulia Calvi, 'Donne in fabbrica: Comunità
femminile e socialità del lavoro in America 1900–1915,' *Quaderni Storici* 51
(December 1982): 817–51.

PART II

Female Immigrants at Work

4 Women Were Labour Migrants Too: Tracing Late-Nineteenth-Century Female Migration from Northern Italy to France

Paola Corti

TRANSLATED BY GABRIELE SCARDELLATO

In the late 1970s, seventy-year-old Margherita, a daughter of peasants in the northwestern Italian province of Cuneo, reported to historian Nuto Revelli: 'My mother went to France to be a *nunù*, a wet nurse. Because she had a son she left him at home with the grandmothers. From here many women went to France to be *la nunù*.'[1] In the study of Italian migrations around the world during the era of mass migrations, the stories of women like Margherita's mother have not yet been recognized or told, let alone analysed.

Why? Invidious gender bias is not the best explanation. As a woman, Margherita's mother belonged to a relatively small minority of migrants, for men formed the overwhelming majority of Italy's emigrants. In addition, Margherita's mother travelled to France, whose considerable importance as an immigrant-receiving country remains submerged beneath veritable oceans of research on the longer-distance transatlantic migrations to the Americas. In fact, throughout the years 1870–1914, migrations to Europe from Italy generally equalled or outnumbered migrations bound for the new world.[2] Finally, Margherita's mother originated in Italy's northwest, a region far better known to historians for its economic development and for its role after 1900 in Italy's industrialization than for its importance as a generator of emigrants abroad. Yet, Piedmont had one of the highest emigration rates in Italy during these years, and female emigration from developing districts was decidedly more important than national statistics suggest.

Most important, the story of Margherita's mother confounds prevailing interpretation of Italy's migrating female minority. When women appear at all in general accounts of Italian emigration, they are participants in family migrations – the daughters and wives who follow the male pioneers and their dictates.[3] Studies of Italy's migrations have not yet taken into account the observation of Mirjana Mirokvasic that women, too, are labour migrants.[4]

This paper draws on research conducted as part of an international collaboration of French and Italian scholars working on borderland migrations along the changing boundary separating southwestern Piedmont and western Liguria (in Italy) from southern France.[5] Although numerous researchers have utilized the records of either France or Italy to explore migration, this international collaboration suggests that a transnational approach by scholars with a shared research program, using records from both countries, may be particularly helpful in bringing to light the lives of women labour migrants.[6]

This case study of female emigration within a specific borderland region – the French Department of the Maritime Alps, and the territories that adjoined it within Italy (mainly southwestern Piedmont) – reveals that alongside the more frequently studied domestic servants moving from countryside to city, there was a migration stream composed of specialized, skilled female vocations and trades. Ever since Ravenstein, scholars have recognized that women, many of them domestics, might dominate short-distance ones while men predominated among migrations over longer distances.[7] In Italy, shorter-distance migrations were not necessarily alternatives to longer-distance ones, but rather existed alongside them. Migrations in this border region were international, but they were relatively short-distance and often temporary.

Our research also reveals the very early presence of females among Italians going abroad.[8] Their migration hints at arenas of both female autonomy and occupational complexity, with several streams of women workers of varying skill levels and family status.[9] The nature of women's skills emerges most clearly when analysed in their districts of origin in Piedmont, Italy. A significant female representation among both seasonal and temporary Italian workers in France also reflected the continued importance into the modern age of the 'life-cycle servants' so common in pre-industrial Europe. These servants included adolescent domestics, older wet nurses, seasonal agricultural labourers of both sexes, male practitioners of itinerant trades, and seasonal workers in construction. Life-cycle migrants often originated in the mountain regions of Europe, including those of Piedmont. By the nineteenth century, life-cycle migrations from alpine valleys also began to feed emerging manufacturing districts, and the exodus of females from mountain communities created remarkable streams of artisanal workers toward new centres of textile production. Migration was thus part of the normal and traditional way of life in mountain communities – something scholars have long recognized, but only in the case of men.

Migration also fully engaged the women of mountain communities, albeit in a variety of ways. By the late nineteenth century, female migration was quite differentiated: it drew women from differing socio-economic backgrounds to differing kinds of jobs abroad, and allowed migrants to meet diverse domestic needs in their home villages. Women's journeys always formed part of a larger system of migration with broad territorial circuits. But the geography of migratory routes and particular trades did not themselves explain women's complex destinies; these were shaped also by an extensive network of personal and family relationships depending on female labour and skills. The proximity of the border, its permeable nature, and the economic opportunities it offered constituted a clear incentive to female mobility and to the development of circuits of temporary migration within female trades. Migration flows of female silk workers directed toward France – originating in an Italian community on which direct surveys have been carried out – not only surpassed those of men, but revealed that women migrants sometimes had higher skill levels than men. For women, too, the development and exercise of particular skills influenced the selection of migration routes. In turn, these depended on the existence of extensive and well-formed informal networks in international labour markets and on the intervention of mediators who recruited women workers for employers abroad.[10] Thus, women's migrations in this border region provide interesting female parallels to the better-known itinerancy of male construction workers from mountain communities.[11] Understanding female migration can provide new insights for discussion of the role, make-up, and geographical origins of migration chains for the development of Italy's worldwide migrations.[12]

Male Predominance in Migrations from Italy

One of the most prominent and studied features of the first waves of Italian migration was the high rate of male participation.[13] For the period 1876–80, men made up some 85 per cent of the emigrants who left Italy, while women formed only 15 per cent of the total.[14] Women's representation reached its highest point (38 per cent of the national total) in 1888, largely as the result of an enormous emigration of Venetian families bound for Brazil. Between 1896 and 1900 the female component hovered around 25 per cent, and between 1901 and 1915 it actually sank to 21–2 per cent of the total migration flow. Scholars generally attribute unbalanced gender ratios to the peculiar character of labour migrations; men left Italy intending to return home again. They were sojourners not settlers.[15]

Only when the First World War reduced migrations from Italy to a small trickle did the representation of women increase sharply – to 59 per cent of total departures. Presumably, women migrating to reunify separated families were unique in risking migration during wartime. But the enlistment of millions of European men in warring armies may also have influenced female migration during these years. France, for example, certainly sought female labour during the war.[16] Gender ratios in Italian migration again were reorganized substantially in the years between the two world wars. Migration from Italy surged sharply after the First World War, but restrictions in the United States encouraged a reorientation of migrations toward Europe, and France became the single most important destination for Italy's migrants by the mid-1920s. Men still dominated, although not as overwhelmingly as they had in the pre-war years. Then, as the great depression and immigration restriction abroad sharply reduced overall migration from Italy, women's representation again rose – to 63 per cent between 1931 and 1935 and to 77.5 per cent between 1936 and 1940.[17]

Historians have also attributed the unbalanced gender ratios apparent in statistical overviews of Italian emigration to the dynamics of family migrations in which men are the pioneer migrants, the most easily detached from family life, and thus the most likely to pursue temporary sojourns abroad. Women follow men only when permanent settlement abroad is seriously contemplated. Yet we also have considerable evidence that migrations from Italy were more complex than this. Early migrations with substantial female participation have been recorded already in the 1800s. Women were well represented among migrants from the rural areas of Italy's northeast, with state-initiated and supported migrations of whole peasant families recruited to work the empty prairie lands of Argentina and the coffee plantations of Brazil, after the gradual emancipation of African slaves there.[18]

Some regional studies replicate national trends. Single males migrated in large numbers because it was their labour that was most often in demand, and recruited, in the labour markets of Europe and North and

South America. For many parts of the Italian south, it was the gender-segmented labour markets of the United States and of Argentina, and their demand for male labour, that discouraged women from entering the broader transoceanic circuits, especially before 1900.[19] Even in those regions where a family-based exodus – like that to Brazil – developed early, male departures generally prevailed for some time. In the mountainous northeastern districts of Italy (from Venice, Friuli, and Trento), male itinerancy had deep and ancient roots. Men from these alpine zones were drawn to the labour markets of the Habsburg empire of which they formed the Italian-speaking periphery prior to 1866 (or in the case of Trento, 1919). Especially important in these districts were the migrations of male construction workers.[20] In fact, throughout both northwest and northeast Italian mountain districts, contemporaries noted the overwhelming importance for local economies of the seasonal and temporary exodus of male labourers and masons. For construction workers in particular, it was the cities of transalpine Europe – Germany, France, Switzerland, Austria – that beckoned with plentiful jobs, especially after 1870.[21]

In some of these districts, male migration was so pronounced that it altered local demographic patterns from the end of the ancien régime until the outbreak of the First World War. Male traditions of seasonal migration thus shaped everyday life for men and women alike. We know, for example, about the impact of male migration from the oft-studied Piedmont villages clustered around the textile centre of Biella, where the emigration of bricklayers to nearby Lombardy was a long-standing tradition. The pattern was repeated in the towns bordering the Italian-speaking parts of Switzerland's Ticino.[22] In Piedmont, births were registered almost exclusively in the summer and fall, while marriage rites and conceptions were celebrated in the winter, with a clear preference for the month of February.[23] In the same region, the opposite situation was also sometimes reported – spring and summer marriages and conceptions – in areas where some of the occupations of male itinerants were more readily compatible with the needs of the pastoral economy of the mountains.[24] The exodus of single men from some districts created 'villages of women' – a pattern noted with curiosity by well-known writers of the late 1800s, and studied more recently by historians in its economic, familial, and other aspects.[25]

Overall, both general studies of Italian migration rates and regional and local monographs suggest that the emigration of women was a statistically restricted phenomenon, associated for the most part with the exodus of families and most limited during the first migratory waves. From this, most historians have also concluded that low levels of skill and of employment also characterized those women who did depart from Italy. While this conclusion is perhaps logical, we need more information about the minority of female migrants before accepting this interpretation. Evidence from receiving countries opens new interpretive avenues.

Female Emigration in the Maritime Alps: The Case of Grasse

In some border areas of the south of France, female immigration was significant enough that it was reported already in the first surveys of rural districts completed after Italy's unification in 1861. According to the French census of 1861 too, there were 5612 Italians resident in the Department of the Maritime Alps, and of these women formed slightly less than half the total – or 2541.[26] After roughly a decade of Italian migration into the department, the numbers increased significantly to reach a total of 15,760 immigrants. Over the same period the sex imbalance also decreased: male Italians numbered 8532 while female Italians numbered 7228.[27]

The female presence was thus substantial and, according to some local authorities, women sometimes outnumbered men. Furthermore, male majorities evaporated in regional urban centres; in the city of Nice, for example, women made up 49.15 per cent of the total of 9336 residents from Italy. In Villefranche, a smaller coastal settlement near Nice, of 202 Italian nationals, women represented 54.45 per cent. In Mentone, a small city even closer to Italy, women formed 50.22 per cent of a population of 1352 resident Italians.[28]

When we reduce the scale of the area studied – from the nation or the region to a single border area – variations in female migration emerge more clearly. Such a framework also permits a more fruitful examination of successive waves of migration. Only thirty years after Italy's political unification, Italians reached such a consistent quantitative level in some French territories that contemporaries began to write of migration in the watery metaphors (flows, streams) that scholars continue to use today. The Maritime Alps soon became the French department with the greatest numbers of Italians. In 1891, 51,867 immigrants in the department came from the nearby peninsula; there were 200 Italians for every 1000 'natives,' and immigrants from Italy formed 80 per cent of the total foreign population of the department.[29]

It is particularly useful to concentrate on one urban centre. The city of

Grasse is one of the few centres for which analytical investigations using familial records from the five-year censuses of the beginning of this century are available.[30] Grasse was somewhat unusual in having a mixed agricultural and manufacturing economy in the midst of the predominantly agricultural region of Nice. The city had become a clear target for immigration from its surrounding region already by the end of the ancien régime.[31] At first the city received in-migrants from other French districts; they followed sojourning migration routes that began in the mountains and directed themselves mainly to the cities of the plain and the coast.[32] Afterwards, with the continuation of the crisis in Italian agriculture after Italy's unification, Grasse also became the goal of emigrants from the neighbouring penninsula. In 1899 Grasse counted 1472 residents from nearby Italy. In the years that followed, the Italian presence increased, and by 1906 they constituted 5000 of Grasse's recorded population of 20,000.[33] Among the Italian immigrants, the female component increased to 50.98 per cent in the census of 1911.[34]

This increase in the number of women in the French city might be attributed, at first glance, to the general stabilization of Italians and to the onset of a family immigration that has been recognized as normal in both sending and receiving districts. For France, for example, it has been noted that, in every period of stable emigration, from 1836 to 1875, the number of males has declined while that of female immigrants has increased.[35] Yet if we analyse in detail the regions of origin of immigrants a different interpretation appears likely.

Many of the Italians of Grasse came from the Italian province of Piedmont. Of 39,000 departures from Italy to France at the beginning of the twentieth century, some 10,000 – or more than 25 per cent – were from this province. That proportion had increased by 1905, when of 58,000 Italians enumerated in the French census, 19,000 were from Piedmont, fully 31.03 per cent of all Italians enumerated. This figure rose to its highest level just before the First World War; in 1911 migrants from Piedmont constituted 41.66 percent of all the Italians living in Grasse.

The high number of immigrants from Piedmont is not surprising when we recognize that many came from the border regions of the Italian district.[36] It is no accident that Cuneo – near the French border in southwestern Piedmont and easily accessible to the French Côte d'Azur – was the Italian city best represented in Grasse. Some 62.2 per cent of immigrants and 93 per cent of the entire Piedmont emigration to Grasse came from this city. Cuneo was followed at a very long distance by migrants from the Ligurian municipality of Imperia (13.13 per cent), by migrants from the much more distant Umbrian municipality of Perugia (3.38 per cent), and from Turin (2.50 per cent), the largest city in Piedmont.[37]

Focusing on Cuneo and female migration to Grasse we not only find high representations of women, but also discover that women migrants from Cuneo to the French city sometimes outnumbered men.[38] As we will see below, the high representation of women from Cuneo in Grasse reflected a distinctively female, yet also autonomous, stream of skilled labour. It is difficult to classify these women as parts of a family migration: of all Italian women enumerated by census takers (including those who were living alone and or with their employer) 28.22 per cent were heads of households. Only 1.17 per cent were married and living with their husband.[39] The same condition applied in the following French census: in 1911, when women formed 51.79 per cent of the total of all Italian immigrants, married females still constituted only 1 per cent of female immigrants from Italy.[40]

Even a brief glance at a few communes in the Maritime Alps reveals a high level of women, and of single women, among migrants arriving in France from Italy. In Grasse, a goodly percentage of the women from the municipality of Cuneo were unmarried yet headed their own households.[41] Women in northwestern Italy, apparently, more often constructed the first links in the migration chains, rather than following a circuit established by husbands or fathers. This pattern is quite different from the one scholars generally associate with family migrations, and may well be an indicator of women migrating independently.[42] Further evidence of female independence and autonomy comes from analysis of the women's occupations. Few of the Italian women of Grasse were housewives and most were recorded as 'domestics' or 'labourers.' The trades exercised by the 223 women from Cuneo in 1888 included 167 manual labourers and 46 domestics; the remainder worked as cooks, seamstresses, hoteliers, gardeners, and (clothes) pressers. Only two women from Cuneo declared themselves to be without work.[43]

Female Migration and Mountain Economies

The work commitments and skills of female immigrants recorded in French censuses are still better understood if we return via more common female migration routes to their southwestern Piedmont home districts. In the case of women immigrants in Grasse this means the communities of the municipality of Cuneo. In fact, women from Cuneo emigrated to the entire southeast of France. Those that were recorded most frequently originated in the mountains; for the lowlands, and for the women living in Grasse, the most common village of origin was Peveragno.[44]

In Peveragno, we are in the middle of a valley that is part and parcel of a pastoral agricultural economy, with long traditions of migration. While the exact skills typical of any given Piedmont valley or village varied, seasonal work on the plains or coastal areas was a constant in the history of all these valleys, as it was in the remainder of the alpine world. Studies of such alpine communities have now eliminated old portraits of traditional communities closed from the outer world, or languishing in backwardness, immobility, and stasis. In these communities, patterns of migration had asserted themselves well before the second half of the 1800s, when population movements were directed toward nearby districts of intensive agriculture or emerging manufacturing enterprises. The residents of these districts had long experimented with circular migrations between mountain and plain that helped to create territorial and social boundaries that were quite permeable and changeable. With so many mountain people on the move, social spaces became woven together into loose, but often quite extensive, systems of human relationships, eliminating the isolation that outsiders typically 'see' in mountain villages. On the contrary, mountain dwellers in the ancien régime were already accustomed to periodic journeys that could range over shorter or longer distances. Nor were their working lives restricted to the skills or work options available in local agriculture or even pastoralism. Instead, many mountain towns developed highly differentiated skilled trades that sent migrants to a variety of far-flung locations. The valleys most involved in movements to France were Maira, Stura, Grana, and Pesio. Over time, the valleys of Varaita and Po also became important sources of migrants for southern France.[45]

Migration streams emanating from these districts involved local artisans as well as beggars, petty street traders, and casual itinerants. Some of these migrations, and local specializations, were evident already in medieval times and persisted into the modern era, providing an element of cultural continuity and normalcy from the era of the Savoy regime, through Italy's unification and the onset of the mass migrations, well into the twentieth century.[46] While some of these migration streams headed for the nearby coastal areas, others stretched around the Mediterranean coast into France. (Border changes also transformed parts of

Italian-speaking Savoy into territories of France, immediately changing 'local' into 'international' migrants without any change in actual human behaviour in the area.)

Female migrations also reached beyond local destinations to bordering villages or valleys toward the more distant targets of the Côte d'Azur or the French Midi. The presence of female domestics from these Italian valleys was reported in the city of Marseilles already during the eighteenth century.[47] Then, at the beginning of the 1800s, observers of mountain communities signalled the onset of female migrations as part of long-standing migrations of artisans who had resided in the highest valleys. Joining the chains of male shoemakers, coopers, knife sharpeners, tailors, and weavers from the highest uplands now appeared female 'spinners,' who travelled to France to 'spin linen and hemp' or to nearby textile workshops on the plain.[48]

From the second half of the nineteenth century, female migrations were recorded with ever-increasing frequency in studies of the mountain areas of the district. For example, in one community of the Maira valley, Roccabruna (whose inhabitants decreased from 3457 in 1881 to 1919 by 1936), a contemporary noted that 'the largest part of the wealth was France, where over one-third of the total population travelled for half of the year, of whom one-half were women.'[49] Priests often commented on female migration, perhaps because it symbolized to them modern decadence. As one Roccabruna priest reported, 'Not only the older men and women emigrate, but also the youth of both sexes.'[50] In certain cases, the female exodus attained such levels that local birth rates plummeted in twenty-five years, reducing annual rates of 130 to 140 births to only 80 to 90. Emigration involved half of Roccabruna's population in 1901, with 1424 emigrants from a total population of 2848 inhabitants.[51] Changes in demographic patterns were similar to those occurring where men migrated in large numbers, but in this case the alteration of the birth rate can be attributed to the widespread migration of women.

Female migration flows from these districts formed a well-known labour stream of servants directed toward the homes and hotels of Savoy, the Côte d'Azur, and other departments of southern France. 'The men go most frequently to Cannes,' wrote Baldioli-Chiorando, an acute observer of the local scene, 'while young women go more frequently to Nice, mainly to serve in the houses of the well-to-do.'[52] Described in detail in the accounts of Italian consuls in France, domestic service absorbed some 14,000 of all Italian women enumerated in the 1901 census.[53] The work was well paid: women working in France received between 30 and 80 francs per month as well as room and board.[54]

The vast seasonal exodus of female labour to temporary agricultural jobs in southern France suggests that women were sojourners, too. This movement became more visible from the beginning of the second half of the nineteenth century, as large-scale agriculture in France increasingly depended on seasonal labour. The demographic pressures of increasing population in some Italian valleys fed the neighbouring lands of southern France that were experiencing a serious depopulation as French birth rates dropped and as 'natives' of the French south began migrating to France's new colonies.[55]

French wages for female agricultural labourers were better than Italy's. In the Bouches du Rhône women's salaries ranged from 1.30 lire in the summer to 1.1 in the winter; in the Var they were 1 lira in the summer and 1.04 in the winter. Young women received 1.25 lire for nine hours of work daily during winter agricultural work, whereas harvesting olives might earn them between 15 and 28 'soldi' daily.[56] In Italy, by contrast, women laboured in agriculture for about 0.75 lire. According to consular estimates in 1903, wages for women in the Department of the Maritime Alps were much lower than those for similar work in nearby French departments, but they nonetheless made possible earnings that could not be made in Italy's local agricultural labour market.[57]

In agricultural migrations, the female presence was sufficiently large that it influenced remittance patterns. A woman migrant often sent or brought home a large share of her earnings. After five or six months of fieldwork – usually completed during the winter – young women from local smallholding families might bring back with them 50 to 80 lire each. By some measures, this sum was relatively modest; it did not, for example, allow a woman worker to live independently.[58] Still, it was a substantial contribution to a household economy, representing about a quarter of the typical annual cash income of a modest peasant household in Piedmont at the end of the nineteenth century. The cash flowing into local economies from female remittances could be significant. In the communities of Dronero, for example, these savings totalled 180,000 lire, an enormous sum.[59] Such savings were possible only if women (like male migrants) rigorously restricted their standards of living during their sojourns abroad.[60]

French and Italian observers noted the impact of higher French wages on women's decisions. Scattered evidence from studies of peasant memory in sending districts – notably the recollections of female peasants collected by Nuto Revelli – demonstrate that women themselves were intensely conscious of the financial advantages of working abroad. One elderly peasant woman, born in 1890, recalled how age and family ties intersected in migration decisions. 'Then when I was a little bit older,' she reported, 'with my sisters Valentina and Maria I began to travel to Hyères. We left in groups, young women and young men, we left contentedly ... I preferred going to France to hiring myself out in my valley, I earned more, sometimes they might even make me a gift of a pretty frock, and we were even better off with our food ... We earned thirty "soldi" a day, they paid us in gold, they paid everyone with gold there, bricklayers did not want to be paid with gold, they were afraid that it would not be of any value, they preferred to be paid with paper money.'[61]

The possibilities for higher salaries also provided the impetus for a type of female migration that, while numerically of less importance, was a traditional specialty of women from mountain villages – that of the wet nurse.[62] Revelli's collection of oral histories, autobiographies, and police records contains ample evidence of this exclusively female trade. Both consular officials and Italian prefects took pains to survey, and control, this type of work because it was believed to threaten family morality, and to lead to crime and imprisonment as peasant families disintegrated. Wet nurses often migrated on their own. As one elderly woman remembered, 'I did not complete third grade in school, which was the destiny of all of us. Because my mother would go to France to be a wet nurse and to Nice every time that she gave birth, so as to earn some money.'[63] Prompted by French wages – 30 to 35 francs monthly, on average, according to the consul in Nice in 1903 – many women even went so far as to call their husbands to join them, thus using their relatively secure wages to stabilize a longer-term earning campaign involving other family members. In some cases, wet nurses from Italy could profit from laws attempting to promote and increase French birth rates: they gave birth in France and became eligible for family benefits offered by the French state.[64]

Migrations of female agricultural workers, domestics, and wet nurses coexisted easily with male-dominated migrations; all were integral dimensions of the rythmns of the pastoral-agricultural economy of mountain districts with their large populations of small peasant landholdings and family economies. Women did not restrict their search for work to the immediate vicinity but, like men, moved toward the best earning opportunities open to them. As for men, too, women's options evolved with the development of French and Italian borderland economies, and with the evolution of political and diplomatic regulation of their common border by French and Italian officials.

The Migration of Female Silk Weavers

Migrations of domestic servants, female agricultural labourers, and wet nurses had deep roots in local circuits and migration extended the female migrants' geographical scope as wage-earning opportunities in southern France surpassed those in northwestern Italy. Over the course of the nineteenth century, a migration of female silk workers also developed in response to the changing economy of this border region. Coexisting with the others, this migration drew highly skilled female workers out of areas of declining domestic or proto-industrial production to emerging centres of industrial production offering more secure work and wages.

The valleys and coastal districts of northwestern Italy had long been the most attractive targets for migration from alpine areas. Both peasants and pastoralists from the mountains descended to the lowlands to pursue a wide variety of agricultural tasks during particular times of the year. At the same time, however, farm labourers resident in the valleys or coast lands often migrated themselves to more-distant locations, including France. It was in the valley that mountaineers often first learned of, and subsequently joined, streams of migrants venturing abroad in the familiar pattern of 'step migration.' As valley towns became targets for mountain artisans, they also launched trade-based migrations connected to local manufacturing specialties.[65]

By the end of the ancien regime, the economy of southern Piedmont had become closely connected with silk-growing. Some of the towns in the district had been known already from the 1400s as centres for the training of silk workers and the manufacture of silk cloth. The skills required for silk-working were complex: while peasants in upland villages more often raised the silkworms – feeding them with mulberry leaves – and oversaw the transformation of worm into silk cocoon, the processing of the silk cocoons more often occurred in workshops in valley locations. Already in the Middle Ages, women formed a substantial component of the labour employed by master silk workers and merchants. Beginning in the 1800s, women came to dominate the silk workforce as the industry itself began to expand, and as centralized manufactures began to replace artisans' workshops. Regarded as highly skilled, female spinners from particular communities that specialized in their training became highly prized workers in silk factories emerging all over Piedmont and beyond.[66]

Contemporaries in the 1800s noted the mobility of female silk workers, and attributed it to increased demand for skilled labour in a decentralized industry. Continuing through the years of the mass migrations, some areas of Cuneo's lowlands became not only reservoirs of female textile labourers but also training grounds where women acquired a highly valued apprenticeship allowing them to migrate as 'highly qualified spinners.'[67] The silk industry thus linked 'in-migration' and 'out-migration,' transforming local into international migrants. Economic development did not undermine international migration and may even have facilitated it. Women workers left from the towns around Biella for silk workshops in Switzerland, the United States, and France; and it was not unusual for female wool workers to emigrate in order to learn silk working. Similar patterns obtained in the silk communities of the Chisone valley in a proto-industrial setting not far from the Piedmont capital, Turin. There, women workers gave up work in local factories and departed for silk workshops in France, where they could earn higher salaries. Emigration to France increased during a crisis in Italian silk production at the end of the nineteenth century.

A highly charged debate about female emigration quickly emerged. Convinced that female migration threatened the morality of women and their families, Italian consuls and others were eager to disseminate news about the dramatic, and negative, consequences of female and child labour abroad. The fact that Italy and France remained locked in trade and imperial competitions throughout this period certainly shaped the bleak picture drawn of female migrations. Scholars are familiar with the many governmental surveys that focused on the 'evil' of women and children's working conditions in France's street trades, glassworks, and textile factories. Women and children migrants from Italy drew the attention not only of Italian but also of French journalists, philanthropists, and reformers who disdained the abuses of industrialization. Equating conditions of work in glass and silk workshops, they saw female and child labourers from Italy as the most reprehensible evidence of the exploitation of workers in modern, industrial factories and 'sweat shops.'[68]

Immigrants from Italy often were sizeable contingents in French factories. In 1902, for example, Italian women immigrants in the industry of Ain totalled some 605; most came from Piedmont and its capital Turin. In the same year, in Lyon, young Italian women totalled 3000; they were 'natives' of Piedmont and of the Lombard town of Brescia. In individual factories, migrant workers outnumbered 'natives.' An investigation of the silk workshop of Permezel undertaken during a large and controversial silk workers' strike in 1906 revealed that of a total of 500 workers, 350 (70 per cent) were from Piedmont.[69]

Obviously, female migrants from Italy flocked to French factories despite their reputations for exploitation and poor working conditions. They seem to have assessed the relative advantages of work in Italian and in French silk shops on rather different terms from government officials and philanthropists. Apparently women who had worked in France also sent positive messages home to their local districts, encouraging other women there to join them.

The Origins of France's Female Silk Workers

That migrants viewed opportunities abroad through the very specific lenses of gender and skill becomes even more apparent when we again return to the Italian districts that sent so many women to work in southern French factories. Here a single silk community in Piedmont – Peveragno with a population of 6871 in 1861 – has been selected for its rich archival documentation and surveys.[70] Particularly useful in studying women's migration from this town were *nulla osta* permits. Piedmont (and later Italian) law required emigrants to obtain a permit from the mayor indicating there were no civil objections (unpaid taxes, unpunished crimes, unfulfilled draft obligations) to emigration.[71]

Because we are examining a borderland that underwent territorial reorganization during the process of Italian unification, interpreting patterns of female migration from Peveragno is somewhat problematic. Between 1857 to 1860, for example, no men at all applied for a *nulla osta*, while small numbers of women – 16 in 1857, 32 in 1859, 10 in 1860 – did so. Perhaps, with military campaigns looming, men could not gain permission to leave as easily as women. These, after all, were the years of the Crimean War, Piedmont's second war with Austria (which resulted in Italy's initial unification under the rule of the King of Sardinia, a representative of the old Savoy dynasty), and the treaties that ceded Nice and Savoy to France.

Of greater importance is the fact that female emigration from Peveragno persisted and increased to a peak during the thirty-year period between 1901 and 1931, when women constituted 63 per cent of all France-bound migrants from the town. During this period women not only outnumbered men but were more highly skilled than the men headed for France. Negative images of migrant women's work in France had little effect on the highly skilled women of the town. Skilled men showed less interest in migrating there, suggesting that these women did not travel together with men from their own families, but rather sought work as individuals of distinctive occupational training and experience. Of women leaving Peveragno unaccompanied, 11 per cent were silk spinners.[72]

The household registration records of local families compiled initially for the census of 1901 (and subsequently updated by municipal record-keepers as individuals joined or departed the family through birth, marriage, death, and migration) provide a more nuanced portrait of female emigration. Of those listed only as 'absent' from the town, men formed the majority, but among Peveragno 'natives' who emigrated to France, women dominated.[73] These records also confirm that women formed 63.87 per cent of the migration flow from the community, and over 80 per cent from some districts. In addition, the family registration files provide a sense of the age of male and female migrants. Women seem to have left Peveragno at an earlier age than men; 17.8 per cent of women migrants from the town were 15 to 19 years of age, while only 7.52 per cent of male migrants were that young. The association of spinning with young unmarried women was a long-standing one, and it appears that women learned the skills with which they could migrate earlier than did their brothers.

Not surprisingly, the male and female migrants from Peveragno had vastly different occupational profiles (see table 4.1). While almost half of male migrants from the town were unqualified day labourers, and about a quarter were peasants, less than a third of women fell into these categories, and the largest group of female migrants – over a quarter – were spinners. Women spinners were not only the largest category of female migrants; given female predominance among migrants, they were also the most skilled component of local migration streams. Given the predominance of peasant backgrounds among men, a reasonable hypothesis is that the daughters of peasants were more successful in acquiring skills, and at an earlier age, than were their brothers. Alternatively, spinners may have been daughters of artisans who had better opportunities to use their skills in France, while their mason or artisan fathers and brothers had better work options locally or in other foreign destinations.

The last strand of qualitative data about this group of female migrants

TABLE 4.1
Occupations of male and female migrants from Peveragno, 1901

	Male	Female
Unqualified labour	47.1	21.8
Peasant	24	8.7
Artisan	11.3	4.7
Student	5	2.2
Petty commerce	2.6	1.4
Mason	2.4	
Spinner		27.3
Worker	1.3	1.4
Teacher/cleric	0.6	
Clerk	0.3	
Housework		12
Domestic servant		12
No occupation	5.4	8.4

Source: Archive of the Municipality of Peveragno, Family registration records (*Fogli di famiglia* of the 1901 census).

concerns their education and training. Piedmont had required the elementary education of both boys and girls since the 1850s, and the common people of this province had better access to basic education than in most other parts of Italy. Women migrants from this town were more often literate than men. The percentages of educated women in the districts of Peveragno were highest in those areas with the greatest numbers of spinners – a possible clue to the spinners' origin in artisanal families, where levels of education were often higher than among peasants. In one of these districts, for example, 99 per cent of all women and men knew how to read; in another district, the literacy level of women migrants – at 89 per cent – was higher than that of men.

Evidence of literacy and education among female spinners is rich. Local archives preserve letters from women migrants as well as a number of labour contracts (from the period 1911–33) that formalized work agreements between female spinners and various French and Italian silk factories. These documents confirm that migration itself provided an incentive for education in humble families, since it allowed family members to remain in touch over long distances, and opened up wider work options for emigrants abroad. The interdependence of skill, occupation, personal contacts, and formal labour recruitment could thus be as important for female as for male migrants.[74]

Spinners thus seem to have held an esteemed, rather than lowly, place within the artisanal realm of silk production, for in other forms of textile production, status and skill more frequently adhere to weaving (a job done by either adult men or women). Producing silk thread is a particularly difficult and challenging process; silk is a relatively hard, brittle, and thin fibre and not easily transformed into thread. Spinners had to possess a 'particular swiftness and intelligence ... as well as ... great precision' in order to produce 'threads of similar size.'[75] Those who were most skilled concentrated on the difficult *getto*, which joined the first fibre from a new cocoon to other threads without leaving visible traces. As a difficult skill, spinning was relatively well paid, even in Italy. In 1905 in a factory in the vicinity of Turin, for example, the pay for this work might range from 0.90 to 2.50 lire, for the spinners, to a maximum of 3.20 lire for supervisors. An experienced spinner could thus earn over twice the wages of a female agricultural labourer.[76]

These particular features of spinning again point us to an interpretation that contrasts sharply with journalists' and philanthropists' portraits of exploitation and misery in industrial work. Indeed, this female migration provides an excellent example, and was considered as such by at least some observers of the liberal era in Italy, of skilled labourers looking for the most profitable employment rather than emigrating to escape economic misery. 'Poverty,' wrote Angelo Mosso, a local doctor and positivist interested in the social problems of his times, 'determines emigration, but by itself it does not suffice to produce it. This is shown by the example of Sardegna, which is much poorer than northern Italy but from where, nonetheless, no one emigrates; it is shown by the women of Lombardy, who go in ever greater numbers to France, because in the spinning mills of Lyon they want only those that have a proven skill in the performance of their trade.'[77] Not surprisingly, when spinners from a town like Peveragno found work in the factories of southern France, they broadcast a rather different picture of work there than did their bourgeois and male contemporaries. Other women spinners proved eager to follow in their footsteps, producing not only a chain of relatively autonomous skilled female labour migrants, but a migrant world where women could acquire the status of teacher and female 'master' as men had traditionally done in their own trades.

The Recruitment of Women Workers and Female Chain Migration

Our picture of female emigration from Peveragno reproduces in a fascinating way a division that scholars of male migration have also found between more and less skilled workers in the proto-industrial regions of the alpine borders. The migratory routes of the least skilled men were determined largely by the recruitment of labour in groups or 'gangs' under the tutelage and mediation of a *capo* (boss) or labour recruiter, often an experienced migrant or artisan. In the female migrations from Peveragno, too, hierarchies of age and skill placed some women under the protection of those with greater skill or experience with work abroad.[78] While it might be presumptuous to label such women *padrone* (female labour 'bosses'), they forged important links in all-female migration chains. Younger spinners more often depended on older women to help them find work in France than on men of their families who – if they migrated – went to other destinations.

Relevant permits and contracts in Italian archives, along with the family registration records, suggest a strongly hierarchical female world stratified according to age and by domestic or family status and clearly bounded by education and skill. Within this female universe, the leader and most important figure was the older woman *maestra*. The term *maestra* (like its male equivalent, *maestro*) is complex, and its meaning has evolved over the past century. Today, many would translate the term as teacher, but in Peveragno in 1900, *maestra* was instead the female counterpart of the male *maestro*, or master craftsman. It was an honorific title used in everyday conversation to address an educated or skilled woman or man, as in 'Mistress Torino' or 'Master Torino.' The 'mistress' spinner (like the master mason in many male migration circuits) was a woman who recruited local children as workers, and directed them first to silk shops for training and then to factories they knew on both sides of the border.

No doubt, most 'mistresses' themselves probably had some experience as migrants. 'The industrialists,' according to Amy Bernardy, the Italo-American journalist, 'employ emigrant women silk workers in their factories, arrange special contracts with adult female silk workers who had previously been employed in the same factory, or with mistresses, who resort to acquaintances or relatives whom they have in their hometowns to bring together the number of female workers required by the industrialist; these contracts are usually arranged through letters.'[79]

These female teachers or 'mistresses' thus served a mixed role. They were highly skilled instructors, but they could also function as leaders of small groups of girls travelling to industrial employment in much the same way that 'bosses' accompanied their 'gangs' of agricultural labourers or that mason contractors travelled with their labourers and hod

carriers. Like their male equivalents, too, these women became interme-
diaries between employers and parents eager to give a daughter a skill
with which she could migrate; in both male and female chains, familial
and work roles often coincided. In the rigid hierarchies of the migration
chains, the mistress spinners often were elder sisters, to whom parents
entrusted the training and control of younger sisters, cousins, and neighbours. The 'mistress spinners' were familiar to all parents in a culture
where apprenticeship had not yet been displaced by formal education as
the most direct route from childhood to adult status as a worker. Both
parents and foreign entrepreneurs praised this system of labour recruitment. In fact, employers seemed particularly reassured that apprenticeship guaranteed order and the perpetuation of family morality.

Clearly identifiable in the documents of Peveragno, the spinner mistresses established both short- and long-distance relations to employers
and recruits; they learned to intertwine various relationships with many
Italian and foreign partners. Through the individual journeys of a few
we can even trace the routes followed by groups of women spinners into
the French Midi; and through the rich local correspondence we can
identify the French workshops that formed the most important stopping
places in spinners' itineraries. These sources also reveal the important
positions that some of the mistress spinners of this community assumed
in the direction and control of factory labour in France. In the Garnier
workshop, for example, the most important silk workshop in Marseille
(or, more precisely, its suburb of Le Cappellette) from 1911 to 1919, the
duty of director was most frequently filled by a woman from a family of
spinners prominent also in the records of Peveragno.[80]

To be sure, as highly skilled female workers, the previously 'hidden'
Italian silk workers uncovered by our research represent an exceptional
group of Italian women migrant workers. The mistress spinners, their
girls, and their 'silk routes' are tangible reminders of how new types of
skilled itinerant trades drew women into broader circuits of migration in
the nineteenth century. They represent the extension of the modest
occupational dynasties of alpine villages. By pushing us beyond the
better-understood migrations of domestics and agricultural labourers,
they also suggest interesting opportunities for further study of female
migration in comparative perspective. In a historiography that generally
emphasizes sharp differences between male and female migration and
experience during the mass migrations, the lives of Italian wet nurses
and mistress spinners suggest some similarities in the structures of male

and female labour migration. Skill, wages, and occupational opportunities, as well as family obligations, shaped the lives of these women who, at times, were not only the pioneer migrants but the majority among migrants from Italy. Even during the mass migrations, Italian women did more than 'wait.'

NOTES

1 Nuto Revelli, *L'anello forte. La donna: Storie di vita contadina* (Turin: G. Einaudi, 1985), 226, 355. For the exodus of wet nurses from the northeast, see Daniela Perco, *Balie da latte: Una forma peculiare di emigrazione temporanea* (Feltre: Comunità montana feltrina, Centro per la documentazione della cultura popolare, 1984); Adriana Dadà, *Lavoro balia: Memoria e storie dell'emigrazione femminile da Ponte Buggianese nell '900* (Lucca: Pacini, 1999).
2 Donna R. Gabaccia, *Italy's Many Diasporas* (London: University College of London Press, 2000), table I.1.
3 Ibid., 72–3.
4 Mirjana Morokvasic, 'Birds of Passage Are Also Women,' *International Migration Review* 28 (Winter 1984): 886–907.
5 For the first results of the research see Paola Corti and Ralph Schor, eds., 'L'esodo frontaliero: Gli italiani nella Francia meridionale – L'émigration transfrontalière: Les Italiens dans la France méridionale,' Special issue, *Recherches régionales* 3 (1995).
6 Donna R. Gabaccia, 'El censo de los Estados Unidos: Fuente para una historia internacional de mujeres immigrantes, familia y genero,' *Estudios Migratorios Latinoamericanos* 33 (August 1996): 267.
7 E.G. Ravenstein, 'The Laws of Migration,' *Journal of the Royal Statistical Society* 48 (1885): 167–277.
8 For the economic, political, and cultural importance of the border see Piero Zanini, *Significati del confine: I limiti naturali, storici, mentali* (Milan: Bruno Mondadori, 1996).
9 On female participation in various Italian peasant economies see the excellent work by Maura Palazzi, 'Famiglia, lavoro e proprietà: Le donne nella società contadina fra continuità e trasformazione,' in Paola Corti, ed., 'Società rurale e ruoli femminili in Italia tra otto e novecento,' special issue, *Annali dell'Istituto A. Cervi* 12 (1990): 25–80. For the application of this methodology to the dynamics of migration see the observations of Maddalena Tirabassi, 'Italiane ed emigrate,' *Altreitalie* 9 (1993): 139–51.

10 Paola Corti, 'L'émigration italienne: Historiographie, anthropologie et recherche comparatiste,' *Revue Européene des Migrations Internationales* 11, 3 (1995): 5–18.

11 Patrizia Audenino, *Un mestiere per partire: Tradizione migratoria, lavoro e communità in una vallata alpina* (Milan: Franco Angeli, 1990).

12 See in particular the conclusions derived from the research promoted by the Fondazione Sella di Biella in the series 'Biellesi nel mondo,' e.g., Valerio Castronovo, ed., *L'emigrazione biellese fra otto e novecento* (Milan: Electa, 1986), and commentary on these by Fernando J. Devoto, *Le migrazioni italiani in Argentina: Un saggio interpretativo* (Naples: Istituto di studi filosofici, 1994).

13 See the tables on male and female emigration in the classic reconstruction by Francesco Coletti, 'Dell'emigrazione italiana,' in *Cinquant'anni di storia italiana*, vol. 3 (Milan: Hoepli, 1911), 49. For an elaboration of this data see Luigi Favero and Graziano Tassello, 'Cent'anni di emigrazione italiana,' in Gianfausto Rosoli, ed., *Un secolo di emigrazione italiana 1876–1976* (Rome: Centro Studi Emigrazione, 1978), 9–63; and Ercole Sori, *L'emigrazione italiana dall'Unità alla seconda guerra mondiale* (Bologna: Il Mulino, 1979), 32.

14 All of the figures cited here and below can be found in Favero and Tassello, 'Cent'anni di emigrazione italiana.'

15 On the temporary nature of Italian emigration, see Franco Bonelli, 'Emigrazione e rivoluzione industriale: Appunti sulle cause dell'emigrazione italiana,' *Bollettino di demografia storica* 12 (1998): 35–44; and Franco Ramella, 'Emigrazioni,' in Bruno Bongiovanni and Nicola Tranfaglia, eds., *Dizionario storico dell'Italia unità* (Bari, Rome: Laterza, 1996), 297–307.

16 Sergio Coletti, 'Condizioni di vita e di lavoro in alcuni bacini carboniferi francesi,' *Bollettino dell'emigrazione* 15, 1 (1916): 21.

17 Favero and Tassello, 'Cent'anni di emigrazione italiana,' 31.

18 Sori, *L'emigrazione italiana*, 32. For emigration from the Veneto see Emilio Franzina, *La grande emigrazione: L'esodo dei rurali dal Veneto durante il secolo XIX* (Venice: Marsilio, 1976) and Silvio Lanaro, ed., *Il Veneto* (Turin: Einaudi, 1984). For emigration to Brasil, see Chiara Vangelista, *Dal vecchio mondo al nuovo continente* (Turin: Paravia, 1997).

19 Andreina De Clementi, *Di qua e di là dall'Oceano: Emigrazione e mercati nel meridione, 1860–1930* (Rome: Carocci, 1999).

20 See, e.g., Casimira Grandi, *Verso i paesi della speranza: L'emigrazione trentina dal 1870 al 1914* (Abano Terme: Francisci, 1987); Alessio Fornosin, 'Una grande trasformazione: Il lavoro migrante in Gruie,' in G.L. Fontana, A. Leonardi, and L. Trezzi, *Mobilità imprenditoriale e del lavoro nelle Alpi un età*

moderna e contemporanea (Milan: CUESP, 1988), 127–46; and Renzo Grosselli, *L'emigrazione del Trentino* (Trento: Museo degli usi e costumi della gente trentina, 1998).

21 Valerio Castronovo, ed., *L'emigrazione biellese tra '800 e '900* (Milan: Electa-Fondazione Sella, 1986); Comune di Cuneo, Assessorato per la cultura, *Migrazioni attraverso le Alpi occidentali: Relazioni tra Piemonte, Provenza e Delfinato dal Medioevo ai nostri giorni. Atti del Convegno internazionale, Cuneo, 1–2–3 giugno 1984* (Turin: Regione Piemonte, 1988); Pier Paolo Viazzo, *Upland Communities: Environment, Population and Social Structure in the Alps since the Sixteenth Century* (Cambridge: Cambridge University Press, 1989); Raul Merzario, *Il capitalismo nelle montagne: Strategie famigliari nella prima fase dell'industrializzazione del Comasco* (Bologna: Il Mulino, 1989); Audenino, *Un mestiere per partire*; Paola Corti, *Paesi d'emigranti: Mestieri, itinerari, identità collettive* (Milan: Franco Angeli, 1990); Dionigi Albera, ed., *Tra il monte e il piano: Tracce di emigranti dalla provincia di Cuneo* (Cuneo: L'Arciere, 1991); Gerard Claude, ed., *Dai due versanti delle Alpi* (Turin: Ed. Dell'Orso, 1991). See also Carlo Brusa and Robertino Ghiringhelli, eds., *Emigrazione e territorio: Tra bisogno e ideale* (Varese: Lativa, 1995), vol. 1; and Fontana, Leonardi, and Trezzi, *Mobilità imprenditoriale e del lavoro nelle Alpi.*

22 Patrizia Audenino, 'Tradizione e mestiere nelle migrazioni dalla Valle Cervo,' in Castronovo, *L'emigrazione biellese tra '800 e '900*, 77–149, 161–234; Paola Corti, 'Gli stagionali di Sala e Torrazzo nella Serra,' in ibid., 161–234; Ada Lonni, 'Edili, boscarini e tessitori nell'emigrazione alla Valsessera,' in ibid., 235–99; Raul Merzario, 'Famiglie di emigranti ticinesi,' unpublished paper presented at the international conference 'Changes in the Family in Western Countries,' Bologna, 6–8 October 1994.

23 Corti, *Paesi d'emigranti*, 75.

24 Dionigi Albera, Manuela Dossetti, and Sergio Ottonelli, 'Società ed emigrazione nell'alta Val Varaita nell'età moderna,' *Bollettino storico bibliografico subalpino* 15, 1 (1988): 117–69.

25 Corti, 'Società rurale e ruoli femminili'; Dionigi Albera, Patrizia Audenino, and Paola Corti, 'I percorsi dell'identità maschile nell'emigrazione: Dinamiche individuali e ciclo di vita individuale,' *Rivista di storia contemporanea* 1 (1991): 69–87; Paola Corti, 'Société sans hommes et intégrations des femmes à l'étranger: Le cas de l'Italie,' *Revue Européenne des migrations internationales* 9, 2 (1993): 113–28.

26 *Statistica generale del Regno d'Italia, Censimento degli italiani all'estero (31 December 1871)* (Rome: Stamperia reale 1874), lxxxvi.

27 Ibid., lxxxvii.

28 Ibid.

29 Anna Maria Faidutti-Rudolph, *L'immigration italienne dans le sud-est de la France* (Nice: Études et travaux de la Méditerranée, 1964), vol. 1, 21–2.

30 Renata Allio, *Da Roccabruna a Grasse: Contributo per una storia dell'emigrazione cuneese nel sud-est della Francia* (Rome: L'Officina, 1984).

31 Paul Gonnet, *Histoire de Grasse et sa région* (Le Coteau: Edition Horvath, 1984), 129. H. Costamagna, 'XVIIIe siècle: Présentation historique et géographique,' in *Aspects de Nice du XVIIe au XXe siècle* (Paris: Les Belles Lettres, 1973), 7–29; Georges Ayache, *Histoire des Niçois* (Paris: F. Nathan, 1978).

32 Abel Chatelain, *Les migrants temporaires en France de 1800 à 1914* (Lille: Publications de l'Université de Lille, 1976), vol. 1, 581.

33 Faidutti-Rudolph, *L'immigration italienne*, vol. 1, 175.

34 Allio, *Da Roccabruna a Grasse*, table 14, p. 44. In 1906 Italian women totalled 2713, the equivalent of 49.73 per cent of the total for all Italians.

35 Gerard Noirel, 'L'histoire des femmes immigrées,' *Femmes immigrées. Quelles chances pour quelles insertions sociales et professionnelles?: Rencontre-débat* (Paris: GRÉC, 1991), 14. In 1836 there were 136 immigrant men for 100 women, in 1891, 113 per 100; in 1931, women formed 64 per cent of the total, in 1936 73 per cent, and, between 1975 and 1981, 76 per cent.

36 *Annuario statistico dell'emigrazione italiana dal 1876 al 1925* (Rome: ISTAT, 1927). The paths out of the Piedmont provinces/municipalities of Cuneo, Turin, and Novara, although statistically less well documented, were sketched according to their social and professional features in the reports of various consuls in southeastern France. See *Emigrazione e colonie. Rapporti dei RR agenti consolari* (Rome: Ministero degli Affari Esteri, 1893); *Emigrazione e colonie. Rapporti dei RR agenti consolari* (Rome: Ministero degli Affari Esteri, 1903); *Bollettino dell'emigrazione* 18 (1910): 245.

37 Allio, *Da Roccabruna a Grasse*, 52.

38 Ibid., 103.

39 Ibid., 120.

40 Ibid.

41 Ibid., 103.

42 Rosangela Lodigiani, 'Donne migranti e reti informali,' *Studi emigrazione* 115 (September 1994): 494–505.

43 Allio, *Da Roccabruna Grasse*, 106.

44 Dionigi Albera, 'Dalla mobilità all'emigrazione: Il caso del Piemonte sudoccidentale,' in Corti and Schor, eds., 'L'esodo frontaliero,' 25–63.

45 Ibid., 29–30.

46 Ibid., 30–4.

47 Michel Vovelle, 'Les piémontais en Provence occidentale au XVIIIe siècle,' in Comune di Cuneo, *Migrazioni attraverso le Alpi occidentali*, 73–91.

48 Giovanni Eandi, *Statistica della provincia di Saluzzo*, vol. 1 *Saluzzo* (Lobetti-Bodoni, 1833), 353–4, and now also in Albera, 'Dalla mobilità all'emigrazione,' 34.

49 ISTAT, *La popolazione italiana (1861–1971)* (Rome: Pubblicazione del centenario, 1971), 94. The quote is from Vincenzo Baldioli-Chiorando, 'L'emigrazione in alcuni paesi della provincia di Cuneo (montagna e collina),' *La riforma sociale* 10, 13 (1903): 847.

50 O. Bonello, 'Le condizioni economiche e sociali della Vale di Maira tra Otto e Novecento' (University of Trento thesis, 1982–3), 146.

51 V. Baldioli-Chiorando, 'L'emigrazione in alcuni paesi della provincia di Cuneo,' 851.

52 Ibid., 849.

53 *Bollettino dell'emigrazione* 20 (1908): 7.

54 *Emigrazione e colonie*, 1903, 323.

55 Robert Foerster, *The Italian Emigration of Our Times* (New York: Russell & Russell, 1968; 1st pub. 1919), 131–4.

56 Baldioli-Chiorando, 'L'emigrazione in alcuni paesi della provincia di Cuneo,' 850.

57 *Emigrazione e colonie*, 1903, 123.

58 *Atti della Giunta per l'inchiesta agraria e sulle condizioni delle classe agraria*, vol. 8 (Rome: Forzani, 1981–5), 188.

59 Baldioli-Chiorando, 'L'emigrazione in alcuni paesi della provincia di Cuneo,' 850.

60 On the budgets of temporary emigrants, see *Emigrazione e colonie*, 1903, 137–8.

61 Revelli, *L'anello forte*, 220–4.

62 Valerie A. Fildes, *Wet Nursing: A History from Antiquity to the Present* (London: Basil Blackwell, 1988); Fanny Fay-Sallois, *Les nourrices à Paris au XIXe siècle* (Paris: Payot, 1980); Carmen Sarasúa, *Criados, nodrizas y amos: El servicio doméstico en la formación del mercado de trabajo madrileño, 1758–1868* (Madrid: Siglo Veintiuno Editores, 1994).

63 Revelli, *L'anello forte*, 226, 355.

64 *Emigrazione e colonie*, 1903, 321.

65 Albera, 'Dalla mobilità all'emigrazione,' 44.

66 Comune di Cuneo, Assessorato per la cultura, *Le fabbriche magnifiche: La seta in provincia di Cuneo tra Seicento e Ottocento* (Cuneo: L'Archiere, 1993); Giuseppe Chicco, *La seta in Piemonte (1650–1800)* (Milan: Franco Angeli, 1995).

67 Amy Bernardy, 'L'emigrazione delle donne e dei fanciulli dal Piemonte,' *Bollettino dell'emigrazione* 10 (1912): 57, 12. See also Paola Corti and A. Lonni,

'Emigration et industrialisation dans la vallée du Chisone (Piémont XIXe siècle),' *Revue Européene des Migrations Internationales* 2, 3 (December 1986): 65–81; and Paola Corti and A. Lonni, 'Da contadini a operai,' in Valerio Castronovo and Patrizia Audenino, eds., *La cassetta degli strumenti* (Milan: Franco Angeli, 1986), 125–266.

68 See the Italian publication of the work written by a secretary of the Italian ambassador in France at the beginning of the century: Raniero Paulucci di Calboli, *Lacrime e sorrisi dell'emigrazione italiana* (Milan: Giorgio Mondadori, 1996; 1st pub. in French, Paris 1909). See also the report of the female secretary for the tutelage of female and child emigrants, Beatrice Berio, *Relazione sull'emigrazione delle donne e dei fanciulli italiani nella Francia meridionale* (Rome: Tipografia Italia, 1912).

69 *Bollettino dell'emigrazione* 9 (1902): 51. See also the contemporary, first-hand account, 'Le témoignage di Lucie Béaud, ouvrière en soie,' *Le mouvement social* 105 (1978): 139.

70 For an assessment of the records, see Paola Corti, 'Nota introduttiva,' in Corti and Schor, 'L'esodo frontaliero,' 7–15.

71 For the use of these records for the study of female emigration, see Romolo Gandolfo, 'Dall'alto Molise al centro di Buenos Aires: Le donne agnonesi e la prima emigrazione transatlantica,' in Corti, 'Società rurale e ruoli femminili,' 325–51.

72 Massimo L. Pistillo, 'Professioni e itinerari migratori nelle richieste di passaporto di Peveragno (1855–1931),' in Corti and Schor, 'L'esodo frontaliero,' 98.

73 In 1901, 71.79 per cent of all emigrants from Peveragno – some 700 emigrants of a population of 7853 – were men. Cf. Archivio Comunale di Peveragno, 'Family Census Records of 1901.' All figures cited below are taken from this source.

74 Corti, *Paesi d'emigranti*, 93.

75 Maria Grazia Codutti, *Bachi e filande nell'economia subalpina* (Cuneo: L'Arciere, 1982).

76 Corti and Lonni, 'Da contadini a operai,' 237.

77 Angelo Mosso, *Vita moderna degli italiani* (Milan: Treves, 1906), 56.

78 Albera, Audenino, and Corti, 'I percorsi dell'identità maschile nell'emigrazione,' 69–87.

79 Bernardy, 'L'emigrazione delle donne e dei fanciulli dal Piemonte,' 57. It is interesting to note the similarity in the organization of the work of migrant bricklayers and the tradition of letter contracts; see, e.g., Corti, *Paesi d'emigranti*, 93.

80 S. Corazza, 'Percorsi professionali femminili: Le setaiole di Peveragno

Francia meridionale,' in Corti and Schor, 'L'esodo frontaliero,' 107–35. An analysis of migratory chains of Piedmont silk workers to Trans-en-Provence, in the vicinity of Marseilles, based on French sources, has been carried out by Karine Lambert and Valérie Pietri: 'La route de la soie: Un siècle des migrations féminines piémontaises vers les filatures de Trans-en-Provence (1830–1930),' *Cahiers de la Méditerranée*, no. 58 (June 1999): 97–118.

5 Gender, Domestic Values, and Italian Working Women in Milwaukee: Immigrant Midwives and Businesswomen

Diane Vecchio

Familiar images of the Italian immigrant working woman in the early-twentieth-century United States include that of home-based worker, factory operative, or cannery worker. Yet, in 1911, the Immigration Commission reported that in Milwaukee, Wisconsin, the largest proportion of households engaged in business for profit were found among the Italians as well as Russian Jews. Among the Italians, immigrant women, whose presence as business 'proprietors' or 'retail merchants' in Milwaukee was recorded in city directories and the state census as early as 1900, were actively engaged in every field of Italian business enterprise during the lengthy period of first-generation settlement, from the 1890s to the 1920s. Another little-studied group of Italian-born women who served the first-generation immigrant community in Wisconsin for several decades were midwives. A distinctive feature of Italian midwifery practice in Wisconsin during the late-nineteenth and early-twentieth centuries is that all the Italian-born midwives were professionally trained and certified.

This chapter examines the working lives of first-generation Italian women in Milwaukee, focusing in particular on two very different occupational groups, businesswomen and midwives. While they differed with respect to educational background and work patterns, these businesswomen and midwives shared a common status as immigrant women and as providers of services critical to first-generation Italians who settled within an ethnic enclave. In Milwaukee, the largest Italian enclave was defined by the boundaries of the Third Ward, and there businesswomen worked as grocers, restaurateurs, saloon keepers, and purveyors of dry goods. Within the same ethnic boundaries, Italian midwives went house-to-house delivering the babies of immigrant women who preferred mid-wife-assisted deliveries by Italian-speaking midwives to the services of U.S. doctors and hospitals.

This chapter attempts to make sense of immigrant women's work experiences by asking several questions. What role did gender and domestic values play in shaping these women's job opportunities? What impact did the life cycle have on immigrant women's work experiences? Were Italian women transient workers? In addressing these questions I explore two models of women's work. The first is that of female entre-preneurs who were motivated to earn an income through businesses enterprises while simultaneously continuing their familial and house-hold responsibilities.[1] This model applies particularly to the women who owned and operated grocery stores at home; their work histories reflect how gender and domestic values shaped their job opportunities and experiences. The second model derives from the work lives of Italian midwives – a small group of women who had been trained in Italy; while these women too had to negotiate family duties and domestic pressures, they also saw themselves as transplanted professionals with heady re-sponsibilities – in contemporary terms, we might call them pioneer 'career' women – and some of them at times put their work careers above family expectations and familial duties. Without wishing to paint too sharp a contrast between the two groups of immigrant women, the discussion particularly of the midwives and their professional ethos is meant as a modest corrective to a scholarship on Italian immigrant working women dominated by images of low-skilled labourers. To recon-struct the lives of these working women, I mined several types of sources. The Wisconsin state census for Milwaukee and the Milwaukee city direc-tories, along with extensive interviews with immigrants and their chil-dren, helped me to profile Italian businesswomen. The Midwives Registration Files in the archives of the Wisconsin State Historical Soci-ety and the Milwaukee Public Health Department records provided critical information on midwives and on their training and certification. The most intimate details concerning birth and midwifery practices came from interviews with women who were assisted in childbirth by Italian midwives and by the midwives' family members.

Italians in Milwaukee

Italians settled in a city that offered an attractive and promising home to immigrants in the late nineteenth century. Several decades earlier Milwaukee had begun its ascent as an important economic centre of the upper Midwest. Rapidly emerging heavy industries and brewing made Milwaukee one of the country's fastest-growing urban centres. In 1850, two-thirds of the city's residents were of foreign birth, with German immigrants forming one-third of the entire population. By century's end Irish, Poles, Bohemians, and Italians combined with Germans to make Milwaukee the most foreign of the twenty-eight largest cities in the United States: the immigrants and their children made up more than half of the city's total population of 300,000.[2]

Italians began migrating into Milwaukee during the late nineteenth century, as the number of manufacturing jobs mushroomed from 8000 in 1870 to 50,000 in 1900. By the turn of the century Milwaukee was a leader in meat-packing, tanning, brewing, and heavy industry; as industry and therefore labour demand expanded, manufacturers turned to immigrants to meet their needs.[3] Southern Italians responded to the job opportunities in large numbers, and by 1910 Milwaukee's Italian population grew to 5000. After 1900, the majority of Italians in Milwaukee were Sicilians from the towns and villages near Palermo (Porticello, Santa Flavia, Sant'Elia, Aspra, and Bagheria) and the provinces of Messina, Trapani, Girgenti, and Siracusa. While northern Italian immigrants settled in the Bay View area of Milwaukee, Sicilians settled in the Third Ward, among the few Irish who remained there after a devastating 1892 fire.[4] Covering nearly five hundred acres, and situated in a geographically important location between Lake Michigan and its harbour, the Milwaukee River, and an expanding business district on East Wisconsin Street,[5] the Third Ward was primarily a business district of warehouses, factories, and stores with residential areas congested around the business core. This congestion led to close living conditions and a tight and cohesive immigrant enclave, one that invited comment from outside observers. As early as 1901, the local newspaper, the *Sentinel*, wrote that the ward's 'corner grocery store and the saloon lend their odors to the mingled smells that float from many kitchens where strange dishes of which garlic is a component part are being prepared. The odor,' it continued, 'is unclassifiable and defies definitions, but it is all pervasive and is a characteristic of the quarter that one remembers long after one has passed into less odoriferous regions.'[6] Within the boundaries of the Third Ward neighbourhoods, Italian women attended church, shopped, and raised their children. They also worked, whether with their spouses or independently, drawing on their varied skills, entrepreneurial talents, training, and homeland practices to become viable wage-earners in America.

Many immigrant women in Milwaukee worked because few immigrant men earned a family wage. While a considerable number of men had been tradesmen and artisans in Italy, most were now reduced to labouring with pick and shovel in the streets or on the railroad. Others found jobs in foundries or steel works, especially with the Allis-Chalmers Company, Falk Manufacturing, and the Rolling Mills of Bay View; some found employment in tanneries, especially with the Pfister and Vogel Company, and others with the electric car lines and Gas Light Company. In Milwaukee, the average Italian male wage was between $1.50 and $2.00 a day, though labourers rarely worked a full year, and even less in the winter months. Indeed, few labourers worked in the winter months, when outdoor work on streets and railroads stopped almost entirely, and Italians (and other recent arrivals) were among the first to be let go.[7] The typical Italian male worked nine months a year and earned an annual salary of about $300 to $400. The average earnings of native-born men in Milwaukee was $539; that of immigrant men was $416,[8] and Italian males earned the lowest wages. Italian women thus usually worked not to pursue careers or independence but to support families.

Milwaukee's heavy industries, however, generated few job opportunities for females. In contrast to New England and New York, Milwaukee had no textile mills and only a tiny number of small garment factories. As a result, only a small minority of immigrant women found paid employment outside the home. Nonetheless, as recent scholarship has documented, Italian women did find ways of earning an income and contributing to the family economy while remaining at home – for example, by taking in boarders, doing homework, and starting small businesses.[9] In Milwaukee, large numbers of Italian women provided boarding services to their countrymen; a study conducted by the Immigration Commission in 1910 revealed that, among Italians, boarders and lodgers constituted a larger proportion of household members than among any other nationality group in Milwaukee.[10] Several years later, in 1915, an Associated Charities survey of 149 Italian households reported that 40 per cent of them were providing services to an average of two to three boarders per household.[11] The Immigration Commission concluded that, in Milwaukee, 'the proportion of families keeping boarders or lodgers among South Italians is so large as to make the proportion of wives who contribute to the family fund higher than in any other race.'[12]

While many Italian women earned an income exclusively from providing boarding services, others combined it with other business activities. Stefana Balistreri, mother of eight, took in boarders but also earned money by preparing meals for her husband's saloon and ran a grocery store in her home.[13] By contrast, few were engaged in homework. Only a few garment factories located in the Third Ward and some downtown department stores generated work that could be finished at home. Few reliable statistics exist on homeworkers in Milwaukee, but a 1915 survey conducted by George La Piana reported that only 'a very limited' number of women 'take outside work into the home, generally sewing and hand embroidering for factories ... either because the work is scarce, or ... poorly remunerated.'[14] Of the 149 households he investigated, La Piana found only five women who contributed to family funds in this way. The most highly paid was a woman who did beautiful hand embroidery and received $5.00 per week, while the most poorly paid was a mother with two daughters who, for mending sacks at two cents each, could not make more than $3.00 per week.[15] Women who had learned fine sewing in Italy commanded the best wages in Milwaukee, including Rose Carini's mother, who had learned to embroider while at convent school in Sicily for ten years. A sample of her work prompted Gimbel's and Chapman's department stores to hire her to do fine embroidery on shirts, blouses, dresses, and baby clothes. Rose picked up the clothing and brought it home, where her mother worked on it in-between cooking meals and caring for the children.[16] Many women who had worked at home while their children were young later abandoned homework for factory labour, as did Giovanna Chirafisi; when her children were older, she entered the men's clothing factory that earlier had supplied her with piecework. La Piana maintained that 'if there was more work and it was better paid, a larger number of Italian women would devote more hours per day to sewing and embroidering, and to assisting the family, especially when the husband is out of work.'[17] But in Milwaukee, homework offered only a limited opportunity for immigrant women who wanted to earn money while remaining at home.

Italian women in Milwaukee also worked as dressmakers. Historian Wendy Gamber has described dressmaking as a business endeavour that many regarded as belonging within the 'women's sphere.' Dressmakers employed other women and totally excluded men.[18] They were part of a larger craft tradition in the United States that provided a lucrative trade for both immigrants and the native-born. Most operated out of their homes, though some were employed in neighbourhood shops. Several Italian dressmakers in Milwaukee, including Francesca Romano and Jennie Gallo, employed their daughters in their businesses with them. Often, immigrant women who were skilled dressmakers in their native land transplanted their skills to America and used them as a means of upward mobility.

Of the immigrant generation, few married Italian women in Milwaukee worked in factories. The Immigration Commission's 1910 survey, based on 86 Italian families, reported that only four wives (4.7 per cent) worked outside the home. It also concluded that Italians (and Russian Jews) had the smallest proportion of Milwaukee wives working outside the home. In attempting to account for this pattern, historians of Italian immigration have argued that Italian women generally avoided factories because of the strong inherited traditions supporting male authority and restrictions upon female work outside the home[19] – an explanation that ignores other factors, particularly the structure of the local economy and the restrictions imposed on married women by childbirth and child-rearing activities.[20]

Milwaukee boasted few light industries that might employ women. Furthermore, work patterns reveal that those Italian women who did work outside the home were either single or newly married with no children. Married women who had children but no relatives or neighbours to care for them simply had to find other means of earning an income. Donna Gabaccia, in her study of immigrant women in the United States, found that 'most immigrant girls worked for about ten years, typically in a variety of short-term, seasonal, and low-paying jobs.' While almost all left factory employment upon marriage, Italians and Poles more typically left after the birth of a child.[21] In Milwaukee too, Italian women earning wages outside the home were transient workers who quit the labour force after marriage or after the birth of their children.

Most Italian female factory workers in Milwaukee were employed at the Jewish-owned garment factories of David Adler and Sons, Cohn Brothers, and Moritz and Winter. Most were young single women who worked in shops located within walking distance of their Third Ward homes. Italian-born girls, generally between the ages of fourteen and seventeen, were employed as packers and dippers at the American Candy Company on Buffalo Street, the Imperial Candy Company on East Water, and the Princess Confectionery Company on Jefferson. These young girls, along with the daughters of immigrants, often quit school at an early age to contribute to the family economy – a pattern consistent with immigrant working patterns in other cities. As John Bodnar observed, '[T]he percentage of wage earners among foreign-born adult females over the age of sixteen was one-third higher than the percentage for all white women, but this could be attributed to the heavier reliance of the immigrant family on the earnings of their unmarried daughters.'[22]

Other examples of Italian women's work experiences in Milwaukee's factories reflect the impact of marriage and family on labour-force participation. Rose Carini, who migrated to Milwaukee with her parents at the age of two, attended schools in the Third Ward, but at age fourteen was allowed to work during summer vacations at Phoenix Hosiery, where she earned fifteen cents an hour.[23] She continued working there until her marriage and the birth of her children. At fifteen, Emma Bellucci set off alone for Milwaukee, after receiving ship fare from her sister. Shortly after her arrival, with the help of other immigrant women, she was hired at David Adler and Sons; she continued there after her marriage, but quit following the birth of her first child. After giving birth to two more children, Emma began taking in homework sewing buttonholes on clothing provided by Adler's garment factory.[24] Vincenza Bartelloni and Conchetta Crivello were sisters who were both widowed in their thirties; they were able to take jobs at Cohn Brothers because they had a mother who willingly cared for their fifteen children while they laboured in the garment factory.[25]

Catherine Balistreri attended school until the eighth grade, but then had to quit to help her widowed mother with finances. She worked at Phoenix Hosiery and handed her weekly pay envelope to her mother, who gave her spending money for an occasional soda or ice cream.[26] The work profile of Balistreri and other women indicates how the family economy shaped immigrant lives. Immigration historians have widely documented the tendency of sons, and particularly daughters, to labour not for individual attainments but in order to pool resources for the economic survival of the entire family.[27]

Gender and domestic values indeed were instrumental in shaping Italian women's working lives in Milwaukee. Nowhere is this clearer than in the case of Italian businesswomen. Immigrants who had been small-business proprietors in Italy founded some of the most profitable produce companies in Milwaukee, and a number of them included the wife and mother as a business partner. Perhaps the most notable example was Mary Pastorino, whose husband Frank was one of the earliest commission merchants in the Third Ward. After emigrating from Italy, Frank and Mary relocated in 1891 from Chicago to Milwaukee, where they bought a wholesale produce business located on Commission Row. Frank and his partner, Louis Schiappacasse, became successful wholesale dealers in domestic and foreign fruits, vegetables, and nuts.[28] Mary frequently accompanied her husband to Central America to advise him on purchases of fruits, dates, nuts, and other produce and she also operated the 'Flora Bon' confectionery shop. In 1910, Frank died, leaving controlling interest of the business to his wife. Sons Harry and Frank worked with their mother in the business until Mary sold her shares to Schiappacasse a few years later, giving him controlling interest. Mary Pastorino had not left the world of business, however; several years later she opened a tea room where she employed several of her daughters.[29]

There were other immigrant women whose contributions to a business enterprise have never been appreciated fully because they too worked alongside their husbands in a family-owned business. The Catalanos also were very successful wholesale producers who in 1911 shifted the centre of their business to their home, most likely because it was more profitable than renting a wholesale house. Mrs Catalano played a key role in the business; she handled the banking and kept the books.[30]

In 1915, La Piana observed that 'generally women attend to the light business, while their husbands are at work on the tracks or in the foundries.'[31] The 'light business' to which La Piana referred included the many small business establishments owned or operated by Italian (mostly Sicilian) women in Milwaukee. One of the earliest female business 'proprietors' or 'retail merchants' in Milwaukee recorded in the city directories and state census data was Theresa Balbi. In 1900, following her husband's murder by the Black Hand criminal organization, Theresa opened a fruit stand in the Chamber of Commerce Building.

Italian-born women who themselves launched various business establishments in Milwaukee exhibited the range of marital patterns. While a minority were single women or widows who had inherited a husband's business, the majority were married women who operated their business independently of their husband's employment or enterprise. Jennie Ferraro, who was twenty-five at the time of the 1920 census, was married to a wagon driver and owned and operated her own bakery. Anna DiMaggio worked as a seamstress while her husband was alive, but took over his butcher shop after his death. Anna's eldest son was employed as manager of the shop and her youngest son was a meat cutter. Fanny Alberti took over her father's butcher shop when he passed away. Anna and Fanny are indicative of female proprietors who surfaced in typically 'unfeminine' pursuits. Often, widows assumed the place of departed husbands, or daughters that of a departed parent, when there was no son to take over the family business.

One of the few northern Italians to live in the Third Ward, Mrs

Rachici owned and operated a small cigar-manufacturing enterprise located within her home. She employed several Sicilian women whose occupations were listed as cigar makers – an occupation that in Milwaukee, as in other U.S. cities, employed large numbers of women.[32]

Most of the above-mentioned businesses were conducted primarily at home, with the family living above or behind the establishment. However, some Italian women ran businesses that were not home-based though still located within the ethnic community. Several of them were the proprietors of confectionery shops in the Third Ward. Jeanette Corti, a single woman who migrated from Italy to Milwaukee in 1905, became the proprietor of a confectionery store. Teresa Balbi, after running a successful fruit stand for several years, became a confectioner in 1908, employing her daughter Lillie as a clerk. As noted earlier, Mary Pastorino, the wife of a leading produce merchant, started a small confectionery shop called the 'Flora Bon,' where she put her nine children to work dipping chocolates.

In 1915, there were twenty-nine Italian saloons in the Third Ward, owned and operated mainly by men. Yet female entrepreneurs emerged even in this predominantly male enterprise; these included Antonia Natoli, Julia Faganelli, Anna Loffredo, and others. Several other Italian women were proprietors and cooks in their own restaurants.

Of the forty-five grocery establishments owned by Milwaukee's Italians in 1915, thirty-eight were crowded into three or four streets of the Third Ward.[33] Mary Maglio, a Sicilian and the first Italian-born female grocer in Milwaukee, had opened one such establishment on Detroit Street in 1905. Many other Italian women followed suit, becoming proprietors of home-based grocery stores. Merely a year later, Angela Azzarello, Isabella D'Amore, Mary D'Amore, and Bella Rodino were all listed as grocery-store owners. This Milwaukee pattern of female Italian-owned businesses became more common in the 1920s and early 1930s as these small concerns proliferated in immigrant neighbourhoods across the country. Bodnar suggests that these enterprises 'were easier to start in an era when monopoly capital had not yet replaced the pattern of commercial capitalism.'[34] With very little capital investment required and virtually no overhead, immigrant families could, in their own homes, start business establishments serving the immigrant community. Kathleen Conzen states that by the 1860s a clear business pattern had emerged in Milwaukee, with immigrants concentrated in local retail and the native-born dominant in regional commerce and wholesale. More specifically, the grocery business was the type of merchandising that most attracted the Irish and

Germans.[35] By the early 1900s, Italians were emerging as business leaders in local retail as well.

Between 1900 and 1920, nearly 130 Italian-owned grocery stores operated in the Third Ward, and forty (32.5 per cent) were owned and operated by women.[36] All forty of these women had been born in Italy, the majority of them in Sicily. They included women like Mary Serio, who migrated to Milwaukee in 1889; the wife of a fruit dealer, she ran a grocery store while she raised her nine children. Similarly, Francesca Maglio, who came to Milwaukee in 1902, operated a grocery store and was the mother of seven children.[37] Proportionately, Milwaukee had a large number of female Italian-owned businesses compared to other regions in the country. Historian Luciano Iorizzo notes that nationwide in the late nineteenth century, by contrast, only 7 per cent of all Italian-American merchants were women.[38]

Italian women who owned grocery stores were either married or recently widowed. The majority of the female proprietors of grocery stores (68 per cent) were married to men gainfully employed; Francesca Maglio's husband was a labourer, for example, and Theresa Sottili's husband a carpenter. Women who operated grocery stores often were married to men who were also in business. Sarah Caravella and Theresa Corso's husbands, for instance, owned saloons, while Mary Serio and Angie Spicuzza were married to fruit dealers.[39]

At least eight women (32 per cent) were widows who took over the grocery business following their husband's death. They included Mary Tornabene, whose husband Beniamino had been a grocer from 1904 through 1910. In 1911, she became a widow and the proprietor of the business. An immigrant in Milwaukee from 1891, Rosa D'Amore took over Agostino's store when he died in 1906 and for years thereafter she was able to support herself and her three children.[40] Another enterprising widow was Catherine D'Aquisto, born in Porticello, Sicily, in 1884. As a young girl she was sent to Palermo to help care for the children of a wealthy family. During her free time, she watched the cook prepare meals and thus began a lifelong love affair with food. In 1900, Catherine migrated alone to America to live and work with her sister who had a bakery in New York City. Several years later she joined another sister living in Milwaukee, where she met and married her husband, Joseph Dentice, a recently arrived Sicilian from Sant'Elia and a fruit peddlar in the Third Ward. While her children were young, Catherine earned extra income by cooking and baking in her home for weddings and baptisms. No longer a fruit peddlar, but a city employee, Joseph's income was still not sufficient to provide for his family, so Catherine decided to start her own grocery store. Shelves loaded with macaroni, tomatoes, oranges, and bananas filled the front room of the family home. Catherine also baked bread every morning and sold it to her customers for a nickel a loaf. While remaining at home and raising her children, Catherine later turned her talents into yet more income by cooking and baking for the immigrant neighbourhood and operating a grocery store specializing in Italian food products.[41]

Gender, Domestic Values, and Home-Based Business

Two case studies of Sicilian women who operated grocery stores in the Third Ward reveal how immigrant women's work lives were shaped by domestic values and the life cycle. Both women operated small grocery stores at home. Front rooms were emptied of furniture and shelving went up where pictures and shrines to the Virgin Mary had once hung; the shelves were stocked with olive oil, imported pasta, olives, tomatoes, homemade bread, and fresh fruits. These enterprising women created the opportunity to run a business while taking care of homes and raising children. Children, however, were not exempt from the responsibilities of the home-based business. In fact, business women frequently encouraged, indeed expected, their children to share the responsibilities of 'running the store.'

Maria Latona exhibits a pattern that scholars have identified as an important component of the Italian family-run business: '[F]amily members were expected to contribute their labor to the family business, thereby maximizing operating hours and minimizing operating costs.'[42] Maria and Salvatore Latona migrated to Milwaukee in 1909 from Bagheria, Sicily, with their four children. Salvatore found work, as did many other Italian men, at the Department of Public Works, while Maria contributed 'a little extra' to the family economy by taking in boarders. Still, the couple could not comfortably support their family, which soon grew to eight. In response, Salvatore and Maria also became small-business owners. In 1914, Salvatore opened a tavern while also maintaining his city job and Maria, who continued to accept boarders, started a grocery store that she operated from six in the morning until eight at night. Maria's work life also was closely intertwined with that of her two daughters, Domenica and Vincenza. The eldest child, Domenica, was thirteen when she arrived in Milwaukee with her parents; a year later she married and at age fifteen gave birth to her first child. She and her husband and their growing family lived upstairs above her parents' grocery store and tavern. In order to help Domenica and her husband provide for their children, Maria turned the grocery store over to her daughter, who expanded the store's inventory with jewellery and children's clothing. In 1932, Domenica's husband died, leaving her a widow with nine children to support. When the grocery store could not sustain her large family, Domenica took a full-time job at Cohn Brothers sewing men's garments and her mother, Maria, returned to the grocery store, giving most of the profits to her daughter. This arrangement allowed Maria to care for her nine grandchildren while her daughter worked in the factory. When the children returned home from school in the afternoon, the older ones were expected to help their grandmother in the grocery store by stocking shelves and relieving *nonna* while she prepared the evening meal and tended to the younger children.[43] Several years later, Maria's youngest daughter, Vincenza, got married, but by this time, Maria and Salvatore were no longer running the tavern or grocery store. Their home, the grocery store, and the tavern had been destroyed when the Black Hand planted a bomb in retribution for Salvatore's refusal to comply with an extortion demand. Maria, Salvatore, Domenica, and her nine children were forced to move in with Vincenza and her husband. One year later, Vincenza's husband died of a heart attack, leaving the young widow with six small children to support. With her sister's help Vincenza was hired at Cohn Brothers, while her mother Maria, still caring for Domenica's youngest children, now had six more grandchildren to tend, the youngest only a year old.[44]

A second case similarly illustrates the influence of gender and family values to Italian immigrant households. In the late 1880s, Conchetta and Joseph Burgerino left their small village near Palermo for Milwaukee's Third Ward and opened a grocery store on Detroit Street. The 1920 census lists Joseph as the store's proprietor, but it was Conchetta who operated the business while raising six children. Unable to read or write, Conchetta nevertheless could keep charge accounts by creating symbols for her customers and marking 'X' next to the symbol each time they paid on their accounts. When Conchetta got too old for the business, her eldest daughter, Anna Torretta, also born in Sicily, took over and repeated her mother's work patterns, running the store while raising her children. Anna walked several blocks to Commission Row every morning to select fresh produce to sell, and in the summer she made Italian ice and sold it on the street in front of her store. Having operated one business successfully, Anna, whose husband was always seasonally employed, opened another grocery on the south side of Milwaukee where, according to her daughter, 'she also did a great business making homemade wine.'[45] Anna took her eldest daughter, Josephine, into the grocery business while proceeding to open two more stores in other locations. When the original grocery store was eventually closed, daughter Josephine operated one of the newer stores with her brother-in-law. Anna also expanded one of the grocery stores to include a butcher shop and did almost all the butchering herself. A tavern was eventually opened adjacent to the grocery store, run by Anna's son-in-law, while daughter Josephine also helped out by serving fish fries on Friday night, chicken on Saturday and potato pancakes on Wednesday.

Anna had taken her daughter out of school at sixteen to start her in the family business. Josephine proudly recalls her busy mother 'running the grocery, making homemade wine, and raising four children.' For her part, Josephine continued working for her mother until her own marriage, and later, when her youngest child was two and one-half years old, she started her own business, a very successful catering operation that she ran for twenty-two years. She credits her business career, and that of her siblings, to her mother; as she put it, '[We] all had this business background from my mom.'[46] In the Burgerino family, the spirit of entrepreneurship passed, with no regard for gender, from one generation to the next. For Italian-born women, the motives for starting a business may have been similar to the entrepreneurial motives of Italian men: limited by education and language, they recognized the needs of the immigrant community and viewed business ownership as a means of achieving economic and familial goals within the boundaries of their ethnic neighbourhoods. Gender, however, helped shape these women's decisions. Operating a business in their home allowed them to combine economic activities with domestic responsibilities. Moreover, small business operations that evolved within the homes of immigrant businesswomen often were a means for upward mobility for themselves as well as their children.

Italian Midwives

If the example of Milwaukee's businesswomen suggests the need for significant revision of conventional portraits of Italian immigrant working women, the case of Italian midwives offers an especially stark contrast to these familiar images. This select group of professionally trained and educated women brought a professional ethos to their working lives, one that in some cases overrode obligations of marriage or family.

For several decades after their arrival in Wisconsin, Italian women called on midwives to assist them in childbirth. This demand allowed the midwife to practise a craft that gave her gainful employment and also a respected position in the immigrant community. Immigrant women, especially those newly arrived from southern and eastern Europe, showed a marked preference for midwives.[47] That Italian women, in particular, preferred midwife-assisted deliveries is supported by data from major cities of Italian settlement.[48]

Midwives were popular with immigrant women and their families for many reasons, including an affordable price. While Milwaukee doctors were charging fifteen dollars for a delivery, Italian midwives cost considerably less.[49] Vincenza Bartelloni, for example, recalls that she paid midwife Pasqua Cefalu five dollars for the delivery of her first child in November 1920.[50] In addition to cost, Italians, who saw childbirth as a natural event, preferred to have their babies at home and were suspicious of hospitals.[51] Like many other immigrants they viewed home births as preferable to hospital births because the home and family life were not disturbed.[52] Finally, as several historians have suggested, Italians were particularly hostile to male attendants because of the 'strong sense of shame associated with permitting a man to attend a woman in confinement.'[53]

Conclusions drawn about midwives, especially immigrant midwives, have ignored their varied backgrounds and their differing levels of education and training.[54] According to Nancy Schrom Dye, in the early decades of the twentieth century the United States saw little in the way of a tradition of professional midwifery.[55] Midwives were described by male physicians as 'filthy and ignorant and not far removed from the jungles of Africa,' 'relics of barbarism,' and 'old grannies with mouths full of snuff, fingers full of dirt and brains full of arrogance and superstition.'[56] With such negative attitudes toward midwives it is even more striking that all Italian midwives in this study were educated and professionally trained.

Current assessments also reflect misperceptions about midwives as well as inappropriate methods of analyses used to examine their working lives. One study of midwives in New York City characterizes the typical Italian midwife as a married woman and the mother of several children.[57] Angela Danzi writes that midwifery was an acceptable way for a woman to supplement the family income. Furthermore, she states that while a small number of formally trained Italian midwives emigrated to the United States, the vast majority were without formal education.[58] Charlotte Borst, a historian who has studied German and U.S.-born midwives in Wisconsin, similarly characterizes midwifery as 'a traditional woman's occupation practiced around the needs of families and communities.' She suggests that midwives, like women who took in boarders, 'could adjust their job schedule to meet the needs of their families, taking fewer cases if they needed the time at home and taking more cases if they needed the extra money.'[59] Borst also concludes that midwives did not incorporate a professional ethos where the occupation itself took precedence over the needs of its practitioners. In the case of midwives, their familial responsibilities took precedence over their occupation.[60]

The assumption that women's domestic values determined entirely the relations of professionally trained midwives to their work ignores the seriousness with which professionally trained midwives conducted their practice. My examination of Italian midwives in Wisconsin leads me to very different conclusions about the professional commitment of immigrant midwives who practised in the early decades of the twentieth century.

Because they have been categorically labelled as uneducated and ill-trained, midwives are often categorized as yet another segment of working-class women who, as Danzi and Borst argue, worked around their family's needs. Yet the women under review were educated and saw midwifery as a career, not simply a job. They also shared other common characteristics: all were born in Italy and began practising midwifery soon after their arrival in the United States. According to the Wisconsin midwife files, Italian midwives in that state practised in Milwaukee and Kenosha, cities with substantial Italian populations located in the southeastern corner of Wisconsin. Each woman chose midwifery as a profession at a young age and, moreover, some of them exhibited patterns of independent behaviour not often observed among working-class Italian women.

The female professionals included Anna Costarella[61] and Rosa Sperandandio,[62] both of whom graduated from the Royal University of Palermo (in 1880 and 1900 respectively). Orsola Casoria completed her training in a hospital in Messina, Sicily, in 1908,[63] while Luisa Giordano was educated at the University of Turin.[64] In 1915, Margerita Ciotti graduated from the University of Camerino,[65] while Rosa Cesario graduated from the Medical University of Naples.[66] The only practising Italian midwife in southeastern Wisconsin who had not been formally trained in Italy was Pasqua Cefalu, who was an apprentice trained by her mother in Porticello, Sicily, but did receive professional training in Milwaukee.[67] One other midwife, Rosa DeStefano, was formally trained but not formally educated; she did not attend formal lectures, but she gained practical experience at the Camerino Hospital in Naples, earning her certificate to practise midwifery on 15 July 1883.[68]

No doubt there were scores of practising immigrant midwives in the early twentieth century who had little or no professional training. Still, Italian midwives in Wisconsin challenge the assumption that all immigrant midwives were poorly trained. There is also evidence that there were professionally trained midwives practising in other cities. According to a New York State study, one supervisory nurse praised the Italian immigrant midwives with whom she worked as 'well-educated, thoroughly trained and scientific women,' adding that 'in Italy none but a well-educated woman can qualify for the training, which covers from two to four years.'[69]

In Italy, as in most European countries, high-quality midwifery schools, usually associated with a lying-in hospital and a clinic of a university medical department, offered the latest instruction in obstetrical science.[70] Midwives learned anatomy, physiology, and elementary pathology as well as practical midwifery, often training alongside medical students. When Kenosha midwife Margerita Ciotti entered the University of Camerino in 1914, her primary textbook was a manual of obstetrics written by highly respected doctors and professors from the universities of Pavia, Rome, and Florence.[71] The nearly five-hundred-page manual clearly illustrated every aspect of pregnancy and delivery, from the anatomy of the pregnant woman to the delivery of multiple births to instructions for performing episiotomies. Midwifery students were often taught by a chief midwife instructor, who typically offered a separate midwifery theory course. To graduate, a pupil midwife took an oral exam in front of her teacher and the members of a government commission.[72]

Successful midwifery applicants were expected not only to be educated but also to be women of good character. As in America, where hospital superintendents maintained strict control over nursing students' work and social lives,[73] the behaviour of a student midwife in Italy was subject to moral regulation. When Margerita Ciotti attended the University of Camerino she lived in town, close to the university, and with a family who exercised parental authority. Another Kenosha mid-wife, Rosa Cesario, was a student at the University of Naples. While there she lived in a convent with the Sacred Heart nuns, who escorted female students to their classes and back to the convent by horse and carriage.[74]

According to Charlotte Borst, the average midwife in Wisconsin was an older, mature woman, and her research suggested that both Ameri-can and German-born women began midwifery at about age forty-eight. By contrast, Italian-born midwives in Wisconsin began formal training at the age of eighteen and began practising in their early twenties. That midwifery was indeed a 'career' that Italian women took seriously is suggested by the dates appearing on their applications for licensing. They allowed no time to lapse after their arrival in America to resume midwifery. All the Italian midwives in Wisconsin registered within a few months of their arrival in America. Pasqua Cefalu arrived in Milwaukee during the summer of 1900 with her husband and three children. The following 10 October she registered with the Milwaukee Health Depart-ment.[75] Luisa Giordano migrated to Wisconsin in 1907, and delivered her first baby in Kenosha one year later. Rosa Cesario and her husband migrated to America in the spring of 1922. On 16 June 1922 Rosa registered with the Wisconsin Board of Medical Examiners to practise midwifery.[76] Margerita Ciotti had practised midwifery for eight years in Montemonaco, Italy, and had already attended 700 women before emi-grating to Kenosha in 1923. In December she applied for a midwifery license.[77]

In 1909, Wisconsin legislation required that midwives be licensed. That did not prevent any one of the Italian midwives from continuing their practice. Pasqua Cefalu would have been the one midwife threat-ened by the legislation, since she did not have the formal training required under Wisconsin law. In addition, she had already been practis-ing midwifery for thirty-two years and thus might also have considered retiring. However, at the age of fifty-two, Pasqua Cefalu enrolled in the Wisconsin School of Midwifery. She graduated and received her Wiscon-sin license on 15 January 1910, and continued her practice for two more decades.

Ethnic patterns of midwifery practice dominated Milwaukee in the late nineteenth and early twentieth centuries. In 1904, for example, 53 per cent of all Milwaukee's babies were delivered by midwives, most of them in immigrant neighbourhoods.[78] German midwives tended Ger-man women and Polish midwives tended Polish women, while Italian midwives tended Italian women.[79] Most of the Italian midwives who attended Italian births lived in the same neighbourhood as, or within close proximity to, the women they assisted.[80] Midwife Pasqua Cefalu delivered 87 per cent of her patients in the neighbourhoods of the Third Ward.

For Italians, midwife-assisted births followed a tradition where women were in control and that centred around the involvement and networking of females. Female kin assisted during childbirth in a number of ways. Carolyn Pontillo, who migrated from Cosenza, Italy, to Kenosha, Wisconsin, in 1915, called for her female relatives when she was ready to give birth. The midwife, Italian-born Luisa Giordano, routinely asked the women in attendance to help her with the delivery by, for example, putting the water on to boil and fetching the clean sheets. After the birth of her daughter, Pontillo recalls that 'female relatives remained to care for the other children, prepare meals, and do household chores.'[81]

As a rule, Italian midwives did not remain in the home of the parturient woman and engage in domestic activities. Elisabeth Crowell noted that Italian midwives in New York City left the household chores to members of the family, 'not considering it part of their duties as midwives.'[82] Immigrant women in Wisconsin similarly noted that the Italian midwives who had attended them had also refrained from domestic activities, which, in turn, reinforced the need to be surrounded and supported by female kin, and also underscores the professional ethos shared by Wisconsin's Italian midwives.[83]

Midwives returned to the home of the parturient woman for seven to ten days following delivery. After Carolyn Pontillo gave birth to her daughter, she recalls, Giordano 'returned to her home every day for one week to bathe and check the baby, and to examine her for infection.' She also advised her what to eat and what activities she could engage in.[84] Margerita Ciotti would visit the parturient woman for one week, bathe the baby, and take care of the mother. Ciotti paid particular attention to the mother, checking her for infection and instructing her on breast feeding.[85]

While the midwife's primary responsibilities revolved around the birth of a child, Italian midwives often became involved with their patients before delivery. Since pre-natal care was almost unheard of at the turn of the century, it was not unusual for Luisa Giordano, who practised in Kenosha from 1908 to 1932, to meet with an expectant woman, give her a complete examination, and determine her date of delivery. Normally, she would not see the pregnant woman again until she went into labour unless something irregular occurred during the pregnancy. Consultation with Giordano was held in her flat, which was arranged like a doctor's office. There, she met her patients in the privacy of her bedroom and examined them on a double bed covered with a huge, white sheet that she cleaned and sterilized following each patient's use.[86] In addition to routine check-ups, Giordano also counselled women on the use of contraceptives.

The work of the midwife was not limited to childbirth. Midwives were consulted about birth control and some performed abortions.[87] Josephine Cialdini, godchild of Luisa Giordano, recalled that 'women came to her for all kinds of advice on birth control. They told Donna Luisa all their problems. One woman said, "if it wasn't for Donna Luisa I would have even more children than I already do."'[88] Giordano showed women how to use contraceptives and reportedly performed abortions. In Milwaukee, women 'who were desperate from so many pregnancies,'[89] or an occasional, unmarried young woman who found herself pregnant, sought help from Orsola Casoria, a Sicilian-born midwife known for her abortionist activities.

Oral interviews with friends and families of midwives suggest a degree of independent behaviour not often observed among Italian immigrant women. Most Italian women emigrated to America as part of family groups, most commonly as wives or daughters. However, Luisa Giordano migrated alone to Wisconsin at the age of twenty-one. She is remembered as 'a very educated, very professional woman.' In America she lived alone, in an upper flat, free from familial supervision. Several oral informants quietly added that Donna Luisa had 'a lot of lovers but was never interested in marriage.'[90]

That these were career women did not mean they did not face enormous difficulty negotiating the demands of family and profession. This was especially true of married women and those with children, yet their evident willingness to place career above family is striking. Married with four children, Margerita Ciotti, for example, found it extremely difficult to balance marriage and children with her career, and her decisions were significantly influenced by her professional commitments. When her husband decided to emigrate in 1920, Margerita chose to remain in Italy and continue practising midwifery. Three years later she decided to join her husband in America, where she gave birth to four children over the next few years, and also ran a limited practice. Discontented with life in the United States, however, Margerita left her husband in Kenosha, and with her four children returned to Italy in 1929, where she resumed midwifery in her home town of Montemonaco. In 1933, she decided to leave her children in Italy with her sister and rejoin her husband in Wisconsin. Once again, she resumed her career as a midwife in Kenosha. Margerita did not see her children again until 1947, when she returned to Italy. A year later, she and her grown children came back to Kenosha, where they were finally reunited as a family. While Italian men frequently made numerous trips back and forth to Italy, it was not as common for Italian women to do so. It was even less common for Italian women to leave their children for considerable periods of time. Ciotti did both. The one thing that remained constant for her was midwifery. Whether in Italy or in the United States, with her husband or with her children, Margerita Ciotti practised her profession.

Rosa Cesario was another midwife who made choices that did not always conform to the usual patterns associated with Italian immigrant women. In June 1922, when she was twenty-five years old, Cesario received her certificate of registration from the Wisconsin Board of Medical Examiners. After only a year in Wisconsin, her husband, Fiorino, became ill and was advised by his doctor to return to the warmer climate of Italy. Rosa, however, chose not to leave her practice in Kenosha. She told her husband to return to Italy himself and she lived alone in a rented apartment in the Italian section of town. In 1927, she returned to Italy to be with her dying mother. Only then did she return to her husband in Cosenza, resuming midwifery there.[91]

Orsola Casoria, a native of Sicily, was trained as a midwife in a hospital in Messina. On 30 June 1914, shortly after her arrival in Milwaukee, she received her licence to practise in Wisconsin.[92] Casoria practised midwifery in Milwaukee for nearly fifty years. This career is all the more remarkable since in 1937 Casoria was charged with second-degree manslaughter in connection with an abortion she performed on a woman who died of peritonitis. Casoria was found guilty and sentenced to six years in Taycheedah prison.[93] Her profession as a midwife might well have ended there, but undaunted, Casoria reapplied for a licence and continued practising until the 1960s, when she was in her late seventies.

Several of the Italian midwives in this study also exhibited independent behaviour by regularly using their birth names instead of their married names. Although married to Joseph Sorci, Pasqua Cefalu was listed as such in the Milwaukee city directories. She advertised under the name Cefalu, registered with the Milwaukee Public Health Department under Cefalu, and received her Wisconsin licence under the name Cefalu. Only after retiring from midwifery did she begin using her married name. Margerita Ciotti also used her birth name while practising midwifery. Her married name was Valeri, but she too appeared in city directories as Ciotti and was licensed and signed birth certificates under that name. The practice of using birth instead of married names reinforces the view of these midwives as professionals.

The practice of midwifery by Italian women suggests that domestic values did not necessarily or entirely shape their relation to work. At an early age, these women made a decision to become midwives and were educated and professionally trained. Midwives were not working-class women who laboured primarily as a means of earning extra money to contribute to the family economy. They did not practise midwifery because it fit in with the rhythms of daily life. If anything, midwifery had a rhythm that could not be controlled. Italian midwives in Wisconsin were women who defined themselves in terms of their education and training as professionals.

Conclusion

Gender and domestic values helped shape immigrant women's work experiences in the early twentieth century. In Milwaukee, the opportunity for women to work outside the home was limited because the city's economic base was primarily heavy industry. Married women were further limited because they were confined to the home with small children. Still, immigrant women found productive ways to contribute to the family economy. In Milwaukee, Italian immigrant women exhibited a spirit of entrepreneurship and self-sufficiency by establishing home-based business enterprises and midwifery practices that served the immigrant community. These ventures allowed Italian women, limited by the parameters of the ethnic enclave and domestic life, to use both to their advantage. Some women combined child-rearing and housework while earning an income from their own home-based businesses, while midwives practised careers that sometimes took precedence over family.

Despite the employment limitations that they faced, Italian women of the immigrant generation in Milwaukee carved out a special niche for themselves within their ethnic community and defined that world according to gender, career, and domestic values.

NOTES

I wish to thank Elliott Barkan, Pamela Mack, Suzanne Sinke, and John Stockwell for reading and commenting on earlier drafts of this chapter.

1 My analysis of Italian female grocers employs a 'gender model' that Ava Baron suggests is typically used by those who focus on family circumstances to explain workers' relation to employment. See Baron, 'Gender and Labor History: Learning from the Past, Looking to the Future,' in Ava Baron, ed., *Work Engendered: Toward a New History of American Labor* (Ithaca: Cornell University Press, 1991), 7.
2 Sally Miller, 'Milwaukee: Of Ethnicity and Labor,' in Bruce M. Stave, ed., *Socialism and the Cities* (Port Washington, NY: Kennikat Press, 1975), 41–71.
3 Adolf Gerd Korman, *Industrialization, Immigrants and Americanizers: The View from Milwaukee, 1866–1921* (Madison, WI: State Historical Society, 1969), 11.
4 Judith Simonson, 'The Third Ward: Symbol of Ethnic Identity,' *Milwaukee History* (Summer 1987): 61–76.
5 Ibid.
6 *Sentinel*, 30 June 1901, sect. 4, 5.
7 George La Piana, *The Italians in Milwaukee, Wisconsin* (New York: Associated Charities, 1915), 8–9.
8 U.S. Immigration Commission, Reports, vol. 26, *Immigrants in Cities*, 738.
9 In the late nineteenth and early twentieth centuries, women frequently earned money at home by taking in boarders and finishing garments. Tamara Hareven and John Modell first examined the economic importance of providing services to boarders in 'Urbanization and the Malleable Household: An Examination of Boarding and Lodging in American Families,' *Journal of Marriage and the Family* 35 (August 1973): 467–79. Eileen Boris and Cynthia Daniels explore the importance of homework in *Homework: Historical and Contemporary Perspectives on Paid Labor at Home* (Chicago: University of Illinois Press, 1989).
10 Reports of the Immigration Commission, *Immigrants in Cities*, 717.
11 La Piana, *The Italians in Milwaukee*, 16.
12 Reports of the Immigration Commission, *Immigrants in Cities*, 748.
13 Interview with Gaetanina Balistreri, 13 April 1991, Milwaukee.
14 La Piana, *The Italians in Milwaukee*, 11.
15 Ibid.
16 Interview with Rose Carini, 23 January 1991, Milwaukee.
17 La Piana, *The Italians in Milwaukee*, 11.

18 Wendy Gamber, *The Female Economy: The Millinery and Dressmaking Trades, 1860–1930* (Urbana, Chicago: University of Illinois Press, 1997), 30.

19 Virginia Yans-McLaughlin argued this position in *Family and Community: Italian Immigrants in Buffalo, 1880–1930* (Chicago: University of Illinois Press, 1982).

20 I analyse the impact of the local economy and women's life cycle on Italian women's work patterns in my dissertation. See Diane Vecchio, 'Family, Community, Culture and Welfare Capitalism among Italian Women in Endicott,' PhD diss., Syracuse University, 1991.

21 Donna Gabaccia, *From the Other Side: Women, Gender, and Immigrant Life in the U.S., 1820–1990* (Bloomington: Indiana University Press, 1994), 49.

22 John Bodnar, *The Transplanted: A History of Immigrants in Urban America* (Bloomington: Indiana University Press, 1985), 78.

23 Carini interview.

24 Interview with Blacky Brocca, 6 October 1992, Milwaukee.

25 Interview with Vincenza Bartelloni, 20 March 1992, Milwaukee.

26 Interview with Catherine Balistreri, 23 March 1991, Milwaukee.

27 John Bodnar explains that family members were continually instructed in the necessity of sharing and notions of reciprocity were constantly reinforced. He explains that 'by working together, pooling limited resources, and muting individual inclinations families attempted to assemble the resources sufficient for economic survival.' See Bodnar, *The Transplanted*, 72.

28 Paul Geib, 'From Italian Peddler to Commission Row Wholesaler,' *Milwaukee History* (Winter 1990): 102–12.

20 Interview with Elizabeth Pastorino Turecek, 4 May 1993, Milwaukee.

30 Geib, 'From Italian Peddlar,' 109.

31 La Piana, *The Italians in Milwaukee*, 9–10.

32 See Gary R. Mormino and George E. Pozzetta, *The Immigrant World of Ybor City: Italians and Their Latin Neighbors in Tampa, 1885–1985* (Chicago: University of Illinois Press, 1987) for a discussion of the prominence of Italian women in the cigar industry.

33 La Piana, *The Italians in Milwaukee*, 9.

34 Bodnar, *The Transplanted*, 131.

35 Kathleen Conzen, *Immigrant Milwaukee, 1836–1860: Accommodation and Community in a Frontier City* (Cambridge: Harvard University Press, 1976), 114.

36 In addition, oral interviews reveal several more women who ran grocery stores but could not be located in either the city directories or the manuscript census.

37 Information derived from Milwaukee city directories and Wisconsin State Census for Milwaukee.

38 Luciano Iorizzo, 'Italian American Merchants as Seen in the R. G. Dunn Collection,' unpublished paper presented at the American Italian Historical Association, Washington, DC, November 1992.

39 Ibid.

40 Ibid.

41 Balistreri interview.

42 Andrew Sanchirico, 'Small Business and Social Mobility among Italian Americans,' in *Italian Ethnics: Their Languages, Literature and Lives*, Proceedings of the 20th Annual Conference of the American Italian Historical Association, November 1987, 208.

43 Interviews with Vincenza Bartelloni and Conchetta Crivello, 20 March 1992, Milwaukee.

44 Ibid.

45 Interview with Josephine Rampolla, 20 April 1991, Milwaukee.

46 Ibid.

47 Judy Barrett Litoff, *American Midwives, 1860 to the Present* (Westport, CT: Greenwood Press, 1978), 27.

48 Italians, more than any other immigrant group, relied on midwives. In her 1906 sample of midwife deliveries in New York City, social worker Elisabeth Crowell found that of 1029 births among Italian women, only 67 (7%) were reported by physicians and the remaining 962 (93%) were reported by midwives. See Elisabeth Crowell, 'The Midwives of New York,' *Charities and the Commons* 17 (January 1907): 667–77. In 1917, Dr Levy reported that in Newark, New Jersey, 'very few Italian mothers are delivered in hospitals, 88% are delivered by midwives.' See Julius Levy, M.D., 'The Maternal and Infant Mortality in Midwifery Practice in Newark, New Jersey,' *American Journal of Obstetrics and Diseases of Women and Children* 77 (1918): 41–53.

49 Milwaukee County Medical Society, Fee Bill, 1 May 1883. Milwaukee County Historical Society, Milwaukee.

50 Bartelloni interview.

51 Elizabeth Ewen, *Immigrant Women in the Land of Dollars: Life and Culture on the Lower East Side, 1880–1925* (New York: Monthly Review Press, 1985), 131.

52 Lee W. Thomas, 'The Supervision of Midwives in New York City,' *Monthly Bulletin*, Dept. of Health, City of New York, 9 (May 1919): 117–20.

53 Litoff, *American Midwives*, 29.

54 Charlotte Borst, 'The Training and Practice of Midwives: A Wisconsin Study,' *Bulletin of the History of Medicine* 62 (1988): 608–27.

55 Nancy Schrom Dye, 'Mary Breckinridge, The Frontier Nursing Service and

the Introduction of Nurse-Midwifery in the United States,' in Judith Walzer Leavitt, ed., *Women and Health in America* (Madison: University of Wisconsin Press, 1984), 327–43.

56 Quoted in Neal Devitt, 'The Statistical Case for Elimination of the Midwife: Fact versus Prejudice, 1890–1935,' *Women and Health* 4, 1 (Spring 1979): 81–93.

57 Angela Danzi, 'Old World Traits Obliterated: Immigrant Midwives and the Medicalization of Childbirth,' in Dominic Candeloro, Fred L. Gardaphe, and Paolo A. Giordano, eds., *Italian Ethnics: Their Languages, Literature and Lives* (New York: The American Italian Historical Association, 1990), 215–30.

58 Ibid., 217.

59 Borst, 'The Training and Practice of Midwives,' 620.

60 Ibid., 47.

61 Physicians Records (midwifery), Milwaukee Public Library, Archives, Milwaukee.

62 Board of Medical Examiners Midwife File, Wisconsin State Historical Society (Madison), box 1, folder 26, #25.

63 *Milwaukee Sentinel*, 25 January 1976, 24.

64 Interview with Josephine Cialdini (Luisa Giordano's godchild), 11 November 1993, Kenosha.

65 Midwife File, box 1, folder 3.

66 Ibid., folder 3.

67 Ibid., folder 16.

68 Ibid., folder 17.

69 Quoted in Doris Weatherford, *Foreign and Female: Immigrant Women in America, 1840–1930* (New York: Facts on File, 1995), 31.

70 Charlotte Borst, 'Catching Babies: The Change from Midwife to Physician-Attended Childbirth in Wisconsin, 1870–1930,' PhD diss., University of Wisconsin, Madison, 1989, 63.

71 Alessandro Cuzzi, *Manuale di ostetricia ad uso delle levatrici* (Milan: Francesco Vallardi, 1914).

72 Borst, 'Catching Babies,' 63.

73 See Barbara Melosh, *The Physician's Hand: Work, Culture and Conflict in American Nursing* (Philadelphia: Temple University Press, 1982), 50.

74 Interviews with Louis Martino, 9 November 1993, and with Annetta Valeri Carlini and Domenica Valeri Domenici, 28 September 1993, Kenosha.

75 Health Department Physicians Register, 1882–1907, vol. 1, Milwaukee Public Library, Archives.

76 Midwife File, box 1, folder 3.

77 Ibid., folder 3, #363.

78 Borst, 'Catching Babies,' 194.

79 Charlotte G. Borst, 'Wisconsin's Midwives as Working Women: Immigrant Midwives and the Limits of a Traditional Occupation, 1870–1920' *Journal of American Ethnic History* 8, 2 (Spring 1989): 47.

80 New York City Clerk, Birth certificates (1904), Manhattan, New York.

81 Interview with Carolyn Pontillo, 24 January 1994, Kenosha.

82 Elisabeth F. Crowell, 'The Midwives in New York,' *Charities and the Commons* 17 (January 1907): 672.

83 Pontillo, Carlini, and Domenici interviews.

84 Pontillo interview.

85 Carlini and Domenici interviews.

86 Cialdini interview. Giordano rented a flat from Josephine's parents. Growing up, Josephine spent much of her time in her godmother's flat, running errands for her and accompanying her to deliveries.

87 In her study of Italians in Greenwich Village during the 1920s, Carolyn Ware observed that 'Italian women who sought to use contraceptives were driven to acquire them secretly through the Italian midwives.' Caroline Ware, *Greenwich Village, 1920–1930* (New York: Harper & Row, 1965), 179.

88 Cialdini interview.

89 Interview with Mary Sorgi, September 1992, Milwaukee.

90 Martino, Amendola, Carlini, and Domenici interviews.

91 Martino interview.

92 Obituary in *Milwaukee Sentinel*, 26 January 1976.

93 State Historical Society of Wisconsin (Madison), Archives, 'Regulation and Licensing,' Medical Examining Board, Complaint and Revocation File, series 1873, box 1; 'Woman Accused in Death of Girl,' *Milwaukee Sentinel*, 10 February 1927; 'Midwife Gets 4 to 6 Years,' ibid., 27 May 1937.

PART III

Fighting Back: Militants, Radicals, Exiles

6 Italians in Buenos Aires's Anarchist Movement: Gender Ideology and Women's Participation, 1890–1910

José Moya

Donna Gabaccia and Franca Iacovetta recently asserted that 'perhaps the least understood aspect of Italian women's diasporic lives is their role as resisters, protesters, and activists.'[1] Various factors make Buenos Aires an optimal setting to attempt a response to the call implied in that statement. The Argentine capital had the largest, and earliest, concentration of Italians in the diaspora during the nineteenth century. Already by 1855, the city's 10,279 Italians made up 11 per cent of the total population and outnumbered their compatriots in New York City by more than ten to one. By the end of the century Italians accounted for one-fourth of Buenos Aires's population and their community was larger than those of New York, Philadelphia, Chicago, Boston, San Francisco, and Toronto *combined* (see table 6.1). Moreover, the maturity of the community gave it one of the most balanced gender ratios in the diaspora. Already by the end of the century (1895), women accounted for four out of every ten Italians in the city. During this period, Argentina's port cities developed some of the most active labour movements in the world and the Italians' early arrival, large numbers, and demographic weight allowed them to play a critical role in the unions' formation.[2] In this chapter I trace Italians' influence in the development of the most important of these movements in Buenos Aires, anarchism. I then examine the movement's gender ideology and the participation of women in it.

Buenos Aires's anarchist movement owed much to Italians from its very beginnings. Although the first section of the International in Argentina was founded by French communards in 1872, within a year there were Italian and Spanish sections[3] – a remarkably early development given that the first sections of the International in Italy and Spain had appeared only four years before, in early 1869.[4] The names of various groups in the Argentine capital during the early 1870s leave little doubt as to their general ideology and national origin: Gli Spostati, Il Malfattori, Sempre Avanti, Gli Internazionali, I Salvatori. We know nothing, however, about their gender composition. At any rate, these groups remained minuscule and Argentina, unlike Italy and Spain, failed to develop a federation of anarchist labour unions during the 1870s.[5]

Italian influence in Argentina's libertarian movement increased in the mid-1880s with the arrival of scores of militants.[6] Although we do not know the nationality of the founders of the Circulo Comunista Anarquista in 1884, most of the surnames that have survived in documents (Garbaccio, Fazzi, Marzoratti, Natta) provide a clue, particularly at a time when Italian patronymics were not as common among Argentine-born adults as they would later be.[7] But none of the forenames that have survived belongs to a woman. A year later, a much more famous figure, Errico Malatesta, arrived. With other compatriots, he published one of the first anarchist periodicals in the country, *La Questione Sociale*, and helped turn the local bakers' mutual-aid association into the first clearly anarchist 'resistance society' in Argentina.[8]

Because this was not a trade with significant female participation, few women, if any, were involved in the union. I have not found any mention of *compañeras* (comrades) in *El Obrero Panadero*, the union's newspaper. Still, this 'resistance society' became a prototype and some of its characteristics had important gender implications for future anarchist labour unions in the country. Administration was as non-bureaucratic and horizontal as possible, which would later facilitate the participation of women workers. The fact that leaders came from the rank and file and received no pay had a similar impact. The retention of mutual-aid practices (the payment of a one-peso monthly fee, about a day's wage, entitled members to medical and disability benefits) provided female and male workers an essential service and gave them an alternative to ethnic or mainstream mutual-insurance associations. At the same time, a whole array of 'direct action' tactics that women could easily engage in – strikes, slowdowns, sabotage, propaganda, boycotts – were added to traditional mutual insurance. As the designation of unions as 'resistance societies' indicated, immediate concerns with 'bread-and-butter' issues were not seen as incompatible with long-term 'resistance' to the state and capitalism. Partial strikes and confrontations with employers served – in this view – not only to gain better wages and working conditions but

TABLE 6.1
Cities with the largest Italian population in the diaspora, c. 1900 and c. 1920
(in rank order)

Year	City	Italians	Year	City	Italians
1904	Buenos Aires	228,556	1920	New York	390,832
1900	New York	145,433	1914	Buenos Aires	312,267
1900	Sao Paulo	48,000	1920	Sao Paulo	91,544
1900	Montevideo	44,120	1920	Montevideo	70,000
1900	Rosario, Arg.	25,676	1920	Philadelphia	67,723
1896	Paris	18,503	1920	Chicago	59,213
1900	Philadelphia	17,830	1914	Rosario, Arg.	45,357
1900	Chicago	16,008	1920	Boston	38,179
1895	La Plata, Arg.	15,547	1920	Newark, NJ	27,465
1900	Boston	13,738	1920	San Francisco	23,924
1901	London	10,889	1920	Rio de Janeiro	21,929
1900	Newark, NJ	8,537	1914	La Plata, Arg.	20,247
1900	San Francisco	7,508			

Note: The only city that may have made it into this ranking, though likely at the bottom, for which I was not able to find data is Algiers.

Sources: Brazil, Directoria Geral de Estatística, Sinopse do Recenseamento, 1900 (Rio de Janeiro, 1905), xii, 101 (for total population; Italian pop. estimated at $\frac{1}{5}$ of total for Sao Paulo) and Recenseamento do Brazil, 1920 (Rio de Janeiro, 1922–30), vol. 4, p. 1, 331; Great Britain, Census Office, Census of England and Wales, 1901 (London, 1902–3), vol. 31, 156, and Census of England and Wales, 1921 (London, 1922–5), vol. 32, 114; Philip Ogden, Foreigners in Paris: Residential Segregation in the Nineteenth and Twentieth Centuries (London, 1977), 22; Rosario (Santa Fe, Arg.), Primer censo municipal, 1900 (Rosario, 1902), 69; United States, Census Office, Twelfth Census of the United States, 1900 (Washington, 1901–2), vol. 1, cixxvii, and Bureau of the Census, Fourteenth Census of the United States, 1920 (Washington, 1921–3). Figure for Montevideo is based on a rough extrapolation from a 1907 census and various estimates.

also as a sort of revolutionary gymnastic that stimulated the workers' rebellious instinct and trained them for the eventual 'general strike,' the harbinger of the social revolution. This ultimate goal may have been shared only by a minority of workers, male or female, but it was not a requisite for radical collective action.

Malatesta's enthusiasm for labour organization had to do as much with his previous experiences in Italy as with his impressions of Argentina. It also had implications for women's participation in the movement. His involvement in the failed insurrections in Puglia (1874) and La Banda de Matese (1877) had cooled his fervour for guerrilla warfare and made him question his anarcho-communist comrades' disdain for labour unions as intrinsically reformist and anti-revolutionary. Malatesta feared that if anarchists rejected trade unions they ran the risk of isolating themselves from the grass roots and degenerating into individual terrorism. The lack of a reserve army of labourers in countries of immigration like Argentina convinced him that unions and strikes had an even better chance there of improving the workers' conditions without dulling their militancy and revolutionary edge. In turn, his experience in the River Plate reinforced his support of this strategy when he returned to Europe in 1889.[9] The absence in nineteenth-century Argentina of rural insurrections concocted by anarchist conspirators was due mainly to the lack of a traditional peasantry in the pampas. Yet the fact that they were not even attempted, as they were in Italy and Spain, may have to do with the early success of the organizational model sponsored by Malatesta, Mattei, and other Italian immigrants in the 1880s. This model would prove more appealing to immigrants, and particularly to immigrant women, than one based on rural insurrection and urban terrorism, and it would help the anarchist movement withstand the challenges of the next decade.

The 1890s began with intra-left conflict in the Old and New Worlds. The Second International held in Paris in 1889 had proposed the celebration of the first May Day the following year in support of the eight-hour workday. What was meant to be a display of international proletariat solidarity became the occasion for anarchist/socialist clashes – an old schism in Italy but a relatively new development in Argentina, where the previous small size of the left had encouraged more concord than separation. The anarchists refused to participate in the parade organized by the socialists, denouncing the latter as authoritarian and unrevolutionary and the event as a futile and unprincipled celebration that should be replaced with violent protest.[10] This started a long and dual practice of peaceful socialist processions and riotous anarchist manifestations. The cleft may have had an ethnic component in the 1890s, as most anarchists were Italians and Spaniards and many of the socialists German. As an Italian immigrant put it: 'Con tutti i socialisti alemanni componenti il circolo *Vorwärts* noi, anarchici qui residenti, non abbiamo niente di comune.'[11] In so far as many women got involved in labour activism through the male members of their family, Italian immigrants' preference for anarchism had significant gender repercussions.

A similar but less visible ethnic component may have been part of the conflict within libertarian circles that surfaced in the 1890s with the increased arrival of radicalized anarcho-communists. They condemned the collectivists' acceptance of organization and involvement in the labour movement as a betrayal of libertarian purity, of the inviolable principles of individual freedom and communal spontaneity. Trade unions and strikes fostered material ambition, contentment, and conservatism among workers who became more interested in reaping benefits from an irredeemably unjust system than in destroying it. The role of anarchists was not to ameliorate the conditions of the working class, and thus blunt their rebelliousness, but to expose the contradictions of the capitalist system and incite the natural hatred of the masses toward their oppressors. The 'propaganda by the deed' of individuals or small groups of devoted revolutionaries – and during the period the term became synonymous with sabotage, bombings, and attentats – not trade unions, would hasten the apocalyptic 'social revolution' and the anarchist utopia right after that. The other anarcho-communist complaint actually regarded the collectivists' vision of the future society as a place where workers would be remunerated with the full value of their labour. Remuneration according to productivity exhibited a lack of human solidarity, perpetuated private property, and would recreate social inequality, claimed the anarcho-communists, who proposed compensation according to need instead. This uncompromising egalitarianism would not simply benefit women in the future utopia but, as we will later see, it served to highlight all sorts of power inequalities, including those based on gender, in present society. While these ideological disputes took place in other countries, the fact is that a disproportionate number of the anarcho-communists arriving in Argentina then were Spaniards, particularly Catalans, at a time (the mid-1890s) when Barcelona was replacing Paris as the world's focus of anarchist terrorism. Many tended to look down upon the less extremist or less 'advanced' Italians.[12] Even Malatesta, an anarcho-communist himself, was attacked as an 'organization maniac' and 'a ridiculous federationist.'

Argentine anarchism weathered the 'propaganda by the deed' tempest of the 1890s with much skill and assurance. It began the decade with a feeble and foiled attempt to form a labour federation based on half a dozen unions, and it began the next century with a permanent federation of thirty-five workers' resistance societies, a figure that doubled to sixty-six affiliates and 33,000 members by 1904, at least 4000 of them women. This was the reverse of the trend in Italy, where anarchism ended the century weakened and losing ground in the labour movement to its legalitarian socialist opponents. For all the talk of dynamite and violence during this decade, Buenos Aires did not experience the cycles of terrorism and state repression common in France, Spain, Italy, and Russia – a circumstance that was likely to encourage stronger female participation. The fact that Argentina was apparently one of only three countries in the world to outlaw anarchist associations had little to do with the lack of terrorist activity, since it did so in 1910, fifteen years later than the other two – which not coincidentally were Spain and Italy.

Other factors account for this relative absence of terrorism and the instrumental, mass-based, and practice-oriented nature of anarchism in Argentina. One was the legacy of Malatesta's pragmatic/militant model, which presented a viable alternative to both individual terror and gradualist syndicalism.[13] After his departure, various compatriots kept those ideas alive through the publication of the pro-organization news-papers *El Obrero Panadero* (1894), *La Questione Sociale* (1894), and *L'Avvenire* (1895).[14] The arrival in 1898 of another influential Italian, Pietro Gori, supporting a radical but institutionalized movement, furthered the tendency toward compromise.[15] The influence of the Spanish doctrine of 'anarchism without adjectives' – which ridiculed the collectivist/communist clash as unbecoming a people who thought of themselves as enemies of all dogmas – had a similar effect, as did the concern of an immigrant population with material well-being and mobility. Indeed, the relatively fluid nature of Buenos Aires's social structure made attainable many of their desires for mobility.

Italians continued to play a key role in Buenos Aires's anarchist movement during the first decade of the twentieth century, as it became one of the largest and most active in the world. In a 1902 registry by the Buenos Aires police of 661 anarchist suspects, 389, or 59 per cent, were Italian-born.[16] Moreover, 35 of the 87 suspects listed as 'Argentines' bore Italian surnames. The only other over-represented groups were the Spaniards (particularly from Catalonia and Andalusia) and, later in the decade, Eastern European Jews. In 1909 *The Times* of London maintained that 'the bomb-throwing party consist[ed] of foreigners recruited from Europe' and that most of the 11,000 militant anarchists known to the police in Buenos Aires were 'Italians, Russians, or Catalonians.'[17]

Women rarely appeared in the police registries of anarchists. For example, only a dozen of the 661 individuals in the 1902 police file mentioned above were women. In part this resulted from the simple fact that women were less likely to occupy positions of leadership in the labour movement and to engage in street violence.[18] But it also reflected a gendered view of dangerousness and violence that resulted in prejudicial police behaviour against males, particularly young ones. Comparing information from anarchist periodicals with police reports and arrest records, I noticed that the police often tagged men as 'zealots' or 'dangerous' and harassed or arrested them for actions, such as writing pamphlets and giving speeches, that their female comrades usually got away with. Furthermore, police hesitancy about arresting women obeyed more than a traditional sense of propriety. At least in two instances, a police sheriff counselled against arresting women in street demonstrations because the public might view such actions as abusive, which might serve the propaganda aims of the anarchists.[19]

Nevertheless, women's participation in the anarchist movement was much greater than police registries and arrest records would indicate. Police informers themselves consistently remarked on the large presence of women in anarchist meetings, where they sometime outnumbered their male comrades. And they were more than passive spectators. Women such as Teresa Marchisio, Virginia Bolten, Ramona Ferreyra, and Teresa Caporaleti became some of the most popular orators in the movement, drawing crowds of over a thousand in indoor conferences. Others organized schools, libraries, theatreer and musical troupes, study groups, labour unions, boycotts, and strikes. Women in Buenos Aires published dozens of propaganda pamphlets and what may have been the first anarcho-feminist newspaper in the Western Hemisphere. Indeed, it is difficult to think of any other contemporary social or political movement (other than feminism and organized charity) where women played such a dynamic role. There are several reasons for this high degree of female participation.

One of these reasons is that anarchism contained a gender ideology that was in many respects more liberationist than that of contemporary mainstream feminism.[20] Like socialism, but unlike liberal and Catholic feminism, it started with a materialist critique of power. Women's inferior social condition resulted in part from their economic subordination. Indeed, anarchists were among the first groups to call not simply for equal pay for equal work but also for women's economic independence, which an Italian woman anarchist in Buenos Aires described as 'the source of personal dignity and liberty.'[21] Women's economic dependence, in turn, was seen as part and parcel of an exploitative system that usurped the surplus value of the majority's labour for the benefit of a minority.[22] This capitalist exploitation, in turn and at a more primary level, rested not on natural individual inequalities (including sexual) but on organized brute force. Laws, religion, and bourgeois morality could barely conceal this primordial fact. Such an unjust and unnatural system could only be maintained through the violence (actual or implicit) of the state and its forces of repression, the army and the police.

Anarchists thus disdained both Catholic feminism's claims of female spiritual superiority and liberal feminism's demands for politico-legal equality. The former was pure mystification; the latter insufficient and immoral, in so far as it simply claimed a share in an unjust system rather than its destruction. Anarchists' aims were more apocalyptic. Libertarian writer Soledad Gustavo phrased it this way in an 1896 pamphlet addressed to women workers: 'The society that has condemned us to be flesh for pleasure, to be indispensable fixtures, to be a hygienic necessity, to be an exploitable thing, is our enemy and as such we should combat it and procure its total and speedy ruin.'[23]

At the same time that anarchists called for women's economic independence, they had a less solemn view of women's work than their ideological competitors. They ridiculed both the original Christian notion of female labour as god's punishment and the Church's revised view of it as 'sacred.' The secular version of the latter view, held by most political groups from conservatives to socialists, received equal scorn. In an 1895 pamphlet addressed to schoolgirls, the Italian-born anarchist Ana María Mozzoni wrote: 'Work is neither a sacrament nor a duty, as they taught you in the stupid school dogma, but simply a necessity that should be constrained within those limits. You will realize that the woman condemned to agitate herself like a gadget all her life, in manual labor to relieve man from even thinking about the small concerns of practical everyday life, is defrauded of four-fifths of her existence. She becomes a eunuch of the mind, turned into such for the splendor and pleasure of her sultan.'[24] Similarly, anarchism's view of technology was less sanguine than that of most other contemporary ideologies. In another pamphlet Mozzoni reminded the 'daughters of the people' that machines had added nothing but toil and trouble for them, enriching only those who speculated with their labour.[25]

Anarchists' rejection of capitalism often sprang from deeper philosophical roots that had feminist implications even if they were not explicitly stated. Their attitude toward social Darwinism is a case in point. Although anarchists accepted the concept of evolution and even championed it as epitomizing the triumph of modern science over obscurantism, they challenged the Darwinist-Spencerian notion of survival of the fittest. In the famous book *Mutual Aid: A Factor in Evolution* (1902), Peter Kropotkin, the principal anarchist ideologue of the late nineteenth century, accepted that struggle was common to all species, but argued that it took the form of a common effort against unfavourable natural conditions rather than competition among members of the same species. Mutual aid and cooperation rather than competition against one another were the key to survival. This emphasis on mutual protection, solidarity, and sociability was clearly more in tune with a feminist ethos than a world view – attacked as phallocentric by many – that exalted individual competition and clashing.

Long before Kropotkin wrote about mutual aid, another famous Russian anarchist, Michael Bakunin, had exclaimed that 'social solidarity is the first human law; freedom is the second law.' Anarchists' gender ideology had as much to do with the second law as with the first. Their insistence on the need to end women's economic dependence reflected, perhaps more than an economic issue, their idealization of individual autonomy in general. Indeed, within libertarian currents individualists seem to have been the most ardent supporters of women's emancipation.[26] The individualist newspaper *Germinal*, for example, defended feminism from the attacks of an Italian seamstress who, in the pro-organization newspaper *L'Avvenire*, dismissed it as an invention of 'elegant little women' (6 March 1898). *Germinal* maintained that feminism emerged out of 'a scientific revolution' (which proved the intellectual equality of the sexes) and from a principle of libertarian justice that vindicated woman's individuality. This individuality had been destroyed by religion, particularly Christianity, which had condemned woman as 'an impure being, an injurious animal, a creature of Satan.' But it had also been denied by the majority of socialists and pseudo-anarchists who wanted her at home, precisely the place where her subjugation was fourfold (economic, paternal, marital, and filial).

Anarchism rejected capitalism, then, not only because it viewed it as inimical to social equality, but also because it saw it as a form of domination detrimental to individual freedom. Its basic tenet regarded hierarchical authority – be it the state, the church, the economic elite, or patriarchy – as unnecessary and deleterious to the maximization of human potential.[27] In this respect, anarchists maintained, the factory system exploited woman, the nation-state drafted her sons to die in wars that enriched the owners of the factories, the law gave her children as property to her husband and made her his slave, religion aimed to keep her ignorant and passive, and morality fettered her sexuality. In 1895 Ana María Mozzoni phrased this notion in more personal terms when she warned young women: 'You will find that the priest who damns you is a man; that the legislator who oppresses you is a man, that the husband who reduces you to an *object* is a man; that the libertine who harasses you is a man; that the capitalist who enriches himself with your ill-paid work and the speculator who calmly pockets the price of your body, are men.'[28]

The last phrase brought attention to another of the evils that, according to anarchists, capitalist society visited upon women: prostitution. Some individualist anarchists viewed condemnations of prostitution as strait-laced and pharisaical, as behaviour more becoming priests and sententious matrons than people who thought of themselves as free-thinkers. Others went as far as to view prostitution, insofar as it was not forced on women by need, as an expression of female biological and economic emancipation.[29] Most, however, simply blamed prostitution on social poverty, need, and exploitation rather than viewing it as either a personal sin or a morally neutral choice. Although expressed in fustian language and revolutionary manifestos, this view of prostitutes as victims reflected in fact the common wisdom of the period, shared by the left, centre, and even much of the right of the ideological spectrum.

Much more iconoclastic was the anarchists' assertion that marriage too was a form of prostitution. Women's lack of economic independence, in this view, turned matrimony into a commercial exchange of sexual and domestic services for pecuniary support. The arrival of children deepened women's dependency, forcing them to put up with boredom and abuse because they could not leave and support the children by themselves. Wives became 'prostitutes,' slaves of their husbands even as these were in turn slaves of their bosses. Marriage was thus an authoritarian institution that replicated at a domestic level the domination and inequity that characterized class relations in the public sphere. Poverty and the insecurity inherent to a market economy added pressure on both partners. Lack of education made women less appealing as intellectual companions. Religion and bourgeois morality inhibited their sexuality and made it more difficult to escape a forced cohabitation in which spouses made their lives mutually miserable. Marriage led then, according to anarcho-feminist Carmen Lareva writing in 1896, to the evils it aimed to prevent: 'alienation, adultery, venereal disease, conjugal onanism, fraud and aberrations in coitus' (apparently, fake orgasms and sodomy).[30]

An Episode of Love

The ultimate solution to this sad state of affairs lay in 'Anarchy,' the future society which most libertarians saw not as a far-away utopia but as an imminent reality that would dawn right after the 'social revolution.' In the eyes of anarcho-communists, who as we saw formed the bulk of the movement in Argentina, this future society would allocate resources according to need, making everyone – including women and children – economically independent. This would turn marriage from a form of prostitution and an authoritarian bond into a free union of equals.

Some tried to create this utopia before the explosion of the social revolution. In 1890 a group of mostly Italian immigrants founded an anarcho-communist commune in southern Brazil, Colonia Cecilia. Soon after, Juan Rossi, one of its founders, wrote a pamphlet titled 'An Episode of Love' that was published in Buenos Aires by *La Questione Sociale*, an association of Italian anarchists. In it, Rossi told the titillating story of his amorous affair with the wife of an Italian comrade who 'placed respect for his companion's liberty above his own passions.' Free love was not 'an animalistic vulgarity but the highest and most beautiful expression of affective life.'[31] Eleda, the wife, was not an amoral nymphomaniac but an intelligent proletarian who had been personally improved by the anarchist ideal. She was thus 'gentle and positive rather than vulgar or romantic' (bourgeois traits). In a questionnaire Rossi sent to the couple for a 'psychological analysis,' the husband admitted to jealousy and Eleda to guilt. But both considered these feelings the unfortunate result of atavistic prejudices and felt secure in their love. They thought that free love fostered a higher anarchist morality not based on conformity and proprietary rights but on human solidarity and liberty, and that it was thus the way of the future.

'Free love,' however, was a rather polysemous term and most libertarians interpreted it in less libertine ways. Many anarchist women feared that unhindered plurisexuality would unshackle male appetites and wreck the family. These concerns must have been common enough, because the editors of an anarcho-feminist newspaper felt the need to address them in the front page of the first issue of their publication.[32] After enumerating the evils of marriage in a capitalist society, they went on to assure their working-class readers that free love did not mean the destruction of the family but the reconstruction of it on the basis of mutual respect and freedom. Freedom, of course, opened up the opportunity for multiple and simultaneous physical or emotional relations. But not everyone had to choose this path.

In contemporaneous pamphlets, Ana María Mozzoni made similar arguments.[33] Betraying the anarchist idealization of natural forces, she maintained that if humans were intrinsically fickle and promiscuous, no dose of social or political restriction could change that fact. For centuries, legal codes, religious commandments, and the canons of polite society had done more to enslave people than to prevent adultery. So if, as she thought, there was a natural tendency to monogamy in humans – a notion that fitted with the anarchist ideal of solidarity – freedom rather than religious and legal restrictions was the most likely incentive to healthy and durable relationships. At any rate, Mozzoni asserted that 'two beings who love each other do not need permission from a third to go to bed.' By the same token, if that love ended they did not require anyone's approval to leave each other. To most anarchists then *amor libre* meant a natural, and normally monogamous, union that was based on mutual consent and required no sanction from state, church, or society.

The Public and the Personal: Ideology and Front-Line Activism

In general, the most distinguishing feature of anarchism's gender ideology was its insistence in linking the public and the personal, in identifying economic and cultural forms of oppression. This characteristic was expressed in a series of tracts published by *La Questione Sociale* in the late nineteenth century that reminded women in the front page: 'You are slaves both in social and private life. If you are a proletarian, you have two tyrants: the man and the boss. If bourgeois, the only sovereignty left to you is that of frivolity and coquetry.' Anarchists included thus a class and economic analysis that was normally absent from mainstream feminism. At the same time, they demonstrated a sensitivity to domestic power relations that eluded the economic determinism of socialists, syndicalists, and Marxists in general. Indeed, syndicalists often chided anarchists for abandoning the principles of dialectic materialism and degenerating into a culturalist analysis that resembled that of bohemians and the liberal intelligentsia.[34]

Anarchism's attraction for women was based not only on its ideological discourse but also on its practices and the fact that it was more inclusive than most other contemporary movements or organizations. Political parties, including the socialist one, addressed the interests of voters, and women obtained the suffrage in Argentina only in 1947. Besides, as foreigners (and naturalization rates in Argentina were lower than 2 per cent), not even the husbands of Italian immigrant women could vote, diminishing the possibility of indirect involvement through other family members. Mainstream liberal feminism was geared toward the middle class and not likely to welcome – or appeal to – immigrant working-class women. Syndicalism, with its emphasis on class struggle and proletarian autonomy, could appeal to them as workers. But its militant ouvrierisme was rather androcentric and unlikely to appeal to them as women.[35] Anarchism, by contrast, incorporated both a labour component and a broader humanistic vision that went beyond the struggle between wage labour and capital.

Even within the labour movement, the anarchists were able to attract more female workers than the socialists, syndicalists, or Catholics because they enjoyed a dominant position in it at least until the outbreak of the First World War. Of the 142 trade unions in Buenos Aires registered by the police in 1907, 66 were federated into the anarchist FORA (Federación Obrera Regional Argentina); 52 into the socialist UGT (Union General de Trabajadores); and 24 were independent, though mostly syndicalist. The unions federated into the FORA accounted for two-thirds of the 212,000 members, with the socialists and syndicalists splitting the remaining third.[36] Moreover, the FORA included at least ten trade unions – such as those of the seamstresses, shoe-binders, textile workers, and shirtmakers – whose membership was mostly female.

Although individual members of labour unions associated with a federation were theoretically free to choose their own political positions, the influence of both the leadership and the rank and file tended to push them toward the ideology of the federation. In this respect, the dominant position of the FORA gave anarchists an edge. Perhaps because they were more committed, or fanatic, anarchists were also more likely to propagandize in labour unions associated with competing ideological groups than vice versa. Police informers often referred to anarchist 'rabble-rousers' who infiltrated unions affiliated with the UGT to disrupt meetings, denounce socialist passivity, and try to convince members to switch to the FORA. But they never mentioned socialists doing the same.

In its fifth annual congress (1905) the FORA voted to make anarcho-communism, the most radical form of the ideology and the most concerned with gender egalitarianism, its official 'philosophy.' Indeed, the preceding article in the manifesto called for women's equality and urged the associated unions to intensify their propaganda efforts among them.[37] The FORA did not see this, however, as a question of feminism (which it rejected as particularist) but as 'a purely human, purely social, question.' Women's economic independence imposed itself as a requirement for them to join men in the struggle for human emancipation. And gender equality appeared as part and parcel of the anarchist notion of social justice and personal freedom rather than as a separate issue.

Labour strikes provided an optimum medium to spread the revolutionary creed among women. The anarchist Virginia Bolten had led in 1889 what was perhaps the first strike by women in the country – that of the dressmakers in Rosario, a city that became known as the 'Argentine Barcelona' because of the militancy of its workers. During the next two decades anarchist men and women played a key role in scores of labour strikes in mostly female trades. Women's involvement was not always restricted to the shop. On 21 November 1902 an English newspaper in Buenos Aires (*The Standard*) observed that the general strike had taken revolutionary characteristics and that 'the strikers wander about the town armed with sticks and shouting "viva la anarquia" – an occupation, as regards the yells, in which they are assisted by their women folk!' The frequent closing by police of labour-union locales during general strikes turned tenement houses into meeting places and narrowed the division between public and domestic spheres, at least temporarily.

Anarchists also fomented strikes that were related to consumption rather than production and that thus incorporated women not involved in the paid labour force or working at home through contracting. Boycotts formed a more common, and effective, weapon in the libertarian arsenal than the proverbial dynamite. Some of the boycotts, such as those on tobacco and beer manufacturers, relied mostly on the consuming behaviour of men. But others, such as those on food and clothing companies, depended on women's commitment.

Rent strikes were another consumer-related activity supported by anarchists that served to involve women in collective action. Again, this was particularly so for those who worked inside their own homes in domestic tasks, doing laundry, ironing, and sewing for pay, or tending small family stores. Since the mid-1890s at least, libertarian newspapers had supported such actions and sporadic tenant leagues were formed. In its 1902 congress, the anarchist labour federation called for an 'energetic agitation to obtain the lowering of rents until we get their complete abolition.'[38] This ambitious communist goal was, of course, never reached. Still, tenant leagues became more numerous and active, and in 1907 a huge, anarchist-led rent strike broke out.[39] It eventually affected 2000 tenements and over 120,000 tenants, or four-fifths of the tenement buildings in the city and one-tenth of its population.[40]

Women played varied and important roles in the strike. An Italian laundress, Josefina Rinaldi, became the treasurer of the Central Strike Committee. Obdulia Mable became the president of a neighbourhood subcommittee. Activists Juana Rouco and Maria Collazo, who had been organizing tenant leagues for the past two years, spoke at various rallies.

On 27 October they led a column of hundreds of women holding aloft the red banners of the Centro Feminista Anarquista, protesting the police killing of Miguel Pepe, an eighteen-year-old Italian striker. In an act of mockery before the situation turned tragic, girls and boys symbolically swept away the landlords during 'broom parades' through the streets of the Italian neighbourhood of La Boca.[41] When striking tenants were evicted during working hours, swarms of women and children would move the furniture back the minute the police left.[42] Juana Rouco, who was seventeen years old at the time, still remembered fifty years later 'this great revolutionary moment' and how women battled police with brooms and by throwing boiling water from second-floor porches.[43] The practice became an anarchist slogan *Desalojos? Agua hirviendo!* (Evictions? Boiling water!) and common enough that just the threat of it could accomplish results.[44] In a letter to the anarchist daily *La Protesta* (2 October 1907), a striker recounted how the landlord and superintendent of the tenement gave up their attempts to collect the rents by force and ran away when the women of the building promised them 'a hot shower.'

What allowed anarchists to lead the rent strike with little opposition from competing ideological groups was their belief in spontaneous popular 'direct action' outside the bounds of organizations. The syndicalists, while sympathetic, were too tied, both institutionally and ideologically, to the trade union to act in a movement that took place not only outside organized labour but also outside the realm of production. Their notion of direct action did not go beyond labour strikes or sabotage in factories. The socialists, while also sympathetic – as were most people except real estate owners – were too tied to the party, rejected the concept of direct action, and shared with the syndicalists the orthodox Marxist disdain for a movement of consumers rather than proletarians.[45]

Anarchists, by contrast, had a broader vision (or 'fuzzier,' according to their detractors) that reached out beyond 'producers' and the organized working class to 'oppressed' people in general. It is telling that while socialists and syndicalists often titled their newspapers 'the worker' or 'the proletariat,' anarchists preferred more inclusive terms: *El Pueblo, El Perseguido, El Oprimido, Los Desheredados, El Rebelde, L'Agitatore, La Nueva Humanidad, La Protesta Humana*. In her 1895 pamphlet directed 'to the daughters of the people,' Ana María Mozzoni expressed this inclusiveness: 'Anarchy defends the cause of all the oppressed, and because of this, and in a special way, it defends your cause, oh! women, doubly oppressed by present society in both the social and private spheres.'

Mozzoni's pamphlet was part of a wider propaganda effort directed toward women. During the last five years of the nineteenth century the Italian immigrant newspaper *La Questione Sociale* published a series of five pamphlets, all but one written by women, dealing with 'women's economic, political, and religious emancipation' and distributed them gratis. In 1900 another Italian anarchist newspaper in Buenos Aires, *L'Avvenire*, published two pamphlets partly addressed to women: *Educazione anarchica, Il nostro dovere* and, in conjunction with the bakers' union, *Lo que quieren los anarquistas / La familia*. That same year Pietro Gori published a talk he had given at a Buenos Aires theatre, *La Donna e la Famiglia*. Four years earlier a group of anarcho-feminists had published *La Voz de la Mujer, periodico comunista-anarquico*.[46] In the first issue, 8 January 1896, they expressed their general purpose: 'Weary of asking and begging, of being the toy, the object of pleasure of our infamous exploiters or vile husbands, we have decided to raise our voice in the social concert and demand, demand we say, our share of pleasures in the banquet of life. The publication of pamphlets and newspaper articles directed to women continued unabated at least during the first decade of the twentieth century.

Anarchists employed a series of propaganda methods to reach women besides the written word, relying on a plethora of 'circles,' often linked to, but independent of, organized labour. In a sense these circles represented the quintessential libertarian association: small, locally based, decentralized, non-hierarchical, and unstructured. They met in cafes and bars, apartments, the offices of anarchist newspapers, or union halls, or on certain street corners that would change when police harassment reached a higher pitch than normal. Their membership ranged from half a dozen to fifty. With the help of an informant, a newspaper reporter writing a series of investigative articles on the anarchist movement in Buenos Aires in 1901 found fifty circles and admitted that there were probably many more.[47] Many were clearly Italian: Ne dio ne patrone, Rivendicatori, L'Avvenire, La nuova civiltà, and Occhi aperti. The nationality of others was undefined, but their apology for violence was not: Bomba Pallás (after the action of Paulino Pallás, who hurled two bombs against the retinue of a general in Barcelona in 1893), Caserio (the Italian anarchist who stabbed the French president a year later), Angiolillo (a compatriot of Caserio who assassinated the Spanish prime minister in 1897), Dinamitardo, La violencia contra la violencia, and La venganza será terrible. These normally secretive groups, with conspiratorial pretensions, were unlikely to attract women. The majority, however, had more serene aims and names (L'Aurora [dawn], Estudiosos, Luz y vida, Libertad y amor, La emancipación humana, El arte por la vida). They attracted a good number of women, and some were founded by them: Feminista, Luisa Michel (the famous French anarchist known as 'the red virgin'),[48] Las ácratas (a synonym for anarchist).

Besides meeting among themselves, these circles developed a series of activities for the general public meant to spread 'the Ideal.' Some gifted orators, including women such as Virginia Bolten, María Collazo, and Ramona Ferreyra, could 'pack the house' by themselves. But normally debates attracted larger crowds, and anarchists began to organize them at least since the early 1890s, consistently inviting both *compañeros* and *compañeras*. They functioned as a sort of Ciceronian cock fight, with speakers for each side trying to score rhetorical points, incite the vociferous crowd, and score a kill. The common opponents were 'legalitarian' socialists rather than the anarchists' true 'enemies' (conservatives, Catholics, government and church officials, capitalists), though it is difficult to tell if this was so because they were not invited or because they would not come. In true libertarian fashion, anyone could speak and the resulting cacophony added to the spectacle. Whether the organizers were aware of it or not, part of the appeal of the debates lay in the histrionics and their entertainment value. The reports from police informers show that these events drew crowds ranging from one hundred and fifty to twelve hundred, with an average of about three hundred. This significantly surpassed the attendance at trade-union meetings, which, with the exception of special occasions such as a strike vote at a large union, normally ranged between forty and eighty.

Veladas (social evenings) drew in even larger crowds and a larger feminine component. Like the debates, these revolutionary soirées dated back to the early 1890s. They originally consisted of a conference and a play, but with time they developed a regular, and more successful, formula. The evening began around 7 to 8 p.m. with the members of a libertarian music society playing *Los hijos del pueblo* (the children of the people), the International, and other anarchist anthems, with the audience, numbering about 400, singing along. This was followed by one or two short comic plays, usually written by local anarchist workers and performed by libertarian theatre societies; a conference on a revolutionary theme ('free love,' being one of the most popular ones), poetry declamation, a longer drama, and a 'family dance' that lasted until 4 a.m.

For various reasons, gender issues appeared often in the plays. Because, unlike in commercial theatre, plays were rarely repeated, just the sheer number of them made the odds of this happening rather high. In 1908 alone, anarchist theatre troupes staged 85 different plays, only 19 of which had more than one presentation.[49] The fact that romantic relations provided a facile plot for amateur playwrights further increased the odds of plays dealing with gender issues. Moreover, sexual melodrama and humour could serve to couch an ideological message in a form that increased its appeal to the public.

Gender issues in the plays, however, consistently appeared linked to issues of socio-economic justice. This reflected the key characteristic of anarchism's gender ideology discussed before: its insistence on connecting the personal and the political (in the broader sense of power relations). The one-act drama *La institución sacrosanta*, by a local anarchist with the nom de plume Pierre Quiroule, offers an example. As the title suggests, it critiques and mocks marriage as an institution. Quirole provides plenty of clues to the leading man's ideology: his apartment is full of books and newspapers; he is independent but solidary; he will not bow to rank but will not lord over others; his love is honest, straightforward, devoid of guile and sentimentality; and just in case some doubts remained, the author names him 'Anarco.' The husband of Honorata, the leading lady, is the petty bourgeois antithesis of Anarco. Instead of being independent but respectful of others, he is simply self-centred and unconcerned – a contrast that serves to highlight the difference between anarchist and liberal individualism. Instead of a fulfilling and egalitarian relationship, his marriage is arid and denigrating. Yet Honorata cannot bring herself to abandon him for Anarco. She feels a sense of marital duty and fears public scandal. Anarco tries to liberate her from these repressive mores. But, as her name indicates, the prejudice of 'honour' is too ingrained in her. The hope apparently lies in the future generation: Honorata's little daughter is named Proleta. The second act of the play involves the attempt of a capitalist (suitably named 'Alcon' [a bird of prey]) to seduce and coerce Honorata, who is forced to give in to his advances out of economic necessity. The unhappy ending thus serves to highlight the link between class and sexual oppression and to kindle the public's indignation and wrath.

The anarchist *veladas* had their Sunday afternoon counterpart in the *asado libertario*. These 'libertarian barbecues' attracted even larger crowds than the soirées because of the lack of space constraints. Advertised as 'family picnics,' they also drew in a large number of women. Besides the juicy Argentine beef, the attractions included games, music and dancing, singing of revolutionary tunes, 'humorous lotteries,' and vinous conviviality. The latter, however, was at times an issue of contention. Some saw alcohol as a curse on the working-class family. They argued that the oppressed should hold higher standards of morality than their oppressors because of their historical obligation to bring about the anarchist utopia. They thus favoured 'dry' picnics. The majority saw this as 'bourgeois moralizing' and as an infringement on personal liberty, so wine continued to flow freely at the libertarian picnics.

Although other working-class groups also organized picnics and soirées, none reached the anarchists' level of activity. The reports of police informers show that of the thirty-two theatre performances held by working-class groups in 1905, two were staged by independent labour unions, ten by socialists, and twenty by anarchists. By 1908 both the number and the gap had increased. Of the fifty-three theatre perform-ances that year, five were staged by socialists, five by independent unions, two by syndicalists, and forty-one by anarchists.[50] This again demon-strates that, compared to other left-wing movements, anarchism repre-sented a broad cultural – or countercultural – phenomenon that transcended formal and labour politics.

The fact that these performances attracted many more women than did union or political-party meetings gave anarchists an advantage in reaching them. This was particularly important because women's lit-eracy rates, although relatively high, were lower than men's. In 1914, for example, 67 per cent of the Italian men in Argentina but only 52 per cent of the women knew how to read and write. The gap was even wider among the other two national groups with high participation in the anarchist movement, Spaniards (79 per cent for males, 55 per cent for females) and Russians (68 and 48 per cent).[51] Of course, pamphlets and newspapers could be, and were, read to people who could not do it themselves. But these performances, with their emphasis on songs, plays, and speeches, reached those women whom the written word could not reach directly.

To spread their ideology among the young, anarchist circles founded a series of 'free' schools and 'popular' libraries. The first of these ap-peared in the late nineteenth century in the Italian enclave of La Boca. In a 1901 article an Argentine journalist described one of these schools. It was in a humble four-room house decorated with portraits of anarchist terrorists (Bresci, Angiolillo, Pini, and Ravachol). It had seventy students of both sexes. The director was a local bookstore owner, and the instruc-tors a professional teacher, a clerk, a tanner, and a barber. They did not teach about the Argentine constitution and history because they claimed that 'history is idolatry and the constitution the foundation of authority.' They taught instead reading, writing, and arithmetic and instilled in the children 'a hatred of power, the notion of social destruction, and the duty to combat all types of government with steel and fire.'[52]

Anarchists made young girls a special target of their propaganda through means other than schools. In 1895, for example, Ana María Mozzoni addressed a pamphlet 'to the girls who study' (*A las muchachas que estudian*) because 'your mothers, divided between the confessor, the pots, fashion, and the *husband who God has given them*, relics of an era that heads toward its twilight, could not understand me.' These relics of a decadent age included the bourgeois notion of an educated and success-ful woman as one who could speak and act with refinement, dress elegantly, play the piano, dance, embroider, and marry a man who could provide her a comfortable life. Despite its apparent appeal, Mozzoni warned her young readers, this life led to an empty existence without ideals, economic independence, and emotional or intellectual fulfil-ment. Young women should reject the 'authoritarian bond of marriage' and live with whomever they wished and only as long as they wanted to.

There is evidence that these propaganda efforts achieved some re-sults. When the police killed an eighteen-year-old Italian boy during the rent strike of 1907, the protest march organized by the anarchist labour federation for his funeral was headed by a column of a thou-sand women, most of them, according to a contemporary observer, 'between the ages of fifteen and twenty.'[53] One of the fiercest anarchist activists during this strike was Juana Rouco, who despite being only seventeen was considered dangerous enough to be expelled from the country. Police informers remarked on the high number of young girls in anarchist soirées and how they often sold pamphlets about 'free love' during the intermission.

Young women not only distributed pamphlets during these meetings but also spoke with amazing verve and self-assurance. On 15 July 1905, for example, Delia Barrozo, a thirteen-year-old girl, fiercely defended women's emancipation in front of 700 people at a conference organized by the carpenters' union. A week later a police informer sent her photo-graph to the division of investigations with the following observations: 'A psychological study is not needed to assert that Barrozo's precocity, and the ardent zeal she has devoted to the study of the idea [anarchism] will make her a primordial factor in the propagation of her creed. She has an uncommon facility of diction, infusing her declamations with so much

color that from the first words she inoculates the audience with a hyp-
notic suggestion, as demonstrated by the ovations they bestow on the
"little Michel," as she is commonly known' (after French anarchist Louise
Michel).[54] The principal anarchist intellectuals flocked to the girl's home,
the informer continued, lured by her fame and aura and by the knowledge that her approval would multiply the value of their literary produc-
tions. She in turn chastised them for their passivity, because 'a real
anarchist should not allow himself to be dragged into jail docilely but
should push a knife into his captor's body instead.'

Not all women were as belligerent as 'little Michel,' and the anarchists'
insistence that violence from above should be repelled with violence
from below surely dismayed many of them. Yet as I explained before, the
anarchist movement in Argentina did not experience the spree of terrorism that afflicted its European counterparts and its use of violence was
mostly rhetorical. Nonetheless, anarchists retained an aura of icono-
clasm and extremism that probably turned away politically progressive
immigrant women with aspirations to middle-class respectability and
drove them toward socialist groups. But it was precisely that aura that
lured their younger and more rebellious sisters. And the same was true
of the anarchist radical sexual discourse.[55]

In terms of Italian women's labour and radical activism, certain methodological limitations allow us to offer only tentative answers to the
inquiries posed by Donna Gabaccia and Franca Iacovetta in the article
cited at the beginning of this chapter. As I explained before, militant
women were much less likely to be arrested by the police than their male
companions. While this was lucky for them, it represents a problem for
historians because much of the personal information on militants other
than the top leaders comes from the state's repression apparatuses. I
have been able to cull hundreds of women's names from newspapers
and other sources, but have little information on them other than the
fact they militated in the anarchist movement. This limited information
does suggest that Spanish women were more active in the movement
than their Italian counterparts, something that resembles the situation
in the United States between Jewish and Italian women but that also
undermines the notion that this gap resulted from a particularly patriarchal form of 'Latin' culture.[56] At the same time, the situation in Buenos
Aires supports Gabaccia's and Iacovetta's hypothesis that Italian men's
relative prominence in the labour and radical movements would increase the participation and activism of their female compatriots.

This fuller activism may also explain the difference between the discourse of Italian women anarchists in Buenos Aires and that of their compatriots in North America as discussed in this volume by Caroline Waldron Merithew and by Robert Ventresca and Franca Iacovetta. In the United States, Merithew – and to a lesser degree Ventresca and Iacovetta – found an emphasis on 'anarchist motherhood,' the notion that the primary role of revolutionary women was to educate the next generation and instil in them libertarian principles. This too was a common idea among anarchist women in Argentina and one that they shared, with different goals of course, with most mainstream feminists in that country. Yet many other Italian anarchist women took a position similar to that of Emma Goldman, Voltairine de Cleyre, and other non-Italian ideologues in the U.S. and stressed economic and sexual liberation and personal autonomy rather than maternity. It seems thus that Italians' greater weight in the labour and anarchist movement of Argentina, when compared to that of the U.S., positioned them over a wider discursive spectrum that ran from the 'anarchist motherhood' notion of most working women and the grass roots to the anti-maternalist positions of radical individualists.

Of course, most Italian women in Buenos Aires (or most men of any nationality for that matter) never became devotees of 'free love' and libertarian militants. Yet thousands of them were induced to take collective action by anarchist activism in the labour movement and beyond. More than 50,000 women participated in the anarchist-led rent strike of 1907. A similar number did so in the general strike of 1909. Thousands marched in the May Day manifestations and attended the anarchist meetings, plays, dances, picnics, schools, and libraries. An unknown number read their newspapers and pamphlets. The anarcho-feminist newspaper *La Voz de la Mujer* printed 3000 issues in 1896, when there was nothing similar in the New World, nor probably in the Old. In terms of gender discourse, anarchism was arguably more liberationist than mainstream feminism. In terms of practice, their emphasis on loosely structured, spontaneous, and neighbourhood-oriented movements based on both work- and household-related issues was particularly in tune with women's inclinations and interests. Donna Gabaccia has found that these community-based and spontaneous forms of protest were the most common among women immigrants in the United States.[57] The same was true of true about their counterparts in Argentina, but there and in most cases the anarchist presence was never not far away.

NOTES

1 'Women, Work, and Protest in the Italian Diaspora: An International Research Agenda,' *Labour / Le Travail* 42 (Fall, 1998): 176.
2 This, regarding host-society institutions and adaptation in general, is part of the main thesis in Samuel L. Baily's seminal comparative study *Immigrants in the Lands of Promise: Italians in Buenos Aires and New York City, 1870–1914* (Ithaca: Cornell University Press, 1999).
3 Dardo Cúneo, *El periodismo de la disidencia social, 1858–1900* (Buenos Aires: Centro Editor de America Latina, 1994), 25. Gonzalo Zaragoza, *Anarquismo Argentino, 1876–1902* (Madrid: Ediciones de la Torre, 1996), 72.
4 Nunzio Pernicone, *Italian Anarchism, 1864–1892* (Princeton: Princeton University Press, 1993), 31. Murray Bookchin, *The Spanish Anarchists: The Heroic Years, 1868–1936* (New York: Free Life Editions, 1977), 12–15.
5 The Italian federation of the IWA was founded in August 1872 with 21 sections, which expanded to 155, and 32,000 members, two years later; see Pernicone, *Italian Anarchism*, 58, 72, 75. The Federación Regional Española was founded in June 1870 with 150 sections (and 40,000 members), which expanded to 320 four years later. George R. Esenwein, *Anarchist Ideology and the Working-Class Movement in Spain, 1868–1898* (Berkeley: University of California Press, 1989), 18, 44; Temma Kaplan, *Anarchists of Andalusia, 1868–1903* (Princeton: Princeton University Press, 1977), 75.
6 The term 'libertarian' is used in this chapter, as it was used at the time, as a synonym of anarchist.
7 Héctor A. Palacios, *Historia del movimiento obrero argentino*, tomo I (Buenos Aires, 1992), 46. For the Italian authorities' views on their nationals' activities in the Argentine anarchist movement see José Luis Moreno, 'A proposito de los anarquistas italianos en la Argentina, 1880–1920,' *Cuadernos de Historia Regional* (Lujan, Argentina) 2 (December 1985): 42–63, and Maria R. Ostuni, 'Inmigración política italiana y movimiento obrero Argentino, 1879–1902,' in Fernando Devoto and Gianfausto Rosoli, eds., *La inmigración italiana en la Argentina* (Buenos Aires: Editorial Biblos, 1985), 105–26. Both works are based on the same Italian diplomatic documents.
8 Gonzalo Zaragoza, 'Errico Malatesta y el anarquismo argentino,' *Historiografía y Bibliografía Americanista* 16, 3 (December 1972): 401–24.
9 For the influence of Malatesta on the anarchist movement in Italy and among Italians in the United States, see chapter 9 by Robert Ventresca and Franca Iacovetta.
10 Although the police feared a radical outburst and prohibited posting mani-

festos calling for a general strike on this first May Day, the event turned out to be rather tame. Most of the groups supporting it were even more moderate than the socialists. They included republican and Mazzinianist clubs; German, Scandinavian, Belgian, and Italian associations; Italian regional societies such as the Figli del Vesuvio and Unione Calabrese; and even such 'subversive' groups as the Circolo Mandolinisti Italiani, an association of Italian mandolin players. See *La Patria Italiana*, 1 and 2 May 1890, and *L'Operaio Italiano* for the same dates. The weather did not prove propitious, leading an English newspaper in Buenos Aires (*The Standard*) to summarize that the event 'amounted to nothing. Rain is more effective in dispersing crowds than horse, foot, or artillery.'

11 'With all the German socialists who make up the Vorwarts circle, we anarchist who reside here have nothing in common.' *El Perseguido, voz de los explotados* (Buenos Aires), 18 May 1890.

12 Because anarchists rejected national identities and because Italians and Spaniards could be found on both sides of the 'organization' issue, the debate was never phrased in explicit ethnic terms – at least I have not found any instance of this. Yet hints appear occasionally in the working-class press. For example, *Germinal*, a newspaper edited by Spanish immigrants, kept a bitter dispute with the Italian-run *L'Avvenire* in the 1890s. In a specific column (3 July 1898), it ridiculed its adversaries in another newspaper by using the ruse of an imaginary telephone conversation between an anti-organizationist, who spoke in Spanish, and a fatuous 'anarchist Minister of Finance,' who spoke in Italian and was too dense to understand the sarcasm.

13 Malatesta's influence continued for decades. The Italian anarchist periodicals in Buenos Aires *Il Pensiero* (1927) and *Sorgiamo!* (1932) headed every front page with quotes from his writings.

14 A measure of the Italians' influence in Argentine anarchism is given by the fact that the International Institute of Social History holds copies of twenty-five anarchist newspapers published by Italian immigrants in that country.

15 P.A. Geli, 'Pietro Gori, o le vicissitudini del pensiero anarchico nell'Argentina moderna,' *Ventesimo Secolo* 11–12 (1994): 377–89.

16 Archivo de la Policía, Buenos Aires, 'División Investigación, Orden Social, Antecedentes de Anarquistas, 1902, No. 1.'

17 *The Times*, 16 and 17 November 1909, 5, c. 6.

18 Housewives' fear of violence and extremism was often seen as an element that encouraged a speedier accommodation of labour disputes, but it could also have the opposite effect. For example, when after a month-long strike in 1902 by port workers in the Italian neighbourhood of La Boca, the owners attempted to open up the workshops, they found themselves sur-

rounded by women who demanded the closing of the shops again because they feared their husbands and sons would be attacked by intransigent strikers if they returned to work. *El Diario*, 28 January 1902.

19 Archive of the Federal Police in Buenos Aires, Policía de la Capital, División de Investigaciones, Sección Orden Social, Copiador de Notas, 22 January 1905 and 17 March 1907. Another example of harsher treatment of male anarchists by police and judges appears in Robert Ventresca and Franca Iacovetta's chapter in this volume about Virgilia D'Andrea. She spent a few weeks in an Italian jail for the same activities for which her two male comrades served nine months.

20 For mainstream feminism see Francine Masiello, ed., *La mujer y el espacio público: El periodismo femenino en la Argentina del siglo XIX* (Buenos Aires: Feminaria Editora, 1994) and Asunción Lavrin, *Women, Feminism, and Social Change in Argentina, Chile, and Uruguay, 1890–1940* (Lincoln: University of Nebraska Press, 1995); and for women in right-wing movements, see Sandra McGee Deutsch, *Counterrevolution in Argentina, 1900–1932: The Argentine Patriotic League* (Lincoln: University of Nebraska Press, 1986) and *Las Derechas: The Extreme Right in Argentina, Brazil, and Chile, 1890–1939* (Stanford: Stanford University Press, 1999).

21 *A las muchachas que estudian* (Buenos Aires: La Questione Sociale, 1895). The pamphlet appeared anonymously, but it was either a translation from, or the original for, Ana María Mozzoni's *Alle fanciulle che studiano*. The only issue of the Italian version that I have found was published in Paterson, New Jersey (one of the most active centres of Italian anarchism in the diaspora), seven years later.

22 In this respect, anarchists adhered to the Marxist labour theory of value. Most contemporary anarchists considered themselves socialists, though 'libertarian' and 'revolutionary' as opposed to 'authoritarian' and 'legalitarian,' the terms they employed to attack their socialist opponents.

23 Soledad Gustavo, *A las proletarias* (Buenos Aires: La Questione Sociale, 1896), 4.

24 Mozzoni, *A las muchachas que estudian*, 8.

25 Ana María Mozzoni, *A las hijas del pueblo* (Buenos Aires: La Questione Sociale, 1895), 10–11. An edition of this pamphlet was published seven years later by Elo Despertar in Paterson, New Jersey, as *Alle figlie del popolo*.

26 The American individualist anarchist Voltairine de Cleyre expressed that libertarian tenet this way: '[A]ny dependence, any thing which destroys the complete selfhood of the individual, is in the line of slavery.' Paul Avrich, *An American Anarchist: The Life of Voltairine de Cleyre* (Princeton: Princeton University Press, 1978), 161.

27 Anarchist Rodolfo González Pacheco expressed this anti-hierarchical ideal with local colour when he wrote: 'The libertarian sense is horizontal, like the pampas.' Cited in Eva Golluscio de Montoya, 'Círculos anarquistas y circuitos contraculturales en la Argentina de 1900,' *Caravelle* [Toulouse, France] 46 (1986): 49.

28 Mozzoni, *A las muchachas que estudian*, 10.

29 Donna J. Guy, *Sex and Danger in Buenos Aires: Prostitution, Family, and Nation in Argentina* (Lincoln: University of Nebraska Press, 1991), 93.

30 *La Voz de la Mujer*, 8 January 1896.

31 Juan Rossi, *Un episodio de amor en la colonia socialista Cecilia* (Buenos Aires: La Questione Sociale, 1896; originally written 1893), 4.

32 *La Voz de la Mujer*, 8 January 1896.

33 *A las muchachas que estudian* and *A las hijas del pueblo*.

34 See, e.g., *La Acción Socialista, Periódico Sindicalista*, 16 April 1906.

35 Unlike in European countries, where syndicalism sprang out of anarchism and was thus often called anarcho-syndicalism, in Argentina it emerged around 1905 as a split from the Socialist party – largely because, as explained earlier, anarchism there had already embraced labour organization. The syndicalists' preoccupation with labour unions left little room for other issues such as gender equality. The movement's organ *La Acción Socialista, Periódico Sindicalista*, published since 1905, rarely included articles on these issues. Moreover, syndicalism may have appealed less to Italian immigrants in general than did anarchism. For example, *La Acción Socialista* of 1 May 1907 ridiculed anarchists who in a debate against syndicalists made their speeches in Italian or broken Spanish and won the controversy simply because the mob drowned 'the voices of reason' by yelling 'nonsense' in Italian.

36 Policía de la Capital, División de Investigaciones, Sección Orden Social, Copiador de Notas, February–April 1907.

37 Federación Obrera Regional Argentina, *Acuerdos, resoluciones y declaraciones; congresos celebrados desde 1901 a 1906* (Buenos Aires, 1908), 18–19.

38 FORA, *Acuerdos, resoluciones y declaraciones*, 5.

39 Police spies sent reports in October–November 1905, that is, two years before the big strike, about thirteen meetings of striking tenants and of a 'central committee' led by known anarchist figures, including María Collazo and Juana Rouco Buela. Policía de la Capital, División Investigaciones, Sección Orden Social, Reuniones Sociológicas, 1905.

40 Hobart Spalding, *La clase trabajadora argentina: Documentos para su historia, 1890–1912* (Buenos Aires: Editorial Galerna, 1970), 453. James A. Baer, 'Tenant Mobilization and the 1907 Rent Strike in Buenos Aires,' *Americas* 49, 3 (January 1993): 343–68.

41 *Caras y caretas*, 21 September 1907, included in the collection of documents compiled by Juan Suriano as *La huelga de los inquilinos de 1907* (Buenos Aires: Centro Editor de América Latina, 1983), 63.

42 Mabel Bellucci and Cristina Camusso, *La huelga de inquilinos de 1907: El papel de las mujeres anarquistas en la lucha* (Buenos Aires: CICSO, 1987), 65, 71.

43 Juana Rouco Buela, *Historia de un ideal vivido por una mujer* (Buenos Aires: own edition, 1964), 16–17.

44 *La Protesta*, 2 October 1907.

45 The socialist daily *La Vanguardia* (24 November 1907) referred to the 'so-called strike' as 'instinctive, impulsive, incoherent, and disorderly' and led by 'the eternal augurs of the imminent catastrophic explosion' (a clear reference to the anarchists).

46 I found eight issues of this newspaper, dated from 8 January to 14 November 1896, at the UCLA Special Collection Archives, but there may have been three more. The 15 July 1897 issue of *La Protesta Humana* included a list of donation-subscriptions for the 11th issue of *La Voz de la Mujer* and also a letter from its editors dated 1 July that stated: '[A]fter a long absence of five months the paper now disappears, but we will repeat it: Without women's emancipation nothing will be durable, all will be fictitious. As we retire, only one phrase, mixture of impotence and rancor, sprouts from our lips: Long live the emancipation of women! Martyr of sorrow, woman of today, till soon!' Surprisingly, this seminal newspaper is just mentioned in one sentence in Marifran Carlson, *Feminismo! The Woman's Movement in Argentina, From Its Beginnings to Eva Peron* (Chicago: Academy, 1988), 127. For an article on this publication see Maxine Molyneux, 'No God, No Boss, No Husband: Anarchist Feminism in Nineteenth-Century Argentina,' *Latin American Perspectives* 48 (Winter 1986): 119–45.

47 *El Diario*, 8–9 October 1901. The informant told the journalist that the immense majority of anarchists in Buenos Aires were Italians, followed by Spaniards and French, and that he only knew of twenty-five Argentines, twenty Uruguayans, just one Englishman, and four Turks.

48 The French-speaking and Italian women in northern Illinois that Caroline Waldron Merithew studies in chapter 7 of this book had also named their association Luisa Michel. This attests to the internationalism of the movement and to the existence of shared anarcho-feminist icons.

49 Policía de la Capital, División Investigaciones, Sección Orden Social, Reuniones Sociológicas, 1908.

50 Ibid., Reuniones Sociológicas, 1905 and 1908.

51 *Censo Nacional de 1914*, vol. 1, 175.

52 *El Diario*, 8 and 9 October 1901.

53 *El Tiempo,* 24 October 1907.

54 Policía de la Capital, División de Investigaciones, Sección Orden Social, Copiador de Notas, 24 July 1905.

55 Hubert Van den Berg, '"Free Love" in Imperial Germany: Anarchism and Patriarchy, 1870–1918,' *Anarchist Studies* 4, 1 (March 1996): 3–26, argues that in Wilhelmine Germany, because of the anarchists' negative view of female wage labour, their antifeminism, and women's low participation in the movement, the concept of 'free love' ended up strengthening the patriarchal order rather than subverting it. As I have argued, this was not the case in Argentina, in large part because the most ideological wing of the movement, anarcho-communism, prevailed and came to dominate the labour movement. But as syndicalist tendencies gained an upper hand in organized labour after the First World War, concerns with matters outside the workshop and union, including gender issues, seem to have diminished, and women's involvement in wage labour began to be seen as benefiting capitalists at the expense of the male working class.

56 In chapter 8 of this volume, Jennifer Guglielmo demonstrates that Italian working women in the United States intensely engaged in labour activism and that this reflected not simply a process of adaptation to the new environment but also the continuation of pre-migratory practices. She also acknowledges, however, that 'unlike the Jewish women who dominated the rank and file of the industry at the turn of the century, Italian women did not join the New York garment unions en masse until the Great Depression.'

57 Donna Gabaccia, *From the Other Side: Women, Gender, and Immigrant Life in the U.S., 1820–1990* (Bloomington: Indiana University Press, 1994), 80.

Italian women harvesting lemons, Mentone, France, c. 1900.

A formal portrait from Cannes, France, of a wet nurse from Città di Castello, Umbria, Italy, c. 1925.

Woman carrying home bundle of sewing (outwork or homework) on her head, New York City, early 1900s.

Maria Mauro, 309 E 110th Street, New York City, and four children around a table working on feathers. The children are Victoria, Angelina (a neighbour), Frorandi, and Maggie. Two of Maria's boys are also shown.

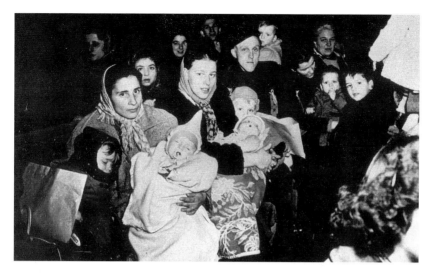

Emigration to a new world: women and children en route to Canada after the Second World War, part of the largest immigration to Canada by Italians in the twentieth century.

Women workers posing in front of the Tip Top Tailors building, Toronto, Ontario, 1936.

Mother and daughter working in Lalli's Grocery Store, corner of Humboldt and Brady Streets (Third Ward), Milwaukee, 1949.

The *Conventillos* strike in Buenos Aires in the Italian quarter of Boca. The strike was also known as the 'strike of the broom' because of the mass participation of women.

A group of women and children in Barre, Vermont, 1915, who had originally emigrated from Piedicavavallo (Prario Tortorelli, Valz), Biella, Italy.

Italian immigrants in Barre, Vermont, 1912, including a group of women, shown displaying socialist newspapers.

Luigi Antonini, Atlantic City, New Jersey, 1937 at the 23rd convention of Local 89 of the ILGWU (International Ladies Garment Workers' Union).

Front page of a 1918 edition (vol. 6, no. 44) of *L'Operaia* (*The Woman Worker*), official publication of Local 25 of the ILGWU, published and edited in New York by the Italian branch of the Ladies Waist and Dressmakers Union.

EDITO A CURA DEL RAMO ITALIANO DELLA LADIES WAIST & DRESSMAKERS UNION LOCAL 25 I. L. G. W. U.

PER L'ORGANIZZAZIONE E LA LOTTA DI CLASSE

— PAL ANTONINI —

VOLUME VI. — No. 44
Saturday, November 2nd, 1918

Abbonamento per un anno 1 dollaro,
" per gli affiliati alla nostra I. L. G. W. U., 50 soldi.

Editorial Office: 16 W. 21 Street.
Telephone: Chelsea 9730

L'UNITY CENTER OSSIA LA NOSTRA UNIVERSITA' DEL LAVORO

LA FELICITA'

Il grande filosofo Spinoza affermò giustamente che la felicità non istà nella ricchezza, o nel potere, o nella soddisfazione delle cupidigie materiali ed ambiziose; la felicità sta invece nelle gioie emozionali ed intellettuali, nell'amore, cioè, nella scienza e nell'arte. Perciò la felicità non è oggettiva, ma tutta soggettiva; e propriamente consiste nel perfezionamento dello spirito ossia della mente e del cuore. La felicità non è il premio della virtù, ma è la virtù stessa elevata a lenimento dell'infelicità, la quale altro non è che il malefico effetto dell'ignoranza delle leggi naturali, onde l'uomo che vuol vivere meno infelice deve conoscere e seguire la natura.

Sono stati gli ingiusti assetti storici della passata e presente Società, che, caselando l'umanità in classi distinte, hanno limitata entro ristretti confini la felicità sociale ed individuale; ma noi possiamo ora affermare che pure il progresso civile in qualche modo abbia attenuata la nostra infelicità e resa possibile un'ombra di felicità sociale. Per questo progresso civile sono sorte le Società di mutuo soccorso, le Cooperative e le Unioni di mestiere, fra le quali si distingue la nostra; che, ben comprendendo come la felicità si forma dei quattro fattori essenziali: Desideri sani, Soddisfazioni lecite, Lavoro ricercatore e Sicurezza del futuro, si è data prima di tutto a procacciare la soddisfazione dei sani desideri del buon lavoratore e della buona lavoratrice; cioè, dopo aver fatto ottenere a chi lavora paghe migliori con più brevi orari di fatica, gli ha aperto l'Università del Lavoro — l'Unity Centre situata al N. 340 East 20.a strada in New York City, nella quale lavoratori e lavoratrici potranno apprendere quanto di più importa alla vita libera, intelligente, cosciente e volente per riscattarsi dalla schiavitù antica e dall'avvilimento attuale degli operai incoscienti.

L'Università operaia (Unity Centre) col 7 ottobre u. s. ha aperto una nuova sessione per istruire ed educare i lavoratori e le lavoratrici dell'Unione ad una nuova vita più attiva, non passiva, e meno infelice, se l'istruzione può dare un po' di quella felicità che è l'effetto della cooperazione di tutti gli affiliati e dell'Unione. E tale felicità sarà ben diversa di quella dei ricchi, ben più serena e più consolante.

I ricchi son felici perchè possono soddisfare i loro desideri ed hanno la certezza del futuro, ma non possono godere il piacere che crea il lavoro libero, cosciente e ristoratore. I borghesi nemmeno, sebben possano avere il lavoro, scende in essi la monotonia del vivere deserto di varietà e di consolanti emozioni. Nei borghesi la loro infelicità accasciante si legge a tratti indelebili

sui loro volti terrei ed anzitempo ingialliti, annoiati e melensi, e si manifesta spesso nella bizzosa inquietudine borghese, la quale li travaglia continuamente. Non così il lavoratore; egli può godere la sua felicità quasi simile a quella dello scienziato che fa una scoperta od a quella dell'artista che riesce a terminare un capolavoro.

Al lavoratore manca per esser felice la certezza del domani; ma l'Unione appunto per procacciarsi tale certezza si agita, freme e sospira e cerca coll'istruzione, coll'Università del Lavoro di dirozzare i suoi affiliati e prepararli all'azione che assicura l'avvenire del nostro benessere.

In alto i cuori! dunque. Approfittiamo dell'Unity Centre e prepariamoci ad essere meno infelici, se la felicità consiste nel perfezionamento dello spirito.

Lo spirito comanda al lavoro ed il lavoro comanda al mondo intero. E' il lavoratore che prepara il futuro buono e cattivo; è dunque necessario che chi lavora sia forte di corpo, illuminato di mente e fermo nei propositi della sua volontà. E perchè divenga tale occorre l'istruzione e l'educazione per le quali ora sorge anche l'Unity Centre. Stolti quindi sono coloro che potendo approfittare vogliono marcire nella loro stoltizia e nella propria ignoranza cagione della loro infelicità.

Affrettiamoci dunque ad inscriverci nel numero dei frequentatori che vanno in cerca di una felicità intellettuale e serena, che nessuno ci potrà distruggere e che conforterà sempre la nostra fatica.

Accorriamo all'Università del Lavoro e non perdiamo un sol punto del suo programma che svolgerà quest'anno e che è così concepito:

— Igiene, nozioni per conservare e ritvigorire la salute fonte di piaceri insaziabili;

— Arte del dire — lezioni di lingua inglese parlata e scritta con correttezza ed efficacia, date da valenti ed esperti insegnanti.

— Sapere è potere — Nozioni di scienze fisiche e positive necessarie alla vita per via di esperimenti;

— La musica è un sollievo della fatica — ed anche infonde coraggio nella lotta della vita. Settimanalmente si eseguiranno canti con accompagnamento di piano forte sotto la direzione di esperto maestro.

— Lettura e drammatica — per meglio far conoscere la vita attraverso la parola dei grandi uomini.

— Sociologia — per conoscere i problemi del lavoro;

— Libreria dell'Unione infine fondata colle cooperazione e colle donazioni affinchè tutti i nostri soci ne approfittino nei momenti di riposo.

L'OPERAIA

Angela Bambace and her mother.

Luigi Antonini at a 'Local 89' installation.

Paternità e maternità *fu Stefano e di Sambasia Nicoletti*

Luogo e data di nascita *Sulmona (Aquila) 12-2-1888*

Professione o mestiere *Insef. elementare* residenza *America Nord* domicilio *Sulmona*

Colore politico **Anarchica**

CONNOTATI

Statura		Naso { forma	Collo { lunghezza
Corporatura		dimensioni	grossezza
Capelli { colore		Orecchio { forma	Spalla
forma		dimensioni	Gambe
foltezza		forma	Mani
Viso { colorito	Baffi { foltezza	Piedi
forma	colore	Andatura
dimensioni	Barba { forma	Espressione fisionomica
Fronte { forma	foltezza	
sporgenza	colore	Abbigliamento abituale
dimenzioni	Mandibola	
Sopracciglia { forma	Mento	Segni speciali (cicatrici, tatuaggi, de-
colore	Rughe	formità, ecc.)
Occhio { forma	Bocca { forma	
dimensioni	dimensioni	
colore		

D'Andrea Virginia 21104

Avuta da *Prefettura Aquila* il *16-7-1928* col N. *024440*

inserita nell' album pericolosi: sì - no

Scheda biografica: sì - no
Munito di carta d'identità (Art. 3 T. U. legge P. S.): sì - no

Page from the Italian police files for Virgilia D'Andrea. She is described as an 'anarchist' on the line for information concerning her *Colore politico* (political colour or persuasion). The annotation next to her photograph suggests that her file was copied to the authorities in Rome on 12 July 1932.

7 Anarchist Motherhood: Toward the Making of a Revolutionary Proletariat in Illinois Coal Towns

Caroline Waldron Merithew

In the winter of 1900, several months before Leon Czolgosz assassinated U.S. President William McKinley for the cause of anarchy and for the love of Emma Goldman, a group of French-speaking and Italian women residing in northern Illinois's coal-mining communities formed a club, Il Gruppo Femminile Luisa Michel, and began to put egalitarian theory into practice. One of the women's first acts of rebellion was a challenge to the all-male Prosperity Club – an anarchist saloon and a key venue of radical culture and activism in the region. With the help of some sympathetic members, Luisa Michel planned an assault on the Prosperity Club to demand that the rules of membership be changed. Unable to enter the saloon themselves, the women had male comrades serve as their proxy voices. Attending a Sunday meeting that was designated as a time to discuss club regulations, one of the Luisa Michel allies suggested that the club rule stating the 'anybody can become a member' be changed because it was unclear regarding 'the sex of those who are allowed to apply.' Why not clarify the wording and state that 'anyone, man or woman, may become a member'? After all, the ally argued, it was 'necessary and even urgent to focus first of all on the emancipation of woman in order to achieve the emancipation of all workers.'

The proposal was not well received. 'The majority of the members at large [believed] "anybody" meant "any man." Women, according to them, should be excluded because they are women.' A debate ensued and the assembly broke out into 'beast-like screams' and 'insults.' One man suggested that 'women should be confined to South America ... [They] are worse than dogs, because they are bitches ... Women have long hair and short brains.' Another quipped, 'If women want a *club* ... they should create their own.' When asked to put the proposal to a vote, the president refused. Outraged by the events and the 'anti-feminist furors,' Luisa Michel and their male sympathizers published an article describing the meeting and articulating their positions regarding female emancipation. They wrote, 'We await without fear, because we know we did nothing but our duty.'[1]

The Prosperity Club episode and the article about it offer key insights into gender relations within turn-of-the-century anarchism and alert us to the ways that transnational ideologies shaped immigrant women's understanding of their class position. Insisting that the membership rules reflect the egalitarian spirit of the movement, the women engaged in an act of maternal rebellion that was based on their experiences within their homes and communities. Although they were unsuccessful at integrating the club itself, Luisa Michel's activism had obviously had an impact. They had raised the consciousness of their male allies who agreed that 'if woman occupies an inferior place in society today, it is because we condemn her to it, not because she is destined to it by nature. It is we who force women to occupy themselves only with cooking, laundry, sewing and housecleaning ... for the only and stupid reason that we are men, that is, because we are animals with a high degree of muscular strength.' Women had the 'intelligence, ability, learning and practical sense' to participate fully in the movement.[2]

This chapter examines the political and social lives of immigrant anarchist women from Italy, Belgium, and France who resided in Illinois's coal communities at the turn of the century. These immigrants challenged the patriarchal assumptions of both the anarchist movement and capitalism by redefining motherhood as a revolutionary activity – what I term 'anarchist motherhood.' The concept of anarchist motherhood was premised on the understanding that women's primary role was to sustain the revolution through the next generation. Their discussions of equality were often expressed through a discourse of the family. In particular, their opposition to male oppression was mediated by an equally clear but distinctively anarchist notion of 'motherhood' and maternal duty. Immigrant women here celebrated their roles as mothers, but as radical mothers and revolutionaries they also sought to undermine the ruling order. In their struggle to do so, they formulated an educational mission to teach their children how to subvert the system's oppressive institutions and thereby create a better world for future generations.[3]

Tracking these lessons and tracing the life histories of Luisa Michel members shed new light on the character of social movements, labour, and radical women. Thanks to scholars like Paul Avrich, Nunzio Pernicone, and Michael Miller Topp, we now have a fairly broad under-standing of the international roots and evolution of anarchism in the United States and in Europe. Topp's efforts to use the construct of masculine identity to explain the limitations of the Italian Socialist Fed-eration and the male domination of the Italian-American left have opened up new possibilities for gender analysis. But because we know compara-tively little about women's commitment to anarchism we are still limited in our ability to do a fully gendered reading.[4] The few but important studies of women – including Margaret Marsh's work on Jewish, Ger-man, and native-born anarchist women in the United States, the expand-ing historiography on Emma Goldman, and work on Voltairine de Cleyre – focus on the female leaders in the international anarchist movement. Marsh's argument that such women were 'representative of the move-ment's rank-and-file' is indicative of the scholarship as a whole, which generally assumes that the ideology of leaders and grassroots organizers were one and the same.[5] This assumption is misleading, and neither Marsh's study nor the volumes analysing Emma Goldman tell us much about the type of grassroots resistance mounted by immigrant women like those who formed Luisa Michel. My research shows that French-speaking and Italian women anarchists in Illinois viewed their world and shaped their ideology differently than did Goldman and other female leaders, who preferred 'sexuality' to 'domesticity' and had little interest in motherhood as revolutionary practice.[6]

Indeed, anarchism as ideology was diffuse, and its adherents were widespread and varied in revolutionary word and deed. While socialists formulated rigid policy regarding the relationship between women's liberation and class struggle on a worldwide level, anarchists avoided such top-down strictures. As the Prosperity Club incident reveals, anar-chists certainly bickered over similar questions locally. Yet it was precisely the less authoritarian nature of anarchism and its loosely constructed ideological tenets that attracted women of various cultural and eco-nomic backgrounds. Indeed, this movement reality created a breach for female resistance. The anarchist women leaders about whom we know the most struggled on various fronts to battle oppression – both societal and individual. Women like Voltairine de Cleyre, Marie Ganz, and Mollie Steimer fought for justice and acted for workers' revolution; others, including Margaret Anderson, were less concerned with changing their class society per se than with securing liberation on a personal level. Emma Goldman's universal appeal and her lessons for both individual emancipation and social revolution made her a heroine for many radical female contemporaries, including those who did not agree entirely with all of her views. Certainly, her visits to Illinois coal towns assure us that immigrant women there came out to hear her message.[7]

Still, unlike Goldman and other female leaders, the French- and Italian-speaking cohort who resided in the upper Illinois valley spent the bulk of their time on the issues of motherhood, children, and equality rather than on birth control and free love. Clearly, their diverse ideologies offered different solutions to the problems of gender inequity and sexual oppression within the family and society. As José Moya argues in this volume (chapter 6), not all female Italian anarchists in the diaspora eschewed the practice of free love as a means for liberation. Revolutionizing sexual relations became a major issue feeding women's radicalism in Buenos Aires. Women in Illinois, however, were responding to a different set of circumstances and a particular movement culture. They used motherhood to rebel because it addressed a specific set of economic circumstances they faced. In the upper Illinois valley, women were barred from coal mining but their labour was essential for survival. They were the caretakers of the community. In family units as well as in boarding houses, women cleaned loads of dirty laundry, cooked for hungry workers, and watched over their children. Thus, it makes sense that their liberation ideology would focus on their point of production. That they viewed motherhood as part of this liberation attests to their emotional connection to their families and to their commitment to the revolution and to a better world for future generations.

Illinois's immigrant women's ideology of anarchist motherhood was essential for their work yet quite distinctive in the anarchist community. In general, however, from the late Gilded Age through the Progressive Era, motherhood was an important component of women's activism in the United States and Europe. Middle-class maternalist reformers, socialist women, and anarchist female activists all used the concept of motherhood to gain power in their respective movements. Maternalists combined the notion of republican motherhood and patriotic duty with political activity in the public sphere. Working on behalf of social welfare goals and the need for state protection for women and children, these women advocated social motherhood.[8] Women in the socialist movement, like maternalists, also fought their battles in the public sphere and argued that political rights had not kept up with changing social relations of production in the industrial era. Parallel beliefs and organizing principles could be found among the maternalist, socialist, and anarchist organizers at the turn of the century. Equal suffrage was particularly important to socialist women and maternalists, for instance, and they used the notion of public housekeeping to win respect for their cause. Socialist and anarchist women alike saw the education of their children as a means by which they would perpetuate their cause and hasten the revolution.[9]

There were also marked differences among maternalist, socialist, and anarchist women. Unlike suffragists and socialists, female anarchists were unconcerned with citizenship and enfranchisement, and rarely talked about women's role in mainstream governmental politics. Rather, they struggled for an overthrow of the state altogether. Anarchist mothers' scathing critiques of their world never held up citizenship as the answer to women's oppression or liberation; as anarchists they saw state authority as innately oppressive. They were not alone. In the 1880s, Jean Grave along with Errico Malatesta and other well-known French and Italian anarchists reaffirmed the principle that voting delayed the revolution. Class position provided one explanation for the different views on voting. Most of the anarchist women who resided in the upper Illinois valley struggled to survive in the face of dire economic circumstances – to vote meant collusion in capitalism's injustices. In contrast, many working-class socialist women believed that suffrage could be justified as part of a broader struggle for proletariat emancipation rather than a more narrowly defined call for 'women's rights *per se.*'[10]

In addition to offering insight into the anarchist movement, this essay also contributes to the scholarship on women's and immigrant working-class history, particularly coal mining studies. With few exceptions (Dorothy Schwieder and Mildred Beik, for example) the literature on coal mine communities has focused on the dominant locus of paid labour and union organizing. Because these were male-dominated, women have been too often cropped out of the historical record.[11] Since many women who resided in mining towns had little time to write about their experiences and only a few of them held jobs outside of the home – thereby making union involvement difficult and public activity limited – their stories often went unrecorded. In part, the deficit of women's histories in coal mining studies of the new labour history reflects the types of sources (such as census data and newspaper) on which these scholars relied. When women did appear in the narrative, they were portrayed as vigilant fighters who attacked scabs, led pickets, and protested violently the high cost of food.

Such portraits are not inaccurate insofar as they reflect women's crucial role in strikes, but they are one-sided because they focus on particular forms of protest that were union- and male-defined.

In point of fact, women's activism was self-made and very much rooted in female experiences. Women's radicalism was forged in contexts well beyond the point of production. The life histories of the women in Luisa Michel suggest that immigrant women in Illinois coal towns were not spontaneous militants alone, but also politicized radicals who understood the meaning of their acts. Their public actions were indeed part of a revolutionary strategy as well as a product of ideology that reached around the globe.[12] Their own writings, for example, allow us to glimpse the realities of poor immigrants as well as their views on the world, their dreams of the future, and their responses to their circumstances in the United States.

In addressing my central themes of grassroots female rebellion and the ideology of anarchist motherhood, this chapter draws on several previously overlooked sources, especially women's newspaper correspondence to the Italian-language press and the Italian government's files on subversives in the United States. The sources I use, unfortunately, also reveal material that has been lost. Italian spies who tracked these emigrants, for example, hint at missing data, including a newsletter that Luisa Michel published. The circular's absence is a reminder of just how precious are the voices that remain. Women correspondents help us retrieve debates that have otherwise been masked because of the historiographical emphasis on male discourse. My sources indicate that radicalism could contain numerous elements, including motherhood, as part of a revolutionary agenda that challenged both economic oppression and traditional familial roles.[13]

Besides recovering important but overlooked sources, my essay's intent is twofold: to define and contextualize the concept of anarchist motherhood and by so doing unearth the as yet untold histories of impoverished Italian, Belgian, and French immigrant women who resided in Illinois coal towns; and to explain how the notion of anarchist motherhood contributed to revolutionary work. This latter exercise will aid in rectifying historiographical gaps by centring women's organizing and ideological contributions to the movement.

Political, social, and cultural conditions informed the radical immigrant women who moved to the coal communities of Illinois. Central to my argument is the view that the formulation of anarchist motherhood was a product of both international and local circumstances. First, the women whose writings remain seem to have been introduced to anarchist thought before their arrival to America. Women's ideas were part of a community that transgressed geographic boundaries and nation-states. Second, immigrant women's understanding of capitalism – which, again, was initiated in Europe – solidified in the United States, in general, and in the Illinois coalfields, in particular. Through the process of migration, the members of Luisa Michel witnessed the breadth of the economic order that oppressed working-class people all across the globe. Finally, anarchist motherhood was a response to male and female roles within the family; clearly, gender relations had a significant impact on the concept of the maternal as revolutionary. It is unclear, however, just how much family structures had been altered by immigration. Depending on a woman's origins – from an industrial or agricultural setting in Italy, for example – her duties may or may not have changed in America. Still, the Italian- and French-speaking women in Illinois at least were aware of some variation. Moreover, they saw anarchist motherhood as a solution to all women's oppression.

Anarchist Motherhood in Context

The backdrop for anarchist mothers' activism was their multi-ethnic community. At the turn of the century, the majority of Italian anarchists in Illinois resided in the northern part of the state, in particular, the upper Illinois valley. After the Civil War, during the period of mass 'new' migration to the United States, this region was the destination of thousands of immigrants from all over Europe as well as a haven for radicals. In the 1870s and 1880s, British and German skilled miners, well versed in trade unionism, arrived in the area and organized the precursors to the United Mine Workers of America. By the end of the 1880s, migration chains directed people from Italy, France, Belgium, and Poland to mining communities all over the state. These southern and eastern Europeans brought to America many forms of radicalism that had been fashioned on the continent and transformed through migration. By the turn of the century, there were over a dozen ethnic groups populating the upper Illinois valley and each had informed ideas about the nature of capitalism and solutions for its injustices. From anarchism to socialism to trade unionism, radical ideology became the mainstay of the area's social, political, and institutional milieu. As the concentration of mining in the state moved south, immigrants migrated again, carrying with them their radical cultures.[14]

The bulk of the vocal female activists who corresponded with the Italian-language press came from the town of Spring Valley. This small but vibrant red town housed a remarkable mix of foreign-born individuals from Italy, France, Belgium, Germany, Ireland, Wales, Scotland, Poland, Lithuania, Turkey, Sweden, Russia, and elsewhere. Smaller communities like Spring Valley, particularly diverse locales demographically, could have significant influences on radicalism. In contrast to big cities such as Chicago or New York, workers in coal mining towns travelled shorter distances to make contact with ethnic and radical others. This multi-ethnic community thus brought Italian- and French-speaking women together. Although they were clearly aware of the inequities of capitalism before reaching their destination, Spring Valley's multi-ethnic residents could see just how entrenched were the economic and patriarchal orders. Neighbours from all parts of the world were living examples that people experienced similar circumstances no matter where they originated.

As in Ybor City, Florida, where radicalism had a distinctly Latin character, there were language and cultural ties among the women who participated in Luisa Michel. In part these ties were based on mutual rejection of Anglo culture. Anarchist immigrant miners and their families in Illinois also were reacting against what they perceived as conservative union ideology. But ideology went beyond the male United Mine Workers of America and became more focused on female experiences in the domestic realm. Luisa Michel thus created the possibility of forging cross-ethnic gender solidarities. There were examples of such inter-ethnic female movements in other mining communities. In Canada's similarly diverse coalfields, for instance, Allen Seager found that Finnish women radicals enlisted the support of Slavic, Italian, and English-speaking immigrants. My sources do not permit me to determine whether the upper Illinois valley women reached out in similar ways to those who did not share their Latin language base, but the possibility was certainly there, given the transnational experiences of motherhood and the demographic conditions of the region. Seager's findings underscore the need for further research on the pan-ethnic bonds women created.[15]

Economic transformations in global capitalism brought these diverse immigrants to Illinois coal towns. Men and women moved for reasons tied to labour demand and economic survival. Similar reasons for moving did not preclude gender differences in the migration experience. Since most of the work in the area required male labour (women were legally barred from the mines), coal towns were filled with single men.

Though linked, women's migration patterns differed from their male counterparts'. In particular, all of the Italian, Belgian, and French women who settled in this region did so in groups.[16] Whether daughters, mothers, or wives, women's main reason for moving was bound to their familial relationships.

Besides the distinct migration experiences, men's and women's labour was quite different. Unlike in agricultural settings, where male and female chores were more fluid and required all family members to work together, labour in coal towns was gender-segmented. Most migrants, whether they were industrial workers or peasants in Europe, were familiar with the features of hard labour that defined a coal-mining livelihood – miserable work, long hours, seasonal lay-offs, and poverty. They also knew that women's work in the domestic realm – cleaning, taking in boarders, and stretching meagre wages to feed many mouths – helped to ensure the survival of mining families.[17] The demographic realities and gendered divisions of labour in the upper Illinois valley coal towns are important for understanding how gender relations, ethnic identity, and class consciousness affected immigrants' histories. Moreover, the structural realities of female migration to the region lays the foundation for understanding the evolution of anarchist motherhood.

Personal histories are also essential for explaining the rise of the maternal in female anarchist ideology. Biographical information is sketchy, but thanks to the Italian government's file on subversives, international spies have left us with some sense of experience. The lives of Ersilia Grandi and Angela Marietti, both of whom were involved in Luisa Michel, serve as examples. It is important to note that while Grandi's and Marietti's life histories vary in terms of their sexual relations, each came to motherhood as a way of changing the patriarchal and economic orders that duly oppressed them. Grandi was born in Bologna in 1864. Married to Giulio Grandi before the 1890s, she and her husband practised 'free love.' During the last decade of the nineteenth century, Ersilia Grandi travelled throughout Italy on tours to spread anarchist propaganda. In 1897, she moved to Paris with her lover, Giuseppe Ciancabilla. The couple soon moved again to the United States and by 1899 were living in northern Illinois. Ciancabilla was the editor of *L'Aurora*, an Italian-language newspaper that had subscribers around the world. Grandi took over the editorship for at least part of the time the two lived in the region. Her understanding of the capitalist system stemmed from her daily experiences with the oppressive labour market in Europe and America. Her ideas were also part of a revolutionary heritage to which she remained true throughout her life. Once she left the upper Illinois valley, the Italian government traced her movements to San Francisco, where she continued her 'subversive' activities. At the age of 68, Grandi was still involved in radical politics, contributing money to the anti-Fascist movement and reading Carlo Tresca's paper, *Corriere del Popolo*.[18]

Angela Terrando Marietti's life history resembled Grandi's in international experience. She was born in the small village of Favria Oglianico in the Piedmont region of Italy. She married Michele Marietti, a *contadino* (peasant) from the nearby village of Comagna, in the province of Turin. The couple was involved in anarchist politics while in Italy and continued their work in the United States. Michele emigrated in the late 1880s; we do not know whether Angela migrated with him or moved later. By the end of the century, they lived in Spring Valley together, and by 1913 had settled in Sacramento. As Ersilia had, the Mariettis kept up their anarchist organizing in California. Unlike Grandi, however, Angela's marriage was one of the pillars of her radicalism. While Grandi's subversive file makes no mention of children, Marietti's notes that she had one son.[19]

Though obsessed with keeping tabs on such women, the government spies paid little attention to their revolutionary roles as mothers. It was in their fashioning of maternal rebellion, however, that they helped their male comrades build a radical stronghold in the upper Illinois valley. Experiences in Europe – in particular, in the Paris Commune, the Italian wing of the International Workingmen's Association, and day-to-day resistance – helped them in their efforts. While men's roles in this radicalization were more readily apparent to late-twentieth-century observers, women's contribution was also key.[20] In each case ideology provided a coping mechanism for the dismal conditions in Illinois. Work, leisure, and even consumption patterns were shaped by the anarchist-socialist community in the region. These activities included attending the many anarchist theatre performances, playing in bands that marched in parades, celebrating May 1 and the Paris Commune, and churning out propaganda at meetings with one's comrades over beer and conversation.[21] Immigrants also shopped at cooperatives they had built.[22] Women participated in all of these activities and were at the forefront of many.

To understand better the meaning of women's lives in Illinois coal towns, and the development of anarchist motherhood, we must also consider the political theory of the anarchists. The anarchist movement at the turn of the century generally can be divided into four wings, although, as Avrich argues, 'these categories overlapped; there were no hard-and-fast divisions between them.' Despite significant theoretical differences, the groups agreed upon one general principle: external authority, including but not limited to the government, was the main impediment to liberation. One wing, anarchist-individualists, believed in the state's destruction but not in the abolition of private property. In contrast, the three other wings, anarchist-socialist, anarchist-collectivists, and anarcho-syndicalists, believed that emancipation required the abolition of private property. Their analysis was steeped in Marx's interpretation of class struggle.[23]

Women were involved in each wing of the anarchist movement in the United States, and the majority of those who joined the socialists, collectivists, and syndicalists were also immigrants or daughters of unskilled immigrant workers. Coal-mining families were clearly part of this economic and ethnic echelon. This immigrant profile distinguished anarchists from socialists, as the latter tended to attract skilled workers and their families. In each case, however, socio-economic realities affected the distinct ideals of motherhood advocated by working-class and bourgeois women.[24] At the turn of the century, both the socialist and anarchist movements believed that women's liberation should be subordinated to the class struggle and workers' emancipation. While male leaders occasionally discussed female oppression, they placed gender egalitarianism in the distant future rather than the present. Ersilia Grandi grew tired of hearing her male comrades 'shout in favour' of women's emancipation 'in the future society,' and even compared them to priests who 'make false promises to the starving masses ... [that] there will be rewards in paradise.' In Italian anarchist circles, such an analogy was a biting insult, as Grandi clearly meant it to be.[25]

In general, anarchist thought was split on the question of the family in relation to female oppression. Peter Kropotkin, Pierre-Joseph Proudhon, Jean Grave, and their followers saw the home as the place for women's contribution to society. Wife and mother were women's natural roles and once society acknowledged this their female comrades in the movement would be liberated within their domestic realms. The revolution, they argued, would re-value women's work as homemakers and highlight their contribution as producers in the home rather than abolish family life altogether. In this future society, women's domestic duties would not be compensated with wages and, according to Proudhon, wives would continue to be subservient to their husbands. By contrast, followers of Michael Bakunin believed that the home was another locus of oppression and, because men and women were equals, they should share in every aspect of production, including domestic labour. For anarcho-syndicalists, who saw the union as the main organizing component in any future anarchist society, the mutual contribution of the sexes outside of the home was essential. As workers in the production of goods, women would begin to play a larger role in unions and thus in culture and society.[26]

Given the male leadership's myopic views about female participation and gender relations in the future anarchist society, women had plenty of reason to theorize their own position. While for some communities theoretical explanations might mean little, for anarchists in the coal towns of Illinois, especially women, theory was enlightening. Indeed, the lively debates in these red towns offered an avenue for women's involvement and encouraged their theoretical formulation of mothers' roles. What evolved from reading anarchist thought was women's own theory. Women combined the male leaders' ideas about the institution of the family with their personal understanding of problems with the systems of capitalism and patriarchy. More specifically, as we shall see, Illinois coal-mining women felt that domestic duties were oppressive not only because they were undervalued but also because they impeded participation in the movement. Anarchist motherhood was a response to this dilemma; it offered a means of gaining some recognition as well as a practical solution. If mothers were already raising children, they could use the time spent in upbringing for revolutionary goals. But only if they were well educated themselves, as the activists of Luisa Michel argued.

In fact, many Italian- and French-speaking women in this region were well read in the movement's ideology. The books available to them through the anarchist libraries and book sellers, as well as their stints at translation, suggest as much. Women who wrote to the radical press from Italy, Illinois, and elsewhere often commented on their own lack of formal education. Yet despite their poverty their knowledge of anarchism's important tracts attests to their commitment. Alba Genisio wrote, 'I am not an intellectual; a daughter of the poor and oppressed ... I spent my days reading and in contemplation of our great book.' Similarly, the government agent who reported in Ersilia Grandi's subversive file noted that she was 'very intelligent, but little educated.'[27]

Anarchist motherhood combined education with emancipation. Its formulation included an analysis of gender and class oppression. In one article written 'to mothers,' the female author argued that 'the principal aim of women is to educate the children. She should make them honest men, virtuous citizens, and hard workers.'[28] Like Black women maternalists, these immigrant women knew poverty. But unlike their African-American contemporaries, whose motto was 'Lifting as We Climb,' French- and Italian-speaking anarchist mothers were not interested in bridging the 'gulf of class.'[29] They believed instead that working-class mothers should combat bourgeois mothers who did not 'inculcate in their children a love for humanity but rather the egoistic love for things.' Anarchist mothers were to teach their children 'the love of their own freedom together with the respect for the freedom of others,'[30] and, as one writer noted, their children should be revolutionaries. 'Don't cry, mothers,' she stated, 'if some of your children rebel against society abandoning the prejudice of their fathers,' because 'Oh! it is a thousand times better to be martyrs with consciousness than victims without dignity.'[31] Becoming revolutionary teachers was the greatest contribution mothers could make to the movement.

In 'The Maternal Mission,' Ersilia Grandi offered some practical lessons for how her comrades could help their children combat society's evils. They should teach their sons the following:

1. that all men are born equal and therefore they have equal rights;
2. that the idea that god exists is absurd, useless, criminal because religious belief serves the boss [and] the government ...;
3. that the boss who is necessary today for the poor to live, will not be necessary tomorrow, when the workers will work and produce for themselves ... so inspire constant rebellion against the bosses and against every exploitation;
4. that laws are made by the government to defend the system of oppression ... thus excite in your young hate for every law, and make them understand that laws are the synonyms for violence;
5. that ... your sons should refuse to don a military uniform since the army ... in reality only serves to defend the rich against the poor who are hungry.[32]

Mothers, she added, 'should inculcate the same ideas in the minds of their daughters, whom they should make understand that the difference in sex does not imply inequality in rights.' 'Besides being rebels against the social system of today,' women 'should fight especially against the oppression of men who would like to retain woman as their moral and material inferior.'[33]

In addition to helping her contemporaries become good teacher-mothers, Grandi's principles offered the basic tenets to which anarchist mothers adhered. Mothers of the movement were to be teachers of rebellion within and beyond the family. The specific lessons for boys and girls should be slightly different though the goal of subversion was the same. The curriculum for male children was clearly focused on exposing the collusion between the state, capitalism, and oppression; for them, emancipation began with their understanding of the class system. Daughters too had to learn about capitalist domination, but also how to combat sexual inequality and to appreciate the need for equal rights.

Raising children was central to anarchist motherhood; preserving the oppressive family was not. Anarchist women expressed their concern for male domination in various ways. Included in their critique was an admonishment of social mores as well as a tendency to blame themselves for abuse. Resistance involved immediate battles against subjugation in the home but also a longer-term strategy. Indeed, many believed that women's emancipation must begin with women. Taking Marx as her inspiration and modifying his words, Grandi wrote, 'The emancipation of women should be made by women themselves.' She believed that liberation would come to women when they realized how to 'conquer freedom' and escape the 'social environment' that suffocated them, 'whether in the family, in intimate relations, in today's hypocritical conventions, or in public life.'[34] Writing seven years later, Alba Genisio agreed particularly with the idea that women needed to emancipate themselves. She asked, 'Why are we afraid to break the chains ... of slavery ...?' Her answer was a double-edged sword: 'Because we are cowards ... Because we bow weakly and defeated to the voice of the priest, to the whips of the government, to the commands of the boss, to the club of the husband, to the prejudice of the people.' Men could be brutes but women colluded in their own oppression by being submissive.[35] Genisio believed that once free of their vegetable-like existence, women would be able to more fully participate in the vanguard of the movement with their male comrades. Joining together to discuss such problems would be the impetus to their own liberation as well as their children's emancipation.

Coinciding with their self-taught understanding of the movement, Italian- and French-speaking women in Illinois had their own revolutionary heroes. In fact, these icons contributed to the formulation of anarchist motherhood. Louise Michel, one of the leading figures in the Paris Commune, became their inspiration. In addition to fighting the government at the barricades, Michel was head of the Women's Vigilance Committee in Paris, which was responsible for caring for two hundred children whose parents were Communards. Upon her arrest and subsequent prison sentence for her Commune activities, she became an anarchist. After her release under the government's general amnesty of 1880, she devoted herself to spreading anarchist propaganda and spoke throughout Europe and England.[36] Some of the women who eventually migrated to Illinois probably had heard of Michel's tours through newspaper accounts and they may even have attended her lectures. In any case, they were moved by her activism. Michel's training as a teacher and her care of children during the Paris Commune were key components of her radicalism. For the Illinois immigrant women the 'valiant French comrade' served not only as a model for organizing but also as a symbol of anarchist motherhood. They drew from her life the importance of educating future revolutionaries and women's indispensable contribution to the movement.[37]

The group Luisa Michel reflected the transnational character of women's participation in anarchism and their concept of anarchist motherhood. For Italian, Belgian, and French women, class emancipation was tied to internationalism as exemplified in their decision to name their group after their revolutionary hero. There were also precedents for choosing the name; in the mid-1880s, the loosely bound federation of anarchists in Florence named themselves Gruppo Anarchico Luisa Michel, and José Moya has found a group with the name in Buenos Aires. While it is difficult to draw direct links between Illinois's Luisa Michel and the groups in Italy and Argentina, indirect connections are evident, including the fact that the famed anarchist Errico Malatesta was an inspiration for each group.[38]

Living like Revolutionaries

Taking their cues from the real Louise Michel, women in Luisa Michel acted upon one of the most fundamental anarchist-socialist tenets, that the revolution would happen when people began living it. They thus transformed themselves into revolutionaries. Initially, Luisa Michel acted largely as a forum in which women discussed their experiences and their responsibilities as anarchists. Its members invited their sisters to participate 'for the emancipation of women ... for the rights of all oppressed humanity ... [and] against the tyranny and prejudice of men ... [who] consider woman inferior and treat her straight away as a slave.'[39] It soon became the centre of women's opposition to patriarchy and capitalism in the upper Illinois valley coal towns.

These anarchist women were as concerned with reordering their domestic roles as they were with gaining respect for their contributions to
the movement. They believed that the Prosperity Club could be a vehicle
for both, which is why the fight over membership was so important to
them. Luisa Michel and their male allies believed that the club should be
a 'vehicle of propaganda' rather than a place to 'drink a good glass of
beer.'[40] Despite their disappointment, they did not give up the fight. In
their letter to the Italian press explaining the episode, they concluded
that the 'weak sex' could take 'satisfaction in being the ruler of life, the
arbiter of human destiny.' Moreover, 'Those who shouted such stupid
anti-women proverbs last Sunday, and thought of being very witty, would
do well to remember another, much wider – if crude – adage, "Women's
hair pulls much further than a hundred oxen."' The article's authors
reminded readers about revolutionary motherhood and argued for investment in their children. 'Now, it is indisputable that all hopes for the
future must rest not on the present generation but on the next,' they
wrote, 'which, born in a more free environment and without prejudice,
will be able to rid itself of the obstacles to its emancipation.' Reiterating
the importance of motherhood, they stressed that 'the education of this
new generation is mostly entrusted to women, who, as everyone knows,
more than men have the power to influence young minds and leave on
them indelible marks.'[41] Anarchist women, if they had given up on their
own generation, could continue their work in the movement rather than
leave their activist responsibilities altogether.

After the disturbing Prosperity Club incident, Luisa Michel continued
to meet together every Wednesday night and to plan new strategies for
living the revolution. Each rebellious moment was a means of translating
theory into practice. For women in Luisa Michel, emancipation was
deeper than abolishing economic inequalities inside and outside the
family. While the disagreements between Kropotkin and Bakunin were
important, they involved only one feature of women's thoughts and
activities. In particular, the debate about the family did not take into
account women's perceptions about mothers' contributions, but rather
focused on the locus of economic oppression. But women were oppressed socially and culturally as well. In their naming of such oppression, Luisa Michel women had begun to define a female-centred position
as revolutionaries.

Defining that oppression, and formulating solutions to it, took different forms. There were overt challenges and more subtle ones. In a letter
she sent to the newspaper L'Aurora in the summer of 1901, Angela

Marietti told readers that women's 'principal duty was ... the education of the family ... and the future generation.' Children, Marietti argued, 'if brought up well, would be able to obtain the fruits of progress and liberty,' thus helping to bring about an anarchist-socialist revolution. She also expressed concern about women's ability to fulfil the special duties required of anarchist mothers. Pondering the state of children's education, she and her comrades worried that Italian mothers lacked the proper tools to teach their children well, making them and their children unable to 'combat the ill-fated influence of all the so-called educational books' in American schools. As there was nothing of merit in Italian for the development of anarchism's next generation, Marietti and her comrades decided to translate from French a 370-page book, Jean Grave's *Les Aventures de Nono*. Reading it would help ensure their children learned the skills to fight what Marietti called 'the poison of state prejudice, country, religion, the respect for private property, authority, and the law, etc.'[42]

In Grave's story, the child protagonist, Nono, dreams that he visits two societies: Autonomy and Monnaia. In Autonomy, people live in freedom, love, and peace, and they share work and the goods they produce together. Liberty and Labour are among the characters Nono encounters. He also meets an ogre from Monnaia who lures him to that frightful country. In contrast to Autonomy, Monnaia is a tyrannical, oppressive, and hierarchical land. The rich look like vultures and tigers and the poor like sheep. In the end, a girl and a boy from Autonomy rescue Nono from Monnaia and deliver the child into his mother's arms. In their decision to translate *Les Aventures de Nono*, anarchist women were preparing their children to combat economic oppression. Their project also reveals the continuing importance of international networks, acquaintance with anarchist literature, and language skills that tied French- and Italian-speaking women together.[43]

Tackling the difficult work of translation also offered an opportunity for men and women in the movement to cooperate. Women believed it was their duty to educate and take responsibility for the project, but also argued that the men were obliged to help – and, further, that doing so was as important as joining the Prosperity Club. As Marietti put it: 'We think we deserve volunteer support from our male comrades in this venture.' A lack of support would 'dishearten' the female companions who had 'taken their first and uncertain steps in our movement' and potentially cripple future initiatives.[44]

As Marietti's intervention and the unpleasant Prosperity Club episode

each reveal, there were problematic gender relations within their movement, though probably it came as no great surprise to Luisa Michel
members. Still, the problems indicated that there were two impediments
to women's liberation. The first was that men and women perceived
living the revolution differently from one another. While fighting capitalism was a common goal for both sexes, undermining patriarchy was
not. For the women in Luisa Michel the two were inseparable. Indeed,
the boss, husband, father, lover who tried to exert authority over them
were thought to be equally oppressive.

Further, male arrogance and lack of respect for women's equality
undermined the women's contribution to the movement and deterred
them from acting. The insulting language men used to describe wom-
en's inferiority at the Prosperity Club meeting was a case in point. There
were other such affronts. In an article written from Trieste, the male
author lambasted women for speaking up too much and discouraged
them from participating in the movement. When women 'have begun to
read some pamphlets and attend conferences, they imagine that they are
the best anarchists of all,' he noted sarcastically. He continued the
demeaning picture: women 'want to make note of their presence taking
advantage of mother nature's mistake of giving them loose tongues, but
haven't they become annoying on many occasions?'[45] While there were a
few male supporters in the anarchist community, such views suggest that
many women lived and interacted with men who viewed them as inferior.

In an article entitled, 'Ma tu sei una donna!' (But you are a woman),
one woman recounted the type of negative experiences that were familiar to her female comrades. 'If we find ourselves in the middle of some
men who are having a discussion of morality, religion or politics and we
hazard to intervene with our opinions,' she wrote, 'father or brother or
husband or companion tells us: – but you are a woman: you should shut
up!'[46] She urged her readers instead to fight back for themselves and all
of humanity – 'to aspire to redeem ourselves, politically and morally ...
and from the terrible economic servitude of all humanity.' She signed
her letter, 'Una donna che pensa' (A thinking woman).[47]

Women also combated patriarchy through their continued development of an ideology of anarchist motherhood. If women were oppressed
in the home, their children were likely to renew the pattern in their own
relationships as adults, thus making the work of future generations 'no
less fatiguing and difficult than how it is now.' Women should use their
'gentle and beneficial influence for the benefit of everyone,' raising 'a
new generation of workers who are class-conscious and free of prejudice.' But it was a continuous struggle, one that was especially difficult

when men marginalized women's commitment and defined their activities. Throughout their lives, husbands, lovers, and other men in the movement had treated women as different, inferior, and subordinate. Luisa Michel members envisioned a revolution that would overturn sexual inequality as well as capitalist domination. While some of the men in their communities supported their ideals, many more did not; articles in the local anarchist press suggest the kind of prejudice that pervaded the movement and that women faced on a daily basis.[48]

In response, the Luisa Michel members began to re-evaluate and define their own contribution to the movement. In particular, they believed that their duty as anarchist mothers extended to all realms of society and included the education of adults. Working-class women, (like their middle-class maternalist contemporaries) extended the home into the public sphere. Through speeches, conferences, dramatic performances, discussion groups, and public action, women enlightened their contemporaries. Ersilia Grandi for years had been an effective orator in Italy and France and she continued to spread the word in the upper Illinois valley. Angela Marietti made her mark performing in anarchist plays. In each medium, this educational process involved the scrutiny of egalitarian rhetoric against its practice.[49]

In addition to these educational forums, whose goals were to root out theoretical inconsistencies, anarchist mothers also took responsibility for schooling their communities in the history of their movement. The curriculum included celebrating radical holidays like the Paris Commune, May Day, and U.S. Labor Day. As the local English-language press noted with alarm, 'some anarchist women have persisted on labor day occasions and at other times in hanging a red flag from their windows.'[50] Through their teaching and celebrations, together with their choice of the name Luisa Michel, the women also confirmed and strengthened international ties among anarchist-socialists. Lessons of the movement, and its geographic breadth, were made clear when internationally renowned visitors came to town. Malatesta visited the upper Illinois valley in January 1900, and his lectures were part of the many bilingual conferences women attended to enlighten themselves and, in turn, their families.[51] Such events clearly reflected the radical heritage that immigrant women brought with them from Europe and how it shaped their U.S. coal community.

Emma Goldman travelled to the region at least twice in 1899 (for May Day and for Labor Day). Her trip was sponsored by the anarchists in cooperation with the United Mine Workers' local. During her second visit, the anarchists made over one hundred dollars on the lectures, twenty-five of which went to pay Goldman's expenses.[52] Among other topics, Goldman spoke candidly to her audience about women's liberation and families. After the march of three hundred immigrant women and men who defied police orders to haul down the 'red flag of anarchy,' Goldman gave a talk and joined in the anarchist picnic.[53] Describing the event in her autobiography, she recalled that, '[a]lthough it was broiling hot, the miners turned out with their wives and children, dressed in their finest ... [T]he comrades brought nineteen babies to be baptized by me in "true anarchist fashion." '[54] Goldman also wrote that she had felt as though 'the ones who needed baptism were really the parents, baptism in the new ideas of the rights of the child.' The anarchist mothers who had gone to her talks would have agreed that the rights of their children included emancipation from capitalist and patriarchal oppression. Carrying their babies to see Emma Goldman was a metaphor for the revolutionary instruction they gave their children on a daily basis.

In 1901 the Luisa Michel circle was also part of a coalition that invited Peter Kropotkin to Spring Valley for a conference during his travels in the United States. Kropotkin was unable to come because of his health and busy schedule, but he wrote to thank them for their valuable commitment to the movement and to educating their communities. 'I don't need to tell you how happy it would make me to come and see comrades in Spring Valley,' he wrote. 'Be secure that it causes me much grief to decline your fraternal invitation.'[55]

Clearly, the lecture series and visits from celebrated guests gave sustenance to Illinois radicals, encouraging local people to give their own speeches and otherwise continue to educate their members. Still, the educational fanfare that accompanied renowned leaders occurred sporadically. In the interim, Italian, Belgian, and French immigrant women and men continued other propaganda activities by relying on the region's own inhabitants. While women participated behind the scenes of lecture tours, they were at the forefront of arranging social events. Producing plays and arranging festivals on radical holidays were two powerful tools for education. In 1901, Luisa Michel along with other French and Italian groups commemorated the Paris Commune by inviting a speaker to talk about the event. The commemoration took place in a local saloon. For May Day of that same year women played a significant role in producing famed anarchist Pietro Gori's *Primo di Maggio* followed by a dance.[56]

Participation in the movement included material and intellectual contributions. In early September 1901, Italian- and French-speaking anarchists put on a big festival and picnic. Among the events was a gift-giving exchange. In order to participate, one bought a 25-cent ticket and, in return, received a prize. Although the festival was held in northern Illinois, gift donations came from all over the country. Included among the items sent were a French conversation book, a bag of flour, and binoculars. Women were generous contributors: the Luisa Michel group donated a pocket watch; Ersilia Grandi gave a woman's blouse that had appliqué work of crochet; Delfina Bertotti furnished a woman's white metal belt, and Domenica Braida a coffee pot that served six. The array of donations suggests that both men and women were invested in the exchange. The types of gifts themselves give us a glimpse of the material culture of the community. Food, language resources, and clothes were all needed for survival in this immigrant community. Moreover, the event exemplified women's work in the public sphere as an extension of their duties as mothers and caretakers.[57]

The festival was one of the many ways that women became involved. Their allegiance to anarchist-socialism and their attempts to build bridges with male leaders continued. Women made one of their most vital contributions to their community after President McKinley's assassination in September 1901. The anarchists in Illinois had always had a precarious relationship with the native-born town leaders of Spring Valley. Their adulation for Leon Czolgosz's actions did not help. Within a few weeks of the assassination, county officials arrested Giuseppe Ciancabilla, the editor of *L'Aurora*. Once Ciancabilla was in jail, Ersilia Grandi took over his post. The transition of editorship reveals not only women's central position in the community but also their commitment to the movement. Interestingly, as editor, Grandi made few changes to the contents of *L'Aurora*. There were not, for example, more articles discussing women's liberation. Instead, the focus remained on the siege of the anarchist community. Did these decisions reflect the limitations or extensions of the ideology of anarchist motherhood? There are no straightforward answers to this question. It seems, however, that Ersilia Grandi was clear about the role of the teacher-mother in the movement. She thus spent the bulk of the space in the paper's columns reporting on the international community and the local crisis. In particular, she gave special attention to Ciancabilla's well-being in jail and the lessons to be learned from the arrest.[58]

Conclusion

My focus here has been on the voices and activities of women whose experiences with capitalism, migration, and family relations brought them to the ideology of anarchist motherhood. The writings and work of Angela Marietti, Ersilia Grandi, Alba Genisio, and their comrades in Luisa Michel make clear that Italian, Belgian, and French women who resided in the coal communities of Illinois were as committed to anarchism as were the men in the movement. Indeed, these women's voices suggest that they viewed their own organizing as both revolutionary and indispensable. The ultimate goal of anarchist motherhood's adherents was a thorough integration of male and female work: men and women would be equal partners in the revolution. They attempted to persuade their husbands, fathers, brothers, and sons to recognize their contribution and its importance for the cause. Sadly, such recognition seldom occurred in radical theory or in practice. Nonetheless, anarchist women in Illinois coal towns continued to chastise male dominance in everything from conversations, political debates, sexual aggression, community politics, education, and leadership.

The members of Luisa Michel believed that, as mothers, women held the tools for creating the future society. Educating their children was one of the first steps in the revolution and in their own emancipation. The curriculum they developed included a critique of both capitalism and patriarchy. By instilling in children their own loathing of these oppressive international systems, they believed they could hasten the revolution and ensure that its character would embody the spirit of all workers around the globe.

Anarchist motherhood remained a crucial part of women's local struggles. It defined rebellion in ways that differed from that of the more nationally renowned female anarchist leaders. The lives of the Italian- and French-speaking immigrants who resided in the upper Illinois valley thus help us to develop a broader and more nuanced understanding of how foreign women with few resources could fight back. These women's writings are precious resources for decoding the myths about, and ending the silences surrounding, immigrant women.

NOTES

I would like to thank Franca Iacovetta and Donna Gabaccia for their insight and constructive criticism and for being model feminist scholars. I am grateful for Jim Barret's many helpful comments and our discussions about the conceptualization of anarchist motherhood. I would also like to thank Nancy Hewett, Carl Weinberg, Grace Palladino, and Jennifer Guglielmo for commenting on the chapter, and Patrizia Sione for her translation help.

1 *L'Aurora*, 22 December 1900, 2, 'L'articolo 2. di tale regolamento dice: "Chiunque può divenir membro,"' 'Chiunque, uomo o donna può divenir membro, ecc."' 'Come si vede, qual'é concepito tale articolo, lascia l'equivoco sullo stabilire il sesso di coloro che possono esser soci, perché chiunque puo riferisi tanto a uomo che a donna.' 'E spiego le ragioni per cui, dal punto di vista dell'emancipazione dei lavoratori, sia necessario, anzi urgente, preoccuparsi, prima di tutto, dell'emancipazione della donna.' 'nella mente del comitato ... il chiunque voleva e vuol dire chiunque uomo. Le donne, seconde questa gente, debbono essere escluse ... perché sono donne.' 'Le donne bisogna relegarle nell'America del Sud ... Le donne son peggio dei cani, perché son cagne ... Le donne hanno i capelli lunghi e il cervello corto.' 'Noi attendiamo sereni perché convinti di aver fatto niente piú che il nostro dovere ...'

2 Ibid. 'Se la donna occupa oggi un posto inferiore nella società, è perché noi ve la condanniamo, non già perché essa vi sia destinata per natura. Siamo noi che alla donna imponiamo di occuparsi solo della cucina, della biancheria, delle calze da rammendare, della casa da spazzare ... per la sola e stupida ragione che noi siamo gli uomini, cioè perché abbiamo ammalescamente qualche grado di forza muscolare in più, per imporci come bruti.'

3 On anarchist women's negative views toward motherhood, see Margaret Marsh, *Anarchist Women, 1870–1920* (Philadelphia: Temple University Press, 1981), 52, 95–8, and for Voltairine de Cleyre's difficulty combining her role as parent and revolutionary, 130–1; Emma Goldman's discussion of motherhood, in 'Marriage and Love,' centres around women's right to have children out of wedlock. See *Anarchism and Other Essays*, 3rd rev. ed. (New York: Mother Earth Publications, 1917), 241–2. See also Martha Solomon, *Emma Goldman* (Boston: Twayne Publishers), 68.

4 Nunzio Pernicone, *Italian Anarchism, 1864–1892* (Princeton: Princeton University Press, 1993); Paul Avrich, *Anarchist Portraits* (Princeton: Princeton University Press, 1988) and his *Sacco and Vanzetti: The Anarchist Background* (Princeton: Princeton University Press, 1991); Michael Miller Topp, 'Immigrant Culture and the Politics of Identity: Italian-American Syndicalists in the U.S., 1911–1927' (PhD diss., Brown University, 1993) and his 'The Transnationalism of the Italian-American Left: The Lawrence Strike of 1912 and the Italian Chamber of Labor of New York City,' *Journal of American Ethnic History* 17 (Fall 1997): 39–63.

5 Marsh, *Anarchist Women*, 22. The following are among the many works about Emma Goldman: Marian J. Morton, *Emma Goldman and the American Left: 'Nowhere at Home'* (New York: Twayne Publishers, 1992); Candace Falk, *Love,*

Anarchy, and Emma Goldman, rev. ed. (New Brunswick, NJ: Rutgers University Press, 1990); Solomon, *Emma Goldman;* B.N. Ganguli, *Emma Goldman: Portrait of a Rebel Woman* (Bombay: Allied Publishers Private Ltd., 1979); Richard Drinnon, *Rebel in Paradise: A Biography of Emma Goldman* (Chicago: University of Chicago Press, 1961); Oz Frankel, 'Whatever Happened to "Red Emma"? Emma Goldman, from Alien Rebel to American Icon,' *Journal of American History* 83 (December 1996): 902–42. Paul Avrich's work on Voltairine de Cleyre is an excellent biography on one of the movement's prominent female leaders: *An American Anarchist: The Life of Voltairine de Cleyre* (Princeton: Princeton University Press, 1978). There are a few good books on anarchist women's involvement in the Spanish Revolution, see Martha A. Ackelsberg, *Free Women of Spain: Anarchism and the Struggle for the Emancipation of Women* (Bloomington: Indiana University Press, 1991) and Temma Kaplan, 'Female Consciousness and Collective Action: The Case of Barcelona, 1910–1918,' *Signs* 7 (Spring 1982): 545–66; for a discussion of women and anarchism in Argentina see Asuncion Lavrin, *Women, Feminism, and Social Change in Argentina, Chile, and Uruguay, 1890–1940* (Lincoln: University of Nebraska Press, 1995).

6 Marsh, *Anarchist Women,* 98. Elliot Gorn's recent analysis of Mother Jones suggests that this legendary leader also had a revolutionary concept of motherhood. See his *Mother Jones: The Most Dangerous Woman in America* (New York: Hill and Wong, 2001).

7 Mari Jo Buhle, *Women and American Socialism* (Urbana: University of Illinois Press, 1983), 11–14; Marsh, *Anarchist Women,* 4–5, 20–43; Avrich, *An American Anarchist,* 15–16.

8 For a comparative perspective on maternalist activism and the creation of welfare states around the world see Seth Koven and Sonya Michel, ed., *Mothers of a New World: Maternalist Politics and the Origins of Welfare States* (New York: Routledge, 1993). On republican motherhood, see Linda Kerber, *Women of the Republic: Intellect and Ideology in Revolutionary America* (Chapel Hill: University of North Carolina Press, 1980). For a delineation of maternalist values for middle-class women during the Progressive Era see Molly Ladd-Taylor, *Mother-Work: Women, Child Welfare, and the State, 1890–1930* (Urbana: University of Illinois Press, 1994), 3–7. On the tension between racism and maternalism see Gwendolyn Mink, 'The Lady and the Tramp: Gender, Race, and the Origins of the American Welfare State,' in Linda Gordon, ed., *Women, the State, and Welfare* (Madison: University of Wisconsin Press, 1990), 93.

9 On social housekeeping see Buhle, *Women and American Socialism,* 218–19, and on educating for the revolution, see xvi, 118; on ideals of motherhood in the Italian socialist community see Virginia Yans-McLaughlin, *Family and*

Community: Italian Immigrants in Buffalo, 1880–1930 (Urbana: University of Illinois Press, 1982), 229–30.

10 Louis Patsouras, *Jean Grave and the Anarchist Tradition in France* (Middletown, NJ: Caslon Company, 1995), 19. Buhle, *Women and American Socialism*, 220. The issue of women's liberation was also bypassed by the socialist movement in Canada. For an example, see Ruth A. Frager, *Sweatshop Strife: Class, Ethnicity, and Gender in the Jewish Labour Movement of Toronto, 1900–1939* (Toronto: University of Toronto Press, 1992). It is interesting to contrast immigrant women's ideological reason for not joining in the suffrage movement with their African-American contemporaries who were using collective expression of the franchise as their voice; see Elsa Barkley Brown, 'Negotiating and Transforming the Public Sphere: African American Political Life in the Transition from Slavery to Freedom,' *Public Culture* 7 (1994): 121–4.

11 For coal mining historiography, see David Alan Corbin, *Life, Work, and Rebellion in the Coal Fields: The Southern West Virginia Miners, 1880–1922* (Urbana: University of Illinois Press, 1981); Michael Nash, *Conflict and Accommodation: Coal Miners, Steel Workers, and Socialism, 1890–1920* (Westport, CT: Greenwood Press, 1982); Joe William Trotter, *Coal, Class, and Color: Blacks in Southern West Virginia, 1915–1932* (Urbana: University of Illinois Press, 1990); John H.M. Laslett, *Nature's Noblemen: The Fortunes of the Independent Collier in Scotland and the American Midwest, 1855–1889*, Monograph and Research Series, 34 (Los Angeles: Institute of Industrial Relations, 1983); Carl Weinberg, 'The Tug of War: Labor, Loyalty and Rebellion in the Southwestern Illinois Coalfields, 1914–1920' (PhD diss., Yale University, 1995); Dorothy Schwieder, *Black Diamonds: Life and Work in Iowa's Coal Mining Communities, 1895–1925* (Ames: Iowa State University Press, 1983); Mildred Beik, 'The Miners of Windber: Class, Ethnicity and the Labor Movement in a Pennsylvania Coal Town, 1890s-1930s' (PhD diss., Northern Illinois University, 1989). For the period of the 1930s, Stephanie Booth's work on women coal-community activists is refreshing; see 'Ladies in White: Female Activism in the Southern Illinois Coalfields, 1932–1938,' in John H.M. Laslett, ed., *The United Mine Workers of America: A Model of Industrial Solidarity?* (University Park: Pennsylvania State University Press, 1996), 371–92. See Gorn, *Mother Jones*, 230, for Mother Jones's opposition to fighting for women's suffrage.

12 Priscilla Long, *Where the Sun Never Shines: A History of America's Bloody Coal Industry* (New York: Paragon House, 1989), 157; Victor R. Greene, *The Slavic Community on Strike: Immigrant Labor in Pennsylvania Anthracite* (Notre Dame: University of Notre Dame Press, 1968); Nash, *Conflict and Accommodation*, 65, 71.

13 Casellario Politico Centrale, busta 3062, Archivio Centrale dello Stato, Rome, 18 January 1907.
14 On statistics for European migration to the U.S., see Roger Daniels, *Coming to America: A History of Immigration and Ethnicity in American Life* (New York: Harper Perennial, 1990), 188. On migration to Illinois, see Grace Abbott, 'The Immigrant and Coal Mining Communities in Illinois,' *Bulletin of the Immigrants Commission No. 2* (Springfield: State of Illinois, Dept. of Registration and Education, 1920), 5, 11–12; for the ethnic make-up in southern Illinois coal towns, see Stephanie Elise Booth, 'The Relationship between Radicalism and Ethnicity in Southern Illinois Coal Fields, 1870–1940' (PhD diss., Illinois State University, 1983), 96–106 and Carl Weinberg, 'The Tug of War: Labor, Loyalty and Rebellion in the Southwestern Illinois Coalfields, 1914–1920' (PhD diss., Yale University, 1995), 51–8. On British miners and union organizing in America, see Laslett, *Nature's Noblemen*, 37–8, 45–7, and Herbert G. Gutman, 'Labor in the Land of Lincoln: Coal Miners on the Prairie,' in *Power and Culture: Essays on the American Working Class* (New York: Pantheon Books, 1987), 117–212; Gutman also discusses the multi-ethnic nature of the area, 134. On French, Belgian, German, and Italian immigrant miners and radicalism in the upper Illinois valley, see Ronald Creagh, 'Socialism in America: The French-speaking Coal Miners in the Late Nineteenth Century,' Marianne Debouzy, ed., in *In the Shadow of the Statue of Liberty: Immigrants, Workers and Citizens in the American Republic, 1880–1920* (Urbana: University of Illinois Press, 1992), 151–3. Because of the destruction of the 1890 manuscript census, it is difficult to quantify specific immigrant numbers for Illinois coal towns for the last decade of the nineteenth century. Government statistics from the 1890 census offer little information for ethnic make-up regionally. Other qualitative sources help. These include city directories for Bureau and LaSalle counties and Knights of Labor meeting minutes. The former are held at the Spring Valley and Peru public libraries. Knights minutes are at the Illinois State University Archives.
15 Allen Seager, 'Class, Ethnicity, and Politics in the Alberta Coalfields, 1905–1945,' in Dirk Hoerder, ed., '*Struggle a Hard Battle': Essays on Working-Class Immigrants* (DeKalb: Northern Illinois University Press, 1986), 312. Gary R. Mormino and George E. Pozzetta, *The Immigrant World of Ybor City: Italians and Their Latin Neighbors in Tampa, 1885–1985* (Urbana: University of Illinois Press, 1990), 11–12.
16 Abbott, 'The Immigrant and Coal Mining Communities,' 12. For details on individual migrants and migration patterns, see microfilm copies of the United States Census, 1900 manuscript schedule, Brown-Bureau 1, reel 238; 1910 manuscript schedule, Boone, Brown and Bureau-1, reel 231; 1920

manuscript schedule, Brown-Bureau, reel 300. Yans-McLaughlin, *Family and Community*, 99–102 analyses family migration patterns.

17 Again, this phenomenon contrasts with that of agricultural families, which relied on female farm labour at home while men left the village and travelled abroad for work. For women's role in agricultural labour see Donna Gabaccia, *Militants and Migrants: Rural Sicilians Become American Workers* (New Brunswick, NJ: Rutgers University Press, 1988), 43; for female migration patterns from Italy as well as more on agricultural families, see her article 'Worker Internationalism and Italian Labor Migration, 1870–1914,' *International Labor and Working Class History* 45 (Spring 1994), 66–7.

18 The Italian government collected information on persons they dubbed subversives. Among the names held in the Casellario Politico Centrale (CPC) is Ersilia Cavedagni in Grandi, busta 1205, Archivio Centrale dello Stato, Rome. The main file, no date, includes Grandi's life history. For information on her activities in San Francisco, see letter from the Regio Consolato Generale d'Italia to the Ministero dell'Interno, Rome, December 1932.

19 CPC, busta 3062, Michele Marietti, Letter from the Prefettura della Provincia di Torino to the Ministero dell'Interno, Rome, 8 February 1912 and 12 July 1935; Angela Marietti, busta 3062, Letter from the Consolato Generale d'Italia to the Ministero dell'Interno, Rome, 14 Dec. 1911 and 14 April 1913. The December letter is in Michele Marietti's file.

20 On Illinois's red towns and coal communities, see Gabaccia, *Militants and Migrants*, 112–20; Creagh, 'Socialism in America,' 151–2; and Avrich, *Anarchist Portraits*, 166, 174. For details on the Italian International see Pernicone, *Italian Anarchism*, 210–12.

21 For information on radical holiday festivities in Illinois coal towns see *Il Grido degli Oppressi*, 17 March 1894, *La Questione Sociale*, 14 October 1899, and *L'Era Nuova*, 26 June 1909.

22 Many of these cooperatives were started by Italians; see John H. Walker Papers, box 3, folder 18, 11 Aug. 1916 (to Walker from Peter Micca Leary), box 4, folder 22, 8 Sept. 1916 (to Walker from Louis Rigotti) and box 1, folder 6, 16 May 1916 (to Walker from Andrew Zuliani). Walker's papers are in the Illinois History Survey at the University of Illinois, Urbana-Champaign.

23 Marsh, *Anarchist Women*, 10–14; Avrich, *Anarchist Portraits*, 171. Note that Margaret Marsh's paradigm includes two groupings of anarchists, while Paul Avrich delineates four categories. What I term anarchist-socialist, Avrich and Marsh call anarchist-communist. For the most part, Italian, Belgian, and French anarchists in Illinois dubbed themselves anarchist-socialists and therefore I adhere to their terminology.

24 Marsh, *Anarchist Women*, 14.

25 *La Questione Sociale,* 15 April 1897: 'il prete quando fa delle bugiarde promesse alle masse affamate ... saranno premiate in paradiso.'

26 Marsh, *Anarchist Women,* 19–20; G.P. Maximoff, ed., *The Political Philosophy of Bakunin: Scientific Anarchism* (New York: Free Press, 1964), 326–7; Martha A. Ackelsberg, *Free Women of Spain: Anarchism and the Struggle for the Emancipation of Women* (Bloomington: Indiana University Press, 1991), 24–5; Louis Patsouras, *Jean Grave and the Anarchist Tradition in France* (Middletown, NJ: Caslon Company, 1995), 13, 94.

27 *La Questione Sociale,* 7 March 1908, 'Non sono un'intellettuale; figlia del popolo diseredato e oppresso ... ho speso i miei giorni alla lettura e alla contemplazione di un gran libro;' CPC, busta 1205, 8 Sept. 1899, 'Molto intelligente, ma poco instruita. Non ha compiuto studi.'

28 *La Questione Sociale,* 30 June 1897, 'La missione della madre ha per scopo principale l'educazione dei figli. Essa deve fare di loro degli uomini onesti, dei cittadini virtuosi, degli operai laboriosi.'

29 Eileen Boris, 'The Power of Motherhood: Black and White Activist Women Redefine the "Political,"' in Seth Koven and Sonya Michel, eds., *Mothers of a New World: Maternalist Politics and the Origins of Welfare States* (New York: Routledge, 1993), 222.

30 *La Questione Sociale,* 30 June 1897, 'La madre borghese non inculchera al figlio l'amore agli uomini, ma bensì l'amore egoistico delle cose'; 'l'amore alla libertà propria unito al rispetto per la libertà altrui.'

31 Ibid., 'Non piangete, o madri, se qualcuno dei figli vostri, ribellandosi alla società intiera abbandonando i pregiudizi dei padri ... Oh! si mille volte meglio essere martiri coscienti, che no vittime senza dignità.'

32 *L'Aurora,* 13 Oct. 1900, 2: '1. che tutti gli uomini nascono uguali e quindi hanno uguali diritti; 2. che l'esistenza d'un dio regolatore dell'universo è assurda, inutile, criminosa, perché la credenza religiosa serve appunto ai padroni, ai governanti ...; 3. che il padrone, oggi necessario ai poveri per vivere, non sarà necessario domani, quando i lavoratori vorranno lavorare e produrre per loro ... perciò ispirar la ribellione costante contro i padroni e contro ogni sfruttamento; che le leggi son fatte dai governanti per difendere il sistema di oppressione dell'oggi ... eccitar quindi nel fanciullo l'odio contro ogni legge, e fargli comprendere che legge; 5. che ... il figlio deve rifiutare di vestire l'ignobile devise del soldato, giacche l'esercito ... in realtà non serve che per difendere i ricchi contro i poveri che hanno fame.'

33 Ibid.: 'E le stesse idee deve la madre inculcare nell'animo delle fanciulle, a cui deve far comprendere in più che la disuguglianza di sesso non implica disuguaglianza di diritti, e che quindi oltre ad essere ribelli contro tutto il sistema sociale di oggi, debbono esserlo specialmente contro l'oppressione

degli uomini, i quali vogliono ritener la donna a un livello morale e materiale inferiore dell'uomo.'

34 *L'Aurora*, 24 Aug. 1901, 1: 'L'emancipazione della donna dev'essere opera della donna stessa,' 'all'ambiente sociale in cui ora soffoca, sia nella famiglia, sia nelle relazioni intime, sia sottraendosi alle ipocrite convenzioni odierne, sia nella vita pubblica.' The letter, signed 'E,' is almost certainly by Grandi.

35 *La Questione Sociale*, 7 Mar. 1908, 'Perché noi abbiamo paura di spezzare le catene ... della schiavitu ...' 'Perché noi siamo vili ... Perché noi preghiamo deboli e vinte alla voce del prete, allo scudiscio del governante, al comando del padrone, al bastone del marito, al pregiudizio della gente.'

36 Bullitt Lowry and Elizabeth Ellington Gunter, eds., *The Red Virgin: Memoirs of Louise Michel* (Tuscaloosa: University of Alabama Press, 1981), viii–xv, 58.

37 *L'Aurora*, 22 Dec. 1900, 3.

38 Pernicone, *Italian Anarchism*, 225; Moya's essay (chapter 6) in this volume.

39 *L'Aurora*, 22 Dec. 1900, 3: 'per l'emancipazione della donna ... per la conquista dei diritti che tutta l'umanità oppressa ... dalla tirannia e dai pregiudizii degli uomini ... considerano la donna come un essere inferiore, quando non la trattino addirittura come una schiava.'

40 Ibid., 2: 'una scuola di propaganda,' 'destinato a consumarvi dei buoni bicchieri di birra.'

41 Ibid.: 'la donna, il sesso debole, si compiace invece di essere nella realtà la signora della vita, l'arbitra dei destini umani'; 'Coloro che domenica lanciavano le loro frasi sciocche, credendole spiritose, a riguardo della donna, perché scordano tanti altri proverbi più veri e più saggi, quello, per esempio, il quale un poco britalmente, se si vuole, ma molto efficacemente dice che "Tira più un pelo di ... donna, che non cento paja di buoi?"'; 'Ora, è un fatto innegabile che tutte le speranze di conquista verso l'avvenire, più che sulla generazione presente, debbono riposare sulla generazione ventura la quale ... Ma, appunto, l'educazione di questa nuova generazione affidata in grandissima parte alle donne le quali più dell' uomo, e tutti lo sanno, hanno potere d'impressionare le tenere menti de' fanciulli, e lasciarvi traccie incancellabili per tutta la vita.'

42 *L'Aurora*, 10 Aug. 1901, 1: 'sia principale compito delle donne quello di preoccuparsi dell'educazione della famiglia ... e ventura generazione'; 'se bene sapremo allevarla, potrebbe ottenere abbondanti frutti di progresso e di liberta'; 'noi potremo soltanto combattere l'influenza nefasta di tutti i libri cosi detti educativi'; 'veleno dei pregiudizii di patria, di religione, di rispetto alla proprietà, all'autorità, alla legge, ecc.' Jean Grave, *Les Aventures de Nono* (Paris: Heidbrinck, 1901).

43 Patsouras, *Jean Grave*, 60.
44 *L'Aurora*, 10 Aug. 1901, 1; 'Noi crediamo di aver ragione di meritare l'appoggio volenteroso dei compagni'; 'il far naufragare questa nostra varebbe a sfiduciare quelle non numerose compagne che muovono i primi ed incerti passi nel nostro movimento.'
45 Ibid., 2 Oct. 1901, 3; 'e quando hanno incominciato a leggere qualche opuscolo e ad assistere a qualche conferenza s'immaginano d'esser più anarchiche degli altri! ... vogliono far notare la loro presenza, approfittando dello sbaglio di madre natura nel lasciar loro lo scilinguagnolo sempre sciolto, ma non s'accorgono come diventan noiose in molte occasioni.'
46 Ibid., 12 Jan. 1901, 3: 'Se ci troviamo in mezzo a dei signori uomini che van discutendo di morale di religione o di politica e ci azzardiamo di interevenire colla nostra opinione, quasi sempre chi ci sta sopra (papa o fratello o marito o compagno) ci dice: – ma tu sei una donna: devi tacere!'
47 Ibid.: 'nell'aspirare alla redenzione nostra, politica e morale: e nella redenzione di tutta la umanità dal terribile servaggio economico.'
48 *L'Aurora*, 22 Dec. 1900, 2–3: 'l'opera dei rinnovatori dell'avvenire, dei rivoluzionarii, sarà non meno faticosa e difficile di quanto lo sia ora'; 'potremo adoprare la sua influenza resa doce e benefica a vantaggio di tutti, per crescer su una nuova generazione di lavoratori conscienti e spogli di pregiudizii.'
49 CPC, busta 3062, 18 Jan. 1907.
50 *Bureau County Republican*, 12 Sept. 1901, 1.
51 For Malatesta's visit, see *La Questione Sociale*, 10 Feb. 1900; for other conferences, see also *La Questione Sociale*, 15 June 1898 and 5 Oct. 1907 and *L'Era Nuova*, 12 Dec. 1908.
52 *La Questione Sociale*, 27 May 1899, 22 Aug. 1899, and 16 Sept. 1899; Records of the Knights of Labor (Spring Valley), 16 May 1899, Illinois State University Archives, Normal, Ill.
53 *Bureau County Republican*, 7 Sept. 1899; *La Questione Sociale*, 16 Sept. 1899.
54 Emma Goldman, *Living My Life* (New York: Alfred A. Knopf, 1931), 245.
55 *L'Aurora*, 9 and 16 Mar. 1901, 'Non ho bisogno di dirvi quanto sarei felice di venire a vedere i compagni di Spring Valley ... Siate sicuri che mi affligge molto di rifiutare il vostro invito fraterno.'
56 *L'Aurora*, 16 Mar., 3, and 4 May 1901, 3. On Gori see also the essays by Moya and Ventresca and Iacovetta in this volume.
57 *L'Aurora* 10 Aug. 1901, 4; 17 Aug. 1901, 4; 24 Aug. 1901, 4; and 31 Aug. 1901, 4.
58 *Bureau County Republican*, 3 Oct. 1901, 1; *L'Aurora*, 2 Oct. 1901, 1; 12 Oct. 1901, 1 and 2; 7 Dec. 1901, 1; CPC, busta 1205.

8 Italian Women's Proletarian Feminism in the New York City Garment Trades, 1890s–1940s

Jennifer Guglielmo

On 19 January 1913 over 4000 striking Italian women garment workers gathered at Cooper Union in New York City to learn that the International Ladies Garment Workers' Union (ILGWU) had signed an agreement with manufacturers without their approval. With jeers and the stomping of feet, the women rejected the union leaders' instructions to return to work. Several women rushed to the stage, forcing speakers off the platform with cries of 'a frame up,' and urged workers to abandon the ILGWU in favour of the more militant Industrial Workers of the World (IWW). A 'storm of protest,' as the *New York Times* called it, spread to the streets as Italian women workers hurled stones at the windows of a nearby shirtwaist factory and sat in the centre of Third Avenue, bringing traffic in lower Manhattan to a halt. Dissent spread throughout Brooklyn and Harlem as workers learned of the settlement and gathered in the streets to defy the court injunction forbidding them to picket garment shops. The next day, in an icy snowstorm and sub-zero temperatures, 20,000 workers, most of them Italian women, marched through the city's garment districts in opposition to the union, the state, and their employers.[1]

The rioting in 1913 erupted after unprecedented numbers of first- and second-generation Italian-American women spent months on a mass organizing campaign in New York City's clothing trades. Alongside Russian, Lithuanian, Polish, German, Greek, Irish, Spanish, Hungarian, and other immigrant workers, Italian women had organized picket lines, convinced others to abandon their sewing machines, and withstood arrest and beatings at the hands of employers and police. Although sceptical of the ILGWU (an affiliate of the American Federation of Labor), they nevertheless hoped the union would bring them union recognition, better wages, and safer working conditions. By late January, 150,000 workers in four sectors of garment production had walked off their jobs, paralyzing the industry and forcing manufacturers into negotiation. As the second largest group of workers in the garment trades, Italian women's solidarity and militancy had been crucial to the union's ability to orchestrate one of the most explosive labour uprisings of the era. Yet, at the height of the strike, Italian women argued, the ILGWU had sold them out. As workers in the most poorly paid and dangerous jobs in the city's dress and shirtwaist factories, they had the most to lose in the settlement, which institutionalized a sex-based division of labour, assigned women to the lowest-paid jobs, and set their minimum wage lower than that of men who held the same jobs. The agreement had won them union recognition, but they had not gained a voice in union affairs. The leaders of the ILGWU, they argued angrily, 'preferred to deal with the employers rather than with their own members.'[2]

The 1913 'riot' encapsulates several compelling themes in the history of Italian women workers in the United States. During the early decades of the twentieth century, the majority of Italian women who migrated to the New York metropolitan area found work in the needle trades and, like other female garment workers, they endured low wages, dangerous working conditions, and inhumane treatment. Yet, unlike the Jewish women who dominated the rank and file of the industry at the turn of the century, Italian women did not join the New York garment unions en masse until the Great Depression. In earlier decades, their political struggles were more often waged outside of and in opposition to mainstream labour and political organizations. Dramas such as the 1913 uprising brought such oppositional grassroots activity to the surface.

The social and cultural world that first- and second-generation Italian-American women created to nurture dissident political activity has remained invisible to scholars of U.S. history, many of whom have heeded the words of the union leaders who argued that 'there was no real discontent among the workers, only a plot by the rival Industrial Workers of the World to destroy the union,' and that Italian women insurgents had been 'easily pacified.'[3] Stereotypes of Italian-American women as docile workers, bound by patriarchal traditions, and confined to their homes to suffer in silence, continue to dominate narratives of U.S. history largely because most of the research on Italian-American women's political activism has relied on English-language sources, and used the more documented histories of Eastern European and Russian Jewish women's militance and class consciousness as the yardstick by which to assess Italian-American women's activity. Stereotypes also abound in the male-dominated literature on Italian-American working-class activism, where narrow definitions of the political have obscured female activism.

The labour activism of Italian-American women garment workers differed from that of Italian-American men and Jewish women. It also differed from the activism of African-American, Chinese, Korean, Puerto Rican, Jamaican, Panamanian, and the other Asian and Caribbean women who entered the U.S. needle trades alongside and after them. Italian women often entered the labour market at a rank below other European immigrants but always above women of colour, and sometimes men of colour too. Their entry level reflected, in part, the moment at which they entered the U.S. garment trades, before foreign competition and the relocation of businesses to lower-wage areas had begun to erode key sectors of the industry. As a result, they did not experience the disadvantages of industry contractions in the same ways as those workers who entered the trades during and after the Second World War. But external factors provide only a partial explanation. When African-American, Puerto Rican, Chinese, and other Asian and Caribbean women and men began to enter the garment trades in the 1930s, Italians held a relative monopoly over the higher-paying jobs, the result of Italian men's shared political leadership with Jewish men in the union's hierarchy, and their special status as the only workers granted autonomy in their own ethnic locals. This privilege meant that Italians could build a solid base of organizational power within the garment unions, gain access to better-paying jobs, and use the locals as a centre of community activism, organization, and protest. They consolidated this autonomy and power during the 1920s and 1930s, when the ILGWU purged its most radical members and grew increasingly unwilling to distribute power and benefits to its newest members, most of them women of colour. On the eve of the Second World War, Italian garment workers had gained control of a movement that not only notoriously restricted women's role but was also increasingly stratified along racial lines.[4]

This essay examines the transition that Italian women garment workers made from waging oppositional struggles from the margins to occupying the privileged spaces at the centre of U.S. labour institutions. The project of recovering the history of protest and collective action of this group of 'unorganized' workers requires that we follow the advice of scholars such as Robin D.G. Kelley, Ardis Cameron, Nan Enstad, George

Lipsitz, Dana Frank, and others, who have demonstrated how we must think differently about politics in order to appreciate those previously hidden spaces where ordinary people have critiqued authority.[5] By reconceptualizing the political to include unorganized, everyday acts of resistance that inform and shape formal working-class movements and institutions, we are able to understand how Italian immigrant women and their daughters confronted systems of hierarchy and domination in the United States, how they claimed and asserted political identities, and the complex implications of their choices.

The Roots of Resistance

Italian women needleworkers first became a discernible part of New York City's garment labour force in the 1880s.[6] As one of the largest sectors of the industrial economy, garment manufacturers had long relied on abundant and cheap immigrant labour, which in turn enabled clothing manufacturers to expand their businesses and make New York City an international centre of garment production.[7] The industry's labour force was characterized by a steady displacement of old immigrant groups by more recent immigrants, and by a continued reliance on the cheap labour of women workers. Of the 29,439 workers in U.S. dress and waist shops in 1913, 24,128 were women and 4711 were men.[8] Whereas earlier migration waves had brought Irish and German seamstresses and tailors into New York City's first clothing shops, the 1880s and 1890s saw large numbers of Jews from Eastern Europe and Russia enter the industry, as well as Italians, who formed the second largest group of labourers. By the 1930s Italian women formed the majority of garment workers in New York City, just as African-American, Chinese, Puerto Rican, and other women from the Caribbean began entering the clothing industries in larger numbers.[9]

· Various factors account for the presence of Italian women in the garment trades, including their active recruitment by New York garment manufacturers who advertised extensively in Italian newspapers, and often with promises of a union job.[10] They were also trained in needlecraft techniques, such as fine hand sewing and embroidery, whether by female kin, the local seamstress, or in convent and public schools in Italy.[11] Such training prepared women for homemaking but also offered a way to earn wages for their family.[12] Between 1900 and 1910, textiles were among Italy's chief exports and the industry relied heavily on women's labour. While textile work varied from region to region, women throughout the peninsula dominated the industry, whether in domestic production, cottage industry, or factory manufacture.[13] Tina Gaeta learned to sew from her mother and grandmother, both seamstresses in Salerno, before migrating to New York City in 1902. She recalled that the *sarta* (seamstress) held a distinguished position in her community; the scissors that dangled at her waist symbolized her status. In New York, a young Tina and her siblings helped their mother with piecework in the men's clothing trade; when they became skilled, they entered the factories in their neighbourhood. The daughter of a Sicilian dressmaker, Antoinetta Lazzaro first learned to sew from her mother and sister and then in a day nursery, where the nuns taught embroidery. A week after arriving in the United States in 1928, Antoinetta began work as an operator on dresses in her East Harlem neighbourhood. As a child, Carmela La Rosa was sent to train with a *sarta* in Palermo; by fourteen, she was training other girls and working as a dressmaker out of her home. Upon arriving in New York in 1912, she found work immediately in a bridal dress shop, where for thirty years she sewed alongside other Italian women.[14]

These stories reflect what federal agencies and researchers also discovered for the early decades of the twentieth century: New York City's garment trades contained large percentages of southern Italian women and many of them had earned wages sewing in Italy.[15] As in Italy, needlework was a skill Italian women could use to earn money in New York City. Those women who had not learned to sew in Italy turned to the simple work of finishing men's and women's tailored garments and were trained in other, less-skilled tasks.

Italian women also brought with them a history of protest and rebellion. During the mass migrations (1890s–1920s), widespread poverty, economic depressions, labour upheavals, and violent state repression shaped the lives of most Italians. In the 1890s Italians throughout the peninsula formed workers' organizations, including *fasci dei lavoratori* (workers' unions), and struggled for a reconstruction of society in which industry and government were brought under the control of workers. The Italian government condemned these actions, shutting down newspapers, arresting leaders, and brutally suppressing workers' protests. Repression intensified after Mussolini came to power in 1922. The Italian labour movement extended internationally, as Italians traversed the globe, transplanting traditions of militancy and rebellion.[16]

As historians such as Donna Gabaccia and Jole Calapso have well documented, women played critical roles in these popular movements,

and their collaborative activities often helped them to carve out autonomous political spaces. Throughout southern Italy and Sicily, in regions
with the highest percentages of migration to the United States, women
often emerged as the most militant activists in popular demonstrations
and neighbourhood movements among farm workers and urban labourers. Gender differences were also important; while men focused on
employers, women targeted the state and resorted more frequently to
direct-action strategies such as looting and rioting. In Sicily women
became the primary bearers of the communal protest traditions (be it
subsistence towns, areas of market cultivation, or towns with large wheat
estates). They formed *sezioni femminili* (women's sections) within local
socialist *fasci* as well as their own *fasci femminili* (women's unions). In
Piana dei Greci, thousands of women participated in a tax revolt, destroying municipal offices while demanding that 'all should have bread
for themselves and their children.' In Monreale, women and children
filled the piazza chanting, 'Down with the municipal government and
long live the union!' After looting the offices of city council, they marched
toward Palermo crying, 'Abbiamo fame!' (We are hungry!) In Villafrati,
Caterina Costanzo led a group of women carrying clubs to the fields,
where they threatened workers who had not joined the community in a
general strike against the repressive local government and high taxes. In
Balestrate, thousands of women dressed in traditional clothes and also
armed with clubs, marched through the streets, demanding an end to
government corruption and high taxes. Many of the Sicilians who later
migrated to the United States, Gabaccia observes, had experienced,
directly or indirectly, this sort of unrest in their hometowns.[17]

Such protests were not limited to Sicily, but occurred in many cities,
including Rome, Bologna, Imola, Ancona, Naples, Bari, Florence, and
Genoa. In Ancona, hundreds of women, men, and children demonstrated for lower bread prices and an end to the flour tax in 1898 with
the cries 'Viva l'anarchia!' and 'Viva la rivoluzione sociale!' [18] Within
months of the nationwide uprisings, Italian prime minister Francesco
Crispi announced a state of siege; workers' movements were suppressed,
and hundreds of women and men were imprisoned and murdered. After
1900, Italian women turned to collective action in trade unions and
radical political parties, participating in organizing drives and strikes in
textile, tobacco, clothing, rice, and hemp industries, and in organizations such as the Unione Sindacale Italiana, the Partito Socialista Italiano,
and the Camere del Lavoro.[19] By 1908, women's membership in the

National Federation of Textile Trades, the union that represented the country's largest industry and the one employing the most women, equalled that of men.[20] And when the need arose, Italian women workers defended their autonomy from union directives.[21] Such stories, experiences, and political lessons were a vital part of what Italian women carried into the Italian-American labour movement, which, as Rudolph Vecoli observes, 'did not simply spring from the American soil,' but was 'in many ways an extension of the labor movement in Italy.'[22]

The turn of the century also saw the beginning of a labour migration in which Italian women entered important sectors of the North American economy, including New York City's garment trades. Among all Italian women working in the United States in 1905, 80 per cent were employed in the fashion industries, which included garments, millinery, and artificial flowers.[23] In 1911, the U.S. Bureau of Labor reported that half of all women workers in the men's garment industry were Italian; for the clothing industry as a whole the figure ranged from one-quarter to one-third.[24] As Miriam Cohen has documented, the numbers of Italian women garment workers continued to grow during the first half of the twentieth century. In 1925, 64 per cent of all Italian women in the United States worked in the fashion industry. By 1950, 77 per cent of first-generation, and 44 per cent of second-generation Italian-American women in New York City were factory operatives, the majority of them in the needle trades. Highly decentralized and with production processes that required little or no machinery, the garment industry offered women and children the opportunity for immediate wage work. Many owners kept their shops and permanent workforce small, while contractors responsible for sewing the garments cut in the manufacturer's shop subcontracted finishing tasks to homemakers during the busy season.[25] As the U.S. Department of Labor reported in 1916, the nature of the garment industry, with its homework, sweating, contract, and subcontracting systems, and concentration of cheap 'casual women workers,' lent itself to the exploitation of its workers, who toiled under 'a condition of deplorable industrial chaos.'[26]

The industry was also stratified rigidly by gender, and Italian women were assigned to the lowest paid 'women's work' as finishers, operators, sample makers, shirtwaist and dressmakers, and employed as home- or pieceworkers.[27] For the early twentieth century, Miriam Cohen found that one-fifth of workers in the men's garment industry were female home finishers, almost all of them Italian women and their children.[28] A

1911 congressional study revealed that homework was done in approximately one-fourth of all Italian households in New York City,[29] while other government surveys found that 95 per cent of all homework was done by Italians. In 1920, the ILGWU estimated that close to 80 per cent of the 10,000 hand embroiderers in New York City were Italian women.[30] For thousands of them work began with bundles of partly constructed garments (dresses, blouses, skirts, undergarments) picked up at an agent's warehouse or a local factory, often in their neighbourhood. With the help of young children and other female kin or neighbours, they then finished the garments at home. As homework was seasonal, families had to maximize their wages in the rush period, which often meant that all available family members, including young children, worked late into the night to increase output. While home-based work allowed mothers to supplement the family income, watch young children, and enjoy some independence in their work schedules, it was highly exploitative. Women often worked as long as eighteen hours a day and earned only four or five cents an hour.[31]

Both younger single women and married women also sought work outside the home in garment factories. They most often found jobs in the 'unskilled' trades as operators and finishers, 'lining garments, sewing on buttons, trimming threads, and pulling bastings by hand,'[32] while employers, trying to fill orders on short notice, continually pushed them to increase the pace. Exhaustion from standing for hours on end, severe eye strain brought on by hours of close work in poor lighting, long-term exposure to filthy work environments, and the sexual abuse of some bosses and male workers made garment work extremely dangerous and difficult.[33]

Employers monitored women closely to maximize production and discourage collective action. They fined workers for being late, talking, singing, and taking too much time in the bathroom, because these activities might help to build an oppositional political culture. When women attempted to organize outside of the factories, employers found other methods of surveillance, including sending spies to union meetings to spot the 'trouble makers' whose lives they would make so 'unbearable, that the worker was forced to leave, if not dismissed.'[34] Italian immigrant women became highly critical of what they termed the *rigorosa sorveglianza* (rigorous surveillance) of garment employers, the dangerous work conditions, and the low-quality of work they were forced to produce rapidly.[35]

Women's Revolutionary Proletarian Culture before
the First World War

From the moment Italian women entered the United States they united to alleviate poverty and exploitation, and asserted and redefined their identities, priorities, and methods of struggle. In the late nineteenth and early twentieth centuries, labour uprisings were a regular feature in Italian immigrant communities. In cities such as Hoboken, Paterson, Newark, Lowell, Passaic, Little Falls, Boston, Hopedale, Rochester, Lawrence, Lynn, Chicago, Tampa, Cleveland, and Providence, Italian women were central actors in workers' movements, and were regularly portrayed in the Italian immigrant radical press as *le più ardenti nella lotta* (the most ardent in the struggle).[36] Indeed, Italian women often entered politics in the U.S. via labour militance. They became pivotal to workplace actions, where they drew on communal protest traditions from Italy and on the urban female neighbourhood networks they had developed. While Italian women rarely held positions of leadership in unions or formal strike committees during this period, their ability to organize co-workers and neighbours often proved crucial in winning labour struggles, especially in the clothing and textile industries, where they outnumbered men in the rank and file.[37]

Stories of Italian female activism on the front lines of U.S. labour struggles are numerous and highlight women's audacity, courage, and inventiveness in confronting abusive and demeaning conditions. Generally, however, these stories have been missing from the scholarship on working women's labour struggles in New York City, with the result that Italian women are assumed absent from such movements. Such conclusions are drawn from sources that portray Italian women as non-militants reluctant to join strikes orchestrated by the Jewish women who dominated the rank and file in garment shops and unions at the turn of the century.[38] Indeed, the history of New York City female garment workers in this period remains almost exclusively focused on the first major garment strike in the city, the famous 1909 'Uprising of 20,000.' During this strike Jewish women workers responded to the reluctance of the ILGWU's male leaders to support them by aligning themselves with middle-class progressives and feminist activists in the Women's Trade Union League (WTUL).[39] Scholars have been quick to assert that Italian women were unorganized and unsympathetic to the union movement on the grounds that only 6 per cent (approximately 2000) of the strikers were Italian women, while they constituted almost 34 per cent of the shirtwaist industry labour force.[40]

This conclusion requires revision. If Italian-language dailies such as *Il Bollettino della Sera* and *Il Progresso Italo-Americano* covered the shirtwaist strike only briefly, they gave considerable attention to another strike that occurred that same month, just across the Hudson River in Hoboken, New Jersey. There, Italian women textile workers engaged in a month-long strike for livable wages, shorter work hours, and improved working conditions, and they did so alongside Italian men, as well as Armenian, Russian, German, Polish, and other immigrant women and men.[41] As a result of their success, Arturo Caroti, an IWW organizer of the strike and manager of a cooperative store owned by the Hoboken silk workers, was recruited immediately by the WTUL to organize Italian female garment workers in New York.[42] But while Caroti gained public prominence as the leader of the Hoboken strike, it was the *pinzettatrici* (pinchers) – Italian women in the worst-paid and most monotonous jobs as piece-workers in the silk industry – who had formed the most militant core of strikers. Their successful efforts at forging cross-ethnic alliances with other textile and clothing workers under the IWW banner before and during the strike explains why immigrant workers in Hackensack, Passaic, Paterson, North Hudson, Jersey City, and New York City walked off their jobs in solidarity with the Hoboken movement.[43]

In each of these struggles Italian women transplanted homeland strategies. When clashes between workers, police, and factory owners grew violent in Paterson, West Hoboken, and elsewhere, Italian women used a tactic from Italy – protecting their children by sending them to stay with *compagne* (women comrades) in New York City and further away. That strikers could entrust their children to a *compagna* for months at a time reflected the women's success in developing these networks in advance. The 'exodus of children' in turn strengthened ties among Italian women in the New York metropolitan area.[44] As in their *paese* (homeland), women's direct-action tactics involved entire communities, not just wage-earners, as demonstrated in the 1912 Lawrence Strike, where the female mob was at the heart of workers' strategies.[45] It also emerged elsewhere; in 1903 'a mob of Italians, a third of them women,' reportedly 'assaulted a gang of Americans and Irish' laying track on the Third Avenue subway line while Italian men were on strike with the IWW.[46] (We saw these same tactics at work in the 1913 ILGWU strike described at the start of this chapter.) These stories suggest the need to challenge the conventional wisdom that Italian women did not join the 'Uprising of 20,000' because, unlike Jewish women, they were isolated from radical political and social movements, lacked militant traditions, and suffered from weak community networks and restrictive families.[47] Rather, Italian women garment workers did not join the 1909 uprising en masse in part because they were not convinced that either the ILGWU or the WTUL were committed to their particular struggles.

Writing about the strike in *Collier's* three years later, journalist Adriana Spadoni explained that while the Italian working woman 'appeared gentle, malleable' in reality, she was 'like a rock.' 'Those at the head of the movement for better conditions,' she continued, 'saw all their efforts about to be nullified by this brown, ignorant, silent woman who would not listen, and, when she did, could not or would not understand.'[48] Italian community organizers, however, discovered another reason for the women's lack of enthusiasm. Within days of the uprising, the IWW, the Federazione Socialista Italiana (FSI), and the Socialist party hastily sent out teams of organizers to mobilize Italian women garment workers because this work had not been done before. Several thousand Italian women did walk off their jobs in solidarity with Jewish women, but the organizers noted that the vast majority were deeply sceptical of the strike since very little effort had been made to include them.[49] Indeed, both WTUL and ILGWU leaders routinely described Italian-American women as 'hopeless' labour activists, who were 'absolutely under the dominance of men of their family, and heavily shackled by old customs and traditions.'[50]

Neglected by mainstream labour movements, Italian women in New York City pursued collective forms of protest and resistance that, as in Italy, were independent of formal organization but embedded in the women's own neighbourhood and kinship networks. Since most women found jobs through family and friends and worked in factories located within or near their neighbourhoods, the garment shop was at the centre of informal systems of female networking. Through such relationships Italian women learned transportation systems, how to communicate with English-speaking employers and co-workers, and, if they had children, how to find care for their young while they worked.[51] In her 1919 study, Louise Odencrantz found that the Italian immigrant woman relied on these networks to learn the rudiments of the trade, 'so she did not feel as "strange" as if she had been plunged into the midst of work,' and 'to make her clothes more presentable according to American standards, so she will look less like a new arrival.'[52] Conversations, songs, jokes, workplace complaints, and shared dreams of a life without such pain also reinforced a sense of collective identity. Ginevre Spagnoletti's dress shop in the Bowery was 'full of Italian women bending over their machines and peering at the needles,' as the El trains roared by, but also was a place where the women were always 'singing and joking together to escape the monotony and beat back the gloom.'[53] Even in shops where singing or talking was prohibited, 'some girl, unable to endure the silence any longer, would begin humming a tune which would be taken up by others near her.'[54] Like other workers, Italian women also colluded to steal time for themselves on the job by slowing down the pace of work and using any opportunity to talk about family, neighbourhood, work conditions, and politics.[55]

Women's networks also facilitated more dramatic episodes of resistance. Strikes often began when one woman was harassed or insulted and her co-workers walked off the job in protest.[56] Adriana Valenti, who learned the power of collective action from her father's stories of peasant uprisings in his *paese*, took action as a teenager after listening to the women in her shop discuss their continual struggle to feed their families. 'I was a fighter,' she recalled of the day she shut off the power in her shop, and signalled workers to leave their machines and hold an outdoor meeting. When the owner came after Adriana with an umbrella, demanding that she leave, all the women operators walked out with her.[57] Such stories fill the oral histories of Italian-American women and also regularly appeared in the radical press. Some English-language labour newspapers also reported these episodes to illustrate that if Italian women were often not sympathetic to unions in the United States, they were adept at collective action and therefore capable of organization.[58]

For their part, Italian-language workers' papers chronicled such stories to encourage oppositional activism. In an effort to build community support for the women in her shop on West 27th Street, Rose Alagna wrote about the indignities they were forced to endure and announced plans to orchestrate a strike against a boss who demanded they stay late without compensation to gather stray pins on the floor.[59] Stories of women's collective action were also retold on the shop floor, around kitchen tables, and on tenement stoops, and passed from one generation to the next. These daily, unorganized, seemingly spontaneous actions formed an important part of Italian-American women's political strategies, as they did for all workers.

Italian seamstresses in New York City also used more formal organizational strategies to build solidarity and political consciousness. Especially important were the workers' *circoli* (clubs); modelled on the mutual-benefit societies that in Italy had become a popular strategy for extending radical movements, these groups spread throughout the Italian diaspora.[60] In the United States, they also forged alliances with radical Spanish, Eastern European and Russian-Jewish, Cuban, Puerto Rican, and other Caribbean-American immigrant workers' groups (which were also transnational in nature).[61] This network was at the heart of New York City's revolutionary working-class subculture in this period. For example, in the handmade cigar industry, such groups coalesced into unions and jointly published radical newspapers. And in Brooklyn, Italian shoe and garment workers built coalitions with Latin-American, Spanish, and Jewish neighbours through a *circolo* called Club Avanti, which was founded by Sicilian anarchists and free-thinkers.[62]

L'emancipazione della donna (the emancipation of women) was a regular topic of conversation within these circles because women kept the issue on the agenda; they invited prominent Italian women radical intellectuals and activists to speak on women's activism in transnational labour movements and to help them mobilize Italian women workers in the U.S.[63] These groups became a primary space for working women's politicization and education. Vincenza Scarpaci discovered that shirtwaist factory workers Angela and Maria Bambace were drawn into labour activism in 1916 by attending meetings sponsored by Italian socialists and anarchists in their neighbourhood in Harlem, where they also met IWW organizers and learned syndicalist strategies.[64] Tina Cacici, a textile worker who would become a notorious leader of a radical faction in the Lawrence strike of 1919 and an organizer for the Amalgamated Clothing Workers of America (ACWA), first became known for her fiery speeches on women's emancipation at a local socialist club in Brooklyn.[65] Feminist discourse and activism also emerged as central themes in festivals, dances, picnics, and theatrical performances, thereby making them an integral part of *circoli* culture.[66] Many of these activities included men, but women also organized their own *gruppi femminili di propaganda* (women's propaganda groups), where mothers and daughters could debate and produce revolutionary theory and strategy.[67] In 1897, Maria Roda, a weaver in a Paterson silk mill, self-described anarcho-socialist, and early organizer of separate activist circles for women, announced that women in New York City and New Jersey were meeting on their own 'because we feel and suffer; we too want to immerse ourselves in the struggle against this society, because we too feel, from birth, the need to be free, to be equal.'[68] A decade later, Italian women in New York City were still building *gruppi femminili di propaganda*, working closely with Italian women's political circles in New Jersey, and corresponding regularly with similar groups in cities such as Boston and Chicago, and in the mining communities of Pennsylvania, Illinois, and Vermont (Barre).[69] They too used community-wide meetings, jointly hosted lectures, and the radical press to publicize their efforts, develop activist networks for women, and bring *l'emancipazione della donna* to the centre of working-class revolutionary debates and practice. As a comrade from the Spring Valley, Illinois, coal town studied by Caroline Waldron Merithew put it, they struggled '[f]or the emancipation of women, together with those struggles that must occur in order to attain the rights that all of oppressed humanity demand.' 'A woman,' she added, 'must struggle with great zeal to emancipate herself from the tyranny and prejudice of men, and from those who foolishly consider women inferior, and often treat her like a slave.'[70]

The *gruppi femminili* also reflected Italian women's desire to assert their commitment to the labour movement, which meant confronting those male comrades who held to notions that a woman could never 'elevate herself from subservience.'[71] In response, they argued, 'You believe that a woman, who takes care of the entire home and the children, is not concerned with education, that she cannot find the time in her long day, to dedicate herself to her emancipation? ... Women also have the capacity, tenacity and perseverance to confront obstacles and elevate themselves to the road of their emancipation ... We agitate, we organize to prove to the world that accuses us, that we too are capable of these things.'[72] The core group of women active in the *gruppi femminili* embraced revolutionary socialist and anarcho-syndicalist ideas, and advocated working-class mobilization and collective action in the context of the industrial union movement. In this way, their propaganda work provided women with a point of entry into the larger American labour movement. The Italian women textile workers in Paterson who formed one of the earliest *gruppi femminili* also participated in forming one of the first IWW locals alongside men in 1906, laying the groundwork for collective action in the years that followed.[73]

In fact, workplace agitation increased dramatically among Italian workers in New York City overall after the founding of the IWW in 1905.[74] The centrality of international working-class struggle and revolution to the *circoli* and the 'virtually disenfranchised status' of Italian workers in relation to the exclusionary and nativist unions of the American Federation of Labor helps to explain why many Italian workers joined 'a militant organization that made unskilled workers the primary subjects of its revolutionary program.'[75] Salvatore Salerno's research has demonstrated how Italian anarchist textile workers in Paterson were among the first to create foreign-language locals of the IWW; that they remained active in the IWW during the critical period (1905–8) when the leadership shifted from socialists to direct actionists; and that Italian women infused these anarcho-syndicalist locals with feminist praxis well into the 1920s.[76] Italian women were particularly drawn to the IWW's emphasis on industrial unionism and direct action, which more closely resembled strategies in Italy. Also, from the start, the IWW backed their labour struggles. Following the 1909 uprising, it was the IWW that demanded that the ILGWU make all of its decisions in mass meetings rather than in committees where Italians were absent or under-represented.[77] The IWW drew its membership from many Italian-American radical circles, and assisted with major organizing drives among Italian shoemakers, and hotel workers, barbers, piano makers, and textile, garment, construction, and dock workers throughout New York City.[78]

The vast majority of Italian garment workers in New York City did not join the ILGWU in the 1909 strike, but they were visible and active participants in the 'Great Revolt' of 50,000 cloak-makers one year later. That strike helped to make the ILGWU the third-largest member of the AFL (1914). More than 2800 Italian workers, many of them inspired by the gains made in the 1909 uprising, joined the ILGWU in the first three days of the 1910 strike.[79] Three of the strikers, Catherine Valenti, Anna Canno, and Sadie La Porta, organized a separate local to mobilize the unprecedented numbers of Italian women that began attending union meetings and joining picket lines, often with their children. Three weeks later, an additional 20,000 Italian workers walked out, including large numbers of Italian women finishers who went on strike in solidarity with the mostly male cloak-makers.[80]

Why had Italian women begun to organize in garment unions at this time? Their dramatic shift from 'scabs' to ILGWU strikers speaks less of their sudden politicization than of an important change in strategy that was then taking form. First, Italian women were willing to join a strike orchestrated by the more moderate, reformist, AFL-affiliated union because it had become increasingly impossible to organize separately from them. As Annelise Orleck has argued, the 1909 shirtwaist uprising produced mixed results, but it 'breathed new life into a struggling immigrant labor movement and transformed the tiny ILGWU into a union of national significance.'[81] In the next decade, the ILGWU would have more success than the IWW in forcing garment employers to the bargaining table, and so began to attract many revolutionary leaders in the Italian immigrant community. Second, the ILGWU became willing to invest time and funds to recruit Italian organizers. Unlike in the 1909 uprising, Italians had been involved in planning and executing the 1910 strike.[82]

Significantly, the initial strategy of both the ILGWU and WTUL, to hire prominent socialist Italian male labour leaders to bring Italian women into the union, was unsuccessful. In the 1909 strike the WTUL turned to Arturo Caroti, hoping that his role in the Hoboken movement would enable him to mobilize Italian women workers. However, his tactics – buying off the strike-breakers and enlisting the support of fathers and husbands – failed to generate substantial union membership among women, and he returned to Italy in 1913. Clearly, the needs of the union or the sympathy and support of the men in their families and communities were not enough to coax Italian women into the ILGWU. They began to enter the ILGWU in 1910 partly because of what they had witnessed in 1909; they hoped that building alliances with Jewish workers might bring them access to higher wages, shorter hours, and safer working conditions. In addition, beginning in 1910, the ILGWU granted Italian workers financial and institutional support and, moreover, self-governing spaces crucial to developing the movement and building internal leadership. But since Italian women's mobilization in the ILGWU came on the heels of a strike dominated by male cloak-makers, the union and the WTUL initially assumed that Italian women could only be organized after and with the support of Italian men. Historians also have assumed that 'until Italian men were made to understand the importance of unionization, Italian women would remain outside union ranks.'[83] As a result, they have failed to recognize Italian women's efforts at building solidarity within their own ranks, their conscious shifts in strategy, and their struggle for representation and voice.

The 1910 strike, which was the first ILGWU mobilization to receive a mass base of support among Italian workers, marked a shift for garment workers. It occurred at a time when Italian migration to the United States was peaking, and when, as Bruno Ramirez observes, 'Italian associational networks had grown in leaps and bounds, and their presence within the American industrial apparatus had consolidated.' Over the next several decades, Italian garment workers, as Vecoli notes, 'found themselves in the midst of one of the most sweeping organizational drives ever to take place in one single industrial sector, where cultural, political, and ethnic dynamics interacted to convert those drives into a truly community-based movement.' In short, New York City's garment unions became a centre of Italian-American labour activism and radicalism.[84]

The movement in the garment trades drew the energies of many Italian men, including prominent radicals, but it was Italian women who at all times composed the majority of workers in the garment industry and unions. From the outset, workers such as the Bambaces, Susanna Angretina, Rosalina Ferrara, Rose De Cara, Giordana Lombardi, Anna Coocha, Laura Di Guglielmo, Lina Manetta, Maria Prestianni, Anna Squillante, Millie Tirreno, and Rosalie Conforti, and countless others, created the first organizing teams that brought thousands of *compagne* (comrades) into the ILGWU.[85] These teams of women were formed after Caroti's campaign, during and after the 1910 strike, and included both immigrants and the American-born. Indeed, union meetings, demonstrations, and picket lines were often multi-generational. Tina Gaeta remembered how her mother, who 'was always against homework,' encouraged her daughters 'to carry the picket sign when her shop went on strike.'[86] Vincenza Scarpaci has documented that Giuseppina Bambace not only let her daughters attend union meetings and participate in organizing activities, but she sometimes joined them on their union rounds with a rolling pin tucked under her arm, just in case there was trouble.[87] A buttonhole-maker and mother of six, Ginevre Spagnoletti, joined the union after she started reading the newspapers and pamphlets of an Italian anarcho-syndicalist *circolo* in her Greenwich Village neighbourhood. Each evening after work, she read them aloud to her children and encouraged political debate at her kitchen table.[88] Families were a central site where Italian women developed oppositional ideologies and strategies of resistance, and the union culture they created would be grounded in such relationships.[89]

The women who formed the first ILGWU organizing teams differed from the rank and file in one significant respect: most did not have children. Yet they often worked in the same 'women's jobs' as their married sisters as operatives, drapers, finishers, hemstitchers, and examiners. They also became radicalized by the deteriorating labour conditions in the factories, exemplified most dramatically by the Triangle Shirtwaist Factory fire in 1911, which claimed the lives of 146 women garment workers in New York City, many of them Italian women and girls. Similarly, the highly publicized and violent labour uprisings in the 1910s, in Lawrence, Paterson, Chicago, Ybor City, and other cities where

Italian women were major components of the labour force, further politicized Italian immigrant women. As many scholars have demonstrated, these events helped to unify the Italian community, and also prompted the mainstream Italian-language press, the community's *prominenti*, and local parish priests to support workers' movements publicly.[90]

After the 1910 strike, Italian women formed the majority in the newly formed Organizational Committee of the Italian Branch of the ILGWU, which became the Italian Branch, or Local 25, after the 1913 strike. With their own organizational space, women could consolidate their activism. From isolated shops spread across the city women contacted the committee each day, reporting on their struggles, methods of resistance, and their need for assistance. Organizers met with workers in community meetings and found work in garment shops that were non-union. They visited women and listened to their grievances, brought them into the union, and encouraged them to shape and direct the movement – all at the risk of arrest and beatings from employers and police. They planned workplace committees, distributed leaflets, and ran educational and publicity programs, cultural activities, demonstrations, strikes, picket lines, soup kitchens, and theatre troupes.[91] Organizers used key newspapers, such as the popular socialist Italian-language weekly *L'Operaia* (to which thousands of women garment workers were subscribers by 1914),[92] to create a community of *lavoratrici coscienti* (politically informed or 'conscious' women workers). They carried the message that 'the inferiority of women is not physiological or psychological, but social,' and advocated instead a *femminismo* that was based on 'the spirit of solidarity between women.' This feminism, they asserted, was not 'a movement against men, but one that is primarily interested in developing intelligence among women.' Rather, it was 'the belief that the woman is exploited doubly, by capitalism and by her companion ... In the labor movement women can find the opportunity to become a militant force for humanity with a clear vision of the world.'[93] In addition, Italian women drew on cultural codes of honour and respect, and an emergent ethnic nationalism, to discourage scabbing and encourage a collective identity that was grounded in labour activism. 'You are not Italians,' wrote Clara Zara, a labour organizer and factory operative, 'you who trample on our revolutionary traditions; you are not Italians who dishonour and betray the holy and sublime cause of our work ... You have massacred our reputation, our dignity, our honour, [and created] the suspicion that Italian immigrant women workers have inherited.' Dismantling this reputation required organizers to demonstrate how the union movement was a legitimate and necessary site of women's activism.[94]

These tactics paid off when unprecedented numbers of Italian women joined the large-scale uprisings among garment workers in 1913 and 1919.[95] It was also due to such efforts that women joined the ILGWU once Italian members had their own autonomous language locals in 1916 and 1919.[96] Colomba Furio's ground-breaking research on this topic showed that 'an overwhelming majority' of Italian women and girls joined the ranks of striking workers during the 1919 strike wave, and 'distinguished themselves on picket lines, at strikers' meetings, and on organizational committees.'[97] As one older Italian woman recounted, she joined the union in this period because 'me sick of the boss, me sick of work, me sick of go hungry most time.' She then raised her deformed finger, the bone worn down into the shape of a hook, and showed the space where her front teeth had once been. With a body damaged from decades of quickly twisting cotton and biting button holes to save time and keep her factory job, she concluded, 'me sick, me tired, me can stand no longer, that's why me all strike.'[98] The first administration of the Italian Dressmakers' Local 89 of the ILGWU (chartered in 1919) included many women 'who had shown particularly outstanding abilities during the strike' that won the 40-hour work week.[99]

The transition from revolutionary industrial unionism to the reform socialism of the ILGWU was neither straightforward nor accomplished quickly. Shifting strategies were continually contested. Scholars have demonstrated how this tension was informed by the 'ideological and organizational cleavages that had marked the development of the leftist movement in their home country,' and was symptomatic of the divided labour movement in the United States.[100] Throughout the U.S.-based, Italian-language radical press, male activists routinely asked, 'Is it compatible for an industrial socialist to also become a propagandist for the AFL?'[101] Although male political leaders dominate the newspapers and the historiography, Italian-American women were also at the centre of these community struggles, and they made themselves highly conspicuous. When ILGWU organizer Pasquale Di Neri tried to speak before a group of Italian women garment workers before the 1913 strike, he was met with the 'loud cynical laughter' of an older Italian woman who yelled out, 'Ha! Ha! you want more 15 cents to pay you fakers!' She then proceeded to 'make [him] look ridiculous in the presence of the other finishers.' Several weeks later, the same woman led an independent strike in her shop when employers demanded an impossible work pace.[102]

Support for the 'new unions' was always tenuous in this period, as Italian women struggled for representation and voice. In 1913, for instance, several thousand Italian-American women joined the ILGWU strike, but one week after the union settled without a vote and the female 'rioting' in Cooper Union took place, close to one thousand of them in twelve factories across New York City abandoned the ILGWU and declared a strike (for better pay and shorter hours) under the auspices of the IWW.[103] In fact, Italian women did not turn to the reformist unions en masse until post–First World War repression against the left caused the defeat of the more radical alternatives. Even then, they continued to combine activism in the union with other strategies and community movements.

Red Scare, Fascism, and Italian-American Women's Radicalism in the Interwar Period

Reform-oriented socialist labour organizations like the ILGWU were adopted more fully by Italian workers in the 1930s as they came to terms with what was possible in the United States. Historians are only beginning to tell the story of how the repression of immigrant radicals, and of pre-war movements like the IWW, preceded the incorporation of Italian-American workers into the mainstream U.S. labour movement and contributed to the making of their national identities both as Americans and Italians. Yet, scholars generally agree that 'the New York clothing industry [was] the theater of a significant political recomposition within the Italian American left.'[104] Ironically, however, there are virtually no studies that consider the Italian-American women who ran the organizational departments and composed the majority of the rank and file in the very garment unions that were so significant to the Italian-American left during this period.[105] Furthermore, as Michael Denning argues, in New York City the 'symbolic center of Popular Front womanhood was the garment industry.' This 'insurgent social movement,' he writes, was '[b]orn out of the social upheavals of 1934 and coincided with the Communist Party's period of greatest influence in US society,' but it was not centred on the Communist party. Rather, the Popular Front emerged as 'a radical historical bloc uniting industrial unionists, Communists, independent socialists, community activists, and emigré anti-fascists around laborist social democracy, anti-fascism, and anti-lynching.'[106] By shifting our focus to the culture of struggle in this period we can locate how second-generation Italian-American women informed working-class politics in these years, and also identify the continuities and departures from pre-war styles of immigrant activism. Moreover, we can assess the dramatic impact that shifting organizational strategies had on gender and inter-ethnic relations within one of the most visible and celebrated working-class movements of the 1930s.

Italian-American historians generally agree that during and after the First World War, the federal government's push for national unity and the repression of radical campaigns caused a massive dislocation in the Italian-American labour movement.[107] As Vecoli writes, the political climate of the First World War 'dealt the first debilitating blow to Italian radicalism. Smashing their presses, shuttering their offices and meeting places, and arresting thousands, federal and state agencies instituted a reign of terror against the *sovversivi* [subversives].'[108] According to Salvatore Salerno, these 'red scare' campaigns targeted those Italian-American radicals who publicly challenged U.S. racist and imperialist ideologies, and thus resulted in the muzzling of a critical oppositional praxis that was developing within Italian America.[109] In addition, during the 1920s, the racism and anti-Catholicism of the Ku Klux Klan, nativist movements for immigration restriction, and the eight-year struggle of anarchists Nicola Sacco and Bartolomeo Vanzetti made it clear to Italian Americans that they were perceived by native-born white Americans as inferior and undesirable.[110] In response, the majority of Italian-American workers began to turn to new methods of organizing.[111]

Italian-American women responded to this repression by 'uniting around a common ethnic identity' in the Italian-language locals of the reformist socialist unions that were less targeted by the government, such as the ILGWU and the newly formed ACWA.'[112] Yet, Vecoli reminds us that this was not a tale of assimilation. Rather, the deradicalization of Italian-American workers was as much due to transnational influences as it was to domestic developments. The Bolshevik and Fascist revolutions had profound impacts upon the Italian labor movement in America.'[113] Demographic changes also mattered. With Italian immigration to the United States drastically limited by restrictive legislation in 1921 and 1924, the economic strategies of many Italian families shifted from seasonal labour migrations and temporary settlement to the expansion of community support systems. Regional loyalties and diasporic identities began to give way to Italian and American nationalisms, as 'ethnic identity, class-consciousness, and workers' demand for respect as "citizens" fused.'[114] In addition, at the national level, unionism was at a low tide; the number of women in garment unions plummeted by almost

40 per cent between 1920 and 1927.[115] The strategy of sustaining ethnic autonomy within the garment unions was thus prompted by a variety of cultural, economic, and political exigencies.

In the ILGWU, women's membership dropped even further when 'civil war' broke out in the 1920s, and the General Executive Board expelled communists and unaffiliated women activists struggling for more democratic representation. Alice Kessler-Harris has demonstrated that the 'civil war' that occurred 'in the context of a defensive and harassed trade union movement,' represented a decisive rejection of the cultural space women had created in the ILGWU the decade before.[116] Since Italian garment workers in the ILGWU had established their own language locals just before this confrontation, the 1920s were spent consolidating and safeguarding ethnic autonomy. Furthermore, to protect their new jurisdiction over Italian-American workers, the Italian locals supported the actions of the ILGWU leadership.[117] This placed Italian-American organizers 'in an ideal position to negotiate theirs and their constituency's ethnicity within the broader labour and political context.'[118] But it came at a great cost. By the late 1920s, the Italian Dressmakers' Local 89 (the largest of the two Italian-language locals in the ILGWU) was heavily bureaucratized, with men in leadership positions over a primarily female rank and file. On the eve of the stock market crash, this 'progressive' union (which unlike other AFL unions, had sought to organize women workers) had become deeply stratified along gender lines.

The response of Italian-American women organizers to these developments varied. Some, such as Angela Bambace and Albina Delfino, opposed the direction taken by the Italian locals and became active in Communist party meetings and strikes, where they formed alliances with Jewish anarchist and communist insurgents in the union, some of whom were Wobblies (IWW members). For such actions both women were denounced by the Italian locals. For the rest of the 1920s, Bambace assisted the ACWA's organizational campaigns in Elizabeth, New Jersey, and then accepted a position to unionize garment workers in Baltimore for the ILGWU. Delfino became a labour organizer for the Communist party. In this capacity, she travelled between Lawrence, Providence, Boston, Paterson, and New York City with Frances Ribaldo, another Italian woman organizer in the party, to assist workers on the verge of, or already on strike, and to combat racial and ethnic antagonism within these working-class communities.[119] Other organizers, such as Margaret di Maggio and Grace de Luise, became virulently anti-communist and committed to the ethnic-based organizing strategy of Local 89. All of these women, however, came together in the anti-Fascist movement.[120]

As Italian-American garment workers became increasingly sympathetic to Mussolini's claims for a 'New Italy,' anarchists, syndicalists, communists, socialists, and other radicals led oppositional movements in their homes, neighbourhoods, workplaces, and unions.[121] Margaret di Maggio, who entered the garment trades at the age of thirteen and joined the ILGWU because of the Triangle Fire, became a renowned organizer of Local 89 by age eighteen. She was also well known in her Sicilian family for challenging those who 'felt drawn by Mussolini's promise of grandeur to the Italian people.' Di Maggio's niece recalled how 'she and my grandfather were always arguing ... She wanted to buy him a round trip ticket to go back to Italy and see how things were.' When the arguments got worse, Margaret bought him a one-way ticket and 'within two months he wrote back here begging her to send him the return ticket.'[122]

Such battles also took place more publicly and suggest that even as Italian workers were changing patterns of migration, settling, and naturalizing in greater numbers, they were still connected to Italy. As Mussolini's propaganda machine stretched across the Atlantic and encouraged Italian women to embrace a new sense of national identity as 'mothers of the race,' thousands of seamstresses participated in the spectacle of sending their wedding rings to Mussolini's coffers and restating their vows in public. Though smaller in number, other women crowded anti-Fascist rallies (many of them sponsored by the garment unions), and disrupted Fascist meetings in their neighbourhoods. A constant stream of political exiles escaping Fascist repression invigorated the radical movement and raised much vocal opposition to the nationalization of Italians and Italian-Americans. They included the anarchist anti-Fascist Virgilia d'Andrea, who eventually settled in Brooklyn in 1928 and, as Robert Ventresca and Franca Iacovetta document (in chapter 9), became a popular and celebrated speaker at Italian workers' demonstrations across the United States.[123] Throughout the 1920s and 1930s, Angela Bambace, Margaret Di Maggio, Lucia Romualdi, Lillie Raitano, Josephine Mirenda, and other leading ILGWU organizers were not only active in anti-Fascist circles in New York City, but also joined the inter-ethnic coalition of radical groups that united to fight for the release of Sacco and Vanzetti and build community support for the Spanish anti-Fascist resistance. The union remained one of many sites of activism.[124]

The garment unions did not become central to the lives of Italian-American women garment workers until the dramatic labour mobilizations of the 1933–4 Depression-era strike wave. In August of 1933, 60,000 dressmakers in New York, New Jersey, and Connecticut walked off their jobs and into the streets.[125] Joined by African-American, East-European Jewish, Puerto Rican, and other Caribbean women dressmakers, Italian women filled strike halls to capacity, stormed non-union shops calling workers to join them, marched through the streets of their neighbourhoods, and formed picket lines outside shops demanding decent wages and working conditions and an end to sweatshops once and for all.[126] The Italian women dressmakers who helped to orchestrate the strike were both veterans from earlier labour struggles and new recruits. They were immigrant and American-born, though predominantly second generation.[127] Together they ushered in an entirely new era that Italian garment workers called *l'alba radiosa* (the radiant dawn).[128]

The five-day strike was the crucial event by which Italian-American garment workers assumed the overwhelming numerical majority within the ILGWU. For the first time, they held a measure of power not only in the industry and union, but before the state, which appeared to support their organizational appeals for economic justice.[129] In fact, many Italian garment workers associated the strike with becoming American. Frank Liberti, a presser and organizer for the Italian Dressmakers' Local 89 recalled, 'I became a Citizen ... during the 1933 Strike.'[130] In March 1934, Margaret di Maggio, Minnie Badami, Dorothy Drago, Yolanda Liguori, Angelina Farruggia, and other prominent organizers of Local 89 travelled to Washington to present President Roosevelt with a bronze plaque and pledge the support of Italian-American garment workers to the National Industrial Recovery Act.[131] While Italian women were still not proportionately represented in the union hierarchy, they represented almost 80 per cent of Local 89 (whose 40,000 members made it the largest local in the nation), and the majority of workers in other large locals.[132]

The acquisition of mainstream organizational space and authority in the U.S. labour movement reconfigured Italian-American women's activism in several significant ways. Following the uprising in 1933, the garment unions became a central site of Italian-American women's community activism. Since they composed the majority of the rank and file, they were called upon by the union leadership to consolidate the gains of the strike. They continued to run the organizational drives and struggled with Italian and Jewish men for a voice in union affairs. Yet, the sheer magnitude of new members propelled the Italian locals into 'an important center around which Italian-American life in New York City revolved.'[133] As tens of thousands of women poured into the local's district offices, spread throughout New York City's Italian neighbourhoods, veteran organizers were needed to mentor and train those new to the movement. The movement thus remained multigenerational.[134] As in earlier periods, women socialized their own children within union culture by bringing their families to workers' halls and meetings.[135] Margaret di Maggio, the manager of Local 89's organizational department, was not only described as a mother figure by the newest recruits, but her twelve-year-old niece was literally at her side during many union meetings. The atmosphere in the local's offices also reaffirmed a sense of family. Di Maggio's niece recalled that in 'the 30s and 40s you couldn't get through the halls for the mobs that were there.' 'They would work on their lunch hours,' she added, 'they would run to the union at 5:00. At 8:00 the halls would still be mobbed ... You become so involved, it's home.'[136] Indeed, during the 1930s, while male leaders of the garment unions emphasized ethnic nationalism in their appeals to Italian-American workers, women organizers of Local 89 more often referred to the union as 'nostra grande famiglia' (our large family),[137] thereby drawing attention to the union as a central community institution that was based on the labour of women. They took the malleable social ideal of *la famiglia* and infused it with political purpose to justify making their union work a priority over their commitments to kin. Indeed, the great flood of new members demanded a new kind of commitment from women organizers. As di Maggio's niece remembered, since union women 'worked until the wee hours of the morning,' and on weekends, 'few knew whether they had families.'[138] Actually, many organizers came from union families; they often delayed marriage, and most left organizing or took a sabbatical during child-rearing years. While some women did their union work in defiance of a husband or parents (and thus talked of being disowned or of 'broken marriages'), most who did marry chose partners within the movement. As Albina Delfino stated, 'You cannot be active, unless your mate has the same opinion.'[139] Such sentiments were prevalent earlier, but during the massive Depression-era organizing drives more women than ever chose to devote their lives to the movement and to redefine their reponsibilities to kin in ways that included community activism. Women were drawn to the ILGWU for many of the same reasons that they joined workers' *circoli*. The union provided a space for them to combine political activism and intellectual pursuits, and as with the *circoli*, the union offered classes in political strategy, including Marxist theories of working-class revolution, vocational and technical training, and social events. Labour organizing provided women with a rare opportunity to achieve both personal and collective advancement, earn an income, and get the education most missed when they entered wage work as children.

Investing in Whiteness: Concluding Comments

As women breathed new life into the labour movement and made careers out of union organizing, they also struggled with increased union bureaucratization, and the resulting entrenched gendered and racial hierarchies. After the civil war of the 1920s, the union offered few avenues for democratic representation and those women who drew attention to inequalities were marginalized, if not removed, from union offices. Women were excluded not only from positions of power in the union, but also from the dominant symbolic system of labour in this period.[140] Ironically, their more common response to this marginalization would be to unite with men around the practice of racialized exclusion, rather than work with other women to democratize the union. In the last few decades, several scholars and labour activists have examined how Italian-American garment workers resented the entrance of new workers into the industry and union (most of whom were Puerto Rican and African-American women) and actively worked to prevent their access to well-paying jobs and positions of power in the union.[141]

Why did Italian-American workers come to see their interests as against rather than in solidarity with the industry's newest recruits? The 1933 strike had dramatically affirmed the logic of working-class solidarity; however, everywhere Italian-American women confronted a society obsessed with the ideology of racial difference. Pronouncements of white racial superiority were widely disseminated in popular radio shows, magazines, vaudeville shows, and movies, and they were used to justify lynchings, immigration restriction, and segregation. Moreover, it was clear that where people lived, which housing they had access to, who was hired, fired, and promoted, who could serve on juries, vote, and become citizens were always mediated by racial privilege. Even in a union like the ILGWU, which claimed to unite workers across the colour line, Italians learned contradictory lessons. At times, union leaders espoused the ideology 'We are all minorities'; at other times, they sought to avoid the issue of race altogether and drew attention instead to the 'culture of unity' offered by a multi-ethnic socialist union.[142] Yet, all workers did not have the same privileges in the union. Only Italian workers were permitted the autonomy of their own language locals, which, in turn, enabled them to acquire leadership positions in the International, and gain access to the higher-paying jobs in the industry. This privilege was denied to other members, despite repeated demands by Puerto Rican and African-American seamstresses for similar rights.[143]

Italian-American women did not possess the formal power to exclude workers of colour from the union, but the evidence suggests that in the 1930s and 1940s they worked to exclude women and men of colour from the workplace. As Altagracia Ortiz has documented, one way was to oppose granting membership to *puerto-riqueñas* and thus keep them out of union shops.[144] It also appears that those Italian-American women who remained in Local 89 throughout their union careers rarely initiated or joined class-based, inter-ethnic coalitions, but focused instead on building soldarity among Italians and on solidifying their alliances with Jewish workers. Differential access to and control over the better-paid and more highly skilled jobs did not lead Italian-American women to disrupt racial inequality. Instead, they used their political stature in the union to counter the nativism and racism that cast *them* as undesirable citizens and members of an 'inferior race,' and distanced themselves from the newcomers.[145]

The types of coalitions that Italian garment workers had forged with other workers in the decades before the First World War were no longer a central part of their workplace organizing strategies. Rather, alliances with Latin- and African-American workers more often developed outside of the union, in local neighbourhood movements that developed to confront the devastation of the Great Depression. In grassroots struggles for better housing, education, and health care, in Popular Front groups such as the United Council of Working Class Women, the International Workers' Order, Congressman Vito Marcantonio's Harlem Legislative Council, and in the few remaining anarcho-feminist circles, Italian-American women continued to collaborate with African-American, Puerto Rican, Cuban, and other Caribbean women.[146] Yet, in the 1940s, Italian-American women also mobilized to keep African and Latin American children out of 'their' schools and 'their' public housing.[147] Decades later Italian-American community activists would recall that tensions between Italians and their Puerto Rican and African-American neighbours increased so dramatically in these decades that it led to new organizing strategies. Vito Magli remembered that in the 1930s 'we had a situation where we had to intervene and explain to the brothers and sisters about racism in the Italian American community ... We had to combat racism, a problem in the progressive movement.'[148] Robert Orsi has suggested that increased tension occurred in part because Italian immigrants and their children learned that 'achievement in their new environment meant successfully differentiating themselves from the dark-skinned other.'[149] His observation also applies to Italian-American women garment workers, whose claims to being different from their African and Latin American co-workers grew more insistent at precisely the same time that the latter group entered the industry in larger numbers. Yet, Italians had lived alongside African and Latin Americans for decades, sharing neighbourhoods, schools, and workplaces. The 1930s and 1940s, then, were a turning point for Italian immigrants and their children. It is no coincidence that they began to distance themselves from racialized 'others' at the same time as they achieved numerical and political power in the garment unions, and gained access to the higher-paying jobs. As Tom Guglielmo's research on Italians and race making in Chicago well demonstrates, 'protecting this powerful and privileged position required that Italian Americans grow increasingly vigilant about policing the color line.'[150] This racial privilege too was the site of continual dialogue and contestation, as Italian-Americans confronted and debated the costs of a white identity.[151]

Italian-American women garment workers entered the age of the Congress of Industrial Organizations, a period historians commonly associate with increased inter-ethnic working-class unity, when mobilization at the site of production offered few spaces to challenge hegemonic systems of power. With an increasingly bureaucratized labour movement grounded in racial and gendered hierarchies, the workplace became an unlikely site for the revolutionary culture of struggle characteristic of the pre–First World War years. Mapping the oppositional political culture that Italian-American women created in this period thus requires us to look beyond the union movement and to recognize that women's activism was not always emancipatory or antagonistic to systems of power. By focusing on the complex and often contradictory messages that were conveyed in different political moments, we might better assess the role that Italian immigrant women and their daughters played in both sustaining and challenging institutionalized privilege. After all, systems of power were never stable, but always reconfigured through debate, contest, and negotiation.[152]

NOTES

I would like the thank the following for sharing their ideas and reading drafts throughout the writing process: the entire Guglielmo family, especially my grand-mother Grace and my brothers Marco and Tom; Franca Barchiesi, Jim Barrett, Philip Cannistraro, Nan Enstad, Edvige Giunta, Nancy Hewitt, Rachel Maxine Kochinski, Todd Michney, Yuichiro Onishi, Kym Ragusa, Danilo Romeo, Joseph Sciorra, and Jane Slaughter; and to the participants at the following meetings, where I presented the findings in this essay: Immigration History Research Center's Research in Progress Series (1996); University of Minnesota Compara-tive Women's History Workshop (1996); Canadian Historical Association (1996); Berkshire History of Women Conference (1996); 'The Lost World of Italian American Radicalism: Politics, Culture, History' Conference (1997); Social Sci-ence History Association (1997); Midwest Labor History Conference (1997); North American Labor History Conference (2001); and American Studies Asso-ciation (2001). I am especially grateful to Donna Gabaccia, David Roediger, and Salvatore Salerno for their wise counsel, and to Franca Iacovetta for her enthusi-astic support and editorial expertise.

1 *New York Evening Post* (20 Jan. 1913); *New York Times* (19, 20, and 22 Jan. 1913); *New York Call* (30 Dec. 1912; 1, 7, 9, 13–16 and 19–20 Jan. 1913; 2 and 5 Feb. 1913); *New York Sun* (4 Jan. 1913); *Il Bolletino della Sera* (3, 4, 10, and 16 Jan. 1913); *L'Era Nuova* (11 and 25 Jan. 1913); *Il Proletario* (18 and 25 Jan. 1913; 1 Feb. 1913); *Il Progresso Italo-Americano* (10 Jan. 1913 to 3 Feb. 1913); Theresa Malkiel, 'Striking for the Right to Live,' *The Coming Nation* 1:124 (25 Jan. 1913). See also Colomba Furio, 'Immigrant Women and Industry: A Case Study, The Italian Immigrant Women and the Garment Industry, 1880–1950' (PhD diss., New York University, 1979), 185–204; Annelise Orleck, *Common Sense and a Little Fire: Women and Working-Class Politics in the United States, 1900–1965* (Chapel Hill: University of North Carolina Press, 1995), 75–6; Melvyn Dubofsky, *When Workers Organize: New York City in the Progressive Era* (Amherst, Mass.: University of Massachusetts Press, 1968), 83; Louis Levine, *The Women's Garment Workers: A History of the International Ladies' Garment Workers' Union* (New York: B.W. Heubsch, Inc., 1924), 226–7; Edwin Fenton, *Immigrants and Unions, A Case Study: Italians and American Labor, 1870–1920* (New York: Arno Press, 1975), 522–5; Philip S. Foner, *History of the Labor Movement in the United States*, vol. 5, *The AFL in the Progres-sive Era, 1910–1915* (New York: International Publishers, 1980), 256.
2 *New York Times* (19 and 20 Jan. 1913) paraphrased in Orleck, *Common Sense*

and a Little Fire, 76. In 1914 the U.S. Department of Labor reported that Jewish women occupied 56% of the dress and waist industry, while Italian women, the second largest group of workers, comprised 34%. See U.S. Department of Labor, Bureau of Labor Statistics, *A Study of the Dress and Waist Industry for the Purpose of Industrial Education, Bulletin 145* (Washington: U.S. Government Printing Office, 1914), 7. See also Furio, 'Immigrant Women and Industry,' 80, 185–204; and Elizabeth Ewen, *Immigrant Women in the Land of Dollars: Life and Culture on the Lower East Side, 1890–1925* (New York: Monthly Review Press, 1985), 260.

3 I am building on the work of Annelise Orleck, who also advances this argument in *Common Sense and a Little Fire*, 76. The second quotation is from Levine, *The Women's Garment Workers*, 226.

4 Altagracia Ortiz, 'Puerto Rican Workers in the Garment Industry of New York City, 1920–1960,' in Robert Asher and Charles Stephenson, eds., *Labor Divided: Race and Ethnicity in the United States Labor Struggles, 1835–1960* (New York: State University of New York Press, 1990); Ortiz, '"En la aguja y el pedal eché la hiel": Puerto Rican Women in the Garment Industry of New York City, 1920–1980,' in Altagracia Ortiz, ed., *Puerto Rican Women and Work: Bridges in Transnational Labor* (Philadelphia: Temple University Press, 1996); Xiaolan Bao, *Holding Up More than Half the Sky: Chinese Women Garment Workers in New York City, 1948–92* (Urbana: University of Illinois Press, 2001); Alice Kessler-Harris, 'Problems of Coalition-Building: Women and Trade Unions in the 1920s,' in Ruth Milkman, ed., *Women, Work and Protest: A Century of U.S. Women's Labor History* (New York: Routledge & Kegan Paul, 1985), 126–9; Herbert Hill, 'Guardians of the Sweatshops: The Trade Unions, Racism, and the Garment Industry,' in Adalberto López and James Petras, eds., *Puerto Rico and Puerto Ricans: Studies in History and Society* (New York: Wiley, 1974); Robert Laurentz, 'Racial/Ethnic Conflict in the New York Garment Industry' (PhD diss., State University of New York at Binghamton, 1980); Roy B. Helfgott, 'Puerto Rican Integration in the Skirt Industry in New York City,' in *Discrimination and Low Incomes: Social and Economic Discrimination against Minority Groups in Relation to Low Incomes in New York State* (New York: Studies of New York State Commission against Discrimination, New School for Social Research, 1959).

5 Robin D.G. Kelley, '"We Are Not What We Seem": Rethinking Black Working-Class Opposition in the Jim Crow South,' *Journal of American History* 80, 1 (June 1993): 112; Kelley, *Race Rebels: Culture, Politics, and the Black Working Class* (New York: Free Press, 1994); Ardis Cameron, *Radicals of the Worst Sort: Laboring Women in Lawrence, Massachusetts, 1860–1912* (Urbana, Chicago: University of Illinois Press, 1993); Nan Enstad, *Ladies of Labor, Girls of Adven-*

ture: *Working Women, Popular Culture, and Labor Politics at the Turn of the Century* (New York: Columbia University Press, 1999); George Lipsitz, *A Life in the Struggle: Ivory Perry and the Culture of Opposition* (Philadelphia: Temple University Press, 1988); Dana Frank, 'White Working-Class Women and the Race Question,' *International Labor and Working-Class History* 54 (Fall 1998): 80–102; Cathy J. Cohen et al., *Women Transforming Politics: An Alternative Reader* (New York: New York University Press, 1997); Patricia Gurin and Louise A. Tilly, eds., *Women, Politics, and Change* (New York: Russell Sage Foundation Press, 1990); James C. Scott, *Domination and the Arts of Resistance: Hidden Transcripts* (New Haven: Yale University Press, 1990).

6 Edwin Fenton, *Immigrants and Unions, a Case Study: Italians and American Labor, 1870–1920* (New York: Arno Press, 1975); Miriam Cohen, *Workshop to Office: Two Generations of Italian Women in New York City, 1900–1950* (Ithaca: Cornell University Press, 1992); Nancy L. Green, *Ready-to-Wear and Ready-to-Work: A Century of Industry and Immigrants in Paris and New York* (Durham, NC: Duke University Press, 1997); Ewen, *Immigrant Women in the Land of Dollars*; Thomas Kessner and Betty Boyd Caroli, 'New Immigrant Women at Work: Italians and Jews in New York City, 1880–1905,' *Journal of Ethnic Studies* 5 (Winter 1978): 19–31.

7 By 1900 close to one-half of the nation's clothing establishments, capital, and product value were located in New York City. See Ben Morris Selekman, Henriette R. Walter, and W.J. Couper, *The Clothing and Textile Industries in New York and Its Environs* (New York: Regional Plan of New York and Its Environs, 1925); Louise Odencrantz, *Italian Women in Industry* (New York: Russell Sage Foundation, 1919), 38; Green, *Ready-to-Wear and Ready-to-Work*; and Levine, *The Women's Garment Workers*.

8 U.S. Department of Labor, Bureau of Labor Statistics, Bulletin 146, *Wages and Regularity of Employment and Standardization of Piece Rates in the Dress and Waist Industry: New York City* (Washington: Government Printing Office, 1914), 8.

9 Local 22, ILGWU, *Our Union at Work: A Survey of the Activities of the Dressmakers' Union Local 22, ILGWU* (New York, 1937), Immigration History Research Center, University of Minnesota (hereafter IHRC); Edith Kine, 'The Garment Union Comes to the Negro Worker,' *Opportunity* 12 (April 1934): 107–10. See also Green, *Ready-to-Wear and Ready-to-Work*, 200–4; and Ortiz, '"En la aguja y el pedal eché la hiel."'

10 Odencrantz, *Italian Women in Industry*, 44.

11 Furio, 'Immigrant Women and Industry,' 67 and reprinted interviews in appendix D; Furio, 'The Cultural Background of the Italian Immigrant Woman and Its Impact on Her Unionization in the New York City Garment

Industry, 1880–1919,' in George E. Pozzetta, ed., *Pane e Lavoro: The Italian American Working Class* (Toronto: Multicultural History Society of Ontario, 1980), 83, 88; Emiliana P. Noether, 'The Silent Half: Le Contadine del Sud before the First World War,' in Betty Boyd Caroli, Robert F. Harney, and Lydio F. Tomasi, eds., *The Italian Immigrant Woman in North America* (Toronto: Multicultural History Society of Ontario, 1978), 7; Judith E. Smith, 'Italian Mothers, American Daughters: Changes in Work and Family Roles,' in Caroli, et al., *The Italian Immigrant Woman*, 207; Ewen, *Immigrant Women in the Land of Dollars*, 244; Fenton, *Immigrants and Unions*, 469; Corinne Azen Krause, *Grandmothers, Mothers, and Daughters: Oral Histories of Three Generations of Ethnic American Women* (Boston: Twayne Publishers, 1991), 18; Odencrantz, *Italian Women in Industry*, 40, 51; Marie Hall Ets, ed., *Rosa: The Life of an Italian Immigrant*, 2nd ed. (Madison: University of Wisconsin Press, 1999).

12   Furio, 'The Cultural Background,' 83. See also Teresa Noce, *Gioventù senza sole* (Rome: Editori Riuniti, 1973), 15–36; Odencrantz, *Italian Women in Industry*, 38–9; Ann Cornelisen, *Women of the Shadows: A Study of the Wives and Mothers of Southern Italy* (New York: Random House, 1977); Noether, 'The Silent Half,' 7; and Smith, 'Italian Mothers, American Daughters,' 207.

13   From 1880 to 1910, in Lombardy and Piedmont, domestic production continued alongside both silk- and wool-spinning cottage industries, at the same time as both silk and wool factories developed. Furthermore, Anna Cento Bull argues that the 'mechanization of the [Italian] textile industry, the spread of the factory system, the lengthening of working hours, and the worsening of conditions of work were accompanied by a leap forward in the employment of women and children.' Bull, 'The Lombard Silk-Spinners in the Nineteenth Century: An Industrial Workforce in a Rural Setting,' in Zygmunt G. Baraski and Shirley W. Vinall, eds., *Women and Italy: Essays on Gender, Culture and History* (New York: St Martin's Press, 1991), 26. Donna Gabaccia discovered that in 1901, spinning and weaving employed almost a third of adult women in Sicily and Calabria. Gabaccia and Fraser Ottanelli, 'Diaspora or International Proletariat?' *Diasporas* 6 (Spring 1997). See also Noether, 'The Silent Half,' 7; Noce, *Gioventù senza sole*; 'Organizing a Women's Union, Italy, 1903' in *European Women: A Documentary History, 1789–1945*, Eleanor S. Riemer and John C. Fout, eds. (Brighton: Harvester Press, 1983), 27; Lucia Chiavola Birnbaum, *Liberazione della donna / Feminism in Italy* (Middletown, CT: Wesleyan University Press, 1986), 15–18; and Elda Gentili Zappi, *If Eight Hours Seem Too Few: Mobilization of Women Workers in the Italian Rice Fields* (Albany: State University of New York Press, 1991).

14   Colomba Furio interview with Tina Gaeta, ILGWU business agent and price

adjuster, New York City, 22 Nov. 1976; with Antonetta Lazzaro, executive board member and organizer, Local 89, Bronx, New York, 29 Mar. 1977; and with 'Mrs. L,' Ridgewood-Bushwick Senior Citizens' Center, Brooklyn, New York, 2 Nov. 1976. Reprinted in Furio, 'Immigrant Women and Industry,' 449–50; 472–3; and 409–11.

15 In 1911, the Immigration Commission reported that 90% of the southern Italian women in New York City's garment trades had worked in lacemaking, embroidery, and sewing in Italy. U.S. Immigration Commission, *Immigrants in Industries*, Senate Document 633, 61st Congress, 1st Session (Washington: Government Printing Office, 1911), 376; Odencrantz reported in 1919 that of 295 Italian women in New York City's garment industry, 133 had worked for wages in Italy. *Italian Women in Industry*, 313–14, 38. For the period 1909–13, Donna Gabaccia found that 94% of Sicilian women living on Elizabeth Street on the Lower East Side worked in the garment industry, and most of them had worked as seamstresses or ladies' tailors in Italy. *Militants and Migrants: Rural Sicilians Become American Workers* (New Brunswick, NJ: Rutgers University Press, 1988), 133.

16 Rudolph J. Vecoli, 'Pane e Giustizia,' *La Parola del Popolo* 26 (September–October 1976); Vecoli, '"Primo Maggio" in the United States: An Invented Tradition of the Italian Anarchists,' in Andrea Panaccione, ed., *May Day Celebration, Quaderni della Fondazione G. Brodolini* (Venice: Marsilio Editori, 1988), 55–83; Vecoli, 'Italian Immigrants in the United States Labor Movement from 1880–1929,' in Bruno Bezza, ed., *Gli italiani fuori d'Italia, gli emigrati italiani nei movimenti operai dei paesi d'adozione, 1880–1940* (Milan: Franco Angeli, 1983); Gabaccia, *Militants and Migrants*; Gabaccia, 'Migration and Militancy among Italy's Laborers,' in Dirk Hoerder, Horst Rössler, Inge Blank, eds., *Roots of the Transplanted* (New York: Columbia University Press, 1994), 245–67; Mario De Ciampis, 'Storia del Movimento Socialista Rivoluzionario Italiano,' *La Parola del Popolo, Cinquantesimo Anniversario, 1908–1958* (December 1958–January 1959): 136–63; George E. Pozzetta and Bruno Ramirez, eds., *The Italian Diaspora: Migration across the Globe* (Toronto: Multicultural History Society of Ontario, 1992); Gianfausto Rosoli, ed., *Un secolo di emigrazione italiana, 1766–1976* (Rome: Centro Studi Emigrazione, 1978); Zeffiro Ciuffoletti, 'Il movimento sindacale italiano e l'emigrazione dalle origini al fascismo,' and Emilio Franzina, 'L'emigrazione schedata: Lavoratori sovversivi all'estero e meccanismi di controllo poliziesco tra fine secolo e fascismo,' in Bezza, *Gli italiani fuori d'Italia*; Franco Andreucci and Tommaso Detti, *Il movimento operaio italiano, dizionario biografico, 1853–1943*, 6 vols. (Rome: Edizioni Riuniti, 1975–78); Nunzio Pernicone, *Italian Anarchism, 1864–1892* (Princeton: Princeton

University Press, 1993); Romano Canosa and Amedeo Santosuosso, *Magistrati, anarchici e socialisti alla fine dell'Ottocento in Italia* (Milan: Feltrinelli, 1981); Ernesto Ragionieri, 'Italiani all'estero ed emigrazione di lavoratori italiani: Un tema di storia del movimento operaio,' *Belfagor* 17 (November 1962): 641–69.

17 Jole Calapso, *Donne Ribelli: Un secolo di lotte femminili in Sicilia* (Palermo: S.F. Flaccovio, 1980); Calapso, *Una donna intransigente: Vita di Maria Giudice* (Palermo: Sellerio Editore, 1996); Gabaccia, *Militants and Migrants* (passim); Franca Pieroni Bortolotti, *Alle origini del movimento femminile in Italia, 1848–1892* (Turin: Einaudi, 1975); Bortolotti, *Femminismo e partiti politici in Italia, 1919–1926* (Rome: Editori Riuniti, 1978); Bortolotti, *Socialismo e questione femminile in Italia* (Milan: G. Mazzotta, 1974); Franca Pieroni Bortolotti, *Sul movimento politico delle donne, Scritti inediti,* ed. Annarita Buttafuoco (Rome: Cooperativa Utopia, 1987); Camilla Ravera, *Breve storia del movimento femminile in Italia* (Rome: Editori Riuniti, 1978); Jane Slaughter, *Women and the Italian Resistance, 1943–1945* (Denver: Arden Press, 1997); Victoria de Grazia, *How Fascism Ruled Women, Italy, 1922–1945* (Berkeley: University of California Press, 1992); Chiavola Birnbaum, *Liberazione della donna*; Claire LaVigna, 'Women in the Canadian and Italian Trade Union Movements at the Turn of the Century: A Comparison,' in Caroli et al., *The Italian Immigrant Woman*; Gentili Zappi, *If Eight Hours Seem Too Few*; Furio, *Immigrant Women and Industry*, 85–6; 57–62, 146, 153. See E.J. Hobsbawm, *Primitive Rebels: Studies in Archaic Forms of Social Movement in the 19th and 20th Centuries* (New York: Frederick A. Praeger, 1959), 183; Francesco Renda, *I Fasci Siciliani, 1892–94* (Turin: G. Einaudi, 1977), 352; and Salvatore Francesco Romano, *Storia dei Fasci Siciliani* (Bari: Giuseppe Laterza e Figli, 1959), 228–30.

18 Chiavola Birnbaum, *Liberazione della donna*, 23.

19 'Organizing a Women's Union, Italy, 1903,' 27; Elizabeth Gurley Flynn, 'Problems Organizing Women (1916),' *Solidarity*, 15 July 1916, repr. in Rosalyn Fraad Baxandall, ed., *Words of Fire: The Life and Writing of Elizabeth Gurley Flynn* (New Brunswick, NJ: Rutgers University Press, 1987), 138; Chiavola Birnbaum, *Liberazione della donna*, 15–18; Gentili Zappi, *If Eight Hours Seem Too Few*; Noce, *Gioventù senza sole*; Bortolotti, *Femminismo e partiti politici in Italia*; Bortolotti, *Socialismo e questione femminile in Italia*; Bortolotti, *Sul movimento politico delle donne, Scritti inediti*; Ravera, *Breve storia del movimento femminile in Italia*; Calapso, *Una donna intransigente*; Calapso, *Donne Ribelli*, 119–38; Gabaccia, *Militants and Migrants*, 150–1.

20 LaVigna, 'Women in the Canadian and Italian Trade Union Movements,' 37.

21 Gentili Zappi, *If Eight Hours Seem Too Few*, 280.

22 Vecoli, 'Pane e Giustizia,' 58.

23 U.S. Immigration Commission, *Reports*, 42 vols. (Washington: Government Printing Office, 1911), 2: 297–313; 11: 660. Large numbers of women workers, however, did paid labour at one time or another that went unrecorded in the census. See Donna Gabaccia, 'Houses and People: Sicilians in Sicily and New York, 1890–1930' (PhD diss., University of Michigan, 1979), 195–6.

24 On men's clothing, see U.S. Congress, Senate, *Report on Condition of Woman and Child Wage Earners*, 2: *Men's Ready-Made Clothing*, S. Doc645, Cong., 2d sess. (Washington: Government Printing Office, 1911), 45. For the clothing industry as a whole, see U.S. Immigration Commission, *Reports*, 11: *Immigrants in Industries*, part 6, 372.

25 Cohen, *Workshop to Office*, 53; table 12, 167; 47.

26 U.S. Department of Labor, Bureau of Labor Statistics, *Woman and Child Wage Earners in the U.S.*, Bulletin no. 175 (Washington: Government Printing Office, 1916), 294.

27 Mable H. Willett, *The Employment of Women in the Clothing Trade* (New York: Columbia University, 1902; repr. New York: AMS Press, 1968), 94–8. See also Luisa Cetti, 'Donne Italiane a New York e Lavoro a Domicilio (1910–1925),' *Movimento Operaio e Socialista* 7, 3 (1984): 291–303; and Cetti, 'Work Experience among Italian Women in New York, 1900–1930,' *Rivista di Studi Anglo Americani* 3, 4–5 (1984–5): 493–505.

28 Cohen, *Workshop to Office*, 48.

29 U.S. Congress, Senate, *Report on Condition of Woman and Child Wage Earners* 2: *Men's Ready-Made Clothing*, 35, 221. See also U.S. Immigration Commission, *Reports*, 26: *Immigrants in Cities*, 1: 20; and Mary Van Kleeck, *Artificial Flower Makers* (New York: Russell Sage Foundation, Survey Associates, 1913).

30 Green, *Ready-to-Wear and Ready-to-Work*, 203, 351.

31 Cohen, *Workshop to Office*, 47–51; Furio, 'Immigrant Women and Industry'; Ewen, *Immigrant Women in the Land of Dollars*, 248–9; Fenton, *Immigrants and Unions*, 468–9.

32 Cohen, *Workshop to Office*, 65.

33 These work conditions have been well documented by historians; my discussion draws on Alice Kessler-Harris, *Out to Work: A History of Wage-Earning Women in the United States* (New York: Oxford University Press, 1982); Philip S. Foner, *History of the Labor Movement in the United States*, vol. 3 (New York: International Publishers, 1964), 25; Cohen, *Workshop to Office*, 66–7; Ewen, *Immigrant Women in the Land of Dollars*, 246–55; Odencrantz, *Italian Women in Industry*, 39, 77; and Furio, 'Immigrant Women and Industry,' 400.

34 Colomba Furio interview with Concetta D., Ridgewood-Bushwick Senior Citizens' Center, Brooklyn, New York, 22 Sept. 1976, repr. in Furio, 'Immigrant Women and Industry,' 408.

35 'Fra I Tessitori, Lo Sciopero di Hackensack,' *Il Bolletino della Sera,* 17 Dec. 1909; Odencrantz, *Italian Women in Industry,* 41. See also Ewen, *Immigrant Women in the Land of Dollars,* 244.

36 *L'Era Nuova,* 13 May 1913.

37 From a vast literature, see Donna Gabaccia, *From the Other Side: Women, Gender, and Immigrant Life in the U.S., 1820–1990* (Bloomington: Indiana University Press, 1994); Cameron, *Radicals of the Worst Sort*; David J. Goldberg, *A Tale of Three Cities: Labor Organization and Protest in Paterson, Passaic, and Lawrence, 1916–1921* (New Brunswick, NJ: Rutgers University Press, 1989); Anne Huber Tripp, *The IWW and the Paterson Silk Strike of 1913* (Urbana, Chicago: University of Illinois Press, 1987); Fenton, *Immigrants and Unions*; George E. Pozzetta, 'Italians and the General Strike of 1910,' in Pozzetta, *Pane e Lavoro*; Gary Mormino and George Pozzetta, *The Immigrant World of Ybor City: Italians and Their Latin Neighbors in Tampa, 1885–1985* (Urbana, Chicago: University of Illinois Press, 1987); Patricia A. Cooper, *Once a Cigar Maker: Men, Women, and Work Culture in American Cigar Factories, 1900–1919* (Urbana, Chicago: University of Illinois Press, 1987); Nancy Hewitt, '"The Voice of Virile Labor": Labor Militancy, Community Solidarity, and Gender Identity among Tampa's Latin Workers, 1880–1921,' in Ava Baron, ed., *Work Engendered: Toward a New History of American Labor* (Ithaca: Cornell University Press, 1991); Nancy Hewitt, 'In Pursuit of Power: The Political Economy of Women's Activism in Twentieth-Century Tampa,' in Nancy A. Hewitt and Suzanne Lebsock, eds., *Visible Women: New Essays on American Activism* (Urbana, Chicago: University of Illinois Press, 1993); Mary H. Blewett, *Men, Women, and Work: Class, Gender, and Protest in the New England Shoe Industry, 1780–1910* (Urbana, Chicago: University of Illinois Press, 1988); Meredith Tax, *The Rising of the Women: Feminist Solidarity and Class Conflict, 1880–1917* (New York: Monthly Review Press, 1981); Philip S. Foner, *The Industrial Workers of the World, 1905–1917* (New York: International Publishers, 1965); Judith E. Smith, *Family Connections: A History of Italian and Jewish Immigrant Lives in Providence Rhode Island, 1900–1940* (Albany: State University of New York Press, 1985), 155; Joan M. Jenson and Sue Davidson, eds., *A Needle, a Bobbin, a Strike: Women Needleworkers in America* (Philadelphia: Temple University Press, 1984); Barbara Mayer Wertheimer, *We Were There: The Story of Working Women in America* (New York: Pantheon Books, 1977); Robert E. Snyder, 'Women, Wobblies, and Workers' Rights: The 1912 Textile Strike in Little Falls, New York,' *New York History,* January 1979:

29–57; Phillips Russell, 'The Strike at Little Falls,' *International Socialist Review* 13 (December 1912): 453–60; Bruno Ramirez, 'Immigration, Ethnicity, and Political Militance: Patterns of Radicalism in the Italian-American Left, 1880–1930,' in Valeria Gennaro Lerda, ed., *From 'Melting Pot' to Multiculturalism: The Evolution of Ethnic Relations in the United States and Canada* (Rome: Bulzoni Editore, 1990); Vecoli, 'Etnia, internazionalismo e protezionismo operaio'; Philip S. Swanton, ed., *Silk City: Studies on the Paterson Silk Industry, 1860–1940* (Newark: New Jersey Historical Society, 1985); Steve Golin, 'Defeat Becomes Disaster: The Paterson Strike of 1913 and the Decline of the IWW,' *Labor History* 24 (Spring 1983): 223–49; James D. Osborne, 'Paterson: Immigrant Strikers and the War of 1913,' in Joseph R. Conlin, ed., *At the Point of Production: The Local History of the IWW* (Westport, CT: Greenwood Press, 1981); James D. Osborne, 'Italian Immigrants and the Working Class in Paterson: The Strike of 1913 in Ethnic Perspective,' in Paul Stellhorn, ed., *New Jersey's Ethnic Heritage* (Trenton: New Jersey Historical Commission, 1978); Delight Dodyk, 'Winder, Warpers, and Girls on the Loom: A Study of Women in the Paterson Silk Industry and Their Participation in the General Strike of 1913' (MA thesis, Sarah Lawrence College, 1979); Paul Avrich, *Anarchist Voices* (Princeton: Princeton University Press, 1995), 97, 107, 497; Brigid O'Farrell and Joyce L. Kornbluh, *Rocking the Boat: Union Women's Voices, 1915–1975* (New Brunswick, NJ: Rutgers University Press, 1996), 34–57; Patrizia Sione, 'Industrial Work, Militancy, and Migrations of Northern Italian Workers in Europe and Paterson, New Jersey, 1880–1913' (PhD diss., State University of New York, Binghamton, 1992).

38 For an insightful discussion of the ways Jewish women have stressed their own militance and class consciousness in contradistinction to the values and behaviour of Italian-American women, see Susan A. Glenn, *Daughters of the Shtetl: Life and Labor in the Immigrant Generation* (Ithaca: Cornell University Press, 1990), 191–4.

39 Enstad, *Ladies of Labor, Girls of Adventure*; Orleck, *Common Sense and a Little Fire*, 41–50, 57–63; Glenn, *Daughters of the Shtetl*, 177, 213; Ann Schofield, 'The Uprising of the 20,000: The Making of a Labor Legend,' in Jenson and Davidson, *A Needle, a Bobbin, a Strike*; Maxine Seller, 'The Uprising of Twenty Thousand: Sex, Class and Ethnicity in the Shirtwaist Makers Strike of 1909,' in Dirk Hoerder, ed., *Struggle a Hard Battle: Working Class Immigrants* (DeKalb: University of Northern Illinois Press, 1986): 280–303; Nancy Schrom Dye, *As Sisters and As Equals: Feminism, Unionism and the Women's Trade Union League of New York* (Columbia: University of Missouri Press, 1980); Mary Jo Buhle, *Women and American Socialism, 1870–1920* (Urbana, Chicago: Univer-

sity of Illinois Press, 1980). See also Helen Marot, 'A Woman's Strike: An Appreciation,' *Proceedings of the Academy of Political Science* 1 (October 1910): 119–28.

40 For a summary of this scholarship, see Donna Gabaccia, 'Immigrant Women, Nowhere at Home?' *Journal of American Ethnic History* 10, 4 (1991): 61–87; Gabaccia, 'Italian Immigrant Women in Comparative Perspective,' *Altreitalie* 9 (1993): 163–75; J. Vincenza Scarpaci, '*La Contadina*: The Plaything of the Middle Class Woman Historian,' *Journal of Ethnic Studies* 9, 2 (Summer 1981); Maddalena Tirabassi, 'Bringing Life to History: Italian Ethnic Women in the United States,' in George Pozzetta and Bruno Ramirez, eds., *The Italian Diaspora, Migration across the Globe* (Toronto: Multicultural History Society of Ontario, 1992).

41 *Il Bolletino della Sera*, 2, 23, 24, 26, and 27 Nov. 1909; 4, 8, 9, 10, 14, and 17 Dec. 1909; 2 Feb. 1910); *Il Progresso Italo-Americano*, 25 Nov. 1909;

42 Adriana Spadoni, 'The Italian Working Woman in New York,' *Collier's*, 23 Mar. 1912, 14. See also Fenton, *Immigrants and Unions*, 490; and Furio, 'Immigrants and Industry.'

43 *Il Bolletino della Sera*, 2 Nov. 1909; 4, 9, 10, 14, 17 Dec. 1909.

44 *L'Era Nuova*, 17 Feb. 1912; 2 and 10 Mar. 1912; 10 and 17 May 1913); *Il Proletario*, 16 Feb. 1912. See also Fenton, *Immigrants and Unions*, 350–3; Furio, 'Immigrant Women and Industry,' 176–7; Cameron, *Radicals of the Worst Sort*, 142–3, 154; Foner, *The Industrial Workers of the World*, 324–6.

45 Cameron, *Radicals of the Worst Sort*, 111–16.

46 *Evening Sun*, 18, 22 and 29 May 1903. See also Fenton, *Immigrants and Unions*, 215.

47 For discussion of this literature see Glenn, *Daughters of the Shtetl*, 191–4.

48 Spadoni, 'The Italian Working Woman in New York,' 14.

49 'Sciopero generale di lavoratori in Camicette, 40,000 scioperanti,' *Il Proletario*, 3 Dec. 1909; 'Le Sartine, Noi e L'A.F.L.,' *Il Proletario*, 24 Dec. 1909.

50 Quotes from WTUL leaders are reprinted in Glenn, *Daughters of the Shtetl*, 190–3. For ILGWU attitudes toward Italian women in this period see Furio, 'Immigrant Women and Industry,' 99–104; Jean A. (Vincenza) Scarpaci, 'Angela Bambace and the International Ladies Garment Workers Union: The Search for an Elusive Activist,' in Pozzetta, *Pane e Lavoro*, 102; and Fenton, *Immigrants and Unions*, 483–5.

51 Cohen, *Workshop to Office*, 60–4; Scarpaci, 'Angela Bambace,' 101. See also Colomba Furio interview with Gaeta, Lazzaro, and 'Mrs. D' in Furio, 'Immigrant Women and Industry,' 453, 473, 397; Josephine Roche, 'The Italian Girl,' in *The Neglected Girl* (New York: Russell Sage Foundation, Survey Associates, 1914), 95–8; and Odencrantz, *Italian Women in Industry*, 273. This

was also the case in other cities. For example, Robert Park and Herbert Miller observed that in Chicago, Italian women travelled in groups on the streetcars to and from garment shops. In *Old World Traits Transplanted* (New York: Harper and Brothers, 1921), 152.

52 Odencrantz, *Italian Women in Industry*, 43, 25.

53 Patrick Watson, *Fasanella's City: The Paintings of Ralph Fasanella with the Story of His Life and Art by Patrick Watson* (New York: Ballantine Books, 1973), 99; Paul S. D'Ambrosio, *Ralph Fasanella's America* (Cooperstown, NY: New York State Historical Association, 2001). See note 55 below.

54 Maria Ganz, *Rebels: Into Anarchy and Out Again* (New York, 1920), 73.

55 Furio, 'Immigrant Women and Industry;' Ewen, *Immigrant Women in the Land of Dollars*, 250. Ginevre Spagnoletti's son, Ralph Fasanella, worked as a steam-iron operator, among other jobs, before becoming an artist. His painting *Dress Shop* (1970) depicted the NYC factory where his mother worked as a buttonhole maker while he was growing up; to signify the women's worries, he placed newspaper headlines on the walls of the factory that stated, 'These women, lots of women, Italian women, Puerto Rican women, black women, Jewish women, sweating away ... did not go through their days in a state of narcosis, but carried the news of the day with them, and worried about their families in the context of current affairs.' Watson, *Fasanella's City*, 99–100.

56 Furio, 'Immigrant Women and Industry'; Ewen, *Immigrant Women in the Land of Dollars.*

57 Ewen, *Immigrant Women in the Land of Dollars*, 253–4.

58 One such story told of several Italian women finishers who grew impatient with a demanding forelady after she continually screamed at them to quicken their pace. When an older worker who 'could not stand the nagging any longer' got the 'courage to tell the forelady to "Shut Up,"' the forewoman, 'with one hand, snatched the garments from her and with the other gave her a good strong push and told her to "Get out of the shop."' In response, 'every worker walked out of the shop in a body, in protest against the action of the forelady and in defense of the abused finisher.' P. Di Neri, 'When Is the Next Meeting?' *The Message*, 15 Oct. 1915.

59 *L'Operaia*, 18 Apr. 1914.

60 Ramirez, 'Immigration, Ethnicity, and Political Militance,' 116. For instance, *Regeneración*, the newspaper of the Partido Liberal Mexicana, and one of the most important papers of the Mexican Revolution, included an Italian-language column, as well as graphics and cartoons by Ludovico Caminita, a prominent anarchist activist and organizer of workers' circles in New Jersey. See Salvatore Salerno, '"Odio di Razza?" ("Race Hatred"): The Beginnings

of Racial Discourse in the Italian American Anarchist Community,' paper presented at the American Italian Historical Association conference, New York City, 12–14 Nov. 1998.

61 Julia Blodgett interview with Antonino Capraro, 11 Sept. 1969, tapes 4, 6, and 7, Capraro Papers, IHRC; Emma Goldman, *Living My Life* (New York: Dover Publications, [1931] 1970). See also Gabaccia, *Militants and Migrants*, 139–41; Fenton, *Immigrants and Unions*, chap. 9; Ewen, *Immigrant Women in the Land of Dollars*, 259; Scarpaci, 'Angela Bambace'; Vecoli, 'The Italian Immigrants in the United States Labor Movement,' 274–5; Michael Miller Topp, 'The Italian-American Left: Transnationalism and the Quest for Unity,' in Paul Buhle and Dan Georgakas, eds., *The Immigrant Left in the United States* (New York: State University of New York Press, 1996); Glenn, *Daughters of the Shtetl*, 198; and De Ciampis, 'Storia del movimento'; Bernardo Vega, *Memorias de Bernardo Vega: Contribucion a la historia de la comunidad puertorriqueña en Nueva York*, ed. Cesar Andreu Iglesias (Buenos Aires: Ediciones Huracan, 1977), 115; Virginia Sánchez Korrol, *From Colonia to Community: The History of Puerto Ricans in New York* (Berkeley: University of California Press, 1983); Roberto P. Rodriguez-Morazzani, 'Linking a Fractured Past: The World of the Puerto Rican Old Left,' *Centro: Journal of the Center for Puerto Rican Studies* 7, 1 (1995); Winston James, *Holding Aloft the Banner of Ethiopia: Caribbean Radicalism in Early Twentieth-Century America* (London: Verso, 1998); Enstad, *Ladies of Labor, Girls of Adventure*; Orleck, *Common Sense and a Little Fire*, 26–7; and Buhle, *Women and Socialism*, 298–9.

62 Vega, *Memorias de Bernardo Vega*, 115; Cooper, *Once a Cigar Maker*. Club Avanti 'supported education, sponsored lectures on peace, religion, and sexual and family questions, on women's emancipation, nationalism, imperialism, major immigrant strikes, the Mexican Revolution, the problems of political prisoners in Italy, and, more generally, current events.' Cited in Gabaccia, *Militants and Migrants*, 139–41.

63 For example, the intellectual Bellalma Forzato Spezia came to the Bronx; Concettina Cerantonio went to Newark. *L'Era Nuova*, 27 May 1911; 'Nostre Corrispondenze,' *Il Proletario*, 1 Dec. 1907. The Italian anarchist newspaper *L'Era Nuova* contains much information on women's participation in NYC workers' circles.

64 Scarpaci, 'Angela Bambace,' 101. See also 'Notes to interview questions dictated by Angela Bambace to Marian,' 18–20 Feb. 1975. My thanks to Philip Camponeschi, Angela's son, for sharing this and other documents with me. They are now included in the Bambace Papers at the IHRC. For more on the Bambace sisters' activism within these *circoli*, see Blodgett interview with Capraro, 11 Sept. 1969, tape 7, Capraro Papers, IHRC.

65 Blodgett interview with Capraro, 12 Sept. 1969, tape 5, Capraro Papers, IHRC; *Il Proletario*, 17 Feb. 1911; Rudolph J. Vecoli, 'Anthony Capraro and the Lawrence Strike of 1919,' in Pozzetta, *Pane e Lavoro*, 14–5.

66 See, e.g., 'Per Maria Barbera,' *La Questione Sociale*, 15 Aug. 1895; Club Femminile di Musica e di Canto, 'XI Anniversario della Festa della Frutta,' *La Questione Sociale*, 3 Sept. 1904; 'Una importantissima riunione,' *Cronaca Sovversiva*, 10 Feb. 1906; *Il Proletario*, 8 Nov. 1911; 6 Jan. 1911; Blodgett interview with Capraro, 11 Sept. 1969, tape 7, and 12 Sept. 1969, tape 2, Capraro Papers, IHRC; for other cities see Avrich, *Sacco and Vanzetti*, 54–6, 107–8; Avrich, *Anarchist Voices*, 107–11, 129, 139.

67 Maria Roda, 'Alle operaie,' *La Questione Sociale*, 15 Sept. 1897; Luigia Reville, 'Ai Rivoluzionarii, in nome del gruppo "L'azione femminile" di Parigi,' *La Questione Sociale*, 5 May 1900; 'I gruppi femminili di propaganda,' *La Questione Sociale*, 23 Nov. 1901; 'Le nostre compagne,' *La Questione Sociale*, 6 and 23 Nov. 1901; 14 Dec. 1901; 4 and 11 Jan. 1902; 5 Apr. 1902; Il Gruppo Anarchico Femminile, Paterson, 'Il Gruppo Anarchico femminile,' *La Questione Sociale*, 12 July 1902; Gruppo Emancipazione della Donna (GED), Paterson, 'Comunicati,' *La Questione Sociale*, 26 Jul. 1902; GED, 'Pubblicazione di Propaganda,' *La Questione Sociale*, 10 May 1902; GED, *La Questione Sociale*, 16 Aug. 1902. See also Carey, '"La Questione Sociale,"' 292. For a more detailed discussion of these anarcho-socialist and feminist *gruppi* see my essay 'Donne Ribelli: Recovering the History of Italian Women's Radicalism in the United States,' and that of Salvatore Salerno, 'No God, No Master: Italian Anarchists and the Industrial Workers of the World,' forthcoming in Philip Cannistraro and Gerald Meyer, eds., *The Lost World of Italian American Radicalism* (Albany: State University of New York Press).

68 Maria Roda, 'Alle operaie,' *La Questione Sociale*, 15 Sept. 1897. See also Salerno, 'No God, No Master.'

69 'Cronaca di Spring Valley, Il Gruppo Femminile' and Il Gruppo I Nuovi Viventi, Il Gruppo Femminile Luisa Michel, 'La questione della donna,' *L'Aurora*, 22 Dec. 1900; Gruppo Emancipazione della Donna, Paterson, 'Pubblicazione di Propaganda,' *La Questione Sociale*, 10 May 1902; Il Gruppo Anarchico Femminile, 'Il Gruppo Anarchico femminile,' *La Questione Sociale*, 12 July 1902; Gruppo Emancipazione della Donna, Paterson, 'Comunicati,' *La Questione Sociale*, 26 July 1902; GED, *La Questione Sociale*, 16 Aug. 1902; 'I gruppi femminili di propaganda,' *La Questione Sociale*, 23 Nov. 1901; 'Nostre Corrispondenze,' *Il Proletario*, 26 Nov. 1909. See also Gianna S. Panofsky, 'A View of Two Major Centers of Italian Anarchism in the United States: Spring Valley and Chicago, Illinois,' in Dominic Candeloro, Fred L.

Gardaphé and Paolo A. Giordano, eds., *Italian Ethnics: Their Languages, Literature, and Lives* (Staten Island: American Italian Historical Association, 1990), 275–6; and Caroline Waldron Merithew's essay on 'anarchist mother-hood' in chapter 7 of this volume.

70 The quotation is from 'Cronaca di Spring Valley, Il Gruppo Femminile,' *L'Aurora*, 22 Dec. 1900. On the activities, see 'I gruppi femminili di propa-ganda,' *La Questione Sociale*, 23 Nov. 1901; Il Gruppo I Nuovi Viventi, Il Gruppo Femminile Luisa Michel, 'La questione della donna,' and 'Cronaca di Spring Valley, Il Gruppo Femminile,' *L'Aurora*, 22 Dec. 1900. See also the regular postings under 'Le nostre compagne' in *La Questione Sociale*, 6 and 14 Nov. 1901; 23 Dec. 1901; 4 and 11 Jan. 1902, and 5 Apr. 1902; Luigia Reville, 'Ai Rivoluzionarii, in nome del gruppo "L'azione femminile" di Parigi,' *La Questione Sociale*, 5 May 1900; Il Gruppo Anarchico Femminile, Paterson, 'Il Gruppo Anarchico femminile,' *La Questione Sociale*, 12 July 1902; Gruppo Emancipazione della Donna, Paterson, 'Comunicati,' *La Questione Sociale*, 26 July 1902; GED, 'Pubblicazione di Propoganda,' *La Questione Sociale*, 10 May 1902; GED, *La Questione Sociale*, 16 Aug. 1902; and 'Movimento Sociale, Dagli Stati Uniti, Paterson, N.J.,' *La Questione Sociale*, 15 Nov. 1902. See also Carey, '"La Questione Sociale,"' 292; Sione, 'Indus-trial Work, Militancy, and Migrations,' 169; and Waldron Merithew's essay in this volume.

71 Alba, 'Eguali diritti,' *La Questione Sociale*, 5 Oct. 1901. See also 'La famiglia, la donna,' *La Questione Sociale*, 6 Nov. 1901.

72 Roda, 'Alle operaie.' For other essays by women that defend their commit-ment to the movement see Alba, 'Eguali diritti,' *La Questione Sociale*, 15 Oct. 1901; Caterina Sebastiani, 'L'Ultima Parola,' *La Questione Sociale*, 8 Dec. 1906; 'I gruppi femminili di propaganda,' *La Questione Sociale*, 23 Nov. 1901; Una Sartina, 'Ma tu sei una donna!' *La Questione Sociale*, 24 Aug. 1901.

73 Salerno, 'No God, No Master.' For strike activity among Paterson's silk workers after the formation of the IWW locals see Goldberg, *A Tale of Three Cities*; Huber Tripp, *The IWW and the Paterson Silk Strike of 1913*; Fenton, *Immigrants and Unions*; Foner, *The Industrial Workers of the World*; Swanton, ed., *Silk City*; Golin, 'Defeat Becomes Disaster'; Osborne, 'Paterson: Immi-grant Strikers and the War of 1913'; Osborne, 'Italian Immigrants and the Working Class in Paterson'; and Dodyk, 'Winders, Warpers, and Girls on the Loom.'

74 Gabaccia, *Militants and Migrants*, 140; Fenton, *Immigrants and Unions*; Cartosio, 'Gli emigrati italiani e l'Industrial Workers of the World'; Ramirez, 'Immigration, Ethnicity, and Political Militance.'

75 Ramirez, 'Immigration, Ethnicity, and Political Militance,' 128.

76 Salerno, 'No God, No Master' and 'Odio di Razza.' See also George Carey, 'The Vessel, the Deed, and the Idea: Anarchists in Paterson, 1895–1908,' *Antipode* 10–11 (1979); Rudolph Vecoli, '"Free Country": The American Republic Viewed by the Italian Left, 1880–1920,' in Marianne Debouzy, ed. *In the Shadow of the Statue of Liberty: Immigrants, Workers and Citizens in the American Republic* (Saint Denis, France: Presses Universitaires de Vincennes, 1988).

77 *Il Proletario*, 16 and 22 July 1910. See also Furio, 'Immigrant Women and Industry,' 156–7, 242–6; and Fenton, *Immigrants and Unions*, 498–9.

78 Salerno, *Red November, Black November*, 48–9, 58, 89; Salerno, 'No God, No Master'; Cartosio, 'Gli emigrati italiani e l'Industrial Workers of the World'; Furio, 'Immigrant Women and Industry,' 156–7, 242–6; Charles Zappia, 'Unionism and the Italian American Worker: A History of the New York City "Italian Local" in the International Ladies' Garment Workers' Union, 1900–1933' (PhD diss., University of California, Berkeley, 1991); Zappia, 'Unionism and the Italian American Worker: The Politics of Anti-Communism in the International Ladies' Garment Workers' Union,' in Rocco Caporale, ed., *Italian Americans through the Generations* (Staten Island: American Italian Historical Association, 1986); De Ciampis, 'Storia del Movimento Socialista Rivoluzionario Italiano,' 154; Gabaccia, *Militants and Migrants*, 117, 140–2; Rudolph J. Vecoli, 'The Making and Unmaking of an Italian-American Working Class, 1915–1945,' paper presented at the European Social Science History Conference, Noordwijkerhout, The Netherlands, 9–11 May 1996, 25; Vecoli, 'The Italian Immigrants in the United States Labor Movement'; Vecoli, 'Italian American Workers, 1880–1920: Padrone Slaves or Primitive Rebels?' in Silvio Tomasi, ed., *Perspectives in Italian Immigration and Ethnicity* (New York: Center for Migration Studies, 1977), 28–9; Fenton, *Immigrants and Unions*, 479–91; Foner, *The Industrial Workers of the World*, 67; Orleck, *Common Sense and a Little Fire*, 76; Collomp and Debouzy, 'European Migrants and the U.S. Labor Movement,' 363–73; Ramirez, 'Immigration, Ethnicity, and Political Militance.'

79 'Cloak Makers Vote to Strike,' *New York Call*, 5 July 1910. See also Foner, *The Industrial Workers of the World*, 66; Furio, 'The Cultural Background of the Italian Immigrant Woman,' 93; Furio, 'Immigrant Woman and Industry,' 154; Green, *Ready-to-Wear and Ready-to-Work*, 364–5.

80 'Lo Sciopero dei Sarti,' *L'Araldo* (21 July 1910). See also Furio, 'Immigrant Women and Industry,' 154–6, 162. Unfortunately, we know very little about women's participation in the Amalgamated Clothing Workers of America at this time, an organization that was founded in the aftermath of the clothing workers' uprisings in the 1910s, and drew the support of Italian immigrant

women in New York City, Chicago, Philadelphia, Rochester, and other cities.

81 Orleck, *Common Sense and a Little Fire*, 63.

82 Fenton, *Immigrants and Unions*, 495.

83 Furio, 'Immigrant Women and Industry,' 121.

84 Ramirez, 'Immigration, Ethnicity, and Political Militance,' 130, 139; Fenton, *Immigrants and Unions*; Vecoli, 'The Making and Unmaking'; David Montgomery, 'The "New Unionism" and the Transformation of Workers' Consciousness in America, 1909–1922,' *Journal of Social History* 7, 4 (Summer 1974). Between 1900 and 1910 the numbers of Italians in the United States tripled.

85 Angela Bambace, 'Notes to interview questions dictated by Angela Bambace to Marion,' 18–20 Feb. 1975, Bambace Papers, IHRC; *L'Operaia*, 13 Sept. 1913; 4 Apr. 1914; 13 Aug. 1914; 3 Sept. 1914; 17, 24, and 31 Oct. 1914; 2 Jan. 1915; 27 Feb. 1915; Furio, 'Immigrant Women and Industry,' 192, 196, 251–2; Furio, 'The Cultural Background of the Italian Immigrant Woman,' 96.

86 Colomba Furio interview with Tina Gaeta, ILGWU business agent and price adjuster, New York City, 22 Nov. 1976; repr. in Furio, 'Immigrant Women and Industry,' 456.

87 Scarpaci, 'Angela Bambace,' 103.

88 Watson, *Fasanella's City*, 137.

89 For examples of scholars who have demonstrated the importance of family to working-class resistance and struggle see Donna Gabaccia, 'Kinship, Culture, and Migration: A Sicilian Example,' *Journal of American Ethnic History* (Spring 1984): 39–53; Smith, 'Our Own Kind'; Elsa Barkley Brown, 'Mothers of Mind,' *Sage* 6 (Summer 1989); Kelley, '"We Are Not What We Seem"'; Alice Kessler-Harris, 'Treating the Male as "Other": Redefining the Parameters of Labor History,' *Labor History* 34 (Spring-Summer 1993): 190–204; and Cameron, *Radicals of the Worst Sort*.

90 Ramirez, 'Immigration, Ethnicity, and Political Militance,' 134. See also Fenton, *Immigrants and Unions*, 320–66; Furio, 'Immigrant Women and Industry'; Topp, 'The Italian-American Left,' 131; and Montgomery, *Workers' Control in America*, 93–5.

91 Una Compagna, 'Interessi Femminili,' *Lotta di Classe*, 27 Dec. 1912; *Lotta di Classe*, 13 Apr. 1912; *L'Operaia*, 13 Sept. 1913; 4, 18 and 23 Apr. 1914; 13 Aug. 1914; 3 Sept. 1914; 17, 24, and 31 Oct. 1914; 2 Jan. 1915; 27 Feb. 1915; and 24 Apr. 1915; Bambace, 'Notes to interview questions dictated by Angela Bambace to Marion'; Furio, 'Immigrant Women and Industry'; Ewen, *Immigrant Women in the Land of Dollars*.

92 Circulation figures are estimated in *The Message*, 25 Dec. 1914.

93 *L'Operaia*, 4 July 1914; 24 Apr. 1915.

94 Clara Zara, 'Alle Krumire della Liptzin & Co.,' *L'Operaia*, 24 Oct. 1914. See also Bambace, 'Notes to interview questions'; *L'Operaia*, 13 Sept. 1913; 4 Apr. 1914; 4 July 1914; 8 and 13 Aug. 1914; 3 Sept. 1914; 17, 24, and 31 Oct. 1914; 28 Nov. 1914; 2 Jan. 1915; 27 Feb. 1915; 24 Apr. 1915); *Lotta di Classe*, 27 Dec. 1912; 25 Feb. 1912; 13 and 27 Apr. 1912; Furio, 'Immigrant Women and Industry.'

95 Furio, 'Immigrant Women and Industry'; Fenton, *Immigrants and Unions*; Zappia, 'Unionism and the Italian American Worker.'

96 There were two Italian-language locals in the ILGWU: The Italian Cloak, Suit, and Skirt Makers' Union Local 48 received its first charter in 1916, and the Italian Dressmakers' Local 89 was chartered in 1919. Local 48-ILGWU, *'48' Libro Ricordo del XXV Anniversario della Unione dei Cloakmakers Italiani* (New York: International Newspaper Printing Co., 1941), 25–30; John S. Crawford, *Luigi Antonini* (New York: Educational Dept. of Italian Dressmakers' Union, 1950); Furio, 'Immigrant Women and Industry'; Furio, 'The Cultural Background'; Zappia, 'Unionism and the Italian American Worker'; Glenn, *Daughters of the Shtetl*; Fenton, *Immigrants and Unions*, 526; Green, *Ready-to-Wear and Ready-to-Work*, 366.

97 Furio, 'Immigrant Women and Industry'; Furio, 'The Cultural Background of the Italian Immigrant Woman,' 94–5. See also Scarpaci, 'Angela Bambace,' 101–2; Fenton, *Immigrants and Unions*, 526; on Italians in the 1919 strike wave in the steel, coal, textile, and clothing industries, Vecoli, 'The Making and Unmaking,' 10; and Vecoli, 'Anthony Capraro and the Lawrence Strike of 1919.'

98 This quote, taken from Theresa Malkiel, 'Striking for the Right to Live,' *The Coming Nation* 1, 124 (25 Jan. 1913), is reprinted in Furio, 'Immigrant Women and Industry,' 188.

99 Furio, 'Immigrant Women and Industry,' 251; Zappia, 'Unionism and the Italian American Worker'; Fenton, *Immigrants and Unions*, 526; Scarpaci, 'Angela Bambace,' 101–2. See also 'Amministrazione dell'Unione delle Sartine Italiane No. 89, ILGWU,' *Guistizia*, 6 Dec. 1919, 2.

100 Ramirez, 'Immigration, Ethnicity, and Political Militance,' 116.

101 *Il Proletario*, 31 Mar. 1911.

102 P. Di Neri, 'When Is the Next Meeting?' *The Message*, 15 Oct. 1915.

103 *Il Progresso Italo-Americano*, 1 Jan. 1913.

104 Ramirez, 'Immigration, Ethnicity, and Political Militance,' 137. See also Fenton, *Immigrants and Unions*; Vecoli, 'The Making and Unmaking'; Montgomery, 'The "New Unionism"'; Zappia, 'Unionism and the Italian American Worker.'

105 The only book-length studies are still unpublished dissertations: Furio,

'Immigrant Women and Industry' and Zappia, 'Unionism and the Italian American Worker.'

106 Michael Denning, *The Cultural Front: The Laboring of American Culture in the Twentieth Century* (New York: Verso, 1996), 138, 4.

107 Fiorello B. Ventresco, 'Crises and Unity: The Italian Radicals in America in the 1920s,' *Ethnic Forum* 15, 1–2 (1995): 12–34; Rudolph J. Vecoli, 'The Making and Un-Making of an Italian Working Class in the United States, 1915–1945,' keynote address, 'The Lost World of Italian American Radicalism,' New York City, 14 May 1997; Vecoli, 'Ethnicity, Internationalism, and Worker Protectionism'; Vecoli, '"Free Country"'; Vezzosi, 'Class, Ethnicity, and Acculturation'; Vezzosi, *Il socialismo indifferente*; Cartosio, 'Gli emigrati italiani e l'Industrial Workers of the World'; Avrich, *Sacco and Vanzetti*; Topp, 'The Italian-American Left,' 135.

108 Vecoli, 'The Making and Un-Making of an Italian Working Class.' Also important is Vecoli's argument that Italian-American radicals were not only targeted by government agencies, but also by their own *prominenti*, whose 'patriotic fever' was 'vented against the anti-war *sovversivi*.' See Vecoli, 'Ethnicity, Internationalism, and Worker Protectionism,' 14.

109 Salerno, 'Odio di Razza?'

110 Vecoli, 'The Making and Un-Making'; John Higham, *Strangers in the Land: Patterns of American Nativism, 1860–1925* (New Brunswick, NJ: Rutgers University Press, 1963), 264–330.

111 Elisabetta Vezzosi has argued, for example, that after the war, Italian workers turned to strategies that embraced ethnic nationalism, since 'life in the United States fostered the development of ethnic identities and solidarities, even among radical internationalists.' See her 'Radical Ethnic Brokers: Immigrant Socialist Leaders in the United States between Ethnic Community and the Larger Society,' in *Italian Workers of the World: Labor Migration and the Formation of Multiethnic States* (Urbana, Chicago: University of Illinois Press, 2001). See also Ramirez, 'Immigration, Ethnicity, and Political Militance' and Vecoli, 'The Making and Un-Making.'

112 Vezzosi, 'Radical Ethnic Brokers.'

113 Vecoli, 'The Making and Un-Making.'

114 Vezzosi, 'Radical Ethnic Brokers.'

115 Furio, 'Immigrant Women and Industry,' 267.

116 Kessler Harris, 'Problems of Coalition-Building,' 133. See also Ruth R. Prago interview with Albina Delfino, 9 Jan. 1981, 'Oral History of the American Left,' Wagner Archives, Tamiment Collection, New York University; Scarpaci, 'Angela Bambace'; Zappia, 'Unionism and the Italian American Worker'; David Gurowsky, 'Factional Disputes within the ILGWU,

1919–1928' (PhD diss., State University of New York, Binghamton, 1978); and Green, *Ready-to-Wear, Ready-to-Work.*

117 Zappia, 'Unionism and the Italian American Worker.'

118 Ramirez, 'Immigration, Ethnicity, and Political Militance,' 139.

119 Scarpaci, 'Angela Bambace'; Furio, 'Immigrant Women and Industry'; Ruth R. Prago interview with Albina Delfino.

120 Furio, 'Immigrant Women and Industry.'

121 Vecoli, 'The Making and Unmaking,' 19; Vecoli, 'Italian Immigrants in the United States Labor Movement'; John P. Diggins, 'The Italo-American Anti-Fascist Opposition,' *Journal of American History* 54, 3 (December 1967): 582; Diggins, *Mussolini and Fascism: The View from America* (Princeton: Princeton University Press, 1972), 112; Philip V. Cannistraro, 'Luigi Antonini and the Italian Anti-Fascist Movement in the United States, 1940–1943,' *Journal of American Ethnic History* 21 (Fall 1995); Cannistraro, 'Fascism and Italian-Americans,' in S.M. Tomasi, ed., *Perspectives in Italian Immigration and Ethnicity* (New York: Center for Migration Studies, 1977); Cannistraro, *Blackshirts in Little Italy: Italian Americans and Fascism, 1921–1929* (West Lafayette, Ind.: Bordighera, 1999); Zappia, 'Unionism and the Italian American Worker'; Gaetano Salvemini, *Italian Fascist Activities in the United States, 1940–1943* (New York: Center for Migration Studies, 1977); Fiorello B. Ventresco, 'Italian-Americans and the Ethiopian Crisis,' *Italian Americana* 6, 1 (Fall/Winter 1980); Nadia Venturini, *Neri e Italiani ad Harlem: Gli anni Trenta e la guerra d'Etiopia* (Rome: Edizioni Lavoro, 1990); Furio, 'Immigrant Women and Industry'; Scarpaci, 'Angela Bambace.' For a description of Italian garment workers' support for Fascism see Vanni B. Montana, *Amarostico: Testimonianze euro-americane* (Lovorno: V. Bastogi, 1976).

122 Colomba Furio interview with Diane Romanik, ILGWU officer and niece of organizer Margaret di Maggio, New York City, 1 Apr. 1977, repr. in Furio, 'Immigrant Women and Industry,' 417–26.

123 For information on Italian-American women's mass donation of wedding rings to Mussolini's regime, see *New York Times*, 8 Jan. 1936, 8; 25 Apr. 1936, 19; 25 May 1936, 21. My gratitude to my brother, Tom Guglielmo, for helping me to locate these sources. See also Ventresco, 'Italian-Americans and the Ethiopian Crisis,' 18–19. For evidence of anti-Fascist rallies among garment workers, see the photographs in the Capraro Papers, IHRC. For discussion of d'Andrea, see Robert Ventresca and Franca Iacovetta, chapter 9 of this collection.

124 Scarpaci, 'Angela Bambace,' 104–7; Furio, 'Immigrant Women and Industry'; Romualdi, 'Storia della Locale 89'; Philip Camponeschi, 'Speech prepared for Oscar,' 15 Nov. 1908, Bambace Papers, IHRC.

125 *New York Times*, 16 and 17 Aug. 1933); Fannia M. Cohn, 'The Uprising of the Sixty Thousand, The General Strike of the Dressmakers' Union,' *Justice*, 1 Sept. 1933; *Daily Worker*, 17, 18, and 19 Aug. 1933); *Il Progresso* 16, 17, 18, 19, and 20 Aug. 1933). See also materials on the 1933 strike in box 28, file 5, Papers of Charles Zimmerman and in box 69, file 2, Papers of David Dubinsky, ILGWU Archives, Labor-Management Documentation Center, Cornell University (hereafter LMDC). See also Max Danish, *The World of David Dubinsky* (Cleveland: World Publishing Co., 1957), 77; Gus Tyler, *'Look for the Union Label': A History of the International Ladies' Garment Workers' Union* (Armonk, NY: Sharpe, 1995); Furio, 'Immigrant Women and Industry,' 290; Irving Bernstein, *The Turbulent Years: A History of the American Worker, 1933–1941* (Cambridge, MA: Riverside Press, 1960), 37; Sharon Strom, 'Challenging "Woman's Place": Feminism, The Left, and Industrial Unionism in the 1930s,' *Feminist Studies* 9 (Summer 1983).

126 *New York Times*, 16 Aug. 1933; *Daily Worker*, 17, 18, and 19 Aug. 1933); *Il Progresso Italo-Americano*, 18 and 19 Aug. 1933. During the strike thousands of handbills were distributed by the strikers that read, 'We are calling this strike for the purpose of establishing humane and orderly working conditions in our great industry. The present situation of the dressmakers is unbearable. This general strike is being called to make an end to the misery and chaos in the dress shop, to introduce union concerns in the entire industry, and to enable the dressmakers to work ... and live like human beings.' *New York Times*, 17 Aug. 1933.

127 From the Zimmerman Papers, ILGWU Archives, LMDC: 'Joint Board Dress and Waistmakers Union, General Strike (1933) Hall Committee Assignments,' box 45, file 1; 'Tentative Instructions and Information for Hall Chairmen, Secretaries, and Deputies (1932),' box 45, file 1; Letter from Luigi Antonini to Charles Zimmerman, 8 Aug. 1933, box 28, file 5; 'Assignments, Strike 1933,' box 28, file 5; 'Information and Directory of the General Strike Committee, Joint Board Dress and Waistmakers' Union, General Strike, August, 1933,' box 28, file 5; 'Women Speakers List, Strike Meetings, 1932,' box 8, file 15, Papers of the Research Dept. *Giustizia*, January 1932, April–May 1932; August 1932. See also Furio, 'Immigrant Women and Industry'; and Scarpaci, 'Angela Bambace.'

128 Serafino Romualdi, 'Storia della Locale 89,' in *Local 89 Fifteenth Anniversary Commemoration Pamphlet* (1934).

129 Serafino Romualdi made a direct connection between *l'alba radiosa* and the strike, the collective power of Italian workers, and state support of the union through Franklin Delano Roosevelt's National Industrial Recovery Act (inaugurated in June 1933); Romualdi, 'Storia della Locale 89.' For

similar sentiments see the speech by Antonino Crivello at the fourth anniversary of the 1933 Strike, ILGWU Local 144, Newark, NJ (1937), box 1, file 1, Papers of Antonino Crivello, IHRC; 'Compagne e Compagni della Local 89!' address by John Gelo, Ratification Meeting, Madison Square Garden, 2 Apr. 1937, box 15, file 8, Antonini Papers, ILGWU Archives, LMDC; Local 48–ILGWU, *Libro Ricordo*; 'Il Sindicato dell'Abbigliamento Femminile-ILGWU,' *La Parola del Popolo*, 50th Anniversary Publication, 1908–1958, 195; Local 89, ILGWU, *We the Italian Dressmakers Speak* (New York, 1944); *Giustizia*, October 1933. See also Furio, 'Immigrant Women and Industry'; Zappia, 'Unionism and the Italian American Worker'; Bernstein, *The Turbulent Years*, 34, 87–9; and Green, *Ready-to-Wear and Ready-to-Work*.

130 Letter from Frank Liberti to David Dubinksy (1962), Liberti Papers, Botto House National Landmark, Haledon, NJ.

131 *Giustizia*, April 1934. The NIRA, which was passed in the first 100 days of Franklin Delano Roosevelt's administration, sought to stimulate production and competition in business by establishing the National Recovery Administration, which set industrial codes to regulate prices, production, and trade practices.

132 At no point during the 1930s and 1940s were women proportionally represented in the hierarchy of their locals. In 1934, 41 women and 79 men held positions within the administration of Local 89. In 1944 women held 75 of the offices, while men held close to 125. Only occasionally were Italian women permitted entrance into the male-dominated positions of price adjuster, district manager, and business agent in Local 89. The business agent and district manager were particularly important since they increasingly set the priorities of the local by controlling union meetings. Price adjusters also held a certain degree of prestige since they had their own offices, and were in charge of negotiating prices with manufacturers. They also assisted workers with their price complaints. In 1934 there were no women district managers and women only held two of the twenty-one business agent positions. In 1944 women still held only four of the thirty-one business agent positions. See 'Administration of Local 89, 1934' in *Local 89 Fifteenth Anniversary Commemoration Pamphlet* (1934), and 'Administration of Local 89, 1944–46' in ILGWU, *Jubilee, 1919–1944* (1944). See also 'New York: Our City-Our Union, 24th Convention of the ILGWU, Fortieth Anniversary' (1940), box 1, Crivello Papers, IHRC. See also Colomba Furio interviews with Tina Catania, Grace de Luise, and Tina Gaeta reprinted in Furio, 'Immigrant Women and Industry,' 427–35, 436–45, 446–57; Scarpaci, 'Angela Bambace'; and Green, *Ready-to-Wear, Ready-to-Work*.

133 Zappia, 'Unionism and the Italian American Worker,' 87.
134 *Giustizia*, October 1933, November 1933, December 1933, February 1934, March 1934, and April 1934; ILGWU, 'Administration of Local 89,' *Commemorative Pamphlet, Local 89, XV Anniversary of the Formation of the Italian Dressmakers' Local 89* (New York: ILGWU, 1934); Romualdi, 'Storia della Local 89'; Local 89, *Jubilee, 1914–1944*. See also Furio, 'Immigrant Women and Industry,' 293.
135 Furio, 'Immigrant Women and Industry.'
136 Colomba Furio interview with Diane Romanik, ILGWU officer and niece of organizer Margaret di Maggio, New York City, 1 Apr. 1977; repr. in Furio, 'Immigrant Women and Industry,' 425.
137 Romualdi, 'Storia della Locale 89,' 63.
138 Furio interview with Diane Romanik; repr. in Furio, 'Immigrant Women and Industry,' 423.
139 Letter from Maria Rosaria Cimato to Luigi Antonini, 9 June 1939, box 16, file 6; Letter from Lucia De Stefano to Luigi Antonini, 9 Feb. 1940, box 15, file 9; Letter from Lina Richeri to Luigi Antonini, 19 Mar. 1942, box 16, file 7; Letter from Lucia Romualdi Lupia to Luigi Antonini, 18 Aug. 1942, box 16, file 7. All letters are from Antonini Papers, ILGWU Archives, LMDC. Quotation is from Ruth R. Prago interview with Albina Delfino. See also Furio, 'Immigrant Women and Industry'; Ewen, *Immigrant Women in the Land of Dollars*; and Scarpaci, 'Angela Bambace.'
140 For an in-depth study of gender and the iconography of labour in the 1930s, see Elizabeth Faue, *Community of Suffering and Struggle: Women, Men, and the Labor Movement in Minneapolis, 1915–1945* (Chapel Hill: University of North Carolina Press, 1991).
141 Ortiz, 'En la aguja y el pedal eché la hiel'; Robert Laurentz, 'Racial/Ethnic Conflict in the New York City Garment Industry, 1933–1980' (PhD diss., State University of New York, Binghamton, 1980); Will Herberg, 'The Old-Timers and the Newcomers: Ethnic Group Relations in a Needle Trades' Union,' *Journal of Social Issues*, Summer 1953; Roy B. Helfgott, 'Puerto Rican Integration in the Skirt Industry in New York City,' in New School for Social Research, ed., *Discrimination and Low Incomes: Social and Economic Discrimination against Minority Groups in Relation to Low Incomes in New York State* (New York: Studies of New York State Commission against Discrimination, 1959); Herbert Hill, 'Guardians of the Sweatshops: The Trade Unions, Racism, and the Garment Industry,' in Adalberto López and James Petras, eds., *Puerto Rico and Puerto Ricans: Studies in History and Society* (New York: John Wiley and Sons, 1974); Labor Subcommittee of the House Committee on Education and Labor, testimony of Herbert Hill, 17 August

1962, 88th Cong., 1st sess., *Congressional Record* 109, 2 (31 Jan. 1962), 1569–72; Elaine Gail Wrong, *The Negro in the Apparel Industry* (Philadelphia: University of Pennsylvania Press, 1974); Green, *Ready-to-Wear and Ready-to-Work*.

142 Romualdi, 'Storia della Locale 89'; speech given by Antonino Crivello, organizer and district manager for Italian Dressmakers' Local 89 at 4th anniversary of 1933 strike, ILGWU Local 144, Newark (1937), box 1, file 1, Crivello Papers, IHRC. 'We are all minorities' is from Green, *Ready-to Wear and Ready-to-Work*, 379. The 'culture of unity' discourse was not confined to Italian-American workers; see Lizabeth Cohen, *Making a New Deal: Industrial Workers in Chicago, 1919–1939* (Cambridge: Cambridge University Press, 1990), and 'A Symposium on *Making a New Deal*: Industrial Workers in Chicago: 1919–1939,' *Labor History* 32 (Fall 1991): 562–96.

143 In order to maintain power in the union, Jewish and Italian leaders in the ILGWU established exclusionary electoral processes that prevented other groups from occupying important decision-making positions. The eligibility rules for candidates for president, secretary-treasurer, or membership on the general executive board were the strictest among all the labor unions in the nation. This severely limited the number of challengers, especially among the newcomers to the union. In addition, since political groups or caucuses were not allowed to convene until three months before the annual convention, it was difficult for contending candidates to meet with the rank and file to present their platforms. Those in office, however, could meet with the members as often as they wished. Ortiz, 'En la aguja y el pedal eché la hiel'; Herbert Hill, 'Guardians of the Sweatshops'; Laurentz, 'Racial/Ethnic Conflict'; Green, *Ready-to-Wear and Ready-to-Work*.

144 Ortiz, 'En la aguja y el pedal eché la hiel,' 58.

145 For an elaboration on this positioning in another context see Robert Orsi, 'The Religious Boundaries of an Inbetween People: Street *Feste* and the Problem of the Dark-Skinned "Other" in Italian Harlem, 1920–1990,' *American Quarterly* 44 (September 1992).

146 Letter from Esta Pingaro to Vito Marcantonio, 5 Oct. 1941, box 67, file 6, Papers of Vito Marcantonio, New York Public Library (NYPL); Letter from John W. Sutter to Vito Marcantonio, 24 Oct. 1938, box 3, file 3, Papers of Vito Marcantonio, NYPL; Paul Buhle interview with Vito Magli, 15 Mar. 1983, 'Oral History of the American Left,' Wagner Archives, Tamiment Collection, New York University. See also in the Papers of the International Workers' Order, LMDC: Letter from Natalina Arcangeli to Constantino Lippa, 16 Aug. 1950, box 10, file 14; Letter from Constantino Lippa to 'Sorella Geraci,' 18 Apr. 1950, box 10, file 14; Letter from Constantino

Lippa to Salvatore Geraci, 22 Aug. 1950, box 10, file 14; 'Conferenza dei Delegati Sezione Italiana alla Quarta Convenzione Nazionale, 28–9 Apr. 1938,' box 10, file 14. For evidence of *circoli* see 'Communicazioni: New York, NY,' *L'Adunata dei Refrattari*, 26 and 30 Apr. 1932. See also Guglielmo, 'Donne Ribelli,' forthcoming in Cannistraro and Meyer, *The Lost World*; Keeran, 'The Italian Section of the International Workers' Order'; Meyer, *Vito Marcantonio*; and Venturini, *Neri e Italiani*.

147 Jennifer Guglielmo, 'Italian American Women's Dialogue on Race in Labor and Neighborhood Coalition Movements in New York City, 1930–1945,' paper presented at American Italian Historical Association, 12–14 Nov. 1998, New York City.

148 Paul Buhle interview with Vito Magli.

149 Orsi, 'The Religious Boundaries,' 317.

150 Tom Guglielmo, *White on Arrival: Italians, Race, Color, and Power in Chicago, 1890–1945* (New York: Oxford University Press, forthcoming).

151 For examples of this see the recollections of Vito Magli in his interview with Paul Buhle (15 Mar. 1983) and the Ruth R. Prago interview with Albina Delfino (9 Jan. 1981), in 'Oral History of the American Left,' Wagner Archives, Tamiment Collection, New York University; Angela Bambace, 'Notes re Civil Rights Meeting, July 9, 1963,' Bambace Papers, IHRC; Bambace, 'Radio Address, WBMD' on racism of Governor Wallace, (10 May 1964), Bambace Papers, IHRC; and 'Statement by Mrs. Angela Bambace' (n.d.), Bambace Papers, IHRC. See also Gerald Meyer, 'Italian Americans and the American Communist Party: Notes on a History' and Keeran, 'The Italian Section of the International Workers Order,' papers presented at 'The Lost World of Italian-American Radicalism: Labor, Politics, and Culture' conference, City University of New York, New York City, 14–15 May 1997; and Guglielmo, 'Italian American Women's Dialogue on Race.'

152 There are many scholars who have provided theoretical models for such work, including: Elsa Barkley Brown, 'Polyrhythms and Improvisation: Lessons for Women's History,' *History Workshop Journal* 31 (Spring 1991); Evelyn Brooks Higginbotham, 'African-American Women's History and the Metalanguage of Race,' *Signs* 17, 2 (1992): 251–74; Evelyn Nakano Glenn, 'Racial Ethnic Women's Labor: The Intersection of Race, Gender, and Class Oppression,' *Review of Radical Political Economies* 17, 3 (Fall 1985): 86–108; and Frank, 'White Working-Class Women.'

9 Virgilia D'Andrea: The Politics of Protest and the Poetry of Exile

Robert Ventresca and *Franca Iacovetta*

On 16 November 1929, Italian immigrant anarchists in Chicago crowded into Meldazis Hall under the banner of Italian anti-Fascism to avoid police harassment. Paid informants of the Italian Consulate moved anonymously through the crowd. At the podium was a revolutionary anarchist considered by Rome's Fascist authorities to be one of the more dangerous anti-Fascist exiles. 'We will exterminate all capitalists because they suck the blood of the working class,' the speaker declared. 'We must use violence. We must shed our own blood for our cause, and we must avenge our brothers who died for it.'[1]

The speaker was Virgilia D'Andrea, best known in anarchist circles and to Italian and North American authorities as the female companion of noted anarcho-syndicalist Armando Borghi. With Borghi, D'Andrea fled Mussolini's Italy in 1923 to Germany, then France, Canada, and, finally, the United States. D'Andrea was closely linked to the major events of Italian anarchism and to international leaders like Errico Malatesta and Luigi Galleani during the 1920s and 1930s. Shifts in her politics – from socialist to anarchist and anti-Fascist, and from an anarcho-syndicalist committed to mass-based organization to one more sympathetic to terrorist acts – reflected the permeable boundaries among Italian left movements (where shifts in allegiances among parties and organizations on the left were not unusual) and the shifting fortunes and highly fractured nature of anarchism in Europe and North America. D'Andrea had achieved notoriety in her own right, and by the time she entered the United States in 1928 (a year after the death of Sacco and Vanzetti) she was known across North and South America as a bright light among beleaguered Italian anarchist exiles. In the United States, she earned respect and affection as a poet, propagandist, and radical anti-Fascist, while all the time struggling with debilitating illnesses and a life of imposed exile.

In this chapter, we attempt an initial biography and, like the relevant feminist scholarship on radical women, we aim to satisfy the social historian's demand for the specificity of a life lived in a particular time and place.[2] A cultural and intellectual biography of D'Andrea sheds light on some fascinating but still under-studied topics in the history of women leftists, international proletarian struggles, and inter-war Italian-American radicalism. As a political exile, D'Andrea belonged to a global network of Italian migrants who lived in expatriate communities and forged ties with comrades in radical and labour movements in Europe, the Americas, and elsewhere. She was one of a long line of radicals forced by their politics to flee Italy, highlighting the transnationalism of Italian radicalism.[3]

Anarchist migrant women like D'Andrea helped to define what radicalism meant for the much larger group of immigrant women entering American labour movements. Italian radicals had provided critical leadership to emerging labour movements in France and Brazil. In the United States, they more often provided alternatives to the conservative American Federation of Labor in major strikes that, as in the case of Lawrence, Massachusetts, Paterson, New Jersey, or Tampa, Florida, included significant female participation.[4] Similar observations apply to multi-ethnic strikes in Canadian mining and industrial communities.[5] D'Andrea's activism among Italian immigrant workers in the late 1920s and the 1930s challenges established wisdom that the executions of the Italian immigrant anarchists Sacco and Vanzetti (1927) marked the death of Italian-American radical movements. While their death was a crisis for anarchists, D'Andrea's career as an anti-Fascist points to important continuities in the history of Italian-American radicalism. At the same time, her relationship to immigrant workers, including women, differed markedly from that of Italian-American women radicals and labour organizers who were more firmly integrated into working-class immigrant communities.[6]

Furthermore, D'Andrea's free love (*amore libero*) union with Borghi demands a gendered analysis, inviting comparisons to Emma Goldman and revisiting the connection between the personal and the political. As historians we are forced repeatedly to see D'Andrea through the gaze of her male comrades, yet this also allows us to pursue another important but still underdeveloped theme of how male allies gendered radical women.

Finally, a biography of D'Andrea must explore links between her literary and political work. Successive generations of Italian radicals have combined literary aspirations and politics, yet the role of poetry and prose remains a neglected topic in the history of Italian radicalism. Poets played a special role in Italian nationalism and internationalism. D'Andrea had many predecessors, from the early-nineteenth-century nationalist romantic poet Ugo Foscolo to famed Industrial Workers of the World (IWW) poet Arturo Giovanitti and the lawyer-turned-playwright-poet, anarcho-syndicalist Pietro Gori. Literature allowed anti-clerical, anti-state, and anti-nationalist radicals to come to terms with Italian cultural nationalism.[7] D'Andrea's ever-present nostalgia for Italy is thus best understood not as a rejection of internationalism but as a reflection of a complex, transnational life rooted in attachments to Italian internationalist ideologies and to a beloved homeplace.[8] By considering D'Andrea's poetry we complement existing social histories of Italian leftists and remind historians of radicalism of such long-neglected themes as cultural nationalism.

'Maestrina del popolo, Young teacher of the people'

Virgilia D'Andrea was born in Februrary 1880 in the Abruzzo town of Sulmona, a centre of working-class radicalism among railway workers and the birthplace of Italian-American anarcho-syndicalist Carlo Tresca.[9] Apart from some allusions in her poetry to a difficult childhood, D'Andrea left no record of her early years. Borghi's memoirs tell us she 'was raised in pain.'[10] D'Andrea's father was a civil servant, her mother a homemaker. Orphaned before reaching her teens – her mother died young and her father's new wife's lover then murdered him – she was sent to a convent. Her two brothers died while she was there. She enrolled at the University of Naples, earned a teaching certificate, and began teaching in her native Abruzzi.[11]

Her brief career as an elementary school teacher proved transformative. 'La maestrina del popolo,' wrote Borghi, 'entered the classroom with pony-tails still in her hair, and her heart embittered by rebellion and the need for justice.' Her rebellion may have been nurtured by close contact with impoverished students; she herself endured relative poverty as a self-supporting teacher in one of Italy's poorest regions. She also witnessed the region's great earthquake of 1915, which devastated the capital town of Avezzano where D'Andrea taught and which killed thousands of people – mainly women at home – in the surrounding towns and villages. The state's inadequate response and indifference sharpened D'Andrea's sense of injustice.[12]

D'Andrea was still at the convent in 1900 when she learned about anarchism. Gaetano Bresci had assassinated Italy's king, Umberto I, after returning from Paterson, New Jersey, to avenge the brutal repression of the *fatti di maggio* (uprising of May) 1898, when hundreds of Milanese rioted over high bread prices, local taxes, and other grievances.[13] His act gave huge notoriety to Italian anarchists like Malatesta, Gori, and Galleani, all of whom fled Italy to avoid harassment and arrest. At the convent, the nuns told children to pray for the soul of the dead king. When D'Andrea asked for an explanation of the assassination, they told her it was the crazy act of an insane and evil man.[14]

D'Andrea's first act of political defiance came during the First World War, when she left teaching to join the anti-militarist campaign against Italy's intervention in the war. Like many young Italians of her generation, D'Andrea's opposition to war evolved into a broader critique of capitalism and imperialism. To them, Italy's decision to join a war while Italians suffered from lack of food, clothing, or housing exposed the moral shortcomings of the state. A critique of the bourgeois nation-state became a central tenet of D'Andrea's radicalism.

Morally Shameful and Dangerous

By 1917, state security authorities in Rome had already created a file on D'Andrea, whom they dubbed a highly skilled and dangerous agitator, in the Casellario Politico Centrale (CPC). A 1919 report from the prefect in Bologna described her as a 'morally shameful' woman with 'the gift of the gab' and a 'loud and violent ... disposition,' yet also 'modestly intelligent and cultured.' Her strength in public speaking is suggested by the prefect's ominous reference to D'Andrea's ability to manipulate 'the masses' with ease.[15]

The moral denunciation of D'Andrea reflected her new relationship with the journalist Armando Borghi. It was as Borghi's 'companion' that D'Andrea first attracted the attention of the political police in summer 1918.[16] The couple had met in 1917 in Milan at a meeting of the syndicalist union that Borghi headed – the USI (Unione Sindacale Italiana). When D'Andrea appeared in Borghi's police file, she was still affiliated with socialists in her hometown of Sulmona. She had joined the Italian Socialist Party (PSI) and had helped establish a local women's section of the party. We cannot trace precisely her shift from socialism to anarchism, but as noted earlier, given the fluid character of Italian left politics it was not unusual.

Taking their lead from Malatesta, anarcho-syndicalists sought to foster revolutionary consciousness within the labour movement and were committed to building a revolutionary mass movement. While defending revolutionary violence, they condemned individual acts like bombings, assassinations, and sabotage as damaging to the cause. By contrast, other Italian anarchists were highly suspicious of unions or other centralized, bureaucratic structures. Anarcho-communists like Galleani, whose American base was Barre, Vermont, rejected both the state and private property; they denounced the syndicalists' acceptance of organized labour activism as a betrayal of the libertarian and communal values central to anarchism. Individualist anarchists distrusted both the communal arrangements of the anarcho-communists and the labour organizations of the anarcho-syndicalists, preferring terrorism ('propaganda of the deed') aimed at critical targets of oppression to expose the evil of capitalism and facilitate mass unrest.[17]

In joining Borghi and the USI, D'Andrea embraced labour activism. During the 1890s and early 1900s, anarchists had been a minority group in Italy, but, as Peter Marshall notes, anarchists like Malatesta and Borghi made syndicalism a serious alternative to socialism for workers and their USI at first joined the socialist and reformist General Confederation of Labour (CGL). In 1912, the USI broke away from the CGL and quickly gained strength, attracting members from central Italy and the Ligurian coast.[18] In 1914, Malatesta called for a general strike after the shooting of anti-militarist demonstrators in Ancona. The call triggered Italy's dramatic red week (*settimana rossa*), during which trains ground to a halt, violence erupted in many areas, and small towns in the Marches declared themselves autonomous republics. Marshall has argued that the anarchists and the USI 'seemed poised to overthrow the monarchy' until the CGL ordered its members back to work, crushing the movement.[19]

D'Andrea's politics were greatly influenced by Malatesta, who was in exile when she first joined the anarchists.[20] Malatesta had argued for working 'as anarchists within the unions, advocating and practising as far as possible direct action, decentralization and individual initiative.'[21] In D'Andrea's words, anarchists were 'a banner' and 'flame' fuelled by the 'fire of secular revolt.' 'Our Idea,' she insisted, 'represents a revolt of permanent innovation based on truth and therefore rejects an official limit, a sacramental seal, a single creed, a priestly interpretation of any creed.' D'Andrea believed that an anarchist-led social revolution could

forge a society in which free will would be the sole guiding ethos. Like
Malatesta, she envisioned a society composed of federations of free
associations of producers and consumers acting harmoniously in mutual
self-interest. For anarchists, 'freedom and justice' meant not merely civil
rights but 'the abolition of suffering, of superstition; the abolition of
man's oppression of man, that is the abolition of government and private property.' D'Andrea had little tolerance for the 'fatalistic theories'
of Russian anarchist Kropotkin, who argued that the revolution was
preordained.[22] Impatient with waiting 'in vain' for 'the saviour or sav-
iours,' D'Andrea declared: 'We alone are the vehicle for our Idea, and
only through our work will it one day become an indispensable part
of life.'[23]

Internationalism and anti-clericalism were other major tenets of
D'Andrea's anarchism, which largely conformed to the anarchist program laid down at Bologna in 1920. It called for the abolition of private
property, monarchies, and even republics, of parliaments and police
forces, and any other 'coercive powers.' Her comrades vowed to wage
'war' on all 'rivalries and patriotic prejudices' and promote a 'brotherhood among all peoples.' Italian anarchists, unlike their comrades
elsewhere, did not denounce the family, but instead envisioned a 'recon-
structed' family based on 'the practice of love, freed from every legal tie,
from every economic and physical oppression, from every religious
prejudice.' This was the closest anarchists came to calling the traditional
nuclear family a source of women's oppression.[24]

Nor did D'Andrea explicitly address the issue of marriage and family,
although she, like many Italian radicals, was an ardent anti-cleric. 'Convinced as we are that man will never be free as long as he remains
spiritually tied to the prejudices of God, of morality,' she wrote, 'we want
to free man from the restrictions of these terrible moral [and] intellectual constrictions.' History showed, she added, that good sprang from
human effort when 'man fought against the idea of God, of owner and of
government.' D'Andrea's position on the 'woman question' perhaps
resembled that of many other Italian anarchist women who, rather than
attack marriage and family, sought a role for anarchist mothers as revolutionary educators of children.[25]

On the Road to Exile, 1919 and After

As opponents of Italy's entry into the First World War Borghi and
D'Andrea were placed under house arrest until the armistice. Amid the

revolutionary fervour unleashed by the war, D'Andrea and Borghi then worked hard to spread the USI's anarcho-syndicalist message of proletarian revolution,[26] and to bring Malatesta home.[27] Malatesta did return, in December 1919, to find a renewed anarchist movement. He also immediately joined the fray of labour and peasant activism against the established order.[28]

The *biennio rosso* (two red years) of 1919–20 witnessed the widespread occupation of factories and land by workers and peasants, especially in the north of Italy. The USI leadership did its part in the occupation by leading its metalworkers and other affiliated members in a national strike.[29] During a 1920 metalworkers' strike in Milan, city authorities accused Borghi and Malatesta of arming workers for an impending revolution.[30] They were arrested along with eighty other anarchists, and spent almost nine months in prison awaiting trial. D'Andrea was also arrested, on charges that ranged from conspiring to overthrow the government and inciting insurrection, to 'moral complicity' in terrorist bombings committed by third parties.[31] As a woman, D'Andrea spent less time (a few weeks) in prison than the men; while there she wrote poems, including one dedicated to the late Rosa Luxemburg.[32]

D'Andrea became associated with a critically important event in the history of Italian anarchism – the bombing of Milan's Diana theatre, on 24 March 1921, by two young anarchists unconnected to the USI. The blast killed twenty people, injured many more, and provoked a severe backlash.[33] The revolutionary moment of 1919–20 was brutally crushed and fear of further disorder gripped parts of the country. Fascists promising order began attacking working-class institutions, including the USI, and life quickly became unbearable for radicals. It was amid this brewing crisis that D'Andrea and her male comrades agonized over the Diana bombing.

Borghi later wrote that his 'beloved' Virgilia faced the trying period with tenacity and determination.[34] Those attributes well describe D'Andrea's decision to defend the Diana bombers despite her distaste for random violence. Malatesta too thought the bombing a 'stupid' mistake but refused to vilify the bombers, calling them instead 'saints and heroes.'[35] Writing in 1922 in Malatesta's newspaper *Umanità Nova* (which Borghi now edited), D'Andrea implored her readers to consider the young terrorists as victims too. These were disillusioned young men, without hope, dehumanized by a war that an avaricious, uncaring bourgeois state had forced them to fight. Her plea provoked the angry response of the husband of a woman (a twenty-nine-year-old mother of two) killed in the bombing.[36] D'Andrea responded as one who knew 'the pain' of losing a parent at a young age. Of the surviving children, she wrote, 'I run my hands through your children's hair so that their life might be easier and to brighten all of life's colours and to rekindle all of life's hopes for the solitary little sprouts.'[37] Still, D'Andrea clung tenaciously to her argument that the true murderer was the bourgeois state that had turned innocent caring young men into killers by sending them to fight in a brutal war.[38] By supporting the bomb-throwers, D'Andrea became an enemy of the Fascist state established by Mussolini in 1922.

Once convinced they could not remain safe in Italy, D'Andrea and Borghi chose to continue the fight against Fascism from abroad.[39] The couple travelled to Berlin in December 1922 to attend a meeting of European anarcho-syndicalists. The Berlin sojourn lasted less than one year, and by late 1923, the couple had moved to Paris to a large Italian anti-Fascist exile community. In the company of like-minded Italian exiles, Borghi felt at home.[40] In Paris, there was also food on the table. Although initially opposed to the move,[41] D'Andrea found in France a vibrant expatriate community peopled by some of the most revered figures of Italian socialism (Filippo Turati, Claudio Treves, Anna Kuliscioff), scores of liberal democrats, communists, and republicans, and a small contingent of Italian anarchists concentrated in Paris and Marseille.[42] Malatesta, aging and tired of living in exile, chose to remain in Italy and, under house arrest, to agitate against the regime.

D'Andrea quickly resurfaced in police files as an anti-Fascist exile worth watching. In 1926 she led a large commemoration ceremony in memory of the foremost anarchist writer, poet and dramatist (and D'Andrea's literary 'mentor'), Pietro Gori, in Marseilles. She contributed regularly to Italian- and French-language anarchist and anti-Fascist newspapers[43] and, like other critics of Mussolini, she denounced the murder in 1924 by Fascist thugs of the socialist parliamentarian Giacomo Matteoti. Radicals like D'Andrea mounted a serious if ultimately unsuccessful challenge to Fascist rule.[44] The Matteoti affair awakened Mussolini to the vulnerability of his rule, leading him to impose new authoritarian and repressive measures. It also alerted Mussolini to the political threat of exiled anti-Fascists living in relative safety in foreign countries. In response, Mussolini intensified surveillance of expatriate anti-Fascists like D'Andrea, and even impounded copies of D'Andrea's *Tormento*, a volume of provocative poems written during the *biennio rosso*.

Radical Anti-Fascist in America, 1928–33

As D'Andrea wrote her second volume of poetry, *L'Ora de Maramaldo*, in Paris, Nicola Sacco and Bartolomeo Vanzetti languished in a U.S. prison. Italian immigrants and committed anarchists, they were arrested in April 1920 for robbing and murdering two men in Massachusetts. Despite the absence of concrete evidence linking the two to the crime, Sacco and Vanzetti were convicted of murder, and sentenced to death. After several years of appeals, they were executed. One poem, 'Mentre il Boia Attende' ('Executioner Awaits'), is dedicated to the pair, who, for D'Andrea, embodied 'the story of all immigrants' who had been 'betrayed' by their native Italy. Two innocent emigrants awaited death abroad, wrote D'Andrea, 'but did their country remember them?'[45] In fact, Italy had not forgotten Sacco and Vanzetti; Mussolini used their imprisonment to fan the flames of anti-Americanism. The Italian anarchists tried to come to their aid. In May 1927, Borghi left on a speaking tour of Massachusetts and New York on behalf of Sacco and Vanzetti. D'Andrea made immediate plans to follow him, but by the time she arrived, they were already dead, electrocuted by the state of Massachusetts in August 1927. D'Andrea arrived in November 1928 amid much legal wrangling over Borghi's immigration status.[46] U.S. authorities had advance warning of her arrival. The Italian embassy in Rome told Washington that though purportedly coming to the United States to join her partner Borghi, D'Andrea was a 'dangerous propagandist and organizer of radical activities,' which 'she disguises under the cover of anti-Fascism.'[47]

D'Andrea's subsequent activism in the United States reflected the beleaguered state of Italian-American anarchism and the new exiles' deep-seated desire to defeat Fascism in Italy. In the red-scare era of the 1920s, anarchism in North America had come under serious attack. D'Andrea was entering a country where a once-vibrant syndicalist movement within the IWW, led in part by Italian anarchist exiles like Tresca and Malatesta, had been crushed by a repressive state. By the 1930s, the anarchists, though highly committed anti-Fascists, had become a marginal voice on the Italian-American left, where communist and socialist voices dominated as they did in other countries, narrowing the range of action for anarchists like D'Andrea.

According to her male comrades, D'Andrea felt emotionally drained by the experience of the new exile. Leaving behind friends and allies in France, she tended increasingly towards melancholy or depression. She had also begun to suffer from the disease that would kill her five years later. Borghi observed that her pain was tempered by her love for political work. 'She liked propaganda work,' he noted, 'and she was dearly loved by all the comrades. But her strength would not help her as she would have liked.'[48] D'Andrea's years in the United States would bring long, exhausting, but fulfilling speaking engagements followed by periods of almost complete inactivity as she lay bed-ridden.

Borghi saw D'Andrea's main problem as 'the inertia of exile,' which strongly hampered her need to 'feel useful to someone.' Yet, in short time D'Andrea became much celebrated among Italian radical exiles in the Americas. Her male comrades held her in high regard, but also expressed considerable fraternal – or was it paternal? – concern for her welfare. Osvaldo Maraviglia's report of a 'successful' New York conference held by 'our dear Virgilia,' written in a letter to Malatesta just months before his death, contained a typical mix of admiration and worry. The hall was 'filled to capacity' and 'she enthused the young while reminding the old comrades of friends that had been in this country to plant the seeds of the "Eighth Day."' 'Poor Virgilia,' Maraviglia added, 'as delicate as she already is, it was too much for her, but every time she speaks, she leaves behind seeded ground.'[49]

D'Andrea did have occasional pangs of doubt about the utility of her work. Writing Malatesta from White Plains in 1932, she noted: 'I continue to work, though my health remains fragile, but I alone continue to carry on with oral propaganda, and these United States are immense. How to please everyone?' Her letter might also suggest a frustration with her male comrades for not doing enough. 'At times,' she writes, 'I am so physically tired but unfortunately no new speakers have yet to emerge even though they are so badly needed.'[50]

As a migrant and dangerous foreigner who spoke little English, D'Andrea had few contacts outside her community of exile intellectuals. Most Italian-American women radicals began their political work among the women of their shop and neighbourhood. D'Andrea was not similarly rooted. Her speeches were less about local workers' struggles than about international proletarian struggles, and her approach was historical, argumentative, and theoretical, though the purpose remained essentially educational. D'Andrea's experience also differed from that of other revolutionary émigrés who, like Maria Barbieri and Maria Roda, spearheaded organizing campaigns of Italian-American workers in this period. As Jennifer Guglielmo shows, such women spent years living and working alongside the Italian workers. Wedded to communities of workers, whether in the Illinois mining towns studied by Caroline Waldron Merithew or (to move outside North America) the immigrant community of Buenos Aires examined by José Moya, such anarchist women initiated workplace protest and consumer boycotts and boisterous rent strikes led by housewives.[51]

The last years of D'Andrea's life seemed lonely and full of death. In Boston in July 1932 she learned of Malatesta's death. Borghi left their Brooklyn home to join her, but found her in hospital, where internal bleeding had prompted emergency surgery, performed by Ilya Galleani, the daughter of anarchist-communist and defender of violent propaganda of the deed, Galleani. The crushing defeat of anarcho-syndicalism in the United States had rendered even old ideological disputes among anarchists irrelevant.[52]

When D'Andrea returned to New York, she began work on *Torce nella notte*, a good part of which would be devoted to what she called *l'anarchismo eroico* (heroic anarchism), a veiled reference to the use of violence by individual anarchists. Such a book was now desperately needed, she wrote to the editor of *L'Adunata dei Refrettari*, given that 'Ghandist ideas ... are infiltrating our ranks more than you might think.' Revisiting the Diana bombing from the relative safety of the United States, D'Andrea issued a still stronger defence of the bomb-throwers, arguing that the act, when measured against the backdrop of Fascist thuggery, was an 'attack of rebellion and of desperate retaliation.'[53]

No sooner had D'Andrea returned home than illness struck again. She asked the comrade writing the preface to her book to say nothing. 'Illness is not nice to look at,' she wrote, 'and those poor and modest pages contain the little bit of good and beautiful that remains in my soul.'[54] For a time, the book was a helpful distraction from the disease and she managed to submit it before her death. In spring 1933, after months of what Borghi called bouts of 'atrocious pains' and many 'terrible nights,' when 'I feared she would lose all reason,' D'Andrea entered a New York City hospital for the last time. Borghi's memoir provides his detailed memory of her last days, noting her struggles and her refusal to accept a priest's ministrations. Terrified of being arrested, he did not leave her side, and she warned him to 'be careful.' Then, on 11 May, he reported, 'the publishers gave me the first copy of her book. I caressed and kissed it. She died in the night.' In a testament to his own difficult life as a political exile, Borghi added: 'I had mourned the death of my mother in 1929, of my father in 1930 and of Malatesta in 1932. In these painful moments, I had always had her by my side to help me. Now, I was alone.'[55]

Italian consular officials in New York informed Rome of D'Andrea's death, from abdominal cancer, on 13 May 1933 at Fifth Avenue Hospital.[56] Comrades were eloquent in expressing their sense of loss.[57] Friends, allies, and workers paid their final respects to D'Andrea in a New York City cemetery. Her friend Osvaldo Maraviglia said a few words over her open grave and comrade Nino Crivello recited a poem he had written for the occasion as the casket was lowered into the ground – a fitting farewell for *la poetessa*. As news of her death spread, *L'Adunata dei Refrettari* was inundated with letters and telegrams from Italy, Europe, Africa, and elsewhere.[58] *L'Adunata* paid tribute to D'Andrea by publishing posthumously several of her writings and speeches.[59] Writing from Toronto in July 1933, Borghi shared his sense of loss and expressed gratitude for the kind words of so many comrades for D'Andrea – 'Lei, grande e buona, senza confronti' ('She, great and good, incomparable').[60]

Free Love, Male Comrades, and Sexual Politics

No doubt Borghi loved D'Andrea, his life-long partner. In his memoir, he recalled their first encounter and his instant attraction to her. 'She shared my own opinions,' he wrote, and was 'an exceptional creature' and 'kind soul' who 'gave colour and poetry and sympathy to anything close to her.' 'Spiritually,' he added, 'she was an indomitable fighter,' though physically, 'it was as if her soul was trapped in a tiny cage from which it was impossible to escape.' 'This conflict,' Borghi concluded, 'reduced her to pieces.'[61]

D'Andrea and Borghi entered into a free-love union shortly after they met. Police authorities in Milan attributed her 'distaste' for the institution of marriage to an irresponsible preference for 'losing herself body and soul in *amore libero*.'[62] This link between sexual and political liberation calls to mind Emma Goldman, who first gained attention as the partner of Alexander Berkman (would-be assassin of U.S. steel magnate Henry Clay Frick) and then became a major anarchist leader and anarchist-feminist.[63] As Margaret Marsh observes, anarchist-feminists believed that inequality between women and men was the product of the nuclear family and traditional sexual relations. Hence, their call for the abolition of marriage and family and their support for sexual varietism, or free love, as an act of sexual liberation. In anarchist circles, Goldman developed a reputation for a strong sexual appetite and she attracted numerous lovers, many of them younger men and the husbands and brothers of comrades. But the 'one great love of her life,' as biographer Alice

Wexler observes, was Ben Reitman, the Chicago-born doctor who prac-tised among vagabonds and prostitutes in a world quite apart from Goldman's tight circle of European and Jewish intellectual radicals. Goldman wrote that in Reitman she had finally found a man who could both 'love the woman in me' and 'share my work.' While Reitman proved an 'effective manager' for Goldman's career, the most striking feature of their relationship was its sexual intensity.[64]

The intersection of the political with the personal arises too in D'Andrea and Borghi's union, but the eroticism about which Goldman loved to write is absent from the written record on D'Andrea's partnership with Borghi. While Borghi appears to have been D'Andrea's great love, he also appears to have been the only lover she ever had. For D'Andrea, free love evidently meant a monogamous relationship between loving partners, not sexual 'promiscuity.' For Italian male radicals, by contrast, free love more often meant sexual variety. Carlo Tresca, for example, carried on a passionate affair with Elizabeth Gurley Flynn and, later, had a child with Flynn's sister. As Michael Miller Topp observes, such behav-iour nurtured the men's reputation as 'womanizers' who had many sexual affairs, including with wives of comrades and very young women.[65] In D'Andrea's many writings, some of them intensely personal, there is hardly mention of Borghi let alone commentary on his sexual politics or her sexual life with him.

Borghi wrote much about his life with D'Andrea but nothing about sexuality. He described their relationship with words of friendship, com-panionship, and respect rather than sexual passion. In his memoir, he writes: 'We were together for fifteen years of work, struggle, fear, ostra-cism, persecutions, imprisonment, exile, unchanged and forever tied one to the other by affection and respect.' Borghi stressed the inherent equality of their rapport, their mutual intellectual and political interests, and above all the emotional tie that bound them to each other under the most trying circumstances. 'Virgilia was my confidante,' he wrote, 'giving and trustful, never suspicious, insinuating or malicious.'

Yet, it appears he still saw himself as chief dissident, claiming, for example, that 'Virgilia reinforced my work.'[66] Although D'Andrea was early dubbed a dangerous subversive, she did not initially command the same degree of notoriety as Borghi. Writing to security forces in Rome, the local prefect described D'Andrea as Borghi's 'most trustworthy col-laborator in the illegal diffusion of his revolutionary ideas.'[67] In the end, D'Andrea proved as 'dangerous' as Borghi, and perhaps was even better respected. While Borghi spent many years in hiding or on the run to escape arrest, D'Andrea diligently carried out key tasks, circulating Borghi's pamphlets and delivering speeches.[68]

D'Andrea also became the more prolific writer, and mutual friends and comrades would later recall D'Andrea with greater admiration and affection than Borghi. An acquaintance who hid the couple briefly in 1929, Valerio Isca, claimed that Borghi played a 'small role' in the American anarchist movement. Although a 'good speaker and good actor on the stage,' he lacked the 'charm' or 'bearing' of famed anarchists Malatesta and Tresca. By contrast, Isca remembered D'Andrea as 'a marvelous person,' 'gentle,' and 'a fine speaker' whose speeches were 'masterpieces of eloquence.' Her poems, Isca added, were 'beautiful ... every one of them.'[69]

Apart from her brief experience helping to organize a women's section of the Italian Socialist Party in the red region of Abruzzo, D'Andrea was largely silent on gender politics in the movement. She did not rage against the sexism of male comrades, although she did criticize comrades who opposed women's participation in actual physical violence. As an anarcho-syndicalist, D'Andrea was prepared not only to support a strategy of organized, class-based violence but to participate in it. She developed no sustained critique of the oppressive nature of marriage or the nuclear family and made no explicit call for female liberation. D'Andrea never saw sexual varietism as a strategy for women's liberation nor did she appear to engage in sexual experimentation. This is not to say that D'Andrea did not take seriously the issues of women's oppression and liberation; her commitment to free love and her friendships with female comrades suggest otherwise. By committing to a life as a radical activist, D'Andrea sought to change the world and to carve out a space for herself in defiance of prevailing gender norms. Her decision to eschew formal marriage and motherhood reflected in part a search for personal autonomy.[70]

D'Andrea's personal life, political work, and poetry suggest the need to define more broadly the nature of female political activism. Officially unmarried and without children, D'Andrea differs from the Italian anarchist women of Illinois coal mining towns, though she might well have supported their concept of 'anarchist motherhood.'[71] No doubt D'Andrea shared their calling as an educator. Her poetry suggests she was happiest when filling the void of loneliness, isolation, and emptiness with the anarchist 'Ideal' of the betterment of humankind.

D'Andrea's male comrades offered varying versions of this model of woman as educator. Auro d'Arcola said of D'Andrea after her death that she 'was born for the classroom and for the home.' In the schoolroom, she would have taught generations of young people 'in the cult of liberty and love.' In the home, she would have been 'an inextinguishable source of grace and light of the family.' Denied by 'fate' from having a classroom or family, claimed d'Arcola, she instead took her message directly to the people, making the 'piazza' and the streets her classroom. Indeed, in the writings of her male comrades, she appears at times as a Christ-like figure that suffers courageously for the greater good.[72]

While clearly intended as expressions of admiration for her political skills and genuine concern for her health, the comments about D'Andrea made by male comrades prompt us to consider the real or apparent paternalism of radical men toward even their dearest female comrades. Do their observations reveal gendered notions of womanhood that resemble bourgeois ideals? The men commented constantly on D'Andrea's fragility. Yet Borghi also marvelled that so much energy and force could come from one so small and frail. Borghi stressed the physical and emotional toll of exile on D'Andrea. He offers us the anguished recollections of a man uncertain about whether he had done the right thing in 'bringing [Virgilia] with me to Berlin,' yet convinced that had saved her from the 'torment' of 'arrests' and 'persecutions' that would have awaited her had she stayed in Italy. When describing D'Andrea's transfer to the United States, he again stresses her courageous suffering and his angst as her male protector. 'When I finally managed to bring [Virgilia] from overseas,' he wrote, 'I found that I had done the right thing, for her sake and for mine,' as 'her condition seemed to improve.' But D'Andrea's nagging health problems grew worse. 'I tried to alleviate her sadness,' he wrote in the melancholic manner he often adopted when describing D'Andrea, and 'with what heart she would thank me for making her laugh just like when she was a child, she would say.'[73]

These passages offer critical glimpses into D'Andrea, and into Borghi's concern for his partner. But do they tell us more about Borhgi's romantic image of the suffering D'Andrea and of the protective, even fatherly, sense of responsibility he felt for guarding her health and safety? One might argue that men's recurring references to D'Andrea's 'grace,' 'light,' and 'smile' conjure up bourgeois images of the 'angel in the house.' Absent are vibrant images, and tougher notions, of femininity and motherhood found in other working-class accounts. Topp has noted the highly sexualized, and masculinist, image of a virulent female comrade described by syndicalist Edmondo Rossoni in 1915 as 'a strong woman with strong breasts and a strong voice, with fire in her eyes, who becomes drunk at the sight of bloody conflicts amidst the clamour of the populace, the smell of gunpowder and the rumblings of the cannon. And she offers her sturdy pelvis only to men as strong as she is, and she wants to be embraced only by arms covered with blood.'[74] How different, too, D'Andrea's portrait from that of the Irish-born 'hell-raiser' and organizer Mother Jones, who, as Donna Gabaccia notes, 'used the suffering, angry, and pungent language of a working-class womanhood rooted in hard lives of European peasants and artisans transplanted to the U.S.'[75] Given the lack of attention paid in this period to questions of sex equality and to gender relations, we caution against easy generalizations. As Moya suggests, adjectives like frail do accurately describe a small, thin, chronically ill person who suffered from periodic fainting spells and depression and died young of cancer. In addition, similar words were sometimes used to describe male leaders – Che Guevera, Lenin, José Marti, and Gori, for instance – who, compared with D'Andrea, seemed 'exemplars of physical fortitude.'[76] In short, the role of gender in shaping radical politics remains an open question.

Poetry of Exile, Cultural Nationalism, and Workers' Internationalism

Final clues to D'Andrea's life and politics are in her poetry. D'Andrea devoted much of her last years not to political or feminist analysis or to autobiography, but to poetry. Even when she first went into exile, suffered the disruptions of repeated moves, and devoted herself to political propaganda on the lecture circuit, she found time to write, as is evident from *L'Ora di Maramaldo*. In D'Andrea's first published volume of poems and writings, exile loomed large as a theme. The preface, written in Paris in June 1925, speaks of the pieces she composed while still in Italy, 'between the severe rage of the Fascist disease,' while others were composed abroad, 'in the sad, painful and bitter silences of exile.'[77] In France, she found her muse in the 'long and slow chants of refugees without exile, pungent songs of unspoken and secret nostalgia' of Italian workers in Paris and the countryside, and in the 'blackened and threatening throats' of Italian miners in the north.[78]

Much of D'Andrea's poetry is intensely personal but virtually devoid of references to her private life; she describes herself almost always as a member of a group, whether of exiles, poets, or Italian cultural nationalists. In 'Life of Exile,' written in April 1923, D'Andrea writes of the squalor, isolation, and hunger that haunted her in Berlin, and her feelings of disorientation and nostalgia: 'A wind of memories beats at the pained doors of my soul,' she says, 'and the painful moment of the nostalgic good-bye lifted the gloomy silence of shattered dreams.' In exile she is alone, 'without a home,' without the companionship even of a 'sweet brother,' and deprived of human affection and basic material comfort. She writes that exile has drained and exhausted her: 'her arms are tired and her face is withered.'[79]

In the poem 'Paris,' the City of Lights and a city of refuge for courageous Italian leftists becomes a 'den of refugees.' Seen through refugee eyes, Paris is less glorious. Amid it's architectural splendour, vibrant intellectual culture, and outward expression of wealth and energy D'Andrea sees its dehumanizing quality: 'Paris/ city of intensity, of work,' she writes, 'where the siren rings at six in the morning, and ignites the pistons, the wheels, the machinery/ where the lives and colours of the human face have changed, and the large, frightened eyes have the expression of uncertainty, of desire, of emptiness.'[80]

It is perhaps not surprising that Paris provoked such melancholy. Everywhere D'Andrea saw Europe's uprooted, destitute, persecuted, banished. The Italian exiles she encountered were a constant reminder of her own situation, and she wrote of 'the thousands of tired and exhausted faces of the Italian refugees that wander – unremovable expression of infinite pain – through the streets of the Sparkling city, mute and foreign.' In D'Andrea's literary depictions of life in exile, there is little room for laughter and joy, no appreciation for the beauty of Paris, or for the relative freedom provided the refugees by French democracy. Instead, there is 'infinite pain' born of the anguished recognition that the condition of exile lay in the ease with which Italy had led itself into the arms of Mussolini. 'O Italia!' D'Andrea cries, 'so much of your own blood, spilled by your own hand, is dispersed throughout the world, and it gushes forth from the darkest homes, from the places of hard work, from all the corners of pain.'[81]

In her poems of exile, D'Andrea identified herself with a long line of radical poets and writers, particularly anarchists, forced by their politics into exile. Most of Italy's anarchist leaders had spent some time exiled abroad or imprisoned under house arrest in Italy, often in remote mountain villages or on small islands off the coast. Many also turned to literature to reconcile their longing for home and their internationalism, as did the poet Pietro Gori, a leading Italian anarchist in Latin America.[82] For D'Andrea, Gori embodied both Italian anarchism and the marginal life of radical exiles.[83] Moreover, the two shared a history of physical illness.[84] As both a poet and an activist, D'Andrea felt Gori's story could inspire others. At Cooper Union Hall in New York City in 1929, D'Andrea urged her mostly Italian immigrant working-class audience to read Gori so that they, too, so far from home and family, might find the same comfort and inspiration that she had found in his work. 'To all of you, who roam the streets of the world, because you do not have safe refuge in your own country, a country you render great and noble with your work,' she told Italian expatriots, 'that you render glorious and admirable with your struggle.'[85]

For D'Andrea and other anti-Fascists, Fascism was a betrayal of the 'real' Italy, of Italian history, and of its humanist traditions. Fighting Fascism, even from abroad, was thus a 'great and noble' goal even for internationalists. D'Andrea never wasted an opportunity to chastise the Fascists for locating national pride in imperialistic ambitions. In its place, D'Andrea appealed for an international struggle to forge a new kind of citizen, a 'citizen of the world, child of father Sun and mother Earth.'[86] At the same time, she wrote admiringly of Italian civilization, of national identity and pride, of belonging to a particular place called Italy, and of being the descendant of a rich cultural, artistic, and intellectual tradition.[87]

Successive generations of prominent anti-state, anti-nationalist Italian radicals, including anarchists like D'Andrea, used literature as a way to come to terms with Italian nationalism. Italian cultural nationalism had emerged from the re-discovery in the early nineteenth century of a secular and humane Italian civilization that had spread throughout the West, supposedly civilizing 'barbarian' Europe and lifting it from the 'dark ages' in the late Middle Ages. Cultural nationalism supported a movement for a national state, but also differed from the state-centred nationalism that emerged after Italy achieved independence and unification. It differed even more from the racist and imperialist nationalism of Mussolini. At a November 1929 anti-Fascist gathering of more than 500 people at Chicago's West Side Auditorium, D'Andrea typically railed against Mussolini, insisting that the operating principles of the Fascist regime were completely contrary to the humane traditions of Italian art, culture, and thought.[88] Still, cultural nationalism was a form of nationalism, and one that coexisted in uneasy tension with radicals' internationalism.

Central to D'Andrea's radicalism, and to anti-Fascism, were competing definitions of nationalism: a disdain for the competitive and oppressive character of the bourgeois nation-state and a love for the country of their birth, the *patria*. In a rare reference to private desire for personal fulfilment, D'Andrea wrote at one point about her *paese natio* (birth-place) – where 'our own "ME" was formed,' where 'the dear face of our mothers smiled at us,' where 'in that courtyard we took our very first steps toward a longer journey.' She contrasted her deeply felt sentiment for her homeplace (*luogo nativo*) to the political unity of the bourgeois nation-state, which was by definition 'too big and artificial' to be genu-inely loved by all its citizens, yet 'too small' for the love of all humankind. The narrow, prejudiced nationalism of the modern bourgeois nation-state had to be replaced by 'the fatherland of humankind,' born of social revolution.[89]

D'Andrea, like her comrades, tried to avoid jingoistic praise of Italy's dazzling contributions to Western civilization. The point, she argued, was not to search for Italian greatness in the conquests of the Roman Empire, but, instead, in the secular, humanist, civic traditions that first emerged about the twelfth century and dominated the variegated politi-cal life of the city-states and kingdoms of the Italian peninsula until the Risorgimento[90] of the nineteenth century. This was the Italy of Dante Alighieri, the 'father of the Italian nation,'[91] who spent twenty years in exile from his own city of Florence for condemning the factionalism of thirteenth-century Italy. It was the Italy of Savonarola, the religious reformer of the late fifteenth century who was burned at the stake for his republican experiment. In modern times, D'Andrea held up Giuseppe Mazzini[92] as the embodiment of a revolutionary patriotism that equated social revolution with democratization and saw patriotism as the prism through which oppressed national groups like Italians would achieve the self-expression needed to forge a true brotherhood of nations. Then there was Giuseppe Garibaldi, whom Italian anti-Fascists praised for his internationalism, anti-imperialism, and humanitarian socialism, and his willingness to bear arms for the cause of Italian unification.[93]

The anarchists' celebration of Italian writers, artists, political thinkers, and radicals who embodied internationalism, anti-imperialism, and in-tellectual independence offered them a way to reconcile their national-ism and internationalism. It also served as an inspiration for a poetry of human liberation from suffering. For D'Andrea, Italian history and tradition was in some fundamental respects the history of free-thinkers, revolutionaries, humanists, internationalists, and secular reformers, many of whom had suffered the same torment of exile for their beliefs and struggles. The history of the Risorgimento and of Italian unification was at base the struggle against tyranny, ignorance, and the mystical religious faith that gave the church so much temporal power. In that regard,

D'Andrea saw Fascism as equally pernicious: under the false guise of restoring Italy to its former greatness, it sought to replace 'reason' with 'superstition,' 'truth' with 'dogma,' 'civility' with 'fetishism,' and thereby soiled the great universalist and free Italian traditions.[94] D'Andrea's grand inheritance of a history of Italian humanists, internationalists, radicals, and great prophets of humanity forced into exile was always a font for her poetry. Yet it did not entirely relieve the personal pain of living in forced exile, as is eloquently captured in poems such as 'Primo Maggio in Solitudine,' written in May 1932 as she was undergoing her treatment for cancer. It combines her zeal for anarchism – the 'fighting spirit' – and her physical pain, fatigue, and fear of death. As she stares down the face of death, D'Andrea writes that her one and truly faithful companion, the one that will not betray, will not desert her, is the 'Ideal,' nothing or no one else. The mood is inescapably funereal, as she speaks of wishing to rest 'my tired head' with this *drappo* (flag), of *sogni e primavera* (springtime and dreams) as her pillow. At the same time, her place alongside prophets like Gori confirmed for her, and her comrades, a sense of their rightful place in human history.[95]

Conclusion

Like most Italian expatriate radicals, Virgilia D'Andrea had planned to return to Italy once Mussolini's regime had been toppled. Her transnational status as a political exile conjures up the words of that other Italian-American anarchist from Sulmona, Carlo Tresca, who said of his early years in the United States, 'with my heart and mind I still lived in Italy.'[96] D'Andrea's political career, like that of other Italian radical exiles, confirms the value of a transnational and gendered approach to the history of anarchism, anti-Fascism, and radical women. Her status as a refugee conditioned the nature of her activism abroad. Unlike other Italian women labour organizers and anti-Fascists in the United States, D'Andrea was not wedded to a given community or neighbourhood. She did not put roots down in one place for a while and participate in building a labour organization or leading a strike from the ground up. Her activism was more detached from the workers she addressed on her many lecture tours. Indeed, many of her lectures were historical, philosophical, theoretical – more intellectual and cultural history than political propaganda. Above all, D'Andrea loved teaching and was most happy when on the political trail carrying out her role, forged years earlier in Italy's Abruzzo region, as the teacher of the people. So doing, she played an as yet unacknowledged role in the history of Italian and Italian-American radicalism during the interwar years.

A twentieth-century radical whose career suggests some important continuities in Italian-American radicalism, D'Andrea as poet nevertheless possessed an idealistic and romantic quality reminiscent of nineteenth-century Italian cultural nationalists. Her notion of the 'Ideal' as harkening back to a more perfect world that needs to be retrieved linked her to the nineteenth-century romantics at the same time that it helped to define her anti-Fascist politics. D'Andrea's radical career also raises some important gender patterns. Throughout her life, she remained largely reticent to talk about herself as a woman, lover, and sexual being. She was a woman who suffered tremendous emotional and physical pain, yet persevered in her political work and writing, all the while refusing to direct attention to herself as an individual. There were a few exceptions, as when, dying, she wrote about her exhaustion and loneliness: 'Alone, all alone is the little girl now/ Nothing remains of her past/ But something strange hits her/ And against pity, she rages, and rebels.' But such stanzas and poems are rare, and serve to underscore D'Andrea's collectivist spirit. It may well have been an exaggerated notion of female self-sacrifice, one accentuated by her own Christ-like suffering and her abilities as a writer and orator, that enabled D'Andrea to speak not for herself but for all exiles, workers, refugees, and Italian radicals. A childless woman, D'Andrea took on the role of self-sacrificing mother for the 'Ideal.' In the process, her radicalism, like that of many other Italian women radicals but in sharp contrast to anarchist-feminists like Goldman, acquired some decidedly maternalist components.

NOTES

Our heartfelt thanks to José Moya, Fraser Ottanelli, Jennifer Guglielmo, Michael Miller Topp, Salvatore Salerno, and especially Donna Gabaccia for their suggestions and feedback on this project and for kindly sharing with us their own research findings and expertise.

1 From a report in the file of Virgilia D'Andrea (who is sometimes incorrectly referred to as Virginia) in the Casellario Politico Centrale (hereafter CPC), busta 1607, Archivio Centrale dello Stato, Rome (hereafter ACS).

2 On radical women, such path-breaking feminist works as Alice Wexler, *Emma Goldman: An Intimate Life* (New York: Pantheon Books, 1984) remain

crucial reading, while recent excellent contributions include Andrée Lévesque, *Scènes de la vie en rouge: L'Epoque de Jeanne Corbin 1906–1944* (Montreal: Les éditions du remue-ménage, 1999). For a more detailed discussion of the relevant literatures, consider Donna Gabaccia and Franca Iacovetta, 'Women, Work, and Protest in the Italian Diaspora: An International Research Agenda,' *Labour / Le Travail* 42 (Fall 1998): 161–81; and Franca Iacovetta, 'Manly Militants, Cohesive Communities and Defiant Domestics: Writing about Immigrants in Canadian Historical Scholarship,' *Labour / Le Travail* 36 (Fall 1995). On the value of feminist biography more generally, consult such fine recent contributions as Natalie Zemon Davis, *Women on the Margins: Three Seventeenth-Century Lives* (Cambridge: Harvard University Press, 1995) and Deborah Gorham, *Vera Brittain: A Feminist Life* (Cambridge: Blackwell Publishers, 1996; paperback ed., University of Toronto Press, 2000).

3   Michael Miller Topp, 'The Transnationalism of the Italian-American Left: The Lawrence Strike of 1912 and the Italian Chamber of Labor of New York City,' *Journal of American Ethnic History* 17 (Fall 1997): 39–63.

4   Relevant North American studies include Topp, 'The Transnationalism of the Italian-American Left'; Nancy Hewitt, 'In Pursuit of Power: The Political Economy of Women's Activism in Twentieth-Century Tampa,' in Nancy A. Hewitt and Suzanne Lebsock, eds., *Visible Women: New Essays on American Activism* (Urbana: University of Illinois Press, 1993); and Rudolph J. Vecoli, 'Italian Immigrants in the United States Labor Movement from 1880 to 1929,' in Bruno Bezza, ed., *Gli italiani fuori d'Italia: Gli emigrati italiani nei movimenti operai dei paesi d'adozione, 1880–1940* (Milan: Franco Angeli, 1983), 157–306.

5   Allan Seager, 'Class, Ethnicity and Politics in the Alberta Coalfields,' in Dirk Hoerder, ed., *'Struggle a Hard Battle' – Working Class Immigrants* (DeKalb: Northern Illinois University Press, 1986); Carmela Patrias, 'Relief Strike: Immigrant Workers and the Great Depression in Crowland, Ontario 1900– 1935,' in Franca Iacovetta ed., *A Nation of Immigrants: Women, Workers and Communities in Canadian History* (Toronto: University of Toronto Press, 1997).

6   See, e.g., the essays by Jennifer Guglielmo (chapter 8) and Caroline Waldron Merithew (chapter 7) in this volume.

7   On the themes of *civiltà italiana* and Italian cultural nationalism see Donna Gabaccia, *Italy's Many Diasporas: Exiles, Elites, and Workers of the World* (London: University College; Seattle: University of Washington Press, 2000), and Maurizio Viroli, *For Love of Country: An Essay on Patriotism and Nationalism* (New York: Clarendon Press, 1995).

8   In making this point, we are not advocating a postmodern approach to our subject, but instead highlighting the great complexities of identities in the

past, with particular reference to Italian migrant workers and radical exiles who, as Donna Gabaccia and Fraser Ottanelli have noted, could be simultaneously class-conscious, family-oriented, emotionally tied to a hometown or region, and yet develop ethnic, national, international, and transnational loyalties and networks; see, e.g., the introduction to their edited *Italian workers of the World: Labor Migration and the Making of Multi-Ethnic States* (Urbana and Chicago: University of Illinois Press, 2001).

9 On Tresca, see Peter Marshall, 'Errico Malatesta: The Electrician of Revolution,' in *Demanding the Impossible: A History of Anarchism* (London: HarperCollins, 1992); Paul Avrich, *Anarchist Portraits* (Princeton, NJ: Princeton University Press, 1988); and Vernon Richards, ed., *Errico Malatesta: His Life and Ideas* (London: Freedom Press, 1965).

10 Armando Borghi, *Mezzo secolo di anarchia (1898–1945)* (Naples: Edizioni Scientifiche Italiane, 1954). See also Robert D'Attilio's biographical sketch, 'Virgilia D'Andrea (1890–1933): Maestra, poetessa, anarchica,' in *Memoria storica*, supp. to 'La Protesta' (1994). Our thanks to Salvatore Salerno for this valuable source.

11 D'Attilio, 'D'Andrea.' Her mother died when she was not yet a teenager. In his autobiography, Borghi suggests that D'Andrea did indeed have one brother left living, in Italy, with whom she had not spoken for years.

12 Borghi, *Mezzo secolo*, 173–4. The great quake remains alive in local memory and is memorialized in huge cemeteries erected outside the small rural towns of the region.

13 Official statistics recorded 80 civilian deaths and 450 people wounded, but actual numbers were probably higher.

14 Years later, D'Andrea sought a fuller explanation and, as Robert D'Attilio suggests, the poet Ada Negri, celebrated by Mussolini for her contributions to Italian culture yet also published in the left-wing press, offered the first major clues. Quite possibly, Negri's poetry convinced D'Andrea, for whom Bresci became a 'mythical figure,' that the assassination of Umberto I was morally justified. It is not clear which of Negri's poems influenced D'Andrea, but a good guess is her 'Sette Maggio 1898' (7 May 1898), which does not refer directly to the events but nevertheless laments, in evocative ways, the use of force against the masses: 'Fin ch'io vivro' mi restera' ne l'ossa/ quell'angoscia ... su gente inerme del suo sangue rossa,' she writes, recalling the sight of 'quel fanciul, senza soccorso/ morente – un bimbo – in mezzo la via.' From her collected works, *Opera Omnia: Tutte le poesie* (Catanzaro: Carello, 2001). D'Attlio, 'Virgilia D'Andrea.' See also D'Andrea's reference to Bresci in a published lecture in *L'Adunata dei Refrettari*, 19 Aug. and 2 Sept. 1933, where she writes 'La violenza degli oppressori e la rivolta degli oppressi.' On Negri, see Santo L. Arico, ed., *Contemporary Women Writers in*

Italy: A Modern Renaissance (Amherst: University of Massachusetts Press, 1990); Beverly Allen, Muriel Kittel, and Keala Jane Jewell, *The Defiant Muse: Italian Feminist Poems from the Middle Ages to the Present* (New York: Feminist Press, 1986).

15 CPC, ACS, D'Andrea file.

16 CPC, ACS, Armando Borghi, 755.

17 Avrich, *Anarchist Portraits*, 171–4, chap. 12; see also José Moya's essay in this volume (chapter 6).

18 Marshall, *Demanding the Impossible*, 450.

19 Ibid.; Nunzio Pernicone, *Italian Anarchism, 1864–1892* (Princeton, NJ: Princeton University Press, 1993), 293–4.

20 Marshall, *Demanding the Impossible*, 442.

21 Ibid., 356.

22 Her lecture, 'Chi siamo e che cosa vogliamo / Who We Are and What We Want,' is in Pernicone, *Italian Anarchism*, 6.

23 CPC, ACS, D'Andrea; the speech 'Chi siamo e che cosa vogliamo' was originally delivered at the Rand School in New York, and was printed in *L'Adunata dei Refrettari*, 26 Mar. 1932.

24 'Il Programma Anarchico,' Bologna, 1920, in Richards, *Errico Malatesta*, 27–8. On anarchist critique of the family, see, e.g., Margaret Marsh, *Anarchist Women, 1870–1920* (Philadelphia: Temple University Press, 1981).

25 For example, see Waldron Merithew's essay in this volume.

26 Borghi, *Mezzo secolo*, 178; see CPC, ACS, D'Andrea, for summary of D'Andrea's speaking engagements and articles ca. 1919–21.

27 Marshall, *Demanding the Impossible*, 'Malatesta'; Richards, *Errico Malatesta;* Paul Avrich, 'Sacco and Vanzetti: The Italian Anarchist Background,' in *Anarchist Portraits*, 162–75.

28 Borghi, *Mezzo secolo*, 201. Speaking of the long-awaited reunion, Borghi recalled: 'Errico hadn't changed since the days of the red week.' D'Andrea and Malatesta became 'instant friends.'

29 On *biennio rosso*, see Paolo Spriano, *Occupation of the Factories: Italy 1920* (London: Pluto Press, 1975).

30 CPC, ACS, Errico Malatesta, 2949–53.

31 CPC, ACS, D'Andrea.

32 'É Forse Un Sogno?' (Is It a Dream?), in *Tormento* (Paris: La Fraternelle, 1929), 79–81.

33 Manlio Cancogni, *Gli Angeli Neri: Storia degli anarchi italiani* (Pontealle Grazie: Mondadori Editore, 1994), 95–101.

34 Borghi, *Mezzo seccolo*, 286.

35 By contrast, violence aimed against a target or enemy guilty of 'a greater

violence,' such as Fascism, could be justified. See Malatesta, *Umanità Nova*, 21 Oct. 1922, in Richards, *Errico Malatesta*, 58–9; Pier Carlo Masini, *Storia degli anarchici italiani da Bakunin a Malatesta (1862–1892)* (Milan: Rizzoli, 1969), 83–4.

36 D'Andrea's article, 'Un anno dopo,' in *Umanità Nova* is cited in Richards, *Errico Malatesta*, 53–9.

37 'E passo la mano fra i capelli dei vostri figliuoli, perché mite sia la vita per essi e addolcisca attorno ai due solitari germogli tutti i suoi colori e rinverdisca tutte le sue speranze.' In addition, 'Il dolore dá la virtù' della comprensione. Io possó, perció,' intendere tutto quanto mi avete scritto.' Ibid., 165.

38 D'Andrea, 'Fate il Processo Al Fulmine: Polemiche sulla bomba del Diana,' in *L'Ora di Maramaldo* (University of Minnesota, Immigration History and Research Center, n.d.), 163–90 (168). See also D'Andrea's 'Il Diritto alla Rivolta,' published posthumously in *L'Adunata dei Refrettari*, 19 Aug. 1933, 5–6.

39 'In Milan,' recalled Borghi, 'we could no longer live. No one wanted us in their home. At the hotel, they pleaded with us to leave after a day.' *Mezzo secolo*, 353–4.

40 Ibid.

41 Ibid. Borghi attributed her reluctance to a tendency to 'attach herself to her spot and to fear the unknown of anything new' – an interesting comment about a committed internationalist.

42 On the Italian *fuorusciti* (exiles) in France, see Simonetta Tombaccini, *Storia dei fuorusciti italiani in Francia* (Milan: Mursia 1988); Charles Denzell, *Mussolini's Enemies* (Princeton, NJ: Princeton University Press, 1961).

43 Such as *Monito* and the French-language *La Libertaire*.

44 See CPC, D'Andrea. Even Mussolini later admitted that if there had been a moment when his regime could have been easily toppled, the controversy surrounding Matteotti was it.

45 'E li ha mai ricordati la patria?' in *L'Ora di Maramaldo*, 137.

46 Borghi, *Mezzo secolo*.

47 CPC, ACS, D'Andrea.

48 Borghi, *Mezzo secolo*, 353–4.

49 CPC, ACS, Malatesta.

50 Written in White Plains, NY, March 1932 under the alias 'De Cicco'; CPC, ACS, D'Andrea.

51 Jennifer Guglielmo, 'Donne Sovversive: The History of Italian-American Women's Radicalism,' in *Italian America* (September 1997), 8–11; see also essays by Guglielmo, Moya, and Waldron Merithew in this volume.

52 CPC, ACS, D'Andrea, Borghi; Borghi, *Mezzo secolo*, 355–6 (Borghi later wrote that Ilya had 'saved Virgilia'); Avrich, *Anarchist Portraits*, and *Anarchist Voices: An Oral History of Anarchism in America* (Princeton, NJ: Princeton University Press, 1995).

53 D'Andrea's 'Il Diritto alla Rivolta' was published posthumously in *L'Adunata dei Refrettari*, 19 Aug. 1933, 5–6.

54 'le malattie sono una cosa antiestetica, e quelle povere e modeste pagine raccolgono quel pó di buono e di bello che é nell'animo mio.' Ibid.

55 Borghi, *Mezzo secolo*, 355–6.

56 CPC, ACS, D'Andrea.

57 See, e.g., CPC, ACS, John Camillo, Elena Melli, busta 3211–12.

58 See 'Medio-Evo' in *L'Adunata dei Refrettari*, 27 May 1933, 1; see also 'Dopo la morte di Virgilia d'Andrea,' *L'Adunata*, 15 July 1933, 6.

59 For example, 'Medio-Evo,' *L'Adunata*; Auro d'Arcola, 'Virgilia d'Andrea, Poetessa dell'Amore,' in ibid., 23 Dec. 1933, 5–6.

60 'Dopo la morte di Virgilia d'Andrea,' *L'Adunata*, 15 July 1933, 6.

61 Borghi, *Mezzo secolo*, 174–6.

62 CPC, ACS, D'Andrea.

63 Wexler, *Emma Goldman*, xv, xvi; Marsh, *Anarchist Women*.

64 Wexler, *Emma Goldman*, 145, 146–7; Avrich, *Anarchist Portraits*; Marsh, *Anarchist Women*, introduction and passim.

65 Michael Miller Topp, 'I Senza Patria (Those without a Country): The Transnationalism of the Italian American Movement' (PhD thesis, Brown University, 1996), esp. chap. 3 and 4. See also Ardis Cameron, *Radicals of the Worst Sort: Laboring Women in Lawrence, Massachusetts, 1860–1912* (Urbana: University of Illinois Press, 1993).

66 Borghi, *Mezzo secolo*, 173–4.

67 CPC, ACS, Borghi. While doubtful that she alone could lead 'an anarcho-syndicalist movement,' the writer also felt that she 'represents the central point in the most loyal diffusion of [Borghi's] activities.'

68 Giovanni De Luna, *Donne in oggetto: L'antifascismo nella società italiana, 1922–1939* (Turin: Bollati Boringhieri, 1995) is perhaps the only Italian source that sheds light on the gender dimensions of anti-Fascist activity and police/state repression.

69 Avrich, *Anarchist Voices*, part 3, 'Sacco and Vanzetti'; see recollection of Valerio Isca, 143–50 (146–7).

70 Marsh, *Anarchist Women*, especially introduction.

71 See Waldron Merithew's essay in this volume.

72 Auro d'Arcola, 'Virgilia d'Andrea, Poetessa dell'Amore,' *L'Adunata dei Refrettari*, 23 Dec. 1933, 5–6.

73 Borghi, *Mezzo secolo*, 353–4.

74 *Il Proletario*, January 1915, cited in Topp, 'I Senza Patria,' 261–2. Our thanks to Michael Miller Topp for sharing his important research with us.

75 Donna Gabaccia, 'Mother Jones and Working Men and Women in the Progressive Era,' in Ballard Campbell, ed., *The Human Tradition in the Gilded Age and Progressive Era* (Wilmington, DE: Scholarly Resources, 2000).

76 Our thanks to José Moya for this and other insightful comments.

77 'fra il crudo infierire del morbo fascist/ nei silenzi tristi e penosi ed amari dell'esilio.' Containing poems written in Italy, Germany, and France, the book was published in Paris in 1928. *L'Ora di Maramaldo* (1st ed., Libreria Editrice, Lavoratori del Mondo, New York), Immigration History Research Center, University of Minnesota. Many thanks to Jennifer Guglielmo for this and other D'Andrea materials; they made it possible to write this article.

78 'canti lunghi e lenti dei profughi senza asilo, canti pungenti di inconfessata e segreta nostalgia.' Ibid.

79 Ibid.

80 In *L'Ora di Maramaldo*, 'Parigi/ paese di intensità, di lavoro,' she writes, 'dove la sirena squilla alle sei del mattino e da l'impuslo ai cilindri, alle ruote, alle macchine/ dove il viso umano ha mutato linea e colore e gli occhi, larghi, spauriti, hanno l'espressione della incertezza del desiderio e del vuoto.'

81 'mi fa rivedere i mille e mille volti stanchi ed esentuati dei profughi italiani che si aggirano – espressione incancellabile d'infinito dolore – fra le vie della scintillante città muta e straniera.' 'O Italia! e quanto tuo sangue da te discacciato é disperso per il mondo ed esso sgorga a fiotti da tutte le case più buie, da tutti i luoghi di fatica, da tutti gli angoli di pena!' Ibid.

82 See P. Avrich, *Anarchist Voices*, 498 n. 229. On Pietro Gori, see the following important, but obscure sources: Pietro Gori, *Opere*, ed. Pasquale Binazzi (La Spezia, 1912) and Gori, *Scritti scelti*, 2 vols. (Cesena: L'Antistato, 1968); Carlo Molaschi, *Pietro Gori* (Milan: Il Pensiero, 1959); Sandro Foresi, *La vita e l'opera di Pietro Gori nei ricordi di Sandro Foresi* (Milan: Editrice Moderna, 1948); *Commemorando Pietro Gori nel 40' anno della sua morte* (Rome, 1950); *Rosignano a Pietro Gori: Raccolta di saggi e testimonianze a cura del comitato cittadino cosituitosi per le onoranze a Pietro Gori* (Cecina, 1960); Gigliola Dinucci, 'Pietro Gori e il sindacalismo anarchico in Italia all'inizio del secolo,' *Movimento Operaio e Socialista* 13, 3–4 (July–December 1967): 289–99; see also Pernicone, *Italian Anarchism*, 238–9, 259.

83 D'Andrea dedicated to Gori a poem she wrote to mark her first year in exile, 'Un Anniversario in Esilio / One Year in Exile.'

84 When Gori was granted amnesty to return to Italy in 1902, he was dying

from tuberculosis. Upon return, he went into semi-retirement, first in Tuscany, then eventually on the island of Elba, where he died in 1910. As he lay sick and dying, Gori captured the inner struggle between the desire to continue to agitate for the cause and the enormous physical resistance put up by a body slowly being consumed by disease. Gori, 'O mio pensier tenace,' in *Prigioni*; quoted by Virgilia D'Andrea in 'Pietro Gori' in D'Andrea, *Richiamo all'anarchia* (Cesena: Edizioni L'Antistato, 61–2 (Immigration History Research Center, University of Minnesota).

85 D'Andrea, 'Pietro Gori,' delivered at Cooper Union, NYC, 6 Jan. 1929; in *Richiamo all'anarchia*, 51–70.

86 *L'Ora Maramaldo.*

87 D'Andrea, 'I Delitti della Patria Borghese, I Diritti della Patria Umana,' lecture delivered at Somerset Hall, Sommerville, Mass., 3 Dec. 1891; in *Richiamo all'Anarchia*, 147; Immigration History Research Center Print Collection.

88 CPC, ACS, D'Andrea.

89 D'Andrea, 'I Delitti della Patria Borghese,' n. 86.

90 The term refers to an early-nineteenth-century nationalist movement, inspired partly by the French Revolution, that aimed at establishing a united, independent state of Italy. See Donna Gabaccia, 'Class, Exile and Nationalism at Home and Abroad,' in Gabaccia and Ottanelli, *Italian Workers of the World.*

91 Giuliano Procacci, *History of the Italian People* (London: Weidenfeld and Nicolson, 1970), 63.

92 On Mazzini, the nineteenth-century Italian revolutionary nationalist, see, e.g., Marshall, *Demanding the Impossible*, 255, 276, 300, 345–6, 446–7, 637.

93 D'Andrea, 'Le Tradizioni Italiane Rinnegate e Tradite dal Fascismo,' lecture delivered at the Casa del Popolo, Philadelphia, 19 April 1929; in *Richiama all'anarchia*, 95–116.

94 Gabaccia and Ottanelli, *Italian Workers*, 116.

95 Published in *L'Adunata dei Refrettari*, 14 May 1932.

96 Cited in Delzell, *Mussolini's Enemies*, chap. 2.

10 Nestore's Wife? Work, Family, and Militancy in Belgium

Anne Morelli

TRANSLATED BY GABRIELE SCARDELLATO

Soon after the Second World War ended, a nineteen-year-old Calabrian girl named Enza became engaged, via a written correspondence, to Nestore Rotella, a fellow villager working as a miner in Belgium. Enza lived at home and regularly attended church. At age sixteen, she had joined Catholic Action, a group seeking to counter the political and cultural influence of communists among land-hungry peasants. Nestore, for his part, was completely open with Enza about his convictions as a communist. In theory, political differences as sharp as Nestore's and Enza's should have precluded marriage and a harmonious life together. But Enza's desire to leave the misery of the Calabrian countryside was so strong that she accepted a number of conditions that Nestore placed on their marriage.

In an interview, many years later, Enza noted, 'He had warned me: "If you accept me in marriage, no more Catholic Action, and no church marriage, nothing of all that! And when we have children, they will not be baptized."' Enza continued to hope that 'at the last moment he would change his mind and agree to a Catholic church marriage.' His only accommodation, however, was a religious ceremony at a Waldensian (Protestant) church in addition to the civil service.

The couple then went to Seraing, near Liège, in Belgium. There, political activity among foreign workers was forbidden. Nestore worked in the mine and held clandestine Italian Communist party (PCI) meetings in his home on Sundays. He later founded an Italo-Belgian 'cultural' association named 'Leonardo da Vinci' as a party front. When political activity for foreigners became legal in Belgium, Nestore moved to Brussels and in 1974 he became secretary of the PCI in Belgium.

And what of his wife and her youthful commitment to Catholic Action? Years later, Enza told the story of her marital and political struggles to Myrthia Schiavo in a lengthy interview.[1] Although Nestore Rotella did not want his wife to work in Belgium, Enza took jobs (for a farmer and a florist, and in a confections factory) without her husband's knowledge, to overcome her solitude and to save to buy a small house. At the same time, Nestore also considered it his duty as a communist militant to have Enza participate in party activities.

Thus, Enza Nestore began what appeared at first to be a reluctant transformation from a Catholic into communist activist. She noted, 'I attended meetings from the beginning, as soon as I arrived in Belgium because generally, they were held in our home.' At first, she acknowledged, 'I was a little resentful,' even though 'theoretically I was already a communist because, when we had gotten married, the first thing that he had made me do was to sign up with the party.'

Soon, however, Enza pursued these activities more willingly. She even developed her political formation alone during two weeks of party school in Italy. She remembered this as a positive experience not so much because of the courses that she attended, but for the contacts that she made 'with comrades who arrived from everywhere, from all of the countries of Italian emigration.' As she concluded to her interviewer, 'Over time through my experiences with immigration and with factory work ..., finally, I also became a true communist!'

Nestore and Enza Rotella both appear as paradoxical figures in a history of women's activism in the Italian diaspora. Although Nestore prohibited Enza from working, he also forced her into other public activism in communist meetings. Enza may have obediently become a communist, but she never obeyed Nestore's prohibition against working. And Nestore apparently never challenged her wage-earning as he had her Catholic activism. Enza herself believed she gained in autonomy because of both work and political activism. Later, in her village of origin, she would encourage others to break with tradition.

Paradoxical links among work, activism, family, and community ties are a common theme in the lives of Italian women activists in Belgium before and after the Second World War. While some women became politically active in Italy, more – like Enza Rotella – became activists as a result of family and work experiences during migration and life abroad. The history of Italian women's activism in Belgium cannot be reduced to that of 'Nestor's wife,' but neither can women's activism easily be severed from their family, work, and community lives.

Women and Labour Migration to Belgium

In the nineteenth century, almost as many Italian migrants sought work in Europe as in the Americas. But fewer sought permanent homes there. While the typical migrant to the United States in the nineteenth century was a southern Italian male, some of whom called for family members to follow, the typical migrant to Europe was a north Italian man who returned home again.

The First World War significantly altered nineteenth-century migrations from Italy. During the 1920s economic hardship persisted in Italy, while political repression under Mussolini's Fascist dictatorship created a new motive for emigration. Meanwhile, U.S. restrictions on immigration made European destinations more popular with Italians. As a result, Italian migration to Belgium became a mass phenomenon.

Like France, Belgium had lost much of its young male population to the war; many feared for the country's demographic future and looked favourably on immigration. Indeed, the 30,000 Italians recorded in this small country in about 1930 already constituted the second-largest foreign community (after the Poles) that had travelled great distances to work. (Larger numbers of French, Germans, and Dutch still lived in Belgium's border territories.)

In the interwar years Italian immigration to Belgium included only a few women. Italian men worked in construction, mining, and industry even though many had been peasants and agricultural workers in Italy. Most were temporary migrants with little incentive to call for their wives and daughters. Family unification motivated female migration. For example, of forty-seven women who left Italy for Belgium in August 1925, thirty-nine described themselves as housewives, five as agricultural labourers, and only three as workers and two as domestics.[2] Once in Belgium, some Italian women provided housing for Italian bachelors, for whom they cooked and washed in return for payment, or ran a canteen or restaurant, or sometimes a café.[3] They worked as seamstresses,[4] tailors,[5] cleaning women, maids, or occasionally as agricultural workers. While few had factory experience in Italy, small numbers of Italian women also worked in Belgian factories, often in industries like textiles and food preparation.[6]

By 1970, 300,000 people of Italian nationality formed the largest group of foreigners in Belgium, a country of less than ten million inhabitants. They lived in Brussels and in old mining centres where they, their parents, and grandparents had settled in large numbers under

Italian-Belgian bilateral agreements facilitating labour migration. Beginning in 1946, Italy agreed to provide, on a weekly basis, some 2000 young men for Belgian mines. Belgium in return sold to Italy fixed quantities of coal. The agreement contributed to the recovery of Italy's postwar economy, and became one of the first steps toward the subsequent formation of the European Community.

Until 1953, Italian immigrants in Belgium were primarily from northern Italy; thereafter the trend reversed and the largest number came from southern Italy and the islands. Most were men who worked in mining and the heavy industries covered by the bilateral treaties. Still, the sex ratio quickly adjusted during the 1950s, because the agreements also provided for family reunification. In contrast to Switzerland (which insisted on 'rotating' male workers), Belgium's policy makers wanted Italian workers to settle permanently in mining (which was unpopular with native workers). By admitting women as family dependents, they hoped to keep migrants' expenditures within the Belgian economy, and to bolster Belgium's aging population and declining birth rate. After 1946, Italian miners like Nestore Rotella could bring their wives to Belgium after six months or call for a fiancée to marry immediately upon arrival. Once men and their wives succeeded in finding a home, permanent residence rights were guaranteed. Furthermore, if Italian husbands wanted wives to join them abroad, Italian law obligated wives to move.

Not all husbands wanted their wives to follow them, however. Some preferred temporary emigration to pay off their debts, to accumulate a sister's dowry, or to buy a piece of land or a house. Many left their wives in their villages of origin for many years. The lives of the men in Belgium and their wives in Italy could not have been more different. In Belgium, young Italian men benefited from seeming unattached in a country where women were morally freer than in Italy and viewed Italian men as particularly attractive, virile, and exotic. Fifty years later, while being interviewed in Italy, men told of the dance halls they frequented, and of the Belgian districts where brothels concentrated. Still others, despite being married, reported having Flemish 'fiancées' they visited on their motorcycles in their free time.

Meanwhile, the 'white widows' – the women whose husbands had emigrated – remained the objects of careful surveillance within their families. Rural codes of honour forbade them any entertainment. They could neither divorce (it was forbidden in Italy until 1980) nor decide to join their husbands. (Only the male émigré had the legal right to acquire the necessary documents from his employer.) The emigration of

Italian women to Belgium depended almost entirely on men's choices. A few female domestic servants, who travelled alone to Belgium, provide the only exceptions and even domestics typically followed a father, brother, or brother-in-law already in Belgium.

Although their migration was motivated by family ties, many of the Italian women migrating to Belgium – like Enza Rotella – nevertheless took jobs. Beginning in the 1950s, Italians crowded into heavy industries like the National Munitions Factory in Herstal. Then they also moved into the commercial sector, notably as cashiers and clerical workers in large businesses. As was true for Enza Rotella, the experiences of migration, family, and work all shaped women's lives as political activists in twentieth-century Belgium.

The Interwar Years: Exiles and Politicized Workers

While the vast majority of male and female migrants went to Belgium to work or to unify families, some were already political activists before they left home. Exile has been a continuous theme in the history of Italy's migrations since the late Middle Ages. Still, it is often difficult, if not impossible, to distinguish between 'labour' (or 'economic') migrants and 'political' migrants (exiles or refugees). Immigrants to Belgium included both women who fled Italy because of their activism there and those who became politically active after beginning life and work abroad. As the life of Enza Rotella revealed, furthermore, activism motivated by family solidarity did not inevitably render women submissive to men.

Beginning with liberal refugees from the period of the Risorgimento, then followed by socialists who fled Italy during the revolts of 1893 and 1898, Belgium attracted small numbers of Italy's 'subversives.' The early refugees included men like Count Sforza and Arturo Labriola. The first was the former ambassador of the king of Italy and future minister of the Republic and the second had been the mayor of Naples and a socialist and former minister of labour.[7] Of the well-known Italian exiles of the nineteenth century almost all were men. The only female name to emerge in the group of political refugees in Belgium is that of Isabelle Gatti de Gamond, who was the daughter of an Italian exile. In Belgium she became celebrated as a socialist and feminist, but above all as the founder of the first lay establishment for the secular education of young women.[8] By the early twentieth century, small numbers of women appear among Italy's refugees and exiles. The best-known woman in this group was the prominent socialist Angelica Balabanoff.[9]

It is in the interwar years that female activism in Belgium can first be explored with any confidence.[10] In many respects, the Italian police archives, especially the dossiers of the Casellario Politico Centrale, provide richer sources than those of Belgium.[11] Police sources are problematic, of course. Police informants rarely were skilled political analysts and they frequently confused communists and anarchists. Since informants were paid for the information they passed to the police, they also had a strong incentive to manufacture information. But sources in the receiving country were even more problematic. The very active anti-Fascist press in Belgium faced political pressures that made it quite secretive about the identities of activists.[12] Belgium prohibited political activities among its foreign workers, and the mere possession of an anti-Fascist newspaper was sufficient grounds for expulsion. Fascist diplomatic personnel in Belgium read the anti-Fascist press to alert Italian agents, who in turn informed their Belgian counterparts, leading to the expulsion from Belgium of hundreds of Italian anti-Fascists. Consequently, anti-Fascist newspapers used pseudonyms for men and women alike. Slender published materials in newspaper articles and interviews give some insight into the life of the female activists of the interwar years.[13]

Whether in Italy or abroad, harsh controversies over Mussolini and his Fascist dictatorship shaped the lives of Italy's political activists. A significant number of Belgium's women activists were themselves political migrants, if not forced into exile by Mussolini's policies, then at least politicized before their departure. For some women, political activism was part of a family tradition in Italy. Thus, anti-Fascist activist and resistance fighter Noemi de Tomi had seen her father beaten bloody by Fascists. A communist sympathizer in Belgium, she became a supporter of the republicans in the Spanish Civil War and joined the armed partisans, working in the Resistance after Germany occupied Belgium. Distinguishing herself by her courage, she was arrested in 1943 and deported to Ravensbrück, where she was sterilized.[14]

For other women, activism originated in wage-earning experiences in Italy. Linda Carrà Gagliardi, for example, was one of a small group of women who had participated in agricultural uprisings in the rice fields of northern Italy before her migration. In such districts, women's combativeness had long been strong enough to attract attention from Italy's left, and it provided a foundation for continued activism abroad.

For still other women, activism seems to have been an individual choice, linked to neither work nor family. For example, Maria Simonetti, born on 4 September 1896 in Trieste, well educated, slender and very beautiful, had already organized women's protests for the radical left in Italy during and after the First World War. Exiled to Paris in 1925, she then presented herself in Belgium with a false passport. She was quickly implicated in many anarchist illegal activities, including stealing and breaking into safes. In 1928 she was falsely implicated in the assassination of a Fascist provocateur known as Castri in Liège. By then, however, she was already serving a prison term for other crimes at Versailles and the French government refused the Belgian demand to extradite her.[15]

Emigrated women did not leave behind controversies over Fascism when they left Italy, whether their goal was to work or to reunify families. During the interwar years, the rift between Fascists and anti-Fascists divided Belgium's immigrants into two camps, with little possibility for political apathy or neutrality. Men and women alike either favoured or opposed Mussolini. The Fascists gathered around official Italian representatives and consular organizations (Italian schools, leisure programs, sports clubs, and the Italian Cultural Institute). Diplomats and Italian civil servants (teachers, employees of the office of tourism) recruited to Fascism mainly immigrant shopkeepers and those who were independently employed. In opposition, anti-Fascist refugees sought support mainly among intellectuals and workers. Political exiles secretly recreated the political parties (republican, socialist, communist) outlawed in Italy; they produced and supported an anti-Fascist press; they encouraged workers to join Belgian unions. The only 'meetings' between the two Italian political factions occurred on those occasions when they fought each other.[16] This violence grew with the invasion of Belgium by the Nazis in May 1940. Since workers were the largest group of immigrants in Belgium, accounts by both sides admit that anti-Fascists generally predominated.

The majority of Italian women activists were anti-Fascists. Women born into activist families in Italy often married activists, and continued their activism alongside their husbands after migration. Thus, the married woman Paola Cansini initially attracted attention in 1930 as the promoter of a community celebration raising funds for the Italian communist journal of Belgium, *Il Riscatto*.[17] Her husband was also a communist, but well before that Mussolini's police already described her in Italy as belonging to 'a family of subversives.'[18] She was a communist agitator in Italy, where she disseminated propaganda. The police described her as violent in nature and a voluble talker who worked effectively for the formation of the red guards of S. Croce sull'Arno before

Mussolini's take-over. In Belgium, Cansini encouraged the Italian communist women of Seraing to organize collections for the Red International Aid Association. She later joined her exiled husband in Luxembourg, where informants again found her missing no opportunity to make propaganda for communism.[19]

More women, however, resembled Enza Rotella in following their husbands into activism in Belgium. For example, Giuseppina Marcon had emigrated to join her husband, a miner in Belgium, in 1931. On 1 January 1933 she became a member of the Communist party of Belgium, as her husband had already done, and was responsible for the trusteeship of the Communist Federation of the Precinct of Thuin. She also quickly became chairwoman of the feminine section of the communist cell of Bray (in which her husband was the treasurer). In September 1936, according to the Italian consul in Charleroi, this housewife, known under the pseudonym 'Palmina,' transported into her house 'subversive newspapers under her clothing or in her bosom.'[20] In a period of clandestine activity, women's domestic world, far from being a sphere separated from politics, was one of the few places where political organization could occur.

Whether Fascist or anti-Fascist, many of Italian women's political activities in the interwar years strike the modern reader as traditionally feminine because they emerged from women's responsibilities for everyday family and community life and for caring for and supporting children and male relatives. Fascist women held parties for the 'Fascist Befana' (a gift-giving holiday for children). Anti-Fascist women organized community celebrations that were often fund-raisers, and then gave the funds to political comrades in poor health and to the families of those who had been expelled or imprisoned. While Fascist women sent poor children on free vacations to Italy, in 1929 the Italian communist women of Belgium developed a 'free summer camp' on the North Sea for children of comrades who were experiencing financial difficulties.[21] They repeated their initiative in 1930, and held a series of social gatherings to raise money for the camp in the intervening year.[22]

Another political domain where women's leadership seemed traditional to both Belgians and Italian immigrants was pacifism. Immigrant Teresa Bosco had remained in Belgium after the expulsion of her husband, the communist Teresio Testa, in 1932. Shortly thereafter she created an 'Anti-war League of Women.'[23] In 1933, she helped establish the first alliance among anti-Fascists of various persuasions, forming a 'Women's Peace Group.'[24] Their movement peaked in 1935 during the

'Brussels Convention against the War in Ethiopia,' which was united under a classically female logo depicting a white mother and a black mother holding their children in upraised arms so that they might kiss. The slogan from the poster published for this conference is eloquent: 'Mothers of Italy, mothers of Abyssinia, mothers of the entire world shout: We don't want war.'[25]

In their quasi-traditional roles as fund-raisers and supporters of male initiatives, anti-Fascist women also developed a relief association called the Red International Aid Association. Its goal was to provide support for male comrades who went to Spain to help defend the democratically elected Republican government against Fascist insurgents led by General Franco. The women also mobilized to collect funds for the families of Italian volunteers who had left Belgium to fight in the ranks of the International Brigades in Spain's civil war.

Sewing the red flags that decorated the windows of anti-Fascists on May 1st,[26] or baking a cake for the celebration by the Belgian Antifascist League may have reflected some women's obedience to the political leadership of their fathers and husbands. But it would be a mistake to dismiss such political activism as a form of female submission or to deny its political content. As the women of the Red International Aid Association all agreed, they acted out of genuine 'anti-Fascist fervour';[27] their motivation was political, not just familial. Militant communist women used the meetings of the aid association to explain the political motivations behind their initiative.[28] While traditional, women's activities could have consequences little different from those of other political actions. When, for example, the children returned from their 'free' summer camp of 1930, Bernardina Sernaglia, who had been the camp's creator, soon afterward was branded as a communist activist and expelled from Belgium.

Nowhere was the move of immigrant activists out of the domestic sphere into more conventional forms of autonomy clearer than in the life of Giuseppina Marcon, who had followed her husband to Belgium, and then transformed her home into a site for communist recruiting. For Marcon, the Spanish Civil War became an opportunity to develop previous political activities outside her home. Marcon's husband left for Spain with the first Italian volunteers in early 1937; he was subsequently captured by Franco's followers and executed.

Giuseppina Marcon's response was to pour even more energy into the cause of the Spanish Republic. After her husband's death, the Italian communists of the region continued to meet in her house, and she was involved actively in distributing a 'money-raising subscribers' list in support of the women and children of those volunteers from the region who are fighting in Spain.'[29] According to reports of the Italian consulate in Charleroi, the political activities of 'Palmina' continued at least until the end of 1939, when, they reported, she 'continues to disperse communist propaganda and subversives still find refuge with her.'[30] Another Italian International Brigade volunteer, Sanzio Gambara, left a wife in Belgium, Maria Filippini, who during the war distributed clandestine newspapers, collected funds and stamps to finance the resistance fighters, helped Soviet prisoners, and served as an agent for the partisans. Other women travelled even farther from their homes to maintain their political collaborations with activist husbands. After working and agitating in Belgium, Guiseppe Bifolchi went to fight in the Spanish Civil War for the Republicans. There, he was joined by his wife.[31]

The Necessity of Female Equality

Not surprisingly, some women activists moved from political action motivated by family loyalties and traditional female responsibilities to a critique of women's place in left-wing movements. The wife of Paolo Moschelli, Carolina Gioachino, at first wrote under the pseudonym of Rina Valera, for the communist press in Belgium.[32] She later attempted to form anti-Fascist feminist leagues. Expelled from Belgium in 1931, some months after her husband, she had already created an all-female anti-Fascist section in the province of Liège. In the weekly *Il Riscatto*, she exhorted the women of Mons and Charleroi to do as much as she had. She described for them the situation of female workers in Italy and assured her companions that 'children, the home, socks were the concerns of the followers of the village priest' – not of communist women.[33]

At least in theory, the Italian communists of Belgium adopted as positive the general principle of female emancipation and political autonomy. During LIABS (Anti-fascist Italian League in Belgium) congresses, male activists regularly expressed regrets about the small number of women delegates and talked about increasing women's participation. The communist press also regularly included articles on the necessity of female equality[34] and it explained to comrades the specific motives that pushed women towards anti-Fascism.[35]

One of these motives was Fascist opposition to labour initiatives. A significant number of Italian women became active in Belgium, not at home or in their marriages, but as wage-earners in their workplaces. On 27 January 1930 Italian women took part in a demonstration in Brussels in support of the 48-hour work week. The conservative newspaper *La Libre Belgique* described the group as a communist cortege that sang 'Bandiera rossa.' The paper called it 'a composite of doubtful elements, young people and girls singing verses in Italian, in Slavic [*sic*], etc. ... "Mussolini," someone shouts and everyone howls in chorus "Boo! boo!"'[36]

In May Day marches in the early 1930s, Italian anti-Fascist women sold badges for the Red International Aid Association and portraits of the martyred Italian socialist Giacomo Matteotti. During strikes in 1932, Italian women on the picket line attracted the attention of consulate informers and were expelled from Belgium.[37] A Fascist informant also reported on a woman, Teresina Capellazzo, who carried a large red flag in the May Day parade of 1937.

The life of Teresina Capellazzo reminds us of the Italian women who found independent paths to political activism. Born into a very poor family in Italy, Teresina had only one year of schooling and began to work as an embroidress at the age of ten.[38] She married at seventeen, and immediately bore her only child. Upon arrival in Belgium, she was still young, beautiful, free in her moral behaviour (informers insisted), and of a happy and calm temperament. Informers reported her first as an anti-Fascist propagandist in the pasta factory where she worked, but she also engaged in traditionally female activities – ordering drinks, organizing a tombola (raffle), and hiring musicians for a dance that brought together men, women, and families in a communist festival.[39] Mussolini's informant was certain that the communist sympathies of her husband (from whom she would later separate) were 'primarily the result of his wife's influence on him.'[40]

From Brussels, Capellazzo travelled to mining regions to hold meetings in cafés frequented by Italians. She disseminated propaganda material and distributed *Noi Donne*, the PCI organ published for women. Later, during the Spanish Civil War, she held special meetings for women 'to discuss politics.' Capellazzo was the delegate for Italian anti-Fascist women of Belgium to the 'Congress of Italian Anti-Fascist Women' held in Paris in October 1937. There, she delivered a fiery speech despite the fact – as she reported fifty years later – that she had never before spoken into a microphone.[41]

During the war, Capellazzo maintained her contact with communists in hiding. She took in two children whose father had been executed by the Germans, and she continued with political activities as she had for twenty years. She produced and distributed clandestine anti-Fascist propaganda material. At the time of Belgium's liberation, Capellazzo was named representative of the 'Unione delle Donne Italiane' (Union of Italian Women), and in this capacity she joined other anti-Fascists in occupying Italy's consulate. Her job was to assist the large number of Italian prisoners who flowed toward Brussels.[42]

Capellazzo was thus one of many immigrant women activists who moved, along with immigrant men, from anti-Fascist activity rooted in political struggles in Italy into resistance alongside Belgian colleagues against German Fascist occupation. While Italian Fascists in Belgium benefited initially from the German invasion by encouraging their allies to stop the activities of the Italian anti-Fascists, hundreds of Italian anti-Fascists, including women, resisted the new repression to join the ranks of the Resistance.[43]

The price paid by Italian Resistance members was heavy. In fact it was in the resistance that many women anti-Fascists first became visible and began a sometimes violent and cruel transition to postwar activism. Elda Vellar, an armed resistance fighter, was the only surviving member of her family when she was deported to Ravensbrück. Pierina Spagnolo was an armed resistance fighter who had transported weapons and dynamite, and subsequently was tortured and died in Ravensbrück. Among other Italians deported to Germany were the armed resistance fighters Albina Fassio, Maria Filipini, and Rosa Grimaldi. Elda Pozzebon and Noemi de Tomi survived incarceration in Ravensbrück, while Elisa Mattei died there. Of those who succeeded in remaining in Belgium, Esterina Ceccarina distributed tracts, collected funds, and harboured Russian prisoners, while Onolinda Cunaccia became an armed partisan widely acclaimed in Belgium. Sixteen-year-old Henriette Marinoni was tortured by the Germans for her resistance activities. Maria Meneghinotto was incarcerated. The hardships and suffering of these immigrant Italian women highlight the degree to which immigrant women had become autonomous political beings, independent of men. Whether they took up arms or not, all risked their lives for their political beliefs, and they suffered as individuals, not as daughters, wives, or sisters within politically active families.

The Generation of 1946 and After

The Liberation of Belgium from Fascist occupation began a complex political transformation of Europe that shaped the lives of immigrant activists of both sexes. During the Liberation, Italian anti-Fascists took possession of Italy's diplomatic offices and began to hunt down those Italian Fascists who had represented Italy's Fascist regime. But the cold war quickly reshuffled the political cards in Belgium, as it did also in France and Italy. Many Italian immigrant heroes of the Belgian resistance were quickly expelled from the country as communists, the group that had – in fact – dominated the country's anti-Fascist press. Christian Democrats – the supporters of Catholic Action in Italy – took over diplomatic positions vacated by the Fascists, and they imposed their own press monopoly and began their own hunt for communists within the immigrant community. Not surprisingly, Italian missionaries in Belgium played a central role in these events.[44]

Although the Italian communist party had succeeded in maintaining a continuous presence in Belgium from 1923, it remained suspect and semi-clandestine after the fall of Fascism. Belgian law continued to prohibit political activism among foreigners and most immigrant workers maintained their Italian citizenship. Italian immigrant workers quickly became the most radical elements in Belgium's postwar labour movement, however, especially in the unions of the steel-making centres and in the extreme-leftist movement known as 'Union Renewal.' Indeed, the director of this movement was Roberto D'Orazio, the son of immigrants who was himself still an Italian citizen.

In this context, the PCI enjoyed considerable support among postwar migrants like Nestore Rotella and his wife. In 1984, when European elections justified tallying the Italian vote in Belgium separate from that of other Belgians, 41 per cent of Belgium's Italian immigrants had voted communist. This number suggests that the sharp division typical of immigrant communities during the interwar years of Fascism persisted in Belgium's growing Italian immigrant community after the war. Communities divided between left and right supporters of the USSR and the United States forced new female arrivals from Italy – like Enza Nestore – into a highly politicized world.

With tape recorder in hand, Myrthia Schiavo has rescued from oblivion the political militancy of women who made the transition into postwar activism and formed a new generation of immigrant women activists in Belgium. Many were women never seen at party meetings, who nonetheless expounded harsh political critiques of the bilateral treaties that brought them, and Italian men, to Belgium to work. Italy, some of these women reported, 'sold its men for a few sacks of coal,'[45] while it could not nurture or support the white widows enduring interminable separations from their husbands before being forced, like the men, to leave for the north.

Schiavo's 1000 pages of interviews reveal women's perspectives on this massive postwar migration.[46] For them, 'emigration is not essentially a masculine problem: for decades, it has involved the dreams, sacrifices, the ability to work, the intelligence, imagination, plans, and the dignity of millions of women.'[47] And this was true despite the fact that the emigration of women was neither recorded nor understood.[48] To this day, Schiavo's work remains one of only a very few treatises on the lives, work, and activism of the postwar women migrants.[49]

Not surprisingly, Italian women who had become politically active during the anti-Fascist agitation in Belgium quickly turned their attention to welcoming, and recruiting, the new postwar Italian immigrants. Noemi de Tomi appeared in person at the train stations where this human 'livestock' was deposited, and she protested loudly and strongly against the conditions under which they were transported. According to de Tomi, officials used physical blows to encourage workers to get off at the right station. Women like de Tomi often met leftist activists among the newly arrived men, but the women immigrants they encountered more often resembled Enza Rotella, many of whom were predisposed to see Catholic missions, with their religious services and pilgrimages, as sources of support while adjusting to the new country.

Many of the new women immigrants, like Enza Rotella, were from rural backgrounds, and from the south; many still lacked a strong sense of belonging to a nation of Italians and regarded the older immigrants with suspicion. In Belgium they met for the first time women from other regions of Italy, often beginning in the camps that were their first homes in Belgium. Abandoning Italian regionalism was a first step toward greater autonomy.

The many women who had married communist men did not necessarily submit to their husbands' political expectations as Enza Nestore did. Instead, many seemed to assume that politics was a male activity, and that their husbands would take care of politics while they took care of the family. Italy's women, after all, had only recently obtained the right to vote, and Fascist repression in Italy had not only discouraged all forms of political activity for twenty years but had also glorified women in their familial and maternal roles. For thirty years, PCI celebrations of International Women's Day were observed mainly by men, with occasional female speakers invited as guests. Trains organized by the PCI to transport immigrants back to Italy to vote (even for the referenda on divorce and abortion) almost always carried men voters. Women remained behind in Belgium to look after children, the elderly, and daily problems.

They also remained behind because they now had jobs there. Far more than in the interwar years, work transformed the lives of the most traditional immigrant women. Most, as we have seen, worked in factories, with smaller numbers managing cafés, canteens, and restaurants, or working as cleaning women or servants. Even this last task, which might be seen as the most traditionally female because it restricted women even as wage-earners to the domestic realm, held emancipatory potential. It allowed for both financial autonomy and daily contact with another social class, and thus mediated immigrant women's introduction to Belgian society, with its differing gender ideology.[50] Domestics were freer to choose their future husbands than girls who worked while living at home. On occasion they even unionized. Thus, during the 1950s and 1960s, a Belgian union wrote employment contracts for domestics in both French and Italian.

Women's activism was even more obvious in industry. The workers who, in 1966, launched a noteworthy and successful strike in the national munitions factory in Herstal under the slogan 'Equal pay for work of equal value' were for the most part Italian immigrant women. At this time, immigrant Italians did not emerge as leaders of the movement. It was their daughters who later became leaders, as seen for example during the strike in the Coras department stores in the 1980s led by Carla Nona.

Immigrant women themselves associated wage-earning work, however laborious, with autonomy and viewed it as positive. An Italian woman, trained as a stenographer, but who had been the proprietor of a canteen, and had worked as a domestic and a sales clerk, summed up her experience as follows: 'What bothered me the most is not being able to work. For a woman, it is like a handicap to remain home all the time: she must defer to her husband for a yes, for a no. The wife who works has more autonomy, more ideas, more contacts with life.'[51] Today, 25 per cent of Italian workers (mainly former industrial workers) claim Belgian social security, freeing them from financial dependence on their families in old age.

Changing Notions of Women's Emancipation

Women's emancipation in the interwar years had often meant revolutionary activity, albeit in distinctively female forms, and had been closely tied to movements aimed at transforming the governments of Italy and Europe. In the postwar era, by contrast, women's emancipation has been more often associated with changes in domestic life. For immigrant families, this sometimes generates marital conflict, most notably over whether to remain in Belgium or to return to the home village. The large majority of men favour a return, while their wives – remembering the difficulties of daily life and the concomitant social control that marked their youth – prefer to remain in Belgium.

Having been exposed, sometimes initially against their wishes, to the larger world around them, the white widows too have had contact – direct or indirect – with a new world of ideas and goods. The new autonomy and transnational identities of the women who emigrate are even more pronounced. They are revealed in a thousand details – changes in the language spoken, in their clothing, in food preparation, in house-keeping habits,[52] and in social behavior. Nowhere is this transformation more obvious than in the lives of the emigrated women who returned home again. There, they report, they are treated as strangers. When Linda Carrà and Ida Zecchini returned to their villages after thirty years, their neighbours called them 'the Belgians.'

Even Nestore's wife, who at first seemed so submissive, knew when she returned that she was not the same girl who had left Calabria thirty years before. In her oral history, Enza Rotella reported becoming a conscious agent of feminist change in her own right. On her return home, she introduced the 'Festa dell'Unità' – a celebration organized by and for the communist newspaper – to the women of her village. 'Do you under-stand, the women who lived in the village always thought: "What would they say about you if you were to work for the celebration?" The fear of what others might say still ruled! Those women who had been immi-grants, on the other hand, they could care less! They said: "Me, I am going to work for the Festa dell'Unità, that is all!"'

Enza Rotella became a new model of womanhood in other ways too. She explained that, back in her village in Calabria, she attended party meetings, as she was accustomed to doing. 'I was the only woman present and they looked at me askance. One day, there was a comrade who said to me, "Why are you here?" "Well, there is a meeting of the party and I am a comrade like the others and I don't see why I can not participate." And this individual insisted: "This is not Belgium, you know, this is Falerna," by which he meant that in Falerna, women don't go to party meetings. So I told him: "I don't care, I'm not leaving," and that was it, I remained in my place. But then, over time, women, and even more young women rather than older ones, began to participate in meetings and now, no one pays any more attention.'

'Nestore's wife' ignored what others might say and she became, perhaps in spite of herself, simply 'Enza.' This was an essential transformation for one Catholic, peasant woman, and a transformation that often escapes the scrutiny of historians. Her experience has parallels throughout the Italian diaspora, especially in North America, where to date much of the social-history scholarship on women in the immigrant left has been concentrated. The story of 'Nestore's wife' is one part of a hidden history of female activism, and it deserves a place not just alongside but as part of accounts of working-class institutions, radical newspapers, and anti-Fascist struggles, and of heroic tales of the suffering of resistance heroes.

NOTES

1 Myrthia Schiavo, *Italiennes au coeur de l'Europe: Des femmes italiennes immigrées se racontent* (Brussels: L'incontro dei lavoratori, 1990), 100–13 (also published as *Italiane in Belgio: Le emigrate raccontano* [Naples: Tullio Pironti, 1984]).

2 *Bolletino dell'emigrazione,* October 1925.

3 Interview with Giuseppina Marcon.

4 Interview with Teresa Capellazzo (12 July 1995), who embroidered for the decorator Vanderborght in Brussels.

5 Interview with Linda Carrà Gagliardi (various conversations 1974–82).

6 Teresa Capellazzo worked in the Toselli pasta factory.

7 Mario Battistini, *Esuli italiani in Belgio 1815–1860* (Florence: Brunetti, 1968).

8 For Isabelle Gatti de Gamond, see Anne Morelli, 'Isabelle Gatti de Gamond hors du féminisme bourgeois,' *Sextant: Revue du groupe interdisciplinaire d'études sur les femmes,* Winter 1993: 57–62.

9 Angelica Balabanoff (1876–1965) was an Italian socialist of Russian origin, and editor of the newspaper *Avanti.* She was a collaborator of Lenin and Trotsky and first secretary of the Third International. Her disagreements with Soviet rule forced her into exile in the France and the U.S., but she returned to Italy after its liberation from Fascism.

10 See Anne Morelli, 'Fascismo e antifascismo nell'emigrazione italiana in Belgio, 1920–1940' (unpublished PhD thesis, University of Brussels, 1985). A short version was published as *Fascisme et antifascisme dans l'immigration italienne en Belgique, 1920–1940* (Rome: Bonacci, 1998). For the dissertation I used a wide variety of Belgian archives, notably Ministère Belge des

Affaires Etrangères – Bruxelles, 'Correspondance politique Italie 1922–
1940+,' dossiers 2637 bis, 2647 bis, 4344, 11.382/3, 11.382/4, 2669 bis I/A,
4404; Ministère de la Justice – Bruxelles, 'Police des étrangers'; Ministère de
la Santé Publique – Bruxelles, 'Dossiers de réparation aux victimes de la
guerre'; Archives générales du royaume – Bruxelles, 'Papiers de Broque-
ville, Paul Hymans, Henri Jaspar, Marcel-Henri Jaspar, Prosper Poullet';
Parti communiste de Belgique – Bruxelles; Institut Emile Vandervelde –
Bruxelles; Archives Louis Bertrand, Emile Vandervelde. In Italy, especially
useful archives included the Archivio Storico del Ministerio Affari Esteri –
Roma, 'Affari politici Belgio'; Archivio centrale dello Stato (ACS) – Roma,
'Casellario politico centrale (CPC)'; Ministerio cultura popolare; Ministero
dell'Interno, 'Pubblica Sicurezza, Affari generali e riservati, Segreteria
particolare del Duce'; Istituto Antonio Gramsci – Roma, 'Carteggio Luigi
Sturzo'; Istituto per la storia della resistenza in Toscana, 'Archivi di Giustizia
e Libertá, carteggio Rosselli.'
11 On recent scholarship using the CPC files on 'subversives' to reconstruct
Italian immigrant radicalism, see, e.g., Donna Gabaccia and Fraser Ottanelli,
eds., *Italian Workers of the World: Labour, Migration, and the Making of Multi-
ethnic States* (Urbana and Chicago: University of Illinois Press, 2001) and the
essays by Caroline Waldron Merithew (chapter 7) and by Robert Ventresca
and Franca Iacovetta (chapter 9) in this volume.
12 See Anne Morelli, *La presse italienne en Belgique, 1919–1945* (Paris, Louvain:
Nauwelaerts, 1981).
13 I interviewed Noemi de Tomi (3 Feb. 1978), Linda Carria Gagliardi (various
conversations 1974–82), Elvira Lattanzi, Ida Zecchini and, afterward, Teresa
Capellazzo (12 July 1995).
14 Interview of 3 Feb. 1978.
15 ACS, 'Casellario politico centrale' (hereafter, CPC), no. 3.297.
16 I have recorded dozens of acts of violence between Italian Fascists and anti-
Fascists in Belgium in the interwar period. See Morelli, *La presse italienne en
Belgique*, 138–53.
17 ACS, CPC, 83811.
18 Report of 15 Jan. 1931.
19 ACS, CPC, 83811, Luxembourg report, dated 7 June 1935.
20 ACS, CPC, 122.719, b3043, report of 27 Sept. 1936.
21 *Il Riscatto*, 14 July, 25 Aug. and 1 Sept. 1929. Those interested in comparative approaches to Italian immigrant Fascists and anti-Fascists might consider some recent contributions, including Donna Gabaccia and Fraser
Ottanelli, eds., *Italian Workers of the World*; Franca Iacovetta, Roberto Perin,
and Angelo Principe, eds., *Enemies Within: Italian and Other Internees in*

Canada and Beyond (Toronto: University of Toronto Press, 2000); and the other essays in part III of this volume.

22 *Il Riscatto*, 25 May, 1 June 1930.

23 This communist leader died in 1938, victim of an assassination. See Mario Montagnana, *Ricordi di un operaio torinese* (Rome: Ed. Rinascita, 1952), 316–17.

24 ACS, CPC, 36293, Carlo Gagliazzo. The police informant reported the presence of Ida Zecchini (wife of Ottorino Perrone) amongst communist women of the center including Teresa Reversi, Carolina Guelpa, and Teresa Bosco.

25 Postcard seized by Italian censors (ACS, PS, 1935, b28, J4F).

26 *Il Riscatto*, 18 May 1930.

27 Cf. Anne Morelli, 'La solidarité active des femmes laïques en faveur de l'Espagne républicaine,' in Y. Mendès da Costa and Yolande Anne Morelli, eds., *Femmes – Libertés – Laïcité* (Brussels: Editions de l'Université de Bruxelles, 1988), 112–18.

28 ACS, Polizia politica (1927/45), envelope 13.

29 Ibid., report of 20 Oct. 1937.

30 Ibid., report of 8 Aug. 1939.

31 Archives du Fonds de l'Indépendance, file III 12.758.

32 *Il Riscatto, La Voce dei Proscritti.*

33 *Il Riscatto*, 22 July 1928; see also the issue for 8 Apr. 1928.

34 See, e.g., *Il Riscatto*, 31 Mar. 1929, where delegates to the fourth convention of the LIABS regret the absence of women and include a translation of Lenin's text on the emancipation of women in *Drapeau rouge, bandiera rossa* 21 (2 Feb. 1926).

35 *Il Riscatto*, 6 June 1928. The themes evoked were often familial (small children in Italy went hungry because their father was in jail), as well as linked to women's traditional roles.

36 *La Libre Belgique*, 28 Jan. 1930.

37 A. Gilly, rue de la Plature, 23 July 1932 (ACS, PS, 1933, b25, klb). The report focuses in large part on Maria Maruzzo and Innocenza Doni.

38 Interview of 12 July 1995.

39 Ibid.

40 ACS, CPC, 126.891.

41 *Nuovo Avanti*, 23 Oct. 1937.

42 I had the great pleasure of meeting Capellazzo when she was in her nineties. She had not lost any of the passion of her youth. In the home for the elderly where she lived, she regularly received marriage proposals from her male co-habitants and she also counselled the young nurses to insist on their professional status and helped them to organize a strike!

43 See Anne Morelli, *La participation des émigrés italiens à la Résistance belge* (Rome: Ministero Affari Esteri, 1982).

44 The situation was described masterfully by a priest who himself was sickened by these activities. See Gianfranco Monaca, *Une réflexion sociologique politique, théologique et pastorale sur cinq ans de vie en migration* (Louvain: Faculté de Théologie, 1970).

45 The reference is to a bilateral agreement between Belgium and Italy in the early 1950s. Italy agreed to provide, on a weekly basis, some 2000 young men for Belgian mines, while Belgium in return sold to Italy specified quantities of coal for each young man recruited.

46 Myrthia Schiavo, in a very friendly gesture, gave me all of her interviews.

47 Schiavo, *Italiennes au coeur de l'Europe*, xiv.

48 Ibid.

49 Bernadette Bawin-Legros, 'La mobilité sociale des femmes: De la (re)production à la production' (unpublished PhD, Sociology, Université de Liège, 1979), includes some interviews with Italian women. On Italian youth in Brussels, see the study by Bruno Ducoli and Silvana Panciera, *Entre souvenir et avenir: Enquête sur les jeunes Italiens de Bruxelles* (Brussels: Barbiana éditions, 1990).

50 See the Bawin-Legros's interviews, some of which have been published by Etienne Hélin: 'Vivre ensemble n'est pas s'intégrer,' *Vie Wallonne* 70 (1996): 41–51.

51 'Giulia,' interviewed by Schiavo, *Italiennes au coeur de l'Europe*, 48.

52 Italian-Belgian women subsequently introduced push-mops (which free women from scrubbing on their knees) and absorbent dishcloths.

PART IV

As We See Ourselves, As Others See Us

11 Glimpses of Lives in Canada's Shadow: Insiders, Outsiders, and Female Activism in the Fascist Era

Angelo Principe

Donne, da voi non poco
La patria s'aspetta; e non in danno e scorno ...

Giacomo Leopardi

As Donna Gabaccia and Franca Iacovetta observe in their introduction, and this volume demonstrates, family, work, and struggle were important sites in the formation of Italian immigrant women's complex and transnational identities. Furthermore, identity formation does not occur in a vacuum, but is the product of complex negotiations, including between how 'outsiders' saw or wished to shape the Italian women they observed or addressed, and how the women, the 'insiders,' saw themselves. Whether responding to the bourgeois image-makers and reformers from either the sending or receiving societies, or to their political and class allies in their immigrant communities, Italian immigrant women developed their identities in contexts that both appealed to their maternal qualities and imposed certain obligations or constraints on how they were expected to behave.[1]

This essay seeks to make a modest contribution towards examining the complex but under-studied subject of Italian immigrant women's identities in late-nineteenth- and early-twentieth-century Canada and, most particularly, the Fascist era of the 1920s and 1930s. It offers some suggestions for writing women into a national historiography that with important exceptions has neglected women or relegated them to the subaltern role of helpmate, social convener, and loyal wife. In contrast to the post-

1945 literature, which focuses on the single largest migration wave of Italians into Canada, and considers women's high rates of waged work in this era,[2] the scholarship on Italian immigration to Canada for the period from the 1880s to the 1920s focuses on the men – particularly male sojourners, ethnic leaders, and labourers engaged in spontaneous forms of militancy – who dominated the migration streams. This emphasis is entirely understandable, though, alas, even the treatments of family economies and community pay insufficient attention to Italian women's lives or offer reductionist portraits of them as helpmates. The few direct assessments of women's income-earning activities acknowledge women's contributions to family survival, but tend to downgrade female wage-earning as producing merely supplemental incomes that never challenged a husband's status as chief breadwinner, when it is possible that women's earnings, though meagre, might have kept families from abject poverty in situations when male incomes were seasonal, risky, and insecure.[3]

Although fragmentary, my evidence, which covers a long historical sweep up to 1945 and offers examples from across Canada, is drawn from a wide range of archival records and oral interviews, as well as from a relatively recent source, the work of second- and third-generation Italian women whose published family histories and autobiographical and literary works permit us rare glimpses of the lives of their grandmothers, mothers, aunts, and sisters during the first half of the twentieth century. In highlighting the Fascist era in Canada, a period that played an influential, if contradictory, role in the shaping of Italian immigrant women's ethnic, gender, and class identities, I note how Fascists and anti-Fascists appealed to women and describe the experiences of women in both camps. More generally, my efforts to catch glimpses of Italian women in the Canadian shadow before 1945 suggest that the identities of Italian immigrant women emerged more from their encounters with the often conflicting Italian discourses over what constituted the most appropriate form of 'womanhood' and 'motherhood' than from their responses to Canadian models. Significant differences characterized the models of womanhood through and against which different groups of Italians perceived and assessed the lives of immigrant women – including Italian bourgeois observers sent out to report on the situation of Italians in North America, immigrant male workers and militants, and the Fascist and anti-Fascist activists, liberals and radicals, who competed in Canada, as they did elsewhere, for the support and loyalty of the women within the immigrant communities.

Overall, I argue that Italian women, though often designated to a subaltern and subordinate position relative both to their men and to national projects (such as war work), did not always passively accept that role. At times, women resisted, and on occasion they challenged their subaltern position in the family and community. Always they were resourceful.

Women and Familial Roles, 1890s–1920s

Most Italian immigrants to Canada before the First World War were male: for the period 1890–1920, the ratio was 77.1 males to 22.9 females, or more than three men for every woman – though by 1931 the gap had narrowed: 55,141 Italian males to 43,032 Italian females, or about five men for every four women. The closing gender gap reflected changes in postwar immigration policy in Canada and abroad, and the high birth rate among Italians settled in Canada. In the 1920s, policies regulating the movement of workers, which were implemented on both sides of the ocean, drastically curtailed migration patterns worldwide. While Fascism discouraged emigration from Italy, in Depression-era Canada, as in the United States, restrictions were introduced for 'less preferred' immigrants such as Italians. Only immediate relatives of Canadian residents (as well as bona fide agricultural labourers) were admitted into Canada, so that during the 1930s most immigrants from Italy were women and dependent children entering the country to join men. By 1941, roughly 64 per cent of Canada's Italian population (112,625) were Canadian-born.[4] In considering both the representations and experiences of Italian women and their daughters, I begin with the immigrant generation's role as reproducers. The increase in the number of second-generation Italians in these early decades reflected the large size of immigrant families – prompting both Canadian and Italian observers to attribute the matter to the migrants' Roman Catholic background, and to assert (erroneously) that they neither knew of nor practised birth control but, fatalistically, accepted children *come Dio li manda* (as God sends them). To be sure, there were plenty of marriages and children,[5] which reflected the youthfulness of the immigrant population, but public attention, when focused on Italian women, usually stressed their unusually large families. In cities across the country, Canadian reporters noted that the Little Italies teemed with children. Writing about the 'Ward,' in Toronto, the location of Toronto's earliest Little Italy, Kenneth Douglas was amazed to see so many children of any age in the streets, who 'manage to escape disaster from passing wheels, careless pedestrians and the bugaboo of the health authorities.'[6] Italian women's association with big families also emerged in the coverage of the so-called Stork Derby, held in Toronto (1926–36), to reward the city's most prolific mother. A Toronto lawyer, Charles Millar, had left an unusual will in 1926, which directed his executors to let his estate accumulate interest for ten years and then pay it 'to the mother who has since my death given birth in Toronto to the greatest number of children.' Of the twelve women who joined the contest, three were Italians: Grace Bagnato, who had married at the very young age of 13 and given birth to twenty children, Hilda Graziano, and a Mrs Darrigo.[7]

This volume cautions against treating the Italian family, whether in Italy or Canada, as a static and monolithic institution in which fathers ruled and mothers and children cowered in silence. Fathers did enjoy much authority, but women could both recognize that authority and also challenge and defy it even as they worked tirelessly to improve the family's well-being. Upon arrival in the new land, Italian women, most of them unschooled and unable to speak the new language,[8] faced many challenges. At least initially, some felt trapped in their homes – a dilemma that writer Maria Ardizi captured in her novel *Made in Italy*; the protagonist Nora, once active and articulate, becomes so paralysed that she goes mute and ends up in a wheelchair.[9] Yet, many Italian women proved resourceful, even if it meant relying on their children to communicate with the outside world. In their recollections, daughters tend to stress their mother's vulnerability. Carmela Galardo-Frascarelli of Montreal observed that her mother 'did not speak the language of the country, and so I did the shopping and took care of household affairs.' According to Penny Petrone of Thunder Bay, Ontario, her mother Luisa, though she had had some schooling in Italy, relied on her daughter. 'Mamma's English,' recalls Penny, 'was not proficient enough for her to manage her business affairs, especially over the phone ... I became Mamma's interpreter when I was about seven years of age ... climbing a chair to reach the wall telephone.' But we might also see in these actions the resourcefulness of immigrant women with few skills. For example, Maria Labella, in hunting for a job in the garment industry in Toronto, took her oldest son along because, as she put it, 'I don't know where to go, [which] streets.' Equally significant, however, she was very active about getting a job, first locating ads in the newspaper and then instructing her son to accompany her 'as I don't know whether to take a streetcar, where is that place.'[10]

The most prominent image of Canada's Italian immigrant women is an urban one, and indeed most of them did live in cities, usually joining sojourners who had migrated from frontier jobs to the city. But some women joined their men in the bush, sharing with them the challenges of pioneer life. In 1884, Rosa Bevilacqua Casorso travelled with three children to British Columbia's Okanagan Valley to join husband Giovanni, who was working in the agricultural community established by the Oblate Order in the BC 'interior.' After a twenty-day ocean voyage, Rosa arrived at the harbour in San Francisco with an address scribbled on a piece of paper: 'Father Pandosy, Okanaga [*sic*] Mission.' No one knew how she might reach her destination, but somehow Rose learned that a large crate containing a bell was destined for the mission and, as she later recalled, she sat by the bell and 'I never took my eyes off [it] ... for the entire trip to Okanagan Mission.' At the mission, Rosa raised her family, which in time grew to nine children, and worked in the kitchen, cooking for over a dozen men. During the first hard winter, their food supplies all gone, a Native neighbour gave them venison and saved them from starvation. Her husband remembered Rosa as a tireless, helpful, and cheerful woman who 'held the fort, managing both ranch and home.'[11] Warm memories of growing up in communal living arrangements in northern Ontario lumber camps have also been published recently.[12]

In the crowded Little Italies of Montreal, Toronto, Vancouver, and smaller industrial cities, Italians attracted the attention of the health inspectors and social workers who investigated over-crowded quarters and unsanitary conditions. In their efforts to change Italian women's way of life – in everything from eating habits and dress to religious practice – Canadian reformers shared with their U.S. counterparts a bourgeois assumption that the small, nuclear family where 'the father earns enough to support wife and children, and where the mother can devote her time to the care of them, and where neither she nor the children go out and help in the support of the family' was 'superior' to the large family 'where the wife and often the older children must slave.'[13]

This idealized model of the bourgeois family was shared as well by Italian middle-class professionals who toured abroad, including Amy Bernardy, the journalist and ambassador's daughter who was sent by the Italian government to report on the conditions of Italians in North America. U.S. historians are well acquainted with Bernardy's tour of the United States,[14] but she also visited Canada. Diverted northward into

British Columbia from Washington state when bad weather impeded her progress across America by train, Bernardy made some negative observations on the Italians of Vancouver. She wrote: 'Little Italy is along Westminister Street and surroundings, on the East End, near the cemetery, in the poorest part of the city. Italians crowd these poor houses, sleeping ten or twelve in a room. Hence houses are very dirty inside.'[15] We cannot directly evaluate this specific assessment, but class prejudice, and a particular disdain for households not confined to nuclear families, likely influenced her judgment. Unable to afford 'better' housing, many immigrants bought small rundown houses and, to help pay the mortgage or rent, set aside a room or two for boarders, generally relatives, friends, or *paesani* (old-country friends). It was not unusual to have twelve to fifteen, or more, living in a five-room house with poor or nonexistent toilet facilities. Other kinds of evidence, however, suggest that women worked hard to keep up their interiors. A Toronto journalist, reporting on a case of domestic violence in the 'Ward' in 1921, wrote: '[T]he house, although scantily furnished, was spotless clean with snow white linen in every room.'[16] As Maddalena Tirabassi and Linda Reeder's contributions here suggest, we should regard with similar suspicion the Italian middle-class critics who moralized about the 'adulteries, infanticides, and vendettas' supposedly unleashed at home by male migration overseas, even while we can acknowledge that on both sides of the ocean, some married men and women temporarily separated by migration found lovers. But few women would have seen themselves in the caricatured images drawn by social conservatives who, acting as the self-appointed guardians of rural Italy's morality, branded women with husbands away as 'whores.'[17] The following poem, *I mugghiere d'i 'm'r'cane* (The Americans' Wives), first written in the Molisan dialect, suggests how local prudes saw these women.

> The wives of those gone overseas
> Eat pasta from flour so fine,
> They won't eat potatoes, and please,
> With each meal bring a bottle of wine.
> They go to the church and pray to God
> 'Keep him healthy, that husband of mine:
> For the money he sends, the poor sod,
> Keeps both me and my lover divine.
> I enjoy never having to work,
> Send me money, you cuckolded jerk.[18]

Gossip did migrate with people, and like the customary rules and rituals of courtship, it was revived but also renegotiated in Canadian cities. The streets of Little Italy also served as a playground where children met and mingled and negotiated contradictory cultural principles: the individualism of the bourgeois instruction they received in school, and their parent's family-defined work ethos that, as the great Sicilian author Giovanni Verga put it, stressed that family members worked together, 'united like the fingers of the hand.' Strict sex codes were central to church teachings and the fear that country priests had tried to instil in the supposedly naive – and earthy – peasants and rural workers was also transplanted to immigrant communities, with mixed results. Italian conservative lay culture, too, was imbued with such notions. In Verga's popular novel, *I Malavoglia*, the young Sicilian Lia, after being seen a few times meeting a local police chief at night, must leave for the city of Catania, where she is later spotted in *una di quelle case* (one of those houses).[19]

In his autobiography, *L'orfano di padre*, Joseph Ricci (unknowingly) addresses the subject of gender conflicts between tradition and change in immigrant contexts. Alone and depressed during his first months in Canada, Ricci later made friends with some young people, among them the Canadian daughters of Italian immigrants, who had been born in Toronto and spoke no Italian. On Saturday nights, the group gathered in one of their homes to dance and socialize. 'From then on,' writes Ricci, 'knowing that after work I could enjoy myself as I desired, my morale was high.' But when it came time to find a bride he never considered any of these Canadianized women, confessing that as he then saw it, they 'were not adaptable to my character still purely Italian with all the tradition and moral and familial values of Abruzzo.' Other young men acted likewise.[20]

Other evidence points to the defiance of teenage girls schooled in Canada who began to challenge their parents' authority in matters of dating, socializing, and marriage. Not all parents were the same, some being more strict than others. One father was particularly strict and would not allow his seventeen-year-old daughter to be a bridesmaid as it meant going to the church arm-in-arm with a boy. In a clash with her father in the summer of 1940, Rosa Meschino, whose sister described her as 'a very independent and strong-minded person,' packed her bags and left home for good.[21] Canadian-born Giuseppina Gatto was twenty-five when she confronted her father, a well-known grocer in Toronto, about never having been to a dance. One evening, she asked her father if she could be a nun, and when he refused, she promptly responded, 'Then, let me participate in the community's events.' He agreed and took her to a dance (organized by the Fascists), where a young man, Tommaso, asked her to dance. 'I looked at my father,' she recalls, and 'he said yes,' making Tommaso the first man, other than a close relative, who had spoken to her before 'this moment.' He became her husband. Avoiding direct clashes, other women circumvented their parents' authority with cunning. Lucia Marotta enlisted her brother's help as a fictitious chaperone for an evening and then they parted ways once out of their parents' sight. Anne Altilia, 'went out' with a group of girls and then, at a 'safe' distance from home, left the group as prearranged to meet her boyfriend, a Foggiano from a relatively more 'liberated' family. Had she brought him home, she would have faced family pressure to marry him.[22]

Some Italian girls did marry very young, for a variety of reasons – to escape home, out of economic concerns, or to assuage parents' fears that they might otherwise 'go astray.' The small number of women in relation to men made marriage easy, even for those women who, according to Amy Bernardy, would not have had a chance back home. On this point, the labour reformer (and future Canadian prime minister) Mackenzie King, observed that 'it is natural to find that, with the exception of a few very young girls, nearly all [Italian] women are married.'[23] Anecdotal references to the preponderance of very young Italian brides[24] must be viewed with caution (the subject demands more research), but, certainly, young brides caught the eye of observers, including Bernardy, who noted: 'Boys for some time now reveal a worthy tendency to further their education by completing high school. Girls "wisely" chose to get married instead.'[25] Bernardy disapproved of the North American mores that allowed girls to date and experience life before marrying, calling it a 'waste' of time. Some fathers agreed, even refusing to allow girls who wanted to study to pursue an education.[26] And at least a few women were married to men many years older than them. Gioconda Bartolini, twenty-two, married forty-seven-year-old Domenico Maglio, who was two years older than her own father. A devout Roman Catholic, she rationalized the marriage with a prophetic dream in which she saw 'the Blessed Virgin walking towards her and leading Domenico by the arm. When she reached Gioconda, the Blessed Virgin said, "this is the man you will marry."'[27]

While priests might encourage or cajole Italian women to heed their heady responsibilities as moral paragons and self-sacrificing mothers, the left's challenge to dominant codes of sexual morality also crossed the ocean. Italian leftists in North America upheld women's equality in theory if not always in practice.[28] In 1906, *Il Proletario*, a socialist weekly published in Philadelphia and read by Italian-Canadian workers, attacked priests for accusing socialists of harbouring 'vile intentions' towards women and instead proclaimed themselves as great supporters of gender equality. They also offered their own model of the emancipated woman under socialism, and urged women to join the class struggle. 'In a socialist society,' the paper proclaimed, 'women shall be both socially and economically independent' and never 'subjected to tyranny nor to exploitation.' 'Being free and equal to men,' women would be 'masters of themselves and of their destiny,' and '[g]iven equal opportunity,' would be 'neither less capable nor less skilful than men.' Moreover, in love they would be 'as free to choose as men; they may ask in marriage or be asked and they can tie the knot without any other regard but their own inclination.' After asking, rhetorically, whether this is 'a condition of life that wise women should reject?' the paper cried: 'Women! This new morality, against which the bourgeois priests rant, is also your redemption!'[29] A 1918 editorial in the anarchist monthly *Il Martello*, published in New York, similarly argued that 'nothing is so unjust as the artificial inequality between man and woman.' 'The inequality,' it added, 'begins with schooling so limited for women ...[,] continues in the domestic life where the woman has to serve her man ... [and] goes on in the social sphere in which the woman is considered inferior and unworthy of certain occupations or positions. Everything is geared to keep the woman in a condition of moral and economic dependence [upon] the man. Her imperfect and partial education, her more or less servile jobs, her low salary and, when she cannot find a man to support her, prostitution attends her.'[30] Only a minority of Italian-Canadian women embraced the arguments advanced by left-wing radicals, and though we still know far too little about these female activists, preliminary research suggests that, like their counterparts elsewhere, they could find themselves having to fight not only bosses and capitalist exploitaton but the paternalism, if not outright chauvinism, of their male comrades.[31] Still, for centuries, Italian women, regardless of political persuasion, had found ways to circumvent the obstacles posed by the power of husbands, even if their everyday defiance did not approach the domestic revolution as envisioned by *Il Proletario*, *Il Martello*, and other left-wing newspapers.

From the vantage point of both Italian and Canadian bourgeois outsiders, the reassembled family in Canada turned sojourning men without women into settled immigrants and also began the process of restoring to them their rightful place as fathers, breadwinners, and patriarchs. But if, from the outside, reunited families appeared to approximate (or move more closely towards) the idealized bourgeois institution, from the inside the matter was more complicated. For one thing, children who saw their father for the first time ever or who could barely remember a father they had not seen in years, hardly experienced the intimacy conveyed by the phrase 'reunited family.' In their published recollections, the daughters of Italian mothers who were far from being submissive or idle housewives agree that mamma worked endlessly, but offer differing assessments of their mother's status within the family. According to Penny Petrone, her mother for years had 'controlled the family's budget, her husband's paycheque, and the earnings of her boys,' yet she always 'displayed, as required by custom and church law, deference and obedience to her husband.' Eleonora Maglio described her mother's similarly demanding work regime – 'mother' was the 'first to rise in the morning and usually the last to go to bed at night. Even when seated, she was active – either darning socks, or crocheting something, or reading her prayer book, or saying her rosary.' She also insisted that the respect her mother enjoyed in the family was not merely given to her; she earned it with affection, hard work, and devotion.[32]

As these memoirs and other sources attest, Italian mothers differed little from the Canadian working-class mothers who 'managed and stretched the wages of other family members, shopped with care, scrimped on their own nourishment so that others would eat better, or took in boarders or even a whole extra family to stretch the rent.'[33] Italian women, like all poor women, practised recycling long before any municipality implemented such a policy: 'a pair of Pa's discarded abundantly large trousers were expertly transformed into maybe three pair for his male offspring. Unbleached cotton flour sacks were sewn together to make bed sheets, and items of outer clothing, no longer wearable, were neatly and efficiently dissected and subsequently reappeared as crazy quilts or floor mats.' Nothing was just thrown away: glass jars were used for preserves; cans became spare utensils for the kitchen or for fetching water.[34] In families that owned a cart from which they sold bananas or other fruit, or a small grocery or convenience store, women were as involved as men in the business; men generally looked after the outside dealings, while women managed the business at home. And many women took in sewing work at home to bring in much needed cash.[35] It seems clear that the majority of the adult Italian women of the immigrant generation did not work outside the home for factory or other industrial wages, though some did so.[36] The Italian female factory operatives in these years were more likely to be young and single daughters, whether Italian- or Canadian-born. Government enquiries into female factory work reveal familiar depictions of immigrant women workers as wage depressors. The 1889 Royal Commission on Capital and Labour reported on Italian women's very low wages, and also recorded the complaints of artisans in Toronto, who accused Italian tailors of unfair competition because they had women 'slaves' working for them cheaply.

Q. Are there any Italians doing labouring work?
A. They take the work home, and they run what are known as sweating shops. They are making quite a pile of money and have a few slaves under them in the shape of women.
Q. Do they work cheaper than regular men?
A. They do the work cheaper, and they get women to do the work cheaper still.[37]

However modest, those wages could make a significant difference to their family's well-being, but until further research is conducted, we cannot draw meaningful comparisons with the United States or other places.[38] Some young women spent their teenage years in the garment industry or in a food or tobacco factory. 'When I was thirteen,' recalled Miss E., 'my father took sick and I had to start work in a macaroni factory to help support the family.' It was hard work: 'I used to get up at five o'clock as it took an hour to reach work on the streetcar. We worked from seven to five and though I was supposed to weigh macaroni in the boxes, I had to do much other work and this was very hard.'[39] On the same subject, Frascarelli recalled: 'I had to quit school because my family was poor. We had three *paesani* boarding with us. With these three people and five children, my mother needed me at home.'[40]

Perhaps the most demanding work performed by mothers who 'stayed' at home was taking in boarders – whether they ran a large boarding house or provided space in rented homes. In large lodging houses, the *ambiente* (ambience) was more impersonal than in private homes, where boarders often were kin or *paesani*. Boarding provided economic and social benefits to both parties involved, and for women, it also meant long, exhausting days all week. One woman recalled how she accommodated ten boarders in her house in Timmins, Ontario: 'They were all relatives and I had to cook and clean for all of them ... [T]here was no running water, no hot water, no bathrooms ... On top of all that work I already had two children to take care of and then I had another two.'[41] Not so surprisingly, Bernardy did not approve of what she called 'the servitude of the board system.' 'The lives of most Italian women,' she argued with moral concern, 'swings between two poles: Corruption and economic exploitation.'[42] By 'corruption' she no doubt meant moral corruption – thereby reflecting the bourgeois preoccupation concerning women living in the same house with men other than their husbands or sons. As for serious economic exploitation, Bernardy, of course, shared with her middle-class co-nationals a deep dislike for the physically hard labours that so-called housewives from humble and impoverished backgrounds performed as a matter of daily practice.[43]

In trying to rescue Italian immigrants from pathological portraits, immigration scholars, including feminist historians of Italian women, perhaps have been reluctant to discuss domestic violence. As feminist scholarship on the subject shows, however, domestic violence shows no respect for class or social-ethnic boundaries. It also documents that men who resort to physical abuse often justified their actions by claiming to have a stubborn, disobedient, or inferior wife who failed to fulfil her wifely duties.[44] Italian wife abusers were no different. In 1908, one Italian mother of seven children, and pregnant with an eighth, ran away from home in Vancouver because her husband beat her and forced her to keep 'thirteen men boarders.' A fifteen-year-old son was also implicated. When arrested, the husband lamented that there was no justice in America, because 'a husband cannot teach his wife a lesson.'[45] Joe C. recalls that on his wedding day, his father-in-law took him aside and advised, 'If she [the new bride] does not behave, "daglieli" (beat her).'[46] Mary Giordano remembered her own fears and those of her siblings every time their parents had a heated argument; afterwards, 'they would not speak to each other for a few days or a week, and then everything would be peaceful until the next time.' 'During these arguments,' she added, 'we lived in fear and imagined all sorts of terrible things. So if we thought there was an argument brewing we would plead with mother not to antagonise my father. He had a very bad temper.'[47]

Most cases of domestic violence never became public, but when violence led to murder, the resulting court cases attracted media attention. On occasion, it was the victims who turned to violence. In 1911 Angelina Napolitano killed her husband with an axe while he was sleeping, and Mary Ciccalone received five years in Kingston Penitentiary for attempting to murder her husband in 1921. A pregnant Angelina was abused and beaten regularly by her husband because she refused to become a prostitute. One day she exploded in a violent rage and killed him, putting an end to her misery. She was sentenced to death by hanging, but a worldwide clemency campaign forced the authorities to commute the death sentence to one of life imprisonment. As Karen Dubinsky and Franca Iacovetta have documented, the Napolitano case garnered enormous international attention from first-wave feminists, religious and reform groups, and the left. The portrait that detractors and supporters alike drew of Napolitano ranged from a pathetic and demented woman, to an innately violent foreigner (like all Italians!), to a feminist heroine who had killed a brute. In the Italian socialist newspaper *Il Proletario* of New York, the famed labour militant, anarchist, poet, and playwight Arturo Giovannitti stressed the weakness and hypocrisy of the law. Noting that Napolitano's execution date had been held over until she gave birth, and that she was even given an additional month to nurse her newcomer, Giovannitti argued that since no physician could ever know with certainty whether she might again be pregnant at any given moment, she should not go to the noose.[48]

In Toronto, Mary Ciccalone did not succeed in killing her husband, Cenzo (Vincenzo) Ciccalone, in June 1921, although she certainly tried – by shooting and stabbing him. Evidently, her motive was abandonment. Mary and Cenzo ran a rooming house in Brantford, Ontario. They sold it in 1920 and deposited the money ($3000) in a joint bank account. According to Mary's declaration to the police, her husband took the money and went to Italy, leaving her in Ontario with two young children (aged five and six) and no financial resources. Undaunted, she moved from Brantford to Toronto, and with some local assistance bought a small house in the 'Ward.' She turned part of the house into a small grocery store and, on the side, ran a bootlegging business. When he returned, she stabbed and shot him. The jury found her guilty of attempted murder and the judge, while sentencing her to five years in Kingston Penitentiary for Women, sternly declared: 'Not withstanding your children [I] must impose some penalty, which will be *a warning against bringing such ideas into the country*' (emphasis added).[49]

Notwithstanding the violence that erupted from time to time, Italian-Canadian families and Little Italies were not the evil places imagined by middle-class critics – where violence, corruption, crime, and degradation allegedly flourished. For many Italian-Canadians, their neighbourhoods were the source of friendship, community sentiments, and sharing and solidarity. Speaking of Toronto's west-end Little Italy in the late

1920s Mary Giordano recalled that 'Clinton was a fascinating Street to live on' and described her neighbours as poor emigrant women who were nonetheless kind and supportive. 'The women [would] bake or cook meals for one another when there was a celebration, death or illness. Most women gave birth at home and their neighbours would help look after the household until the new mother was strong enough to get back on her feet.'[50]

Charity and Community Work

Although Italian women became involved in charity and community activities, the First World War, in which Canada and Italy were allies, drew many Italian-Canadian women, as well as men, into the Canadian war effort. Even when unemployment was widespread and many families were surviving on public assistance, Italian immigrants responded positively to the efforts of Italian diplomats and Italian-Canadian community leaders, and their respective cronies, to induce men of military age to volunteer for war. Opposed to Italy's entry into the war, local Italian socialists ran a strong anti-war campaign in which women were enlisted to the cause, at one point circulating widely among Italians in North America a letter written by an Italian mother to her son living in America, in which she tells him to desert. Perhaps the letter had its intended effect – the number of volunteers, though large, was nowhere close to what Italian authorities had expected. Across the country, Italian volunteers were celebrated in parades and escorted to railroad stations.[51] During these events the women were relegated to cooking and serving dinners, while younger women in costumes adorned the parades.[52]

In Montreal, a new weekly newspaper, *L'Italia*, was created to spearhead the pro-war campaign in the community.[53] The New York–based daily *Il Progresso italo-americano*, which was read widely in Canada, joined the campaign, and after the United States entered the war in 1917, it stepped up its propaganda efforts, at one point issuing a public plea to middle-class and working-class women that they use their 'generous heart' and love of 'our Patria' (Italy) to good effect by joining the war effort:

> We appeal even to women, 'signore' and 'signorine' [married and single], who being favoured by their social positions can devote many hours of the day to the holy cause and to charity work. We appeal also to women and

girls who work in thousands of factories where they may ask their co-workers for a contribution. Men can do and have done much, but women can do as much as men. For no one would deny a contribution to a woman, who, as an angel of charity, asks for a donation to help our unfortunate brothers. It is only a question of will, gentleness of heart, and love for the Fatherland. All women, as apostles and angels of charity, take on this task.[54]

Large numbers of Italian women joined community campaigns in Vancouver and elsewhere[55] to collect money for the Italian Red Cross. In a single 'Italian Tag Day' in Toronto some 2200 young women and children, some of them dressed in 'traditional costumes,' reportedly raised $15,448.10 by approaching people heading to work. In return for donations they pinned an Italian flag on their garments. The coverage portrayed a scene of 'perfect order and harmony' as the 'Canadian and Italian ladies worked together marshalling the younger women.' Evidently, the Italian teams collected about as much as the 'Anglo-Saxon ladies.'[56] After the war, the Italian government and the Croce Rossa (Red Cross) recognized the war effort of Canada's Italians, but only men, it appears, were singled out for a special 'attestato di benemerenza' (certificate of merit).[57]

If some priests might be seen as Italian-speaking 'outsiders' vis-à-vis the humble immigrant women they sought to lead, it would be inaccurate to portray the immigrant church entirely in these terms. Many Italian women, however they defined their religious beliefs, took church life seriously. In the Italian parish churches of Montreal and Toronto, male and female religious confraternities had long histories, and women clad in their sodality robes took part in church processions. They also offered their volunteer labour, cleaning the church, setting up the altars, placing candles and flowers, and changing linen.[58]

In the 1920s and 1930s, lay female auxiliary associations appeared in cities across Canada. The Order Sons of Italy (OSI) of Quebec and Ontario, the largest Italian-immigrant mutual-benefit organization in North America, included several female lodges, which organized social events, such as dances and dinners, and served coffee during OSI conventions. They also raised funds for good causes by selling crocheted and embroidered items and baked goods at bazaars, and administered the mortuary funds for members of their lodges. From 1927 to 1940, the Ladies' League of Vancouver was very active. In 1927, it contributed to the Christmas Chest Fund of the *Province*, the *Sun* and the *Morning Star*, three Vancouver newspapers. In 1929, the annual ball, organized with the Sons of Italy Society, donated the funds raised to the local *scuola italiana* (Italian-language school). In the Depression, these groups used the funds raised during its annual ball and a bazaar to give every needy Italian family a Christmas turkey.[59]

These kinds of community organizations also illustrated the subaltern role of women in the wider community. Throughout the 1930s, when Fascists dominated the OSI, no woman was elected to the grand council (governing body) of Quebec or Ontario. In the 1920s, two women had held such positions on the Ontario Grand Council;[60] but when, in 1940, most of the male leaders and one woman, Venera Lobosco, were interned for having compromised with Fascism, the organization's administration fell to some of its women members, who took over the vacated posts and carried on.[61] By contrast, the anti-Fascist and socialist-leaning Order of Italo-Canadians had always been open to women. On its first executive council, five of thirteen members were women.[62] The Independent Order Sons of Italy, which had been created in 1927 by two lodges, the Mazzini and the Piave, became the Order of Italo-Canadians (OIC) in 1937. Both lodges had left the Quebec branch of the OSI because the latter had gone Fascist. The OIC obtained a federal charter (when it was renamed as such in 1937); included in the growth were several very active female lodges.[63]

Among the Italian-Canadian female associations that proliferated between the two world wars, Toronto's Società Femminile Friulana (Friulan Women's Society) well illustrates women's disenchantment with the subordinate role generally assigned them in male-dominated associations. In response, these women in 1938 organized their own society, and it collaborated with the male association on an equal basis. Although Friulan women organized themselves late in relation to their male counterparts, they have successfully run their own affairs without male interference to the present. In 1939, they organized a banquet and dance for 'women only,' for which women provided everything, including the musical entertainment. In her presidential speech, Maria Cristante thanked her women 'associates' for a successful celebration.[64]

Engendering Fascist Rivalries: Fascist and Anti-Fascist Immigrant Women

From 1929 on, Fascists officially dominated the social-political life of Italian-Canadian communities; every sizeable Little Italy had its Fascist club (*fascio*), usually led by bold individuals who tolerated neither opposition nor criticism. Until the Ethiopian war (1935–6), Fascist clubs prospered in part because of their anti-communist stance. They were supported by conservatives such as Roman Catholic church leaders, leading journalists, businessmen, and right-wing intellectuals. Furthermore, before Italy's invasion of Ethiopia, all governments in Canada and elsewhere supported Mussolini and his local followers. In this atmosphere, Fascists enjoyed prestige and favour in their community and in the society at large and also took over some of the immigrant organizations, such as the Order Sons of Italy in Quebec and Ontario. In Montreal, they established an umbrella association, named Fronte Unico Morale Italiano (FUMI), intended to control small Italian-Canadian mutual-benefit and social societies. In the early 1930s, women and youth Fascist clubs followed. An 'Italian Week,' organized across the country in 1934, brought to Canada a group of Fascist intellectuals who enthused over the 'tremendous achievements' of Fascist Italy. That same year, Piero Parini, the highest Fascist party official to travel to Canada, visited Toronto. Local male Fascists, hoping to be knighted by Mussolini, and the appointed Italian government consuls, with both eyes on their careers, sought to impress their powerful guest by creating branches of the female and youth institutions created in Italy. They mobilized their wives, daughters, and sisters and otherwise encouraged the establishment of female Fascist organizations.

Two key organizations were the Opera Nazionale Balilla (ONB), 1926–37 (a Fascist Scouting association), which was superseded in 1937 by the Gioventù Italiana del Littorio Estero (GILE; Italian Lictorial[65] Youth Abroad), and the Opera Maternità e Infanzia (OMI). The latter was created to channel married women's energies into what the regime considered their primary function – procreation. With the full support of the Roman Catholic church, the OMI encouraged women to reproduce and rear children, whom the regime recognized as Italy's future soldiers. The girls organized into the ONB and then into the GILE were divided into four age groups: Figlie della lupa (Daughters of the She-wolf, ages 2–8), the Piccole italiane (Little Italians, ages 8–14), the Giovani italiane (Young Italians, 14–18), and Giovani fasciste (Fascist Youth, 18–21). (There were corresponding groups for boys.) In Canada's immigrant communities, the young women who joined fascist groups were very active; they attended classes to learn Italian and, in the process, were indoctrinated in the 'Fascist mystique.' They organized dances, joined athletic events, and dressed in their Fascist uniform (black skirt and white blouse) to march in parades and sing Fascist songs. Furthermore, like other immigrant children abroad, those girls who most distinguished themselves were rewarded with the trip of their dreams – a summer vacation on the Italian coast, where they were housed with youths from around the world in summer resorts normally reserved for the well-to-do, and given *un tuffo nell'ideologia fascista*, literally a plunge into or total immersion in Fascist ideology. To what extent these indoctrination techniques worked remains open for debate, but anecdotal evidence shows that Fascists succeeded in making these vacations a memorable event in these young people's childhood.[66]

In seeking to turn Italian women into good Fascist women, the Fascist state and the Church were in part seeking to stem the tide of 'modernism,' often defined in terms of industrialization and democracy, which had catapulted women into the job market and political arena. Regarding the franchise, Mussolini said dismissively in 1925, '[I]n my peregrinations I never met a woman who asked me for the right to vote,' adding that it 'reflects honorably on Italian women.'[67] In the 1931 encyclical *Quadragesimo Anno*, Pope Pius XI similarly stated that 'Mothers' place is in the home' and their main duty is 'looking after their families.' 'That a mother is compelled to go out to work because of father's inadequate salary' was 'a disorder' to be 'eliminated with every means.' Some high-level Fascist party officials even declared that 'women ... should not mix promiscuously with men on the streets, on public transportation, or in factories and offices.'[68]

The female Fascist groups in Canada aimed also at silencing or neutralizing feminist and socialist criticism, a situation that alarmed some Canadian women. In a 1935 report sent to his superiors in Rome, the Italian consul in Montreal, Giuseppe Brigidi, charged Canadian intellectuals of slandering Fascism when they claimed that it was an anti-Semitic and war-mongering regime, and that Italian women were in a grave condition of moral, social, and political inferiority. In the consul's opinion, the most destructive critique was that regarding women, because Canadian women 'are more intelligent than men and, by customs and laws, they enjoy more protection and privileges than men.' Thus, he concluded, 'they have a powerful influence on the social, intellectual, and political life of the country.'[69]

Leading Fascist women, in Canada as in Italy, had the delicate task of convincing immigrant and working-class Italian women to embrace the role that Fascism cast for women in the social life of the nation. From Italy, these 'outsiders' included Amy Bernardy, who, as part of a group of Italian dignitaries involved in a special Fascist social event dubbed Italian

Week, spoke to the Canadian Female Club in Toronto. In Montreal, Consul Bridigi's wife, Giovanna, who was well educated and fluent in both English and French, 'initiated a series of conferences, speaking in many Canadian woman associations and clubs.' The pro-Fascist weekly *L'Italia* reported that at one of these conferences, held at Senator Rodolfe Lemieux's residence, 'Signora Brigidi spoke in Italian in a meeting of ladies from the best sector of Canadian society,' during which she discussed the work undertaken by the regime to promote *Maternità e Infanzia* (motherhood and childhood), and stressed the great value of women to the regime. This high mission that Mussolini assigned to Italian women reached its apex in 1935–6 during the Ethiopian war, when Italian women at home and abroad were asked to give, or indeed were stripped of, their wedding bands for the glory of the regime. It was a graphic illustration of how, to paraphrase Victoria De Grazia, Fascism ruled Italian immigrant women by propagating a nationalist ideology that appealed to women as reproducers of the race while denying them full political rights.[70]

A major paradox regarding female activism within right-wing political parties is that women become activists within a movement that preaches domesticity and family values. Some of them also emerge as prominent and forceful leaders. Leading Italian-Canadian Fascists organized conferences and meetings that were less intellectual in tone than those mounted by visiting dignitaries and more geared to action. Among the many women active in the various associations, clubs, and OSI lodges (directly or indirectly) under Fascist control, Carmela Galardo-Frascarelli symbolizes these women's commitment as well as their ideological confusion. She was a remarkable woman, but though bright and dynamic, she did not see through the profound contradictions that she lived. A 1940 report by the RCMP (Royal Canadian Mounted Police) called Frascarelli 'a fanatic Fascist' and 'strongly recommended' her internment because she had been very active in the Fascist party in Montreal and had held high positions in Fascist clubs and satellite associations, including the Girls' branch ONB (1934–5) and the Ville-Emerald Feminine Fascio (1935–40).[71]

In a recent lengthy interview, Galardo-Frascarelli carefully avoided speaking of her Fascist past (and apparently was not prompted on this subject by her interviewer, literature professor Filippo Salvatore). Instead, she highlighted her association with Thérèse Casgrain, a Quebec feminist and civil-rights activist. Yet the evidence shows Galardo-Frascarelli as an active, indeed, leading woman Fascist. In addition to the activities noted above, she was involved in the OSI (and in the FUMI that orbited round the Fascio and the Italian consulate). In the OSI, she founded the Anita Garibaldi Lodge in 1923; with 300 members, it was one of the most influential and active lodges in the Order. At the same time, Frascarelli's association with Casgrain was linked to the struggle to obtain the right to vote for women in Quebec. (Women had had the right to vote federally since 1918, but it was not until 1940 that Quebec women could vote in provincial elections, more than two decades after women in Canada's other provinces had gained that right.) Ironically, the Catholic clergy urged women to vote federally while insisting that fighting for political rights provincially was opposed to God's will.[72] According to Frascarelli, she had been elected president of the Italian section of the suffrage committee in Quebec. At meetings, she recalled, 'Mme Casgrain spoke an excellent French,' but 'it was I who used to explain things in the English and Italian languages.' 'I was convinced,' she added, 'that universal suffrage would have given women substantial social and economic weight.' Frascarelli also claimed to have struck up a good friendship with Casgrain as they travelled together on the political trail, 'to Quebec City, to Ottawa, to Rouyn, Rivière-du-loup.' Their relationship 'cooled off,' however, when Casgrain decided to join Canada's social democratic party, the Co-operative Commonwealth Federation (CCF, later the New Democratic Party (NDP)).[73] Frascarelli's pro-Fascist and pro-female suffrage sentiments reflect her naive and contradictory politics.

When Italy entered the war in June 1940, of more than twenty Italian-Canadian women considered for internment,[74] four were actually interned: Maria Egilda Fontanella, Luisa Guagnelli, Venera Lobosco, and Maria Pressello.[75] Carmela Galardo-Frascarelli avoided internment, but her husband, Leonardo Frascarelli, was sent to Camp Petawawa, as were other prominent Italians involved with Fascism. Leonardo was a successful contractor who had built the Casa d'Italia (a social centre under Fascist control) in Montreal. Using her political connections in the ruling Liberal party, Carmela obtained a permit to visit her husband – a privilege not extended to other Italian-Canadian women. When her twenty-year-old son, Leo, received an order to join the Canadian army, the Canadian-born Carmela proved equally resourceful. She, not her son, went to the enrolment centre, where she argued successfully that since her husband was considered a potential 'traitor,' their son Leo could not join the army. As she put it, 'Ainsi mon fils n'a pas fait son service militaire' (thus, my son did not do his military service).[76] Clearly, Frascarelli could see the contradictions at work in Canadian government action in wartime, but failed to see (or to acknowledge afterwards) the contradictions at the core of her own political life. She tenaciously promoted Fascism, which denied freedom to both men and women in Italy, while vigorously fighting for the right of Quebec women to vote. She and her comrades on the suffrage committee were riding two horses, running in opposite directions.

Italian immigrant and Italian-Canadian women could also be found in the anti-Fascist forces, both liberal and radical, and they too found themselves turned into female icons for the cause. The radical anti-Fascists, though far fewer in number than their political enemies and constantly under the watchful eye of both the Fascists and the RCMP, produced one of the most dedicated female comrades, Maria Cazzola, a worker and socialist in Montreal. In recognizing her dedication, moreover, her male comrades used the gendered language of motherhood, dubbing her, quite literally, *la mamma dell'anti-fascismo italo-canadese* (the mother of Italian-Canadian anti-Fascism).[77]

Unfortunately, Cazzola too remains hidden in darkness, but even the all too brief references to her in workers' newspapers and the anecdotal stories recounted by a former male comrade, the late Anselmo Bortolotti (who was the source of Cazzolla's nickname), suggest that Cazzola deserved her reputation as a dangerous woman. No doubt the reference to Cazolla's motherly status is due in part to the fact that, as Bortolotti explained, she was considerably older than most of the anti-Fascist radicals in her networks. According to Bortolotti, her age placed limitations on what Cazzola could actually do, but like the male comrades who showed respect but also concern for the Italian-American anarchist anti-Fascist exile Virgilia D'Andrea,[78] they nonetheless commented on her strong political presence. In Bortolotti's words, she 'attended all our meetings and *diceva la sua* (forcefully expressed her views).' A native of the Marche region in central Italy, Cazzola hailed from Italy's *cinghia rossa* (red belt), which included the Italian socialist strongholds of Parma, Piacenza, and Ancona.

We do not know exactly how Cazzola, a widow without children, earned a living in these years, but we know that she was active in the female Concordia Lodge of the OSI in 1926 – a significant date in the history of Fascist/anti-Fascist struggles. That year, the OSI of Quebec held its Grand Convention, which was attended by the Supreme Venerable of the Order in the United States, the Fascist Giovanni di Silvestro, who used his influence to convince the Quebec Order to go Fascist. In response, four opposing lodges – Mazzini, Piave, Diaz, and the female

Concordia – voted a motion of 'vigorous protest' and requested that the newly elected Grand Officials declare that 'they praised Fascism and Mussolini only as individuals and not as Officers of the Order.'[79] According to Bortolotti, Cazzola played a leading role in the Concordia Lodge and perhaps influenced the decision to renounce Fascism. All four lodges left the Order in protest; two of them (Diaz and Concordia) later returned to the Order and the other two (as noted) founded the Independent Order Sons of Italy.

With the financial and organizational support of the two anti-Fascist Lodges, Mazzini and Piave, Antonino Spada published *Il Risveglio* in 1926, the first Italian-language anti-Fascist paper in Canada.[80] There are indications that Cazzola was involved in assembling the newspaper. She was also probably in contact with anti-Fascists back home. Indeed, Spada claimed that she hid in her own home Mafaldo Rossi, an anti-Fascist exile from Bologna, who entered Canada illegally by deserting the cargo ship on which he worked. In Montreal, he assumed the name Nello Vergani. Rossi-Vergani later died in the Spanish Civil War fighting both Spanish and Italian Fascists. In his commemorative article on Rossi-Vergani, Spada recalled how he had met Vergani:

> The good, the dear comrade Maria [Cazzola] spoke to me about him. She said, 'comrade, you know, at my place lives a young man. He is here illegally. He works at the Windsor [Hotel]. He is a comrade. Do you want to meet him?' 'Are you sure he is a comrade?' Her affirmative answer wiped out all my doubts. It was the period [when] we were publishing the first *Risveglio Italiano* in Lagauchetiere. The time when all our activities, thoughts and every effort aimed at making sure that *il Risveglio* was published.[81]

Cazzola supported *Il Lavoratore* and *La Voce degli italo-canadesi* and also actively aided the volunteers enrolled in the Italian Garibaldi Battalion fighting Fascism in Spain. A 1937 issue of *Il Lavoratore*, reporting on contributions for the paper, noted that Maria Cazzola had sent a modest amount ($7.05), but it had been collected from thirty-three workers and supporters of the paper in Montreal. In many cases, the use of initials rather than first names makes it impossible to know which contributors were women, but there is reference to another active anti-Fascist, Adele Galante, whom the editor 'deeply thank[ed] ... for generously supporting the paper.' He also singled out 'the indefatigable comrade Maria Cazzola, who distinguishes herself in helping the workers' press.'[82] Further *La Voce*, on 30 April 1940, reported a party given by Montreal comrades on her eightieth birthday. She 'generously offered the profits of the festivities, $37.53, to the paper' and the paper's editor 'thanked the comrade Maria Cazzola for her noble gesture.'

Final references to Cazzola occur in two letters: one from Spada to Bersani and in Bersani's reply. On 25 August 1941, on the letterhead of the Order of Italo-Canadians, Spada wrote:

Dear Mr. Bersani,

Some months ago our mutual friend Maria Cazzola expressed her desire to spend winter in an institution for older people. It is understood that she should be in an institution where she is free, within some general rule, to go in and out as she wishes even if it is necessary to pay *qualche soldo* (a small amount of money). For reasons that I tell you by voice, I believe that we should do everything possible to find her a decent accommodation for this person who is close to our hearts. We believe that you are the only person who could suggest what to do by sending us either a letter or instruction how to proceed.

When the letter arrived in Toronto, Bersani was on vacation. He answered on 2 September 1941 as follows:

Dear Spada,

I answer yours of the 25th u.s. Re: Maria Cazzola and I am sorry for not being able to suggest for the moment the name of an institution that fits the need of our dear and mutual friend. Most probably I shall be in Montreal within days or, for sure, on the 17th c.m.; and I promise you that I look after this matter as soon I got there.[83]

Even these glimpses of Cazzola's life as a radical anti-Fascist underscores the need for more research on Italian-Canadian women radicals, whose lives offer us alternative images and identities of Italian women as resisters and militants. Relevant material is scattered in small community newspapers, union records, local archives, and in police files on both sides of the Atlantic. Preliminary research suggests that Italian-Canadian women were as radical as the situation allowed them to be. As in North and South America, immigrant women in Canada supported their men when they went on strike or joined struggles for social emancipation even while they fought their sexism. *Il Martello* recognized women's role in the struggle for the emancipation of the working class and, apropos, wrote: '*Salve* noble and generous companions, comrades of our struggle, staunch supporters of our sacred claims. Look up in the sky at the rising sun and forge ahead. Triumph belongs to daring people.'[84] In the mining camps of Alberta and British Columbia, militant Italian women joined Finnish women in the Canadian Communist party and, as Allen Seager notes, sought to 'take politics from the union hall into the home and school, where the "bourgeois influence" combined with traditional paternalism to create a condition for mining wives and children equally oppressive as the "slavery" of the workplace.'[85] Regarding anti-Fascism, T. Boschi, curator of the Concordia female lodge in Montreal, in 1923 wrote to the Grand Council of Quebec and the Supreme Council in New York to protest 'the Fascist behaviour' of the Grand Venerable, Ottorino Incoronato, and Grand Orator, Liborio Lattoni, who, she explained, 'adhered' to the Fascist paper *Le Fiamme d'Italia*,[86] sang Fascist songs in public, and had saluted in Fascist mode at the banquet honouring the famous tenor Beniamino Gigli.[87]

Italian-Canadian women's anti-Fascist activities also reveal that women could be as militant as men. When the first biweekly anti-Fascist newspaper, *La Voce operaia*, appeared in Toronto in 1932, the Circolo Femminile A. (Anita) Garibaldi sent hearty congratulations. Women were notably active in Windsor, Ontario, where anti-Fascist forces were particularly strong owing to the presence of an anarchist group. (It might also have given the exiled anarchist couple Armando Borghi and Virgilia D'Andrea temporary refuge before they entered the United States following the executions of Sacco and Vanzetti.)[88] Windsor also boasted a Società Giovanile Italiana (Italian Youth Society), and an energetic group of women in the female Società Venezia, founded in 1928. A model women's volunteer organization, the Società Venezia in 1938 organized a Christmas party for over 300 children, who enjoyed music, a clown, and entertainment, along with Santa Claus and a small pack of *confetti* (almond candies). The presence of Miss White of the Board of Control, of Mrs Croll, the mayor's wife, and Miss Derma Serafini, president of the Youth Society, suggests the popularity that the Società Venezia enjoyed in Windsor's Italian community and beyond.[89] Following Canadian tradition, the anti-Fascists' children's Christmas party also provided an antidote to the pro-Fascist associations that held their childrens' parties on the Epiphany (when Italians traditionally treated their children with gifts) and turned the *Befana* (fairy) into a *Befana fascista*. The Società Venezia became Venezia Lodge of the anti-Fascist OIC in 1938.[90]

As this volume documents, Italian women's activism often developed

within familial and community contexts, and the surveillance files of the
Fascist police certainly reveal that subversive women were usually identified as members of radical families. Only a handful of women, among
them D'Andrea, were considered notorious enough to warrant their
own police file.[91] For Canada, the Fascist security forces determined that
at least four Italian-Canadian housewives were dangerous women in
need of watching. Rome ordered the Italian consulate in Canada to
investigate Elisabetta Presot in Windsor, and, in Toronto, the sisters
Rosina and Giovannina (Annina or Anna) Rossi and Rosa Pomanti.
Their files show us the movements of political exiles and the assessments
of state officials. Elisabetta Presot Piccinato and husband Antonio had
emigrated to France in 1922 and, later, Canada, where Antonio's three
brothers joined them in 1930. Accused of being in sympathy with *partiti
estremi* (extremist parties), Italian police monitored the Piccinatos' mail.
In May 1938, Italy's Ministry of Foreign Affairs requested the Consulate
General in Ottawa to report on the anti-Fascist activities of the four
Piccinato brothers and of Antonio's wife Elisabetta Presot, and provided
a photograph of the woman for the police record.

In a 1938 letter that Elisabetta sent to her sister Teresa in Pasiato,
Pordenone, Italy, the Fascist censor noted what he considered to be
some incriminating statements, and so investigators set out to discover
why a couple that had displayed good moral and 'political' behaviour in
Italy had changed their ways in Canada. In a dispatch from Ottawa dated
14 September 1938, the consulate forwarded information from the vice-
consul in Toronto to the effect that the Piccinatos had indeed 'changed'
their 'moral and political conduct'; they were 'mak[ing] their living
from illegal bootlegging activities ... etc.' Moreover, 'politically they speak
against Italy.'[92]

Like others who appear in the police files, it took little to prompt the
Fascist regime to monitor Rosa and Annina Pomanti of Toronto. Their
file was opened in 1929, when an anonymous letter from Toronto arrived at police headquarters in Teramo, Italy, accusing the women and
their husbands of being 'fervent communists.' The police commu-
nicated this allegation to the *Prefetto* (political of the province), the
Ministry of the Interior, and the Ministry of Foreign Affairs. A long
correspondence between staff in Italy and the consulates in Canada
appears to have produced little information or other results.[93]

Giovannina (Annina) Rossi's file was created as a result of a letter she
sent to her brother Nicola (residing at S. Elpidio a Mare, Ascoli Piceno),
in which she complained about Italy's economic situation and the high

cost of taxes and repairs she had to pay on a house she owned in S. Elpidio a Mare. 'I believe that in Italy the time has arrived that people can no longer live,' she wrote.

> Even we can see it. All that tax that is imposed on people who have some piece of property and the interest: *fa veramente schifo* (it is truly disgusting). Think about it: in tax, interest, and repairs we spent over L.6,000 and it was not enough; and us here [Canada], should we work for keeping a house [in Italy]? I am so mad that you cannot even imagine it. Couldn't we have a bit of luck and succeed in selling it? After all, we don't intend to return to Italy for good. For a month vacation, it is possible. But to reside there, forget about it. If it should happen that we would return we would lose the house in no time, for it is impossible to earn enough money to keep it.[94]

In the end, the Italian consul in Toronto cleared her of an anti-Fascist reputation. In a report from Ottawa to Rome, dated 13 October 1939, the Consul General A. Rossilonghi passed on information gathered by the vice-consulate in Toronto, which reported that 'Rossi, Giovannina [daughter] of the late Fabio residing at 102 Peterboro [*sic*] Street, Toronto, Ontario, is of good moral and political conduct. I am told that the above mentioned person shows patriotic sentiments.'[95]

All four women listed as anti-Fascist in the Fascist police records were housewives and married to working men, and not to political leaders or members of the elites in the immigrant communities. Their files reveal the degree to which the Fascist regime monitored Italians at home and abroad. That an anonymous letter or the violation of private correspondence between siblings could put into motion two ministries and their investigative apparatus reveals just how pervasive was Fascist and state surveillance in these years. It also reveals how hard it was for anti-Fascists to operate even in a liberal democratic country like Canada. Both the RCMP and Italian consular agents watched Italian anti-Fascists closely. Even when Canada was at war against Fascist Italy and Italian anti-Fascists supported the Canadian war effort, the Canadian authorities did not fully accept them. When the anti-Fascist newspaper *La Vittoria* appeared in 1942 in Toronto, both the Canadian government and the RCMP refused to approve it as it did not have the support of the Italian Catholic priests, who were enthusiastic supporters of Mussolini's regime. In short, Italian anti-Fascist women, especially leftists, were considered to be dangerous and found themselves in dangerous situations on both sides of the ocean.

Conclusion

The Fascist era offers a particularly graphic illustration of the complexity of Italian women's identities and experiences, and also shows how differing groups of both outsiders and insiders within the Italian-speaking community mobilized the gendered language of womanhood and motherhood to enlist women to their cause. For their part, Italian women's involvement in community affairs, even in subaltern roles, spoke to their desires and demands for greater respect from men. Ultimately, only a minority of Italian-Canadian women publicly advocated emancipation for all women, while those women who were pro-Fascist experienced the conundrum of being female activists in a movement that regarded women merely as reproducers of the race.[96] Furthermore, the socially active women who joined this or that political camp often did so in part out of loyalty to their men, though that did not necessarily free them from age-old sexism and internalized patriarchy. Still, the evidence underscores women's absolutely critical roles in their family and community, especially in tough economic times, such as the Depression, when women's resourcefulness was stretched to the limit. Perhaps only the tiny number of Italian-Canadian women who enjoyed relative economic comfort could afford the freedom – or aspire to the middle-class model of 'modern' homemaker – that Canadian society promised. As the political theorist and communist leader Antonio Gramsci put it, 'Each Lira you have is a bit of freedom you enjoy.' Economically stretched and politically oppressed, many Italian-Canadian families survived even the stresses of the war-time internment of men (approximately 600) largely because of women's actions. Some families reached the critical point, but few of them disintegrated.[97]

NOTES

I would like to thank Franca Iacovetta, Roberto Perin, and Gabriele Scardellato for their suggestions and encouragement.

1 See the editors' introduction to this volume and their discussion of national and female identities in Donna Gabaccia and Franca Iacovetta, 'Women, Work and Protest in the Italian Diaspora: An International Research Agenda,' *Labour / Le Travail* 42 (Fall 1998) 161–81; and essays by Maddalena Tirabassi (chapter 3) and Roslyn Pesman (chapter 12) in this volume.

2 Notwithstanding a long history of Italian immigration, Canada, like Australia (see Pesman in this volume) experienced its 'mass migration' of Italians after the Second World War. See, e.g., Franca Iacovetta, *Such Hardworking People: Italian Immigrants in Toronto* (Montreal: McGill-Queen's University Press, 1992) and, for a very recent effort to deal with a group of women workers in Canada who have been largely ignored, domestic workers, Stephanie Weisbart Bellini, 'The Kitchen Table Talks: Immigrant Italian Domestic Workers in Toronto's Post-War Years' (MA thesis, Memorial University of Newfoundland, 2001), which builds on Iacovetta, 'Primitive Villagers and Uneducated Girls: Canada Recruits Domestics from Italy, 1951–52,' *Canadian Woman Studies* 7, 4 (1986): 14–18.

3 A sample of this important body of work includes Robert F. Harney, 'Men without Women,' in Betty Boyd Caroli, Robert F. Harney, and Lydio F. Tomasi, eds., *The Italian Immigrant Woman in North America* (Toronto: Multicultural History Society of Ontario, 1977), 79–102; Bruno Ramirez, 'Brief Encounters: Italian Immigrant Workers and the CPR, 1900–30' *Labour / Le Travail* 17 (1986): 9–27; his *On the Move: French-Canadian and Italian Migrants in the North Atlantic Economy* (Toronto: McClelland and Stewart, 1991); Bruno Ramirez and Michelle Del Balso, *The Italians of Montreal: From Sojourning to Settlement, 1900–1921* (Montreal: Les Editions du Courant, 1980); John Zucchi, *Italians in Toronto: Development of a National Identity, 1875–1935* (Montreal: McGill-Queen's University Press, 1988); the Canadian essays in Caroli et al., *Italian Immigrant Woman in North America*, including Luigi Pautasso, 'La donna italiana durante il periodo fascista in Toronto, 1930–1940,' 168–90; Franc Sturino, *Forging the Chain* (Toronto: Multicultural History Society of Ontario, 1991); Angelo Principe, 'Note sul radicalismo tra gli italiani in Canada (1900–1915),' in Valeria Gennaro Lerda, ed., *Canada e Stati Uniti* (Venice: Marsilio Editore, 1984), 147–56; John Potestio and Angelo Pucci, *The Italian Immigrant Experience* (Thunder Bay, ON: Italian Canadian Historical Association, 1988); and Gabriele Scardellato, 'Italian Immigrant Workers in Powell River, BC: A Case Study of Settlement Before World War II,' *Labour / Le Travail* 16 (1985): 145–63. See also Franca Iacovetta, 'Writing Women into Immigration History: The Italian-Canadian Case,' *Altreitalie* 9 (1993): 24–47.

4 John Murray Gibbon, *Canadian Mosaic* (Toronto: McClelland and Stewart, 1975), 386; a more detailed quantitative analysis of Italian migration to Canada, 1860–1940, is in my PhD dissertation, 'The Concept of Italy in Canada and in Italian-Canadian Writings from the Eve of Confederation to the Second World War' (University of Toronto, 1989), chap. 1, 15–36.

5 E.g., the two Italian Roman Catholic churches of Montreal, Mount Carmel
   and Notre Dame de la Défense, celebrated 1525 marriages and 8056 baptisms between 1906 and 1923. See Bruno Ramirez and Michael Del Balso,
   The Italians of Montreal, 26.

6 Kenneth Douglas, quoted by Enrico Carlson Cumbo, 'As the Twig Is Bent,
   the Tree's Inclined': Growing Up Italian in Toronto, 1905–1940' (PhD
   thesis, University of Toronto, 1996).

7 Mark M. Orkin, *The Great Stork Derby* (Don Mills, ON: General Publishing
   Co., 1981), 78; Vince Bagnato, *Half-a-Buck: Nobody and Me* (Erin, ON:
   Boston Mills Press, 1984), 12; Angela Baldassare, 'Grace Bagnato,' in
   Tandem-Corriere Canadese, 12 Mar. 2000; and my letter in ibid., clearing up
   some historical misconceptions concerning how the name Grace Street, in
   Toronto, was derived.

8 Emiliana P. Noether claims that illiteracy rates in the regions of southern
   Italy 'declined very slowly' in this period, and that 'the illiteracy rate for
   women remained particularly high.' Noether, 'The Silent Half: Le Contadine del Sud before the First World War,' in Caroli et al., *Italian Immigrant
   Woman*, 11, n. 8.

9 Maria Ardizzi, *Made in Italy* (Toronto: Toma Publishing, 1982).

10 Quoted in Filippo Salvatore, *Le fascisme et les Italiens a Montréal: Une histoire
   orale* (Toronto: Guernica, 1995), 233 (translated from French); Penny
   Petrone, *Breaking the Mould* (Toronto: Guernica, 1995), 104, quoted in
   Charlene Gannage, *Double Day Double Bind: Women Garment Workers* (Toronto: Women's Press, 1986), 48. While this last example is taken from a
   post-1945 immigrant woman, it illustrates a theme that is nonetheless
   relevant to the earlier period.

11 Victor Casorso, *The Casorso Story: A Century of Social History in the Okanagan
   Valley* (Okanagan Falls, BC: Rima Books, 1983).

12 See the stories in Leopolda Dobrzensky, *They Worked and Prayed Together:
   Italians in Haliburton Country* (Haliburton, ON: 1988).

13 Adolphus Knoph, 'The Smaller Family,' *Survey* 37 (1916): 161, cited in
   Elizabeth Ewen, *Immigrant Women in the Land of Dollars* (New York: Monthly
   Review Press, 1985), 87; on Canada, see, e.g., Nancy M. Forestell, 'Bach-
   elors, Boarding-Houses, and Blind Pigs: Gender Construction in a Multi-
   Ethnic Mining Camp, 1900–1920,' in Franca Iacovetta et al., eds., *A Nation
   of Immigrants: Women, Workers and Communities in Canadian History* (Toronto:
   University of Toronto Press, 1998); Harney, 'Men without Women.'

14 On this subject, see the editors' introduction and Tirabassi's essay (chapter
   3) in this volume.

15 Amy A. Bernardy, 'Relazione sulle condizioni delle donne e dei fanciulli italiani negli Stati del Centro e dell'Ovest della Confederazione del Nord-America,' in *Bollettino dell'Emigrazione* (1911): 70.

16 *The Evening Telegram*, Toronto, 13 June 1921; Jean Scarpaci, 'La Contadina, The Plaything of the Middle Class Woman Historian,' *Journal of Ethnic Studies* 9 (1981): 21–38.

17 'Adulteries, infanticides, and vendettas are the order of the day,' reported De Nobili in his survey of Calabria in 1907, quoted by Robert F. Harney, 'Men without Women,' 154. Also, 'anche contro le donne che lavoravano nel terziario veniva indirizzata l'accusa di prostituzione, che in precedenza era stata rivolta contro le operaie' (middle-class women holding jobs were, like their working-class sisters, accused of prostitution as well). Gloria Chianese, *Storia Sociale della donna italiana (1800–1980)* (Naples: Guida editori, 1980), 29.

18 Michele Colabella, *Bonefro. 'Gente foretana'* (Isernia: Cosmo Iannone Editore, 1999), 65, trans. Celestino De Iulis. See also Reeder's discussion of the 'vedove bianche' (white widows) in this volume (chapter 1).

19 Both quotations from Giovanni Verga, *I Malavoglia* (The House by the Medlar Tree) (Milan: Mondadori, 1951).

20 See Giuseppe Ricci, *L'orfano di padre: Le memorie di Giuseppe Ricci* (Toronto: Astra, 1981), 134–5. See also the young man who explained to sociologist Charles M. Bayley that 'we go out with French-Canadian girls until we are ready to get married and then we look for an Italian girl'; 'The Social Structure of the Italian and Ukrainian Immigrant Communities, Montreal, 1935–1937' (MA thesis, McGill University, 1939), 284.

21 Cited in Mary Giordano, *The Banana Bunch* (n.p., n.d.), 71.

22 Interview with Giuseppina Gatto-M., Angelo Principe collection; cited in Cumbo, 'As the Twig Is Bent,' 113. About Italians on the west coast, Amy Bernardy wrote: 'When it was necessary for an [Italian] girl to go to work in a factory, her mother took her to work [in the morning] and walked her home [in the evening].' 'Relazione sulle condizioni delle donne,' 39.

23 The *Mail and Empire*, 2 Oct. 1897.

24 According to one source, the age of marriage for Italian girls in these years was 'fourteen to sixteen years old'; 'Entretien avec Carmela Galardo-Frascarelli,' in Salvatore, *Le fascisme*, 234.

25 Bernardy, 'Relazione sul condizioni delle donne,' 88.

26 Giordano, *The Banana Bunch*, 33, 34–5.

27 'Gioconda Maglio, *A Biography by Her Family*' (n.p., n.d.), 7; my thanks to my colleague, Gabriele Scardellato for placing this, and other material on Italians in western Canada, at my disposal.

28 On male sexism in the Italian left see, e.g., the essays by Caroline Waldron Merithew (chapter 7), Jennifer Guglielmo (chapter 8), and Robert Ventresca and Franca Iacovetta (chapter 9) in this volume; Michael Miller Topp, 'The Lawrence Strike: The Possibilities and Limitations of Italian American Syndicalist Transnationalism,' in Donna R. Gabaccia and Fraser M. Ottanelli eds., *Italian Workers of the World: Labor Migration and the Formation of Multiethnic States* (Urbana and Chicago: University of Illinois Press, 2001).

29 *Il Proletario* (Philadelphia), 10 June 1906.

30 *Il Martello*, 16 Apr. 1918, 5. In 1920, the anarchist Carlo Tresca, editor, transformed the paper from a monthly to a weekly.

31 See, e.g., the discussion of Maria Cazzola below.

32 Petrone, *Breaking the Mould*, 58; 'Gioconda Maglio,' *A Biography*, 24.

33 Bettina Bradbury, *Working Families* (Toronto: McClelland and Stewart, 1993), 13.

34 Maglio, *A Biography*, 27.

35 More research is required before we can usefully compare Toronto to Wisconsin, where Diane Vecchio (see her essay, chapter 5) found wives who ran both outside and inside aspects of the family grocery store or business, as well as widows who took over the family shop. On the point that discussions of 'family' businesses or small entrepreneurs usually ignore women, see also Iacovetta, *Such Hardworking People*.

36 On this point, wives and mothers played a similar role; for example, one woman recalled that when her construction worker father was unemployed in winter, her mother sought factory work so they could survive. 'Entretien avec Maria De Grandis-Marrelli,' in Salvatore, *Le fascisme*, 209.

37 *Report of the Royal Commission on the Relations of Labour and Capital* (Ottawa: Government of Canada, 1889), 828.

38 Italian women are virtually invisible in Canadian feminist studies of working women and the left; see the relevant discussion in the editors' introduction.

39 Bayley, 'Social Structure of the Italian and Ukrainian Immigrant Communities,' 279.

40 'Entretien avec Carmela Galardo-Frascarelli,' 233.

41 Cited in James Louis Di Giacomo, 'They Live in the Moneta: An Overview of the History and Changes in Social Organization of Italians in Timmins,' in *Polyphony: The Bulletin of the Multicultural History Society of Ontario*, special issue on Italians in Ontario, vol. 7, 2 (Fall/Winter 1985): 83.

42 Bernardy, 'Sulle condizioni delle donne e dei fanciulli,' 78.

43 The essays in part I offer plenty of relevant examples of rural women's waged and non-waged labours. Here I add an extreme example: some

female seasonal harvest workers in the south were sent to work quite literally 'muzzled' (like dogs affected by rabies) so they would not consume the fruits they were hired to harvest. Camilla Ravera, *Breve storia del movimento femminile in Italia* (Rome: Editori riuniti, 1978), 63.

44 See, e.g., Annalee Golz, 'Uncovering and Reconstructing Family Violence: Ontario Criminal Case Files,' in Franca Iacovetta and Wendy Mitchinson, eds., *On the Case: Explorations in Social History* (Toronto: University of Toronto Press, 1998); Kathryn Harvey, 'To Love, Honour and Obey': Wife-beating in Working-Class Montreal, 1869–1879,' *Urban History Review* 19, 2 (October 1990): 128–40; and Linda Gordon, *Heroes of Their Own Lives: The Politics and History of Family Violence* (New York: Penguin Books, 1989).

45 Bernardy, 'Sulle condizioni delle donne e dei fanciulli,' 78

46 In conversation with relatives and friends, Joe C., who is now 85 years old, spoke freely about this episode, but did not want his full name published.

47 Giordano, *The Banana Bunch*, 33. For a contemporary example that refers to a post-1945 immigrant family, see Gianna Patriarca, *Daughters for Sale* (Toronto: Guernica Press, 1997), 21–2.

48 See 'La donna e la Forca,' *Il Proletario* 15, 25 (30 June 1911); Karen Dubinsky and Franca Iacovetta, 'Murder, Womanly Virtue, and Motherhood: The Case of Angelina Napolitano, 1911–1922,' *Canadian Historical Review* 72, 4 (1991): 503–31. On Giovanitti, see also Topp, 'The Lawrence Strike,' 151–2.

49 *Evening Telegram*, 13 June 1921; *Globe*, 13 June 1921; *Daily Mail and Empire*, 13 June 1921. One week before the shooting and stabbing, Mary Ciccalone had been found guilty of selling alcoholic beverages and had received a suspended sentence. On later developments, *Evening Telegram*, 31 Oct. 1921 and *Toronto Daily Star*, 29 Oct. 1921.

50 Giordano, *The Banana Bunch*, 22. For a male example, see Vince Bagnato's warm memories of growing up in a large family. Bagnato, *Half-a-Buck*, 12.

51 See Angelo Principe, 'Note sul radicalismo tra gli italiani in Canada (1900–1915),' 155–6; Nicoletta Serio, 'L'emigrato va alla guerra: I soldati italiani nel corpo di spedizine canadese (1914–1918),' in Luigi Bruti Liberati, ed., *Il Canada e la guerra dei trent'anni* (Milan: Edizioni Angelo Guerini e Associati, 1989), 109–38; and Camille Lauriente, *The Chronicles of Camille* (New York: Pageant Press, 1953), 203–7.

52 See National Archives of Canada, MG 30, C 94, Eugenio D'Angelo Collection, which contains photographs of the 'reservists' dining (including a dinner described as having been 'given by the ladies of the Italian Red Cross'), marching to Toronto's Union Station, and getting ready to leave for

Italy. The parades gave rise to a myth known as 'il treno degli italiani' (the train of Italians). When Gian Gasparro Napolitano, a journalist for the Italian newspaper *La Stampa*, visited Canada in 1932, he was driven around Toronto in a taxi owned by Mr Scandiffio, an Italian-Canadian supporter of Mussolini and Fascism, who described the First World War parades. Napolitano probably embellished the story, since it fit well with Fascist Italy's agenda. In his book *Troppo grano sotto la neve* (Milan: Casa editrice Ceschina, 1936), 36–8, he describes a train that crossed Canada from Vancouver to the east, stopping at every station to pick up Italian volunteers and reservists.

53 Evidently, community leaders did not think the two existing Italian-language papers, *L'Araldo del Canada* (Montreal) and *La Tribuna Canadiana* (Toronto), were enough; on the editorial policy in *L'Italia*, see Angelo Principe, *The Darkest Side of the Fascist Years, 1920–1941* (Toronto: Guernica, 1999), 63–84.

54 *Il Progresso italo-americano* (New York), 14 Jan. 1918.

55 See *L'Eco italo-canadese* (Vancouver), June 1940.

56 The team led by Mrs Armstrong collected $1688.17; Mrs Reynolds's team raised $1686.50; Miss Romanelli's and Mrs C. Muto's teams collected $1079.63 and $795.90 respectively. The provincial government donated $10,000 and Toronto City Hall $7500. Principe, 'The Concept of Italy in Canada,' 100–1; Il Carroccio (New York), September 1918, 282; Toronto *Daily Star*, 22 Aug. 1918; Toronto *World*, 23 Aug. 1918; Toronto *Globe*, 22 Aug. 1918.

57 Vangelisti, Guglielmo *Gli italiani in Canada* (Montreal: Chiesa italiana di N.S. della difesa, 1958), 201.

58 For example, some middle-class women *patronesse* organized and ran L'Orfanotrofio, an orphanage that opened in the Madonna del Carmine parish in Montreal in 1922, in the wake of the many deaths caused by the postwar Spanish influenza epidemic. Although the orphanage was administered by nuns of the Compassionate Order under Mother Camilla Boffa, many women did a great deal of fund-raising and visited it. Italian Protestant women were active in promoting the welfare of needy Italians; their organizations were active during the Depression in Montreal, Toronto, and Hamilton. On Italian parishes in Montreal, see Vangelisti, *Gli italiani in Canada*; for Toronto, see Zucchi, *Italians in Toronto*; and on Hamilton see Diana Brandino, 'The Italians in Hamilton' (MA thesis, University of Western Ontario, 1977).

59 For details, see Marino Culos (a founder) in *L'Eco italo-canadese* of Vancouver (23 Mar. 1940), who notes that the League continued its 'precious social

and charitable activities' for some years, never forgetting to support the Italian school or the Sacred Heart Italian church.

60 They were Maria Dora, Grand Orator, 1920–4, and Maria Della Giustina, Grand Administrative Secretary, 1926–30; Gabriele P. Scardellato, *Within Our Temple: A History of the Order Sons of Italy of Ontario* (Toronto: Order Sons of Italy of Canada, 1995), 77–8.

61 The women who led the Order in Ontario in the critical years 1940–3 were Giulietta Galasso, Gemma Galasso, Tonietta Irwin, Clementina Sauro, and Delfina Vistorino. Ibid., 75. On the internment, see Franca Iacovetta, Roberto Perin, and Angelo Principe, eds., *Enemies Within: Italians and Other Internees in Canada and Beyond* (Toronto: University of Toronto Press, 2000) especially the essays by Luigi Bruti Liberati and Michelle McBride.

62 The women were Antonietta Volpe, Teresa Anselmo, Fernanda Vottero, Giuseppina Bortolotti, and Lauretta Ivone; the men were Vigilante Nidata, president, August Mei, Antonino V. Spada, Raffaele Rossi, Carlo Peressi, Luigi Palermo, Anselmo Bortolotti, and Sabino Bozzer. See Spada, *Italians in Canada* (Ottawa: Canada Ethnica VI, 1969), 100.

63 Ibid., 100–2.

64 *Il Bollettino italo-canadese* (5 May 1938); Angelo Principe and Olga Zorzi Pugliese, *Rekindling Faded Memories: The Founding of the Famee Furlane of Toronto and Its First Years* (Toronto: Famee Furlane, 1996), 32; *La Nostra storia (Our History) 1938–1988* (Toronto: Società Femminile Friulana, 1988).

65 In ancient Rome, the lictorial fasces were symbols of authority, as the sceptre is today.

66 See, e.g., the photos taken by one of these young women of Hamilton, in Iacovetta, Perin, and Principe, *Enemies Within*, 101; and, for more details, the essay by Luigi Pennacchio and others in *ibid.* See also the letter by Ersilia Sauro (one of the young women who went on the trip to Italy) sent to *La Nuova Italia* (Montreal) in Principe, *The Darkest Side*, 222–3.

67 Benito Mussolini, *Opera omnia*, vol. 21: 302 (Florence: La Fenice); Maria Antonietta Macciocchi, *La donna 'nera': 'Consenso' femminile e fascismo* (Milan: Feltrinelli, 1976). In 1925, Italian women obtained the right to vote in the municipal election. They, however, never had the chance to vote because the following year, 1926, the Fascist government abolished civic elections.

68 Macciocchi, *La donna 'nera,'* 49, 111.

69 Brigidi dispatch to Rome, 9 May 1935 (Archivio Storico, Ministero Affari Esteri, Inventario Serie Affari Politici, Sezione Canada, 1931–45).

70 *L'Italia*, 2 Mar. 1935; Victoria DeGrazia, *How Fascism Ruled Women* (Berkeley: University of California Press, 1992); Rosella Isidori Frasca, *E il duce le volli sportive* (Bologna: Pátron Editore, 1983).

71 NAC, Memorandum to the Inter-Departmental Committee, Ottawa, 23 Sept. 1940; 40 D 269-1-D-754; MWJ/LIJ; Re: Mrs Carmela Frascarelli (female), Montreal, PQ.

72 Sylvie D'Augerot-Arend, 'Why So Late? Cultural and Institutional Factors in the Granting of Quebec and French Women's Political Rights,' *Journal of Canadian Studies / Revue d'études canadiennes* 26, 1: 143.

73 The information and quotations in this paragraph, if not otherwise indicated, come from Filippo Salvatore's 'Entretien avec Carmela Galardo-Frascarelli.' To date, no one has explored the role of Italian-Canadian women in the struggle for the right of Quebec women to vote.

74 They included Dr Laura D'Anna, Giuseppina Di Ioia, Carmela Galardo-Frascarelli, Fosca Gibilei, Etelvina Frediani, Filomena Riccio, Maria Spaziani, Francesca Olivieri, and Antonietta Mancuso. See RCMP Headquarters, 'C' Department, Ottawa, 4 Oct. 1940, to the Hon. E. Lapointe, PC, KC, Minster of Justice and Attorney General of Canada, Ottawa, Ontario; NAC, RG 18, vol. 3563, file N, C 11-19-2-3.

75 These women, along with some German and Canadian women, were taken to Kingston Penitentiary, where a special section, away from the ordinary inmates, was reserved for female political internees. See Michelle McBride, 'The Curious Case of Female Internees,' in Iacovetta, Perin, and Principe, *Enemies Within*.

76 'Entretien avec Carmela Galardo-Frascarelli,' 242.

77 When I first mentioned Cazolla's activities in my 'Note sul radicalismo tra gli italiani in Canada dalla Prima Guerra Mondiale alla Conciliazione,' I hoped that someone would take the lead and carry out further research, but to date this still remains only a hope. It appears that Cazzola left behind no writings or personal information about herself. My information is derived from a long interview with the now-deceased Anselmo Bortolotti of Ottawa, who had met her several times, and from the brief references made to her in a commemorative article, 'Nello Vergani – Mafaldo Rossi, un Martire!' by Antonino Spada (which appeared in *Il Lavoratore*, a socialist paper published in Toronto, 18 Sept. 1937), and in *Il Lavoratore* and *La Parola degli italo-canadesi* and Italian-American left-wing newspapers.

78 See the essay by Robert Ventresca and Franca Iacovetta in this volume.

79 See Angelo Principe, 'The Difficult Years of the Order Sons of Italy (1920–1926),' *Italian Canadiana* (Centre for Italian Canadian Studies, Dept. of Italian Studies, University of Toronto) 5 (1989): 104–16.

80 How *Il Risveglio* was silenced is described by Antonino Spada in his *The Italians in Canada*, 113–14.

81 Spada explains (*Il Lavoratore*, 18 Sept. 1937) that Rossi had to leave Canada

and take refuge in the U.S. because his Italian boss, a Fascist at the Windsor Hotel, reported him to the police and he was being sought by immigration officials.

82 *La Voce,* 11 Mar. 1939; 10 and 20 Jan., 2 and 15 Feb., 23 Mar., and 29 Apr. 1940. For the Italian anti-Fascists fighting in Spain in the Italian Garibaldi Battalion, Cazzola collected $6.10. On Cazolla, see also *Il Lavoratore,* 20 Mar. 1937. The modest but important donations were as follows: 'Montreal, Quebec, A mezzo Maria Cazzola: T. Beretti 25c.; M. Cazzola 50c.; De Simone 25c.; L. Talarico 25c.; P. Nobile 25c.; I. Rossanigo 25c.; N. Vigilanti 25c.; Augusto 20c.; R.C. 25c.; G. Lonzo 10c.; G. Rastelli 10c.; Piatti 10c.; Pavone 25c.; Monferant 10c.: V. Galante 10c.; Gianpaolo 10 c.; L. Cottelesi 10 c.; C. Rapattoni 10 c.; Ciro Frabbro $1.00; L. Londei 10c.; A. Sandelli 10c.; m. Prato 25 c.; P Lorenzetti 25c.; L. Bennero 25c.; F. Talevi 10c.; Marfoglio 10c.; G. Pellini 25c.; Volpi 25c.; G. Cantoni 10c.; A. Iannacci 25c.; Delonzo 10c.; Sebastiano 25c.; G. Galiardino 10c.; Adele Galante 10c.'

83 Augusto Bersani's papers (not catalogued yet), Multicultural History Society of Ontario.

84 See *Il Martello* (New York), 1 Mar. 1920.

85 See Allen Seager, 'Class, Ethnicity, and Politics in the Alberta Coalfields, 1905–1945,' in Dirk Hoerder, ed., *Struggle a Hard Battle* (DeKalb: Northern Illinois University Press, 1986), 312.

86 On its editorial policy and its editor and publisher, Nanni Leone Castelli, see Angelo Principe, *The Darkest Side.*

87 See *Il Martello,* 29 Dec. 1923.

88 See the essay by Iacovetta and Ventresca in this volume.

89 See *La Voce degli italo-canadesi,* 3 June 1939. Over the years Signora V. Bocchini, Angelina Carpenti, Assunta Zuana, Nina Bortolotti, Rosina Menchini, and others headed the society.

90 See *Il Lavoratore,* 8 Jan. 1937.

91 See Ventresca and Iacovetta's essay in this volume; and Franca Iacovetta and Robert Ventresca, 'Italian Radicals in Canada: On Sources in Italy,' *Labour / Le Travail* 37 (Spring 1996): 205–20.

92 See Elisabetta Presot's file, Archivio Centrale dello Stato (ACS), Casellario Politico Centrale (CPC), b4121. Unfortunately, the letter discussed here is no longer in the CPC file.

93 Unaware of their own consular structure in Canada, the Ministry of Foreign Affairs requested from the consulate in Montreal information on the Po-mantis. This office sent the minister the following note: 'I have the honour to inform His Excellency that the three notes (N. 7548/25525.S., N. 7548/25526–S) have been transmitted to the Royal General Consulate in Ottawa,

the Province of Ontario being under its jurisdiction.' We don't know if the consulate in Ottawa answered the ministry's request and there is no answer from Ottawa in the Pomantis' files.

94 See Rosa and Anna Pomanti, ACS, CPC, b4072.
95 For Rossi, Giovannina, see ACS, CPC, b4446.
96 See DeGrazia, *How Fascism Ruled Women.*
97 See, 'Entretien avec Carmela Galardo-Frascarelli,' 243.

12 Italian Women and Work in Post–Second World War Australia: Representation and Experience[1]

Roslyn Pesman

While from the time of the arrival of the First Fleet in 1788, the Australian population was composed of people from every part of the world and while today's ethnic communities filio-pietistically trace their founding fathers to the first days of white settlement, the history of white Australia until 1945 is primarily that of the transplantation of Anglo-Celtic peoples, law, religions, institutions, and customs.[2] Migration from Continental Europe was a central event in the history of the Americas from the mid-nineteenth century; it was not until a century later that it became of equivalent significance in the history of Australia. In the late nineteenth and early twentieth century, emigrants from the Italian peninsula showed little inclination to move so far from home as the 'America' in the south; the Australian Commonwealth census for 1901 records fewer that six thousand Italians resident. Thirty years later, the Italian-born still only numbered 26,756.[3] It was not until after the signing of the Migration Agreement between Italy and Australia in 1951 that Italians moved to Australia in significant numbers; between 1947 and 1971 the Italian-born in Australia rose from 33,756 to 289,476.[4] The migrants came overwhelmingly from the north-east and south of Italy and from Sicily as yet another wave in the global movements that drove and sucked the denizens of declining and impoverished rural worlds into the maws of the industrialized and industrializing centres.

The great European exodus to the United States of the 1890s was characterized by a conspicuous female presence (even though overall, men clearly outnumbered women), but few women participated in the

Italian emigration to Australia before the Second World War.[5] At the end of the nineteenth century, women constituted only some 11 per cent of the Italian-born; by the mid-1930s, they numbered about a quarter, and on the eve of mass migration, about one-third. Yet almost as many women as men arrived in the 1950s and 1960s, so that by 1971 women accounted for 45 per cent of the Italian-born population.

As an event in Australian history, Italian mass migration was over almost as soon as it had begun. From the early 1970s, the rate of emigration dropped rapidly, so that the Italian-born component of the population was slightly less in 1981 than it had been a decade earlier. According to the 1981 census, 80 per cent of the Italian-born had lived in Australia for more than fifteen years. When an event is over, its history begins. The Italian-born women of Australia are still awaiting their history. They make but fleeting appearances in histories of women; in the first feminist history of Australia published in 1994, the postwar women immigrants are disposed of in two pages.[6] And they have received equally scant treatment in the few general histories of Italian migration, none of which treat gender as a major category of analysis.[7] Indeed, a recent collection of documents on Italian migration carries the masculinist title of *Migrants and Mates* – 'mates' in Australia being the signifier *plus outré* of male bonding.[8]

The most visible work on Italian women in Australia has been done by sociologists such as Ellie Vasta, the daughter of Italian immigrants,[9] as well as anthropologists, social workers, and activists rather than by historians, and most often in general studies of women of non-English-speaking background with little 'Italian' specificity.[10] The predominance of sociologists has meant that the focus is on the postwar immigrant women.[11] Also, as Donna Gabaccia has noted, sociologists remain more concerned with structure, theory, and measurement than with interpretation and lived experience.[12] Thus, enlightening as much of past and current research is, what is usually missing are the dimensions of time, of place – the diverse and diverging Italies that the women left – and of comparison – with the experience of the women who migrated elsewhere, including to other parts of the peninsula and of Europe and with those who remained behind – and the dimension of migration itself as a process alongside departure and settlement. The neglect of the Italies which the women left may also explain another feature of research and writing on Italian women in Australia, and that is the focus on their lives in the paid workforce. In contrast to North America, there have been no

Australian case studies of women's roles in ethnic communities or in ethnic-group formation[13] 'Family' and 'community' are even more complex and nuanced processes than 'work.'

During the postwar decades of heavy immigration, both public authorities and private citizens expected their 'New Australians' to forget the 'old,' to assimilate, and hence to disappear from sight. As one young woman has written of her mother's generation: 'They grew up in a country that did not acknowledge their presence, that provided no information for them, a country that allowed my mother to sit in Casualty for 12 hours because no one could tell her to go home.'[14] Official discourse was gender-blind; migrants were single males; women were appendages, as in the phrase 'migrants and their families.' Although the majority of the women did arrive as wives, daughters, mothers, *fidanzate* (fiancés), and proxy brides, not all of them did so.[15]

The Australian government had encouraged and sponsored the migration of Italian women from the early 1960s to redress the gender imbalance in the migrant population, to provide wives for the large number of single males of so-called Latin temperament who were seen as a potential threat to social order, and to create family units for the reproduction of workers and consumers.[16] The women immigrants fulfilled the state agenda: according to the 1971 census, just under 5 per cent of the Italian-born women over the age of nineteen had never been married, in contrast to some 17 per cent of the Australian-born. In addition to their role as reproducers, however, Italian women were producers in the public sector.

Despite the prevailing ideological campaign of the 1950s and 1960s pushing women to the domestic world of home and family, despite the stereotypes that confined Italian women as domestically devoted servants to their husbands and children, large numbers of Italian immigrant women in Australia, including wives and mothers, took on wage-earning jobs. In 1966, 34 per cent of Italian-born women were in the workforce as opposed to 23 per cent of the Australian-born, and 33 per cent of the married Italian-born as opposed to 24 per cent of their Australian counterparts. This pattern is all the more important when we consider that Italian women were more notably clustered in the child-bearing age range, dropping out of the workforce from their mid-forties.[17] Those reproducing were also producing.

The bulk of Italian women were working in manufacturing, and they were concentrated in the clothing, textile, and footwear industries, at the lowest levels of the labour hierarchy, a concentration that has characterized female migration to the industrialized world.[18] According to the 1954 census, 62 per cent of Italian migrant women in the workforce were employed in manufacturing and, in 1966, 55 per cent.[19] Countless studies have documented that official figures by no means account for the working lives of immigrant women or their contribution to the economy of their adopted home,[20] and Australia is no exception. Omitted from official labour statistics were the Italian mothers of Mariella Vallesi and Rita Price; the former did dressmaking at home, the latter worked in the kitchen of the family's waterfront cafe in Port Melbourne.[21] Official statistics ignore the work done by the women in family small-business enterprises, such as in food shops, and in the farming sector, on the cane fields of Queensland, on tobacco farms, and in orchards, a sector where the pre-war women had also worked. The literature of international migration shows an increasing emphasis on the role of women in ethnic business enterprise and capital accumulation, and the argument is now being made in the Australian context.[22] Also hidden in the official statistics is the paid work done by women at home, outwork for the clothing industry, child-minding, and cooking and cleaning for boarders. We might also figure in the women who wanted to work but were prevented by their inability to find satisfactory child care.[23] As one woman said of her grandmother, 'Nanna would have liked a job to make a little money and relieve the boredom of the day, but she didn't know where to find one, and had nobody to look after the children.'[24]

Ironically, little notice was taken of Italian-born women in the decade when their participation in the workforce was highest, when they were in their child-bearing years, when their children were young, and when the pressures of double time were greatest. It was precisely at the time when Italian migration was tapering off that they began to attract attention. By the early 1970s it had become obvious that Australia's migrants were not going to assimilate and, with the abandonment of the White Australia policy and the arrival of Vietnamese refugees, Australia's population base had become far more complex. At the same time, again undoubtedly under the influence of events overseas, of the 'new ethnicity' in the United States, the ethnic middle classes were beginning to flex their muscles. Other strategies beyond assimilation for the incorporation of immigrants into Australian society were now required. And after an integrationist phase, multiculturalism was adopted. In 1975 Ethnic Communities Councils were appointed in the two most populous states, New South Wales and Victoria.

It was not, however, the male leaders of the ethnic communities now in the process of being constructed who drew attention to the women immigrants, but rather radical and/or feminist activists, social workers, and reformers within the bureaucracies, trade unions, and welfare organizations. As Jean Martin argued in 1978, acknowledgment of the migrant presence coincided with the re-emergence of feminism.[25] The Italian women, alongside other migrant women of non-English-speaking background (NESB), became visible in a plethora of reports that add up to a literature of disadvantage, studies of exploitation and neglect in the workplace, of mental and physical breakdown, of the failure of medical and hospital systems to serve those whose English was non-existent or minimal.[26] Workplace studies revealed that the women were employed in the heaviest and dirtiest jobs, in repetitive boring work, in factories that often operated with poor sanitation, ventilation, and lighting and substandard equipment. Migrant working women were subjected to speed-up practices and were vulnerable to sexual harassment and to racist prejudice on the part of bosses and other workers. Working mostly in industries where compulsory unionism applied, the women were union members, but in the 1950s and 1960s they were of little interest to monolingual Australian and British-born male trade-union organizers who shared the ignorance of the wider community.[27] As one woman recalled: 'The organizer comes and talks always in English, he talks and talks and I don't know a thing.'[28] In their lack of militancy in the workplace in these years, the women were no different from their Italian sisters also newly arrived in Canada or their Australian-born co-workers.[29]

The inquiries and reports of the mid-1970s were unashamedly interventionist and partisan, and intended to provoke action. The authors of one such study characteristically declared that their efforts 'to systematically describe the perceptions and needs of migrant women workers from some Melbourne factories regarding their everyday work situation' were 'only one part of a wider project, which was primarily concerned to develop ways of assisting migrant women workers to organize themselves so that they could more easily articulate their situation and their needs.' These various inquiries also set the agenda for the construction of knowledge about immigrant women of non-English-speaking background for the next twenty years, an agenda that concentrated on documenting exploitation and disadvantage and called for action to improve conditions by the introduction of such measures as proper child care, language instruction and training on the job, adequate interpreter services, and more control over outwork. Furthermore, the spokespersons about and for the women remained for the most part feminists and activists, including by the 1980s women from ethnic backgrounds, working in the bureaucracies, welfare sector, and in agencies established to deal with ethnic affairs. Research report followed research report and conference followed conference on the problems of women of non-English-speaking background.[30]

The activists and reformers of the 1970s did make Italian immigrant women and their disadvantage visible, but their constructions need to be examined. The focus on Australian agencies and policies diverted attention from the process of emigration and the inherent losses, disadvantage, and displacement regardless of destination. Their work also tended to perpetuate the image of the women as a problem, as helpless, passive victims without the capacity for choice or action.[31]

The same comment might be made about the very small amount of academic scholarship on NESB women that has been done from the early 1980s by sociologists and anthropologists, particularly academic women who were both feminists and critics of capitalism. Their discussions quickly became centred on the relative roles of class, gender, and ethnicity in disadvantaging immigrant women, but their work did not lead to in-depth studies of the lives of Italian-born women.[32] It could be argued that the investigation of the 1970s and 1980s represented Italian and other immigrant women as objects to be championed and as evidence in a critique of immigration and settlement policies intended to precipitate widespread structural reform. What is missing from the studies and reports are the Italian women in the role of actors and agents in their own lives, their lived experience, their perspectives, their agendas.

In the early 1980s a new stage in the construction of non-English-speaking women immigrants in Australia took place, again in line with developments in North America and Britain. Immigrant women and their daughters began to speak out and to accuse Australian feminists of ethnocentricity.[33] Among the first were women in the Federation of Migrant Workers and Families (FILEF), an international organization of Italian migrants affiliated with the Italian Communist party. The *donne* (women) of FILEF, a group formed in 1975, were very active, with some success in the areas of child care and English language lessons on the job and in the election of migrant women as officials in the Clothing and Allied Trades Union in New South Wales. They were among those who formed the Migrant Women's Caucus after the 1981 Australian Council of Trade Unions Conference.[34] FILEF was also the first organization to encourage immigrant men and women to tell their stories and to publish them.[35]

The women of FILEF prioritized class over gender and were anxious to defend Italian women and their culture from what they saw as Anglo-Australian disabling stereotypes. Confronting views that attributed the failure of Italian-born women to participate in community life to Italian patriarchy, FILEF women argued that Italian patriarchy was less a problem for the immigrant women than was their class position, the isolation and loneliness intrinsic in the migration process, and Australian racism and structural patriarchy. With regard to the family, Italian women might have agreed with Australian feminists that the family is the site of female oppression, but they also argued that it was an ambiguous and contradictory site; for immigrant women the family could also be a sphere of validation and a base of opposition from which they could act.[36] Gabaccia's observation that modern Americans, including feminists, have difficulty in accepting a concept of self or identity that is created primarily through relations to others within families also applies in the Australian context.[37]

By the mid-1980s other Italian women in Australia were forming and joining associations to put their needs on the public agenda and secure action. In 1985 the Italian-Australian Women's Association was formed under the leadership of Franca Arena, who was later to be appointed as a Labour member of the New South Wales Parliament. In the same year the association held its first conference on the contribution of Italo-Australian women to Australian society, a conference attended by 800 women at its Sydney session and 600 when it met in Melbourne.[38] Beyond specifically Italian groups, immigrant women were also banding together in such organizations as the Association of Non–English Speaking Background Women of Australia and the Immigrant Women's Speakout Association of NSW, founded in 1985, which received government funding to establish the Immigrant Women's Resource Centre to develop services for NESB women. The association also monitors government policy, conducts research in relevant key areas, and holds conferences.[39]

Shifting Constructions, Continuing Conundrums

The moves over the past decade by Italian women in their own organizations and now in collaboration with other NESB women have been directed towards representing their own interests, speaking and acting as pressure groups for themselves. The leaders tend to be women of the second generation, educated women who are working in bureaucracies, welfare agencies, research units and, like Vasta and Caroline Alcorso, in universities. Yet they too can fall into the trap of speaking for or objectifying the lives of their mothers or of their working-class sisters.

In the late 1980s under the impact of international debates that emphasized the need to restore agency to subaltern groups, the focus in constructions of immigrant women shifted from their representation as victims to their representation as agents.[40] The aim of a paper that Vasta published in 1991 was 'to outline not only the discrimination suffered by migrant women, but also their struggles and resistance against such oppression.'[41] She has argued that Italian immigrant women 'do not experience discrimination passively, but often construct new cultural forms, articulate their own ideas and rely on their own historical and cultural traditions as a means of support,' and that 'second generation Italo-Australians have used the cultural practices of their ethno-histori-cal past and developed new cultural competencies to deal with discrimi-natory and marginalizing practices of Australian society.'[42] Further research needs to be done on the precise ways that the women deployed their cultural practices to adapt to the present and future. There is no work being done comparable to that in North America on the multiple and changing links among those who emigrate and those who stay, on the concept of a mobile community spread across a variety of sites.[43]

To write about the way the Italian women deployed their past to take charge of their futures requires an encounter with that past. A major weakness in all discussion and argument about the Italian women from the 1970s to the 1990s is ignorance of the backgrounds and culture of the women and reliance on uninformed stereotypes. This was in part the protest of the FILEF women. Typical of representations is the following extract from the agenda-setting 1978 Galbally report on migration and settlement: 'The Italian marriage is, in its southward manifestation, dominated by the husband who appears to carry full authority and full responsibility. To ensure the husband's status and honour a dutiful wife will foster, in public, the image of a submissive wife ... The public image is balanced by the "Madonna Complex" which places the mother on a pedestal where she is regarded as all-loving, all-giving, warm, compas-sionate and stoic.'[44]

When the migrants from the Italian peninsula arrived in Australia, most of them acquired two new identities; they were 'New Australians' and in most cases also 'New Italians' or 'New Southern Italians.' The women were homogenized into Mediterranean women, southern Euro-pean women, southern Italian women, Italian women. There was little recognition that they came from several Italies not Italy, and that their identity and customs were formed not by nation, nor even by region, but by locality, and that there was a considerable variety in customs and practices, in women's work outside the home, in the relationship between the public and the private, in gender relations, kin and community networks. As Lidio Bertelli suggested, the contradictory views as to whether the Italian family is patriarchal or matriarchal reflect regional variations.[45]

To take one example: contrary to Australian stereotypes, a recent study of one Calabrian village points to a society where, because of inheritance customs, it is women who own the land, who work the land alongside men, who participate in decisions about what to grow, and how to grow, and how to market. It is a village where the concept of honour does not appear to represent a dominant value, does not have the same importance it may have in other Calabrian villages.[46] It is the absence of the local perspective that marred the work of Constance Cronin on Sicilians in Australia. She did indeed live in a Sicilian village to observe customs and mores, but the lives of the inhabitants of the village of her fieldwork were compared with a random group of Sicilians in Australia who came from all over the island, and she too wrote in terms of southern Italian women and the southern Italian family. More attuned to the regional nuances of the Italian peninsula, Helen Andreoni in her investigation of a Sardinian community in rural New South Wales journeyed back to the home *paese*, lived among the women, and learned their traditional weaving techniques.[47]

Australians' ignorance about the pre-migration lives and culture of the women they studied in the 1970s is understandable. If the women of rural Italy were invisible in Australia in the 1950s and 1960s, they were equally invisible in research projects and scholarly literature in Italy.[48] Ignorance is less justified today in view of two decades of research on rural women in Italy.[49] Ignorance continues to discourage researchers from posing widely canvassed questions in the international literature on migration, such as on the impact of entry into the industrial workforce on the lives of the women, on family structures and interaction, and on gender relations.

But as Constance Cronin pointed out a generation ago, immigrants do not carry an entire culture on their backs.[50] They bring their own lived experience and myths and culture. This culture is not some timeless tradition but a process in the making. And the act of migration itself brings changes and adaptations. Culture is transmuted and adapted in the new world, so that what may appear to the outsider to be traditional is something already transformed in response to the migration experience.[51] For example, anthropologist Jeannie Martin observed that because of inadequate child care, the guilt induced in working mothers by local ideologies and by their own fears that their children might adopt different values and habits meant that immigrant women may have considered personal care of their children more important than would have been the case in their countries of origin.[52]

From the late 1980s new voices have joined the debate about Italian women in Australia, namely those of the women themselves who, in response to the new interest in gathering subjective experiences, and in encouraging living subjects to 'fight back' by telling their own life stories and those of their mothers and grandmothers, have participated in autobiographical writing, oral history projects, and interviews.[53] To statistics and ideology is added the much needed element of subjective experience, though, of course, the stories are not 'uncontaminated.' They absorb prevailing discourses and agendas, and depend on what the women remember and on what their collaborators and interviewers prompt them to remember.[54]

The women immigrants are now middle aged and elderly and create the pattern of the past from a present position – of satisfaction or of unhappiness. The life stories that have so far emerged by no means come from a random cross-section of the women. It is the resilient, the confident, and the comfortable who are more likely to tell their stories and seek publication. It was Emma who approached historian Michal Bosworth to help write her story. The stories in the volume *Forza e Coraggio (Give Me Strength)* were written in response to a competition organized by the Italian-Australian Women's Association. The interviews published recently by the women of FILEF in Adelaide document only success in the public world or resilience and triumph over adversity in the private. The children of the majority of women interviewed in the New South Wales FILEF oral history project had received university education. This is not surprising given that the women interviewed were found through the network of young, educated members of FILEF. The life stories can and have been, like all evidence, deployed selectively; in a recent literature review on the health of Italian-Australian women, for example, only those expressing the subjective experience of disadvantage are quoted.[55] In a context where the focus has been primarily on disadvantage and its elimination, life stories or interviews that do not conform to this theme can be disconcerting to reformers; the absence of expressions of dissatisfaction by mature women whose lives have involved constant hard work and who have low expectations has been explained away by culture, the fatalism of peasant women.[56]

There is both consistency and diversity in the stories that the women are telling. There are tales enough of exploitation in the workplace, of the stresses of double time, of regret and unhappiness. Yet many of the women nevertheless are very clear about their goals and aspirations. Almost a generation ago now, Joan Scott and Louise Tilly argued that women's working lives needed to be understood in the context of the economies of the family units upon which their survival depended.[57] It was financial necessity that placed the women in the workplace, but their working lives were fuelled by aspirations for a better standard of living for the family and the liberation of children from the poverty cycle. Often such desires were accompanied by a recognition that sacrifice, hard work, and tough times were the price to be paid for economic mobility. Dora Pallotta, an immigrant from Sicily, suffered all the indignities of immigrant life in Australia – separation from parents and home, living for years in a tin shed in the backyard of domineering relatives, a lifetime of factory and cleaning work while caring for her children. She used to tell her baby daughter: 'I'm going to work so hard and do what I can but you will have your own home when you get married.' 'You will be free and independent and your own boss when you are grown-up,' she promised, 'and no one's slave.'[58]

Another woman interviewed by an Italian journalist in 1977 had no doubt that her hard life – farming, working in a bar, running a fruit shop – had yielded its goals. Those goals, as she put it, were 'il lavoro, la terra per mio marito e me, lo studio per i nostri due figli' (work, the land for myself and my husband, education for our two children).[59] The goal of home ownership is a constant in these stories, just as census data have long born out the importance of property and home ownership to the rural Italians who entered Australia. The 1976 census indicates that just under 80 per cent of the Italian-born owned or were paying off their own homes, as opposed to 66 per cent of the Australian-born.[60]

Education for the children was also a goal. A child of immigrant parents remembered 'the money spent on the *Encyclopedia Britannica*, because it was the best, and because it would help us study. The money spent on private, almost inevitably Catholic, schools because the nuns and the brothers would keep us safe and ensure that we would not take drugs, and would do well in the HSC (NSW school matriculation certificate).'[61] All this explains 'the overtime, the bonus rates, the shift work' that working immigrant parents endured. Notwithstanding the money spent on the *Encyclopedia Britannica*, second-generation Italians, it has

been argued, do not attend university or occupy places in the professions at the same levels as their cohorts with Australian-born parents.[62]
Still, those considering the place of the second generation in the
workforce need again to pay attention to the agendas of the immigrants.
The aspirations of many Italian immigrant parents may not have gone
beyond pushing their children from blue-collar into white-collar jobs;
that is, material security may have been a higher priority than education.
Rina Huber found in her 1974 study of Italian immigrants that daughters were expected to become secretaries, teachers, or hairdressers, and
to work in offices, banks, or shops.[63] 'In keeping with that tradition,'
Maria Pellizzari recalled, 'I would finish high school, obtaining good
marks, of course, and work in the local bank, like all the other Italian
girls in the neighbourhood.'[64] Sonia Cousins said of her mother, 'Mum
had made up her mind she was not going to work in a fruit shop. She
had noticed an Italian girl who had started at the local bank, and
decided that she would like to do that.'[65]

What makes these stories so valuable is that they reveal the diversity
and variety of women's work and family experience in Italy and in
Australia. They also point to a considerable repertoire in ways of confronting, coping, resisting, and adapting within the structural constraints
of class, gender, and what in this context might better be described as
outsider status rather than ethnicity. The stories indicate not only that
many women had worked in their earlier lives in Italy, but also that the
workers in family groups included women with small children. One
woman recalled that her daughter was 'more happy' in Australia because
'I was always home with her all day long,' whereas in Italy 'I would have
to leave her and be out in the fields with the cows.'[66] Rita Price recalled
that her grandmother had worked long hours in Italy in the family
grocery shop.[67] As the contributions to this volume suggest, the very
patterns of Italian migration in the nineteenth and twentieth centuries
should have long ago alerted historians of migration and immigration to
the fact of women's work in rural Italy. Given that it was usual for males
to emigrate alone, whole *paesi* must have been for long periods virtually
denuded of men. It has been suggested that in parts of the south of Italy
at the beginning of the twentieth century some 70 per cent of households were headed by women.[68] One immigrant woman described her
life after the men had gone in the following manner: 'I was harvesting
maize, potatoes, wheat, and cutting trees. We would go up into the
mountain, cut the trees, we use a saw and axe, put the logs on the bullock
and cart them home.'[69]

Also in need of revision are the stereotypes that portray working

women in Australia as tragic victims. In the autobiographies and recorded oral testimonies we find many women who claim to have found
satisfaction in their work as an escape from isolation, as a source of
sociability and meaning. 'On days when I was more in touch with the
world,' recalled one woman, 'I felt an urge to do something worthwhile
with my life, and get out of the domestic walls that were starting to feel
like prison walls.' 'I looked around for some practical answers,' she
added, 'and found a job as a waitress in the nearby Veneto club two
nights a week.'[70] The prison metaphor is invoked by another Italian
working woman, who declared: 'I am sick of staying upstairs like a
prisoner, I want to meet people. I want to learn something more than
just keeping house ... There is one good thing about working in the
shop: I am so busy I forget my problems ... I am also enjoying learning
how to run a business.'[71]

Dora Pallotta spoke of the 'confidence' that she gained from her
workplace experiences, where she learned 'how to talk to all sorts of
people, learning English really well. And I learned a lot about things and
life from the people I've met.'[72] 'Even with the babies,' noted yet another working woman, 'I liked to stay in business [because] [o]nce you
are out of the business you don't talk to anyone in English.'[73] These
comments suggest that at least for some women work was a contribution
not only to the family economy but also to individual self-esteem. This
theme also emerges as a strong one in other studies of post-1945 Italian
immigrant working women, including Franca Iacovetta's work on
Canada.[74]

As to the impact of migration and work on family life, the role of men
in the stories told by Australia's Italian working women also receives
serious consideration. The portrayals range from men who opposed the
participation of their wives in the paid workforce to men who expected
it, to men who encouraged it. Still other men helped in the house and
with the children, as did the husband of the woman who explained, 'At
first I used to leave the children with a cousin, but they were always sick.
My husband decided to work at night so we can watch the children
ourselves.'[75] Similarly, women's responses to their husbands' views varied. While some women gave in to their husband's opposition to their
working, others ignored or defied it or negotiated compromises. The
following recollection speaks volumes on the complicated topic of gender politics in immigrant working-class households: 'After our honey-
moon, I started looking for a job ... In fact, my husband didn't want me
to work. According to him, a wife should stay at home ... But I was living

in Australia now and this was a good reason to reject the old mentality that women should stay at home and wash and cook, iron and embroider, clean and polish ... Finally I found a job in an aluminium processing factory.'[76]

If there is much variety and diversity in the women's responses to their working lives, in their move from rural to urban worlds, from agricultural to factory work, they were nevertheless willy nilly undergoing the processes of modernization. Interviewed in her eighties, Giuseppina Stalitari recalled the hardship of her life – as a day agricultural labourer in Calabria where she picked olives, as a pieceworker, as a *vedova bianca* (white widow) for eleven years, and as the wife of a man too stressed to work in Australia. She reflected: 'In the past, we were all in the same ancient condition. But with the passing years life changed and now life is modern and wonderful.'[77] From her study of fifty-six middle-aged and older women from the south of Italy who had been in Australia more than twenty years, Vasta concluded that despite disadvantage and exploitation, many women felt that migration to Australia had provided them with the freedom to accomplish their aspirations – the aspirations of peasant women – and that their participation in the paid workforce had given them independence and pride in their ability to help the family financially.[78] The Australian experience thus conforms to the commonly adopted view that migration and the incorporation of women into the waged workforce brings both gains and losses. Exploitation may be intensified, but women gain independence, respect, and possibly also an awareness that their lives and futures can be changed.[79]

The stories that the women are telling have as yet to be incorporated into the stories that are told about them. Research that seeks to capture the immigrant perspective, that tries to reconstruct the motives, strategies, and experiences of the immigrants themselves still has a long way to go in Australia. There are no social histories comparable to those that have been done for North America by Rudolph Vecoli, Robert Harney, Virginia Yans-McLaughlin, Donna Gabaccia, John Zucchi, and Franca Iacovetta. Sociologists with critical and reformist agendas continue to predominate in the literature on immigrant women in Australia. Academics working at the Centre for Multicultural Studies at the University of Wollongong, directed by Stephen Castles, where Ellia Vasta and Caroline Alcorso have been based, emphasize the past and continuing disadvantage of NESB women in the workforce and their generally oppressed condition in Australian society. Radical critics of capitalism, like their counterparts in the 1970s, see their work as interventionist.

They look askance at the work of a group of demographers, statisticians, and sociologists who are primarily located at the Australian National University in Canberra, who apply quantitative and statistical methods to census data and argue that immigrants do as well as can be expected given the human capital that they bring and the length of time they have lived in Australia.[80] These social scientists include Mariah Evans who, for example, has argued in a study of immigrant women in the workforce based on the 1981 census that the labour market appears to be 'nearly blind' to ethnicity and that length of residence in Australia is all important in influencing labour-market position.[81]

The work of the demographers in Canberra suggests the emergence of new approaches to the construction of knowledge about immigration in Australia. It has recently been argued that the reformist agendas of the 1970s were ahistorical in their representation of the Australia to which the immigrants came. While the Australian government could and should have paid more attention to informed critiques of assimilation, such as that being made by Jean Martin as early as the 1950s, the Australia of that time was a provincial society with little experience of other peoples and cultures.[82] The very acceptance of widespread non-British immigration was in itself revolutionary, and in the early days the government deliberately concealed its extent from the public at large. The immigrants were sought not to develop an ethnically and culturally diverse society but for the economic benefits that they would confer. They were let in as an unskilled and low-skilled labour force. The immigrants themselves came for work, as part of the global process of the movement of the rural work-less to the places with demand for their labour.

The question now being asked is where immigrants of low formal educational levels and no English, and with skills developed in a rural context, were to work on arrival. According to the 1976 census, 45 per cent of Italian-born women had left school before the age of 12, 68 per cent by the age of fourteen.[83] It has been rightly argued that the women often became de-skilled after arrival and that the human capital they brought was ignored.[84] Many had received considerable training in sewing and dressmaking as young women in Italy. But in an era when the making of clothing had been industrialized, when consumer demand was being directed to the ready-made, where was the outlet for the hand skills of these women? What were the real-life – not Utopian – options open to the women in the world of the 1950s and 1960s: a lifetime of the *miseria* that has been so poignantly evoked in the writing of the women themselves – migration to the factories and service industries of northern Europe where, since migrants were guest workers, women faced problems in gaining entry into the workforce and in achieving security of settlement, or to northern Italy where they also suffered exploitation, isolation, and alienation?[85] There are degrees of oppression. And I would suggest that the immigrant women themselves have been less sentimental about their lives than their Australian champions, infected with new-world beliefs about the inevitability of the good life.

Lou Soccio has told the story of his family's migration to Australia.[86] His mother, Michelina, was born in the province of Foggia. She married in 1933, but saw little of her husband, Michele, who was conscripted into the Italian army the year after their marriage. The end of the war was not the end of their separation, since in 1947 Michele went to work for two years in the coal mines of Belgium, and then in 1949 emigrated to Australia. Michelina followed with their four children a year later. Two more children were to be born in Australia. By dint of joint labour, the family was able to buy a fruit shop and achieve some degree of material security, and the three youngest children went to university. Michelina did not enter the paid workforce, and she also remained the least adapted to the new world; her loneliness and alienation was accentuated by the passage of the three youngest children, with their Australian university degrees and spouses, into the middle class. Her social life was confined to visits with *paesani* and to her 'Italianized' parish church. Yet while Michelina maintained her links with her past, she had no desire to return to Italy. When her husband made a return visit, she refused to accompany him, because 'Italy was to her a place where she had suffered terribly for years on end, always in search of food ... Italy was not the beautiful architecture of Rome or Florence, nor the endless art galleries, churches and museums nor the fine foods. Italy was the memory of bombing, hunger, dirt and despair. There was no idyllic charm in the rustic setting of her village for Michelina. The grotty little house she lived in, the muddy streets, the cold winters were all things she wished to forget.'

The Italian-born women in Australia are now an aging cohort in the population; according to the 1986 census 90 per cent of them had been resident for more than fifteen years. In that census 36 per cent of the women were over the age of fifty-five. Five years later, the proportion was 48 per cent.[87] The 1986 census also indicated that the Italian-born women were moving out of the labour force: 61 per cent were not in official employment and only 2 per cent were in the figures of the official unemployed.[88] Yet the problems they faced as NESB women in the workforce still exist. A recent study argues that the similarities in the lives of women immigrants arriving in Australia in the 1950s and 1960s and those arriving today are more marked than the differences, and that their place in the economy has altered little.[89] If the struggle is over for the Italian-born women in Australia, it continues for the next generations of NESB migrants, as it also continues for women of non-Italian-speaking background in Italy. A FILEF study noted that 'la donna immigrata in Italia è tra i deboli la più debole' (is the weakest of the weak) and that legislation relating to immigration took no account of gender specificity. Thai, Filipino, and Bangladesh immigrant women in Italy were isolated, lonely, exploited in the workplace, and stressed by the problems of child care.[90]

As I have argued on a number of previous occasions, during the past four decades, representations of Italian women in Australia have changed in accordance with prevailing ideologies. The Italian women have progressed from being invisible to becoming victims then protagonists, and from being overseas examples of eternal, passive earth mothers to individuals of widely varied experiences and perceptions. While it may be better to be a protagonist rather than a victim, the recent images need to be regarded as critically and sceptically as their predecessors. Present-day conservative agendas that look to lean economies and the cutting of welfare programs prefer to downplay exploitation and to emphasize the role of individual effort and responsibility in the making and success of lives. I wonder if my own exasperation with ahistorical and sentimental representations of the immigrant women and my admiration for what I choose to view as immigrant realism about their life chances are not also infected with the conservatism of my time and age. And I wonder too if recent studies like that of Catherine Hakim in Britain, which suggest that women prefer the domestic and private worlds and the so-called traditional female cultures and values, will not in the near future turn little old ladies in black into icons and role models.[91] We go on constructing the past as well as the present and we need to be as sceptical about the knowledge that we create in our time and place as we are about that of the past.[92]

The time has now come to historicize the lives of Italian immigrant women in Australia.[93] The story when it is told must begin in Italy, in the pre-migration experience of the women, in the Italies of time and place that they left, and it must be placed in the comparative context of their sisters who stayed behind or travelled to other places and must focus on the event of immigration itself as well as on departure and settlement. The settlers and the birds of passage have to be situated in the Australias of time and place, full employment or recession, assimilationist or multicultural, garlic-hating or cappuccino-crazy. And the question must be constantly asked – who is speaking, for whom, and from where?

NOTES

1 Some of the material in this paper has appeared previously and is enlarged upon in Roslyn Pesman, 'Voices of Their Own: Italian Women in Australia,' in George E. Pozzetta and Bruno Ramirez, eds., *The Italian Diaspora: Migration across the Globe* (Toronto, 1992) 155–71; 'Italian Women and Mass Migration,' in R. Bosworth and R. Ugolini, eds., *War, Internment and Mass Migration: The Italo-Australian Experience 1940–1990* (Rome, 1992) 191–206; and 'Immagini delle donne italiane in Australia: Passato e futuro,' *Altreitalie* 9 (1994): 58–68.

2 In the Australian colonies and later the nation, state policies regarding admission deliberately excluded Asians. Such measures became known as the 'White Australia Policy.'

3 See tables in W.D. Borrie, *Italians and Germans in Australia* (Melbourne, 1954), 51.

4 Commonwealth of Australia, Census, 1954, 1971.

5 Maddalena Tirabassi, 'Bringing Life to History: Italian Ethnic Women in the United States,' in Pozzetta and Ramirez, *The Italian Diaspora*, 135.

6 Patricia Grimshaw et al., *Creating a Nation* (Melbourne, 1994).

7 Women feature most conspicuously in one academic study of Italians in Australia as the 'Big Mother' who 'looms large in the life of the Deep South'; Robert Pascoe, *Buongiorno Australia: Our Italian Heritage* (Melbourne, 1988). A more sensitive awareness of all the nuances of the Italies is evident in Michal and Richard Bosworth, *Fremantle's Italians* (Rome, 1993), but women do not loom large in the study.

8 Gianfranco Cresciani, *Migrants or Mates: Italian Life in Australia* (Sydney, 1988).

9 Among Vasta's articles, see 'Gender, Class and Ethnic Relations: The Domestic and Work Experiences of Italian Migrant Women in Australia,' in *Intersexions* (see below, n. 10), 159–77; 'Italian Migrant Women,' in Stephen Castles, Caroline Alcorso, Gaetano Rando, and Ellie Vasta, eds., *Australia's Italians: Culture and Community in a Changing Society* (Sydney, 1992); and 'Immigrant Women and the Politics of Resistance,' *Australian Feminist Studies*

18 (1993): 5–23. See also Deborah Kasnitz, 'Work, Gender and Health among Southern Italian Immigrants in Australia' (PhD thesis, University of Michigan, 1981).

10 For recent bibliographies on immigrant women in Australia, see Department of Immigration and Ethnic Affairs, *About Migrant Women: Bibliography* (Canberra, 1984); Gill Bottomley, Marie de Lepervanche, and Jeannie Martin, *Intersexions: Gender, Class, Culture, Ethnicity* (Sydney, 1991); Caroline Alcorso, *Non-English Speaking Background Women in the Work Force* (Wollongong, 1991) Centre for Multicultural Studies, University of Wollongong; *Settlement and Employment of Migrant Women in Australia: An Annotated Bibliography* (Canberra: 1993) Library Bibliography Series, Bureau of Immigration, Multicultural and Population Research; *Times of Change: The Social Context of Italo-Australian Women's Health. Literature Review* (Melbourne: 1994) Mercy Public Hospitals. Two earlier studies with considerable information on women are Constance Cronin, *The Sting of Change: Sicily and Australia* (Chicago, 1970) and Rina Huber, *From Pasta to Pavlova: A Comparative Study of Italian Settlers in Sydney and Griffith* (Brisbane, 1977). For the Canadian comparison, see Franca Iacovetta, *Such Hardworking People: Italian Immigrants in Postwar Toronto* (Toronto and Montreal, 1992).

11 For one of the few attempts to look at the history of Italian women in Australia before the 1950s, see Angela Diana, 'Italian Women in Australia,' *Affari sociali internazionali* 16 (1988): 65–80.

12 Donna Gabaccia, 'Immigrant Women: Nowhere at Home?' *Journal of American Ethnic History* 10, 4, (1991): 72.

13 Such as Virginia Yans-McLaughlin's *Family and Community: Italian Immigrants in Buffalo 1880–1930* (Ithaca, 1977) or Donna Gabaccia's *From Sicily to Elizabeth Street: Housing and Social Change* (Albany, 1984).

14 Joanne Travaglia, 'The Memories File,' in *Growing Up Italian in Australia. Eleven Young Australian Women Talk about Their Childhood* (Sydney, 1993), State Library of New South Wales, 15.

15 For the definition of the migrant as male, see, in general, Miriana Morokavasic, 'Birds of Passage Are Also Women,' *International Migration Review* 18 (1984): 132–41.

16 Jeannie Martin, 'Non-English Speaking Migrant Women: Production and Social Reproduction,' in Gill Bottomley and Marie de Lepervanche, eds., *Ethnicity, Class and Gender in Australia* (Sydney, 1984), 112.

17 Katy Richmond, *The Participation of Married Women in the Work force*, La Trobe Sociology Papers, Women in the Work Force, Paper no. 2 (Bundoora: 1973), La Trobe University, table 17, p. 44. On descriptive/prescriptive

stereotypes associating Italian women with devoted motherhood and family-centred life, see Pesman, 'Italian Women and Mass Migration,' 195.

18 Silvia Pedraza, 'Women and Migration: The Social Consequences of Gender,' *Journal of American Ethnic History* 10, 4, (1991): 315.

19 Vasta, 'Italian Migrant Women,' 149–51.

20 Rather than list the numerous studies I refer readers to the introduction of this volume, which cites many relevant works, and to the essays in this volume that focus on work.

21 Mariella Vallesi, 'Seasons' and Rita Price, 'The Cafe at the End of the Bay,' in *Growing Up Italian in Australia*, 71, 19–21.

22 Vasta, 'Italian Migrant Women,' 149–51; on Italian immigrant business-women, see also Diane Vecchio's essay on early-twentieth-century Wisconsin in this volume.

23 Kasnitz, 'Work, Gender and Health,' 153.

24 Sonia Cousins, 'I Am an Australian,' in *Growing Up Italian in Australia*, 193.

25 Jean Martin, *The Migrant Presence* (Sydney, 1978), 203.

26 See, e.g., Katrina Brown and Des Storer, *A Preliminary Survey of Migrant Women in the Clothing Trade* (Fitzroy Vic.: Fitzroy Ecumenical Centre, 1974); Des Storer et al., *But I Wouldn't Want My Wife to Work Here: A Study of Migrant Women in Melbourne Industry* (Fitzroy: Centre for Urban Research and Action, 1976); *Commission of Inquiry into Poverty*, Welfare of Migrants (Canberra, 1975); ACOSS, *Immigrants and Mental Health* (Sydney, 1976); Co.As.It., *Study on Depression amongst Italian Women in Melbourne* (Melbourne: 1976); E. Cox, S. Jobson, and Jeannie Martin, *We Cannot Talk Our Rights* (NSW Council of Social Services and Dept. of Sociology, University of New South Wales, 1976).

27 Jan Pettman, *Living in the Margins: Race, Sexism and Feminism in Australia* (Sydney, 1992), 49. See also Vera Zaccari, 'FILEF, Migrant Women and Australian Trade Unions,' Multicultural Australia Papers, no. 56, 1986; Loucas Nicolaou, *Australian Unions and Migrants Workers* (Sydney, 1992), 265–9; and Santina Bertone and Gerard Griffin, 'Immigrant Women and Trade Unions,' paper for Women and Migration Conference, Bureau of Immigration Research, Melbourne, 1992.

28 Morag Loh, *With Courage in Their Cases: The Experience of Thirty Five Immigrant Workers and Their Families in Australia* (Melbourne, 1980), 64.

29 On the Canadian experience, see Iacovetta, *Such Hardworking People*, 99.

30 Examples can be found in the bibliographies cited above in note 10.

31 For a critical view of the victim image, see esp. Helen Andreoni, 'Le donne italiane nell'Australia multiculturale,' *Il Veltro* 32 (1988): 224.

32 See the articles by Jeannie Martin, Gill Bottomly, and Marie de Lepervanche in *Ethnicity, Class and Gender in Australia* and in *Intersexions*.
33 S. Pieri, M. Risk, and A. Sgro, 'Italian Migrant Women, Participation, and the Women's Movement,' in M. Bevege, M. James, and C. Shute, eds., *Worth Her Salt: Women at Work in Australia* (Sydney, 1980), 389–99; P. Suvendrini, 'How Long Does It Take to Get It Right? Migrant Women and the Women's Movement,' *Refractory Girl* 28 (May 1985); Vera Zaccari, 'Italian Women's Movement Strategies Needed in Australia,' *Scarlet Woman Issues* 24 (1988): 29–33. See also the strong critique of feminist attitudes in Andreoni, 'Le donne italiane nell'Australia multiculturale,' 215–27.
34 Zaccari, 'FILEF, Migrant Women and Australian Trade Unions.'
35 Loh, *With Courage in Their Cases.*
36 Martin, 'Non-English Speaking Migrant Women,' 245.
37 Gabaccia, 'Immigrant Women: Nowhere at Home?' 70.
38 *Noi on Donne Italo-Australiane*, Proceedings of the First Conference of Italo-Australian Women in Australia, Sydney-Melbourne, 1985.
39 Ellie Vasta, Introduction, *Australian Feminist Studies* 18 (1993), Special issue, Gender and Ethnicity: 2. See also *The Politics of Speaking Out: Immigrant Women Ten Years On*, Conference proceedings, Sydney, 1992.
40 Andreoni, 'Le donne italiane'; for similar developments in Canada, see Iacovetta, *Such Hardworking People.*
41 Vasta, 'Gender, Class and Ethnic Relations,' 159.
42 Vasta, 'Cultural and Social Change: Italo-Australian Women and the Second Generation,' paper delivered at the conference *500 Years of Italian Immigration to the Americas* (New York, 1992).
43 See, e.g., Roger Rouse, 'Mexican Migration and the Social Space of Postmodernism,' *Diaspora* 1, 1 (Spring 1991). 8–23.
44 Frank Galbally (chairman), *Report of the Review of Post-Arrival Programs and Services for Migrants* (Canberra, 1978): 39.
45 Lidio Bertelli, 'Italian Families,' in Des Storer, ed., *Ethnic Family Values in Australia* (Sydney, 1985), 33–71.
46 Maria Minicuci, 'Notes on the Condition of Women in a Southern Italian Village,' in Monique Gadant, ed., *Women of the Mediterranean* (London, 1986), 171–3.
47 Helen Andreoni, 'Non-English-Speaking Women in an Isolated Rural Community,' Armidale Papers, 7: 6–7.
48 Amalia Signorelli, 'La condizione femminile nel tramonto della società rurale tradizionale (1945–1960),' in *Le donne nelle campagne italiane del Novecento* (Istituto 'Alcide Cervi' Annali 13, 1991), 255.

49 See, e.g., the collection of articles in *Le donne nelle campagne italiane* (n. 48).

50 Cronin, *The Sting of Change*, 9.

51 For the North American example, see Gabaccia, *From Sicily to Elizabeth Street, Housing and Social Change*, 111.

52 Martin, 'Non-English Speaking Women,' 116.

53 See, e.g., Lou Soccio, 'A Family in Italy and Australia,' in *Melbourne Studies in Education* (Melbourne, 1977), 1–25; 'Maria: A Migrant Woman's Story,' *Social Alternatives* 1, 2 (1978): 57–9; Nina Nelli, *Australia: Un paese che ha nome Speranza. Il contributo del lavoro italiano* (Florence, 1979); Loh, *With Courage in Their Cases*; Chiara Ferronato, *Australia non avrai il mio cuore* (Padua, 1988); *Give Me Strength – Forza e Coraggio: Italian Women Speak*, ed. Anna Maria Kahan-Guidi and Elizabeth Weiss (Sydney, 1989); Valeria Gorrlei Aliani, *Le mie avventure in Australia* (Melbourne, 1989); Emma Ciccotosto and Michal Bosworth, *Emma: A Translated Life* (Fremantle, 1990); *Stories from the Northcote Elderly Citizens Club (Circolo di Pensionati Italiani di Northcote)*, ed. Carmelina Di Guglielmo (Northcote, Vic., 1990); *Le signore di Albion Street: Interviste sull'esperienza migratoria di un gruppo di donne italiane di Sydney*, ed. Roberto Pettini (Sydney, 1991); *Growing Up Italian in Australia*; Maria Berton et al., *Immagini di donne italiane nel Sud Australia* (Adelaide, 1994); Celestina Mammone, *The Calabrian Dilemma* (Mildura, Vic., 1994); Olga D'Albero-Giuiliani, *Piccolo quercia: la vita di Olga* (West Brunswick, Vic., 1994); and 'Mondi Diverse, Le Donne Venute in Australia,' unpublished tapes and transcripts, FILEF, Sydney. Since the completion of this manuscript in 1996, life stories have continued to appear in increasing numbers. See, e.g., Adele Bentley, *Between Two Cultures: An Italian-Australian Autobiography* (Roleystone, WA, 1996); Diana Ruzzene Grollo, *Growing Through the Brick Floor* (Melbourne, 1997): Zita Carew, *From Capers to Quandongs* (Salisbury, SA, 1997); *La Pioggia nelle scarpe: Anedotti di una protagonista*, compiled and written by Marietta Rossetto (Adelaide, 1997); Anna Maria dell'Oso, *Songs of the Suitcase* (Sydney, 1998); Marie Alaface, *Savage Cows and Cabbage Leaves: An Italian Life* (Sydney, 1999); Maria Pallotta-Chiarolli, *Tapestry* (Sydney, 1999).

54 Paula Hamilton, 'The Knife Edge: Debates about Memory and History,' in Kate Darian-Smith and Paula Hamilton, eds., *Memory and History in Twentieth Century Australia* (Melbourne, 1994), 9–32.

55 Jacques Boulet et al., *Times of Change: The Social Context of Italo-Australian Women's Health* (East Melbourne, 1994).

56 Alcorso, *Non-English Speaking Background Women*, 17.

57 Louise Tilly and Joan Scott, *Women, Work and Family* (New York, 1978), quoted in Gabaccia, 'Immigrant Women: Nowhere at Home?' 69.

58 Maria Pallotta-Chiarolli, unpublished interview with her mother Dora.

59 Nelli, *Australia*, 29.

60 Helen Ware, *A Profile of the Italian Community in Australia* (Melbourne, 1981), 35.

61 Travaglia, 'The Memories File,' 9.

62 See below, n. 77.

63 Huber, *From Pasta to Pavlova*, 88–90, 159.

64 Monica Pellizzari, 'A Woman, a Wog and a Westie,' in *Growing Up Italian in Australia*, 134.

65 Sonia Cousins, 'I Am an Australian,' in ibid., 200. For the diversity in the backgrounds of women who emigrated, see Iacovetta, *Such Hardworking People*, 81–6.

66 Loh, *With Courage in Their Cases*, 18.

67 Price, 'The Cafe at the End of the Bay,' 23.

68 Paola Corti, 'Donne che vanno, donne che restano. Modelli migratori e ruoli femminili,' paper to the conference *Le donne nelle campagne italiane del Novecento*, Ravenna 31 May–2 June 1990.

69 Loh, *With Courage in Their Cases*, 17.

70 Oriella Rigoni in *Give Me Strength*, 176.

71 A. Marino, in ibid., 19.

72 Pallotta-Chiarolli, interview with Dora Pallotta.

73 Anne Henderson, *From All Corners: Six Migrant Stories* (St Leonards, 1993), 20.

74 *Such Hardworking People*, esp. chap. 4.

75 Ibid., 151.

76 Lucy Romy in *Give Me Strength*, 96.

77 *Immagini di donne italiane nel Sud Australia*, 22–3.

78 Vasta, 'Gender, Class and Ethnic Relations,' 168.

79 Morokvasic, 'Birds of Passage Are Also Women,' 893.

80 The ongoing debate over how the place of immigrants in the workforce should be interpreted can be sampled in the pages of the *Journal of Intercultural Studies* 7, 3 (1986), 8, 2 (1987), 9, 1 (1988), and 10, 3 (1989). For a summary from one side, see Alcorso, *Non-English Speaking Background Women*, 32–3.

81 M.D.R. Evans, 'Immigrants in Australia: Resources, Family and Work,' *International Migration Review* 18, 2 (1984): 1089. The debate now extends to the workplace position of the second generation. There is no disagreement with statistics that show that the women of the second generation occupy higher positions in the labour market than those taken by their immigrant mothers. According to the 1976 census, whereas 37.8% of Italian-born women worked in the blue-collar labour force and only 14.5% in the cleri-

cal sector, only 6.2% of the women on the next generation were found in the category of trades and labourers and 42.9% in the clerical sector. Still, their upward mobility is lower than those of their generation with Australian-born parents and representation in the professions and their participation in post-secondary education is less. The 1981 census points to the continuation of this pattern. And in the now frequently recurring periods of recession, their unemployment rates are higher. The interpretation of the statistics remains the problem. Is mobility in itself enough? Ellie Vasta would argue that the failure to achieve the occupational distribution of the total workforce is evidence for continuing disadvantage, whereas F.L. Jones would counter that when labour-market characteristics are taken into account, 'difference evaporates' (F.L. Jones, *Ethnicity in the Australian Labor Market: The Immigrant Experience* [Canberra: Australian Bureau of Statistics Occasional Papers, 1992]).

82 John Lack and Jacqueline Templeton, *Bold Experiment: A Documentary History of Australian Immigration since 1945* (Melbourne, 1995), 39.
83 Ware, *A Profile of the Italian Community*, 35.
84 Alcorso, *Non-English Speaking Background Women*, 56–7.
85 Graziella Bonnansea, 'Tra immaginario contadino e realtà operaia: Donne a Torino negli anni cinquanta,' paper to *Le donne nelle campagne italiane del Novecent* (see n. 68), 329–44.
86 Soccio, A Family in Italy and Australia,' 1–25.
87 Ros Wood, *About Migrant Women: Statistical Profile, 1986* (Canberra: Depart. of Immigration, Local Government and Ethnic Affairs, 1989); Bureau of Immigration and Population Research, *Community Profiles, 1991 Census, Italy Born* (Canberra, 1994).
88 Wood, *About Migrant Women*, table 5.3.
89 Alcorso, *Non-English Speaking Background Women*, 8.
90 *Immagini di donne italiane nel Sud Australia*, 6.
91 Catherine Hakim, 'The Sexual Division of Labour and Women's Heterogeneity,' *British Journal of Sociology* 47 (March 1996): 178–88.
92 See also Gill Bottomly, 'Representing the "Second Generation": Subjects, Objects and Ways of Knowing,' in *Intersexions*, 94–5.
93 The task is becoming possible in part because projects for the collecion of material relating to Italians in Australia have now been under way for some time under the direction of Co.As.It in Melbourne and the State Library of New South Wales. A project for the development of a large-scale search and preservation effort led by Ilma Martinuzzi O'Brien at the Victoria University of Technology in collaboration with several universities and public libraries is now gaining momentum with grants from the Australia Research Council.

Contributors

Paola Corti is professor of contemporary history in the Department of History, University of Turin. She has contributed to and collaborated with various Italian and other journals and cultural institutions and has written articles and monographs on rural society and migration in Italy. Hr more recent publications include *L'emigrazione* (Rome: Editori Riuniti, 1999); D. Albera and Paola Corti, eds., *La montagna mediterranea: Una fabbrica d'uomini?* (Gribaudo: Cavallermaggiore, 2000); and *Emigranti, esuli, profughi: Origini e sviluppo dei movimenti migratori nel novecento* (Turin: Paravia, 2001).

Andreina De Clementi is professor of contemporary history at the Istituto Universitario Orientale of Naples. Her most recent research has focused on Italian migration and her most recent publications include *Di qua e di là dell'oceano: Emigrazione e mercati nel Meridione, 1860–1930* (Rome: Carocci, 1999). She also has been president of the Italian Women Historians' Society.

Donna R. Gabaccia is the Charles H. Stone Professor of American History at the University of North Carolina at Charlotte, where she teaches courses on comparative social history and the twentieth-century world. She is the author of many books and articles on international migration and immigrant life in the United States, including *Immigration and American Diversity* (Oxford: Blackwell Publishers, 2002); *Italy's Many Diasporas* (London: University College of London Press, Seattle: University of

Washington Press, 2000), and *We Are What We Eat: Ethnic Food and the Making of Americans* (Cambridge: Harvard University Press, 1998).

Jennifer Guglielmo is a doctoral candidate in history at the University of Minnesota. She is completing her dissertation, 'Negotiating Gender, Race, and Coalition: Italian Women and New York City's Working-Class Politics, 1890–1945,' and co-editing *Are Italians White? How Race Is Made in America* (forthcoming). She teaches history and women's studies at the State University of New York, New Paltz.

Franca Iacovetta is a professor of history at the University of Toronto, co-editor of the Studies in Gender and History at University of Toronto Press, and the recent recipient of the Thérèse Casgrain fellowship from the Social Sciences and Humanities Research Council. She is the author or editor of several books in immigration, labour, social, women's and gender history, including, most recently, *On the Case* (Toronto: University of Toronto Press, 1988) and *Enemies Within* (Toronto: University of Toronto Press, 2000). Her forthcoming monograph is on immigrant and refugee reception work in cold-war Canada.

Caroline Waldron Merithew is Visiting Assistant Professor at Cornell University's School of Industrial and Labor Relations. Her article '"Lynch-law Must Go!" Race, Citizenship, and the Other in an American Coal Mining Town' appeared in the Fall 2000 issue of the *Journal of American Ethnic History*. She is currently revising a book manuscript that explores the hybrid culture of immigrant miners and their families, and has initiated a new research project on immigrant widows.

Anne Morelli is a professor at the University of Brussels. Her earlier work focused on Italian political emigration in the interwar period: *Fascismo e antifascismo nell'emigrazione italiana in Belgio 1922–1940* (Rome: Bonacci, 1987). She has since pursued more general interests in religious and ethnic minority history and has written or edited several works on these themes, including *Lettre ouverte à la secte des adversaires des sectes* (Brussels: Labor, 1997) and *Les émigrants belges* (Brussels: EVO, 1998).

José Moya is an associate professor of history at the University of California at Los Angeles. His book *Cousins and Strangers: Spanish Immigrants in Buenos Aires, 1850–1930* (Berkeley: University of California Press, 1998) won five awards including the Bolton Prize for best book on Latin

American History from the American Historical Association and the Social Science History Association's Sharlin Memorial Award for outstanding book. His current book project is a sociocultural history of anarchism in Buenos Aires during the belle epoque.

Roslyn Pesman is professor of history and pro-vice-chancellor of the College of Humanities and Social Sciences at the University of Sydney, Australia. She has written on Florentine Renaissance politics, Italian–Australian relations, Italian migration to Australia, and on women and travel. Among her recent publications are *Duty Free: Australian Women Abroad* (Melbourne: Oxford University Press, 1996) and the co-edited *Oxford Book of Australian Travel Writing* (Melbourne: Oxford University Press, 1996). She is currently engaged on a short study of migration to Australia from the Veneto.

Angelo Principe is a veteran Italian-Canadian journalist and activist who also obtained his PhD in Italian Studies from the University of Toronto, and has been an instructor there, as well as at York University. He is the author of *The Darkest Side of the Fascist Years: The Italian Canadian Press 1920–1942* (Toronto: Guernica, 1999) and co-editor of *Enemies Within: Italians and Other Internees in Canada and Beyond* (Toronto: University of Toronto Press, 2000). He is completing a book on anti-Fascism and the anti-Fascist press in Canada.

Linda Reeder is an assistant professor of history at the University of Missouri. She has published articles on Sicilian women and transnational migration. She is the author of the book *Widows in White: Male Migration and the Transformation of Rural Sicilian Women, 1880–1930* (University of Toronto Press, 2002). She is currently at work on a study of female insanity and nation-building in Italy, 1880–1930.

Gabriele Scardellato currently holds the Postdoctoral Fellowship of the Mariano A. Elia Chair in Italian Canadian Studies at York University, Toronto, and teaches part time in the Department of Italian Studies at the University of Toronto. He was director of Research Resources for the Multicultural History Society of Ontario for ten years and has written several studies on Italian immigrants in Canada and on other aspects of Canadian ethnic history, including *Within Our Temple: A History of the Order Sons of Italy of Ontario* (Toronto: Order Sons of Italy of Canada, 1995). More recently he edited (with Manuela Scarci) *A Monument for*

Italian-Canadian Immigrants: Regional Migration from Italy to Canada (Toronto: University of Toronto, Dept. of Italian Studies, 1999). His current research project for the Elia Chair is the compilation of a historical atlas of Italian settlement in Ontario.

Maddalena Tirabassi is a researcher at the Fondazione Giovanni Agnelli, Turin, and the managing editor of *Altreitalie, International Journal of Studies on the People of Italian Origin in the World* (published by the Fondazione Giovanni Agnelli). She has been a consultant on intercultural education for the city administration of Turin and other private foundations. A Fulbright scholar at the University of Minnesota in 1979, she is the author of numerous essays on Italian emigration published in Italian and foreign journals, and author of *Il faro di Beacon Street: Social workers e immigrate negli Stati Uniti, 1910–1939* (Milan: Franco Angeli, 1990). A specialist of Italian immigration to the United States, she is Professor of American Studies at the University of Teramo.

Diane Vecchio is associate professor of history at Furman University in Greenville, South Carolina. She has contributed biographical entries on eminent Italian-Americans (including Mother Francesca Cabrini, Angela Bambace, and Helen Barolini) for Elliott Barkan, *Making It in America: A Source Book on Eminent Ethnic Americans* (Santa Barbara: ABC CLIO, 2001), and recently completed a manuscript, 'Work, Family and Tradition: Italian Migrant Women in Urban America, 1900–1935.'

Robert Ventresca is assistant professor in the History Department at King's College, University of Western Ontario. A recipient of several senior graduate student awards at the University of Toronto, his thesis, a social history of Italy's historic 1948 election, won the CHA's John Bullen prize for the best dissertation. He has also published in Canadian immigrant working-class history and is a co-editor of *A Nation of Immigrants* (Toronto: University of Toronto Press, 1998).

Illustrations Credits

Aldich Public Library (Barre, Vermont, USA): Italian immigrants in Barre, Vermont.

Archivio centrale dello stato, Ministero dell'interno, Casellario politico centrale, Rome: Page from the Italian police files for Virgilia D'Andrea.

Archivo General de la Nacion de Buenos Aires: The *Conventillos* strike in Buenos Aires.

Center for Migration Studies (New York): Luigi Antonini, Atlantic City; front page of a 1918 edition of *L'Operaia*.

Editori Riuniti (Rome, Italy): Italian women harvesting lemons; a wet nurse from Città di Castello.

Famee Furlane collection (Toronto): Women and children en route to Canada; Women workers posing in front of the Tip Top Tailors building.

Fondazione Sella, Biella, Italy: A group of women and children in Barre, Vermont.

Immigration History Research Center, University of Minnesota: Angela Bambace and her mother (Angela Bambace papers, Box 1, Folders 11, 12); Luigi Antonini at a 'Local 89' installation (Alberto Cupelli Papers, Box 15, Folder 13).

Italian Community Center, Milwaukee: Mother and daughter working in Lalli's Grocery Store (Mario Carini).

Library of Congress (Washington): Maria Mauro, 309E 110th Street (Lewis Wickes Hine).

New York Public Library: New York City, early 1900s, woman carrying home bundle of sewing (Lewis Wickes Hine, Courtesy of Javitz Collection MFZ Hine 93-6223 91 PH056.133).

Index